Writing Early China

SUNY series in Chinese Philosophy and Culture
———————
Roger T. Ames, editor

Writing Early China

EDWARD L. SHAUGHNESSY

Cover Credit: Calligraphy by Zhang Bofan

Published by State University of New York Press, Albany

© 2023 State University of New York

All rights reserved

Printed in the United States of America

No part of this book may be used or reproduced in any manner whatsoever without written permission. No part of this book may be stored in a retrieval system or transmitted in any form or by any means including electronic, electrostatic, magnetic tape, mechanical, photocopying, recording, or otherwise without the prior permission in writing of the publisher.

For information, contact State University of New York Press, Albany, NY
www.sunypress.edu

Library of Congress Cataloging-in-Publication Data

Name: Shaughnessy, Edward L., 1952– author.
Title: Writing early China / Edward L. Shaughnessy.
Description: Albany : State University of New York Press, [2023] | Series: SUNY series in Chinese philosophy and culture | Includes bibliographical references and index.
Identifiers: LCCN 2023002623 | ISBN 9781438495224 (hardcover : alk. paper) | ISBN 9781438495231 (ebook) | ISBN 9781438495217 (pbk. : alk. paper)
Subjects: LCSH: China—History—To 221 B.C.—Sources. | China—History—To 221 B.C.—Historiography. | Inscriptions, Chinese—History and criticism. | Manuscripts, Chinese—History and criticism. | China—History—Qin dynasty, 221–207 B.C.—Sources. | China—History—Qin dynasty, 221–207 B.C.—Historiography.
Classification: LCC DS741.15 .S54 2023 | DDC 931/.03—dc23/eng/20230214
LC record available at https://lccn.loc.gov/2023002623

10 9 8 7 6 5 4 3 2 1

Dedicated to the memory of my friend and 同鄉

DAVID TOD ROY

Born 5 April 1933, Nanjing

Attended Sewickley High School, 1947–1948

Died 31 May 2016, Hyde Park

文質彬彬

Contents

List of Illustrations — ix

Acknowledgments — xi

Introduction — 1

Part I: Inscriptions

Chapter One
History and Inscriptions — 13

Chapter Two
The Bin Gong Xu Inscription and the Origins of the Chinese Literary Tradition — 47

Chapter Three
The Writing of a Late Western Zhou Bronze Inscription — 57

Chapter Four
On the Casting of the Art Institute of Chicago's Shi Wang Ding: With Remarks on the Important Position of Writing in the Consciousness of Ancient China — 89

Part II: The Classics

Chapter Five
A Possible Lost Classic: The *She Ming or *Command to She — 113

viii | Contents

Chapter Six
Varieties of Textual Variants: Evidence from the Tsinghua
Bamboo-Slip *Ming Xun Manuscript   141

Chapter Seven
Unearthed Documents and the Question of the Oral versus
Written Nature of the Shi Jing   169

Chapter Eight
A First Reading of the Anhui University Bamboo-Slip Shi Jing   203

Part III: Manuscripts

Chapter Nine
The Mu Tianzi Zhuan and King Mu–Period Bronzes   237

Chapter Ten
The Tsinghua Manuscript *Zheng Wen Gong wen Tai Bo and the
Question of the Production of Manuscripts in Early China   253

Chapter Eleven
The Eighth Century BCE Civil War in Jin as Seen in the
Bamboo Annals: On the Nature of the Tomb Text and Its
Significance for the "Current" Bamboo Annals   265

Chapter Twelve
The Qin *Bian Nian Ji and the Beginnings of Historical
Writing in China   297

Notes   319

Bibliography   383

Index   405

Illustrations

1.1	*Heji* 36481, *left* front, *right* back	21
2.1a & b	*Bin Gong xu* 豳公盨 vessel and inscription	55
4.1	*Shi Wang ding* 師望鼎 vessel	90
4.2	*Xiao Ke ding* 小克鼎 vessel	91
4.3	Rubbing of *Shi Wang ding* 師望鼎 inscription	91
4.4	*Shi Wang gui* 師望簋 vessel	95
4.5	*Shi Wang xu* 師望盨 vessel	95
4.6	*Shi Wang hu* 師望壺 vessel	96
4.7	X-ray of the back wall of the *Shi Wang ding* (i.e., the wall bearing the inscription)	99
4.8	X-ray of the front wall of the *Shi Wang ding* (i.e., the wall opposite that bearing the inscription)	99
4.9	Diagram of the mold assemblage for a round caldron	100
4.10	Diagram of the right rear wall of the *Mao Gong ding* 毛公鼎	103
4.11	Diagram of the left front wall of the *Mao Gong ding* 毛公鼎	104
5.1	*Da Yu ding* 大盂鼎 inscription	136
7.1	*Shi Qiang pan* 史牆盤 inscription.	198

| 8.1 | Qin Stone Drums poem "Tian che" 田車 | 229 |
| 10.1 | Slip 1 of the two *Zheng Wen Gong wen Tai Bo 鄭文公問太伯 manuscripts | 261 |

Acknowledgments

As always, my greatest debts are to the archaeologists and paleographers of China, without whose diligence and creativity none of my understanding of early China would be possible. I am particularly grateful to colleagues at Fudan 復旦, Jilin 吉林, Nankai 南開, Peking 北京, Tsinghua 清華, and Wuhan 武漢 universities, with whom I have discussed most of the contents of this book. Since the chapters of this book have all been previously published with more or less the same content, I will reserve for those chapters my thanks to other colleagues who made valuable suggestions that contributed to my writing of them. For now, I would like to thank Andrew West of BabelStone Fonts, who created numerous archaic characters for this book in a very timely manner, and my students Wu Fang, Yang Qiyu, and Zhang Bofan, the first of whom brushed the calligraphy on the cover and the latter two of whom helped with various aspects of the book's production.

In addition, I wish to dedicate this book to my dear friend David Tod Roy, who passed away five years ago. Although David devoted the greater part of his life to the study of a single work written some two thousand years later than most of the texts studied in this book, one of my great joys was talking with him about writing. If anyone deserves the sobriquet "supremely literate," it was David—a *junzi* 君子 to the end.

Introduction

Over twenty-five years ago, I published my first volume in the SUNY series in Chinese Philosophy and Culture, *Before Confucius: Studies in the Creation of the Chinese Classics*, which, as the subtitle indicates, was a collection of studies concerning how (some of) the Chinese classics—principally parts of the *Yi* 易 *Changes*, *Shu* 書 *Scriptures*, and *Shi* 詩 *Poetry*—were composed and how they may have been understood in their earliest contexts. The volume was generally well received in the scholarly press, though a short review by David Schaberg in the *Journal of Asian Studies* hinted at important reservations on his part.

> The essays share a simple and effective intellectual plot. Shaughnessy believes strongly in the widespread use of writing during the Western Zhou period, and often seeks, in opposition to the skepticism of recent centuries, to discover authentically early materials in or behind the texts transmitted from before the Han. . . . Agreeing with Shaughnessy means accepting his belief in the ubiquity of writing as early as the beginning of the first millennium B.C.E. This collection will be useful and exemplary both for those who agree with him and for those who want to argue the point.[1]

Schaberg's reference to "to the skepticism of recent centuries" vis-à-vis "the widespread use of writing during the Western Zhou period" would doubtless call to the mind of many readers familiar with the study of early Chinese history the sort of historiographical iconoclasm that goes back to the work of Yan Ruoqu 閻若璩 (1636–1704) and Hui Dong 惠棟 (1697–1758) on the authenticity of the "Ancient Script" (*guwen*

古文) *Shang shu* 尚書 *Exalted Scriptures*, the *Kao xin lu* 考信錄 *Record of Examining the True* of Cui Shu 崔述 (1740–1816), and especially the *Gu shi bian* 古史辨 *Discriminations of Ancient History* spearheaded by Gu Jiegang 顧頡剛 (1893–1980). Although such iconoclasm has been largely rejected in today's China, its critics arguing that the remarkable archaeological discoveries of the last 120 years—including especially hundreds of thousands of written documents—have provided indubitable evidence of the antiquity of writing in China, it has remained influential among numerous Western Sinologists. In a lengthy review of another book of which I was the coeditor, Schaberg did go on to "argue the point," presenting in detail the sort of disagreements with my work that he had only hinted at in his review of *Before Confucius*.

> If archaeological studies of the second millennium have shown the influence of textualist prejudices, "traditional historical" work on the Shang and later periods has too often been defined by such prejudices. To bring this charge is not merely to repeat the truism that history begins with received texts; the problem lies deeper. For the most part, the texts that historians work with are of late or poorly understood provenance. Either they are known to have been written centuries after the events they recount (as in the case of the *Shiji* 史記) or, worse, they come down to us with no certain information about when and where they were written, or by whom. Even archaeologically recovered writings, like oracle-bone and bronze inscriptions, carry with them precious little information about the circumstances of their composition and use, or about the relation of the instance of writing to surrounding historical realities. Further, the rare cases in which archaeology has yielded documents that unambiguously corroborate a received text's account (as in the famous case of the *Shiji*'s list of Shang kings) cannot, on any logical grounds, be taken to demonstrate the general accuracy of the received text's narratives. If "traditional history" is defined as historical research based in part on received texts, then it seems to begin either with radical uncertainty or with credulity. Historians derive both the framework of history (including the chronology of all but a few rulers) and information about its particulars from received texts that are either late or unprovenanced, and they

will, therefore, never be able to speak about the narrated past with the precision that characterizes many of archaeology's reconstructions.

The best historians, when they use received texts, routinely treat them as artifacts of dubious provenance. They note the doubts that surround them, cite and critique the best theories about their origins, and then take care not to reach conclusions more precise than the data will support. . . . A received text has, by definition, lost many of the material characteristics that it had when it was first made. It has undergone recopying, editing, compilation—we do not know when, or by whom—and it is practically impossible to reconstruct its first form, whether we imagine it starting as a manuscript on bamboo strips, as a spoken pronouncement, or as a performance in some other medium.[2]

According to this argument, not only is historical research based on received texts, such as the Chinese classics, inevitably characterized by "radical uncertainty or with credulity," but even archaeologically recovered writings provide "precious little information" about historical realities. One might think that the Chinese written tradition of the first millennium or more before the common era is essentially null.

I suspect that Professor Schaberg would not wish to argue that all study of ancient Chinese texts is ultimately hopeless (after all, his own work has been resolutely focused on those texts). Instead, the last two clauses of the long quotation from his review hint at a second critique of writing in early China, which—at least at the present in the Western world—has become even more widespread than the earlier Chinese skepticism concerning the dates and authenticity of ancient texts: the notion that ancient China was a fundamentally oral culture and that the contents of the literature that has come down to us were originally communicated orally, and that writing—when it was employed at all—was of only secondary significance. As I will have occasion to recount in chapter 7 of this book, this viewpoint has been particularly pervasive vis-à-vis the *Shi jing* 詩經 *Classic of Poetry*, with such luminaries of contemporary Sinology as Stephen Owen, David Knechtges, Christoph Harbsmeier, and Martin Kern all voicing their support for some version of it.[3] In particular, over the course of the last twenty years Kern has published numerous studies in which he argues forcefully that literary expression in ancient China was largely oral. Perhaps his most mature statement regarding the putative oral nature of the *Shi jing*, and indeed of all the classics, has come in his contribution to *The Cambridge History of Chinese Literature*.

> Quoting and reciting the *Poetry* was primarily a matter of oral practice. Regardless of the writings excavated from a small number of elite tombs, the manuscript culture of Warring States China must have been of limited depth and breadth. The available stationery was either too bulky (wood and bamboo) or too expensive (silk) for the extensive copying of texts and their circulation over vast distances. References to writing and reading, as well as to the economic, material, or educational conditions of textual production and circulation, are extremely scarce in the early literature, which instead consistently depicts learning in personal master–disciple settings (likely supported by writing as aide-mémoire and educational practice). While local writing of technical, administrative, legal, economic, military, and other matters existed in the different regions of the Warring States, the extensive circulation of the Classics probably did not depend on writing. No pre-imperial source speaks of the circulation of the Classics as writings, or of the profound difficulties involved in transcribing them among distinctly different calligraphic and orthographic regional traditions. Not one of the numerous invocations of the *Poetry* in the *Zuo Tradition* and the *Discourses of the States* mentions the use of a written text; invariably, they show the ability of memorization and free recitation—in the literary koine mentioned above—as the hallmark of education.[4]

Given Kern's statement that "the manuscript culture of Warring States China must have been of limited depth and breadth," my own claim made in the introduction to *Before Confucius* that "ancient China was a supremely literate culture," even with the added qualification "at least at the royal court and among the social elite,"[5] must surely seem naïve at best, if not totally mistaken. While I admit that my use of the expression "supremely literate culture" doubtless owed more to my own youthful exuberance than to any sort of sustained survey of the relevant evidence, even now, tempered by quite a few additional years,

I would suggest that there is a powerful evidential basis in support of it: over 160,000 pieces of inscribed oracle bones from the Shang dynasty, upward of twenty thousand inscribed bronze ritual vessels from the Zhou dynasty, and some three hundred thousand bamboo and wooden slips bearing textual records from the Warring States, Qin, and Han periods, all unearthed in China over the course of the last 120 years. These have been found in almost every province of China from Xinjiang and Gansu in the west, Liaoning and even as far as Korea in the north, Shandong and Jiangsu in the east, south as far as Hunan and Guangdong, and of course in every province of central China.

These are just the text-bearing artifacts that happen to have been unearthed; this must be just the tip of the figurative iceberg that was once put in the ground, and that too must have been a miniscule percentage of the writings that were produced but were disposed of above ground. Consider the thirty-six thousand bamboo-slip documents unearthed in 2002 in the village of Liye 里耶, Longshan 龍山 county, in far western Hunan Province. Salvage excavations undertaken in advance of the construction of a hydropower station turned up a Warring States town that apparently had been established by the ancient state of Chu 楚 to defend against the state of Qin 秦. With the Qin conquest of Chu and then subsequent unification of all other states, it became a local jurisdiction on the periphery of the Qin state. The bamboo-slip documents, produced over the course of about fifteen years beginning in 222 BCE and ending with the downfall of Qin, were discovered in the mud at the bottom of an ancient well, where they had been discarded by the vanquished administrators of the town.[6] They show that even this relative backwater was thoroughly integrated into the Qin bureaucracy, exchanging regular correspondence and files with neighboring jurisdictions, and it is clear that those jurisdictions were also producing similar records. We have every reason to believe that local jurisdictions throughout the realm were engaged in the same sort of textual production; indeed, the Liye records show that they were required to do so. This would seem to call into question the claim that the manuscript culture of ancient China "must have been of limited depth and breadth."

Of course, it might be objected first that the Liye records are "local writing of technical, administrative, legal, economic, military, and other matters," and second that they date to the Qin and not to the Warring States period. Both of these points are certainly true, but there was no dramatic difference in the skills required to produce these sorts of records and other kinds of texts or in the technology available to produce the bamboo slips over the course of these two periods.[7] Although no similar Warring States government archives have been unearthed as of yet, thousands of Warring States slips of all kinds—including texts of the *Shi jing* and also other classics—have been unearthed in just the last twenty years. The most important of these texts, at least as of the present, are doubtless those in the collection of Tsinghua (Qinghua) University, three or four of which will be taken up in the following chapters.[8] According to the Tsinghua editors, there are at least sixty other texts, some quite substantial, the publication of which, already ongoing for the last ten years, is expected to take another six or seven years. I suspect that the original effort involved in writing and reading the texts was considerably less labor intensive than the modern work to read and understand them. Moreover, as I will note in chapters 5 and 9, contra Kern's assertion, there is good evidence that some of the texts, including those of the Classics, certainly circulated over very long, if not "vast," distances, at least over the course of the second half of the first millennium BCE.

With regard to still earlier periods, in his review of *Before Confucius*, Schaberg attributed to me a "belief in the ubiquity of writing as early as the beginning of the first millennium B.C.E." I doubt that I have ever believed in the "ubiquity" of anything, much less writing, and certainly would not wish to characterize it as such at the beginning of the Western Zhou. Nevertheless, even then writing was growing ever more widespread. This is not the place to argue the point, and it is certainly not the place to attempt a comprehensive survey of all the sorts of writings currently known from this time, a survey that, given the pace of archaeological discovery in China nowadays, would doubtless be out of date by the time it was published in any event. However, it might suffice to note that such a survey of Western Zhou bronze inscriptions, the primary source upon which I drew when writing *Before Confucius*, was recently given by Li Feng. He describes writing as central to the Zhou government: "Although writing was elite-oriented, its role in Western Zhou society was far more central than marginal or inconsequential. Particularly in the sphere of administration, writing was the indispensable means by which the Zhou government operated, and scribal activities constituted a constant path to political-administrative authority."[9]

Li has demonstrated that writing not only "had a routine place in the operation of the Zhou government," being used in such diverse capacities as official appointments, the validation of property transactions, territorial concessions, lawsuits, and military activities, but it "was also used extensively in local administration beyond the central court."¹⁰

My own preferred style of research, whether in *Before Confucius* or in the present book, might best be described as pointillist, employing specific case studies from which I attempt to draw broader conclusions. While the discussion in *Before Confucius* drew to the extent possible on the paleographic record available at that time, this was largely limited to bronze inscriptions of the Western Zhou period and, to a much lesser extent, to the oracle-bone inscriptions of the earlier Shang dynasty. The twenty-five years since that book was published have witnessed a dramatic change in the type of paleographic sources available. The year after *Before Confucius* was published brought the publication of the Guodian 郭店 manuscripts,¹¹ the first significant discovery of texts from the Warring States period that resembled in type China's traditional classical literature. Since then, many more corpuses of Warring States manuscripts have been unearthed, attracting the attention of scholars the world over, and making possible consideration of a host of new questions, including not least the ways that knowledge was transmitted over the course of China's first millennium of literacy.

The present book, *Writing Early China*, has attempted to take advantage of these new sources to consider these new questions. I have not forgotten by any means my early interest in how the classic literature was created, and so the first four chapters discuss what Shang oracle-bone and especially Western Zhou bronze inscriptions show about record-keeping and literary creativity at that early time. I continue to believe that by the mid- to late Western Zhou—the mid-tenth to the early eighth centuries BCE—the literary record was quite extensive, with a corps of scribes, both at the royal court and among the elite families distributed across the Chinese world of the time, fully capable of producing the kinds of texts seen in the earliest parts of the Chinese classics.

Western Zhou bronze inscriptions also inform several of the chapters that make up the second two-thirds of the book, but here attention turns more and more to the Warring States manuscripts written on bamboo strips. The chapters in this part of the book address very different types of manuscripts, most of them newly unearthed, each reflecting different aspects of the literary and scribal culture of the time. Taken in the aggregate, I am increasingly confident that this new evidence shows that culture to have been wide-ranging; one might even say "supremely literate."

While I would not wish to anticipate any future reviews by Professors Schaberg and Kern,[12] I suspect that they would continue to resist this view of early Chinese literary culture. Since the time of Schaberg's review of my book *Before Confucius*, I have been a very interested reader of both his and Professor Kern's scholarship. Although I have disagreed with many of their viewpoints, I admire the rigor and clarity with which they have argued their position. Over the course of the last twenty years, much of my own scholarship has been stimulated, at least in part, by their arguments, if only to argue against them. None of this is to deny that there was a vibrant and pervasive oral culture in early China. Singers sang, teachers taught, and speakers surely spoke. Nevertheless, it was just as surely the case that writers wrote, and did so in a script that represented the contemporary language, not some sort of secret code shared only by the corps of scribes and the gods. We may not ever see bamboo slips with writing from the Western Zhou period, not to mention from the still earlier Shang. But it is good to keep in mind that it was only some sixty years ago that original bamboo slips from early China were first seen—at least in modern times.[13] With advances in excavation techniques, the next sixty years are likely to turn up many more such writings, at which time we will surely be better able to understand both how they were composed and how they are to be read. The present volume should be viewed as just an interim report, based on some of the presently available evidence. I very much look forward both to new evidence and also to critiques of my own understanding of it.

Most of the chapters in the present book have been previously published over the course of these last twenty years. The versions presented here have been modified somewhat for the purposes of this book: I have unified the conventions concerning presentation and citation; I have updated some of the contents to accord with my present views; I have deleted some sections that were redundant between chapters, retaining the presentation in the chapter where it is most germane to the overall argument; I have deleted most archaic characters, retaining for the most part only current standard characters; and I have deleted many references to secondary sources that were originally supplied for the sake of completeness, but which were not specifically cited. Any reader wishing to consult the more complete published versions of the studies can find them using the citations at the bottom of the first page of each chapter.

Full bibliographic citations of other references will be given at the first mention in the book; thereafter, sources will be cited by author's name, abbreviated title, and page number. Characters will be given for all proper names and terms at the first mention in each chapter, as will reign years and birth and death years for individuals.

This book includes eleven such case studies, treating such diverse early Chinese texts as Western Zhou bronze inscriptions, various types of Warring States bamboo-strip manuscripts, and ending with a Qin period bamboo-strip manuscript. Only the first chapter, "History and Inscriptions," is in the nature of a broader survey, examining both Shang dynasty oracle-bone inscriptions and also a broad array of Western Zhou bronze inscriptions, especially for what they reveal about writing practices over the course of the first several centuries that writing was used in China. I divide the twelve chapters of the book into three major sections: "Inscriptions," led off by the first chapter and including also three case studies of individual bronze inscriptions; "The Classics," in which I examine first two texts, written on bamboo strips, that have some claim to being "scriptures" (shu 書) of the sort that were included in the Shang shu 尚書 Exalted Scriptures, and then follow this with two further chapters discussing recent manuscript evidence related to the Shi jing 詩經 Classic of Poetry; and "Manuscripts," in which I discuss four different manuscripts of different sorts of texts, including especially a study of two manuscripts of a single text copied by one and the same scribe, but certainly based on two different source texts. In this third section, I also examine two different annals, one the Zhushu jinian 竹書紀年 Bamboo Annals and the other the Qin 秦 *Bian nian ji 編年記 *Annalistic Record from Shuihudi 睡虎地, and discuss the important role they played in the development of Chinese historiography.

Part I
Inscriptions

Chapter One

History and Inscriptions

The earliest writing currently attested in China's archaeological inventory comes from about 1200 BCE, during the reign of the Shang dynasty (ca. 1500–1045 BCE) king Wu Ding 武丁 (r. ca. 1220–1190 BCE).[1] This writing comes in two forms: inscriptions carved into turtle shells or ox bones, generally known in the West as oracle-bone inscriptions; and inscriptions cast into bronze vessels, usually referred to as Bronze inscriptions. The oracle-bone inscriptions recorded prayers intended to determine a wide range of future events, including—but by no means limited to—warfare, hunting, agriculture, weather, illness, birth-giving, and so on. Some of these inscriptions also included the king's prognostication of whether the prayer would be successful and/or a post facto record of whether the event had indeed turned out as desired or as predicted. The earliest bronze inscriptions included only the name of the person for whom the bronze vessel, presumably intended to be used in ritual activities (especially

---

This chapter was originally published as "History and Inscriptions, China," in *The Oxford History of Historical Writing, Volume 1: Beginnings to AD 600*, ed. Andrew Feldherr and Grant Hardy (Oxford: Oxford University Press, 2011), 371–93. Contributors to this volume were discouraged from adding citations to secondary scholarship or from using Chinese characters. I reprint the study here without citations but with added Chinese characters. I omit some lengthy bronze inscriptions that will be taken up in other chapters of this book, and introduce certain other changes intended to bring the information up to date or to reflect my current thinking; these latter changes will be noted. Finally, the last section, "The Significance of Inscriptions for the Chinese Historical Tradition," is entirely new.

sacrifices to the ancestors), was cast. Over time the inscriptions evolved to record a momentous occasion to be commemorated, usually a royal award to the person for whom the vessel was made. Both oracle-bone and bronze inscriptions continued to be produced well into the Zhou dynasty (1045–256 BCE), though both sorts of inscriptions underwent important changes. For the purposes of this chapter, I will survey the inscriptional record only through the eighth century BCE, at which time other sorts of written records begin to appear in the historiographical inventory. Indeed, in both the oracle-bone and bronze inscriptions, there is already evidence—both direct and indirect—for other sorts of contemporary written records, presumably written on more perishable materials such as wood or bamboo. Although none of these other sorts of written records has yet been discovered for the period under consideration in this chapter, their importance as historical records may be even greater than the inscriptions presently known.

In China, historians routinely refer to the oracle-bone and bronze inscriptions as the fountainhead of China's long historiographical tradition. In the West, on the other hand, some scholars have recently begun to argue that because both sorts of inscriptions were produced within the context of religious ceremonies, the one in anticipation of events to come and the other in commemoration of events already past, they should not be interpreted as historical records per se. This latter argument is based on the premise that records, just because they are written, do not reflect history *as it really was* but rather were influenced by their context and the subjective intentions of their creators. Important—indeed, essential—as this premise is, it is one that pertains to all written records, not just those pertaining to religious activities, and is well known to historians. With suitable qualifications, the oracle-bone and bronze inscriptions of ancient China can certainly be used both to write, or perhaps better to rewrite, the history of their period and also to divine some of the core historiographical tendencies that would develop in China's later historiographical traditions.

Oracle-Bone Inscriptions

Although the practice of using turtle shells to perform divinations, which would eventually come to be phrased as prayerful statements of one's hopes for the future, continued in China until at least the Qing dynasty (1644–1911), and while there was always some intimation that the kings of the Shang dynasty had also performed such divinations, it was not until nearly the end of the Qing dynasty, in 1899, that the earliest inscribed bones and shells now known were finally unearthed and recognized as records from the Shang dynasty. The story of how the noted antiquarian and paleographer Wang Yirong 王懿榮 (1845–1900) had his servant purchase "dragon bones" from the apothecaries in Beijing in an attempt to treat the malaria from which he was suffering, and how he then recognized the inscriptions on them as examples of China's earliest writing, has now entered into the legend of modern Chinese historiography. The publication in 1903 of Wang's collection of these inscriptions set off a hunt to find where they were buried. This hunt led quickly to the village of Xiaotun 小屯, just outside of the city of Anyang 安陽, in north-central China's Henan Province. This was significant because Anyang was known from historical records as the site of the Shang dynasty's last capital. Xiaotun village would eventually be the first site to be excavated, beginning in 1928, by the Institute of History and Philology of the Republic of China's Academia Sinica, and in 1950 it would become the first archaeological site to be protected by the newly established People's Republic of China. Excavations continue there to the present time. In addition to numerous discoveries of building sites and tombs and manifold examples of the material life of the Shang dynasty, these excavations have also turned up tens of thousands of pieces of inscribed turtle shell and ox bone.

Three discoveries have been particularly important: Pit YH127, excavated in June 1936, which produced seventeen thousand pieces of turtle shell dating to the time of King Wu Ding and bearing inscriptions pertaining to royal activities; an area called "Xiaotun Locus South" (Xiaotun *nandi* 小屯南地), excavated in 1972, with about six thousand pieces of ox bone that proved crucial for arriving at a correct periodization of all Shang oracle-bone inscriptions; and a site at the village of Huayuanzhuang 花園莊, excavated in 1990, that produced almost six hundred intact turtle plastrons bearing inscriptions more or less contemporary with those from YH127, but apparently from a different family or cultural context. Different from all of these Shang oracle bones was the discovery in 1977 at Fengchu 鳳雛 village in Qishan 岐山 county, Shaanxi Province—the heartland of the subsequent Zhou dynasty—of a significant cache of inscribed turtle shells, decisively showing that oracle-bone divination continued to be performed even after that dynasty had overthrown the Shang. Over the course of the last century, the study of these inscriptions has developed into a highly specialized field, generally referred to in the West as oracle-bone studies. Although the specificity (and the difficulty) of the many tens of thousands of individual inscriptions now known make oracle-bone studies a daunting field, their place at the beginning of China's written tradition ensures their historiographical significance. In the following section, I will describe in brief how oracle-bone inscriptions were produced, what they reveal about the history of their period, and what they may show about its historiography.

The Production of Oracle-Bone Inscriptions

In China, the term for oracle-bone inscriptions is *jiaguwen* 甲骨文, "writing on shell and bone," which reflects the material into which this writing was usually inscribed: the plastron (the flat underbelly) of a turtle shell and the scapula bones (the long smooth bones that run from the shoulders down the front legs) of oxen. These materials were probably chosen in the first place for their ritual and mantic significance; the oxen were probably first sacrificed to the ancestors, and turtles—famous for being long-lived—have long been regarded in China as particularly numinous amphibians, able to walk on land but also to descend into the watery depths, the Yellow Springs where the deceased were thought to dwell. However, they both also afforded another advantage: relatively large, smooth surfaces on which to write, a feature that the Shang diviners exploited to the full. Both bones and shells were first prepared with a series of hollows carved and drilled into the rougher of the two sides (in both cases, the side facing inward on the animal), almost but not quite penetrating through to the other side. In the act of divination, a "command" or charge (referred to in later Chinese texts as the *ming* 命) would be addressed to the turtle or bone concerning some future topic, usually quite specific, and then a hot brand was inserted into one of these hollows, causing a stress crack to appear on the reverse side of the shell or bone. These cracks took the shape of ⼘, which in the inscriptions is also the pictograph for the word *bu* "to divine by crack-making" (the pronunciation *bu* is probably also onomatopoeic; the original pronunciation of the word would have been something like *puk).

The king, or in rare cases another officer, would then examine these cracks to determine their auspiciousness for the topic divined. At some later date, an inscription would be carved into the shell or bone beside the relevant crack. These inscriptions would usually include the day on which the crack had been made (indicated as one of a cycle of sixty days used in ancient China) and/or the name of the diviner who had presided over the divination; in oracle-bone studies, this portion of the inscription is generally referred to as the Preface. Then follows the Charge. In the earliest inscriptions known (those of the Shi 師 Group), these were phrased as positive-negative questions, but there are very few of these inscriptions, and they seem to have been produced only in the early years of King Wu Ding's reign. In the most common inscriptions of the Shang dynasty (the Bin 賓 Group), from later in the reign of Wu Ding, the Charge evolved into paired divinations, with a positive statement on the right-hand side of the shell (from the reader's perspective) and a negative statement on the left-hand side. This was perhaps akin to the daisy-picking form of divination "she loves me, she loves me not" performed by small children in America. By the end of the Shang dynasty, these paired Charges gave way to a single, conceptually positive statement ("in the next ten-day week, there will be no misfortune" and "the king will go to XYZ; going and coming there will be no disaster" are by far the two most common statements). In the subsequent Zhou dynasty, divination Charges were routinely concluded with a prayer ("would that there be no misfortune," "would that it can be done," etc.). The Charge could be followed by a Prognostication, usually introduced by the phrase "The king read the crack and said." In a curious theological reversal, whereas prognostications by King Wu Ding were almost always negative or pessimistic (predicting some misfortune), by the end of the Shang dynasty, when the scope of divination had become much reduced, prognostications were invariably positive (simply "The king read the cracks and said: 'Auspicious'"). Finally, in some cases, inscriptions also include a Verification, almost always indicating that the king's prognostication had in fact turned out to be correct. However, it is important to note that the Preface, Prognostication, and Verification are often not present; only the Charge seems to have been essential.

History as Seen in Oracle-Bone Inscriptions

Oracle-bone inscriptions from the reign of Shang king Wu Ding are not only the earliest writing presently known in China, but they also comprise well over half of all Shang dynasty oracle-bone inscriptions, and an even higher percentage of those that would be regarded as historically significant. As mentioned earlier, these inscriptions touch on virtually every aspect of the king's state and personal affairs (indeed, there would seem to be no separation of state and self when it came to the king). The king routinely divined about sacrifices to his ancestors (these inscriptions show that the genealogy of Shang kings preserved in traditional sources was generally correct, with the exception of certain minor details), the weather and the harvest, his travels and hunts, and so on. He also divined about more specific events, including warfare, opening new agricultural lands, establishing new cities, the birth-giving of his numerous wives and consorts, as well as about various aches and pains of his own and other members of the royal family. In a sketch such as this, it is not possible to document all of these royal interests. However, it is possible to show, if only in the most general terms, how inscriptions about warfare can be used to reconstruct something of the history of the period.

According to the very sketchy traditional historical record of the Shang dynasty, Wu Ding's uncle Pan Geng 盤庚 (r. ca. 1250 BCE) first moved the capital to the vicinity of Anyang, and there is certainly ample, if circumstantial, archaeological evidence to support this. There are intimations that in the period immediately preceding this move, the Shang kings had been weak and besieged with a number of problems, and that the move to Anyang was intended to buy them some security. There is better evidence that by the middle period of Wu Ding's reign (the early stage of the period covered by the Bin Group inscriptions, perhaps about 1210 BCE), the Shang were firmly in control of the area around Anyang and stretching west as far as the Taihang 太行 mountain range, south to beyond the Yellow River, and east well into the Shandong peninsula. Oracle-bone inscriptions show Wu Ding allying with various local lords to push Shang hegemony still further west, with numerous inscriptions about Shang attacks on polities located in the southwestern portion of present-day Shanxi Province, and farther north across the Fen 汾 River, perhaps even as far as the north-south stretch of the Yellow River separating the present-day provinces of Shanxi and Shaanxi. Some of these attacks were led by a Shang officer or ally (perhaps a royal son-in-law) named Que 雀, attacking enemies named Fou 缶 and Xuan 亘, among many others.

庚申卜王貞：獲缶。

Crack-making on *gengshen* (day 57), the king affirming: (We) will capture Fou.

貞：雀弗其獲缶。

Affirming: Que might not capture Fou. (*Heji* 6834a)[2]

戊午卜㱿貞：雀追亘㞢獲。

Crack-making on *wuwu* (day 55), Ke affirming: Que will pursue Xuan and have a capture. (*Heji* 6947a)

Although these inscriptions simply record the Shang proposal to carry out these attacks, with very few Verifications to indicate that the attacks were in fact successful, other inscriptions from later in Wu Ding's reign suggest that at least some of the targets of Shang attack, including Fou and Xuan, had subsequently become Shang allies.

己未卜㱿貞：缶其來見王。一月

Crack-making on *jiwei* (day 56), Ke affirming: Fou is expected to come to see the king. First month. (*Heji* 1027a)

壬辰卜貞：亘亡禍。

Crack-making on *renchen* (day 29), affirming: Xuan will not have misfortune. (*Heji* 10184)

In these two inscriptions, the Shang king divined about Fou and Xuan in the way used for friends or allies, seemingly indicating that their previous adversarial relationship with the Shang court had changed.[3]

By the last two reigns of the Shang dynasty, those of Kings Di Yi 帝乙 (r. ca. 1105–1087 BCE) and Di Xin 帝辛 (r. 1086–1045 BCE), Shang military attention seems to have turned closer to home. By then, most inscriptions had become quite routine, as shown by the following example from a series of about 150 inscriptions from a lengthy campaign against the Renfang 人方 people of the Huai 淮 River valley:

癸酉卜在攸，泳貞：王旬亡禍。王來正人方。

Crack-making on *guiyou*, at You, Yong affirming: In the next ten-day week, the king will have no misfortune. It was when the king was coming from attacking the Renfang. (*Heji* 36494)

By comparing the date and place notations in the Prefaces of these inscriptions, it is possible to reconstruct in considerable detail the route and calendar of the army's march. Indeed, from this reconstructed calendar, stretching over as many as nine months, it is also possible to determine that the campaign took place from the autumn of 1077 through the spring of 1076 BCE, a date that can serve as one of the cornerstones of the attempt to reconstruct the political chronology of ancient China.

However, some inscriptions at this time were much longer and much more complex. One of these, probably from the preceding reign of Di Yi (and very possibly from the ninth year of his reign) seems to propose marshalling the many allies to attack one Yan 炎, the ruler of the Yufang 盂方, a state probably located along the Qin 沁 River in southeastern Shanxi Province, not far from the Anyang basin. The inscription is extremely difficult, with numerous expressions that appear in it for the first time (and since it comes toward the very end of the dynasty, also for the last time). I present it, with just a couple of minor revisions, in the translation of David Keightley (1932–2017), the dean of oracle-bone scholars in the West:

丁卯王卜貞：今骨巫九降禍。余其从多田于多伯征盂方伯炎。惠衣翌日步，亡尤。自上下于歔示，余受又又，不蔑戋禍。告于茲大邑商。亡害在毗。 . . . 引吉。在十月，遘大丁翌。

(*Preface:*) On *dingmao* (day 4), the king made cracks and affirmed. (*Secondary Preface:*) Today, the bone and divining stalks have nine times brought down omens (?) (about the following topic:) (*Charge:*) I will ally with the Many Fieldsmen and the Many Elders to march to attack Yan, the leader of Yufang. When (I) end the *yi*-day ritual (I, we, they?) will march to attack (the Yufang); there will be no obstructions.

From the Upper and Lower (Ancestors) to the sacrificial (?) Ancestors, I will receive abundant assistance. (I) will specifically not be struck. (I can) [make an announcement] to (at?) this great settlement Shang that there will be no harm in the omens. (*Prognostication*:) [The king read the cracks and said:] There will be prolonged luck. (*Postface*:) In the tenth month, (at the time in the weekly cycle when, on the day *dingmao*, we) performed the meeting ceremony for the *yi* ritual of Da Ding (the 2nd Shang king). (*Heji* 36511[4])

What must originally have been an even longer inscription, though now unfortunately quite fragmentary,[5] from about the same time, records the results of such an attack (though probably not the same attack; fig. 1.1). As far as we can tell, this is not the record of a divination (though the Charge may be among the portions of the inscription no longer extant), but rather the record of a great victory. Although even many of the characters that remain are susceptible to different readings, it appears that the Shang defeated at least three enemies, capturing their leaders and numerous soldiers and armaments, and then executed the leaders (sacrificing them to royal ancestors) (see fig. 1.1).

Figure. 1.1. *Heji* 36481, *left* front, *right* back. From Guo Moruo 郭沫若, ed. in chief, Hu Houxuan 胡厚宣 ed., *Jiaguwen heji* 甲骨文合集, 13 vols. (N.p.: Zhonghua shuju, 1982).

... 小臣牆比伐，畢危柔 ... 人二十人四，而千五百七十，
繁百 ... 丙、車二丙，󠄀百八十三，函五十、矢 ... 用又白鹿
于大乙，用䖒白印 ... 繁于祖乙，用柔于祖丁。儕曰京易 ...

... Minor Vassal Qiang allied to attack, capturing Rou of Wei ... 24 men, 1,570 of Er, 100+ of Fan ... horses, 2 chariots, 183 ?, 50 quivers of arrows, ... herewith offering a white deer to Da Yi, sacrificing Yin, the leader of Shen ... Fan to Zu Yi, and sacrificing Rou to Zu Ding. Ran said: The capital bestows ... (*Heji* 36481a)

As we will see in the case of bronze inscriptions, there is a general tendency in these inscriptions to accentuate the positive, always proposing to defeat the enemy and, of course, never commemorating their own defeats. In the case of the Shang dynasty, despite the victories won against these enemies, within another generation there would emerge a more formidable enemy, the Zhou, which would bring the dynasty to an end.

Oracle-Bone Inscriptions as Secondary Sources

David Keightley, whose translation of the longest Shang oracle-bone inscription was quoted earlier, began one of his last studies of the general nature of these inscriptions, a study with the provocative title of "The Diviners' Notebooks: Shang Oracle-Bone Inscriptions as Secondary Sources," with the following admission: "I had, for many years, assumed that these divination inscriptions were primary sources—carved into the bones as records of what had actually transpired, shortly after the moment of divination. While this may have been true in some cases, I now believe that a significant number of the divination inscriptions represent a secondary version—sometimes abbreviated or adjusted—of an original record that is now lost to us."[6] Keightley presents various sorts of evidence demonstrating that many inscriptions could not have been carved immediately after the divination, while others refer to specific information from well before the moment of divination. An example of this can be seen in the three inscriptions on an ox scapula from the reign of Wu Ding, the first two of which are nondivinatory in nature (what Chinese scholars term "inscriptions recording events" [*ji shi keci* 記事刻辭]).

癸卯宜于義京羌三人，卯十牛。右

On *guimao* (day 40), (we) *yi*-offered, at Yijing, Qiang (victims), three men, and split open ten cows. On the right (?).

戊戌婦喜示一屯。岳

On *wuxu* (day 35), Lady Xi ritually prepared one (scapula) pair. (Recorded by) Yue.

丁亥卜永貞：王比䤔。

Crack-making on *dinghai* (day 24), Yong affirmed: The king will ally with (Zhi) Guo (on campaign). (*Heji* 390)

Based on the dates in the Prefaces to these three inscriptions, Keightley argued that over one hundred days would have elapsed between the original butchering of the ox and its eventual use in divination; in between, a royal consort apparently prepared the pair of scapula bones so that they could be so used.[7] According to Keightley, given the scores of oxen butchered at the Shang court on at least a weekly basis, the hundreds of scapula bones in use, often concurrently, and the considerable amount of time elapsed, it is unreasonable not to assume that some sort of account book was used to keep track of each individual bone.

A similar conclusion can be drawn from the following single divination inscription, which includes a two-part Verification, the first part twelve days after the initial divination, and the second 175 days later.

[甲]申卜貞：蜀克興生疾。旬生二日[乙]未，蜀允克[興]。百又七十[五]日[戊]寅，蜀亦生疾[乙未夕⭑丙申[蜀]死。

Crack-making on [*jia*]*shen* (day 21), affirmed: Shu will successfully recover from his sickness. On the twelfth day, [*yi*] *wei* (day 32), Shu really did [successfully recover]. On the 17(5)th day, [*wu*]*yin* (day 15), Shu again had a sickness. In the night when [*yiwei*] cleaved into *bingshen* (day 33), [Shu] died. (*Heji* 13753)

Evidence shows that the Preface and Charge as well as the Prognostication and/or Verification of oracle-bone inscriptions were all carved at the same time. That this divination bone remained available for at least 175 days led Keightley to conclude: "Not only does this suggest the presence of some kind of filing system for retrieving the bone over this extended period, but it also suggests that, if the charge and verification had indeed been carved at the same time, the diviner had kept a "notebook" record of his charges and prognostications which the engravers presumably consulted when they finally recorded the divination scenario after Shu's death."[8]

This is a particularly far-reaching conclusion for the beginning of record-keeping, and thus for the beginning of historiography, in China. If it is correct, and I think it surely is, the previously noted argument that in ancient China writing was originally restricted to religious uses would seem to have little basis. The evidence from the oracle-bone inscriptions suggests that already in the Shang dynasty there was a well-developed system for keeping records. As we will see in the following section, this was certainly true of the subsequent Zhou dynasty.

Bronze Inscriptions

Before the discovery of oracle-bone inscriptions, bronze inscriptions were the earliest artifactual writings known in China.[9] These inscriptions, generally cast into the insides of bronze ritual vessels (in the cases of bells, they were cast on the outside; in rare cases, at least in the early period that concerns us here, they could also be carved into the bronze), have been unearthed in China since at least the second century BCE, the discoveries always being regarded as auspicious omens. The archaeological interests of scholars in the Northern Song dynasty (960–1126) resulted in the collection and publication of over one thousand ancient bronze vessels, many of them bearing inscriptions. The linguistic turn in the scholarship of the Qing dynasty subsequently focused even greater attention on the inscriptions as invariant instantiations of ancient writing. With the development of modern archaeology in China in the twentieth century, thousands more bronze vessels, both inscribed and uninscribed, have been excavated from ancient tombs and storage caches. The most recent published collections, up to date through the end of 2015, include over eighteen thousand individual bronze vessels from the Shang and Zhou dynasties that bear inscriptions;[10] new discoveries continue to appear almost every month. As we will see, the inscriptions are wonderfully rich historical sources, especially for the Western Zhou period (1045–771 BCE). And like oracle-bone inscriptions, the bronze inscriptions also contain important evidence for how historical records may have been kept in ancient China.

Although bronze tools appeared as early as 3000 BCE in northwestern China, whence the technology was doubtless imported from areas still further west, present archaeological evidence suggests that bronze casting did not appear in the central area of China proper until the first centuries of the second millennium BCE. One of the first uses of bronze there was for the casting of ritual vessels that had theretofore been made of pottery. None of these early bronzes bears an inscription. However, with the reign of the Shang king Wu Ding, there begin to appear simple inscriptions of the family name or, in rarer cases, the personal name of the individual for whom the vessel was cast. Thus, inscriptions on the numerous bronzes in a tomb excavated in 1975 near the Shang royal palace at Xiaotun allowed it to be identified as that of Fu Hao 婦好 (d. ca. 1195 BCE), known from contemporary oracle-bone inscriptions as one of the three principal consorts of Wu Ding. By the end of the Shang dynasty, inscriptions began to be somewhat longer, usually commemorating an award for some meritorious service, as in the case of the *Xiao Chen Yu zun* 小臣俞尊 (*Jicheng* 5990), better known in the West as the *Brundage Rhino*. Its brief inscription mentions a Shang campaign against the Renfang, though its fifteenth-year date would suggest that this was a different campaign from that recorded in the oracle-bone inscriptions examined in the previous section; perhaps it dates to the reign of King Di Yi, about 1090 BCE.

> 丁巳王省夔京。王賜小臣俞夔貝。惟王來征人方。惟王十祀又五肜日。

> On *dingsi* (day 54), the king inspected the Kui Temple. The king awarded Minor Vassal Yu cowries from Kui. It was when the king was coming from attacking the Renfang. It was the king's fifteenth ritual cycle, the *rong*-sacrifice day.

With the Zhou conquest of Shang some fifty years later, casting inscriptions into bronze vessels became much more prevalent. One such inscription, on the *Li gui* 利簋 (*Jicheng* 4131), commemorates an award made by King Wu of Zhou 周武王 (r. 1049/45–1043 BCE) to an officer named Li 利 just eight days after the conquest.

> 武王征商，惟甲子朝，歲鼎克聞，夙又商。辛未，王在闌師賜又事利金，用作檀公寶尊彝。

> King Wu rectified Shang; it was *jiazi* (day 1) morning. (King Wu) *sui* and *ding* (caldron)-sacrificed and was able to make known that he had routed the Shang. (On) *xinwei* (day 8), the king was at Jian Encampment and awarded Chargé d'affaires Li metal. (Li) herewith makes for the Duke of Zhan this treasured offertory vessel.

While the inscription on the *Li gui* 利簋 is not different in kind from that on the *Xiao Chen Yu zun*, others soon became longer and included new sorts of information. The *He zun* 何尊 (*Jicheng* 6014), dated to the fifth year of a reign that is almost certainly that of King Wu's son, King Cheng 周成王 (r. 1042/35–1006 BCE), includes portions of a royal address to the princes of the newly established dynasty.

> 佳王初遷宅于成周，復禀武王豐，祼自天。在四月丙戌，王誥宗小子于京室，曰：昔在爾考公氏，克弼玟王，肆玟王受茲大命。惟武王既克大邑商，則廷告于天，曰：余其宅茲中或，自之乂民。烏虖，爾有唯小子亡識，視于公氏有爵于天，徹令敬享哉。惠王恭德，欲天順我不敏。王咸誥。何賜貝卅朋，用作㺇公寶尊彝。惟王五祀。

> It was when the king first moved (his) residence to Chengzhou and again received King Wu's abundant blessing from heaven. In the fourth month, *bingxu* (day 23), the king addressed the ancestral young princes in the Capital Chamber, saying: "Formerly, with your deceased-fathers, the elders were capable of assisting King Wen. And so King Wen received this great mandate. It was after King Wu had conquered the great city Shang, then (he) respectfully reported to Heaven, saying: 'I shall reside (in) this central state (and) from it govern the people.' *Wuhu*! Although you are but young princes without experience, look upon the elders' merit with respect to Heaven, and carry

out the commands and reverently make offerings! Help the king make firm his virtue so that Heaven may look favorably upon our indolence." The king completed the address. He was awarded cowries, thirty strands, and herewith makes for Duke X this treasured offertory vessel. It is the king's fifth ritual cycle.

Some generations later, either late in the reign of King Kang 周康王 (r. 1005/03–978) or two generations later still during the reign of King Mu 周穆王 (r. 956–918),[11] a man who had served as the royal tutor cast a vessel with an inscription that is reminiscent of early chapters of the *Shang shu* 尚書 *Exalted Scriptures*, a collection of texts that eventually came to be regarded as one of the Chinese classics; in addition to its historical interest, the inscription on the *Da Yu ding* 大盂鼎 (*Jicheng* 2837) is often studied in histories of Chinese literature and philosophy as one of the earliest exemplars of these genres.

> 唯九月，王在宗周，令盂。王若曰：盂，丕顯文王，受天有大令；在武王嗣文作邦，闢厥匿，敷有四方，畯正厥民。在于御事𢼸 酒，無敢酖；有紫蒸祀，無敢䮸 。故天翼臨子；法保先王，...有四方。我聞殷墜令：惟殷邊侯、甸粵殷正百辟，率肄于酒，故喪師。已！汝昧晨有大服。余惟即朕小學，汝勿尅余乃辟一人。今我惟即型稟于文王正德，若文王令二三正，今余惟令汝盂紹榮，敬雍德堊。敏朝夕入諫，享奔走，畏天威。王曰：而，令汝盂型乃嗣祖南公。王曰：盂，紹夾死司戎，敏諫罰訟；夙夕召我一人烝四方，粵我其遹省先王，受民受疆土。賜汝鬯一卣、冕、衣、巿、舄、車馬。賜乃祖南公旂，用狩。賜汝邦司四伯，人鬲自馭至于庶人六百又五十又九夫。賜夷司王臣十又三伯，人鬲千又五十夫：亟寁遷自厥土。王曰：盂，若敬乃正政，勿廢朕令。盂用對王休，用作祖南公寶。惟王廿又三祀

It was the ninth month; the king was at Ancestral Zhou and commanded Yu. The king approved of saying: "Yu, illustrious King Wen received the Heaven-blessed great mandate. At (the time) King Wu succeeded Wen and made the state, (he) ridded its evil, extended over the four quarters, and governed their people. Among the managers of affairs, he suppressed wine; none dared to get flushed. Having offerings and sacrifices, none dared to get sloshed. Therefore, heaven respectfully looked down and treated (him) as a son, and greatly protected the former kings . . . to have the four quarters. I have heard that Yin's losing the mandate was due to the Yin border lords and fieldsmen and the Yin governors and hundred officials indulging often in wine, and that (they) therefore lost the troops. Yi![12] You early had great service. It was when I attended to my minor learning; you did not press me, your ruler, the one man. Now it is that I assume the model and follow King Wen's upright virtue, and as King Wen commanded the two and three governors, now it is that I command you, Yu, to assist Rong respectfully to secure virtue's continuance. Diligently morning and evening enter to remonstrate, and making offerings hasten to fear heaven's awe." The king said, "Er! (I) command you, Yu, to take as model your ancestral grandfather Nangong." The king said, "Yu, then assist and stand beside me overseeing the Supervisors of the Military. Be diligent and quick in punishments and lawsuits; morning and evening assist me, the one man, to uphold the four quarters and when I inspect the people and borderlands received by the former kings. I award you fragrant wine, one flask; a cap and jacket; kneepads and slippers; and a chariot and horses. (I) award you Grandfather Nangong's pennant; use it in procession. (I) award you states' supervisors, four lords, and human retainers from charioteers as far as common men, 659. (I) award you Yi supervisors and king's vassals, 13 lords, and human retainers, 1,050. Move . . . from their lands." The king said, "Yu, accordingly respect your governance; do not neglect my command." Yu herewith responds to the king's grace, herewith making for grandfather Nangong this treasured *ding*-caldron. It is the king's twenty-third ritual cycle.

By the middle of the Western Zhou period, as the government became organized along more bureaucratic lines, and as royal award and investiture ceremonies became more routine, so too did bronze inscriptions become both more common and, for the most part, more formulaic. An early example of an inscription commemorating an appointment to office, of which there would be hundreds more similar examples over the next century and a half, is that on the *Qiu Wei gui* 裘衛簋 (*Jicheng* 4256), the full date notation of which shows that it was cast in 930 BCE.

惟廿又七年三月既生霸戊戌，王在周，各大室即位。南伯入右裘衛入門立中廷北嚮。王呼內史賜衛巿、朱衡、鑾。衛拜稽首，敢對揚天子丕顯休，用作朕文祖考寶簋。衛其子子孫孫永寶用。

It was the twenty-seventh year, third month, after the growing brightness, *wuxu* (day 35); the king was at Zhou. (He) entered the Great Chamber and assumed position. The Elder of Nan entered and at the right of Qiu Wei entered the gate, standing in the center of the court facing north. The king called out to the Interior Scribe to award Wei purple kneepads, a scarlet demi-circlet, and a jingle bell. Wei bowed and touched his head to the ground, and daring in response to extol the Son of Heaven's illustrious beneficence, herewith makes (for) my cultured grandfather and deceased-father (this) treasured tureen; may Wei's sons' sons and grandsons' grandsons eternally treasure and use (it).

The formulaic nature of the *Qiu Wei gui* inscription does not by any means reflect all later Western Zhou bronze inscriptions. Three inscribed bronzes (the *Hu gui* 㝬簋 [Jicheng 4317] and two *Hu zhong* 㝬鐘 [Jicheng 260, 358]) were cast for a Zhou king, King Li 厲王 (r. 857/52–842/27 BCE), and their inscriptions are addressed in the personal name of the king. The longest inscription known from the period, on the famous *Mao Gong ding* 毛公鼎 (Jicheng 2841), records an address by King Xuan 宣王 (r. 827/25–782 BCE), the penultimate king of the dynasty, to his "uncle" bemoaning some of the troubles that beset the onset of his reign. Two notable inscriptions, on the *Shi Qiang pan* 史牆盤 (Jicheng 10175) and the *Qiu pan* 逑盤,[13] present sketch histories of the dynasty (as well as of the families of the two men for whom the vessels were cast), in the first case only through the reign of Qiang's king, King Gong 共 (r. 917/15–900 BC), but in the second case very nearly to the end of the dynasty. Several inscriptions record court cases between individuals and, in one case (the *San shi pan* 散氏盤 [Jicheng 10176]), between two warring territories,[14] while many others commemorate marriages.

As can be imagined, success in battle was a frequent occasion for royal awards, and the inscriptions commemorating these awards often recount memorable scenes of battle. The inscription on the *Jin Hou Su bianzhong* 晉侯蘇編鐘, arrayed across a double chime of sixteen bells, has a particularly dramatic effect.[15]

惟王卅又三年，王親遹省東域南域。正月既生霸戊午，王步自宗周。二既既望癸卯，王入各成周。二月既死霸壬寅，王償往東。三月方死霸，王至于蕢，分行，王親令晉侯：率乃師左洀氵蒦北洀...，伐夙夷。晉侯蘇折首百又廿，執訊廿又三夫。王至于釁城。王親遠省師。王至晉侯蘇師，王降自車，立南嚮。王親令晉侯蘇：自西北隅敦伐釁城。晉侯率厥亞旅小子、或人先陷入，折首百，執訊十又一夫。王至淖列。淖列夷出奔。王令晉侯蘇率大室小臣車僕從，捕逐之。晉侯折首百又一十，執訊廿夫；大室小臣車僕折首百又五十，執訊六十夫。王惟反，歸在成周。公族整師宮。六月初吉戊寅旦，王各大室即位。王呼膳夫召召晉侯蘇入門立中廷。王親賜駒四匹。蘇拜稽首，受駒以出，返入，拜稽首。丁亥旦，王御于邑伐宮。庚寅旦王各大室。司工揚父入右晉侯蘇。王親儕晉侯蘇䥯鬯一卣、弓矢百、馬四匹。蘇敢揚天子丕顯魯休，用作元穌揚鐘，用卲各前文人。前文人其嚴在上，翼在下，豐_泉_，降余多福，蘇其萬年無疆，子子孫孫永寶茲鐘。

It was the king's thirty-third year; the king personally went on procession inspecting the eastern regions and southern regions. In the first month, after the growing brightness, *wuwu* (day 55), the king walked from Zongzhou. In the second month, after the full moon, *guimao* (day 40 [sic]), the king entered into Chengzhou. In the second month, after the dying brightness, *renyin* (day 39 [sic]), the king continued going to the east. In the third month, at the dying brightness, the king arrived at Huan and divided his ranks. The king personally commanded Su, Lord of Jin: "Lead your armies leftward crossing X and to the north crossing . . . to attack the Su Yi." Su, Lord of Jin, cut off 120 heads and captured 23 prisoners. The king arrived at Xun Citadel. The king in person inspected the armies from a distance. The king arrived at the Lord of Jin's camp. The king descended from his chariot and standing facing south personally commanded Su, Lord of Jin: "From the northwest corner ram and attack Xun Citadel." Su, Lord of Jin, led his Secondary Legion, the Young Nobility, and the spearmen to be the first to go down and enter, cutting off one hundred heads and capturing eleven prisoners. The king arrived at Naolie. The Yi of Naolie went out fleeing. The king commanded Su, Lord of Jin: "Lead the Grand Chamber's Minor Vassals and charioteers to follow and catch and drive them out." The

Lord of Jin cut off 110 heads and captured 20 prisoners; the Grand Chamber's Minor Vassals and charioteers cut off 150 heads and captured 60 prisoners.

It was when the king was going back, returning to Chengzhou. The noble kinsmen put in order the Military Palace. In the sixth month, first auspiciousness, *wuyin* (day 15), at dawn the king entered the Grand Chamber and assumed position. The king called out to Provisioner Ke to summon Su, Lord of Jin, to enter the gate and stand in the middle of the court. The king personally awarded four colts. Su bowed and touched his head to the ground, and accepted the colts in exiting. He went back and entered, bowed and touched his head to the ground.

On *dinghai* (day 24), at dawn the king presided at the City Attack Palace. Supervisor of Works Yangfu entered at the right of Su, Lord of Jin. The king personally presented Su, Lord of Jin, with one bucket of black millet sweet wine, a bow and one hundred arrows, and four horses.

Su dares to extol the Son of Heaven's illustriously beautiful beneficence, herewith making these prime concordant *yang* bronze bells with which to summon the past cultured men; may the past cultured men be strict on high and respected below, abundantly sending down on me much good fortune. May Su for ten thousand years without bound have sons' sons and grandsons' grandsons eternally to treasure these bells.

These bells, used by Su 蘇, the lord of the important state of Jin 晉, then located in the southwestern part of present-day Shanxi Province (the area fought over by the Shang during the reign of King Wu Ding), are as interesting for their archaeological provenance as for their inscription. Throughout the 1980s, archaeologists from Peking University and from the Shanxi Provincial Institute of Archaeology had been engaged in excavations of a giant cemetery just outside of the Jin capital, located at present-day Tianma-Qucun 天馬曲村. They stopped just before reaching a separate cemetery area containing the tombs of the state's rulers and their consorts. Unfortunately, late in 1992 or early 1993, tomb robbers, doubtless attracted by the efforts of the archaeologists, found this cemetery first and opened several of the tombs. In the case of the tomb of Su, otherwise known by his posthumous reign title of Lord Xian of Jin

晉侯獻,[16] numerous inscribed bronzes, including the fourteen largest bells of the set translated earlier, soon appeared on the Hong Kong antiques market. After the Shanghai Museum bought the bells and publicized the find, archaeologists secured this second cemetery and reopened Su's plundered tomb. They found therein the two smallest bells of the second chime, as well as other vessels and artifacts that had been missed by the robbers. This archaeological provenance was particularly important in the case of the inscriptions on the bells because, unlike almost all other Western Zhou bronze inscriptions, these were carved into preexisting bells. Before the discovery in situ of the two smallest bells, some had suspected that this extraordinary inscription was a modern forgery.

With the fall of the Western Zhou in 771 BC, Jin and other states that had been established at the beginning of the dynasty by relatives of the early Zhou kings (the first Lord of Jin was a younger brother of King Cheng of Zhou) became essentially independent (many of them were doubtless semi-independent even before the fall of the western capital). By the end of the eighth century BC, the Zhou kings, newly installed in an eastern capital at present-day Luoyang 洛陽, Henan, had virtually no de facto power. Bronze vessels from this period come more and more to reflect regional tendencies. Fortunately or unfortunately, because this later period is far better documented in the traditional historical record than is the Western Zhou, the bronze inscriptions from this time are often regarded as having relatively less historical value.

Western Zhou History as Seen in Bronze Inscriptions

The Western Zhou period is usually regarded as the high tide of bronze inscriptions. This is due in large part to the great number and intrinsic interest of its bronze inscriptions but is doubtless due in some part too to the relative paucity of other historical sources from the period. Events surrounding the Zhou conquest of Shang and the establishment of the dynasty are reasonably well represented in the traditional historical record, as are events from the last two or three reigns of the dynasty, before the western capital was sacked. It almost goes without saying that the narratives of these respective periods have a strong didactic purpose to show, on the one hand, that it was through the peculiar virtue of the early kings that the dynasty came to be established and through the moral failings of the later kings that it fell. The bronze inscriptions from the period are by no means immune to this subjective view of history; indeed, in some ways they are even more prone always to reflect in the most favorable light the people for whom the vessels were cast and the Zhou kings, who were their patrons. Nevertheless, because inscribed vessels were cast throughout all periods of the dynasty, including those not well represented in other sources, the inscriptions offer an indispensable contemporary view of affairs.

Inscribed bronze vessels from the first century or so of the Western Zhou have been discovered all over northern China. While there is of course a preponderance of vessels from the northwestern province of Shaanxi, which was the homeland of the Zhou people and the site of its primary capital, numerous bronzes have also been found in areas to the east—from Hebei in the northeast to the Shandong peninsula along the eastern seaboard and throughout the central province of Henan. These bronzes were by and large cast by the founders of the colonies that the Zhou established there to rule the newly conquered indigenous peoples: the descendants of Shao Gong Shi 召公奭, a son of King Wu and—with King Cheng and the Duke of Zhou 周公—one of the triumvirate that consolidated Zhou rule after Wu's death, who ruled Yan 燕 in the vicinity of Beijing; Bo Qin 伯禽, the eldest son of the Duke of Zhou and the first ruler of Lu 魯 at Qufu 曲阜, Shandong; Kangshu Feng 康叔封, another son of King Wu, who was deputed to rule the capital region of the defeated Shang dynasty; and so on. However, by the middle of the tenth century BCE, there is a noticeable falloff in the number of bronze vessels that have been discovered in these areas. This may have been a consequence of one of the defining events of the early Western Zhou.

In 957 BCE, King Zhao 昭王 (r. 977/75–957 BCE), seeking to extend Zhou control into hitherto unconquered areas of the south, apparently met with a disastrous defeat. Traditional historical sources also mention this defeat, although usually in euphemistic terms. Numerous bronze inscriptions were also cast during the period leading up to the climax of the campaign and allude to it in positive terms. The two contemporary sketch histories also attempt to portray it in the most favorable of lights. But it seems clear that King Zhao not only lost his own life, but he also decimated the Zhou standing armies. This seems to have been the end of the Zhou expansionist impulse. From the next hundred years or so of Zhou history, bronze vessels have been found primarily in the Zhou capital region.[17]

King Zhao was succeeded by his son, King Mu, a ruler with a rather ambiguous profile in the traditional historical record. For instance, he is praised for having initiated a systematic law code but condemned for being unable to control his people solely through the force of his own personal virtue. Whatever the value of these traditional evaluations, bronze vessels from his reign do attest to a thoroughgoing reform of government and social institutions. One inscribed vessel, the *Li fangyi* 盠方彝 (*Jicheng* 9899), from the early years of his reign appears to commemorate the reorganization of the Zhou military, placing a member of an old Zhou family in supreme command of both the western and eastern armies.

唯八月初吉，王各于周廟，穆公右盠，立于中廷北嚮。王冊令尹賜盠赤市、幽衡、攸勒，曰：用司六師王行、參有司：司土、司馬、司工。王令盠曰：兼司六師眔八師執。盠拜稽首，敢對揚王休，用作朕文祖益公寶尊彝。盠曰：天子不叚不其萬年 / 保我萬邦。盠敢拜稽首曰：烈朕身，賡朕先寶事。

It was the eighth month, first auspiciousness; the king entered into the Zhou Temple. Duke Mu at the right of Li stood in the center of the courtyard, facing north. The king in writing commanded Yin to award Li red kneepads, a black girdle pendant, and bit and bridle, saying: "Herewith supervise the royally enacted Three Supervisors of the Six Armies: the Supervisor of Lands, Supervisor of the Horse, and Supervisor of Work." The king commanded Li, saying: "Concurrently supervise the Six Armies' and the Eight Armies' seals." Li bowed and touched his head to the ground, daring in response to extol the king's beneficence, herewith making for my cultured grandfather Yi Gong this treasured offertory vessel. Li says: "The Son of Heaven is very blessed and very well founded, for ten thousand years protecting our ten thousand states." Li dares to bow and touch his head to the ground, saying: "Array my person to continue my predecessors' treasured service."

It was also during this reign that court audiences came to be standardized, as seen in the *Qiu Wei gui* inscription translated above. This seems to bespeak a growing bureaucratization of the government; whereas a relative handful of particularly important figures seemed to act in various capacities at the beginning of the dynasty (as seen, for instance, in the *Da Yu ding* inscription), now officers were appointed to specific posts with more or less well-defined responsibilities.

Another manifestation of these important reforms is found in the bronze vessels themselves. Whereas sets of ritual vessels from the early Western Zhou were quite small and prominently feature wine vessels, beginning about the time of King Mu vessels came to be cast in sets, with multiple versions of the principal meat and grain vessels graduated according to size. Significantly, wine vessels all but disappear from the archaeological inventory. Numerous modern scholars have called attention to this feature, with Jessica Rawson giving a particularly compelling analysis of the ritual reform it reflects. According to Rawson, whereas rituals with sets of vessels from the early Western Zhou could be performed conjointly by all-male members of a family, the proliferation and nature of vessels after the mid–Western Zhou Ritual Reform suggests that rituals came to be performed by one or more ritual specialists, with the family members looking on as spectators.[18] It is likely that this ritual reform was influenced to at least some extent by the importation of chime bells from south China; these also appear for the first time in Zhou during the reign of King Mu. Chime bells can only produce music when arrayed in sets graduated according to size; this may explain the new vogue in producing grain and meat vessels in graduated sets. And a certain expertise is required to play chime bells; this too may explain the apparent professionalization of the corps of ritualists. However this reform took place, and it was surely a gradual development that took as much as a century to reach its mature manifestation, there can be no doubt that the reign of King Mu brought about a manifold change in the Zhou state.

King Mu's reign was followed, apparently without incident, by that of his eldest son, known by the title of King Gong. However, something seems to have gone awry during the reign of his grandson, King Yih 懿王 (r. 899/97–873 BCE). In the traditional historical record, we learn that King Yih was anomalous for being succeeded not by his son—at least not immediately—but rather by his uncle, yet another son of King Mu; this was King Xiao 孝王 (r. 882?–866). Other statements hint at other troubles. Poets are said to have begun to compose critiques of the royal court, while an annalistic history mentions that King Yih moved his capital to a place that translates as Waste Mound (Feiqiu 廢丘). This is a period that is particularly well represented with inscribed bronze vessels. Indeed, in some ways it is too well represented. For instance, there are a great many inscriptions that bear full date notations: the year of reign, the month, the phase of the moon, and the name of the day in the traditional Chinese cycle of sixty. Unfortunately, there appears to be no way to accommodate all of these dates in a single regnal calendar, and many attempts to reconstruct the absolute chronology of the Western Zhou have foundered on this evidence. David Nivison (1923–2014), who devoted many years to studying this chronology, seems to have been the first to suggest that King Yih's problems may have led to his exile—with his uncle reigning in the capital—and arrogating the title of king, such that there were two "kings" reigning simultaneously.[19] Support for this insight may have now surfaced in the form of one of the two bronze inscriptions that provide histories of the dynasty: the *Qiu pan*. In it, King Yih is treated in the same way as King Li, another king who was forced into exile, with another ruler—Gong Bo He 共伯和—in the capital. Moreover, King Xiao is praised for having "again succeeded in the Zhou country" (又成于周邦).

Whatever the actual historical situation was at this time, the Zhou ruling house continued to decline for another two generations, through the eventual reign of King Yih's own son, King Yi 夷王 (r. 865–858 BCE), and then that of King Li, whose own reign, as aforementioned, was cut short. After King Li died in exile, his own son, to be known as King Xuan, was installed as king. King Xuan went on to a very long reign, forty-six years (r. 827/25–782 BCE), and is credited—at least for the beginning of his reign—with restoring the fortunes of the Zhou government. Scores of lengthy bronze inscriptions from his reign attest to his active involvement in many aspects of this restoration, from launching military campaigns to both the northwest and southeast to fend off incursions from enemies there, to restructuring the market system around the eastern capital at Luoyang, to more philosophical discussions about the nature of government. It seems that it was he who, in his thirty-third year of reign, personally led the months-long campaign described in the *Jin Hou Su bianzhong* inscription translated earlier as far to the east as Shandong. This inscription describes the campaign as a victory over enemies there. However, correlations with the traditional historical record suggest at least the possibility that it was also intended to meddle in the internal politics of one of the important Zhou colonies there, Lu 魯. This is but one hint that toward the end of King Xuan's reign royal control began to deteriorate once again. The dynasty survived for less than a quarter of a century after this campaign before its western capital was overrun and King Xuan's son, known as King You 幽 (r. 781–771 BCE), ended as the last king of the period.

Bronze Inscriptions as Tertiary Documents

In the same way that David Keightley has recognized that oracle-bone inscriptions are secondary documents, based on original records written on some other medium, so too did Herrlee Creel (1905–1994), one of the pioneers of bronze inscription studies in the West, long ago note that bronze inscriptions are based primarily on written commands given out in the course of the royal audience.[20] A good example of this is found in the introductory portion of the *Forty-Second Year Qiu ding* 逑鼎 inscription, one of three lengthy inscriptions sponsored by a person named Qiu 逑 toward the end of King Xuan's lengthy reign. While these inscriptions will be the focus of chapter 3, their significance for historiography warrants consideration here as well, even if only briefly.[21]

After indicating the date and place of the audience, and who Warden Qiu's sponsor had been (Supervisor of Works San 司工散), the prefatory paragraph goes on to state:

尹氏受王釐書。王呼史淢冊釐逑。

Yinshi received the king's award document. The king called out to Scribe Huo to make the award to Qiu in writing.

Then, at the end of the king's address, the inscription continues:

逑拜稽首，受冊釐以出。

Qiu saluted and touched his head to the ground, received the award slips, and went out.

It is clear that the intervening text, introduced with the words "The king approved of saying" (*wang ruo yue* 王若曰) represents the royal "command document" (*ming shu* 命書) written on bamboo or wooden slips.

Two other inscribed bronzes cast for Warden Qiu provide further insight into the compositional process of bronze inscriptions. The first of these, known as the *Qiu pan* 逑盤, has been alluded to earlier. It provides a sketch history of virtually the entire Western Zhou period, from the founding of the dynasty by Kings Wen (d. 1050 BC) and Wu down to the reigning Son of Heaven, King Xuan. Interspersed with brief comments on the achievements of the various Zhou kings are praises of Qiu's own ancestors, members of the Shan family. For the purpose of the discussion of bronze inscriptions as historical records here, I cite just the king's command to Qiu.

王若曰：述，丕顯文武膺受大令，匍有四方。則繇惟乃先聖祖考夾召先王，爵堇大令。今余惟堊乃先聖祖考申重乃令，令汝胥榮兌司四方虞林，用宮御。

The king approved of saying: "Qiu, illustrious (Kings) Wen and Wu received the great mandate and extended it over the four quarters. Then because it was your past wise ancestors and deceased-father who accompanied and assisted the past kings to have merit and care with the great mandate, now it is that I recall your past wise ancestors and deceased-father and extend and increase your command, commanding you to assist Rong Dui, and concurrently to supervise the four quarters' game and forests, to be used for the palace's supply."

Although not stated in this particular inscription, this command would have been given to Qiu in writing, written on bamboo slips, as made explicit in the *Forty-Second Year Qiu ding* inscription quoted earlier. Moreover, this command document was apparently a copy of a document preserved at the royal court. This is clear from yet another vessel with a lengthy inscription made by Qiu one year after his *Forty-Second Year Qiu ding*. This vessel, usually referred to as the *Forty-Third Year Qiu ding*, commemorated Qiu's promotion to be in charge of people at a place called Li 歷. The command document quoted in its inscription in turn quotes the command made previously to Qiu and commemorated by the *Qiu pan*.

王若曰：述，丕顯文武膺受大令，匍有四方，則繇佳乃先聖考夾召先王，爵堇大令，莫周邦。肆余弗忘聖人孫子。昔余既令汝胥榮兌。兼司四方虞林，用宮御。今余惟堊乃先祖考有爵于周邦，申重乃令，令汝官司歷人。

The king approved of saying: "Qiu, illustrious (Kings) Wen and Wu received the great mandate and extended it over the four quarters. Then it was because of your prior wise deceased-father's assisting the prior king to have merit and care with the great mandate that they stabilized the Zhou state. And so I have not forgotten the wise men's grandson. *Formerly, I had already commanded you to assist Rong Dui, and concurrently to supervise the four quarters' game and forests, to be used for the palace's supply.* Now it is that I recall your prior ancestors and deceased-father's having had merit in the Zhou state and extend and increase your command, commanding you to officiate over and supervise the men of Li."

The command continues with the king's exhortation that Qiu carry out his duties faithfully, even at the pain of death, before then awarding him an extensive set of gifts, followed by another exhortation that Qiu "respectfully from morning to night not neglect my command" (敬夙夕勿廢朕令). The inscription then says:

逨拜稽首，受冊佩以出，反入堇圭。

Qiu saluted and touched his head to the ground, received the award slips and suspended them in his sash to go out; returning, he entered and presented a jade tablet.

It is clear that the royal secretariat, charged by the king to produce a new command to Qiu, went into the royal archives and consulted the command given to him previously, quoting it verbatim in the new command document. From this, we can infer that they would have produced two copies of this new command document, one for the royal archives again, presumably placed in Qiu's dossier, and one given to Qiu. In turn Qiu had this copy copied into the inscription on the *Forty-Third Year Qiu ding* made for him, making that inscription not even a secondary document but rather a tertiary document.

The Significance of Inscriptions for the Chinese Historical Tradition

The oracle-bone and bronze inscriptions of Bronze Age China deserve the attention of historians not only because they are the earliest extant examples of writing in China's long literary tradition, but because they also provide enticing glimpses of still more writing that lay behind them. When David Keightley writes, "Shang writing was not limited to the oracle bones, it was not limited to the king's use, nor was it limited to the Xiaotun area,"[22] or when Herrlee Creel wrote, "We simply have to accept the fact that the Chous were a people who liked to write books,"[23] they have highlighted a significant feature not only of ancient Chinese statecraft but also of the development of historiography in ancient China. Both of these eminent historians saw in their respective sources the existence of royal archives, a supposition that the most recent discoveries of bronze inscriptions have fully confirmed. We can surmise with Keightley that the Shang archives held at least simple records of the oxen sacrificed and divinations performed on behalf of individuals, while the Zhou archives certainly contained copies of the thousands of command documents quoted in bronze inscriptions from the period. How much more the archives contained we can only imagine. To me, it is not at all unreasonable to suppose that the Zhou archives, at least, contained copies of the sorts of royal addresses found in the *Shang shu*.[24]

One chapter in the *Yi Zhou shu* 逸周書 *Leftover Zhou Scriptures*, entitled "Chang mai" 嘗麥 "Tasting the Wheat," purports to be an address by King Cheng of Zhou to a Great Governor (*Da zheng* 大正) to put in order a penal scripture (*xing shu* 刑書). While the contents of the *Yi Zhou shu* are particularly complicated, with a few chapters probably dating more or less to the period to which they purport to date (i.e., the Western Zhou) but with most chapters being from the later Springs and Autumns or even Warring States periods, the "Chang mai" reads very much like a contemporary bronze inscription, at least in large part, and may well reflect Western Zhou scribal practices. It concludes with the record:

太史乃藏之于盟府以為歲典。

The Grand Secretary then stored it in the Covenant Repository to serve as a canon of the years.[25]

The "Covenant Repository" (*Meng fu* 盟府) is identified in later sources as the archive of the Zhou court. It stands to reason that a text such as the "Chang mai," with a discussion of penal canons, would be stored in the Zhou archive.

There is evidence from a few centuries later that other royal addresses were certainly in the Zhou archive. The *Zuo zhuan* 左傳 *Zuo Tradition*, at the fourth year of Lord Ding of Lu 魯定公 (r. 509–495 BCE; i.e., 506 BCE), includes a long speech by one Invocator Tuo 祝佗 of Wèi 衛 that the recent translation by Stephen Durrant, Wai-yee Lee, and David Schaberg introduces as "a dazzling speech on historical precedents that contains much information on early Western Zhou history, including the founding of Lu, Wei, and Jin." The speech is too lengthy to quote in its entirety, but it certainly deserves extended consideration. Upon the occasion of an interstate meeting at Shaoling 召陵, convened by the Lord of Jin 晉, the Lord of Wèi objected to Wèi being ranked after Cai 蔡 in terms of protocol since the founding ancestor of Cai was an elder brother of the founding ancestor of Wèi. Invocator Tuo argued that the virtue of the ancestors should be paramount, in which case the founder of Cai would be outranked by the founders of both the states of Lu 魯 and Wèi, as well as by Tangshu 唐叔, the founder of Jin, even though all three of those founders were "younger brothers" (*shu* 叔). In making this argument, he apparently drew on the original "command scriptures" (*mingshu* 命書), that is, appointment documents, for these three different states, contrasting them with that for Cai. He concluded by quoting a more recent appointment document, explicitly said to be stored in the "Zhou Repository" (*Zhou fu* 周府). I will here quote just the entirety of the appointment of the Duke of Zhou 周公, as well as the mention of the other four documents.

分魯公以大路、大旂，夏后氏之璜，封父之繁弱，殷民六族，條氏、徐氏、蕭氏、索氏、長勺氏、尾勺氏，使帥其宗氏，輯其分族，將其類醜，以法則周公。用即命于周。是使之職事于魯，以昭周公之明德。分之土田陪敦、祝、宗、卜、史，備物、典策，官司、彝器；因商奄之民，命以《伯禽》而封於少皞之虛。
　　…命以《康誥》而封於殷虛。
　　…命以《唐誥》而封於夏虛。
　　…其命書云：「王曰：胡！無若爾考之違王命也！」
　　…其載書云：「王若曰：晉重、魯申、衛武、蔡甲午、鄭捷、齊潘、宋王臣、莒期。」藏在周府，可覆視也。

To the Lord of Lu was allotted a grand chariot, a grand banner, the jade half disk of the Xia ruling line, the Fanruo bow of Fengfu, and six houses of Yin people, the Tiao, Xu, Xiao, Suo, Changshao, and Weishao lineages. These six houses were made to lead those who shared their ancestral lineages, to gather together their collateral houses, and to guide their many dependents in following the Duke of Zhou's models. With that, the Lord of Lu assumed his command from the Zhou ruling house, and in this way he was appointed to take up his duties in Lu, in order to display the notable virtue of the Duke of Zhou. To him were allotted lands and fields and dependents, invocators, lineage ritualists, diviners, scribes, regalia, statutory documents, officials, and sacrificial vessels. Taking the people of Shangyan as his own soldiers, our lord was given his command in the "Elder Qin" and enfeoffed at the Mound of Shaohao.

... He was given his command in the "Proclamation to Kang" and enfeoffed at the Mound of Yin.

... He was given his command in the "Proclamation to Tang" and enfeoffed at the Mound of Xia.

... The command scripture said, "The king said, 'Hu! Do not, like your father, defy the king's command!'"

... The covenant scripture begins, "The king said, 'Chong of Jin, Shen of Lu, Shuwu of Wei, Jiawu of Cai, Jie of Zheng, Pan of Qi, Wangchen of Song, Qi of Ju.'" They are stored in the Zhou repository and can be consulted.[26]

In a recent discussion of this passage, David Schaberg, one of the translators of the *Zuo zhuan*, argues that while the "Announcement to Kang" "the *Zuo zhuan* authors had in mind was similar or identical to the *Shu* chapter of the same name," nevertheless, "the speaker does not refer to it or the others as *Shu* chapters or indeed as written texts of any sort and does not aver that they are preserved in an archive."[27] Instead, he suggests that a document such as this was created well after the time of its purported announcement by "stitch[ing] together in memory, and ultimately in transcription" "various remembered components of a famous address."[28] Insisting on the primacy of speech over writing almost certainly reverses the process of composition of not only the "Announcement to Kang" and other *shu* documents but also of the "command scripture" to Hu, the "covenant scripture" of the lords of the various states, and indeed the investiture inscriptions seen on bronze vessels. Sarah Allan has succinctly summarized how these texts were composed:

> We may hypothesize, then, that *shu* were originally the scripts of speeches composed for the purpose of delivery by

officials on behalf of the ruler or high minister in a formal ceremony. Since they were the scripts of speeches delivered by someone other than the person to whom the words were attributed, they were necessarily written down in advance of the performance. The expression *ruo yue*, "seemingly said," marked the fact of their performance by someone other than the purported author; the king or minister "seemed" to say them, but did not actually voice them. Presumably a copy would have been kept in the royal archives, with a record as to the date, place and circumstances of delivery, and the bronze inscriptions indicate that a bamboo slip manuscript of the speech was given to the person to whom the speech was addressed.[29]

Indeed, I would suggest instead that the lists of regalia and dependents seen in the first three command scriptures (and especially in the "Elder Qin" and "Proclamation to Kang") are precisely the sorts of records that would have been put in writing. They were doubtless originally read out orally, but this is not how they were conceived or how they were preserved. As noted earlier, Western Zhou bronze inscriptions show clearly that the text of the appointment document, written on bamboo slips, was handed to the recipient at the end of the investiture ceremony. If that were true of something as routine as the *Qiu pan*'s command to Qiu that he "assist Rong Dui, and concurrently to supervise the four quarters' game and forests, to be used for the palace's supply," I think we can assume that something as momentous as the command establishing a state would be put in writing. The recently unearthed *Feng Xu zhi ming* 封鄦之命 *Command Enfeoffing Xu*, one of the Warring States manuscripts in the collection of Tsinghua University, provides a particularly good example of just such a command document. Unfortunately, the text's first slip is missing, but the remainder of the text is complete, including a still more extensive list of regalia presented to the first lord of Xu 鄦/許.

. . . 越在天下。故天勸之無斁，饗振厥德，膺受大命，允尹四方。則惟汝呂丁，肇牽文王，毖光厥烈。武王司明型，釐厥獻，祇事上帝，桓桓丕敬，嚴將天命。亦惟汝呂丁，扞輔武王，勴敦殷紂，咸成商邑。□□余小子。余惟彊文王明型，非敢荒怠，畏天之非忱，冊羞哲人，審民之若否。今朕永念乃勳，命汝侯于許。汝惟臧耆爾獻，虔恤王家，簡乂四方不虞，以勤余一人。

錫汝蒼珪、秬鬯一卣、路車、䯼衡、玉𨱑、鑾鈴、素旂、朱軒轐、馬四匹、鋚勒、氀毡羅纓、鉤、膺、鑣、弁、匴。贈爾薦彝、盉□、燧珧，龍𦨴、璉、鐘、鐙、𣝓、勺、盤、鑒、鎣、𠨐、雕禁、鼎、簋、鈗、鎥、閣。

王曰：「於呼，丁，戒哉！余既監于殷之不若。稚童在憂，靡念非常。汝亦惟就章爾慮，祇敬爾猷，以永厚周邦。勿廢朕命，經嗣世享。」

... and in all under heaven. Therefore, Heaven encouraged them tirelessly, enjoying and arousing their virtue, to accept and receive the Great Mandate, truly ruling the four quarters. Then it was you Lü Ding, who began helping King Wen, carefully radiating his valor. King Wu inherited the Bright Model, and regulated his plan, reverently serving God on High, vigorously and greatly respectful, sternly upholding the Mandate of Heaven. It was also you Lü Ding, who guarded and assisted King Wu, hitting and striking Shou of Yin, completely pacifying the Shang city, ... me the young son. It is that I extend King Wen's bright model, not daring to be wastefully dilatory, but awed by Heaven's unreliability, make presentation in writing to the wise man to examine the people's approval or not. Now I eternally recall your merit, commanding you to be lord in Xu. It is that you should well present your plans, assiduously care for the royal house, and thoroughly govern the four quarters' unsubmitted, in order to assist me the One Man.

I award you a green scepter and one bucket of black millet sweet wine; a highway carriage with jade-ornamented yoke and jade tailboard, rein bells and plain pennant, maroon shaft tip, four horses with metal-studded bridles and blankets with net tassels, snaffles, girth straps, bits, headpieces, and blinders. I grant you serving vessels: a serving tray ..., a presentation platter, a chalice, ... a deep pot, a dragon *li*-caldron, a *lian*-casserole, a *guan*-jar, a *zheng*-soup bowl, a ladle, a spoon, a *pan*-basin, a *jian*-reflecting-basin, a *ying*-pitcher, a *dou*-decanter, an engraved *jin*-stand, a *ding*-caldron, a *gui*-tureen, a *gong*-sauce-server, a *dao*-cannister, and a storage chest.

The king said, "*Wuhu*, Ding, be on guard, indeed. I have reflected on Yin's disapprobation. I am young and worried, never not recalling the inconstancy. It is that you also should extensively display your deliberations and reverently respect your counsel, in order eternally to strengthen the Zhou country. Do not discard my command, but always pass this on for generations to enjoy.[30]

Whether this command scripture dates to the beginning of the Western Zhou, as it purports to do, or if, as seems more likely, it was composed toward the end of the Western Zhou or even into the early Springs and Autumns period,[31] it was most certainly written, as stated explicitly in its opening portion (*ce xiu zhe ren* 冊羞哲人 "make presentation in writing to the wise man"), and it was almost certainly preserved in one archive or another before being copied for whatever purpose the Tsinghua manuscript originally served. These archives did not survive above ground, but it is fortunate for the historians of ancient China that at least some of the bamboo-slip manuscripts in them were copied into less perishable media (such as bronze) or were buried in less precarious contexts under the ground, and that thanks to the archaeologists of China they have again seen the light of day. I think we can be quite confident in supposing that only a portion—and perhaps just a small portion—of ancient China's writing has yet surfaced.

Chapter Two

The *Bin Gong Xu* Inscription and the Origins of the Chinese Literary Tradition

Recent discoveries of manuscripts from China's Warring States period (480–222 BCE) have stirred renewed debate over the nature of writing and the book in ancient China. Among several important such discoveries,[1] it is the bamboo-slip texts unearthed in 1993 at Guodian 郭店, Hubei, that have attracted the greatest attention.[2] This is because three separate texts, differentiated on the basis of their physical properties, are made up entirely of material found in the received text of the *Laozi* 老子. Just a month after the first publication of the manuscripts, an international conference was held in the United States to discuss these so-called Guodian *Laozi* manuscripts and their relationship with the received text of the *Laozi*.[3] Perhaps the most notable result of this conference was the contrast it showed between the attitudes of Chi-

---

This chapter was originally prepared for the seventy-fifth anniversary of the founding of the Harvard-Yenching Library in 2003 and was subsequently published as "The *Bin Gong Xu* Inscription and the Beginnings of the Chinese Literary Tradition," in *The Harvard-Yenching Library 75th Anniversary Memorial Volume*, ed. Wilt Idema (Hong Kong: Chinese University Press, 2007), 1–19. For the present volume, I omit some of the documentation provided in footnotes that is now out of date. I have not attempted to update other references to the state of the field, which should be understood to pertain to the period prior to 2003. The contrast between the "Doubting Antiquity" (*yi gu* 疑古) and "Believing Antiquity" (*xin gu* 信古) attitudes discussed in the opening section of the chapter is still relevant today, twenty years later.

nese and Western participants. Among Chinese scholars, there was a strong consensus that an author or authors at Jinan cheng 紀南城, the capital of the ancient state of Chu 楚 and the ancient site of which is just south of Guodian, composed these texts by making selections from the *Laozi*, suggesting that the five-thousand-character classic was already complete by no later than the late fourth century BCE, when the manuscripts were put into the tomb. Indeed, many in China have argued that these manuscripts, as also the Mawangdui 馬王堆 manuscripts discovered twenty years earlier, suggest that the composition of the *Laozi* must go back to the fifth or even sixth century BCE, the date some early Chinese traditions ascribe to it. Among Western participants at the conference, on the other hand, there seems to have been just as strong a consensus that the three Guodian *Laozi* manuscripts mark but a stage in the gradual coalescence of the five-thousand-character classic, the presumption being that it did not achieve its final shape—that of the received text—until well into the third century BCE. Doubts about the antiquity of the *Laozi* are not at all new in Western sinology, going back at least more than a century to the work of Herbert Giles (1845–1935), the first professor of Chinese at the University of Cambridge in England, though the arguments adduced by most contemporary scholars derive, explicitly or implicitly, from iconoclastic scholars working in China during the 1920s.[4]

The debate over the date and nature of the *Laozi* text is part of a wider debate concerning the origins of China's literary tradition. As seen in the case of the *Laozi*, in China today there is a broad consensus that the paleographic discoveries of the last generation have served to not only show that the "Doubting Antiquity" (*yi gu* 疑古) scholars of the 1920s went too far in their critiques of Chinese traditions but indeed show that those traditions are generally valid. This new historiographical view is usually termed "Believing Antiquity" (*xin gu* 信古).[5] By contrast, among Western scholars of early China, the critical spirit of the Doubting Antiquity school seems still to reign supreme, as suggested by the great acclaim accorded E. Bruce and A. Taeko Brooks's recently published translation and study of that other foundational text of the Warring States period, the *Lunyu* 論語 *Analects* of Kongzi 孔子 or Confucius (551–479 BCE). Dedicating their study to Cui Shu 崔述 (1740–1816), a figure who might be described as the patron saint of iconoclasm in China, the Brookses argue that the *Lunyu* coalesced over the course of some three centuries, not achieving its final shape until the middle of the third century BCE.[6] In absolute terms, this "accretional theory" is unexceptionable. Not even the most ardent believer in antiquity would deny that early texts changed over the course of their transmission and transcription into new styles of Chinese orthography. But it is as a general approach to China's early literature that the continuing iconoclasm of Western scholars parts company with scholarship in China today.

When we turn to the literature traditionally believed to be even older than the *Laozi* or the *Lunyu*, the *Yi* 易, *Shu* 書, and *Shi* 詩, the classics of *Changes*, *Scriptures*, and *Poetry*, some Western scholars have made even more extreme claims in recent years, stating that these texts were not written at all until many centuries after the dates Chinese traditions assign to their composition. For instance, Bruce Brooks has argued that the *Yi* was not put into writing until late in the fourth century BCE.[7] As for the *Shi*, Stephen Owen's statement "the *Shi* probably existed as orally transmitted texts long before they were ever committed to writing, and even after their commitment to writing (when we cannot be sure, but I would guess late Chunqiu at the earliest), their primary mode of transmission was probably oral until (another guess) the late Warring States,"[8] though properly qualified as guesswork, is nonetheless representative of the view of many Western scholars who have addressed the issue. The *Shu* is, of course, perhaps the most vexed text in all of Chinese tradition and is thus deserving of somewhat more comment. There is no need here to rehearse the legend of the aged Fu Sheng 伏勝 (fl. ca. 215–165 BCE) retrieving the text that he had secreted away at the time of the Qin proscription of literature, or the better documented efforts by Chinese scholars of the seventeenth and eighteenth centuries who demonstrated the spurious nature of later additions to Master Fu's text.[9] Even that core of the text that can be attributed to Master Fu reflects a curious mixture of genres and grammars, much of which was certainly written much later than tradition would suggest. But there is a core of the core, the five *gao* 誥 or "proclamation" chapters of the *Zhou shu* 周書 section and a few related documents, that are written in a language so demonstrably archaic that even the leader of the "Doubting Antiquity" scholars, Gu Jiegang 顧頡剛 (1893–1980), regarded them as contemporary records of Western Zhou (1045–771 BCE) events.[10] Nevertheless, Western sinologists from David Keightley to David Schaberg have criticized historians for using any parts of the *Shu* in writing the history of the Western Zhou period.¹¹ Schaberg concludes his review of the "Western Zhou History" portion of *The Cambridge History of Ancient China* with the pronouncement: "without a clearer understanding of the origins of the received texts, it may be necessary to suspend their status as authorities, and to treat them as a singularly mysterious sort of artifact,"¹² and returns to this theme in the conclusion to his review of the entire book:

> At another extreme—and here I would admit my own sympathies—such texts are presumed less than perfectly reliable, and unsuitable for direct citation as historical authorities, until it be demonstrated that they stem from circumstances in which it was possible and desirable to produce highly accurate records of words and deeds. . . . I suspect that faith in early accounts is likely to remain, for a long time or forever, unsubstantiated by any convincing account of the provenance of the texts, and that an approach resembling Keightley's—in which, to repeat, texts are treated as artifacts rather than as authorities, will always make for more persuasive, more durable historical reconstructions.¹³

The desire that before received texts are "cited as historical authorities" that "it be demonstrated that they stem from circumstances in which it was possible and desirable to produce highly accurate records of words and deeds" is certainly reasonable, but this raises the question of what constitutes such a demonstration. As mentioned previously, the *Zhou shu* chapters of the *Shu* are written in an idiom demonstrably older than that of the classical sources of the Warring States period,¹⁴ and for this reason they have generally been accepted as dating to the Western Zhou period, as they purport to do. More important, they share this idiom with that used in thousands of inscriptions in bronze vessels that were certainly cast during that period, inscriptions that we can now read in essentially the same form as when they were first made.¹⁵ Just the number of inscribed bronze vessels now extant, surely only a small fraction of those produced during the Western Zhou,¹⁶ suggests that writing was widespread at the time. Perhaps more important, the content of the inscriptions shows that they do "stem from circumstances in which it was possible and desirable to produce highly accurate records of words and deeds." Several inscriptions reveal that the bronze inscriptions themselves were only secondary, or even tertiary, records, based on primary documents written on bamboo or wood, one copy of which was stored in royal archives and another given as a royal gift to the person for whom the bronze vessel was cast. This suggests that both scribes at the Zhou court and at least a certain stratum of Western Zhou society were quite literate and very often engaged in the production of written documents. Given these circumstances, it is hard to disagree with Herrlee Creel's pithy statement: "We simply have to accept the fact that the Chous were a people who liked to write books."[17]

Of course, the content of the *Zhou shu* chapters of the *Shu* and the content of Western Zhou bronze inscriptions are quite dissimilar. The *Shu* chapters generally purport to record royal pronouncements and/or court discussions of policy, while bronze inscriptions tend to be both more local and more formulaic. Those with the longest inscriptions generally open with the record of a specific event in the life of a specific individual and close with a prayer meant for the ancestors and descendants of his own family. Even those inscriptions with lengthy narratives describing the events that led to the award commemorated by the making of the vessel are of a different genre from the texts of the *Shu*; it would be difficult to characterize them as "books" or even chapters or other such portions of literary works.

At least, such a characterization of Western Zhou bronze inscriptions would have been valid until the autumn of 2002, when the Poly 保利 Museum of Beijing exhibited and published a bronze vessel that it had recently purchased on the Hong Kong antiques market (see fig. 2.1 for the vessel and its inscription).[18] The *Bin Gong xu* 豳公盨 has an inscription of ninety-eight characters that is entirely anomalous within the inventory of Western Zhou bronze inscriptions. It mentions no occasion for the casting of the vessel, no meritorious deeds of the person for whom it was cast, nor any prayer to his ancestors. Indeed, it is not even clear what relationship the apparent patron, a figure named Bin Gong 豳公, has with the main text of the inscription, which reads very much like a chapter of the *Shu*, even if a short chapter. Although, as might be expected with such an unprecedented inscription, there are numerous problems with its interpretation, the broad outlines of the inscription are clear. A tentative translation would read as follows.[19]

天令禹敷土隨山濬川，迺疇方設征。降民監德，迺自作配嚮民，
成父母，生我王作臣。厥沬唯德，民好明德。憂在天下，用厥邵
好益求懿德，康亡不懋。孝友、盂明、經齊、好祀無期。心好
德，婚媾亦唯協，天釐用考，神復用福祿，永孚于寧。豳公曰：
民唯克用茲德，亡悔。

Heaven commanded Yu to spread out the soil, and to follow the mountains to dredge the rivers, and then to divide the regions and set up their tribute. Descending to the people to examine their virtue, then of itself making a mate to direct the people and be their father and mother, (heaven) gave birth to our king to serve as (its) minister. What he bathes in is only virtue, and the people love (his) bright virtue. Concerned for all under heaven, he uses his radiant goodness to increase and seek fine virtue, calmly but never not diligently. Filial and friendly, expansive and bright, constant and even, he loves the sacrifices without limit. When the heart loves virtue, marriage relations are also concordant, Heaven favors with longevity, and the spirits requite with blessings and wealth, eternally accordant in tranquility.

Bin Gong said: "If only the people can use this virtue, there will be no regret."

The inscription begins with heaven (*tian* 天) commanding Yu 禹 to control the floodwaters, which he does by dredging river channels in accordance with the topography of the land. With the land once again habitable, Yu divides it into definable regions. Heaven then descends to examine the people's virtue (*de* 德), and "of itself" (*zi zuo* 自作) gives birth (*sheng* 生) to the king (*wang* 王), so that he might lead the people, serving as their "father and mother" (*fu mu* 父母), and also be minister (*chen* 臣) to heaven. The inscription then continues with a discussion of the role of virtue in government. It seems to say that virtue is a characteristic of the king, but that the people are able to love (*hao* 好) it, and that when this becomes manifest throughout society, even marital relations will be concordant. For the king and the people's maintenance of good social relations and proper sacrifices, heaven and the spirits bestow longevity and wealth, leading eventually to a state of tranquility. The brief conclusion to the inscription is perhaps in the nature of the appreciations (*zan* 贊) seen in later standard histories; Bin Gong states: "If only the people can use this virtue, there will be no regret." It is unclear if Bin Gong is to be understood as the author of the inscription, or if he has copied a text that was already in circulation, lending it his imprimatur both by casting it in bronze and by adding this appreciation.

Not only is the general form of this inscription comparable to chapters of the *Shu*, but its wording is often identical to wording in various such chapters and other classical texts. For example, the opening line of the inscription, "Heaven commanded Yu to spread out the soil and to follow the mountains to dredge the rivers, and then to divide the regions and set up their tribute" (天令禹敷土隨山濬川，迺嚋方設征), is reminiscent of the opening line of the "Yu gong" 禹貢 chapter of the *Shu*: "Yu spread out the soil, and following the mountains and cutting down trees established the heights and enlarged the rivers" (禹敷土,隨山刊木，奠高大川).[20] Even more striking is its similarity with the synopsis of this chapter given in the *Shu xu* 書序 Preface to the Scriptures: "Yu divided the nine regions, following the mountains to dredge the rivers, relying on the earth to make their tribute" (禹別九州，隨山濬川，任土作貢).[21] The inscription's description of Heaven "descending to the people to examine their virtue" (降民監德) has parallels in numerous chapters of the *Shu* (as well as poems in the *Shi*); the "Gao zong rong ri" 高宗肜日 is but one: "Heaven examines the people below" (天監下民).[22] And Heaven's "making a mate to direct the people" (作配嚮民) is echoed by the "Lü xing" 呂刑 chapter: "Now heaven guides the people, making a mate below" (今天相民，作配在下).[23]

Brief though the inscription on the *Bin Gong xu* is, I think there can be no question as to its importance. Indeed, when I forwarded the inscription and my own preliminary translation of it to colleagues, including some who have contended that no parts of the *Shu* could have been written during the Western Zhou, they uniformly acknowledged that the inscription would be important *if* it were authentic, apparently implying thereby that they suspected it was not. Even if the inscription were not so unusual, the circumstances of the Poly Museum's acquisition of the vessel might well cause one to question its authenticity. The decades since the 1990s have seen Hong Kong flooded with antiques, many of them recently robbed from tombs in China,[24] but including also not a few very well-crafted forgeries. The Poly Museum was established only in 1999, and though it has been very active in acquiring early Chinese bronzes, its "track record" was not yet extensive enough to engender automatic trust. However, after acquiring the *Bin Gong xu*, the Poly Museum sent it for cleaning and restoration to the Shanghai Museum, a museum with the world's finest collection of Chinese bronze vessels. The museum completed its restoration work just before I arrived there for an extended research stay. I spoke with all of the curators in the museum's bronze department about the vessel, and every one of them, including the late Ma Chengyuan 馬承源 (1927–2004), who probably examined more Chinese bronze vessels than anyone in history, confided to me that they were also initially very skeptical that an inscription such as this could be genuine. But, after careful scrutiny, they all became convinced that the vessel and its inscription were produced together toward the end of the middle Western Zhou, roughly the first half of the ninth century BCE. The shape and ornamentation of the vessel fit this period, as does the calligraphy of the inscription. Ma Chengyuan also suggested that the vessel's patina is consistent with long burial in the soil of the Zhou homeland, north of present-day Xi'an 西安, Shaanxi, and a local archaeologist there confirmed to me that he too suspects that the vessel was unearthed there.[25] Perhaps more important than even this sort of expert opinion, technical considerations of the vessel's casting leave no doubt that it was cast in a piece mold; as for the inscription, bronze "spacers" arranged symmetrically about it attest that the inscription was indeed cast into the vessel.[26] If there are no doubts about the vessel's authenticity, and I think there can be none, then we are left to conclude that its inscription is very important indeed—important for our understanding of Western Zhou bronze inscriptions, to be sure, but perhaps even more so for our understanding of the origin of the Chinese literary tradition.

If someone in the first half of the ninth century BCE were capable of writing the inscription on the *Bin Gong xu*, and its materiality leaves no doubt that it was indeed written, then there would seem to be no reason to doubt that other contemporaries were capable of writing the sorts of similar texts that are preserved in the *Shu*. This does not mean, by any means, that all of those texts were in fact written in the Western Zhou; each text must still be judged independently, primarily on the basis of its linguistic usage. But it does mean that anyone who discounts, ipso facto, the possibility that such texts were written at the time, does so in the face of very hard evidence to the contrary (see fig. 2.1a and b).

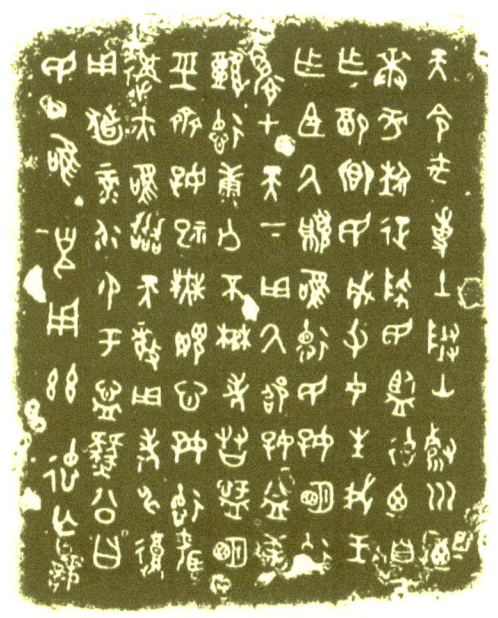

Figure 2.1a and b. *Bin Gong xu* 豳公盨 vessel and inscription. From *Sui Gong xu: Da Yu zhi shui yu wei zheng yi de*, 10–11, 13. Used with permission.

Chapter Three

The Writing of a Late Western Zhou Bronze Inscription

On the evening of January 19, 2003, five peasants collecting soil at Yangjiacun 楊家村, Meixian 眉縣 County, Shaanxi, unearthed a cache containing twenty-seven Western Zhou bronze vessels, all of them bearing inscriptions. This was immediately hailed as one of the great archaeological discoveries of the new century.[1] Its significance is multi-faceted: the intrinsic interest of the inscriptions, including one, on the *Qiu pan* 逑盤,[2] 373 characters long, which provides a sketch history of almost the entire Western Zhou period much like the famous inscription on the *Shi Qiang pan* 史墻盤 (*Jicheng* 10175), discovered three decades earlier in the neighboring Zhou Yuan 周原 or Plain of Zhou, and two others, the *Forty-Second Year Qiu ding* 逑鼎 and *Forty-Third Year Qiu ding*, both also very long (281 characters and 316 characters), which provide important information on military and legal matters near the end of the Western Zhou; the full-date notations in the two *Qiu ding* inscriptions, which require a radical rethinking of late-Western Zhou chronology;[3] the cache's relationship with three previous discoveries of Western Zhou bronze vessels in the same area that allow the makers' family—the Shan 單 family—to be mapped both historically and geographically;[4] and for

---

This chapter was originally published as "Shilun Xi Zhou tongqi mingwen de xiezuo guocheng: Yi Meixian Shan shi jiazu tongqi wei li" 試論西周銅器銘文的寫作過程: 以眉縣單氏家族銅器為例, in *Chutu wenxian yu Zhongguo sixiang yantaohui lunwenji* 新出土文獻與先秦思想重構論文集, ed. Guo Lihua 郭梨花 (Taipei: Taiwan Guji chuban youxian gongsi, 2007), 119–30; the English version was originally published as "The Writing of a Late Western Zhou Bronze Inscription," *Asiatische Studien / Études Asiatiques* 61, no. 3 (2007): 845–77.

the rewarding and public lionizing of the peasants who discovered the cache, which it is to be hoped may help to turn the tide on the tomb robbing that has plagued China for the last decade or more.[5] As the scholarship mentioned in the preceding notes attests, these topics have already stimulated a great deal of discussion and will certainly repay attention for years to come. However, in the present chapter I propose to examine the Shan family bronzes for a different purpose—for the evidence they shed on the writing of a Western Zhou bronze inscription.

The Two *Qiu Ding* Inscriptions

As mentioned before, the *Forty-Second* and *Forty-Third Year Qiu ding* inscriptions both have considerable historical significance, the *Forty-Second Year* inscription providing information about a campaign against the Xianyun 獫狁, and the *Forty-Third Year* inscription narrating a command to Qiu to be in charge of the people of Li 歷, including broad judicial responsibilities. Structurally, both of these inscriptions are typical of late Western Zhou court-audience inscriptions, with a three-part structure: prefatory remarks setting the time, place, and participants in the audience; the king's address; and the donor's dedication of the vessel. What is of particular interest for my purposes here is that both of the inscriptions explicitly mention that the king had the text of his address written on bamboo or wooden slips, which were presented to Qiu at the end of his audiences. This feature, seen previously on the *Song ding* 頌鼎 (*Jicheng* 2827–29) and *Shanfu Shan ding* 膳夫山鼎 (*Jicheng* 2825) inscriptions, both also late Western Zhou vessels, is an important key to understanding the process by which bronze inscriptions were written. It seems desirable to begin with complete translations of both the *Forty-Second Year* and *Forty-Third Year Qiu ding* inscriptions. For clarity of presentation, I will break the translations into constituent parts. Since the purpose of this essay is not strictly paleographical, I will forego detailed notes substantiating each transcription and translation.

Forty-Second Year Qiu Ding 四十二年逑鼎

惟卅又二年五月既生霸乙卯，王在周康穆宮。旦，王各大室即立。司工散右虞逑入門立中廷北卿。尹氏受王釐書。王呼史淢冊釐逑。

The Writing of a Late Western Zhou Bronze Inscription | 59

It was the forty-second year, fifth month, after the growing brightness, *yimao* (day 52); the king was in the Mu Palace of the Kang (Palace) in Zhou. At dawn, the king entered the Great Chamber and took position. Supervisor of Works San at the right of Warden Qiu entered the gate and stood in the center of the courtyard, facing north. Yinshi received the king's award document. The king called out to Scribe Huo to make the award to Qiu in writing.

王若曰：逑，丕顯文武膺受大令，匍有四方。則繇惟乃先聖祖考夾召先王，爵堇大令，奠周邦，余弗遐忘聖人孫子，余惟閘乃先祖考有爵于周邦。肆余肇作囗沙詢。余肇建長父侯于楊，余令汝奠長父休。汝克奠于厥師，汝惟克型乃先祖鬭玁。出蔵于井阿、于曆巖。汝不畏戎。汝蔽長父以追搏戎。乃即宕伐于弓谷，汝執訊獲職，俘器車馬。汝敏于戎工，弗逆朕親令。

The king approved of saying: "Qiu, illustrious Wen and Wu received the great mandate and extended it to the four quarters. Then it was because of your prior wise ancestors and deceased-father's assisting the prior kings to have merit and care with the great mandate and stabilizing the Zhou state that I have not forgotten the wise men's grandson, and it was that I remembered your prior ancestors' and deceased-father's having merits in the Zhou state, and so I made . . . court interview. When I initially established Changfu to be lord in Yang, I commanded you to stabilize Changfu's benefices. That you were able to bring stability among his troops is because you were able to take as model your prior ancestors' and deceased-father's stopping the Xianyun, and went out to defeat (them) at Jing'a and at Liyan. You were not wearied by the warfare, and you accompanied Changfu to pursue and hit the belligerents. Then engaging and broadly attacking (them) at Bow Valley, you manacled prisoners to be interrogated and caught chiefs, and captured weapons, chariots, and horses. You have been diligent in military work and have not transgressed my personal command.

釐女瓚鬯一卣，田于鄭卅田，于犀廿田。

"I award you one *you*-bucket of black millet wine and (the following) fields: at Hui thirty fields, and at Xi twenty fields."

述拜稽首，受冊釐以出。述敢對天子丕顯魯休揚，用乍𢆷彝，用喜孝于前文人。其嚴才上，翼才下。穆秉明德。豐_泉_降余康𩁹屯祐、通祿永令、眉壽繛綰，畯臣天子。述其萬年無彊，子_孫_永寶用喜。

Qiu saluted and touched his head to the ground, received the award slips, and went out. Qiu dares in response to the Son of Heaven's illustriously fine beneficence to extol (it), herewith making this ritual vessel to use to offer filial piety to the prior cultured men; may they be stern on high and respected below, beautifully holding to bright virtue and abundantly sending down on me peaceful harmony and pure blessings, penetrating wealth and an eternal mandate, and long life everlasting to serve the Son of Heaven. May Qiu for ten thousand years without bound have sons' sons and grandsons' grandsons eternally to treasure and use (it) to make offerings.

Forty-Third Year Qiu Ding 四十三年述鼎

惟卌又三年六月既生霸丁亥。王在周康宮穆宮。旦，王各周廟即立。司馬壽右虞述入門立中廷北卿。史淢受王令書。王乎尹氏冊令述。

It was the forty-third year, sixth month, after the growing brightness, *dinghai* (day 24); the king was in the Mu Palace of the Zhou Kang Palace. At dawn, the king went to the Zhou Temple and assumed position. Supervisor of Horse Shou at the right of Warden Qiu entered the gate and stood in the center of the court facing north. Scribe Huo received the king's command document. The king called out to Yinshi to command Qiu in writing.

王若曰。述。丕顯文武膺受大令。匍有四方。則繇惟乃先聖夾召先王，爵菫大令，奠周邦，肆余弗忘聖人孫子。昔余既令女疋榮兌。兼司四方虞林，用宮御。余惟𦔻乃先祖考，有爵于周邦，申重乃令，令女官司歷人；毋敢妄寧。虔夙夕更雝我邦小大猷。雩乃専政事，毋敢不尃不井。雩乃訽庶又粦，毋敢不中不型。毋龏橐，龏橐惟又宥從。廼孜侮鰥寡。用作余一人咎。不雀死。

The king approved of saying: "Qiu, illustrious Wen and Wu received the great mandate and extended it to the four quarters. Then it was because of your prior wise deceased-father's assisting the prior kings to have merit and care with the great mandate and stabilizing the Zhou state that I have not forgotten the wise men's grandson. Formerly, I had already commanded you to assist Rong Dui, and concurrently to supervise the four quarters' game and forests, to be used for the palace's supply. Now it is that I recall your prior ancestors' and deceased-father's having had merit in the Zhou state and extend and increase your command, commanding you to officiate over and supervise the people of Li. Do not dare to be negligently complacent, but diligently morning and evening help and support our country's small and great plans. In the government affairs in which you assist, do not dare not to be square or a model. In your questioning of the commoners and neighbors, do not dare not to be centered and a model. Do not enrich yourself; if you enrich yourself, it will only be because there are bribes and indulgences, and then you take advantage of widows and widowers, and therewith make resentment for me the one man; those not good will die."

王曰。述，賜汝𩰫鬯一卣、玄袞衣、赤舄、駒車、萃較、朱虢𮅕 靳、虎冟熏裏、畫轉、畫輯、金甬、馬騏、攸勒。敬夙夕勿灋朕令。

The king said: "Qiu, (I) award you one *you*-bucket of black millet wine, a black hemmed jacket, red slippers, and a colt chariot (with) an ornamented siderail, a crimson leather-covered front rail, a tiger-skin canopy with a smoky-black lining, painted yoke-bar bindings and axle couplings, and bronze jingle bells, and four horses with bits and bridles. Be respectful morning and night and do not neglect my command."

述拜稽首。受冊佩以出。反入堇圭。

Qiu saluted and touched his head to the ground, receiving the award slips and suspending them in his sash to go out. In return he entered and presented a jade tablet.

述敢對天子丕顯魯休揚。用作朕皇考龏叔龢彝。皇考其嚴在上。廣在下。穆秉明德。豐㝬，降余康虢屯祐、通祿永令、眉壽綽綰，畯臣天子。述萬年無疆，子孫永寶用享。

Qiu dares in response to the Son of Heaven's illustriously fine beneficence to extol (it), herewith making for my august deceased-father Gongshu this ritual vessel. May (my) august deceased-father be stern on high and respected below, beautifully upholding bright virtue and abundantly (sending down upon) me peaceful harmony and pure blessings, penetrating wealth and an eternal mandate everlasting to serve the Son of Heaven. May Qiu for ten thousand years without bound have sons' sons and grandsons' grandsons eternally to treasure and use (it) to make offerings.

It would seem that what I have demarcated as the second and third paragraphs of the two inscriptions are more or less verbatim quotations of the award documents presented to Qiu upon his departures from the court audiences.[6] Certainly the text of the king's commands must be as he had them read in the audiences, and there is at least one feature that suggests different authorship for these paragraphs (i.e., the king's commands to Qiu, and the king's awards of gifts to him, perhaps also including the first paragraphs—those describing the time and place and participants in the ceremonies) as opposed to the last paragraphs of the inscriptions (the dedicatory prayers): whereas the opening paragraphs refer to the king simply as *wang* 王, the last paragraph in each inscription calls him *tianzi* 天子 "Son of Heaven." This distinction, which became common in these portions of late Western Zhou inscriptions,[7] seems to reflect a neutral archival impulse in the use of *wang*, as opposed to the deliberately honorific *tianzi*. Presumably the patron of the vessel, Qiu, used the text on the slips given to him as the basis for the composition of the text to be cast into the bronze vessel, making use also of standard formulas to add his own personal dedication as a conclusion. When we turn next to examine the much more elaborate *Qiu pan* inscription, it will be well to keep this compositional process in mind.

The *Qiu Pan* Inscription

As previously mentioned, the *Qiu pan* inscription resembles that on the famous *Shi Qiang pan* in juxtaposing a sketch history of the Zhou kings down to the time of the patron, Warden (*yu* 虞) Qiu, with laudatory comments about corresponding generations of his own ancestors. It differs from the *Shi Qiang pan* inscription in that, whereas that inscription segregated the two histories, first narrating the generations of the kings and then following it with those of Qiang's ancestors, the *Qiu pan* inscription combines the two narratives into discrete textual units, first mentioning Qiu's own ancestor and how he was able to serve a particular Zhou king or two, and then, in most cases, continuing with a comment about the accomplishments of that king or kings. I will try to illustrate this structure in the following presentation, placing the transcription of the inscription and its translation side by side and making systematic use of indentations.

逑盤	Qiu Pan
逑曰。丕顯朕皇高祖單公：	Qiu said: "Illustrious was my august high ancestor Shan Gong:
趨 克明哲厥德，夾召文王武王	Radiantly capable of making bright and wise his virtue, he accompanied and assisted King Wen and King Wu,
達殷應受天魯令，匍有 四方，竝宅厥堇彊土，用配上帝。	who pierced the Yin, received Heaven's fine mandate, extended it to the four quarters, and widely inhabited the lands that they opened and bounded, therewith serving as mates to God on High.
雩朕皇高祖公叔：	With my august high ancestor Gongshu:
克逑匹成王	He was capable of joining and aiding King Cheng,
成受大令。方狄不享，用奠四或萬邦。	who successfully received the great mandate; when the regional enemies did not make offerings, he therewith settled the four regions and the ten thousand countries.

雩朕皇高祖新室仲： 克幽明厥心，䚅遠能狱。 會召康王， 方裏不延。	With my august high ancestor Zhong of the New Chamber: Capable of making both somber and bright his heart, he was gentle with the distant and enabling with the near, and met with and assisted King Kang, who just embraced the unsubmitted (i.e., the enemy states).
雩朕皇高祖惠仲盠父： 盭龢于政，又成于猷， 用會邵王穆王， 盜政四方，撲伐楚荊。	With my august high ancestor Huizhong Lifu: Bringing harmony in government and also being successful in his plans, he therewith met and assisted King Zhao and King Mu, who extended government to the four quarters, and struck and attacked Chu and Jing.
雩朕皇高祖零伯： 粦明厥心，不豕口服， 用辟龔王、懿王。	With my august high ancestor Ling Bo: Making clear and bright his heart, he did not fail in his . . . duties, and therewith served King Gong and King Yih.
雩朕皇亞祖懿仲𣪘： 諫＿克匍保厥辟孝王夷王 又成于周邦。	With my august secondary ancestor Yihzhong Kuang, Remonstratingly, he was capable of advising and protecting his rulers King Xiao and King Yi, who again succeeded in the Zhou country.
雩朕皇考龔叔： 穆趩＿，龢旬于政， 明陵于德，宫辟剌王。	With my august deceased-father Gongshu: Beautifully and respectfully, harmonious and compliant in government, bright and equable in virtue, he obeyed and assisted King Li.

The Writing of a Late Western Zhou Bronze Inscription | 65

逑肇䌛朕皇祖考服，虔夙夕敬朕死事。	Qiu has begun by continuing my august ancestors' and deceased-father's duties, diligently morning and evening respecting my sworn service.
肆天子多賜逑休。天子其萬年無疆耆黃耉，保奠周邦，諫辪四方。	And so the Son of Heaven has much awarded Qiu benefices. May the Son of Heaven for ten thousand years without bound enjoy a yellowing longevity, protect and settle the Zhou country, and rule the four quarters.
王若曰： 逑，丕顯文武膺受大令，匍有四方。則繇惟乃先聖祖考夾召先王，爵堇大令。	The king approved of saying: "Qiu, illustrious (Kings) Wen and Wu received the great mandate and extended it to the four quarters. Then because it was your past wise ancestors' and deceased-father who accompanied and assisted the past kings to have merit and care with the great mandate,
今余惟巠乃先聖祖考申重乃令，令汝疋榮兌兼司四方虞林，用宮御。	now it is that I recall your past wise ancestors and deceased-father and extend and increase your command, commanding you to assist Rong Dui, and concurrently to supervise the four quarters' game and forests, to be used for the palace's supply.
賜汝赤市、幽黃、攸勒。	I award you red kneepads, a black belt, and a bit and bridle."
逑敢對天子丕顯魯休揚，用作朕皇族考寶尊盤，用追言孝于前文人。前文人嚴在上，廙在[下]。豐泉降逑魯多福、眉壽、䵼綰。受余康虢屯祐、	Qiu dares in response to the Son of Heaven's illustriously fine beneficence to extol it, herewith making for my august ancestors and deceased-father this treasured

通彔永令霝終，述畯臣天子_孫_永寶用言。	offertory *pan* basin, with which to send offerings of filial piety to the past cultured men. May the past cultured men be stern on high and respected below, abundantly sending down on Qiu fine and many blessings and long life everlasting, giving me peaceful harmony, pure aid, penetrating wealth, an eternal mandate and a numinous end, so that Qiu may serve the Son of Heaven. May sons and grandsons' grandsons eternally treasure and use it to make offerings.

From this inscription, it can be seen that Qiu was the scion of a family that traced its heritage back to the founding fathers of the Zhou dynasty. Indeed, there is evidence that confirms at least in part that Qiu's account of his family is not necessarily exaggerated. His fourth generation ancestor, Huizhong Lifu 惠仲盠父, described in this inscription as having served the Zhou kings Zhao 昭 (r. 977/75–957 BCE) and Mu 穆 (r. 956–918 BCE), was the patron of another group of vessels discovered in the same village of Meixian in 1955. Two of these, the *Li fangzun* 盠方尊 (*Jicheng* 9899) and *Li fangyi* (*Jicheng* 9900), bear a lengthy inscription that seems to commemorate a command by King Mu making Li supreme commander of the Zhou armies.[8]

A Possible Saga of the Zhou Kings

While the historical narratives of the *Qiu pan* inscription command the greatest attention, I propose to focus first on the relatively brief quotation of the king's remarks to Qiu that follows them. This quotation is introduced by the phrase "the king approved of saying" (*wang ruo yue* 王若曰):

> Qiu, illustrious (Kings) Wen and Wu received the great mandate and extended it to the four quarters. Then because

it was your past wise ancestors' and deceased-father who accompanied and assisted the past kings to have merit and care with the great mandate, now it is that I recall your past wise ancestors and deceased-father and extend and increase your command, commanding you to assist Rong Dui, and concurrently to supervise the four quarters' game and forests, to be used for the palace's supply. I award you red kneepads, a black belt, and a bit and bridle.

Bearing in mind the example of the *Forty-Third Year Qiu ding* inscription, in which the text of the king's address, written on bamboo or wooden slips, formed the basis for the composition of the bronze inscription, we might surmise that in this case, too, the king's address was instrumental in the writing of this inscription. Note that the king began by extolling the dynastic founders kings Wen 文 (r. 1099/57–1050 BCE) and Wu 武 (r. 949/45–943 BCE) and their receipt of "the great mandate" (*da ming* 大命), and then immediately gave credit also to Qiu's "prior wise ancestors and deceased-father" (*xian sheng zu kao* 先聖祖考), who, he said, "accompanied and assisted the past kings to have merit and care with the great mandate." I would suggest that Qiu's decision to juxtapose the accomplishments of his ancestors with those of the Zhou kings was validated, at least in part, by these remarks of the king. Indeed, much of the wording of the encomium for Qiu's high ancestor Shan Gong 單公 can be seen to have been inspired by those remarks (here putting the encomium on the left and the opening of the king's command on the right).

[單公]夾召文王武王達殷應受天魯令，匍有四方，竝宅厥堇疆土，用配上帝。	不顯文武應受大令，匍有四方。則緐惟乃先聖祖考夾召先王，爵堇大令。
[Shan Gong] accompanied and assisted King Wen and King Wu, who pierced the Yin, received Heaven's fine mandate, extended it to the four quarters, and widely inhabited the lands that they opened and bounded, therewith serving as mates to God on High.	Illustrious (Kings) Wen and Wu received the great mandate and extended it to the four quarters. Then because it was your past wise ancestors' and deceased-father who accompanied and assisted the past kings to have merit and care with the great mandate.

Qiu effectively quoted the king in saying that his high ancestor Shan Gong "accompanied and assisted" (*jia shao* 夾召) King Wen and King Wu to "receive" (*yingshou* 應受) the "mandate" (*ling* 令; i.e., *ming* 命) and then "extend it to the four quarters" (*fu you si fang* 匍有四方). It is perhaps notable that the phrases he has added to the king's own wording, "pierced the Yin" (*da* Yin 達殷), "inhabited the lands that they opened and bounded" (*zhai jue jin jiang tu* 宅厥堇彊土), and "therewith served as mates to God on High" (*yong pei* Shang Di 用配上帝), have precedents in only three other inscriptions: the *Shi Qiang pan*, the *Hu zhong* 猷鐘 (also known as *Zongzhou zhong* 宗周鐘; *Jicheng* 0260), and *Hu gui* 猷簋 (*Jicheng* 4317), the latter two of which were both made for Zhou king Li 厲 (r. 857/53–842/28) and thus are exceptional for representing in their entirety the wording of a Zhou king.

史墻盤：索圉武王：遹征四方，達殷。

Shi Qiang pan: Capturing and controlling was King Wu: He proceeded and campaigned through the four quarters, piercing the Yin.

猷鐘：王肇遹眚文武堇彊土。

Hu zhong: The king for the first time proceeded through and examined the lands that (Kings) Wen and Wu had opened and bounded.

猷簋：王曰：有余惟小子，余亡康晝夜，巠雍先王，用配皇天。

Hu gui: The king said: "Although I am but the little son, I have no leisure day or night, but always recall and support the past kings, therewith serving as a mate to august Heaven."

Although the third of these precedents, that of the *Hu gui*, mentions serving as a mate to "august Heaven" (*huang tian* 皇天) rather than Shang Di, it is noteworthy that, with but two exceptions, the *Hu gui*, *Hu zhong*, and *Shi Qiang pan* are the only inscriptions in the entire inventory of Western Zhou bronze inscriptions that mention Shang Di specifically (as opposed to unmodified mentions of *di* 帝 alone).⁹ Perhaps this suggests that a cult dedicated to Shang Di was reserved exclusively to the Zhou kings, as opposed to a more widespread cult of Heaven. Whatever the merit of this suggestion, that the wording of this encomium to King Wen is found only in inscriptions composed by or for Zhou kings perhaps points to a common derivation for them: a saga of the Zhou kings, from which they all quoted. An early version of such a saga might be seen in the "Zhou Song" 周頌 poem "Capturing and Competitive" ("Zhi jing" 執競; Mao 274):

執競武王，	Firm and stalwart martial King Wu,
無競維烈！	Without compare was his valor!
不顯成康，	Illustrious were Cheng and Kang,
上帝是皇。	The God on High made them august.
自彼成康，	Since the time of those Cheng and Kang,
奄有四方。	We have covered the four quarters.

A more elaborate version might be seen in the *Da Ya* 大雅 *Greater Odes* poem "Wen Wang" 文王 "King Wen" (Mao 235). For reasons of space, I will quote just the first stanza, though the entire poem furnishes numerous parallels with the wording and sense of the *Qiu pan* inscription.

文王在上，	King Wen is up on high,
於昭于天。	Oh, radiant in heaven.
周雖舊邦，	Although Zhou is an old country,
其命維新。	Its mandate, it is renewed.
有周不顯，	The Zhou lords are illustrious,
帝命不時。	God's mandate is very timely.
文王陟降，	King Wen goes up and down,
在帝左右。	To the left and right of God.

It is possible that there existed a more developed saga or sagas of all of the Zhou kings from which all of these poems and inscriptions drew, however sketchily. As is the case with so much traditional literature from the Western Zhou, the *Shi jing* has preserved only that portion dealing with the founding fathers, especially Kings Wen and Wu. With the *Shi Qiang pan* and now the *Qiu pan* inscription, the saga of the following kings is finally coming into focus. The following comparison of their narratives of the Zhou kings might give some idea as to what such a saga was originally like (the inscription of the *Qiu pan* is to the left, that of the *Shi Qiang pan* to the right).

Qiu pan 逑盤	Shi Qiang pan 史墻盤
文王武王：達殷應受天魯令，匍有四方，並宅厥堇彊土，用配上帝。 King Wen and King Wu: who pierced the Yin, received Heaven's fine mandate, extended it to the four quarters, and widely inhabited the lands that they opened and bounded, therewith serving as mates to God on High.	曰古文王：初龢穌于政。上帝降懿德大甹。匍有上下。迨受萬邦。 Accordant with antiquity was King Wen: He first brought harmony to government. The Lord on High sent down fine virtue and great security. Extending to the high and low, he joined the ten thousand states. 索圉武王：遹征四方達殷。畯民永不巩狄。虘。岂伐尸童。 Capturing and controlling was King Wu: He proceeded and campaigned through the four quarters, piercing Yin and governing its people. Eternally unfearful of the Di, oh, he attacked the Yi minions.
成王：成受大令。方狄不享，用奠四或萬邦。 King Cheng: who successfully received the great mandate; when the regional enemies did not make offerings, he therewith settled the four regions and the ten thousand countries.	憲聖成王：左右索敼剛鯀。用肇融周邦。 Model and sagely was King Cheng: To the left and right he cast and gathered his net and line, therewith opening and integrating the Zhou state.
康王：方襄不延。 King Kang: who just embraced the unsubmitted (i.e., the enemy states).	淵哲康王：分尹啻彊。 Deep and wise was King Kang: he divided command and pacified the borders.
邵王穆王：盜政四方，撲伐楚荊。 King Zhao and King Mu: who extended government to the four quarters, and struck and attacked Chu and Jing.	宖魯邵王。廣能楚刑。惟寏南行。 Vast and substantial was King Zhao: he broadly tamed Chu and Jing; it was to connect the southern route.

	顯倗穆王：井帥宇誨。 Reverent and illustrious was King Mu: he patterned himself on and followed the great counsels.
龏王、懿王。 King Gong and King Yih.	申寍天子：天子圕屖文武長剌。天子𩁹無匃䇂卲上下。亟獄逨慕。 Continuing and tranquil is the Son of Heaven: the Son of Heaven strives to carry on the long valor of Wen and Wu; the Son of Heaven is diligent and without flaw, faithfully making offerings above and below, and reverently glorifying the great plans.
孝王夷王：又成于周邦。 King Xiao and King Yi: who again succeeded in the Zhou country.	
剌王。 King Li.	

While isolating the praises of the various Zhou kings in this way reveals most clearly the quasi-historical nature of the *Qiu pan* and *Shi Qiang pan* inscriptions, the comparison also reveals that the two inscriptions share primarily the tone of their language and style of phrasing; the historical information per se is sketchy at best. The only direct correlation between the praises of individual kings is in the mention of King Zhao's campaign against Chu 楚 and Jing 荊. As I have mentioned elsewhere,[10] the bare mention of this campaign, without any explicit resolution, seems to be an oblique reference to the disastrous defeat inflicted on Zhou forces, as if the historian felt obliged to mention the event but could not bring himself to spell out the defeat.

Elsewhere in the *Qiu pan* inscription, there are two more explicit absences that seem to me to be even more significant. Eight of the eleven kings mentioned are supplied with some sort of praise, whether individually or in pairs. However, in two cases—the joint mention of

Kings Gong 共 (r. 917/15–900 BCE) and Yih 懿 (r. 899/97–873 BCE), and the single mention of King Li—the kings' names are left without any elaboration. In the case of King Li, it is perhaps not hard to see why he would be left without praise. Condemned in the traditional historical record as a paradigmatically evil king, he is said to have been driven into exile by the Zhou people, an event that seems to be reflected as well in the contemporary bronze inscriptional record.[11] The case of Kings Gong and Yih may derive from a similar context. The *Shi ji* 史記 *Records of the Historian* states that the decline of the Western Zhou began during the reign of King Yih:

懿王之時，王室遂衰，詩人作刺。

During the time of King Yih, the royal house thereupon declined and poets composed satires.[12]

The *Zhushu jinian* 竹書紀年 *Bamboo Annals* records also external incursions in the seventh and thirteenth years of his reign, and follows this with a terse mention of the king leaving the Zhou capital at Zongzhou 宗周 and moving some fifty kilometers west to Huaili 槐里.

十五年，王自宗周遷于槐里。

Fifteenth year, the king moved from Zongzhou to Huaili.[13]

Traditional histories also state that at this time there was a break in the regular succession of Zhou kings: King Yih was followed not by his son, the eventual King Yi 夷 (r. 865–858 BCE), but rather by his uncle, Bifang 辟方, who reigned as King Xiao 孝 (r. 882?–866 BCE). Finally, the chronology of the period during which Kings Yih and Xiao reigned is particularly confused, with fully dated bronze inscriptions showing several different and mutually incompatible regnal calendars. All of this led David Nivison to suggest that King Xiao's interregnum may have begun even before King Yih's death, and that King Yih, like King Li after him, had been forced into exile.[14] While this remains but an interesting hypothesis, the absence of any praise for King Yih in the *Qiu pan* inscription would seem to be yet further indication that something went very wrong in the course of his reign.[15]

The Shan Family as Seen in the *Qiu Pan* Inscription

The importance of the *Qiu pan* inscription is doubtless greater for the information it provides regarding Qiu's own Shan family than it is for the historical information it provides concerning the Zhou kings. It provides a narrative of seven ancestors, beginning with the high ancestor Shan Gong 單公 and continuing generation by generation until Qiu's own deceased-father Gongshu 龔叔. As mentioned earlier, at least one of these ancestors, Li 盠, here given the apparently posthumous appellation Huizhong Lifu 惠仲盠父, was already known from a previous discovery of inscribed bronze vessels. Although it does not seem possible to identify any of the other ancestors with other bronzes made for members of the Shan family, and so this family cannot serve as a yardstick for the development of Zhou bronze styles in the way that the Wei 微 family of the *Shi Qiang pan* does, the manner in which the ancestors are described in the inscription may still reveal some features of the Zhou lineage structure. Isolating this time just the portions of the inscription describing Qiu's ancestors, and here taking the liberty of arranging the individual descriptions in two separate columns by alternating generations, I believe that at least a couple of different patterns reveal themselves.

丕顯朕皇高祖單公：趩趩克明哲厥德，夾召文王武王。 Illustrious was my august high ancestor Shan Gong: 　Radiantly capable of making bright and wise his virtue, he accompanied and assisted King Wen and King Wu.	
	雩朕皇高祖公叔：克逑匹成王。 With my august high ancestor Gongshu: 　He was capable of joining and aiding King Cheng.
雩朕皇高祖新室仲：克幽明厥心，䩗遠能狱。會召康王， With my august high ancestor Zhong of the New Chamber:	

Capable of making both somber and bright his heart, he was gentle with the distant and enabling with the near, and met with and assisted King Kang.	
	秉朕皇高祖惠仲盨父：龢穌于政，又成于猷，用會邵王穆王。 With my august high ancestor Huizhong Lifu: Bringing harmony in government and also being successful in his plans, he therewith met and assisted King Zhao and King Mu.
秉朕皇高祖零伯：粦明厥心，不家口服，用辟龏王、懿王。 With my august high ancestor Ling Bo: Making clear and bright his heart, he did not fail in his . . . duties, and therewith served King Gong and King Yih.	
	秉朕皇亞祖懿仲徵：諫克匍保厥辟孝王夷王。 With my august secondary ancestor Yihzhong: Remonstratingly, he was capable of advising and protecting his rulers King Xiao and King Yi.
秉朕皇考龏叔：穆㛮，穌甸于政明陵于德，亯辟剌王。 With my august deceased-father Gongshu: Beautifully and respectfully, harmonious and compliant in government, bright and helpful in virtue, he offered service to King Li.	

All of the ancestors are described as assisting past kings, the various verbs used all being synonymous: *jiashao* 夾召 "to accompany and assist," *qiupi* 逑匹 "to join and aid," *huizhao* 會邵 "to meet with and assist" (used two times), *bi* 辟 "to serve," *fubao* 匍保 "to advise and protect," and *xiangbi* 亯辟 "to offer service." It would seem that there is little to differentiate these terms. However, in the phrasing before these descriptions of service to past kings, that is, in the portion of the description dedicated just to the virtue of the ancestor himself, at least two patterns emerge from this division of the epithets by alternating generations. First, ancestors in the first, third, and fifth generations (i.e., the first three ancestors on the left-hand side of the preceding display) are all described as being able to make "bright" (*ming* 明) their "virtue" (*de* 德) or "heart" (*xin* 心):

單公：趩_克明哲厥德

Shan Gong: Radiantly capable of making bright and wise his virtue

新室仲：克幽明厥心

Zhong of the New Chamber: Capable of making both somber and bright his heart

零伯：燊明厥心

Ling Bo: Making clear and bright his heart

In the case of the other ancestor on the left-hand side of the display, Qiu's deceased-father Gongshu 龏叔, although the description in this inscription does not share this pattern, it may be notable that in the inscription on the *Qiu zhong* 逑鐘, a set of bells also cast for Qiu (and which, I will show later, was cast at the same time as the *Qiu pan*), we find him described in the same way:

丕顯朕皇考：克燊明厥心

Illustrious was my august deceased-father: Capable of making clear and bright his heart.

One of the three ancestors in the even generations (i.e., those on the right-hand side of the preceding display), Gongshu 公叔 of the second generation (not to be confused with Qiu's deceased-father Gongshu 龔叔), is lacking any personal description at all, while another is described as simply being "Remonstratingly" (*jian jian* 諫諫). Even the redoubtable Huizhong Lifu 惠仲盠父 of the fourth generation, who as previously mentioned was made commander in chief of all Zhou armies by King Mu, is praised for his successful governance and planning, but not for his personal virtues:

> 惠仲盠父：盠穌于政，又成于猷
>
> With my august high ancestor Huizhong Lifu: Bringing harmony in government and also being successful in his plans.

On the other hand, as we see here in the case of Huizhong Lifu, in which Li 盠 is the ancestor's personal name, it is only with ancestors in even generations for whom personal names are mentioned; another case is in the ancestor of the sixth generation, Yizhong Kuang 懿仲䟽. Perhaps this usage of personal names indicates a degree of closeness since this latter ancestor was Qiu's grandfather, with whom he would have been most closely identified in the Zhou ritual system.[16]

I would like to suggest that these sorts of similarities between ancestors of alternating generations may have something to do with the composition of the Zhou ancestral temple. Ritual texts describe the Zhou kinship system as having been organized according to alternating generations, the so-called *zhao* 昭–*mu* 穆 system. This system was manifested in the ancestral temple by ancestors of the *zhao* generations being arrayed on the left-hand side of the temple, and those of the *mu* generations on the right-hand side.[17] If this observation has any validity, perhaps the shared phrasing about the ancestors in the odd-numbered generations being capable of making bright their virtue or heart derives from the personal epithets written on their spirit tablets in the temple.

The Royal Command

Having considered how the beginning of the king's command to Qiu may have inspired in part the composition of the historical survey that opens the *Qiu pan* inscription, it is now time to examine again the royal command in its entirety. Comparisons between it and the other vessels cast for Qiu will show, I believe, that this was the initial command given to Qiu at the royal court. The command of the *Qiu pan* inscription reads:

王若曰：逑，丕顯文武膺受大令，匍有四方。則緐惟乃先聖祖考夾召先王，爵堇大令。今余惟巠乃先聖祖考申重乃令，令汝胥榮兌司四方虞林，用宮御。

The king approved of saying: "Qiu, illustrious (Kings) Wen and Wu received the great mandate and extended it to the four quarters. Then because it was your past wise ancestors' and deceased-father who accompanied and assisted the past kings to have merit and care with the great mandate, now it is that I recall your past wise ancestors and deceased-father and extend and increase your command, commanding you to assist Rong Dui, and concurrently to supervise the four quarters' game and forests, to be used for the palace's supply."

The first part of the king's address to Qiu is a recounting of his ancestors' assistance to Kings Wen and Wu, which has already been examined. This serves as the immediate context for the command proper, which is an extension (*shen* 申) of Qiu's hereditary position as assistant to Rong Dui 榮兌, simultaneously increasing his responsibilities to include also supervising the provisioning of the royal palace (*gong yu* 宮御) with the game and forests of the four quarters (*si fang yu lin* 四方虞林). As tokens of these responsibilities, he was awarded three insignia.

Let us now compare this command to the other commands that Qiu received or recorded in the *Forty-Second Year Qiu ding*, *Forty-Third Year Qiu ding*, and the *Qiu zhong* inscriptions. I will give only the first portions of the commands in the two *ding* inscriptions, the final portions not being directly comparable.

Qiu pan 逑盤	*Forty-Second Year Qiu ding* 逑鼎	*Forty-Third Year Qiu ding* 逑鼎	*Qiu zhong* 逑鐘
王若曰：逑，丕顯文武應受大令，匍有四方。則緐惟乃先聖祖考夾召	王若曰：逑，丕顯文武應受大令，匍有四方，則緐惟乃先聖祖考夾召先	王若曰：逑，丕顯文武應受大令，匍有四方，則緐惟乃先聖考夾召	

先王，爵菫大令。 The king approved of saying: "Qiu, illustrious (Kings) Wen and Wu received the great mandate and extended it to the four quarters. Then because it was your prior wise ancestors and deceased-father who accompanied and assisted the past kings to have merit and care with the great mandate,	王，爵菫大令，奠周邦。 The king approved of saying: "Qiu, illustrious (Kings) Wen and Wu received the great mandate and extended it to the four quarters. Then it was because of your prior wise ancestors' and deceased-father's assisting the prior kings to have merit and care with the great mandate and stabilizing the Zhou state,	先王，爵菫大令，奠周邦。 The king approved of saying: "Qiu, illustrious (Kings) Wen and Wu received the great mandate and extended it to the four quarters. Then it was because of your prior wise deceased-father's assisting the prior kings to have merit and care with the great mandate and stabilizing the Zhou state,	
今余惟坙乃先聖祖考，申重乃令，令汝疋榮兌司四方虞林，用宮御。 now it is that I recall your prior wise ancestors and deceased-father and extend and increase your command,	余弗遐忘聖人孫子。余惟閘乃先祖考有爵于周邦。肆余作口沙詢。余肇建長父侯于楊，余令汝奠長父休。女克奠于畢僮。 I have not forgotten the wise men's grandson, and	肆余弗忘聖人孫子。昔余既令女疋榮兌，兼司四方虞林，用宮御。余惟坙乃先祖考，有爵于周邦，申重乃令，令女官司歷人。 and so I have not forgotten the wise men's grandson.	天子坙朕先祖服，多賜述休，令兼司四方虞林。 The Son of Heaven recalled my prior ancestors' service, and greatly awarded Qiu benefices, and commanding concurrently to supervise the four quarters'

commanding you to assist Rong Dui, and concurrently to supervise the four quarters' game and forests, to be used for the palace's supply.	it was that I remembered your prior ancestors' and deceased-father's having merits in the Zhou state, and so I made . . . court interview. When I initially established Changfu to be lord in Yang, I commanded you to stabilize Changfu's benefices.	Formerly, I had already commanded you to assist Rong Dui, and concurrently to supervise the four quarters' game and forests, to be used for the palace's supply. Now it is that I recall your prior ancestors' and deceased-father's having had merit in the Zhou state and extend and increase your command, commanding you to officiate over and supervise the men of Li.	game and forests.

In the *Forty-Third Year Qiu ding* inscription, the king's command to Qiu includes a verbatim quotation of his command recorded in the *Qiu pan* inscription.

昔余既令汝疋榮兌，兼司四方虞林，用宮御。

Formerly, I had already commanded you to assist Rong Dui, and concurrently to supervise the four quarters' game and forests, to be used for the palace's supply.

This shows beyond question that both of these court audiences took place during the same reign, and that the audience commemorated by the *pan* inscription took place before the forty-third year of this *ding* inscription. Since the historical narrative of the *pan* inscription shows that it was composed during the reign of King Xuan, with mention of the reigning *tianzi* or "Son of Heaven" coming after the reign of King Li, there can be no doubt that this forty-third year also refers to the reign of King Xuan. This of course has crucial implications for the chronology of the late Western Zhou, as many scholars have already noted.[18] It also has important implications for the question concerning us here—the process by which inscriptions were written—since it shows beyond question that the king could make reference to commands that he had previously issued. This corroborates previous evidence that the royal secretariat maintained archives of royal commands.[19]

The preceding comparison also shows, I believe, that the inscription on the *zhong* refers to the same command as that on the *pan*, implying therefore that the two inscriptions were composed at the same time. Although the *zhong* inscription is much attenuated, it does contain the crucial information that Qiu was "simultaneously to supervise the game and forests of the four quarters" seen already in the *pan* inscription. When we now go on to examine the entirety of the *zhong* inscription, I believe we will find considerable other evidence relating the two inscriptions. Moreover, a comparison of the two inscriptions will go still further to illustrate the process by which bronze inscriptions were composed.

The *Qiu Zhong* Inscription

In August 1985, sixteen bronze bells were found by brickworkers in Yangjiacun, Meixian County, the same village in which the *Qiu pan* and other vessels were discovered in 2003. Like the *Qiu pan* and the twenty-six vessels with which it was discovered, these bells had been placed into a storage pit, presumably at the same time, the two pits being less than sixty meters apart. Unfortunately, after discovery some of the bells were subsequently stolen and smuggled to Hong Kong, there being sold on the antiques market; only thirteen bells now remain in the Meixian County Cultural Relics Control Station (*wenwu guanlisuo* 文物管理所).[20] Three of the bells there have identical inscriptions of 117 characters, while one other has just the final 23 characters of the complete inscription.[21] At the time of their discovery, these bells did not attract a great deal of attention, since even the complete 117-character inscription had seemed quite formulaic, and before the discovery of the *Qiu pan*, there was no way to discern the identity or family background of the patron Qiu.[22] With the 2003 discovery of Qiu's second cache, however, numerous studies have pointed out its connection with this earlier cache and have shown that the two derive from the same individual. I would like to go further to argue not only that the inscription of the bells was composed at the same time as that of the *pan*, but also that a comparison of the two inscriptions shows still further the process of their composition. Let us begin with a translation of the bells' inscription.

Qiu Zhong 逑鐘

逑曰。不顯朕皇考克諆明厥心，帥用厥先祖考政德，宫辟先王。逑御于厥辟，不敢茶，虔夙夕敬厥死事。天子巠朕先祖服，多賜逑休，令兼司四方虞林。逑敢對天子不顯魯休揚，用作朕皇考龏叔穌鐘，鎗恖，雍錯，用追孝卲各喜侃前文人嚴才上，豐泉降余多福降余康娛屯祐、永令。逑其萬年眉壽畯臣天子孫永寶。

Qiu said: "Illustrious was my august deceased-father, capable of making his heart clear and bright, he followed and used his prior ancestors' and deceased-father's governance and virtue to offer service to the prior king. Qiu makes supplies to his ruler, not daring to fail, assiduously morning and evening respecting his sworn responsibility. The Son of Heaven recalls my prior ancestors' duties, greatly awarding Qiu benefices, commanding simultaneously to supervise the game and forests of the four quarters. Qiu dares to respond to the Son of Heaven's illustriously fine beneficence and to extol it, herewith making for my august deceased-father Gongshu these harmonic bells. *Cangcang congcong, yangyang yongyong*, herewith sending filial piety to, summoning to approach, and gladdening the former cultured men. (May) the former cultured men, stern on high, abundantly send down on me many blessings, peaceful harmony, pure aid, and an eternal mandate, and may Qiu for ten thousand years have longevity to serve the Son of Heaven, and have sons and grandsons' grandsons eternally to treasure them."

Lothar von Falkenhausen presciently selected this inscription to illustrate what he termed the "subjective mode" of inscriptions, which he describes as taking "the form of a proclamation from the donor's mouth, which sometimes paraphrases the contents of investiture records without quoting them directly."²³ The opening of this inscription, which quotes the patron as "saying" (Qiu yue 逑曰) the contents of the inscription, is one feature of this mode. It occurs in only about ten mid- to late Western Zhou inscriptions, and it is noteworthy that half of these are on bells.²⁴ It may be that the aural nature of the bells led to a focus on orality in the inscriptions on them. On the other hand, their inscriptions were, of course, very much written, and in the case of the *Qiu zhong* it is possible to demonstrate direct precedents for virtually all of its phrases in the *Qiu pan* inscription. Some of these phrases were more or less transformed as they were adapted for the *zhong* inscription, and it is especially in these transformations that we can see the scribe at work.

On the basis of a comparison of the inscription on the *Qiu zhong* with that on the *Liang Qi zhong* 梁其鐘, another late Western Zhou set of bells, Noel Barnard made the interesting suggestion that some places in it "possibly stem from textual attenuation."²⁵ The discovery now of the *Qiu pan* allows us to demonstrate far more precisely just how this textual attenuation was produced. The inscription of the *Qiu zhong* can be divided into some seven discrete sentences, as in the following comparison. In the comparison, I provide also relevant parallels in the *Qiu pan* inscription.

Qiu pan 逑盤	*Qiu zhong* 逑鐘
雩朕皇考龏叔：穆趩＿，龢訇于政，明陵于德，宣辟剌王。 With my august deceased-father Gongshu: Beautifully and respectfully, harmonious and compliant in government, bright and equable in virtue, he obeyed and assisted King Li.	逑曰。不顯朕皇考克溓明厥心，帥用厥先祖考政德，宣辟先王。 Qiu said: "Illustrious my august deceased-father, capable of making his heart clear and bright, he followed and used his prior ancestors' and deceased-father's governance and virtue to offer service to the prior king.

The Writing of a Late Western Zhou Bronze Inscription | 83

逑肇䎽朕皇祖考服，虔夙夕敬朕死事。 Qiu has begun by continuing my august ancestors' and deceased-father's responsibilities, diligently morning and evening respecting my sworn service.	逑御于厥辟，不敢家，虔夙夕敬厥死事。 Qiu makes supplies to his ruler, not daring to fail, assiduously morning and evening respecting his sworn service.
肆天子多賜逑休。…王若曰…今余惟堅乃先聖祖考申重乃令，令汝疋榮兌兼司四方虞林，用宫御。 And so the Son of Heaven has much awarded Qiu benefices. … The king approved of saying: … now it is that I recall your past wise ancestors and deceased-father and extend and increase your command, commanding you to assist Rong Dui, and concurrently to supervise the four quarters' game and forests, to be used for the palace's supply.	天子巠朕先祖服，多賜逑休，令兼司四方虞林。 The Son of Heaven recalls my prior ancestors' duties, greatly awarding Qiu benefices, commanding simultaneously to supervise the game and forests of the four quarters.
逑敢對天子丕顯魯休揚，用作朕皇族考寶尊盤。 Qiu dares in response to the Son of Heaven's illustriously fine beneficence to extol it, herewith making for my august ancestors and deceased-father this treasured offertory *pan* basin,	逑敢對天子不顯魯休揚，用作朕皇考龔叔龢鐘。 Qiu dares to respond to the Son of Heaven's illustriously fine beneficence and to extol it, herewith making for my august deceased-father Gongshu these harmonic bells.
用追亯于前文人。 with which to send offerings of filial piety to the past cultured men.	鎗鎗恖恖，雄雄鎗鎗，用追孝卲各喜侃前文人。 *Cangcang congcong, yangyang yongyong,* herewith sending filial piety to, summoning to approach, and gladdening the former cultured men.

前文人嚴在上，廙在[下]。豐泉降述魯多福、眉壽、𩔖綰。受余康娛屯祐、通彔永令霝終， May the former cultured men be stern on high and respected below, and abundantly send down on Qiu fine and many blessings and long life everlasting, giving me peaceful harmony, pure aid, penetrating wealth, an eternal mandate and a numinous end,	前文人嚴才上，豐泉降余多福降余康娛屯祐、永令。 (May) the former cultured men, stern on high, abundantly send down on me many blessings, peaceful harmony, pure aid, and an eternal mandate.
述畯臣天子孫永寶用言。 so that Qiu may serve the Son of Heaven. May sons and grandsons' grandsons eternally treasure and use it to make offerings.	述其萬年眉壽畯臣天子孫永寶。 May Qiu for ten thousand years have longevity to serve the Son of Heaven, and have sons and grandsons' grandsons eternally to treasure them.

There is no need to point out the numerous similarities between these two inscriptions; reading across the rows of this display should leave no doubt as to the relationship between them. More interesting, perhaps, are the divergences between the two inscriptions.

The most obvious difference between the two inscriptions, viewed as wholes, is in their length: the *Qiu pan* inscription has 373 characters while the various complete *Qiu zhong* inscriptions have only 117 characters.[26] To some extent, this can be attributed to the differences in the bronzes that carry the inscriptions.[27] The *Qiu pan* is a round basin affording a flat writing surface with a diameter of fifty-three centimeters. The three *Qiu zhong* with the 117-character inscription stored at the Meixian County Cultural Relics Control Station are larger (reported heights of the entire bells are 65.5, 65, and 61 cm), but the surface area available to carry the inscription is much more limited. It would seem that space alone was responsible for some decisions about what could be included in this inscription. Thus, the long historical narrative of the *pan* inscription could not possibly fit on a single bell. In its place, we find an opening sentence praising just Qiu's father Gongshu, some of the language being identical with language in the *Qiu pan* inscription.[28]

One other sentence reveals a subtle rewriting. Qiu praises his father for having followed and used his prior ancestors' and deceased-father's *zheng de* 政德. Although this compound is perfectly understandable as an adjective-noun construction meaning "governing virtue," a comparison with the *Qiu pan*'s praise of Gongshu suggests that it should be read instead as an abbreviation of the epithet applied to him there: *he jun yu zheng, ming qi yu de* 龢訇于政, 明陵于德 "harmonious and compliant in government, bright and equable in virtue," in which "government" (*zheng* 政) and "virtue" (*de* 德) are both nouns.

Another abbreviation can be seen in Qiu's prayer for blessings from the "former cultured men" (*qian wen ren* 前文人). Whereas the prayer in the *pan* inscription includes thirty-two characters, the *zhong* inscription makes do with only eighteen characters. This sort of abbreviation may have been impromptu; since the *zhong* inscription fills all available space on all three of the bells that carry it, it may have been determined at the last minute that some portions of the prayer simply would not fit. On the other hand, it is also likely that the choice of what to delete—from the former cultured men being "respected below" (*yi zai xia* 廙才下),[29] to the desire for "penetrating wealth" (*tong lu* 通录) or a "numinous end" (*ling zhong* 霝冬)—indicates some scale of priorities.

It is in the presentation of the king's address to Qiu that we find the *zhong*'s scribe taking the greatest liberties. Whereas in the *pan* inscription, the entire address is quoted, presumably from the bamboo slips presented to Qiu at the end of his audience, the *zhong* inscription provides a highly attenuated paraphrase, quoting verbatim only the new command "simultaneously to supervise the game and forests of the four quarters." In paraphrasing the preamble of the king's address, the scribe begins by changing the person of the speech: in the verbatim quotation in the *pan* inscription, the "king" (*wang*) speaks in the first person "I" (*yu* 余) and refers to Qiu's ancestors as "your" (*nai* 乃); in the *zhong* inscription, the king is referred to honorifically as "Son of Heaven" (*tianzi*) and Qiu's ancestors become "my" (*zhen* 朕). Despite the personal touch here, the following clause awkwardly reverts to referring to Qiu by name rather than by a transformation of the pronoun that the king used: "you" (*ru* 汝).

More important, two other transformations in this clause introduce grammatical ambiguity. Whereas in the *pan* inscription, the king "recalls" (*jing* 巠) Qiu's "prior wise ancestors and deceased-father" (*xian sheng zu kao* 先聖祖考), the *zhong* inscription changes this to the Son of Heaven's recalling his "prior ancestors' duties" (*xian zu fu* 先祖服). Although this is perfectly grammatical in English, and may also have been grammatical in the language of the Western Zhou, I suspect that the *fu* 服 "duties" marks contamination from a previous sentence in the *pan* inscription: Qiu's characterization of his own accomplishments seen in the second row of the preceding comparison: Qiu *zhao zan zhen huang zu kao fu* 逑肇纘朕皇祖考服, "Qiu has begun by continuing my august ancestors' and deceased-father's duties."

The following five characters are also ambiguous: *duo ci Qiu xiu ling* 多賜逑休令. Should the object of *ci* 賜 "to award" be *xiu* 休 "beneficence" or *ling* 令 "command"? Although either reading is possible,[30] and *xiu ling* 休令 "beneficent command" is common in mid- and late Western Zhou bronze inscriptions,[31] such a reading here would leave the following direct quotation of the king's new command to Qiu without a verb. Unless we posit the inadvertent omission of a duplication mark after *ling* 令 "command," the reading I have given in the translation, awkward though it may be ("greatly awarding Qiu benefices, commanding simultaneously to supervise the game and forests of the four quarters"), seems to be obligatory.

Another example of awkward phrasing, this time produced by the presence of a duplication mark, is to be seen in the final sentence of the *Qiu zhong* inscription. When Qiu prays that for ten thousand years he will have longevity to serve the Son of Heaven and will have descendants eternally to treasure the vessel, the juxtaposition of the *zi* 子 "son" of *Tianzi* 天子 "Son of Heaven," and *zi sun* 子孫 "sons and grandsons," with duplication marks after both *zi* 子 and *sun* 孫 (i.e., 天子₌孫₌ or 天子子孫孫) produces the awkward phrasing "to serve the Son of Heaven, and sons (*sic*) and grandsons' grandsons eternally to treasure" the vessel.[32] In this case, the wording is taken over verbatim from the final prayer of the *Qiu pan* inscription, and so is not the result of editorial transformation. I would suggest that in this awkwardness we see the trace of a writer struggling to reconcile wording that he has cut and pasted from different phrases,[33] even if they are phrases that he may have written originally (assuming that the same scribe was responsible for both the *Qiu pan* and *Qiu zhong* inscriptions).

Conclusions

In this study, I have examined four bronze inscriptions written for a single individual named Qiu, who lived during the last years of the Western

Zhou dynasty. Given the location where these bronze vessels and bells were found, Yangjiacun of Meixian County, Shaanxi, and given Qiu's office of game and forest warden, it seems reasonable to assume that he lived about one hundred kilometers outside of the Zhou capital, though evidence in the inscriptions shows that he was also temporarily posted to other locations and other duties. On at least three occasions, he was received at royal audiences in the capital, and the awards he was given at these audiences served as the occasion for his casting of the commemorative bronzes.

Two of these inscriptions, those on the *Forty-Second* and *Forty-Third Year Qiu ding*, describe these audiences in some detail: Qiu was ushered into the king's presence; the head of the royal secretariat handed the king the prepared text of Qiu's award, written on bamboo or wooden slips; the king called on another scribe to read the text on the bamboo slips to Qiu; and then Qiu was given these slips as he exited the court. This coincides with descriptions of royal audiences in other late Western Zhou bronze inscriptions and was probably the norm for all audiences, even those described in abbreviated fashion. The award documents given to Qiu then served as the basis for the inscriptions cast into the vessels commemorating these audiences and their awards. In the case of the *Forty-Second Year Qiu ding* inscription, the award document is quoted verbatim and comprises the great bulk of the inscription, more than 200 of its total 281 characters. The remaining portion, added by Qiu or by a scribe in his employ, is a formulaic dedication of the vessel to Qiu's ancestors and a prayer for blessings for himself and his descendants. Differences in wording, especially in the mode of reference to the king, reveal the different authorial hands in these two portions of this one lengthy but structurally simple inscription.

The inscription on the *Qiu pan* is far more sophisticated; indeed, there is only one other precedent for it in the entire inventory of Western Zhou bronze inscriptions, the famous *Shi Qiang pan*. I have suggested that this vessel commemorated Qiu's initial appointment at court, in which he was commanded to "continue" his "august ancestors' and deceased-father's duties." In making this command to Qiu, the king recalled how Qiu's ancestors had aided the Zhou kings Wen and Wu in establishing the dynasty and caring for the great mandate. In this inscription, Qiu again quoted the royal appointment verbatim, the text of which must also have been given to him on bamboo or wooden slips. However, in the case of this inscription, the text of the royal appointment constitutes only a minor portion of the entire inscription, just about 65 out of 373 characters, even if it can be presumed to have inspired and legitimated the rest of the inscription. The great bulk of the inscription is comprised of a historical narrative relating—generation by generation—how Qiu's ancestors had aided the Zhou kings; this narrative runs about 240 characters, or two-thirds of the entire inscription. I have suggested that Qiu, or his scribe, may have drawn on a variety of sources in composing this narrative. He certainly drew in the first instance on the text of the royal appointment that had been given to him; he may also have had reference to a saga or sagas of the Zhou kings and their exploits that would have been widely known, either in written or oral form, at the Zhou court; and to this he probably added epithets and encomia found on the spirit tablets of the ancestors in his ancestral temple. He closed the inscription with the obligatory dedication to these ancestors, and the prayer for their blessings on him and his descendants.

At the same time that he cast this *pan* basin and its lengthy inscription, he also had cast a set of bells. Several of these bells carry an inscription obviously related to that on the *pan* basin, but quite abbreviated, with just 117 characters as opposed to 383. Much of the abbreviation was achieved by simply deleting the historical narrative of the *pan* inscription, but other changes required different juxtapositions of phrases taken over from the longer inscription. In at least a few cases, these transformations produced an awkward effect, apparently the result of the cut-and-paste nature of their production.[34]

It is only due to the unique circumstances that two separate caches of vessels and bells, almost all made by a single individual, have been discovered that we can compare and contrast the inscriptions, and in their similarities and differences begin to see something of the process by which the inscriptions were written. Although this is but a single example, it is almost certainly representative of the writing that was taking place throughout late Western Zhou society and thus is an important key to the development of the Chinese literary tradition.

Chapter Four

On the Casting of the Art Institute of Chicago's *Shi Wang Ding*

With Remarks on the Important Position of Writing in the Consciousness of Ancient China

In 2005 the Art Institute of Chicago purchased the important Western Zhou bronze vessel *Shi Wang ding* 師望鼎, its first major purchase of an ancient Chinese bronze vessel since the formation of its Buckingham Collection in the 1920s. A rubbing of the inscription on the *Shi Wang ding* was first published in 1896 in the *Kezhai jigulu* 窓齋集古錄 *Record of Collected Antiquities in the Ke Studio* of Wu Dacheng 吳大澂 (1835–1902),[1] demonstrating that it had been unearthed prior to the end of the Qing dynasty. There are reports that the vessel was obtained by the famous general Zuo Zongtang 左宗棠 (1812–1885) in the course of his 1876–1878 military expedition into Xinjiang. However, it is unlikely that this vessel could have been unearthed in Xinjiang, and much more likely that Zuo

---

The contents of this chapter have been presented to various conferences in both China and the United States, but (as far as I can determine) it is published here for the first time. In the course of writing this chapter, I received help from many friends: Zhou Ya 周亞 and Lian Haiping 廉海萍, both of the Shanghai Museum; Sun Peiyang 孫沛陽 of the Center for the Study of Paleography and Unearthed Documents of Fudan University; Tao Wang 汪濤, Elinor Pearlstein, and Suzanne R. Schnepp of the Art Institute of Chicago; Yung-ti Li 李永迪 of the University of Chicago; and Han Wei 韓巍 of Peking University, and I am happy to acknowledge my debt to them here.

obtained it while he was governor of Shaanxi and Gansu in the decade from 1866 to 1876. According to the *Zhou jinwen cun* 周金文存 *Preserved Zhou Bronze Inscriptions* of Zou An 鄒安 (1864–1940), after Zuo Zongtang's death the vessel was first purchased by a certain Mr. Cheng 程 of Shanghai and then in 1943 sold to Chen Rentao 陳仁濤 (1906–1968) of the same city.[2] In 1946, Chen moved from Shanghai to Hong Kong, taking the *Shi Wang ding* with him. In 1952, he published a catalog of his bronze collection, *Jinkui lun gu chuji* 金匱論古初集 *A First Collection of Jinkui's Discussion of Antiquity*, in which the first photograph of the vessel appeared.[3] From that time until 2005, the vessel remained in the Chen family private collection.

The *Shi Wang ding* is a typical late Western Zhou tripod caldron, with a fairly shallow belly mounted over three solid "horse-hoof" legs, each with an appended mask on the thigh portion of the leg, and two hemispherical ears extending upward from the rim of the vessel (see fig. 4.1). The vessel shape is also very similar to that of such well-known vessels as the *Da Ke ding* 大克鼎 (*Jicheng* 2836), *Xiao Ke ding* 小克鼎 (*Jicheng* 2796–2802; fig. 4.2), *Shi Song ding* 史頌鼎 (*Jicheng* 2787–88), *Forty-Second Year Qiu ding* 逑鼎, and *Forty-Third Year Qiu ding* 逑鼎,[4] with the only difference being that on all of those vessels the belly décor is a wave design (see figs. 4.1 and 4.2).

Figure 4.1. *Shi Wang ding* 師望鼎 vessel. Courtesy of the Art Institute of Chicago.

On the Casting of the Art Institute of Chicago's *Shi Wang Ding* | 91

Figure 4.2. *Xiao Ke ding* 小克鼎 vessel. Courtesy of the Shanghai Museum.

The interior rear wall of the *Shi Wang ding* bears an inscription of ten lines with 91 characters in all (plus three repeating characters; see fig. 4.3).

Figure 4.3. Rubbing of *Shi Wang ding* 師望鼎 inscription. From Zhongguo Shehui kexueyuan Kaogu yanjiusuo, ed., *Yin Zhou jinwen jicheng*, 2812.

This inscription can be transcribed and translated as follows.

大師小子師朢曰不顯皇
考宼公穆_ 克盟氒心哲
氒德用辟于先王得屯
亡敃朢肇帥井皇考虔
夙夜出內王命不敢不
豕不婁王用弗忘聖人
之後多蔑曆易休朢敢
對揚天子不顯魯休用
乍朕皇考宼公尊鼎師
朢其萬年子_ 孫_ 永寶用

The Grand Captain's young son Captain Wang says: Illustriously august deceased-father Duke Jiu was beautifully capable of making accordant his heart and making wise his virtue, with which he served the past kings, gaining purity without flaw. Wang begins to lead on to emulate his august deceased-father, respectfully morning and night taking out and bringing in the king's commands, not daring not to follow through or to manage. Because of this, the king has not forgotten the sagely man's descendant, and has greatly praised his accomplishments and awarded him beneficence. Wang dares in response to extol the Son of Heaven's illustriously fine beneficence, herewith making for my august deceased-father Duke Jiu this offertory caldron; may Captain Wang for ten thousand years have sons' sons and grandsons' grandsons eternally to treasure and use it.

Whether for its artistic merit or its historical interest, the *Shi Wang ding* is surely a most important piece. In the following, I will discuss two topics concerning it: first its date, and second features of its casting. In the past, scholars have commonly dated the *Shi Wang ding* to the Middle Western Zhou (ca. 900 BCE), a dating that is related to—and has in turn influenced—the periodization of a whole series of mid- and late Western Zhou bronze vessels. However, based on numerous bronze vessels that have been discovered in the last decade or two, as well as on advances in our understanding of the periodization of bronze vessels, this date would appear to be too early. Comparisons with other vessels will show that the *Shi Wang ding* should instead be dated to the late Western Zhou (ca. 800 BCE). As for the casting of the vessel, when the Art Institute of Chicago was purchasing it, it subjected the vessel to a complete series of full-body X-rays. Not only do these X-rays reveal crucial features of this one vessel's casting, but they also suggest important information regarding the casting of other inscribed Western Zhou bronzes. Both of these points deserve further discussion.

The Date of the *Shi Wang Ding*

After the inscription of the *Shi Wang ding* had been published, Guo Moruo 郭沫若 (1892–1978) made the first attempt to date it, regarding the inscription's "Captain Wang" 師望 as the same person as the "Wang" 望 of the *Wang gui* 望簋 (*Jicheng* 4272). Because he had dated the *Wang gui* to the reign of King Gong 共 (917/15–900 BCE), he therefore dated the *Shi Wang ding* to the same reign.[5] After this, Shirakawa Shizuka 白川靜 (1910–2006) and Ma Chengyuan 馬承源 (1927–2004) also followed his lead in dating the vessel to the reign of King Gong.[6] Although the book *Xi Zhou qingtongqi fenqi duandai yanjiu* 西周青銅器分期斷代研究 *Studies of Western Zhou Bronze Vessel Periodization* by Wang Shimin 王世民, Chen Gongrou 陳公柔 (1919–2004), and Zhang Changshou 張長壽 (1929–2020) does not include a discussion of the *Shi Wang ding* itself, the very similar *Shi Tangfu ding* 師湯父鼎 *is* dated to "about the time of King Gong." With respect to the similarly shaped *Xiao Ke ding*, they said, "In sum, it dates to the transition between mid and late Western Zhou, about the time of kings Yi 夷 (r. 867/65–858 BCE) and Li 厲 (r. 857/853–842/828 BCE)."[7] Their dating of these two similar vessels to "about the time of King Gong" on the one hand and "about the time of the late Western Zhou king Li" on the other hand would seem to reflect a rather vague sense of periodization. Recognizing that this periodization would seem to be too early for the shape and décor of the vessel, Jessica Rawson related it to eight similar *ding* caldrons showing a development in the caldron through the second half of the mid-Western Zhou, and suggested only somewhat less vaguely that the *Shi Wang ding* "seems rather to resemble vessels of the first part of late Western Zhou."[8]

The 1970s brought some advances in discussions of the periodization of the *Shi Wang ding*. In December 1974, a cache at Qiangjiacun 強家村, Fufeng 扶風 County, Shaanxi, was unearthed with seven bronzes in it. One of these bronzes, a bell called variously *Shi Yu zhong* 師兒鐘 or *Shi Cheng zhong* 師丞鐘 (*Jicheng* 141) bears an inscription that reads:

師兒肇乍朕剌且虢季、眚公、幽叔、朕皇考德叔大林鐘。

Captain Yu for the first time makes for my valorous ancestors Guoji, Duke Jiu, Youshu, and my august deceased-father Deshu this great stand of bells.

Since "Duke Jiu" is the same posthumous name as the "august deceased-father Duke Jiu" of the *Shi Wang ding*'s inscription, Wu Zhenfeng 吳鎮烽 and Luo Zhongru 雒忠如 argued that the *Shi Wang ding* and the bronzes in this cache should be seen as coming from a single family, and that "Captain Wang" should be the great-grandfather of Captain Yu. Based on this identification, they dated the *Shi Wang ding* to the latter portion of mid-Western Zhou, roughly to the time of Kings Yih 懿 (r. 899/97–873 BCE) or Xiao 孝 (r. 882?–868 BCE).[9] After this identification and date were accepted by both Li Xueqin 李學勤 (1933–2019) and Zhu Fenghan 朱鳳瀚, the two most influential contemporary scholars of bronze vessels,[10] it has come to be seen as definitive. Therefore, when displaying the vessel, the Art Institute of Chicago gave its date as "early 9th century," which is to say the latter half of mid-Western Zhou, roughly from the time of King Gong through that of King Yi.

Nevertheless, recent scholarship has presented new views of the periodization of Western Zhou bronzes. Especially after the discovery of the *Forty-Second Year Qiu ding* 逨鼎 and *Forty-Third Year Qiu ding* 逨鼎 in 2003, several scholars have argued that the *Xiao Ke ding* and similar vessels, all of which share the same vessel shape and décor as the two *Qiu ding* vessels, should be dated considerably later than previously thought, and very possibly as late as the reign of King Xuan 宣 (r. 827/25–782 BCE).[11] In line with this, there is also evidence to suggest that the *Shi Wang ding* cannot possibly be dated as early as the reign of King Gong.

Song dynasty catalogs of bronze vessels already contain two bronzes made by a "Captain Wang": the *Shi Wang gui* 師望簋 (*Jicheng* 3682; see fig. 4.4) and *Shi Wang xu* 師望盨 (*Jicheng* 4354; see fig. 4.5).

Although the inscriptions on these two vessels are both quite short, only stating, "Captain Wang, the young son of the Great Captain, makes this offertory vessel" (太師小子師望作尊彝), since the identification of Captain Wang as "the young son of the Great Captain" is the

Figure 4.4. *Shi Wang gui* 師望簋 vessel.

same as that of the *Shi Wang ding*, it is all but certain that these vessels were made by the same person. The vessel shape of the *Shi Wang gui* is a classic example of late Western Zhou *gui* 簋 tureens and could not possibly be dated as early as the mid-Western Zhou. As for the *Shi Wang xu*, unfortunately there is only the Song dynasty line-drawing in which the décor is not entirely clear. However, the vessel seems to be very similar to the *Guo Bi xu* 虢比盨 (*Jicheng* 4466) in the collection of the Palace Museum in Beijing, such that the two vessels should be quite close in date.

Figure 4.5. *Shi Wang xu* 師望盨 vessel. From Wang Fu 王黼 et al., *Bogu tulu* 博古圖錄 (1123), 17.12 Lü Dalin 呂大臨, *Kaogu tu* 考古圖 (1092), 3.38.

The *Guo Bi xu* was doubtless made by the same person who sponsored the *Guo Bi ding* 龢比鼎 (*Jicheng* 2818), which is a classic example of a late Western Zhou *ding* caldron with a hemispherical belly and horse-hoof legs. The *Guo Bi ding* carries an inscription with a date notation of "thirty-first year," which almost certainly refers to the reign of King Xuan. If the *Guo Bi xu* should thus be dated to the very end of the Western Zhou, it stands to reason that the *Shi Wang xu* should also be seen as a late Western Zhou vessel.

In addition to the *Shi Wang gui* and *Shi Wang xu* seen in the Song dynasty catalogs, another vessel made by Captain Wang is the *Shi Wang hu* 師望壺 (*Jicheng* 9661; see fig. 4.6) in the collection of the British Museum.

The *Shi Wang hu*, like the *Shi Wang ding*, was first published in Wu Dacheng's *Kezhai jigulu*,[12] suggesting that the two vessels may have been unearthed at the same time. Wang Shimin, Chen Gongrou, and Zhang Changshou have analyzed the *Shi Wang hu* as a type 2a *hu* 壺 vase, which they describe as having "a round belly inclined outwards with two ears in the shape of snails and ring handles, with the entire vessel decorated with three bands of wave décor."[13] The comparison they cite is the *Fan Ju sheng hu* 番匊生壺 (*Jicheng* 9705), which also bears a complete date notation of "twenty-sixth year, sixth month, first auspiciousness, *jimao*"

Figure 4.6. *Shi Wang hu* 師望壺 vessel. Used with permission of the British Museum.

(隹廿又六年十月初吉己卯). It is almost certain that this vessel too should be dated to the reign of King Xuan.

Based on the characteristics of the four vessels made by "Captain Wang, young son of the grand captain," it is highly unlikely that the *Shi Wang ding* could have been made as early as the time of kings Yih or Xiao, as proposed by Wu Zhenfeng and Luo Zhongru, much less as early as the reign of King Gong, as argued by Guo Moruo, Shirakawa Shizuka, and Ma Chengyuan. Rather, it should date to the late Western Zhou, perhaps even to the time of King Xuan. Of course, this is just a broad periodization that will need further evidence to be fully convincing. In any event, the date given to the vessel by the Art Institute of Chicago—"early 9th c. BCE"—should have at least a question mark after it.

Casting Features of the *Shi Wang Ding*

When the Art Institute was considering buying the *Shi Wang ding*, in order to confirm its authenticity they produced a complete set of X-rays, examining each part of the vessel. It is not at all surprising that the X-rays did in fact confirm that the vessel is unquestionably authentic. However, the X-rays did produce one surprising result: the vessel wall bearing its inscription is the only part of the vessel not marked by gas bubbles produced in the course of its casting. Conversely, the wall opposite that bearing the inscription is marked by numerous gas bubbles. Suzanne R. Schnepp of the Art Institute's Conservation Department described this feature in her "Condition Report on Arrival" of the vessel.

> X-radiographs reveal extensive porosities caused by the entrapment of gas bubbles as the metal cooled. It seems significant that the inscription area is the only section of the sides that is almost free from these porosities. The vessel may have been cast at an angle, with this side lower than the rest, so that as the bubbles rose through the metal they would leave this key area free from blemish.[14]

Based on this report by Ms. Schnepp, I offered the following observation in an occasional essay published in 2012:

> From the x-rays it is possible to observe a very interesting phenomenon. The *Shi Wang ding* is a classic late Western Zhou round caldron, with the inscription arrayed on the interior

back wall, running from the top of the vessel down into the bottom of the belly. The x-rays reveal that the bronze of the wall carrying the inscription is extremely pure, with hardly any gas bubbles. On the other hand, the front wall of the vessel, which is to say the side without the inscription, is marked by numerous gas bubbles. In the casting process, the molten bronze is most dense and most pure in the bottom portion of the mold assemblage, producing more and more gas bubbles as it rises upwards through the assemblage. These gas bubbles invariably leave a trace in the structure of the bronze, and can even occasionally produce blow-holes in the skin of the vessel itself. It would seem that in order to preserve the purity of the side of the bronze carrying the inscription, the casters of the *Shi Wang ding* intentionally placed that side of the mold at the bottom so that the gas bubbles would rise to the opposite wall, even if that was the front wall of the vessel. This is different from our usual understanding of the placement of the mold assemblage and the casting process. The *Shi Wang ding* x-rays demonstrate that the Western Zhou casters were extremely concerned about the inscription and intended that it should display to its best effect. This means that not only was the content of the inscription regarded as important, but its physical display was also regarded as extremely important.[15]

We know that ancient bronze vessels were cast by pouring molten bronze into a piece mold assemblage made up of an inner core and an outer mold. In the process of casting, as the molten bronze cools it naturally produces gas, which rises through the mold assemblage seeking a place to exit. However, as the molten bronze continued to be poured into the assemblage, some of the gas would be blocked and would remain locked within the structure of the bronze itself, taking the form of bubbles and sometimes even producing small blow-holes in the skin of the bronze. Figure 4.7 is an X-ray picture of the wall of the *Shi Wang ding* bearing the inscription, the very few black marks indicating porosities in the bronze (which are the same as gas bubbles).

Compare this with an X-ray of the front wall of the vessel, which is to say the wall opposite that bearing the inscription (fig. 4.8). It can be seen that the entire structure is marked by black marks indicating porosities.

On the Casting of the Art Institute of Chicago's *Shi Wang Ding* | 99

Figure 4.7. X-ray of the back wall of the *Shi Wang ding* 師望鼎 (i.e., the wall bearing the inscription). Courtesy of the Art Institute of Chicago.

As previously noted, Suzanne Schnepp had theorized that the *Shi Wang ding* was possibly cast on its side, such that the wall with the inscription was at the bottom of the casting assemblage. Since the gas would rise upward in the mold, this would seem to be a reasonable hypothesis. However, this is radically different from the way most metallurgists reconstruct the casting method. According to them, a vessel such as the *Shi Wang ding* would be cast in an inverted position, with the mouth of the vessel facing down and the belly and the three legs at the top (as shown in fig. 4.9). Based on this understanding, during casting the three legs would function as sprues and vents. The sprue

Figure 4.8. X-ray of the front wall of the *Shi Wang ding* 師望鼎 (i.e., the wall opposite that bearing the inscription). Courtesy of the Art Institute of Chicago.

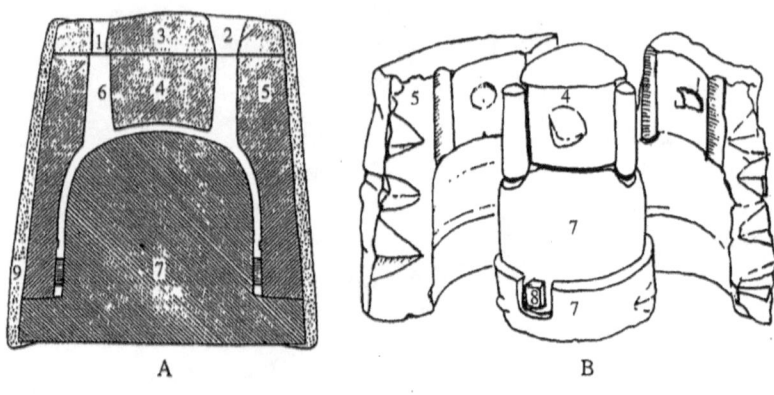

插图七·一三　圆鼎范结构示意图
1. 气孔　2. 浇口　3. 浇口范　4. 顶范　5. 腹范　6. 鼎　7. 鼎腹泥芯和底范
8. 鼎耳泥芯　9. 草拌泥

Figure 4.9. Diagram of the mold assemblage for a round caldron; after Zhu Fenghan 朱鳳瀚, *Zhongguo qingtongqi zonglun* 中國青銅器綜論 (Shanghai: Shanghai Guji chubanshe, 2009), 756. Courtesy of Zhu Fenghan. 1. Vent; 2. Sprue; 3. Sprue Mold; 4. Top Mold; 5. Belly Mold; 6. Caldron; 7. Core and Base of Caldron Belly; 8. Core of Caldron Ears; 9. Straw-mixed clay (not visible).

refers to the ingress point for the molten bronze, while the vent refers to the egress point for the escaping gas.

Still more recently, Su Rongyu 蘇榮譽 has published a long study entitled "Ershi shiji dui Xian Qin qingtong liqi zhuzao jishu de yanjiu" 二十世紀對先秦青銅禮器鑄造技術的研究 "Twentieth-Century Studies of Casting Technology of Pre-Qin Bronze Ritual Vessels," in which he has examined a great quantity of archaeological and technological evidence demonstrating that round caldrons were most certainly cast in an inverted position.[16] After reading Su's essay, it is clear to me that Schnepp's hypothesis that the *Shi Wang ding* was cast at an angle—which is also the idea that I had previously published—is without basis. Nevertheless, there is still a problem that needs to be explained. Although there is no doubt that a round caldron such as the *Shi Wang ding* would have been cast in an inverted position, the metallurgists who have studied the casting of these vessels have not come to any consensus concerning how and especially where the molten bronze was poured into the mold. As noted earlier, the ingress point for the molten bronze is called the "sprue," whereas the egress point for the gas is called the "vent." Most scholars agree that the legs would have served these two functions, but there is no agreement as to which legs or how many of them served which function. Su Rongyu surveys the most influential previous views regarding this question, saying, "In analyzing the *Niu fangding* 牛方鼎, Wan Jiabao 萬家保 discovered that whereas at the top of the vessel there were almost no flaws in the very intricate décor on the vessel, the bottom of the vessel was marred by numerous casting flaws, he surmised that the vessel was cast in an inverted position, with the molten bronze poured in from the top. He thought that the sprue would have been placed in the middle of the belly so as to avoid such flaws as 'turbulence' (*wenliu* 紊流) and 'aspiration' (*xiqi* 吸氣) that could easily be caused by the legs, however he did not indicate whether there was any evidence that could support his notion."[17] Differing from this, Hua Jueming 華覺明 and his colleagues argued that in the casting of both three-legged and four-legged caldrons, the legs would have served as the sprue, that "for a three-legged caldron one leg should serve as the sprue and the other two legs would vent the gas."[18]

Published in the same book as Su Rongyu's study was an essay by Niwa Takafumi 丹羽崇史 entitled "CT jiexi yu zhongguo qingtongqi zhizuo jishu de yanjiu" CT 解析與中國青銅器製作技術的研究 "CT Scans and the Study of Chinese Bronze Casting Technology."[19] Regarding the question of sprues and vents, Niwa observes: "The 'sprue' is the entry point for the molten bronze into the casting assemblage. Aside from the sprue, during casting it is also necessary to allow a 'vent' for the escape of the gas. The sprue manifests on the surface of the vessel as traces of veins, which are visible to the naked eye. However, it is very difficult to differentiate this from the vent."[20]

In order to resolve this question, in the summer of 2015 I visited Zhou Ya 周亞, the director of the Shanghai Museum's Bronze Department, and sought his help. At the museum, we carefully examined both the *Song ding* 頌鼎 (*Jicheng* 2827–29) and the *Xiao Ke ding*, both of which are extremely similar in shape and décor to the *Shi Wang ding*. We were only able to examine these two vessels with the naked eye and could find no trace of any difference between the walls of these two vessels bearing the inscriptions and those opposite to them. This is similar to the situation with the *Shi Wang ding*, for which a naked eye examination also shows no trace of porosity. It is only through the use of X-ray technology that it is possible to see these gas bubbles. Not every Chinese museum has X-ray facilities, and according to Zhou Ya, even those that do, such as the Shanghai Museum, routinely x-ray only the wall of the vessel bearing the inscription.

Fifty years ago, when Noel Barnard proposed for the first time that the famous *Mao Gong ding* 毛公鼎 (*Jicheng* 2841) in the National Palace Museum in Taipei was a forgery, one of the reasons that he cited for this is the numerous porosities visible in the skin of the bronze.[21] Subsequently, in order to defend the honor of the museum, the Palace Museum produced a complete set of X-rays of the vessel and published them in the Summer 1981 issue of the *Palace Museum Quarterly*. Zhang Shixian 張世賢 of the museum staff provided the following discussion of casting technology:

> In producing any handicraft item, it is almost impossible to arrive at perfection without any flaws, and this is especially true in the case of items that require multiple technologies all to be managed at the same time. Ancient Chinese bronze vessels were made by pouring molten bronze into the interstice between a clay mold and its internal core. The quality of its cast products was dependent upon 1) the temperature of the molten bronze; 2) the difference in temperature between the molten bronze and the mold; 3) the time that the different alloys require to melt; and 4) the preparation of the casting materials and tools. In my opinion, these all influence whether any smelting sediments would remain in the molten bronze. Smelting sediments are relatively light and easily floatable. On the bottom of some caldron-shaped vessels, it is possible to see traces of such sediments, and these will sometimes even produce black marks; this is especially true in the case of very large vessels. From this it can be seen that the casting technology available could not entirely eliminate these sediments, and that they would be contained within the structure of the vessels. The structure of the sediments is very different from that of the copper-tin alloy that is bronze, and their location is easily visible in x-rays. Based on the four considerations mentioned above, the gas bubbles produced in the course of casting are even more easily seen as black dots in the x-rays. These are "defects" that could not be controlled at that time.[22]

Zhang's article appended eleven X-ray photographs of the *Mao Gong ding*, which however are not nearly as clear as those of the *Shi Wang ding* produced by the Art Institute. Every X-ray shows numerous "black dots," which suggests that the entire vessel of the *Mao Gong ding* contains gas bubbles, the wall bearing the inscription not necessarily any purer than the wall opposite it. In fact, based on the two diagrams appended to Zhang's article, "Diagram of the right rear wall of the *Mao Gong ding*" and "Diagram of the left front wall of the *Mao Gong ding*" (see figs. 4.10 and 4.11), it would seem that just the opposite is the case, that the wall

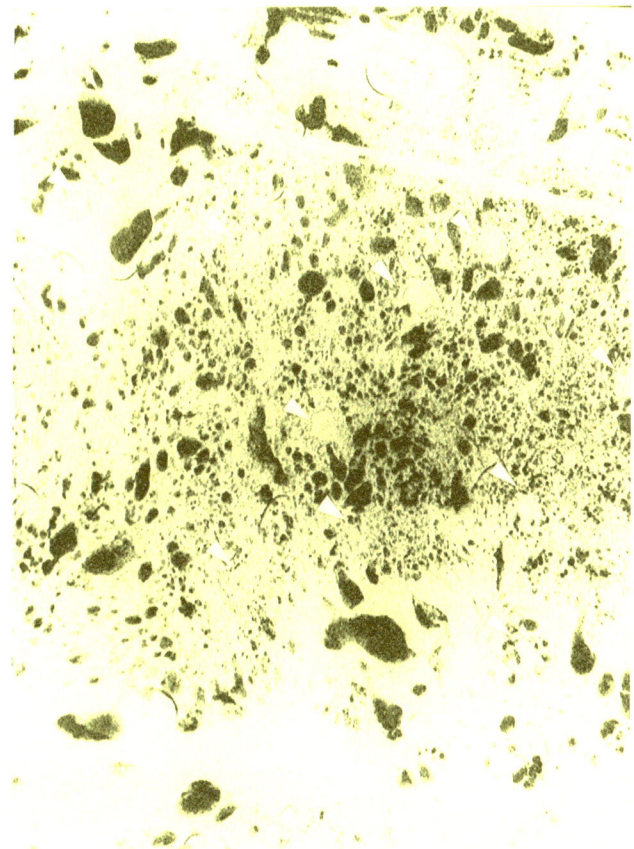

Figure 4.10. Diagram of the right rear wall of the *Mao Gong ding* 毛公鼎. From Zhang Shixian, "Cong Shang Zhou tongqi de neibu tezheng shilun Mao Gong ding de zhenwei wenti," fig. 36b. Courtesy of the National Palace Museum.

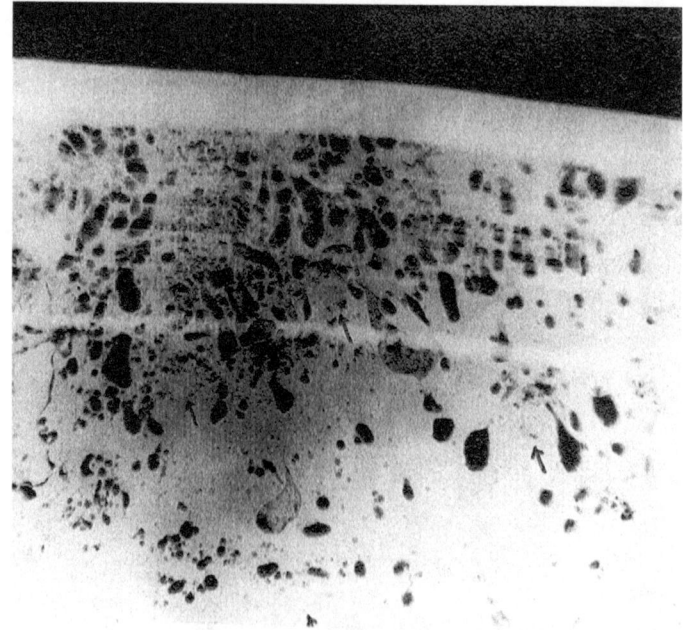

Figure 4.11. Diagram of the left front wall of the *Mao Gong ding* 毛公鼎. From Zhang Shixian, "Cong Shang Zhou tongqi de neibu tezheng shilun Mao Gong ding de zhenwei wenti," fig. 38. Courtesy of the National Palace Museum.

opposite that of the one bearing the inscription has fewer gas bubbles. Zhang Shixian offered the following general conclusion:

> From this it can be seen that with Chinese Shang and Zhou bronze vessels, regardless of whether they were made earlier or later, the chance that larger and heavier vessels would produce flaws was relatively greater. If this type of flaw came to the surface of the vessel, it could be repaired, increasing the vessel's functional and aesthetic value. However, if the flaw was contained within the structure of the vessel and did not detract from its appearance, there was no need to deal with it. These flaws could occur on normal bronze vessels, and could also occur on those bronze vessels that we now regard as extremely important; whether they occurred or not was determined by the conditions at the time of casting, and

there was no way for people to control them by way of their subjective intentions.²³

I am rather skeptical about Zhang Shixian's final statement that "there was no way for people to control them by way of their subjective intentions." For this reason, in the summer of 2015, I also showed the Art Institute's X-rays of the *Shi Wang ding* to both Lian Haiping 廉海萍 of the Conservation Department of the Shanghai Museum and to Sun Peiyang 孫沛陽, a graduate student of the Center for the Study of Paleography and Unearthed Documents at Fudan University, to ask for their advice about this technology. Both of them resolutely hold to the traditional view that vessels were cast inverted, with the mouth of the vessel at the bottom and the belly and legs at the top. They also both explained the difficulty of casting a vessel on an angle. Sun Peiyang also noted that the shape of the gas bubbles apparent in the X-rays shows that they could only have been produced in an inverted mold. After hearing their explanations, I am convinced that the *Shi Wang ding* could not have been cast at an angle. Lian and Sun separately gave the same explanation regarding the distribution of the gas bubbles in the *Shi Wang ding*: the wall bearing the inscription is immediately over the back leg (which is to say the one leg that is not under the two ears), and it was this leg that should have served as the single sprue for the casting. The two legs under the two ears would have both served as vents. After the molten bronze was poured into the mold, it would have flowed toward the vents, pushing gas ahead of it. The bronze would have been at the highest temperature and with the greatest purity while closest to the sprue, which is to say closest to the side bearing the inscription. As it flowed throughout the mold, the temperature of the molten bronze would naturally decrease and gas would be produced, and it is more likely that the gas would be trapped in the wall of the vessel furthest from the sprue. This would certainly help to maintain the purity of the wall bearing the inscription.

On September 25, 2015, my colleagues Yung-ti Li 李永迪 and Han Wei 韓巍 and I visited the Art Institute together, hosted by Dr. Tao Wang 汪濤, the curator of East Asian Art there. We examined the *Shi Wang ding* yet again, paying special attention to its casting features and especially to the location of the sprue and vents. After a very careful examination, we confirmed that the *Shi Wang ding* was cast in an inverted mold. The three legs do not show obvious signs of which was the sprue (or sprues) and which the vents (or vent), but the bottom of the leg beneath the wall bearing the inscription is completely smooth, suggesting that it was indeed the sprue, whereas the bottoms of the other two legs (i.e., the legs under the two ears) both reveal slightly convex lines, which possibly are signs that they served as vents, although it is difficult to be certain about this. If these two legs were indeed the vents, this would coincide with the explanations of the X-rays given by Lian Haiping and Sun Peiyang, and would explain the technique used to cast the *Shi Wang ding*.

The Important Position of Writing in the Consciousness of Ancient China

If this explanation is not mistaken, we can see from the casting of the *Shi Wang ding* that the caster(s) paid special attention to ensuring the purity of the bronze in the portion of the vessel bearing the inscription. This would certainly suggest the importance of the inscriptions both to the elite patrons of the vessels and also to the craftsman charged with producing the vessels. This conclusion is very important not only for the casting technology of bronze vessels bearing inscriptions, but it is also especially important with respect to the social uses of bronze vessels and their inscriptions. The reason that I am interested in this question is because a fairly popular notion among Western scholars holds that ancient Chinese bronze vessels were ritual vessels primarily intended to be used in sacrifices to the ancestors, and that the commemorative nature of the inscriptions was only secondary. For instance, Martin Kern has offered a view of the function of inscribed bronze vessels that is quite at odds with the views of many Chinese scholars. In a review of the book *Writing and Authority in Early China* by Mark Edward Lewis, Kern raised many questions about the nature of bronze inscriptions.

> Following Lothar von Falkenhausen's argument, Lewis notes that in early Zhou times, "wood and bamboo documents were stored in archives for use by the living, while elements of them were reported to the ancestors through inscriptions inside sacrificial vessels" (p. 17). This is most likely correct, but the interesting and important enterprise only begins right here. How were these thousands of texts inside the bronze

vessels "reported" to the ancestors? Did the ancestors read, or did they listen? Did they descend to the texts, or did the texts travel upward? Are these just written texts, or are they texts for oral performances that before or after their recitation were cast into bronze? How should we, in terms of cultural concepts, describe the transformation of archival documents into announcements and prayers directed to the spirits? What precisely should we envision as the particular power of the written—versus the merely spoken—text? What conclusions can we draw from the material aspects of these writings: the resources and technological expertise that went into them, their visual arrangement, their calligraphic style? What is the relation between these writings and those few other texts that we traditionally (and tentatively) date to Western Zhou and Spring and Autumn times, that is, the early layers of the *Changes* (Yi 易), the *Odes* (Shi 詩), and the *Documents* (Shu 書)? And, how, finally, should we perceive the difference between an inscribed and an uninscribed bronze vessel or bell, if writing should be so important for the success and completion of ancestral and other sacrifices?[24]

Following this, Kern offered the following answers to his own questions, saying that it is necessary to differentiate the inscriptions from their original oral production and to treat them as two different entities, such that the text and its carrier are entirely independent.

First, there is no one-to-one relation between a given text and its bronze carrier: a text could be partly or in its entirety repeated on several bronzes or divided across a set of them, especially on bells that were conceived not as singular items but as sets. Second, as it can be demonstrated in the example of the preimperial Qin bronzes, a text of an earlier bronze inscription could be maintained and to a large extent reactivated for a new inscription even a century later, and even though the capital and its ancestral temple had been moved, with the earlier bronzes being left behind. Third, the visual arrangement of the inscriptions does not respect the intrinsic aesthetics of the text, especially their main structuring features of rhyme and meter; it is therefore clear that these elements must have been represented in a different way, and this most likely was in the form of oral performance. Remarkably enough, the practice of rhyming in Zhou bronze inscriptions became more regular over time, probably suggesting that the element of oral representation was not abandoned but continuously practiced, refined, and formalized in Eastern Zhou times.[25]

At the beginning of the first quotation, Kern stated his agreement with Lothar von Falkenhausen, by which he meant Falkenhausen's long 1993 review article "Issues in Western Zhou Studies." In this review article, Falkenhausen stated:

> Their placement on ritual objects in a religious setting implies that the primary function of Zhou bronze inscriptions was probably not an archival one. Rather than aiming at efficient conveyance of information to later descendants, the formulation of the documents and highly selective editing of their contents (an issue on which *Sources* comments on pp. 176–182), strongly suggest that the intended recipients of the texts were the ancestral spirits in heaven. It was arguably their physical association with the offerings to the spirits that made it possible to convey them to the ancestral sphere. Other components of the ceremonies, such as liturgy, singing, and ritual dance, simultaneously contributed to the communication process: rituals were multi-media happenings. We should also not forget the important role that the iconography of bronze decoration may have played—another, "theological" reason why inscriptions should never be considered apart from the bronzes. Being the medium of transmission, the bronzes played a role as important as that of the inscribed texts.
>
>   Supporting this contention is the fact that the texts are usually placed on the bronzes in such a way that they could not conveniently have been read by humans, especially during the time when the objects were in use. Vessel inscriptions, as a rule, are found at the bottom or on the inside walls of the objects, where they would have been covered by the sacrificial foods placed in them; and although the inscriptions of Zhou dynasty bells were placed on the outward sides, that part of an inscription that happened to be on the *verso* face could, at

least on the obliquely suspended *yongzhong* 甬鐘, only be seen if one crouched underneath the bell-rack from behind. The reason for such placement may have been that the contents of the inscription were thought of as physically fused to the ritual offerings, and to the sounds of the ritual tunes.[26]

In my view, if the discussion of the casting of the *Shi Wang ding* that I have given in this chapter is not entirely mistaken, and if the casters of bronze vessels were truly as concerned with the physical properties of the inscription as they seem to have been, then I would suggest that Martin Kern's conclusion that "bronze inscriptions were not primarily written but were essentially oral hymns that at a certain point became cast in bronze; they were intended not to be silently read but to be sung or recited," and Lothar von Falkenhausen's claim that inscriptions did not aim "at efficient conveyance of information to later descendants" and that "they could not conveniently have been read by humans" need to be reconsidered. On the basis of the casting of the *Shi Wang ding*, the Western Zhou casters paid very great attention to the physical appearance of the inscription, and this must have been intended to protect its legibility. Of course, there remains the important question of whether the *Shi Wang ding* is unique in this respect, and to what extent it reflects widespread technical practices during the Western Zhou period. I hope this study will stimulate experts of bronze vessels to do further research into this question.

Part II

The Classics

Chapter Five

A Possible Lost Classic

The *She Ming or *Command to She

Volume 8 of the Warring States bamboo-slip manuscripts in the collection of Tsinghua University was published in November 2018 with eight new manuscripts, none of them ever before seen.[1] The editors present a compelling argument that the first of these manuscripts, to which they have given the title *She ming 攝命 *Command to She, is none other than the original version of a chapter in the "ancient-script" (guwen 古文) version of the received Shang shu 尚書 Exalted Scriptures that is known there as "Jiong ming" 冏命 "Command to Jiong." However, whereas the "Jiong ming" chapter has traditionally been regarded as a command given by King Mu of Zhou 周穆王 (r. 956–918 BCE), the Tsinghua editors suggest that the *She ming should date two generations later, to the time of King Xiao of Zhou 周孝王 (r. 882?–866 BCE), and that "She" 攝 (or Bo She

---

This chapter was originally published as "A Possible Lost Classic: The *She Ming or *Command to She," T'oung Pao 106 (2020): 266–308. This version has been edited for consistency with the format of this book. I have also deleted the original publication's scans of the original characters of the text and their strict transcription as well as many of the supporting notes for the translation. While such presentation is desirable for a full appreciation of the manuscript, for the purposes of the present book it seems unnecessary; interested readers should consult the original publication or Shaughnessy, The Tsinghua University Warring States Bamboo Manuscripts, vol. 2. I have also revised my discussion of the Da Yu ding 大盂鼎 (Jicheng 2837) to represent my current understanding of its date (for which, see, n. 56 in this chapter). Finally, n. 59 is also new to this version.

伯攝; Elder She), the name of the recipient of this royal command, can be identified with Xie 燮, recorded in traditional sources as the name of King Yi of Zhou 周夷王 (r. 865–858 BCE). Thus, according to this interpretation, the text marks a doubly royal decree, from a reigning king to a king-in-waiting. Finally, the editors also note that this Tsinghua manuscript shares much of its format and wording with mid- to late Western Zhou bronze inscriptions, and thus has a prima facie claim to date to that period.

If the editors' identification of the *She ming with the "Jiong ming" chapter of the Shangshu is accepted, it carries important implications for the nature of the ancient-script Shangshu. And if the comparison with Western Zhou investiture inscriptions is accepted, it carries important implications for how such a text may have been composed originally and, just as important, how it may have been transmitted over the course of the half a millennium between the mid- to late Western Zhou period and when the Tsinghua copy was placed into the grave from which it was finally robbed in or shortly before 2006.

The *She Ming Manuscript

The *She ming manuscript is written on thirty-two bamboo slips of about 45 cm in length. The slips were originally bound with three binding straps, which have left vestiges on the slips. Almost all of the slips are intact, with only slips 3, 25, and 29 broken such that there is a loss of text (slips 5, 17, 28, and 32 are also broken above the top binding strap, but this did not result in the loss of any text). The slips are numbered on the back, clearly indicating the sequence of the text (though it has been suggested that slips numbered 12 and 13 were nonetheless transposed). Curiously, the numbers of the first twenty-two slips are written about two-thirds of the way down the back of the slip, while those of the last eleven slips are written just below the midpoint. The title She ming was given by the editors on the basis of the contents and nature of the text (the asterisk used in this essay indicating that the title is not original to the text). The text is divided into two sections. The first section covers the first thirty-one slips, the text being written continuously with between twenty-eight and thirty-one characters per slip, though slip 31 has only twelve characters followed by a text-ending 乙-hook-shaped mark. This section records a continuous royal address by some unnamed king (wang

王) and addressed to She 攝. It is broken into ten different subsections, each of which begins "The king said" (*wang yue* 王曰, though the first subsection begins "The king approved of saying" [*wang ruo yue* 王若曰]). The only punctuation marks in the text are duplication marks, though on slip 4 there are two small characters written in the space between other characters, apparently the result of proofreading. The second section includes only slip 32, which seems to be written in the same hand as the text of section 1 but has distinctly smaller graphs, thirty-nine in all. It too ends with a text-ending 乙-hook-shaped mark, apparently indicating the end of this separate record. This section records the date and place of She's investiture as well as the name of his guarantor and the secretarial official responsible for reading the command to him:

> 隹九月既望壬申，王在鎬京，各于大室即位，咸。士逨右伯攝，
> 立在中廷北鄉。王呼作冊任冊命伯攝：「度。」

> It was the ninth month, after the full moon, *renshen* (day 9); the king was at the Hao Capital and entered into the Grand Chamber, assuming position. Sir Jie at the right of Elder She stood in the center of the court facing north. The king called out to Maker of Slips Ren to command in writing Elder She: "Act."

This record is essentially identical with the typical opening of investiture inscriptions on bronze vessels.[2] As an independent section, it could easily be moved to the beginning of the document, though in the case of this manuscript it obviously was not since the slip is numbered on the reverse as *sa'er* 卅二 "thirty-two."

The Identification of She 攝

As mentioned previously, the *She ming purports to be a royal command addressed to one She 攝. The Tsinghua editors, following an early suggestion by Li Xueqin 李學勤 (1933–2019),[3] identify She as the future King Yi of Zhou 周夷王 (r. 865–858 BCE), whose given name is written in the *Shi ji* 史記 *Records of the Historian* and *Zhushu jinian* 竹書紀年 *Bamboo Annals* as Xie 燮.[4] The editors propose that *she* 攝 (*nhep) and *xie* 燮 (*sêp) were phonetically similar enough to have been written for each other. In addition to this phonetic similarity between the two names, the editors adduce several other points in support of this identification.

In the first line of the *She ming, the king refers to She as *zhi* 姪, which the editors propose to read "as the character itself" (*ru zi* 如字), which they say means "brother's son" (兄弟之子).⁵ Having already identified She as the future King Yi, this allows them to identify the *She ming*'s king as King Xiao. All historical sources say that King Xiao's reign was anomalous for the Western Zhou, in that he was not the eldest son of the preceding king, King Yih 懿王 (r. 899/97–873 BCE). On the other hand, these sources do not agree about his relationship with King Yih. The *Shi ji* once says that he was the younger brother of King Gong 共王 (r. 917–900 BCE), and thus an uncle to King Yih,⁶ but elsewhere indicates that he was King Yih's younger brother.⁷ The editors prefer the identification as King Yih's younger brother and thus suggest that King Xiao's "nephew" would be the future King Yi, the eldest son of King Yih. This identification is not unproblematic, not only because of the conflicting evidence concerning King Xiao's own parentage. The graph *zhi* 姪, said by the editors to mean "nephew," usually denotes either "niece" or the children of one's sisters; it is *zhi* 侄 that ordinarily means "nephew." Of course, it is extremely unlikely that She was female, and it would not violate most principles of Chinese textual criticism to read *zhi* 姪 as *zhi* 侄 (i.e., "nephew"), as I do in the following translation. Nevertheless, the possibility that the graph *zhi* 姪 was used intentionally to refer to a child of the king's sister, and thus in the patrilineal Zhou system not a potential king, remains troubling.⁸

The *She ming*'s king also once seems to refer to She as a "prince" (*wangzi* 王子; lit. "king's son"):

王曰：「攝，乃克悉用朕命，越朕惎朕教，民朋興從顯汝，從恭汝與汝，曰：穆穆丕顯，載允非常人。王子則克悉用王教王學，亦義若時，我小人唯由。

The king said: "She, if you can then in all cases use my commands, and my exhortations and my teaching, the people and associates will . . . rise up consequently to make you lustrous, and consequently support you and join with you, saying: 'So bountiful and illustrious, truly not a common man. If **the prince** is capable in all cases of using the king's teaching and the king's learning, it is also proper in this way that we little men should follow.'" (slips 24–25)

Here too it is not certain that this "prince" refers specifically to She and is not just part of a general saying on the part of the people.

Perhaps the most compelling evidence for the identification of She as a person of special prominence, such as a future king, is seen in the text's repeated reference to him as *chenzi* 沈子, literally "sunken son" but perhaps to be understood as "sincere son" (reading *chen* 沈 as *chen* 訦 or 忱). In the text, it is used three times in this form, and two more times as *chenzi xiaozi* 沈子小子, literally "the (sunken:) sincere son's little son."[9] The Tsinghua editors silently gloss *chenzi* as *chongzi* 沖子 ("young son"), a term frequently seen in Western Zhou texts as a humble or self-deprecatory appellation usually reserved for kings or high-ranking officers, with *chong* 沖 routinely glossed as *tong* 童.[10] Support for the identification of these two terms is seen in the Tsinghua manuscript *Zhou Wu wang you ji, Zhou Gong suo zi yi dai wang zhi zhi* 周武王又疾, 周公所自以弋王之志 *The Record of King Wu of Zhou Being Ill, and the Duke of Zhou Substituting Himself for the King*, which largely corresponds with the "Jin teng" 金縢 "Metal-Bound Coffer" chapter of the *Shangshu*. Whereas the manuscript version of the text uses the term *chenren* 沈人 as a form of self-reference by King Cheng of Zhou 周成王 (r. 1042/35–1006 BCE), the corresponding term in the received text is *chongren* 沖人, "Young Man":

佳余沈人亦弗返智。

It is that I the (sunken:) sincere man had also not come to know of it.[11]

惟予沖人弗及知。

It is that I the young man had not come to know of it.[12]

However, it is also possible that the manuscript's *chenren* 沈人 here is the original reading, and *chongren* 沖人 is the loan word. In Western Zhou bronze inscriptions, *chen* 沈 is used as a modifier for both *zi* 子 ("son") and *sun* 孫 ("grandson") as self-deprecatory references to the patrons of vessels.[13] Whatever the original word, it is clear that the multiple uses of *chenzi* to refer to She in the *She ming* are intended to reflect his elite status.[14] Of course, even this does not require that She be identified as a crown prince; it seems that the usage of *chenzi* is broader than for just royal self-deprecation. We will return to this question later; for now it will have to suffice to conclude that the Tsinghua editors have marshaled considerable circumstantial evidence in support of their argument that She was a crown prince.

Identification of the *She Ming with the "Jiong Ming" Chapter of the *Shang Shu* and Its Implications for the Authenticity of the "Ancient-Script" Version of the *Shang Shu*

The Tsinghua editors' explication of the *She ming text also depends on a relationship between it and the "Jiong ming" chapter of the *Shang shu*, one of the so-called ancient-script chapters of that classic. Whereas the *She ming purports to be the command of some unnamed king to a person named She 攝, the "Jiong ming" purports to be the command of some unnamed king—one whom the later tradition identifies as King Mu of Zhou 周穆王 (r. 956–918 BCE)—to a person named Jiong 囧 in the received version of the text, though the name is written as 臩 in the *Shi ji*.[15] In the *She ming manuscript, *she* 攝 is written as 𦔮, that is, 𦔮, with two "ear" (*er* 耳) components back-to-back over a *da* 大, a character that occurs in the same form in the Guodian 郭店 manuscript of the *Zi yi* 緇衣 *Black Jacket* in a quotation of a line from the *Shi jing* 詩經 *Classic of Poetry*; the corresponding character in both the *Shi jing* and the received "Zi yi" chapter of the *Li ji* 禮記 *Record of Ritual* is *she* 攝.[16] The editors suggest that this is graphically similar to the variant form of the name of the recipient of the "Jiong ming" command: *jiong*: 臩, which features two "minister" (*chen* 臣) components back-to-back (i.e., 𦣝) over a *da* 大 with two further strokes below. In paleographic sources, the "ear" component is frequently almost indistinguishable from the "minister" component; for instance, the bronze inscriptional form of *er* 耳 "ear" is 𦕔, while the "small seal script" (*xiao zhuan* 小篆) form of *chen* 臣 is 𦣝.

The editors note as well that in the Shanghai Museum manuscript of the *Zi yi*, the graph that corresponds to the 臩 of the Guodian manuscript of that text is written as 囧.[17] This leads them to propose that the character *jiong* 囧, the seal form of which was written as 囧, could well have derived from this alternative form of *she*. Jiong 冏 is, of course, the name of the recipient of the king's command in the received text of the *Shang shu*. Whereas either one of these graphic similarities might be dismissed as mere coincidence, that the two together may be two (or four) ways of writing the same name is hard to dismiss. However, this only serves to complicate the explication of the text.

As discussed in the preceding section, the editors identify the name of the recipient of the king's command, She 攝, as a phonetic loan for *xie* 燮, the name of the future King Yi of Zhou. On the other hand, both the *Shu xu* 書序 "Preface to the *Scriptures*" and the *Shi ji* date the "Jiong ming" chapter of the *Shang shu* to the time of King Mu,[18] two or three generations earlier than the time of King Yi. The editors dismiss this dating, suggesting that whoever was responsible for the "Preface to the *Scriptures*" dating was simply mistaken, but their suggestion has not met with universal acceptance.

Cheng Hao 程浩, another member of the editorial team at Tsinghua University, argues that the *She ming text should indeed date to the reign of King Mu of Zhou, saying there are "thousands of threads and myriads of strands" (千絲萬縷) linking the text to that date.[19] In fact, there is pretty much one thread and one strand. The thread concerns the name of the person who serves as Bo She's guarantor (*youzhe* 右者) in the court investiture record at the end of the document; it is written 祭. Although the editors transcribe this graph as Jie 建, Cheng Hao compares it with the graph 祭 seen in many Western Zhou bronze inscriptions and now regularly identified as Zhai 祭. He then identifies this figure with the well-known Duke of Zhai 祭公 who was supposed to be an elderly advisor of King Mu. Inviting though this identification is, Zhai is a state or lineage name, whereas in the context of the manuscript 祭 or 建 should be a personal name or a cognomen (*zi* 字). Cheng's strand of evidence is that the person who reads the command to She in this court investiture is named "Maker of Slips Ren" (*zuoce Ren* 作冊任). Cheng notes that the "Shi ji" 史記 chapter of the *Yi Zhou shu* 逸周書 *Leftover Zhou Scriptures* records that a "Secretary of the Left Rongfu" (*zuoshi Rongfu* 左史戎夫) assisted at the burial of the Duke of Zhai. He says that *rong* 戎 (*nung) and *ren* 任 (*nem) could be used interchangeably in ancient texts, so that Maker of Slips Ren could be none other than Secretary of the Left Rongfu. This seems to be a very slender strand on which to hang such a heavy argument.

Thus, we have one identification of She and Jiong based on graphic similarity and a confusion in the traditional dating of the received text of the "Jiong ming," and another identification based on that dating and on what can only be regarded as very weak threads and strands of graphic and phonetic linkages. While neither identification is fully persuasive, that of the Tsinghua editors is likely to be the most influential reading if only because it is presented in the formal publication of the manuscript. If we accept the identification of the two names—and thus of the two texts *She ming and "Jiong ming"—this discovery would necessarily have important implications for the question of the authenticity of the ancient-script chapters of the Shang shu. Because this has been one of the most important questions in Chinese textual criticism, I propose to consider it here at least in brief.

The received text of the "Jiong ming" chapter is very short, only 237 characters long.[20] It purports to date to the beginning of the reign of an unnamed king, who states the dread with which he approaches his new responsibility and who looks back upon the glory days of Kings Wen 文 (r. 1099/1057–1050 BCE) and Wu 武 (r. 1049/1045–1043 BCE), whose ministers were able to make up for any deficiencies those kings might have had. This king, too, acknowledging his own deficiencies, hopes to have good ministers around him and appoints Jiong to be "Great Governor" (da zheng 大正). In this position, Jiong is enjoined to select good men to be officers under him and to beware "one-sided men and flatterers" (lit., "do not employ those of crafty speech and commanding looks, sycophants and flatterers" 無以巧言令色便辟側媚) and warned against taking bribes (貨). As we will see in the following translation of the *She ming text, this is—in large measure—what the *She ming purports to record as well. However, the similarity is only in large measure; the specific wording of the two texts is quite different. The "Jiong ming" text is composed largely of the sort of four-character phrases familiar from the Warring States period and later.[21] One of these four-character phrases, "crafty speech and commanding looks" (巧言令色), was a standard phrase already in the Warring States period, apparently first being used in the "Gaoyao mo" 皋陶謨 "Consultation of Gaoyao" chapter of the Shang shu,[22] then quoted four times in the Analects of Confucius,[23] and thereafter becoming all but idiomatic. Connoisseurship is an often derided art of textual criticism, but it would be hard not to agree with such traditional readers of the text as Wu Yu 吳棫 (1100–1154) and Wu Cheng 吳澄 (1249–1333) when they suggested that ancient-script chapters of the *Shang shu* such as this are suspiciously easy to read and of a weak style, suggestive of a cut-and-paste composition process.[24]

If we turn to the *She ming* text, it is certainly not easy to read, at least not in its entirety. It begins with the king's exhortation to She, perhaps—as previously noted—identified as his nephew, and then continues with his protestation of the tireless manner with which he rules. This is followed by what would seem to be the command proper to She: that he "take out and report on my commands" 出 [入:] 納朕命, a command also seen in Western Zhou investiture inscriptions on bronze vessels.[25] There then follows the longest of the royal speeches (the third), extending over more than ten bamboo slips, warning She to "sedulously revere your service" 勤祗乃事, and continuing with a litany of moral maxims. Subsequent speeches are more specific: injunctions against alcohol (the fourth), warnings about officials who have "been demeaning to me" 卑于余 (the fifth), injunctions against taking bribes (幣) in court cases (the sixth), and finally concluding with another admonition "not to cause disgrace for me the One Man" 弗為我一人羞. While the general tenor of the text is clear enough, there are any number of passages that remain quite opaque (at least to me). Some of this opacity may derive from the Chu script in which the text is written, though the editors at least seem to be confident regarding their basic transcription.[26] The translation that follows generally adheres to the transcription provided by the editors, though I frequently adjust the modern punctuation that they have added. The translation offered here should be regarded as a tentative first attempt to make sense of a difficult text.

She Ming 攝命 (*The Command to She*)[27]

王曰:"勤侄恖攝:亡丞朕卿,余弗造民康,余亦嬛窮,亡可使。余一人無晝夕 [1] 勤恤,湛圂在憂。余亦橫于四方,宏乂亡斁,甚悸我邦之若否,于小大命。肆余 [2] 囊猷卜乃身休;卜吉。"

The king said: "Be careful nephew, I exhort you, She: Without the support of my officers,[28] I have not created the people's rest, and I too am lonely and exhausted, with no one to be able to employ. I the One Man without regard to day or night [1] am diligent and concerned, sunken and stymied in worries. I have also gone throughout the four quarters, expansively ruling tirelessly, extremely anxious about our country's approval or not, as well as the minor and great commands. And so I [2] have planned and contemplated, divining by crack-making about your person's suitability; the cracks were auspicious."

王曰:"攝,今余既明命汝曰:'肇出納朕命。戲'。今民丕造不康,囗囗囗 [3] 怨,于四方小大邦,于御事庶百又告有各。今是亡其奔告,非汝亡其協,即行汝"。

The king said: "She, now I have already clearly commanded you saying: 'Begin to take out and (bring in:) report on my commands. Act!' Now the people have greatly created unrest,[29] . . . [3] resentment, and the minor and great countries of the four quarters, as well as the hundreds of drivers of service also report there are criminal cases. Now if these will not rush to report, if not for you, there will be no cooperation, and so I mobilize you."

王曰: [4] "攝,敬哉,毋閉于乃佳沈子小子,毋遞才服,勤祗乃事。有曰:'女佳衛事衛命',女佳 [5] 沈子小子,女威由覝由望。不啻;女威則由蔑,女訓言之譔。女能歷,女能并命,并命勤 [6] 肆。女其敬哉,虔恤乃事。汝毋敢枯遏余,曰乃毓。有曰:'四方大羸,亡民亦斯欽我 [7] 御事'。今亦脅肱勤乃事。乃事亡他。女唯言之司,唯言乃事。我非易。矧行墮敬懋。惠 [8] 不惠,亦乃服。雖民攸協弗恭,其旅亦勿侮其聰童,痛懷寡鰥。惠于小民,翼翼畏 [9] 小心,恭民長長。女亦毋敢豢在乃尸服,敬學咨明,勿繇之庶不訓。女亦毋不夙夕經德, [10] 用事朕命。欲女繹繹弗功我一人在位,亦則乃身亡能懆甫非容。汝正命。女有告于 [11] 余事汝有命政。有即政,亦若之容。弜永汝有退進于朕命,乃佳望亡逢,則或即命 [12] 朕,汝毋敢有退于之。自一話一言,汝亦毋敢泆于之。言唯明,毋淫,毋弗節。其亦佳 [13] 乃亦唯肇謀,亦則匃逆于朕。是唯君子秉心。是汝則佳肇咨弜義。乃既誨,女迺敢 [14] 簡極,汝則亦唯肇丕子、丕學、丕啻。汝亦畏獲懃朕心。"

The king said [4]: "She, be warned, indeed! Do not close off by your being the (sunken:) sincere son's little son, and do not make substitutions in responsibilities, but diligently revere your service. It is said: 'You are to defend the service and defend the commands.' You are [5] the (sunken:) sincere son's little son. You are to awe through display and through observation. Not only this. If you awe through praise, you are to instruct with the choicest of the sayings. You are able to calculate and you are able to join in command, jointly commanding to be diligent [6] in presentation. Would that you be warned indeed, assiduously concerned for your service. You ought not dare either to presume upon or to obstruct me, speaking of your parentage.[30] It is said: 'The four quarters are greatly emaciated but even refugees still have respect for our [7] drivers of service.' Now also as legs and arms be diligent in your service. Your service should have no others. You are only to be supervisor of speech and only speech is to be your service. We are not at ease. How much more so if conduct were to lose respect and encouragement. Being kind [8] to the unkind is also your responsibility. Although the people's cooperation does not support it, their ranks also ought not disdain their intelligent youths, and should sympathize with and cherish widows and orphans. Be kind to the petty people, everywhere in awe [9] of minor concerns, supporting the people and treating elders as elder. You also ought not dare to be lazy in your assigned responsibilities,[31] but respectfully study lofty brightness, and do not derive from it many inconsistencies. You also ought not neglect from morning to night to be steadfast in virtue [10], herewith serving my command. And so if you continuously do not support me the One Man in position, then your person will not be able to relax using misdemeanors. You are to make upright the command. You are to report to [11] my service your having command of government. In attending to government, you should also resemble this demeanor. Do not delay your going and coming under my command. If your only desire is to have no encounters, and then attending to command [12] me (sic),[32] you ought not dare to retreat from it. From each statement and each saying you also ought not dare to be neglectful in it. Sayings are to be bright. Do not be licentious, do not fail to moderate them. It is also (sic)[33] [13] it is also that you begin to plan, also then seeking to report back to me. This is the heart to which the lord-son holds tight. This is for you then to begin to inquire and not delay. Your having been instructed, you should then dare [14] to reduce calamities, and then it is that you will also begin to be greatly filial, greatly studious and greatly abundant. You will also awesomely obtain to move my heart."

王曰:"攝,汝有唯沈子。余既設 [15] 乃服。汝毋敢朋酗于酒,勿教人德我。曰:毋朋多朋,鮮唯胥以夙夕敬,罔非胥以堕 [16] 愆;鮮唯胥學于威義德,亡非胥以淫愆。"

The king said: "She, it is that you are the (sunken:) sincere son. I have already set [15] your responsibilities. You ought not dare to associate drunkenly in alcohol, and should not instruct others to ingratiate us. I say: You ought not associate with many associates; few are they who help each other from morning to night to be on guard, none are they who do not help to fall [16] into error; few are they who will help to learn of awesome propriety and virtue, none are they who do not help to dissipate in calamity."

王曰:"攝,余辟相唯御事,余厭既異厥心厥 [17] 德,不延,則俾于余。矧汝唯子。今乃辟余,小大乃有聞知弼詳,汝其有斁有湛。 [18] 乃眾余言,乃知唯子不唯之庸,是亦尚弗逢。乃彝乃作穆穆,唯恭威儀,用辟余在 [19] 位,乃克用之彝。汝不逖是,唯人乃亦無知亡聞于民若否。乃身載唯明唯寅,汝亦毋 [20] 敢畏用不審不允。"

The king said: "She, my ministers and assistants are the drivers of service. I detest that they have already altered their hearts and their [17] virtue, not extending them, and then have caused harm to me. How much more so is it that you are the son. Now in your serving me, the little and great will then hear of and know in double detail; may you have percipience and depth. [18] As for your joining me in speaking, and your knowing that it is the son who is not of this demeanor, in this too we hope not to encounter it. Your constancy will then enact solemnity, and will support awesome propriety, therewith serving me in [19] position, and you will be able to use it constantly. If you are not then correct,[34] it is that others then also will have no knowledge and not hear about the people's approval or not. Your person carrying brightness and caution, you also [20] ought not dare awesomely to use anything not examined or not approved."

王曰:"攝,已,汝唯沈子。余既明命汝,乃服唯寅,汝毋敢囊囊。凡人有 [21] 獄有訟,汝勿受幣,不明于民,民其聽汝。時佳子乃弗受幣,亦尚反逆于朕。凡人無 [22] 獄亡訟,廼唯德享,享載丕孚,是亦引休。汝則亦受幣,汝乃尚祗逆告于朕。"

The king said: "She, enough, you are the (sunken:) sincere son. I have already clearly commanded you, your responsibility is to be careful. You ought not dare to be extravagant. In all cases when others have [21] criminal trials and lawsuits, you ought not accept bribes or be unclear with respect to the people, and the people will listen to you. If at times it is that you then do not accept bribes, would that you also return and report to me. In all cases when people do not [22] have criminal trials or lawsuits, and then it is virtue that is offered, and the offering is carried greatly trustworthily, this also will be extended grace. If you then also accept bribes, would that you then respectfully report back to me."

王曰:"攝,余肇 [23] 使汝,汝毋婪,汝亦引毋好好宏宏劌德。有汝胄子,唯余其恤。"

The king said: "She, now that I begin [23] to employ you, you ought not be covetous, and you also ought extensively neither self-interestedly nor self-aggrandizingly harm virtue. Having you, my nephew, it is that I will be comforted."

王曰:"攝,乃克悉用朕命,越朕 [24] 毖朕教,民朋門與從顯汝,從恭汝與汝,曰:'穆穆丕顯,載允非常人,王子則克悉用 [25] 王教王學,亦義若時,我小人唯由'。民有曰之。余一人曷假不則職知之聞之言;余 [26] 曷假,不則高奉乃身,亦余一人永安在位。所弗克職用朕命朕教,民朋亦則與仇怨 [27] 汝仇讟汝,亦則唯肇不咎逆忤朕命,獲羞毓子。"

The king said: "She, if you can then in all cases use my commands, and my [24] exhortations and my teachings, the people [and associates] will arise and consequently make you lustrous, and consequently support you and join with you, saying: 'So solemn and illustrious, truly not a common man; if the prince is capable in all cases of using [25] the king's teaching and the king's learning, it is also proper in this way that we little men should follow.' The people have said it. How could I the One Man not then recognize it, know it, or make known these sayings? How could I [26] not then raise on high your person, so that I the One Man will also be permanently at ease in position. If you are not able to recognize and use my commands and my teaching, the people and associates will even then arise to oppose and resent [27] you, and opposing and reviling you, will even then begin not to consult but oppose and obstruct my commands, bringing shame on the nurtured son."

王曰:"攝,人有言多,隹我鮮。隹朕 [28] □□□箴教汝,余隹亦功作汝,余亦唯諳燬兌汝。有汝唯沈子,余亦唯肇眘汝德 [29] 行,隹穀罙非穀。"

The king said: "She, the sayings that people have are many, but ours are few. It is my [28] ... admonitions that teach you, it is also I who reward and cause you to act, and it is also I who would break and destroy and overtake you. Having you as the (sunken:) sincere son, it is also that I begin to examine your virtuous [29] conduct, what is good and not good."

王曰:"攝,敬哉,虔聽乃命。余既明啟劼毖女,亡多朕言曰茲。汝毋弗敬 [30] 甚谷女寵乃服,弗為我一人羞。" [31]

The king said: "She, be warned indeed! Assiduously listen to your command. I have already clearly begun by cautioning you; do not regard my words as excessive in saying this. You ought not disregard it. [30] Very much do I wish you to fulfill your responsibilities, and not cause disgrace for me the One Man." [31]

隹九月既望壬申,王才蒿京,各于大室即位,咸。士𢯱右白攝,立才中廷北鄉。王呼作冊任冊命伯攝:"虗。" [32]

It was the ninth month, after the full moon, *renshen* (day 9); the king was at the Hao Capital and entered into the Grand Chamber, assuming position. Sir Jie at the right of Elder She stood in the center of the court facing north. The king called out to Maker of Slips Ren to command in writing Elder She: "Act." [32]

Possible Implications of the *She Ming for Western Zhou History

As previously discussed, the Tsinghua editors have presented a very strong case that the *She ming represents an early version of the "Jiong ming" chapter of the *Shang shu*, and also a strong—if ultimately circumstantial—case that the original command document that it records should date to the reign of King Xiao of Zhou, despite the consistent tradition in the Han dynasty that the "Jiong ming" chapter dates to the reign of King Mu of Zhou, two generations earlier. We might ask whether there is anything in the content of the inscription that would support either of these dates.

While many individual words and even phrases in the *She ming text have not yet been conclusively explained, the general tenor of the text would seem to be quite clear: it is a complaint on the part of the king about general disorder within the state. After an opening protest about his worries that can probably be dismissed as convention, the second royal address moves quickly to the point: "The king said: 'She, now I have already clearly commanded you saying: 'Begin to take out and report on my commands. Moreover, now the people greatly meet with unrest, resentment, and the minor and great countries of the four quarters, as well as the hundreds of drivers of service also report there are criminal cases. Now if these will not rush to report, if not for you there will be no cooperation, and so I mobilize you.'"

After then warning She about joining together with others in drinking alcohol, the king seems to blame his own officers for this sorry state of affairs: "The king said: 'She, my ministers and assistants are the drivers of service. I detest that they have already altered their hearts and their virtue, not extending them, and then have caused harm to me.'" Then, in the most specific of the king's instructions, the king commands She to be judicious in his handling of court cases, and certainly not to accept bribes: "You ought not dare to be extravagant. In all cases when others have criminal trials and lawsuits, you ought not accept bribes or be unclear with respect to the people, and the people will listen to you." Thus, this seems to be a king aware that the situation in his state has grown almost out of control, for which he blames his royal officers. His most serious complaint seems to concern the great number of lawsuits and criminal cases. In this context, the king's command to She not to accept bribes might suggest that he suspected other of his officers to be doing just that.

According to what we can learn from both the traditional historical record and also from contemporary bronze inscriptions, the reigns of both King Mu of Zhou and King Xiao of Zhou were problematic for the Zhou royal court, but they were problematic in very different ways. King Mu came to power after his father, King Zhao of Zhou 周昭王 (r. 977/75–957 BCE), had died in the course of a disastrous Zhou invasion of areas south of the Han River 漢水, probably in present-day Hubei Province. This seems to have led King Mu to reorganize his military and also, at least to some extent, to reorganize his court bureaucracy.[35] He continued to be troubled by external threats from the Zhou's longtime adversary to the southeast, the Huai Yi 淮夷, and at least some of the Huai Yi attacks seem to have penetrated the Zhou eastern territories in present-day southeastern and central Henan Province.[36]

However, as far as we can tell from the historical record, King Mu was not particularly troubled in his relations with his own royal officers. The only note of discord between them comes in the form of a deathbed testamentary charge by one powerful official, Moufu, duke of Zhai 祭公謀父, who in the "Zhai Gong" 祭公 "Duke of Zhai" chapter of the *Yi Zhou shu* 逸周書 *Leftover Zhou Scriptures* is said to warn the king against drawing too close to some, such as favored consorts or ministers, at the expense of others, such as the queen or the great officers of state.

汝無以嬖御固莊后，汝無以小謀敗大作，汝無以嬖御士疾莊士大夫卿 士，汝無以家相亂王室，而莫恤其外。

You ought not because of favored consorts embitter the stately queen. You ought not because of small plans defeat great undertakings. You ought not because of favored relations pain the stately great officers and ministers. You ought not because of the family disorder the king's house, and not be sympathetic to those outside it.[37]

While the apparent lack of any royal concern for malfeasance on the part of his ministers ought not be understood to suggest that there was no such malfeasance, at least it does not show up in what little we know of King Mu's reign.

The reign of King Xiao is still less well known than that of King Mu, especially in the received historical tradition. Nevertheless, what we do know of it from that tradition is altogether different from that of King Mu. As noted briefly earlier in this study, King Xiao's reign was anomalous among all Western Zhou kings in that he did not succeed his father. Rather, he was a younger brother of either King Gong or King Yih. What is more, there is at least some suggestion that his accession to power may have come while his predecessor, King Yih, was still alive. David Nivison, who seems to have been the first historian to make this suggestion, describes the preceding reign of King Yih as follows, paraphrasing the account given in the "Zhou ben ji" 周本紀 "Basic Annals of Zhou" of the *Shi ji*: "The histories do say that Yih was incompetent. He failed to keep the regional lords in order, failed even to keep the calendar of court events in order. He was ridiculed in popular satires."[38]

The *Bamboo Annals* contains a record dated to King Yih's fifteenth year (either 885 or, more likely, 883) that the king relocated from the royal capital to a place called Huaili 槐里.

(懿王) 十五年：王自宗周遷于槐里。

(King Yih) fifteenth year: The king transferred from Zongzhou to Huaili.[39]

There is some reason to think that this may be a veiled reference to the king going into exile, as another source refers to the place variously as either Dog-mound (Quanqiu 犬丘) or Waste-mound (Feiqiu 廢丘).[40] Moreover, though this is speculative, it is possible, and perhaps even likely, that King Xiao's reign began in the very next year: 882 BCE.[41]

Turning to bronze inscriptions, there is one inscription in particular that almost surely dates to the reign of King Xiao and that describes a situation strikingly similar to that described by the *She ming. This is the *Mu gui* 牧簋 (*Jicheng* 4343), which was first published in the *Kaogu tu* 考古圖 of Lü Dalin 呂大臨 (1040–1092).[42] Although the vessel is no longer extant, there is a reasonably good line drawing of the vessel in the *Kaogu tu*, as well as a hand copy of the inscription.[43]

The inscription begins as a typical court investiture, with a full date notation that is consistent with the year 876 BCE.[44] The investiture ceremony is conducted by a figure named Interior Secretary Wu 內史吳, who performed a similar ceremony in two other inscribed bronzes that are surely dateable to the reign of King Yih.[45] The document begins with a mention of a command that Mu 牧, the recipient of the command, had received from the "past king" (*xian wang* 先王) to be supervisor of the land (*situ* 司土), which the current king was revising to put Mu in charge of the "hundred officials" (*bai liao* 百寮). This is all more or less conventional. However, after this, the command proper, which it must be admitted is very difficult to understand in all of its particulars, then launches into a condemnation of the officers, accusing them of "much disorder" (*duo luan* 多亂) and especially of "much abusing the common people in their trials and criminal cases" (多虐庶民厥訊庶右粦). The inscription reads in its entirety:

惟王七年十又三月既生霸甲寅，王在周，在師湯父宮，各大室即位。公尹組入右牧立中庭。王乎內史吳冊令牧。

　　王若曰：牧，昔先王既令汝作司土。今余唯或殷改，令汝辟百寮。厥同事包，迺多亂，不用先王作井，亦多虐庶民厥訊庶右粦。不井不中，迺侯止糦人。今既司匐厥皋召故。王曰：牧，汝毋敢弗帥先王作明井，用于乃訊庶右粦。毋敢不明不中不井乃實政事。毋敢不尹其不中不井。今余惟申重乃命，賜汝秬鬯一卣、金車、貴較、畫輴、朱虢、靷靳、虎冟、熏裏、旂、余馬四匹。敬夙夕勿廢朕令。

　　牧拜稽首，敢對揚王丕顯休，用作朕皇文考益白寶尊簋。牧其萬年壽考，子子孫孫永寶用。

It was the king's seventh year, thirteenth month, after the growing brightness, *jiashen* (day 21), the king at Zhou at the Captain Tangfu Palace approached the Grand Chamber and assumed position. The Duke Governor Dan entered at the right of Mu and stood in the center of the court. The king called out to Interior Secretary Wu to command Mu in writing.

The king approved of saying: "Mu, formerly the past king had commanded you to be Supervisor of Lands. Now, it is that I expand and change it, commanding you to rule the hundred officials. Their collective service is cliquish and then much disorderly, not using the past kings as models, and also much abusing the common people in their trials and criminal cases; unexemplary and immoderate, then they imperiously stop and arrest the people, and now they have compelled their criminals to confess guilt." The king said: "Mu, you ought not dare not to follow the past kings as your bright models, using them in your trials and criminal cases. You ought not dare to be unenlightened, immoderate, or unexemplary, in connecting your government service. Do not dare not to govern their immoderateness or unexemplariness. Now it is that I extend your command, awarding you one bucket of black millet sweet wine, a bronze-fitted chariot, with decorated side rails, patterned axle coverings, a covering of the front rail and chest trappings made of scarlet leather, a tiger-skin canopy with brown lining, a banner, and four northern [horses]. Respectfully from morning to night do not neglect my command."

Mu bowed and touched his head to the ground, daring in response to extol the king's illustrious beneficence, herewith making for my august cultured deceased-father Yibo this treasured offertory *gui*-tureen. May Mu for ten thousand years be long-lived and have sons' sons and grandsons' grandsons eternally to treasure and use it.

The inscription is so similar in tenor to the command of the *She ming* that it is very tempting to view them both as emanating from the same king and pertaining to the same royal court—a court troubled by an antagonistic relationship with the ministers of the preceding reign.[46] If this is so, this would be one further argument in support of the Tsinghua editors' suggestion that the *She ming* should be a command by King Xiao and that She is the name of the crown prince who would become King Yi.

On the Composition and Transmission of the *She Ming

Whether the *She ming can be identified with the "Jiong ming" chapter of the Shang shu or not, the nature of the text, both as a text and as a manuscript, raises a host of questions about both its original composition and also its transmission. The investiture record at the end of the text is so reminiscent of similar records in Western Zhou bronze inscriptions that there is a prima facie case to be made that the text dates to the same period as those bronze inscriptions: perhaps the middle to late Western Zhou. The Tsinghua editors note, moreover, that in addition to this final investiture record, much of the wording of the text proper is similar to language seen in Western Zhou bronze inscriptions or in chapters of the Shangshu that are ordinarily considered to date to the Western Zhou. These similarities include the usage of such idioms and grammatical particles as yu 雩 "and," si 稀:肆 "and so," zhao 肁:肇 "begin," lin 晉:夆 "lofty," buchi 不啻 "not only," yu 谷:欲 "and so," as well as the reduplicative usage of tu 彙 "fulsome." The editors also note phrases that are similar to phrases in those same sources. The following are just a few examples:

余弗造民康

I have not met with the people's rest (slip 1)

我幼沖人 . . . 弗造哲迪民康

I the immature Young Man . . . have not met with wisely leading the people's rest (Shang shu, "Da gao" 大誥)[47]

雩四方少（小）大邦，雩御事庶百又告有晉（夆）

and the minor and great countries of the four quarters as well as the hundreds of drivers of affairs also report there are criminal cases (slip 4)

大誥爾多邦越御事

(I) greatly announce to you many countries and drivers of affairs (Shang shu, "Da gao")[48]

A Possible Lost Classic | 133

惠不惠，亦乃服

Being kind to the unkind is also your responsibility (slips 7–8)

惠不惠，懋不懋。已，汝惟小子，乃服惟弘

Be kind to the unkind, encouraging to the unencouraged. Enough, you are the Little Son, your responsibility is vast. (*Shang shu*, "Kang gao" 康誥)[49]

敬學昚明

respectfully study lofty brightness (slip 10)

昚明亞祖

loftily bright was the Secondary Ancestor (*Shi Qiang pan* 史牆盤 [*Jicheng* 10175])

谷女纍₌（繹繹）弗功我一人在位

And so you ought fulsomely not belabor me the One Man in place (slip 11)

毋童余一人在位

Do not bestir me the One Man in place (*Mao Gong ding* 毛公鼎 [*Jicheng* 2841])

自一話一言，女（汝）亦毋（毋）敢泆于之

from each statement and each saying you also ought not dare to be neglectful in it (slip 13)

時則勿有間之，自一話一言

In this then do not have anything to interrupt it from each statement and each saying. (*Shang shu*, "Li zheng" 立政)[50]

The editors also identify what they regard as a graphic error on slip 10 of the *She ming. In the phrase 汝亦毋敢豙在乃尸服 "you also ought not dare to be lazy in your assigned responsibilities," the graph 豙 is usually used in Warring States manuscripts for the word *sui* 遂 "to succeed,"⁵¹ which would clearly be antithetical to the sense here. For this reason, the editors regard is as a scribal error for *tuan* 彖 (*thôn), which in turn is attested as a phonetic loan for *duo* 惰 (*lôih) "lazy."⁵² *Tuan* is used in this sense in such bronze inscriptions as that on the *Mao Gong ding*: "You ought not dare to be lazy in your responsibilities" (汝毋敢彖在乃服). This seems clearly to be right. Aside from its specialized usage as "hexagram statement" (often translated as "judgment") in the *Zhou Yi* 周易 *Zhou Changes*, *tuan* seems not to occur in any received text from before the Han dynasty. It is understandable that a Warring States copyist unfamiliar with the specialized usage of the word during the Western Zhou period might transcribe it into a graphically similar character that appears in Warring States orthography. If this supposition is correct, this would be the sort of telltale mistake that demonstrates the antiquity of the original text underlying the text of the manuscript.

Parallels and mistakes such as these support the Tsinghua editors' tacit assumption that the *She ming is indeed a lost classic, originally composed in the ninth century BCE or not too much later than that. However, before too readily accepting such a tacit assumption, we ought first to consider whether these parallels might not be merely conscious archaisms embedded into a text composed, if not by the fourth-century BCE scribe responsible for the Tsinghua manuscript of the *She ming, then closer to that time than to the time of the events that it purports to record? Recently, David Schaberg has advanced an argument along these lines to suggest that some chapters of the *Shang shu*, including also some *jinwen* 今文 or "modern-script" chapters, may be such archaistic compositions.

> A bad scholarly habit hallows all the *jinwen* chapters by their association with the few among them thought to date to the Western Zhou: acknowledging the fact of archaism forces us instead to see a sort of continuum, in which the same set of literacy skills that preserved the older pieces in the *Shang shu* probably also allowed the composition of the later pieces and, more importantly, probably also allowed for the citation and composition of much archaic-looking material that would not ultimately be gathered into the fold of an imperially sanctioned *Shang shu*.⁵³

In making this suggestion, Schaberg seems to acknowledge that at least a few of the *Shang shu* chapters do date to the Western Zhou, or at least are "thought to" do so.[54] Schaberg suggests that these texts feature not only a different syntax and vocabulary, but also "a disjointed, haranguing style of address" that is different from the structured arguments of Warring States texts. This "disjointed, haranguing style of address" would certainly seem to be true of the *She ming*; thus, such linguistic criteria would seem to support the Tsinghua editors' assumption about the text's date. But Schaberg proposes still another criterion before accepting that such a text might be as old as it purports to be: that it be consistent with the circumstances of its composition: "*Shu* 書—conceived as the act of writing or as the resulting script—can no longer be understood in isolation from the circumstances (social, religious, ritual) that would have made it meaningful. It can no longer be regarded—as it still is in some quarters—as a natural reflex of ordinary speech or as a widespread, almost unremarkable, aspect of government business."[55] Is it possible that a text such as the *She ming* could have been put in writing during the Western Zhou period? Evidence of this is readily at hand in the form of bronze inscriptions from the period, even earlier than the date to which the Tsinghua editors would ascribe the *She ming*. In addition to the inscription on the *Mu gui*, introduced in the preceding section, consider too the inscription on the *Da Yu ding* 大盂鼎 (*Jicheng* 2837), which is generally dated to the reign of King Kang of Zhou 周康王 (r. 1005/03–979), a full century earlier than the time of King Xiao. Although I have recently argued that this vessel may well date some fifty years later than this time, to late in the reign of King Mu (r. 956–918 BCE),[56] there is no question about the inscription's antiquity. Like the *She ming* text, the *Da Yu ding* inscription is composed of a series of royal pronouncements sandwiched between a very brief introductory statement noting the time and place of the king's command to a senior official named Yu 盂 and Yu's own dedication of the vessel to his own grandfather Nangong 南公. The king's address, which makes up the great bulk of the inscription, is divided into four segments, each introduced by the notation "the king said" (*wang yue* 王曰) or, in the case of the first segment, "the king approved of saying" (*wang ruo yue* 王若曰). The first segment begins by recalling the precedents of the past kings; includes an indictment of the illicit behavior of the Shang; notes the personal contributions of the patron of the vessel, Yu; and then concludes by enjoining him "respectfully to secure virtue's continuance. Diligently morning and evening, enter to remonstrate, and making offerings hasten to fear heaven's awe" (敬雍德經，敏朝夕入諫，享奔走，畏天威). The inscription continues with a second, much shorter, royal pronouncement that Yu should succeed his grandfather, and then a third pronouncement that contains the text of the specific command to him, commanding him to oversee the relocation of various peoples. The fourth royal pronouncement, once again brief, commands Yu to "respect your governance" (敬乃正) and "not neglect my command" (勿廢朕令), all wording extremely reminiscent of wording in the *She ming. The inscription then ends with the notation that this royal audience took place in the twenty-third year of the king's reign (perhaps 934 BCE). From the calligraphy of the inscription (fig. 5.1), as well as the shape and ornamentation of the vessel that carries it, it is clear that this text was composed not long after the royal audience it purports to narrate.

A good part of the reason that the *Da Yu ding* inscription has survived to the present is surely that it was cast into bronze, though it is perhaps paradoxical that another important reason that the vessel that carried the inscription survived is that it was deliberately buried underground.

Figure 5.1. *Da Yu ding* 大盂鼎 inscription. From Zhongguo Shehui kexueyuan Kaogu yanjiusuo, ed., *Yin Zhou jinwen jicheng*, 2837.

The *She ming* too might have been cast into a bronze vessel during the Western Zhou period, but if so it is not among the thousands or even tens of thousands of vessels cast at the time that have been unearthed to date.[57] Instead, the text that has just now been unearthed was written on bamboo slips, though the slips obviously date to some five hundred years later than the time of the royal command to She.

If we can accept the *She ming* as a Western Zhou text in its origin, we might then ask how it could have been transmitted to the Warring States period. Western Zhou bronze inscriptions provide a starting point for this discussion as well. As I have demonstrated in chapter 3, at least the royal command portion of the inscriptions would have been copied, presumably verbatim, from a document written on wood or bamboo slips and presented to the patron of the bronze vessel upon the occasion of the king's command to him. We have seen there that the royal command contained in the *Forty-Third Year Qiu ding* 逑鼎 inscription quotes the previous command to Qiu 逑 commemorated by the *Qiu pan* 逑盤 vessel and inscription.[58] In preparing this new command to Qiu, it would seem that the royal secretarial corps must have consulted the king's past command to Qiu and copied the text of that previous command into the new command. Of course, the original command to Qiu was not particularly long, so it might have been held in the memory of someone at court. However, since the quotation is exact, it seems (to me, at least) more likely that this sort of quotation entails a written original. If there were an archive containing command documents for more or less junior-grade officials (Qiu was a forest warden [*yu* 虞]), then it seems likely that a command document to an officer as important as She obviously was (whether or not he was actually the crown prince, according to the *She ming* he was the intermediary between the king and the other royal officials) might also have been included in that archive. The recipient of the command was also given a copy of the command document, which we may assume he would have made every effort to preserve, not just by casting a bronze vessel or vessels, but also striving to preserve the original bamboo-slip document. This would at least double the chances that such a document might have survived, even if those chances are still almost vanishingly small.

This still does not explain how the text would have been transmitted over the course of about a half of a millennium (from about the middle of the ninth century to the middle of the fourth century BCE) when the manuscript now in the possession of Tsinghua University was likely produced. The evidence that the manuscript was proofread and corrected (by the introduction of two small characters between the original characters on slip 4) suggests that the Tsinghua *She ming was copied from another text, doubtless also written on bamboo slips. But this putative original of the Tsinghua manuscript takes us only one step back along what must have been a multistep process of copying and recopying across not just five centuries but also the distance between the Western Zhou capital and the Chu homeland, where the Tsinghua manuscript was doubtless copied (as evidenced by the Chu script in which it is written).⁵⁹ It is unlikely that we will ever have evidence of these other steps, but then again it was extremely unlikely that we would ever have the evidence of the Tsinghua manuscript. It too survived until today primarily by virtue of having been deliberately buried underground—in some tomb. It is also fortunate that the manuscript came into the possession of Tsinghua University after it was burgled from that tomb.

The history of the text's transmission may not end with the Tsinghua manuscript. If, as Li Xueqin and the Tsinghua editors argue, the *She ming should be identified with the "Jiong ming" chapter of the Shangshu, then we must also ask when and how its subsequent transmission was lost. That the text was known in the Han dynasty by a title that was likely based on a graphic error, either writing 夐 (i.e., 奠) as 弇 or 囧 as 囚, almost certainly points to the role of copying and recopying also between the fourth century and the second century BCE. However, based on the evidence of the ancient-script chapter of the "Jiong ming," whatever text was still available in the second century BCE must have been either very fragmentary already at that time or lost sometime thereafter. While the "Jiong ming" chapter in the received text of the Shangshu is not without some similarities with the *She ming, nevertheless it shows signs of having been recomposed on the basis of fragmentary information and it was clearly rewritten in a much later idiom. This would provide some of the best evidence we have to trace how the ancient-script chapters of the Shang shu were produced.

In one of his first articles about the Tsinghua manuscripts, Li Xueqin had this to say about their implications for the ancient-script chapters of the Shang shu:

所謂作偽，我一再地說并不一定是古人是個騙子在騙我們，而只是整理了一些材料。

> As for the so-called forgeries, I have said over and over again that it was not necessarily that the ancients were tricksters tricking us, but just that they were putting some materials into order.⁶⁰

"Putting into order" (*zhengli* 整理) is a term now usually used to describe the editorial work of teams such as the Tsinghua editors. While the "Jiong ming" ancient-script chapter of the *Shang shu* is not necessarily the result of any sort of trick, if the *She ming manuscript is indeed the original version of this text, then the relationship between the "materials" (*cailiao* 材料) of the two texts is very tenuous. Just how the chapters of the *Shang shu*—the modern-script as well as the ancient-script chapters—may have been produced is still an open question.

Chapter Six

Varieties of Textual Variants
Evidence from the Tsinghua Bamboo-Slip *Ming Xun Manuscript

The fifth volume of the Tsinghua (Qinghua) University 清華大學 Warring States bamboo slips was published with six new manuscripts.[1] As with the first four volumes of this corpus, these new manuscripts can only be described as of startling significance. They are, in the order in which they are presented in the volume: *Houfu* 厚父, which includes a passage quoted in the *Mencius* as coming from the *Shu* 書 *Scriptures* and which has therefore been identified as a lost chapter of the *Shang shu* 尚書 *Exalted Scriptures*;[2] *Feng Xu zhi ming* 封許之命 *The Command Enfeoffing Xu*, which is an example of the *ming* 命 or "command" genre

---

This chapter was originally published as "Varieties of Textual Variants: Evidence from the Tsinghua Bamboo-Slip *Ming Xun Manuscript," *Early China* 39 (2016): 111–44. It is reprinted here with minimal changes in the main body of the text. However, instead of the two appendices in the original article, "Appendix 1: The Complete Text of the Tsinghua University Manuscript *Ming Xun 命訓, in Literal and Exploded Transcription, Together with the Received Text of the 'Ming Xun' 命訓 Chapter of the *Yi Zhou Shu* 逸周書, with Complete Translations" and "Appendix 2: Structured Translation of the Tsing-hua University Manuscript *Ming Xun," I append just the complete text of the *Ming Xun manuscript (in a modified transcription of the Tsinghua editors) and a complete English translation. Readers wishing to see more detail of the orthography of the original manuscript can consult the *Early China* article or, better, Shaughnessy, *The Tsinghua University Warring States Bamboo Manuscripts*, volume 1, chapter 3: "Ming Xun 命訓 *Instruction on Mandates."

that is also represented in the *Shang shu*;³ **Ming xun* 命訓 *The Instruction on Commands*, which corresponds closely with the chapter by that title in the *Yi Zhou shu* 逸周書 *Leftover Zhou Scriptures*; **Tang chu yu Tang Qiu* 湯處於湯丘 *Tang Resided at Tang Mound*, and **Tang zai Di Men* 湯在啻門 *Tang Was at the Di Gate*, both of which share formal features and both of which purport to be conversations between Tang 湯 (i.e., 唐), the founder of the Shang dynasty, and Yi Yin 伊尹, his counselor; and *Yin Gao Zong wen yu San Shou* 殷高宗問於三壽 *Yin Gao Zong Asked the Three Elders*, which purports to be a conversation between the Shang king Gao Zong 高宗 (i.e., Wu Ding 武丁; r. ca. 1210–1190 BCE) and three aged advisers, especially Peng Zu 彭祖.⁴ Each one of these texts merits detailed study and will surely be the topic of much discussion in the years to come.

In the present essay, I propose to study just one of these manuscripts: the **Ming xun* or *The Instruction on Commands*. The manuscript is not titled, but the Tsinghua editors have given it the title because, as previously noted, it corresponds quite closely with a chapter by that title in the received text of the *Yi Zhou shu*. The manuscript is written on fifteen bamboo slips, a complete slip being about 49 cm long by 6 cm wide, and originally bound with three binding straps.⁵ The text is virtually complete and very clearly written in the script of the state of Chu 楚. Slips 1, 2, 3, 7, 9, 14, and 15 are all broken at the top, with the loss of one or two characters each; slip 12 is broken at the bottom with the loss of probably three characters; and slip 14 is also broken in the middle with the loss of one other character. Other than the final slip (15), the slips are numbered on the back, though the number on slip 4 is missing and the number on slip 12 would have come at the point at which the slip is broken and is thus missing. As are all of the Tsinghua manuscripts, the **Ming xun* is beautifully published, first with full-size color photographs, then with enlarged color photographs, followed by transcriptions and notes, and finally with a complete index of character shapes (*wenzi bian* 文字編). The Tsinghua editor of this manuscript is Liu Guozhong 劉國忠, a member of the editorial team assembled by the Research and Conservation Center for Unearthed Texts (清華大學出土文獻研究與保護中心) of Tsinghua University.

The "Ming xun" chapter is the second text in the received text of the *Yi Zhou shu*, following immediately after "Du xun" 度訓 "The Instruction on Degrees" and preceding "Chang xun" 常訓 or "The Instruction on Constancies." As Liu Guozhong points out in his prefatory remarks to the Tsinghua *Ming xun, these three chapters of the Yi Zhou shu all share similar formats, wording, and philosophy. All three discuss heaven's giving birth to the people and the creation of "degrees" (du 度), primarily by "enlightened kings" (ming wang 明王). The texts are marked by explicit parallel structures, both in their overall argumentation and also at the level of the sentence, discussing how good order should be developed to the full (ji 極), but not made absolute, being flexible within certain constancies. As Liu Guozhong notes, all three texts are very much of a piece and must have been composed at the same time. In the past, these three chapters were relatively neglected and even suspected of being Han or later compositions. With the discovery of the Qinghua text of *Ming xun, it is now clear that this one text, at least, dates no later than the fourth century BCE. It stands to reason that the other two texts should also date to the same period.

The three chapters "Du xun," "Ming xun," and "Chang xun" are not the only portion of the Yi Zhou shu that has been relatively neglected in Chinese textual scholarship. Indeed, the entire text has received less attention than it is due. Tradition holds that the Yi Zhou shu was originally a collection of seventy Zhou dynasty texts that Confucius left out (yi 逸) of his collection of the Shang shu, which is supposed to have originally included exactly one hundred chapters. In the "Yiwen zhi" 藝文志 "Record of Arts and Letters" chapter of the Han shu 漢書 History of Han, the Yi Zhou shu (referred to as simply Zhou shu 周書 Zhou Scriptures) is listed together with the Shang shu, and there is evidence that it—or at least some of its chapters—were considered as "scriptures," just the same as the Shang shu.[6] However, beginning with the "Jingji zhi" 經籍志 "Record of Classics and Texts" bibliography of the Sui shu 隋書 History of Sui, the title has been relegated to the category "Miscellaneous Histories" (za shi 雜史). The oldest extant edition is a Yuan-dynasty edition of 1354, but this has rarely been seen in subsequent centuries. In the preface to the earliest critical edition, Lu Wenchao 盧文弨 (1717–1795) cites seven different editions that he consulted, his base text being the Jiajing 嘉靖 era (1507–1567) text of a Zhang Nie 章蘖, which is reproduced in the Sibu congkan 四部叢刊 edition of the Yi Zhou shu. During the nineteenth and early twentieth centuries, the Yi Zhou shu attracted attention from such notable scholars as Wang Niansun 王念孫 (1744–1832), Ding Zongluo 丁宗洛 (1771–1841), Chen Fengheng 陳逢衡 (1778–1855), Zhu Youzeng 朱右曾 (1838 jinshi), Yu Yue 俞樾 (1821–1907), Sun Yirang 孫詒讓 (1848–1908), and Liu Shipei 劉

師培 (1884–1919), all of whom authored commentaries or critical textual studies.[7] Throughout most of the twentieth century, however, the text lapsed into obscurity again, with only certain chapters attracting attention.[8] More recently, Huang Huaixin 黃懷信 has produced both a modern translation and also a collected-commentaries edition that has now become a standard edition, at least in mainland China.[9]

The *Ming xun text, whether of the Tsinghua manuscript or as a chapter of the Yi Zhou shu, is a very tightly structured essay, discussing the methods and aims of governance. It can be divided into three major sections. The first section enumerates six general methods or tools of governance: "commands" (ming 命), "good fortune" (fu 福), "misfortune" (huo 禍), "shame" (chi 恥) or chou 醜 "disgrace,"[10] "rewards" (shang 賞), and "punishments" (fa 罰). According to the text, if these six tools are correctly implemented then "the degrees of good order will reach to the limit" (du zhi yu ji 度至于極). However, the second section introduces a complication: deliberately pushing these methods to their limit produces a countereffect, which results in disorder. The third section then provides a still more detailed list of twelve ways in which the ruler interacts with the people: "soothing" (fu 撫), "harmonizing" (he 和), "gathering" (lian 斂), "entertaining" (yu 娛), "instructing" (xun 訓), "teaching" (jiao 教), "governing" (zheng 正), "mobilizing" (dong 動), "encouraging" (quan 勸), "terrifying" (wei 畏), "looking upon" (lin 臨), and "putting in motion" (xing 行), and the means that he uses to do so: "generosity" (hui 惠), "equality" (jun 均), "sorrow" (ai 哀), "joy" (le 樂), "ritual" (li 禮), "government" (zheng 政), "tasks" (shi 事), "awards" (shang 賞), "punishments" (fa 罰), "centeredness" (zhong 中), and "balance" (quan 權), working forward and backward and then forward again through these lists, counseling their implementation, but always in moderation. Much of the advice to avoid extremes will be familiar from other Warring States philosophical works. For instance, the superior is advised "to harmonize them (i.e., the people) with equality" (he zhi yi jun 和之以均), but "equality is not identical" (jun bu yi 均不一), for "if equality is identical then it is not harmonious" (jun yi bu he 均一不和). This is similar to the dictum in the Analects of Confucius "to harmonize but not to treat as the same" (he er bu tong 和而不同).[11] Being "centered" (zhong) and being "balanced" (quan) are particularly emphasized as the most important of these means.

While the Tsinghua *Ming xun manuscript and the Yi Zhou shu "Ming xun" chapter are extremely similar, such that there can be no doubt that they are simply two versions of a single text, a comparison of the two texts reveals numerous variant readings. Liu Guozhong argues that the variants show the received text to be decidedly corrupt, and it is hard to disagree with this appraisal. I am well aware that much recent scholarship argues that it is misguided to prefer one variant to another.[12] However, not all variants are created equal. It is clear that over the course of the two or more millennia of the text's transmission, one or probably more than one copyist or scribe did not fully understand the fine points of the text and introduced any number of errors into it. Indeed, it is not altogether surprising that the received text of the "Ming xun" text should have been relatively neglected throughout history; it simply does not read as well as it should. However, the Tsinghua manuscript shows that the text was once quite precise and quite subtle.

Some problems in the received text had already been identified by earlier scholars (though some of their suggestions have also proven to be wrong). But many others have come to light only with the appearance of the Tsinghua manuscript. In addition to shedding important light on this one text, the differences between the Tsinghua *Ming xun and the received "Ming xun" provide excellent illustrations of the many different varieties of textual variants found in all received Chinese texts and thus can have a more general significance as well. In this essay, I propose to examine five different types of variants found in the Tsinghua *Ming xun and the received "Ming xun" text. I will give two examples of each: simple writing or copying errors; classifier variation; phonetic loans; variants caused by graphic similarity; and the addition or deletion of words, sometimes apparently for the purpose of making an intended reading more explicit. I will also include one pseudovariant, which may be even more illustrative of editorial practices, both traditional and modern. In most cases (though not necessarily in all), it seems certain, as suggested by Liu Guozhong, that the reading of the Tsinghua manuscript is preferable to that of the received text in the Yi Zhou shu.[13] Most of these variants were doubtless caused simply by the vagaries of traditional textual transmission, exacerbated in the case of the Yi Zhou shu by its noncanonical status and relative neglect by serious editors. However, some seem to have been deliberate attempts to "improve" the text.

Between the Tsinghua *Ming xun and the received text of the "Ming xun" chapter of the Yi Zhou shu, there are of course numerous more or less incidental variants for which a systematic critical edition would need to account, but which will have to pass more or less undiscussed here.[14] These include the systematic variation between the manuscript's cai 才

and the received text's *zai* 在 in the sense of "in" or "at," between the manuscript's *ru* 如 and the received text's *ruo* 若 in the sense of "if," or the manuscript's *wang* 亡 and the received text's *wu* 無 in the sense of "there is none."[15] Other occasional variants that do not seem to affect the sense of the text are between the manuscript's *nai* 乃 and the received text's *ze* 則 in the sense of "then" (as seen on slip 8), or between the manuscript's *jue* 毕 (i.e., 厥) "their; those" and the received text's *ci* 此 "these" (slip 10). The difference between the manuscript's negative *fu* 弗 and the received text's *bu* 不 on slip 8 might be more important, but this variation is extremely common in excavated manuscripts and the present example does not shed any additional light on the usage of the two negatives. I will also not discuss cases of the presence or absence of the pronoun *qi* 其 (for example, on slips 7 and 8) or of the particles *yi* 矣 (slip 8) or *ye* 也 (for example, in the received text corresponding to slip 8). Nor will I discuss the systematic variation between the manuscript's *chi* 恥 "ashamed" and the received text's *chou* 醜 "disgraced,"[16] or between such synonymous locutions as the manuscript's *tong sang* 痛喪 "to be pained by mourning" and the received text's *wu si* 惡死 "to hate death" (slip 4). Instead, I hope that the variations I propose to examine will have more general implications.

In the examples examined in the following section, "T" represents the "Tsinghua" manuscript, while "Y" represents the *Yi Zhou shu* received text. For the manuscript, I provide the transcription into standard Chinese characters provided by the Tsinghua editor. I include the punctuation given by the editor. I indicate in brackets the number of the slip on which the text in question is found. Following this transcription, I give the corresponding text in the *Yi Zhou shu*, as found in the *Sibu congkan* edition of the text. I provide punctuation for this text as well, to make the reading easier to follow, though it was not originally punctuated. I also provide English translations of both the manuscript and received text. I highlight the variation in question with underlining in the Chinese and by italics in the English. I have strived to render the variants explicit in both translations. For the complete context of the manuscript version of the text, see the complete translation given in the appendix to this essay.

Variety 1: Miswriting or Miscopying

The first example seems to be a case of simple miswriting or miscopying on the part of the manuscript scribe. The second example seems to be a simple case of transposition, in which the received text has copied a passage from another portion of the text and inserted it in place of an original passage.

EXAMPLE 1

> T: 夫故昭命以命力(之)曰 [10]
>
> Y: 明王是故昭命以命之曰:
>
> T: Heaven therefore made radiant the mandate in order to command *power* saying:
>
> Y: Enlightened kings for this reason made radiant the mandate in order to command *them* saying:

"To command power" (*ming li* 命力) makes no sense in the context. For this reason, the Tsinghua editor places the pronoun *zhi* 之 "them" in parentheses after *li* 力 in his transcription, indicating that he understands the graph to be miswritten. Of course, his understanding is doubtless influenced by the received text, which does indeed have a *zhi* 之 after the verb *ming* 命. The editor adds a note in which he remarks simply enough that he suspects that *li* is an error. In the manuscript, *li* is written ᗄ, which is not particularly graphically similar to *zhi*, written on the same slip as ᗄ. Nevertheless, although the stroke order is certainly different, perhaps the two characters are similar enough to cause them to be mistaken. Of course, it is also possible that this was just a slip of the brush. In any event, the reading of the received text certainly seems preferable here.

EXAMPLE 2

> T: 福祿在人，<u>人能居，如不居而重義</u>，則度至于極。 [2]
>
> Y: 福祿在人。<u>能無懲乎？若懲而悔過</u>，則度至于極。
>
> T: Good fortune and riches depend on men. *Can men reside in them (i.e., can men be content with them)? If they do not reside in them and yet take seriously propriety*, then degrees will reach to the limit.

Y: Good fortune and riches depend on men. *Can they be without chastisement? If they are chastised and regret mistakes*, then degrees will reach to the limit.

The sentence immediately after this in the manuscript text reads (again marking variants vis-à-vis the received text):

T: 或司不義而降之禍。禍過在人。人口毋懲乎？如懲而悔過，則度至于極。 【2-3】

Y: 夫或司不義而降之禍，在人。能無懲乎？若懲而悔過，則度至于極。

T: [The Overseer of Virtue] also oversees impropriety and sends down on it misfortune. *Misfortune and mistakes* depend on men. [Can] men be without chastisement? *If* they are chastised and regret mistakes, then degrees will reach to the limit.

Y: [The Overseer of Virtue] also oversees impropriety and sends down on it misfortune, *which* depends on men. Can they be without chastisement? *If* they are chastised and regret mistakes, then degrees will reach to the limit.

The topic of the first sentence, "good fortune and riches" (*fu lu* 福祿), elicits different treatment in the two versions of the text, the manuscript asking, "Can men reside in them," whereas the received text asks, "Can they be without chastisement?" This latter phrase is obviously an inappropriate treatment for "good fortune and riches" and has been duplicated from the subsequent sentence, where the topic is "misfortune and mistakes" (*huo guo* 禍過) in the manuscript or "misfortune" (*huo* 禍) in the received text. For this reason, Tang Dapei 唐大培 (fl. 1836) had already suggested in his *Yi Zhou shu fen bian ju shi* 逸周書分編句釋 that the two phrases highlighted were corrupt, having been copied from the following sentence. The manuscript confirms that he was quite right in his intuition and presents us with a better reading of this passage.[17]

Variety 2: Classifier Variation

The next examples are both simple cases of the addition or not of a classifier, in this case a distinction between *zhong* 中 "centered" and *zhong*

忠 "loyal," the latter differentiated by the addition of a "heart" signific. A perhaps similar case of classifier variation is discussed later as a case of a pseudovariant in example 11.

EXAMPLE 3

    T: 臨之以中 [12]

    Y: 臨之以忠

    T: look upon them with *centeredness*

    Y: look upon them with *loyalty*

EXAMPLE 4

    T: 中不忠 [12]

    Y: 忠不忠

    T: *centeredness* is not loyal

    Y: *loyalty* is not loyal

Although in the first of these two cases either reading is perfectly possible grammatically, either "look upon them (i.e., the people) with centeredness" or "look upon them with loyalty," conceptually the manuscript reading would seem to be preferable. Much of the discussion in this chapter, and especially that in the section immediately preceding that in which these examples are found, revolves around the desirability of not going to excess. Being "centered" would seem to be consistent with this. Moreover, *zhong* 忠 "loyalty" is a desired attribute of the people, but not of the superior who here "looks upon" (*lin* 臨) the people. The logic of this seems to be confirmed in the second case: "loyalty is not loyal" seems to be nonsensical, whereas "*centeredness* is not loyal" is not only a striking sort of wordplay but also constitutes a philosophically interesting statement.

Variety 3: Phonetic Loans

The next two examples are both cases of phonetic loans, one of the more common sorts of variation in Chinese texts of all periods. The first example comes from the same slip as the two examples examined earlier and would seem to illustrate the same sort of wordplay on the part of the *Ming xun author.

Example 5

> T: 正之以政 [12]
>
> Y: 震之以政
>
> T: *govern* them with government
>
> Y: *shake* them with government

Although "govern them with government" sounds almost tautological in English, in Chinese the expression sounds quite eloquent. Moreover, the author of the *Ming xun seems to be using the language here in the same way he used the preceding phrase "centeredness is not loyal" (*zhong bu zhong* 中不忠). The variant in the received text, *zhen* 震, apparently a phonetic loan for *zheng* 正 (*zheng* 正 had an archaic pronunciation of something like *teŋh, while *zhen* 震 had an archaic pronunciation something like *[m-]dən[18]) has such meanings as "to shake; to rattle (both literally and figuratively); to bestir; to inspire." In English, many of these meanings sound like they would be appropriate functions for "government." However, while I would not want to be categorical about this, in Chinese texts of this period *zhen* as a transitive verb is not usually attributed to government.

Example 6

> T: 淫祭皮家 [9]
>
> Y: 淫祭則罷家
>
> T: sacrificing excessively will *ruin* their households
>
> Y: sacrificing excessively will *then quit* their households

This phrase comes in the context of doing various activities to excess. The fuller context reads as follows:

T: 極禍則民畏，民畏則淫祭，淫祭罷家。 【8-9】

Y: 極禍則民鬼，民鬼則淫祭，淫祭則罷家。

T: If misfortune is pressed to the limit, then the people will *be terrified*, and if the people are terrified then they will sacrifice excessively, and sacrificing excessively will ruin their households.

Y: If misfortune is pressed to the limit, then the people will turn *to ghosts*, and if the people *turn to ghosts* then they will sacrifice excessively, and sacrificing excessively *then* will quit their households.

Kong Chao 孔晁 (fl. ca. AD 265), the earliest commentator on the *Yi Zhou shu*, commented on the line *yin ji ze ba jia* 淫祭則罷家 "sacrificing excessively then will quit their households":

罷弊其財且無禍也。

Exhaust their resources hoping not to have misfortune.[19]

Clearly, this is more or less what the sentence means. 罷, normally read *ba* and meaning "to quit, to stop" or *bi* "to scatter," also has a reading of *pi* meaning "tired, worn-out; weak; defeated," and it is this latter reading that later editors of the *Yi Zhou shu* have generally adopted, both in Kong Chao's commentary and in the main text. It is also the reading that Liu Guozhong adopts for the 皮 of the manuscript. This is a reasonable, but not a necessary, reading. Perhaps an easier reading of the manuscript character 皮 would be as the protograph of *po* 破 "to smash, to ruin" or of *pi* 披 "to split; to break off": that is, "ruin their households," as I translate it.

Variety 4: Graphic Similarity

The fourth type of variant that I propose to discuss involves differences that develop from graphic similarity between two characters. Again, I will give two examples of this type of variant. I would suggest that both of them derive from serious misinterpretations of the underlying text.

Example 7

T: 夫民生而恥不明，上以明之，能亡恥乎？ [3]

Y: 夫民生而醜不明，無以明之，能無醜乎？

T: When the people from birth are *ashamed* of not being enlightened, and *superiors* because of this enlighten them, can they be *without shame*?

Y: When people from birth are *disgraced* by not being enlightened, and *there is nothing* with which to enlighten them, can they be *without disgrace*?

Although this passage includes three important lexical variants—*chi* 恥 "ashamed" versus *chou* 醜 "disgraced," *shang* 上 "superior" versus *wu* 無 "there is nothing," and *wang* 亡 "there is none" versus *wu* 無 "there is nothing"—I will focus here only on the variation between *shang* 上 "superior" versus *wu* 無 "there is nothing." The focus of the *Ming xun* manuscript, just as it is the focus of the "Ming xun" chapter of the *Yi Zhou shu*, and also the related "Du xun" and "Chang xun" chapters, is the methods by which government can bring about good order. Elsewhere in the text, *shang* 上 is used several times in the sense of political "superiors" (e.g., on slips 4, 8, and 9), and the passage here would seem to make it the responsibility of these superiors to enlighten the unenlightened people. The reading of the received text misses this sense entirely. Moreover, not only is it not consistent with this overall philosophical position, but it is also not very interesting philosophically; after all, if the people are disgraced from birth by not being enlightened, and if there is truly no means to enlighten them, then how indeed could they be without disgrace!

It would seem that the commentary of Kong Chao was based on a text that read more or less as does the manuscript:

不謂醜者，若道上為君。

It does not put this in terms of the disgraced ones, but seems to speak of the superior being the lord.

The only apparent explanation for Kong Chao's mention of a "superior" (*shang* 上) in his comment is that this word was in the text on which he was commenting.

While of course there is no graphic similarity between *shang* 上 and *wu* 無, this variant masks what must have been a different variant earlier in the transmission of the text. *Shang* 上, whether written as 𠄞 (transcribed by the Tsinghua editors as 丄) as here,[20] or as 𠄞 as elsewhere in Warring States manuscripts,[21] is strikingly similar to *wang* 亡, written as 𠃜 in Warring States manuscripts. As noted earlier (n. 12), Chinese readers routinely read 亡 as *wu* and often simply write the character as 無. Some copyist at some point in time must have seen 𠄞 and understood it as 𠃜, and sometime later some other copyist transposed this *wang* 亡 into the *wu* 無 of the received text. Only a couple of commentators seem to have noticed that the received text makes little or no sense.[22]

EXAMPLE 8

A sentence found on slip 8 includes several variants of various kinds. One of these seems to be based on an underlying graphic similarity: between *yi* 弋, read by the Tsinghua editor as the protograph of *dai* 代 "to substitute," and *jie* 誡 "to warn."

T: 極命則民墮<u>乏</u>，<u>乃</u>曠命以<u>弋</u>其上，殆於亂<u>矣</u>。 [8]

Y: 極命則民墮，<u>民墮則</u>曠命，曠命以<u>誡</u>其上，<u>則</u>殆於亂。

T: If commands are pressed to the limit, then the people will let them fall *away* and then lay waste to the commands in order to *replace* their superiors, and will be endangered by chaos *indeed*.

Y: If commands are pressed to the limit, then the people will let them fall, and if *the people let them fall* then they will lay waste to the commands, and laying waste to the commands will *warn* their superiors, *then* they will be endangered by chaos.

Yi 弋 is written in the manuscript as 弋. This could easily have been read by any copyist as *ge* 戈 "dagger-axe," regularly written as 戈 in Warring

States manuscripts, and interpreted as the protograph for either *jie* 戒 "to put on guard" (written in Warring States manuscripts as 𢦏), or that in turn as the protograph for the *jie* 誡 "to warn" of the received text.[23] Once again we have a case of graphic similarity leading to an almost nonsensical received reading. Whereas it is easy to see why the people "replacing" (*dai* 代) their superiors would be perceived to run the danger of chaos, it is very hard indeed to see why their "warning" (*jie* 誡) their superiors should do so. The difference between 弋 and 戈 is tiny, but the significance for the text is great. We have here a classic demonstration of the Chinese proverb *cha zhi hao li, shi zhi qian li* 差之毫厘，失之千里 "missing it by an inch and losing it by a thousand miles."

Variety 5: Added or Deleted Text

The final variety of variants that I propose to discuss involves additional material found in the received text vis-à-vis the manuscript. While of course there is no way to be sure what the underlying cause of such additions may have been, context may allow some explanation to be divined.

EXAMPLE 9

    T: 如有恥而恆行，則度至于極。 [3]

    Y: 若有醜而競行不醜，則度至于極。

    T: If they have *shame* and *constantly behave*, then degrees will reach to the limit.

    Y: If they have *disgrace* and *insistently* practice *not being disgraced*, then degrees will reach to the limit.

    T: 福莫大於行 [10]

    Y: 福莫大於行義

    T: Of good fortune there is nothing greater than behaving.

    Y: Of good fortune there is nothing greater than practicing *propriety*.

These two passages, from different portions of the text, both feature the word *xing* 行, and the parallels between them—both in the manuscript and in the received text—show that the writer or editor was intending an emphatic sense for the word. *Xing* is, of course, a very common verb, with both intransitive and transitive uses, in addition to several nominal uses as well. The normal intransitive use of *xing* is "to walk," and many related senses, while the transitive use normally means "to put into motion, to put into effect" as well as many related senses. In the first passage of the manuscript, *xing* is an intransitive verb, but it surely does not mean just "to walk." Instead, it must mean something like "to behave," that is, "to behave properly," an unusual but not wholly unattested meaning.[24] In the second example, this verbal sense has been nominalized into "behaving" or "good behavior." In the received text, however, both cases of *xing* have been turned into transitive verbs ("to put into effect") by the addition of direct objects (*bu chou* 不醜 "not being disgraced" and *yi* 義 "propriety"). It would seem that some editor of the received "Ming xun" chapter of the *Yi Zhou shu* regarded the intransitive usage of *xing* as incorrect or incomplete. The meaning is essentially the same as "to behave oneself," but in these passages the received text has taken an interesting idiosyncrasy of the text and transformed it into a fairly pedestrian platitude.

It would seem that the intransitive usage of *xing* in the sense of "to behave oneself" was usually a characteristic of the author of the *Ming xun text. It appears also in two other sentences of the text, one of which is preserved essentially without change in the received text, and one of which is completely changed.

T: 正人亡極則不信，不信則不行。 [6]

Y: 正人無極則不信，不信則不行。

T: If in governing men there are *not* limits, then they will not be sincere, and if they are not sincere then they will not behave.

Y: If in governing men there are *not* limits, then they will not be sincere, and if they are not sincere then they will not behave.

T: 弗智則不行 [8]

Y: 不知則不存

T: If they do *not know it*, then they will not *behave*.

Y: If *ignorant*, then they will not *survive*.

On the other hand, there is another occurrence of the verb *xing* that comes just two sentences after this last example. In this case, it is the manuscript that adds a word causing *xing* to have a transitive use in the sense "to put into effect," though this sense is masked to some extent by a preposing of the object *wei* 韋 "disobedience."

T: 極福則民祿，民祿 迁善，迁善韋則不行。 [8]

Y: 極福則民祿，民祿則干善，干善則不行。

T: If good fortune is pressed to the limit, then the people will be enriched; if the people being enriched strive for goodness, then in striving for goodness *disobedience* will not be put into practice.

Y: If good fortune is taken to the limit, then the people will be enriched, and if the people being enriched *then* strive for goodness, then in striving[25] for goodness will not behave.

As can be seen here, the received text does not include the word *wei* 韋, doubtless to be understood as *wei* 違 "to disobey; disobedience." If this sentence were viewed in isolation, the reading of the manuscript would doubtless be preferable; it would serve as an exhortation toward goodness: good fortune enriches the people, which encourages them to improve themselves and not to disobey their superiors. However, this conclusion is out of place in the immediate context of the text, which presents a series of countereffects that are not desirable. The sentences immediately before and after read as follows:

T: 極命則民墮乏，乃曠命以代其上，殆於亂矣。 [8]

Y: 極命則民墮，民墮則曠命，曠命以誡其上，則殆於亂。

T: If commands are pressed to the limit, then the people will let them fall *away* and then lay waste to the commands in order to *replace* their superiors, and will be endangered by chaos *indeed*.

Y: If commands are pressed to the limit, then the people will let them fall, and *if the people let them fall then they will lay waste* to the commands, and laying waste to the commands will *warn* their superiors, then they will be endangered by chaos.

T: 極禍則民鬼，民鬼則淫祭，淫祭則罷家。 【8–9】

Y: 極禍則民鬼，民鬼則淫祭，淫祭則罷家。

T: If misfortune is pressed to the limit, then the people will be terrified, and if the people are terrified then they will sacrifice excessively, and sacrificing excessively will *ruin* their households.

Y: If misfortune is pressed to the limit, then the people will turn to ghosts, and if the people turn to ghosts then they will sacrifice excessively, and sacrificing excessively then will *quit* their households.

It can be seen from these sentences that the conclusions to the sentences are all negative; it stands to reason that the same should be the case in the sentence in question here. This is indeed the reading of the received text, which does not include the word *wei* "disobedience," and so the verb *xing* has to be intransitive, meaning "to behave": "in striving for goodness (the people) will not behave." It is curious that the manuscript mistakes this usage, but it is a clear mistake.

EXAMPLE 10

T: 賞莫大於讓 【11】

Y: 賞莫大於信義，讓莫大於賈上

T: Of awards there is nothing greater than *yielding*;

Y: Of awards there is nothing greater than *trust and propriety*.
Of yielding there is nothing greater than *buying superiors*.

Here some editor of the received text has attempted to correct what he apparently perceived to be a flaw in the text, but in doing so shows that he did not understand the underlying logic of the text. Both the *Ming xun* and "Ming xun" texts are organized in groups of six, and stress this enumeration, as also in the sentence immediately following this one, by referring to "these six things" (*ci liu zhe* 此六者). It is clear throughout the text that these six things are "commands" (*ming* 命), "good fortune" (*fu* 福), "misfortune" (*huo* 禍), "shame" (*chi* 恥) or "disgrace" (*chou* 醜), "rewards" (*shang* 賞), and "punishments" (*fa* 罰). However, in this section of the text (text found on slips 8–11), only five of these topics conclude with the formula "of X there is nothing greater than Y" (X *mo da yu* 莫大於Y); the first sentence, dealing with "commands" has a different structure. Some editor must have counted these five "of X there is nothing greater than Y" sentences, and thought that five cannot equal six. He must also have thought that a sentence such as "of awards there is nothing greater than yielding" does not make sense and so added a different attribute to "awards" (*shang* 賞). But in doing this, he misunderstood the relationship between "awards" and "yielding." Text on slip 9, essentially identical in the received text, shows this:

T: 極賞則民賈其上，賈其上則<u>亡讓</u>，<u>亡讓</u>則不順。 【9】

Y: 極賞則民賈其上，賈其上則民<u>無讓</u>，<u>無讓</u>則不順。

T: If awards are pressed to the limit, then the people will buy their superiors, and if they buy their superiors then *there will be no* yielding, and if *there is no* yielding then they will not be compliant.

Y: If awards are pressed to the limit, then the people will buy their superiors, and if they buy their superiors then *the people will have no* yielding, and if *they have no* yielding then they will not be compliant.

The reason that "yielding" is so important in relation to "awards" is because it is a counterindication that can occur when "awards" are taken too far.

Whoever introduced this error into the received text then went on to compound his error by inventing a wholly new category to the set of six means of governance: "yielding" (*rang* 讓). In doing so, he made matters much worse by adding "of yielding there is nothing greater than buying superiors" (*rang mo da yu gu shang* 讓莫大於賈上), which of course would have been anathema to the author of the *Ming xun.

Variety 6: A Pseudovariant

Example 11

The final example is a seemingly simple case of classifier variation, between *dai* 殆 "danger" and *shi* 始 "beginning," both of which derive from the protograph *tai* 台. However, it reveals much about the editorial process. After listing six examples of excesses in government (excessive "commands," "good fortune," "misfortune," "shame," "awards," and "punishments"), the text relates these to governance:

> T: 凡<u>坒</u>六者，正之<u>所殆</u>。 [10]
>
> Y: 凡<u>此</u>六者，政之<u>始也</u>。
>
> T: All of *those* six things are what *endanger governance*.
>
> Y: All of *these* six things are the *beginnings of government*.

It is easy to see, especially in context, that these six excesses "endanger" government, and it is not easy to see how they could be the "beginnings" of government. Indeed, already in the late eighteenth century Lu Wenchao wordlessly emended the *shi* 始 "beginning" of his source text to read *dai* 殆 "danger," and this emendation has been accepted by all subsequent editors, including now also the Tsinghua editor Liu Guozhong. In a note (n. 25), he says, "Checked against the manuscript text, Lu's emendation is correct, and the manuscript text 台 should also be read as *dai* 殆." Reasonable though this emendation seems at first reading, the evidence from the manuscript is by no means so conclusive. Elsewhere in the Tsinghua manuscripts, 怠 is routinely used to write the word *shi* 始 "beginning," and based on present evidence it is never elsewhere used to write the word *dai* 殆 "danger." What is more, on slip 8 of *Ming xun*, there is what seems to be an unmistakable use of the word *dai* 殆 "danger," and there the graph is written with a "heart" signific: 㥾, that is, 怠. This does not mean that 怠 here could not also be read as *dai* "danger," but any editor should be explicit about his or her reasoning for doing so. On the other hand, if the manuscript's 怠 is in fact to be read as *shi* 始, and given that prior to Lu Wenchao's emendation all versions of the received text read *shi* 始, we might also ask whether these six excesses could be construed as having led to governance in the first place. I think it would not be too hard to develop a political philosophy in which the existence of these problems was viewed as the catalyst for the establishment of government. This is perhaps a chicken-and-egg type of question, and thus an excellent example of how variants can enter into a text.

Conclusion

The *Yi Zhou shu* has truly long been a "leftover" text, throughout the last two thousand or more years having been little read and even less esteemed. The publication in 2010 of the first volume of the Tsinghua University manuscripts provided evidence that at least some texts included in the received text of the *Yi Zhou shu* circulated already in the Warring States period and may well have been regarded as having the same status as texts included in the *Shang shu*. That volume included three separate texts that can be identified with chapters in the *Yi Zhou shu*: *Huang men* 皇門 *August Gate*, which corresponds with the Yi Zhou shu chapter by that title; *Zhai Gong zhi gu ming* 祭公之顧命 *The Duke of Zhai's Retrospective Command*, which corresponds with the "Zhai Gong" 祭公 "Duke of Zhai" chapter; and *Cheng wu* 程寤 *Cheng Awakening*, only the title of which is preserved in the received *Yi Zhou shu* but for which there are numerous medieval quotations that correspond with the Tsinghua manuscript.[26] The *Ming xun* manuscript, included in volume 5 of the Tsinghua manuscripts, presents yet another indication of the importance of these texts. *Ming xun* almost certainly cannot boast the sort of pedigree of either *Huang men* or *Zhai Gong zhi gu ming*, both of which may well be authentic texts of the Western Zhou period, and it does not provide any new historical information. However, it is not for those reasons uninteresting. The text as found in the manuscript is a very tightly argued essay and will surely repay close reading for greater understanding of Warring States political philosophy. Its relationship with the received chapter "Ming xun" will also repay close reading, as I have attempted to demonstrate here, for the varieties of ways in which Chinese texts can be changed in the course of traditional transmission.

Appendix

Transcription and Translation of Tsinghua Manuscript *Ming Xun 命訓 *Instruction on Mandates

［天］生民而成大命，命司德正以禍福，立明王以訓之，曰：

"大命有常，小命日成。日成則敬，有尚則廣。廣以敬命，則度 [一] ［至于］極。

夫司德司義而賜之福。福祿在人。人能居？如不居而重義，則度至于極。或司不義而降之禍。禍過在人，人 [二] ［能］毋懲乎？如懲而悔過，則度至于極。

夫民生而恥不明，上以明之，能亡恥乎？如有恥而恆行，則度至于 [三] 極。

夫民生而樂生穀，上以穀之，能毋勸乎？如勸以忠信，則度至于極。

夫民生而痛死喪，上以畏之，能毋恐 [四] 乎？如恐而承教，則度至于極。

"六極既達，九迂俱塞，達道道天以正人。正人莫如有極，道天莫如亡極。道天有極，則不威，不威 [五] 則不昭。正人亡極，則不信，不信則不行。夫明王昭天信人以度功，功地以利之，使信人畏天，則度至于極。

"夫天道三，[六] 人道三。天有命，有福，有禍。人有恥，有市冕，有斧鉞。以人之恥當天之命，以其市冕當天之福，以其斧鉞當天之禍。六 [七] 方三述，其極一。

弗知則不行。

    極命則民墮乏，乃曠命以代其上，殆於亂矣。
    極福則民祿，民祿迁善，迁善違則不行。
    極禍 [八] 則民畏，民畏則淫祭，淫祭破家。
    極恥則民枳，民枳則傷人，傷人則不義。
    極賞則民賈其上，賈其上則民亡讓，亡讓則不順。
    極罰則民多詐，多詐則 [九] 不忠，不忠則亡復。

"凡厥六者，政之所始。天故昭命以命之，曰：'大命世罰，小命罰身。'

    福莫大於行。
    禍莫大於淫祭。
    恥莫大於 [十] 傷人。
    賞莫大於讓。
    罰莫大於多詐。

"是故明王奉此六者以牧萬民，民用不失。

    撫之以惠，
    和之以均，
    斂之以哀，
    娛之以樂，[十一]
    訓之以禮，
    教之以藝，
    正之以政，
    動之以事，
    勸之以賞，
    畏之以罰，
    臨之以中，
    行之以權。

    權不法，
    中不忠，

Varieties of Textual Variants | 163

罰［不服，
賞］[十二] 不從勞，
事不累，
政不成，
藝不淫，
禮有時，
樂不伸，
哀不至，
均不一，
惠必忍人。

凡此物厥權之屬也。

惠而不忍人，
人不勝 [十三] ［害，
害］不知死，
均一不和，
哀至則匱，
樂伸則亡，
禮［無時］則不貴，
藝淫則害于才，
政成則不長，
事累則不功。

以賞從勞，勞而不至。
以 [十四] ［罰從］服，服而不釙。
以中從忠則尚，尚不必中。
以權從法則行，行不必法。

"法以知權，權以知微，微以知始，始以知終。"[十五]

Heaven gave birth to the people and completed the great mandate, commanding the Controller of Virtue to govern with misfortune and good fortune, and to establish enlightened kings to instruct them, saying:

> The great mandate has constancy and the minor mandates are daily completed. Being daily completed, they are respected; having promotion, it

is expansive. Expansively respecting the mandates, then degrees [1] [will reach to] the limit.

The Controller of Virtue controls propriety and awards it good fortune. Good fortune and riches depend on humankind. Can humans be content with them? If they are not content with them and yet take seriously propriety, then degrees will reach to the limit.

[The Controller of Virtue] also controls impropriety and sends down on it misfortune. Misfortune and mistakes depend on humankind. [Can] humans [2] be without chastisement? If they are chastised and regret mistakes, then degrees will reach to the limit.

When the people from birth are ashamed of being unenlightened, and superiors because of this enlighten them, can they be without shame? If they have shame and constantly behave, then degrees will reach to [3] the limit.

When the people from birth enjoy fresh grain, and superiors use it to pay them, can they be without encouragement? If they are encouraged with loyalty and sincerity, then degrees will reach to the limit.

When the people from birth are pained by death and mourning, and superiors use these to awe them, can they be without fear? [4] If they are fearful and receive teaching, then degrees will reach to the limit.

The six limits all being attained, and the nine strivings all being blocked, one attains the Way and follows heaven to govern humankind. In governing humans, there is nothing as good as having limits; in following heaven, there is nothing as good as not having limits. If in following heaven there are limits, then it will not be awe-inspiring, and if it is not awe-inspiring [5] then it will not be radiant. If in governing humans there are not limits, then they will not be trustworthy, and if they are not trustworthy then they will not behave. If enlightened kings make heaven radiant and humans trustworthy to work by degrees, and to work the land to benefit them, causing sincere humans to be awed by heaven, then degrees will reach to the limit.

The ways of heaven are three, [6] and the ways of humankind are three. Heaven having a mandate, there is good fortune and there is misfortune. Humankind having shame, there are kneepads and caps and there are axes and halberds. By taking humans' shame to match heaven's mandate, by taking their kneepads and caps to match heaven's good fortune, and by taking their axes and halberds to match heaven's misfortune. There are six [7] recipes and three methods, but their limit is unitary.

If they do not know it, then they will not behave.

If commands are taken to the limit, then the people will let them fall away and then lay waste to the commands in order to replace their superiors, and will be endangered by chaos indeed.

If good fortune is taken to the limit, then the people will be enriched, and if the people being enriched strive for goodness, then in striving for goodness disobedience will not be put into practice.

If misfortune is taken to the limit, [8] then the people will be awed, and if the people are awed then they will sacrifice excessively, and sacrificing excessively will ruin their households.

If shame is taken to the limit, then the people will revolt, and if the people revolt then they will harm others, and in harming others then they will not be proper.

If awards are taken to the limit, then the people will bribe their superiors, and if they bribe their superiors then the people will have no yielding, and if there is no yielding then they will not be compliant.

If punishments are taken to the limit, then the people will have many wiles, and with many wiles then [9] they will not be loyal, and not being loyal then they will be without returns.

All of these six things are the beginnings of governance. Heaven therefore made radiant the mandate in order to command them saying: "The great mandate for generations punishes; the minor mandates punish the person."[27]

Of good fortune there is nothing greater than behaving.
Of misfortune there is nothing greater than excessive sacrifice.
Of shame there is nothing greater than [10] harming others.
Of awards there is nothing greater than yielding.
Of punishments there is nothing greater than many wiles.

This is why enlightened kings uphold these six things in order to shepherd the myriad people, and the people are thereby not lost.

Soothe them with generosity,
harmonize them with equality,
gather them in mourning,
entertain them in joy, [11]
instruct them with ritual,
teach them with the arts,
govern them with government,
move them with service,
encourage them with awards,

awe them with punishments,
look upon them with centeredness,
and mobilize them with balance.

Balance is not litigious,
centeredness is not loyal,
punishments are not submissive,
awards [12] are not loosely praising,
service is not toilsome,
governance is not final,
the arts are not excessive,
the rites are timely,
joy is not extended,
sorrow is not all-reaching,
equality is not unitary,
and generosity must be tolerant of others.

All of these belong to the category of the balance of things.

Being generous but not being tolerant of others, others will not overcome [13] [harm, and being harmed] will not know death.
When equality is unitary it is not harmonious.
If sorrow is all-reaching then it is lacking.
If joy is extended then it is lost.
If the rites [are not timely] then they are not honored.
If the arts are excessive then they harm the talents.
If governance is final then it does not grow.
If service is toilsome then it is not effective.

Using awards to accompany praise, there will be praise but it will not be far-reaching.
    Using [14] [punishments to accompany] submission, there will be submission but it will not be sharp.
    Using centeredness to accompany loyalty then there will be promotions, but the promotions will not necessarily be centered.

Using balance to accompany the law then there will be good behavior, but the good behavior will not necessarily be lawful.

Through the law know balance, through balance know the fine points, through the fine points know the beginning, and through the beginning know the end." [15]

Chapter Seven

Unearthed Documents and the Question of the Oral versus Written Nature of the *Shi Jing*

In a widely distributed, recent interview discussing the "unstable" nature of traditional Chinese literature, Stephen Owen opined that the *Shi jing* 詩經 *Classic of Poetry* is "undatable"—that prior to the Han dynasty (202 BCE–220 CE) there is no evidence that there existed an integral written text, and indeed that people of the Warring States era (453–222 BCE) would not have been able to write the text, at least not correctly.[1] Owen concluded that the poems were likely transmitted orally, which would have affected the form in which they were ultimately written.

I agree with many ideas of Martin Kern, as for instance that the *Classic of Poetry* is undateable. First, there is no evidence

---

This chapter was originally published as "Unearthed Documents and the Question of the Oral Versus Written Nature of the *Classic of Poetry*," *Harvard Journal of Asiatic Studies* 75, no. 2 (2015): 331–75. It is reprinted here with minimal revision, except for the systematic replacement of *Classic of Poetry* with *Shi jing*, to conform with usage elsewhere in this book (except in quotations of others), and especially with mention of manuscripts of the *Shi* 詩 *Poetry* unearthed or published after the original publication of this study. For these manuscripts, see n. 14, and see especially chapter 8 in this volume: "A First Reading of the Anhui University Bamboo-Slip *Shi Jing*." Also different from the original published version of the chapter is the deletion of discussion of manuscript-copying practices, mentioned in n. 13, together with its reference to the *Zheng Wen Gong wen Tai Bo* 鄭文公問太伯 manuscript, which is studied in chapter 10 in this volume.

whatsoever that indicates that prior to the Han dynasty an integral text of the *Classic of Poetry* had been recorded; we can guess that it had been recorded, and was lost in the Qin "burning of the books," but it is also possible that no integral text appeared until rather late. I feel that people of that time, before they had ever heard the *Classic of Poetry*, could not write it down; there would had to have been people who remembered the contents of the poetry who explained it to them, and only then could they have searched in their own vocabulary for Chinese characters that corresponded to the sounds that they heard, and it would have been very hard to write it down. Before the Han, it is possible that many people could recite the *Classic of Poetry* to the point that they didn't need a written record. Think about it. If the *Classic of Poetry* were always a type of oral text and also was recited in an archaic dialect, if the language had changed, then the contents of the text would also change along with it; in the process of transmission, if somebody did not understand the meaning of some small parts, he could possibly add something homophonous based on his own understanding. . . . Therefore, this is not a text written at a definite point in time, but rather part of a rather long history of transmission and interpretation.[2]

This interview marks a more assertive statement of Owen's previously published comments on the nature of the *Shi jing*.[3] In arguing for the predominately oral nature of the creation and transmission of the *Shi jing*, Owen is but the most prominent of a long line of Western authorities on early Chinese literature who have expressed similar sentiments.[4]

Given these views, one might assume that there exists firm evidence demonstrating that the *Shi jing* (or simply the *Shi*) was composed and transmitted orally, and that writing played little role in the creation of the text until a very late period. In fact, there is very little direct evidence in the context of ancient China to support these statements, and what evidence exists is susceptible to different interpretations. Instead, there are theories about oral literature, often assumed to be universal but sometimes addressed specifically to China's *Shi jing*.

To say that there is hardly any evidence to support the oral creation and transmission of the *Shi* is not to say that orality played no role in this process. Today we surely hear—and perhaps sing—most of our poetry, in the form of song lyrics; most of us hear much more poetry than we actually read. That was surely true in antiquity as well. I would not want to argue that these performances do not influence the way songwriters and poets compose, either today or in antiquity. Of course, they sound and re-sound their creations as they write them. But today, for the most part, they do write them. In this essay, I show that there is plentiful evidence—some recently discovered and much more that has long been available—to show that writing also played important roles in all stages of the creation of the *Shi*: not only at the time of the initial composition in the first half of the first millennium BCE but also during its transmission over the course of the Spring and Autumn period (722–481 BCE) and the Warring States period (453–422 BCE), and in its final recension during the Han dynasty.

Let me be clear about what I am claiming and what I am not claiming. To argue for the role of writing and written texts in the creation and transmission of the *Shi* is not to suggest that writing and only writing was involved. It would be absurd to imagine the initial creation of this text as the work of a lonely poet—or even 305 lonely poets—scribbling away upon his—or their—scrolls of bamboo slips, or to discount the role of oral performance in their continued existence—their transmission—over the course of the centuries thereafter; after all, these were—in some fashion—songs, and it was in music that they came to life. However, as I show, in the context of ancient China, a period when writing was already developed and becoming increasingly pervasive, it would be just as absurd to imagine that writing did not influence the forms and wording of these poems.

The Theory of Oral Literature and the *Shi Jing*

The thesis that I propose runs counter to much scholarship—especially Western scholarship—addressing the *Shi jing*. There are many different arguments in favor of the orality of the *Shi*, though most of them derive—whether explicitly or implicitly—from studies of the Homeric epics, the New Testament, Malagasy *hain-teny*, Yugoslavian ballads, Old English poetry, and so forth. Few of the arguments have been grounded in the early Chinese literary tradition itself, and even the most influential of them—by Marcel Granet (1884–1940) and C. H. Wang (Wang

Jingxian 王靖獻; 1940–2020)⁵—were developed prior to the discoveries of bamboo and silk manuscripts, beginning in the 1970s, that have so transformed the study of all aspects of early Chinese cultural history.

The one scholar associated with the oral theory concerning the *Shi jing* who has directed more than passing attention to these newly discovered manuscripts is Martin Kern, mentioned by Stephen Owen as a scholar with many of whose ideas he agrees. In a series of studies that bring the paleographic record to bear on the *Shi*, Kern too argues that the transmission of the *Shi* was largely an oral process.⁶ In his most thoroughgoing study of this topic, he examines six different manuscripts that contain text or quotations from the *Shi* and proposes a methodology for analyzing the writing of these manuscripts.⁷ He finds that as many as one-third of all characters in these quotations differ from the received text. He further finds that the great preponderance of these variants are homophonic in nature, characters whose phonetics share the same *xiesheng* 諧聲 (harmonizing sounds) series. Proposing three scenarios for how these manuscripts may have been produced—"the scribe reproduces an earlier written text in front of him and is thus able to compare his own writing to the text he is copying"; "somebody reads a text aloud to the scribe, who then writes it down"; or "the scribe writes the text from memory, or how he hears it recited without any written copy at hand"⁸—Kern concludes that the degree and nature of the variants found in the manuscripts is best explained by a process of transmission without recourse to a written model at hand.

Kern's articles are presented with a thoroughness and clarity of argument that have been persuasive to many readers; unfortunately, there is a basic methodological problem that calls into question his scenario of textual production. Kern states, "The appearance of textual variants . . . affects the *Odes* quotations in the same way as their embedding Warring States philosophical prose."⁹ In other words, there is nothing unusual in the degree of variation found in the quotations of the *Shi*. Rather, the writing of these quotations and also the writing of the texts in which they are found, as well as that of other manuscripts, simply reflect the writing system of the time.

While the incipient bureaucracy of the Qin dynasty (221–207 BCE) certainly began the process of standardizing the writing systems of China, it was not until well into the Han dynasty—and even then only haltingly—that a firm sense of orthography (by which I very much mean "correct writing") emerged. Before this time, the situation is akin to the writing of English before the dictionaries of Samuel Johnson (1709–1784) or Noah Webster (1758–1843); there was simply no "correct" spelling. Kern is well aware of this phenomenon.

> Judging from the manuscripts, it appears that the writing system of pre-imperial and early imperial times was not consistently used to clarify the ambiguities resulting from homophony. Instead, the great number of graphic—homophonous or near-homophonous—variants often perpetuated the problem of homophony on the level of the script. While there definitely was a level of standardization governing the writing system—otherwise, this system could not have been functional—individual scribes, or perhaps groups or schools of scribes, arrived at vastly different choices of characters to write individual words. Evidence that a scribe within a single manuscript could use different graphs to write the same word suggests generous license on his part, which in turns helps to account for the fact that graphic variation affected roughly one-third of all words in any given text.[10]

Nevertheless, Kern's entire analysis is based on a comparison of manuscripts that were written in, or heavily influenced by, the Chu 楚 script of the Warring States through early Han periods, on the one hand, with the received text of the *Shi* written in what we now recognize as standard *kaishu* 楷書 script. It is hard to imagine what he could mean when he says: "The manuscripts under consideration contain different kinds of variants, compared to one another and to their transmitted counterparts. In recognizing such variants, it is not significant whether a text is written in a particular local or regional calligraphic form (e.g., what is summarily called the Chu 楚 script of the manuscripts under discussion) as long as scholars can confidently identify the various graphic elements and transcribe them into standard *kaishu* 楷書 form."[11] Of course it is significant whether a text is written in Chu script or in the *kaishu* of the received text. To compare these two different orthographies (and here I simply mean writing systems; they are certainly not just "calligraphic" forms) is akin to comparing a present-day text of the *Shi* written in "standard characters" (*fantizi* 繁體字) against one written in simplified characters (*jiantizi* 简体字); they would doubtless differ in much the same ways as the manuscripts, and yet such difference signifies nothing about the way or ways in which they were originally written or about their modes of copying or transmission.¹²

Despite the problems with Kern's work, it has had the salutary effect of turning the discussion of the *Shi jing* to the ancient manuscripts discovered in such breathtaking numbers over the last forty years. Although these manuscripts allow for many new insights, they also inform us of just how little we really know about ancient China. In 2005, Kern noted that his conclusions were tentative and could be altered based on new evidence.¹³ The new textual finds do indeed alter the picture. I argue that some of the newest of these finds pertaining to the *Shi*, as well as some other evidence previously available, all show that writing could be—and was—involved in each step in the creation of the *Shi*: from initial composition through transmission to final recension.

Recent Manuscript Discoveries and the *Shi*

In 2001, the Shanghai Museum published the manuscript **Kongzi Shi lun* 孔子詩論 *Confucius's Discussion of the Poetry* as the first title in its corpus of Warring States manuscripts from the state of Chu.¹⁴ The Shanghai Museum editors' attribution of the text to Kongzi 孔子 (Confucius) touched off an initial flurry of debate about the nature of the text; the editors' reading has since been substantiated.¹⁵ Although it is still possible that the text's quotations of Confucius are apocryphal, they certainly reflect a fourth-century BCE understanding of the *Shi* that, for want of a better term, can be called Confucian.¹⁶ The text—especially in its recovered fragmentary state—is more a piecemeal listing of titles of some fifty-eight poems, together with very brief characterizations of the poems' contents, than it is an integral text of the *Shi*. Nevertheless, the text does provide brief characterizations of the different major sections of the *Shi*: the *Song* 頌 *Hymns*, the *Ya* 雅 *Odes*, and the *Guo feng* 國風 *Airs of the States*, referred to in the text as the *Bang feng* 邦風 *Airs of the Countries*. Although many of the titles mentioned in the **Kongzi Shi lun* employ different Chinese characters from those found in the received text of the *Shi*, the Shanghai Museum editors were able to identify fifty-one of them with titles of poems in the received classic. Other scholars have proposed reasonable identifications for the rest.¹⁷ Regardless of whether it is fifty-one or fifty-eight titles, it is clear that the discussion of the *Shi* in **Kongzi Shi lun* is not far removed from the *Shi jing* as we know it. Kern, despite his strong advocacy for an oral transmission of the *Shi*, says that this new manuscript "suggests the existence of a relatively fixed corpus not too different from the received anthology."[18]

In the years since the publication of the **Kongzi Shi lun*, even better evidence for the nature and transmission of the *Shi* in the pre-Qin period has come to light. In 2008, Tsinghua University obtained a significant corpus of Warring States manuscripts written on bamboo slips. No one knew at the time what the contents might be; many of the bamboo slips were still encased in the mud of the tomb from which they had been robbed. Nevertheless, recognizing the potential importance of this cache of texts, the university established a new center to house and publish the texts: Research and Conservation Center for Unearthed Texts. The center, under the leadership of Li Xueqin 李學勤 (1933–2019), set to its editorial work immediately. In late 2010, it published the first volume of texts, and it has issued subsequent volumes on an annual basis.[19] The editors estimate that they will need more than fifteen years before all of the documents will be published. Scholars will doubtless require much more time to digest all of the riches.

The Tsinghua manuscripts, as these documents are known, have already attracted great attention within scholarly circles in China, especially for the light they shed on the early history of the Chinese classics. It is unfortunate that the manuscripts came to the university by way of grave robbing and the Hong Kong antiques market. However, there is no doubt that they are authentic manuscripts of the Warring States period; they are clearly written, for the most part, in the script of the southern state of Chu, which has become familiar to paleographers over the last twenty-five years. Both carbon-14 dating and the best estimates of paleographers place the date of the bamboo slips and the writing on them toward the end of the fourth century BCE. Of the documents published to date, several either are or contain poetry, including versions of two different poems found in the received text of the *Shi jing*. All of these poems bear directly on the question of the nature of the *Shi jing*, and deserve fuller study. Here, I examine just the two poems—or, more precisely, portions of two poems—with received counterparts.

The text *Qi ye* 耆夜, the title of which seems best understood as "Toasting [the victory over] Qi," purports to narrate a drinking party in the eighth year (*sic*) of the reign of King Wu of Zhou (r. 1049/45–43), in which King Wu is joined by several important contemporary figures—Bi Gong Gao 畢公高, Shao Gong Shi 召公奭, Zhou Gong Dan 周公旦, Xin

Gong Quan Jia 辛公諫簷, Zuoce Yi 作冊逸, and Lü Shangfu 呂尚父—to celebrate a Zhou military victory over the state of Qi 耆.[20] Each drinker is required to recite a poem before drinking from the chalice. King Wu's first poem is entitled "Yaoyao zhijiu" 蘖蘖旨酒 "Pleasing the Tasty Brew." It is not particularly memorable but does serve to illustrate the genre:

"Pleasing the Tasty Brew" 蘖蘖旨酒

蘖蘖旨酒，	Pleasing, pleasing the tasty brew,
宴以二公。	Celebrated with the two dukes.
紝仁兄弟，	Trusty and good are my brothers,
庶民和同。	The commoners join in union.
方壯方武，	Very manly, very martial,
穆穆克邦。	Solemnly achieving the state.
嘉爵速飲，	The fine chalice is quickly drunk,
後爵乃從。	Another chalice then follows.

After several iterations of similar poems, just as the Duke of Zhou was about to offer a second poem, a cricket hopped up into the hall. With that, the duke changed tone and extemporized a song in one stanza called, fittingly enough, "Xishuai" 蟋蟀 "Cricket." Unfortunately, there are two places where the Tsinghua manuscript is defective due to broken or missing bamboo slips, but enough of the poem survives to understand its structure.[21] Much of this poem will be familiar to readers of the received Mao 毛 version of the *Shi jing*, who will be reminded of the poem by the same title in the *Tang feng* 唐風 Airs of Tang section of the text.[22] A juxtaposition of the two poems reveals both their similarities and their differences.

Tsinghua Manuscript Version of 蟋蟀 "The Cricket"	*Shi Jing* Version of 蟋蟀 "The Cricket"
蟋蟀在堂，A cricket is in the hall, 役車其行。War chariotlike its movements. 今夫君子，Now we have here the noble sons, 丕喜丕樂。Greatly pleased, greatly amused. 夫日□□，The sun [. . .] □□□忘。 . . . forget.	蟋蟀在堂，A cricket is in the hall, 歲聿其莫。The year-star is about to be dark. 今我不樂，Now we are greatly amused, 日月其除。The sun and moon will be removed. 無已大康，Don't let yourself be too at peace,

毋已大樂，Don't let yourself be too amused,
則終以康。For in the end you will find peace.
康樂而毋忘，Peace and amusement without forgetting,
是唯良士之方。This is the square of the fine man.

蟋蟀在席，A cricket is on the mat,
歲聿云落。The year-star is just now setting.
今夫君子，Now we have here the noble sons,
丕喜丕樂。Greatly pleased, greatly amused.
日月其蒆，The sun and moon will come and go,
從朝及夕。From the morning until evening.
毋已大康，Don't let yourself be too at peace,
則終以祚。For in the end you will be blessed.
康樂而毋[忘]，Peace and amusement without forgetting,
是唯良士之懼。This is the fear of the fine man.

蟋蟀在舍，A cricket is in the house,
歲聿囗囗。The year-star is going. . . .
囗囗囗囗，. . .
囗囗囗囗，. . .
囗囗囗囗，. . .
囗冬及夏。[From] the winter until summer.
毋已大康，Don't let yourself be too at peace,
則終以懼。For in the end you will find fear.
康樂而毋忘，Peace and amusement without forgetting,
是唯良士之懼。This is the fear of the fine man!

職思其居。Only think of where it resides.
好樂無荒，Love and amusement without waste,
良士瞿瞿。The fine man so watchful, watchful.

蟋蟀在堂，A cricket is in the hall,
歲聿其逝。The year-star is about to be gone.
今我不樂，Now we are greatly amused,
日月其邁。The sun and moon will be going.
無已大康，Don't let yourself be too at peace,
職思其外。Only think of what is outside.
好樂無荒，Love and amusement without waste,
良士蹶蹶。The fine man so fleet-footed.

蟋蟀在堂，A cricket is in the hall,
役車其休。War chariot-like its grace.
今我不樂，Now we are greatly amused,
日月其慆。The sun and moon will be past.
無已大康，Don't let yourself be too at peace,
職思其憂。Only think of their worries.
好樂無荒，Love and amusement without waste,
良士休休。The fine man so graceful, graceful.

The differences between these two versions of "Cricket" might be seen as an example of the variable or unstable nature of early Chinese literature.[23] On the other hand, the Tsinghua manuscript certainly shows that it was possible to *write* poems like "Cricket" in the pre-Qin period, contra the assertion of Stephen Owen that "it would have been very hard to write it down."[24] Of course, this evidence does not mean that either version of this particular poem was written at the time of the Duke of Zhou; direct evidence of the poems' date (or dates) of composition, if it (they) should ever be forthcoming, would doubtless be of a different nature. Nevertheless, by providing a written text of a *Shi*-like poem well before the Qin burning of the books, the first volume of the Tsinghua manuscripts already demonstrates the possibility of such writing. Now we need to see just how widespread it may have been.

The third volume of the Tsinghua manuscripts once again contains a suite of poems in which one of the poems corresponds, in this case even more closely, to a poem in the received text of the *Shi jing*. The manuscript is entitled *Zhou Gong zhi qinwu* 周公之琴舞 *The Duke of Zhou's Dance of the Zither* (the title being given on the reverse side of the first bamboo slip). Written on seventeen bamboo slips, the manuscript begins with one poem credited to the Duke of Zhou and then presents a nine-part suite of poems said to have been made by King Cheng of Zhou 周成王 (r. 1042/35–1006 BCE). Although this two-part poem does not bear a title, and it is unclear in the manuscript how the different refrains (*shu* 紑) of the entire piece are meant to be differentiated, nevertheless the first refrain clearly corresponds with the poem "Jing zhi" 敬之 "Be Warned of It" of the "Zhou Song" 周頌 "Zhou Hymns" section of the *Shi jing*.

Placing the two versions of this poem side by side reveals even more similarities than in the case of "Cricket" (making due allowances for the transcription from Chu script into conventional clerical script). Since at least the time of the *Mao zhuan* 毛傳 *Mao Commentary*, the received text of "Be Warned of It" has been divided into two halves, the first half representing an exhortation by the king's ministers, and the second half being the king's response. The Tsinghua manuscript version makes this division explicit, calling the halves the "Opening" (*qi* 啟) and "Ending" (*luan* 亂). In both versions, the opening includes six lines, which correspond with each other almost exactly. The ending of the received text includes six lines, corresponding very closely with the seven lines of the manuscript's ending.

Tsinghua Manuscript Version of "Jing Zhi" 敬之	*Shi Jing* Version of "Jing Zhi" 敬之
敬之敬之。Be warned of it, be warned of it, 天佳㮇帀,Oh, Heaven is so lustrous, 文非易帀。Oh, culture is not easy. 毋曰高高才上,Do not say It is so high above on high, 陟降亓事,Its service goes up and comes down, 卑藍才茲。Giving reflection hereupon. 遹我 夙夜,Leading us morning and night, 不兔敬之。Not with ease do we take warning. 日蹴月將,The sun proceeds and the moon leads on, 孚亓光明。Learn from their shining brightness. 弼寺亓又肩,Assist and hold tight his shoulders, 示告余㮇悳之行。Show and report to me the motion of lustrous virtue.	敬之敬之！Be warned of it, be warned of it. 天維顯思,Oh, Heaven is so lustrous, 命不易哉！Ah, the mandate is not easy. 無曰高高在上。Do not say It is so high above on high. 陟降厥士,Its service goes up and comes down, 日監在茲。Daily reflected hereupon. 維予小子！It is I the young son, 不聰敬止？Who is not wise or respectful. 日就月將,The sun proceeds and the moon leads on, 學有緝熙于光明。We learn from those who bask in the shining brightness. 佛時仔肩,Help these at my shoulders, 示我顯德行！Show me the motion of lustrous virtue.

There are, of course, some differences. The version of the poem in the received text of the *Shi jing* does not explicitly indicate that it should be divided into two stanzas, though this division seems to be implied both by the *Mao Commentary*, which inserts its first comment only after the line "Daily reflected hereupon," and by the "Shi xu" 詩序 "Preface to the Poetry," which states that the poem is a warning to the king on the part of his ministers (群臣進戒嗣王也). In the received text, the following two lines, "It is I the young son, / Who is not wise or respectful," then serve to change the speaker to some unnamed Zhou king ("I the young son" [*yu xiaozi* 予小子] being reserved for the king). By contrast, the Tsinghua manuscript text includes two alternate lines responding to the encouragement to take warning.

There are other differences of a word here or there. In the Tsinghua manuscript text, it is "culture" (*wen* 文) that "is not easy," whereas in the received text, it is "the mandate" (*ming* 命) that "is not easy." The Tsinghua manuscript writes the "service" that "goes up and down" as *shi* 事, whereas the received text writes it as *shi* 士 (but glossed by the *Mao Commentary* as *shi* 事). In the Tsinghua manuscript, "reflection" is "given" (*bei* 卑), while the received text describes the reflection as "daily" (*ri* 日). And the two versions write the word *bi* "to assist" differently: 弼 in the Tsinghua manuscript and 佛 in the received text. However, these are relatively minor differences. Whereas the two versions of "Cricket" might be termed two different poems that share a common topic and a certain amount of phrasing, it would be hard to say that the two versions of "Be Warned of It" are not the same poem. If so, we now have undeniable evidence that at least one poem found in the received text of the *Shi jing* circulated in written form no later than the Warring States period.[25]

Other Evidence for the Written Nature of the *Shi*

There is other evidence—of varying degrees of directness and certainty—suggesting that other poems circulated in writing. Here, I examine the writing of the poems in the *Shi* at three different moments in their history: at the time of their (more or less) final redaction during the Han dynasty; during their early transmission; and at or near the time of the composition of individual poems. For each of these three moments, I draw on what is essentially anecdotal evidence, but evidence that I believe is suggestive of overall trends. In all three moments in the history of the text, I argue that writing—by which I very much mean the physical act of copying characters onto a more or less durable medium—was, or at least could be, instrumental in shaping the text. This claim does not mean that memory, recitation, and/or performance did not also play some role in shaping the text; they doubtless did. But this evidence for the written nature of the *Shi* deserves the attention of all scholars interested in how the *Shi* was created.

Writing and the Redaction of the Shi Jing

It is commonly assumed that all written copies of the *Shi* were burned at the time of the Qin proscription of literature in 213 BCE, but that the collection was reconstituted in its entirety because scholars at the Qin court and elsewhere had committed the text to memory, aided in large part by its rhyming nature.[26] I think there can be little doubt that most scholars, whether at court or elsewhere, had indeed committed the *Shi* to memory, and that this must have played some role in its reconstitution during the Han. However, I think there should be considerable doubt as to just how far the Qin book burning affected the transmission of the text. We have at least some empirical evidence with which to explore this question. In 1977, a manuscript copy of the *Shi*, fragmentary to be sure, was unearthed from Tomb 1 at Shuanggudui 雙古堆, in Fuyang 阜陽, Anhui.[27] This was the tomb of Xiahou Zao 夏侯竈, lord of Ruyin 汝陰, who died in 165 BCE. There seems to be no way to tell whether the Fuyang *Shi* manuscript was copied before or after the onset of the Han dynasty (there is some reason to think that a manuscript of the *Zhou Yi* 周易 *Zhou Changes* found in the same tomb may have been copied during the Qin period,[28] and the script of the two manuscripts is quite similar), but the date of the tomb provides a firm early Western Han *terminus ante quem* for this manuscript.

Unfortunately, the Fuyang manuscript of the *Shi* is so fragmentary that we can gain from it very little direct information regarding the transmission of the text. Nevertheless, the fact that the manuscript was written on bamboo slips should remind us that the standard medium for texts—from at least the Spring and Autumn period through the end of the Han dynasty—was the bamboo slip. A good argument can be made that this medium had a profound effect on the way texts were written.[29] I think an even better argument can be made that it had a profound effect on the way texts were rewritten, which is to say, how early manuscripts were recopied and edited. In the case of the Fuyang manuscript of the *Shi*, characters were written in different sizes to ensure that each individual bamboo slip would carry one—and only one—stanza of any individual poem.[30] This physical nature of the manuscript could have had unintended effects on the presentation and preservation of the content of its own text. If the bamboo slips happened to come unbound—as they apparently did with some regularity in antiquity—it is conceivable that a stanza of one poem might have been grafted onto another poem, especially one that shared a similar topic.

For the question of the oral versus written nature of the *Shi*, it seems to me that such a "misplaced slip" (*cuo jian* 錯簡) would almost necessarily be evidence of copying from one written manuscript to another written manuscript. Of course, we do not have any copies made from the Fuyang manuscript. However, there is other evidence—indirect, to be sure—that at least one such misplaced slip influenced the final text of the received Mao version of the *Shi jing*.

In my book *Rewriting Early Chinese Texts*, I compared two different Warring States manuscript versions of the text *Zi yi* 緇衣 *Black Jacket* with the chapter of the same title found in the received text of the *Li ji* 禮記 *Record of Ritual* (which I refer to as "Zi yi" to differentiate it).³¹ The *Zi yi* makes pervasive use of quotations of the *Shi*, and most of the quotations found in the manuscripts of *Zi yi* closely match not only the received *Li ji* text of "Zi yi" but also the received text of the *Shi jing*. However, there is one case where there is a notable discrepancy between a quotation of the *Shi* found in the manuscripts' version of *Zi yi* and a corresponding quotation of the *Shi* in the received text of "Zi yi," a discrepancy that I think points to an interesting feature in the received text of the *Shi jing* itself.

In the Warring States manuscripts version of *Zi yi*, the *Shi* is quoted as follows:

詩云：其容不改，出言又順，黎民所信。

The *Shi* says: "His countenance does not change, The words he utters can be followed, He is who the black-haired people trust."³²

The corresponding quotation in the received *Li ji* text of "Zi yi" is similar enough to suggest that it should come from the same poem and yet different enough that it should draw our attention:

詩云：彼都人士，狐裘黃黃。其容不改，出言有章。行歸于周，萬民所望。

The *Shi* says: "That great sire of the city, A fox robe so yellow. His countenance does not change, The words he utters have a pattern. On his way back to Zhou, The ten thousand people look to him."³³

The six phrases quoted by the received *Li ji* text of "Zi yi" constitute the entire first stanza of the poem "Du ren shi" 都人士 "Sire in the City" in the received Mao text of the *Shi jing*.[34] However, in his commentary on the *Li ji* "Zi yi," Zheng Xuan 鄭玄 (127–200) notes that these six phrases are found in the Mao version of the *Shi jing* but not in the Qi 齊, Lu 魯, and Han 韓 versions, which were the official versions of the *Shi jing* at the time when Zheng wrote.[35] There are two bits of textual evidence to suggest that the Qi, Lu, and Han versions of the *Shi jing*, long since lost, indeed did not include this entire stanza.

First, the *Zuozhuan* 左傳 also quotes the last two phrases of this same stanza:

行歸于周，萬民所望。

On his way back to Zhou, The ten thousand people look to him.[36]

The *Mao Shi zheng yi* 毛詩正義 edited by Kong Yingda 孔穎達 (574–648) early in the Tang dynasty quotes in turn the *Zuo zhuan* 左傳 commentary of Fu Qian 服虔 (ca. AD 125–195), a contemporary of Zheng Xuan, as providing the following apparently self-contradictory note:

逸詩也；都人士首章有之。

A lost verse; the first stanza of "Du ren shi" has it.[37]

Second, it is clear that the poem titled "Du ren shi" that is included in the Xiping Stone Classics 熹平石經—which were copied 175–183 CE, during Zheng Xuan's lifetime, to serve as the official version of the Classics—did not include this stanza at all.[38]

The Qing scholar Wang Xianqian 王先謙 (1842–1918), in a study of the Han dynasty texts of the *Shi jing*, pointed out that this stanza, although superficially similar to the other stanzas of the poem, really has a different structure and doubtless was an isolated stanza (*gu zhang* 孤章) of some lost poem that was then grafted onto the poem.[39] An examination of the poem shows, I believe, that Wang was certainly correct. I provide the poem here with James Legge's translation (though with his romanization converted to pinyin and with my translation of the title).

"Du ren shi" 都人士 "Sire in the City" (trans. Legge)

彼都人士，	Those officers of the [old] capital,
狐裘黃黃。	With their fox-furs so yellow.
其容不改，	Their deportment unvaryingly [correct],
出言有章！	And their speech full of elegance!—
行歸于周，	If we could go back to [the old] Zhou,
萬民所望。	They would be admiringly looked up to by all the people.
彼都人士，	Those officers of the [old] capital,
臺笠緇撮。	With their hats of Tai leaves and small black caps.
彼君子女，	Those ladies of noble Houses,
綢直如髮！	With their hair so thick and straight!—
我不見兮，	I do not see them [now],
我心不說。	And my heart is dissatisfied.
彼都人士，	Those officers of the [old] capital,
充耳琇實！	With their ear-plugs of *xiu*-stones!
彼君子女，	Those ladies of noble Houses,
謂之尹吉！	Each fit to be called a Yin or a Ji!
我不見兮，	I do not see them [now],
我心苑結。	And my heart grieves with indissoluble sorrow.
彼都人士，	Those officers of the [old] capital,
垂帶而厲！	With their girdles hanging elegantly down!—
彼君子女，	Those ladies of great Houses,
捲髮如蠆！	With their [side] hair curving up like a scorpion's tail!
我不見兮，	I do not see them [now],
言從之邁。	[If I could], I would walk along after them.
匪伊垂之；	Not that they purposely let their girdles hang down;—
帶則有餘。	The girdles were naturally long.
匪伊卷之；	Not that they gave their hair that curve;—
髮則有旟。	The hair had a natural curl.
我不見兮，	I do not see them [now],
云何盱矣。	And how do I long for them![40]

Whereas "Those officers of the old capital" (彼都人士) of the second, third, and fourth stanzas (and implicitly also of the fifth stanza) apparently inspire romantic thoughts ("I do not see them [now], And my heart is dissatisfied" [我不見兮，我心不說], and so on), those officers (or perhaps that officer) of the first stanza are admired for their (or his) statesmanlike appearance, a paragon of virtue for the people. It is the virtuous exemplar—not the romantic nostalgia—that is quoted in the manuscript versions of *Zi yi*: "His countenance does not change, The words he utters can be followed, He is who the black-haired people trust."

These differences in both structure and tone, especially when combined with Zheng Xuan's and Fu Qian's commentaries, suggest that originally there may have been two different poems in the *Shi jing* both entitled "Do ren shi."[41] The first poem probably included both the lines quoted in the Warring States manuscripts' version of *Zi yi* and also the entire stanza quoted in the received *Li ji* text of "Zi yi"—that is, the first stanza of the received text of the poem "Du ren shi." The second poem probably originally consisted of only stanzas 2–5 of the poem "Du ren shi" in the received Mao text of the *Shi jing*.

The differing quotations in the manuscripts' version and the received text version have interesting implications for the editing of "Zi yi." In my earlier study of those manuscripts, I concluded:

> Apparently at some time between the writing of the *Ziyi* ["Black Jacket"] and the Han dynasty, all but the first stanza of the first of these *Du ren shi* ["Sire in the City"] poems was lost; that first stanza was then grafted onto the beginning of the Mao version of the second *Du ren shi* poem. It seems possible that the editor of the *Liji* version of the *Ziyi*, who surely knew the Mao version of the *Shi* well, realized that the quotation in the *Ziyi* was not found in the received text of the *Shi*, but recognizing the similarity between it and the first stanza of the Mao version of *Du ren shi* simply substituted the one for the other.[42]

The conflation of the two poems titled "Du ren shi" in the received Mao version of the *Shi jing* may hold even more interesting implications for the editing of the *Shi*. The first of these poems must have been lost at some time between the writing of the *Zuo zhuan* and *Zi yi*—that is, before the Qin book burning—and the Han redactions of the *Shi*. However, one stanza of the lost "Du ren shi" poem apparently survived, perhaps written on a single bamboo slip. The editor (or editors) of the Mao *Shi jing*, recognizing the superficial similarity between this stanza and the four stanzas of the surviving poem, also titled "Du ren shi," must have simply placed this stanza at the beginning of the other four stanzas.

It seems to me highly unlikely that such a conflation of two different poems could have taken place as a result of faulty memorization. More likely, it came about as a result of copying from one set of bamboo slips that was incompletely preserved and badly ordered onto a new set of slips that was intended to constitute a fair copy. A text such as the Fuyang *Shi jing*, in which individual stanzas of poems were copied on individual bamboo slips, would have made such transposition all the more likely. Granted, this is only a single instance of the role that written texts played in the Han redaction of the received *Shi jing*.[43] Nevertheless, it is explicit evidence and deserves to be considered.

Writing and the Transmission of the *Shi*

As seen in the first section of this chapter, Stephen Owen, Martin Kern, and others have argued that the early transmission of the *Shi* was primarily by way of an oral process. As noted there, Kern concluded that the degree and nature of the variants found in the manuscripts is best explained by a process of transmission without recourse to a written model at hand. However, he acknowledged that the existence of graphic variants—"characters that are graphically similar but otherwise unrelated and therefore appear to be scribal errors, e.g., *ér* 而 (*njə) and *tiān* 天 (*thin)"[44]—in the ancient manuscripts poses a challenge, because such graphic variants would seem to be prima facie evidence for visual copying:

> How does such a scenario account for the existing scribal errors, even if they are only few in number? Even where a manuscript contained just a single mistake that is explicable only as a copyist's error, this singular instance would suffice to prove the process of direct copying. However, scribal errors are not necessarily copyists' errors. They are individual mistakes in writing characters or sequences of characters: confusing graphic forms, transposing characters, leaving them out, or adding them where they do not belong. Such mistakes are not unique to the process of copying but happen under various

circumstances when writing down an internalized text. It is thus exceedingly difficult to isolate copyists' errors from the larger category of scribal errors. This is not to say that there are no copyists' errors; where manuscripts are copied, errors do happen. But we are not free to interpret scribal errors as copyists' errors if we cannot prove them as such, e.g., through circumstantial evidence or information that a manuscript was indeed being copied. Instead, we should actually expect scribal errors in manuscripts generated from memory or oral transmission, especially as the process of writing was not guided and supported by an existing model.[45]

Leaving aside the circularity of using the premise that "the process of writing was not guided and supported by an existing model" as evidence for oral transmission, it is possible to find copyists' errors that have been incorporated into the received text of the *Shi jing*—cases of graphic error that call into question a scenario of "scribal errors generated from memory." It is unlikely that teachers and learners of the *Shi* would misremember words that are graphically similar but phonetically dissimilar unless the error had already entered into the written text. In some cases, it is possible to show that errors probably derived from changes in the way graphs were written over the course of the Zhou dynasty.

These graphic variants are, to be sure, a distinct minority of all of the attested variants in the various texts of the *Shi jing*, but they are not, for that, inconsiderable in number or importance. Yu Xingwu 于省吾 (1896–1984), one of the great Chinese paleographers of the twentieth century, pioneered the comparison of graphic forms in early excavated materials, especially oracle-bone and bronze inscriptions, with readings of the transmitted literature.[46] Let me cite just two among numerous examples of graphic confusions that Yu Xingwu found in the received text of the *Shi jing*.

In the received text of the poem "Huang yi" 皇矣 "August Indeed," we find the following lines describing King Wen of Zhou (r. 1099/1056–1050 BCE):

"Huang yi" 皇矣 "August Indeed"

| 其德克明， | And his virtue, it could be bright, |
| 克明克類， | It could be bright, could be akin, |

克長克君。	He could be head, could be ruler.
王此大邦，	He was king of this great country,
克順克比。	Could be obeyed, could be allied.⁴⁷

During the Qing dynasty, Jiang Yougao 江有誥 (1681–1762) already pointed out that the final word, *bi* 比 (*pih), falls out of the rhyme scheme of this stanza,⁴⁸ and he suggested that the final line here should be reversed to read *ke bi ke shun* 克比克順 "Could be allied, could be obeyed," such that *shun* 順 (*m-luns) "to obey" would rhyme with the final *jun* 君 (*kwən) "ruler" two lines above. This is certainly possible.

However, as Yu Xingwu argues,⁴⁹ a better solution to this textual problem is to see *bi* 比, the archaic form of which is 𠤎, as a graphic error for *cong* 從 "to follow," which was written as 󰀀, that is, 从, during the Shang and Western Zhou (1045–771 BCE) periods. Elsewhere in the *Shi jing*, *cong* (*dzong) rhymes with *bang* 邦 (*prong) "country,"⁵⁰ the final word of the preceding line, and the rhyme scheme of this poem suggests it should rhyme here as well. As Yu further notes, not only does this emendation resolve the problem of the rhyme, but given the use of synonyms in the preceding lines, *cong* "to follow" makes a better match for *shun* "to obey" than does *bi* "to ally." Although Yu had no way of knowing it when he was writing in the 1930s, the mistaking of *cong* 󰀀/从 for *bi* 比 must have taken place by the Spring and Autumn period, since by the Warring States period *cong* was almost invariably written as 從 and thus the graph was written so differently from its earlier form of 从 as to preclude this copying error.⁵¹

We find a different type of copying error in the penultimate line of the poem "Wei tian zhi ming" 維天之命 "It Is Heaven's Command" (Mao 267) from the *Zhou Song* section of the *Shi*. This line reads:

駿惠我文王。

Greatly kind was our King Wen.⁵²

Neither the Mao commentary nor Zheng Xuan's commentary directly remarks on the first two words here, *jun hui* 駿惠, which are hard to construe in the context. Yu Xingwu notes briefly that the compound *jun zhi* 駿疐 "to rule securely" occurs in the final prayers inscribed on two bronzes from the seventh century BCE, the *Qin Gong zhong* 秦公鐘 (*Jicheng* 262–266) and *Qin Gong gui* 秦公簋 (*Jicheng* 4315):

以受純魯多釐, 眉壽無疆, 畯寯在位。

to receive pure aid and many blessings, long life without bound, and to rule securely in position.

Another example of this usage was discovered well after Yu wrote his study; the inscription on the late Western Zhou bronze vessel *Hu gui* 㝬簋 (*Jicheng* 4317) contains the following pair of phrases, ostensibly composed by the reigning King Li of Zhou 周厲王 (r. 857/53–842/28):

畯在位, 作寯在下。

I rule in position, made secure here below.

It seems clear, as Yu suggested, that during the Western Zhou and early Spring and Autumn periods, *jun zhi* 畯寯, "to rule securely," was an idiomatic way of describing a good ruler, certainly fitting for the King Wen of the poem "Wei tian zhi ming." However, this usage is not found in later literature, suggesting that it may have passed out of use (and perhaps even out of understanding) by the Warring States period, at the latest.

If we can agree that *jun zhi* fits the context of the poem "Wei tian zhi ming" better than does the easily intelligible but inappropriate *jun hui* 駿惠 "greatly kind," then we need to ask how the variation came about. Of course, the variation between *jun* 駿 "swift; great" and *jun* 畯 "overseer; to rule" involves only a change of signific and so is textually insignificant. However, the variation between *hui* 惠 (*wîs) and the graphically similar *zhi* 寯 (*tits) would certainly seem to be a classic case of *lectio facilior*—the substitution of a simpler and well-known character for one more difficult (and perhaps, at the time, unintelligible). This type of substitution could only have happened within a written transmission of the text of the poem.

Other scholars have followed Yu Xingwu's lead in pointing out errors in the received Mao text of the *Shi jing* that are similarly based on graphic confusion, many of the suggestions being persuasive.[53] It would perhaps be desirable to provide an exhaustive inventory of all of these different suggestions. However, it seems to me that just the examples presented earlier should suffice to suggest that copying (and miscopying) from one written text to another was instrumental to the transmission of the *Shi* even before the Han dynasty (and perhaps well before the

Han dynasty). This conclusion does not mean that oral transmission was not also instrumental, but oral transmission cannot explain these graphic variants in the *Shi jing*.

WRITING AND THE COMPOSITION OF POEMS IN THE *SHI JING*

I have argued that copying from one written manuscript to another written manuscript was instrumental in shaping the contents of the *Shi jing* in the Han dynasty and also that writing also played an important role in transmitting the *Shi* through much of the pre-Qin period before that. However, even if readers find the evidence adduced for these two moments in the history of the *Shi* convincing insofar as it goes, I suspect that many readers will feel that this evidence does not go to the heart of the oral argument—that the poems were originally *created* in a largely oral context and only put into written form much later. For this stage in the history of the compiled text of the *Shi*, there is no direct evidence of either written or oral sources of the individual poems themselves. However, there is evidence of writing that stems from the same time period when tradition says that the *Shi* was created: roughly the Western Zhou dynasty through the first half of the Spring and Autumn period. Given its importance to the orality argument, whether and when poetry could have been put into writing warrants close attention.

As noted in chapter 2 of this volume, David Schaberg has suggested that written composition would have been anachronistic for the period when the poems were supposed to have been created. "At another extreme—and here I would admit my own sympathies—such texts (i.e., the *Shi* [Poetry] and *Shu* [Documents]) are presumed less than perfectly reliable, and unsuitable for direct citation as historical authorities, until it be demonstrated that they stem from circumstances in which it was possible and desirable to produce highly accurate records of words and deeds."[54] Of course, short of finding a seventh-century BCE manuscript of the *Shi*, it will probably never be possible to prove that the poems of the *Shi jing* were written by the time that tradition suggests they were. Schaberg does not ask for the impossible; he sets the bar of evidence rather lower: simply a demonstration of circumstantial evidence that they could have been written then. This is the demonstration that I take up now.

It has often been noted that the poem "Jiang Han" 江漢 "The Jiang and Han" (Mao 262), the composition of which is traditionally dated to the reign of King Xuan of Zhou 周宣王 (r. 827/25–782 BCE), is similar in both structure and phrasing to some late Western Zhou bronze inscriptions.[55] The protagonist of this poem, Duke Hu of Shao 召公虎, is known from the historical record of the late Western Zhou period and, indeed, figures prominently in the inscriptions on the *Diao Sheng gui* 調生簋 and *Diao Sheng zun* 調生尊, vessels that can be dated with some confidence to the fifth and sixth years of King Xuan's reign—that is, to 823 and 822 BCE.[56] According to the *Zhushu jinian* 竹書紀年 *Bamboo Annals*, 822 is the year that Duke Hu of Shao was commanded to lead the campaign against the Huai Yi 淮夷 that is apparently commemorated in the poem "The Jiang and Han."[57]

"Jiang Han" 江漢 "The Jiang and Han"

江漢浮浮，	The Jiang and Han flow on and on,
武夫滔滔。	The martial men stream on and on.
匪安匪遊，	Neither resting nor sporting about,
淮夷來求。	The Yi of Huai we come to seek.
既出我車，	Having sent out our chariots,
既設我旟，	Having set up our battle flags,
匪安匪舒，	Neither resting nor relaxing,
淮夷來鋪。	The Yi of Huai we come to press.
江漢湯湯，	The Jiang and Han spread out and out,
武夫洸洸。	The martial men shine on and on.
經營四方，	Bringing order to the four quarters,
告成于王。	They announce success to the king.
四方既平，	The four quarters being at peace,
王國庶定。	The royal realm is all settled.
時靡有爭，	Now that there is no more fighting,
王心載寧。	The royal heart can be tranquil.
江漢之滸，	On the banks of the Jiang and Han,
王命召虎：	The king commanded Hu of Shao:
式辟四方，	"Would that you rule the four quarters,
徹我疆土。	All the way to our border lands.
匪疚匪棘，	Not ulcerously, not stabbingly,
王國來極。	The royal realm comes to its peak.

于疆于理，	On the borders, in the hamlets,
至于南海。	As far as to the southern sea."
王命召虎：	The king commanded Hu of Shao:
來旬來宣。	"Come take control, come show yourself.
文武受命，	When Wen and Wu received the mandate,
召公維翰。	The Duke of Shao was their support.
無曰：予小子。	Don't say: 'I am but a young son.'
召公是似。	The Duke of Shao was just like this.
肇敏戎公，	You have opened well the martial work,
用錫爾祉。	For which I award you blessings.
釐爾圭瓚，	"I honor you with a jade ladle,
秬鬯一卣，	One bucket of black millet wine.
告于文人。	I announce to the cultured men.
錫山土田。	I award mountains, lands, and fields.
于周受命，	In Zhou's receiving the mandate,
自召祖命。	From the Shao ancestor's command."
虎拜稽首：	Hu bowed and touched head to the ground:
天子萬年。	Son of Heaven: ten thousand years.
虎拜稽首，	Hu bowed and touched head to the ground,
對揚王休，	In response extolled the king's grace,
作召公考，	Making for father Duke of Shao,
天子萬壽。	Son of Heaven, ten thousand long.
明明天子，	Oh, so bright the Son of Heaven,
令聞不已，	Commanding fame never stopping,
矢其文德，	Arraying his cultured virtue
洽此四國。	Bringing together these four realms.[58]

Another inscription that seems to prefigure the same campaign is recorded on the *Xi Jia pan* 兮甲盤 (*Jicheng* 10174); the full date at the beginning of the inscription corresponds to the year 823 BCE. Even though the structure of this inscription is perhaps not the most representative among all late Western Zhou bronze inscriptions to compare with that of the poem "Jiang Han," there is more reason than just its date and similar content to consider it here: there is some reason to believe that the patron who commissioned the vessel, referred to within the inscription variously as Xi Jia 兮甲 or as Xibo Jifu 兮伯吉父, is the same figure as the Jifu 吉甫 who takes credit for "making" two other poems found in the *Shi jing* from the same context as "Jiang Han": "Song Gao" 崧高 "Song Is High" (Mao 259) and "Zheng Min" 烝民 "Teeming People" (Mao 260).

惟五年三月既死霸庚寅，王初各伐玁狁于䣨盧。兮甲從王，折首執訊，休亡敃。王賜兮甲馬四匹駒車。王令甲政司成周四方責至于南淮尸。淮尸舊我帛畮人，毋敢不出其帛、其責、其進人、其賈。毋敢不即餗、即市；敢不用令，則即刑撲伐。其惟我諸侯、百生，厥賈毋不即市，毋敢或入蠻宄賈，則亦刑。兮白吉父作般，其眉壽萬年無疆，子子孫孫永寶用。

It was the fifth year, third month, after the dying brightness, *gengyin* (day 27); the king for the first time went to attack the Xianyun at Tuhu. Xi Jia followed the king, cutting off heads and manacling prisoners, being victorious without defect. The king awarded Xi Jia four horses and a colt chariot. The king commanded Jia to govern and supervise the taxes of the four regions of Chengzhou as far as the Southern Huai Yi.

The Huai Yi of old were our tribute men. They ought not dare not to produce their tribute, their taxes, their presented men, and their wares. They ought not dare not to approach the encampments and approach the markets. If they dare not to use the command, then enact punishments and strike and attack them. If it be the case of our many lords' and hundred families, of their wares none ought not come to market, nor ought they dare to send in barbarian and illicit wares, for then they too are to be punished.

Xibo Jifu makes this basin; may he have long life for ten thousand years without limit, and sons' sons and grandsons' grandsons eternally to treasure and use it.

I suppose it is a matter of interpretation and degree whether this bronze inscription of Duke Hu of Shao's successful campaign against the Huai Yi demonstrates, as David Schaberg had asked for, "circumstances in which it was possible and desirable to produce highly accurate records of words and deeds." In this regard, it may be worth recalling that Bernhard Karlgren once wrote, "It is important to remember that . . . the early *book* in China was the *ritual bronze*[;] . . . lengthy and important documents were preserved by being inscribed in ritual bronzes. The genuine *Shu ching* chapters and the odes of the *Shih* . . . may well have been cast in bronze long before they were transcribed into ordinary wooden documents."⁵⁹ One need not accept Karlgren's suggestion in its entirety to appreciate the relevance of the inscription on the *Xi Jia pan* vessel vis-à-vis Schaberg's demand for "circumstances" concerning writing. To be sure, the poem "Jiang Han" has a formal structure and rhetorical effect different from the *Xi Jia pan* inscription (which I should add is by no means the most literary of Western Zhou bronze inscriptions). Nevertheless, the inscription surely reflects accurately the message that its patron wished to portray about the campaign—even if it may not be an accurate record of words and deeds according to modern historiographical standards—and it is manifestly written. Writing was clearly possible in 823 BCE.

There is another poem in the Shi jing that I believe is comparable to bronze inscriptions: "Xia Wu" 下武 "Descending from Wu" (Mao 243). By way of demonstrating the traditional understanding of the poem, I present it first in the translation of James Legge (1815–1897), adapting his translation for the title, but in the discussion that follows will also refer to the translation by Arthur Waley (1899–1966):⁶⁰

"Xia wu" 下武 "Successors Tread in the Steps" (trans. Legge)

下武維周。	Successors tread in the steps [of their predecessors] in our Zhou.
世有哲王;	For generations there had been wise kings;
三后在天;	The three sovereigns were in heaven;
王配于京。	And king [Wu] was their worthy successor in his capital.
王配于京,	King [Wu] was their worthy successor in his capital,
世德作求,	Rousing himself to seek for the hereditary virtue,
永言配命;	Always striving to accord with the will [of Heaven];
成王之孚。	And thus he secured the confidence due to a king.
成王之孚,	He secured the confidence due to a king,
下土之式。	And became a pattern of all below him.
永言孝思,	Ever thinking how to be filial,
孝思維則。	His filial mind was the model [which he supplied].

媚茲一人，	Men loved him, the One man,
應侯順德。	And responded [to his example] with a docile virtue.
永言孝思，	Ever thinking how to be filial,
昭哉嗣服。	He brilliantly continued the doings [of his fathers].

昭茲來許，	Brilliantly! and his posterity,
繩其祖武，	Continuing to walk in the steps of their forefathers,
於萬斯年，	For myriads of years,
受天之祐。	Will receive the blessing of Heaven.

受天之祐。	They will receive the blessing of Heaven.
四方來賀。	And from the four quarters [of the kingdom] will felicitations come to them.
於萬斯年，	For myriads of years,
不遐有佐？	Will there not be their helpers?

There is disagreement concerning the subject of this poem. The *Mao Preface* understands it as a praise of King Wu, which is also reflected by the translation of Legge. On the other hand, Waley focuses on the line *San hou zai tian* 三后在天, which he translates as "Three rulers are in Heaven," to suggest that the poem may pertain to King Kang of Zhou 周康王 (r. 1005/03–978 BCE), though he further suspects its composition dates to later than King Kang's time. Others, such as Qu Wanli 屈萬里 (1907–1979),[61] have seen in the last line of the second stanza and first line of the third stanza, *Cheng wang zhi fu* 成王之孚, the temple name of King Cheng—that is, 成王. Legge's translation, "He secured the confidence due to a king," which, it should be noted, accords with the *Mao Commentary* reading of the line, takes the word *cheng* 成 as a verb meaning "to complete, to fulfill," with *wang* 王 "king" as part of its direct object. I think the proper noun interpretation is by far the easier reading of this line, but it is not, I think, the key to understanding the poem.[62]

For that, we need to look to the poem's fourth stanza, and especially the second line of stanza 4: *ying hou shun de* 應侯順德, which Legge has translated, more or less in accord with the traditional interpretation, as "And responded [to his example] with a docile virtue." Here too, it is easy (indeed, far easier, I would suggest) to read the two graphs *ying hou* 應侯 as a proper noun, "the lord of Ying," than as two verbs, as the traditional interpretation does. According to the *Mao commentary*, *ying* 應, which usually means "to respond," here means *dang* 當 "to match; to serve as; to be," while *hou* 侯, which is almost always a noun indicating a social rank (traditionally translated as "marquis," though now more commonly rendered simply as "lord"), is here to be understood as *wei* 維 "to be."[63] As far as I know, there is no support anywhere else in the early Chinese literary tradition for this latter reading of *hou*, but even if there were, the clause as a whole would still not make any sense either grammatically (the king cannot "be" virtue) or conceptually (it is very strange to describe the king as being "obedient" or "docile" [*shun* 順]). I suggest that it is only when we realize that there was a state called Ying 應 that was ruled by "lords" (*hou* 侯) and that had a very special relationship with the Zhou royal family, that we can begin to understand this line and, indeed, the entire poem.

Ying was located at the site of present-day Pingdingshan City 平頂山市 in central Henan. Its founder was a younger brother of King Cheng, and bronze inscriptions show that its rulers continued to have a close relationship with the Zhou kings throughout the Western Zhou dynasty. The *Ying Hou Xiangong zhong* 應侯見工鐘 (*Jicheng* 107, 108) is a set of mid- to late Western Zhou bronze bells that carry an inscription commemorating an award to Xiangong 見工, Lord of Ying 應侯. It is dedicated to Xiangong's "august ancestor" (*huangzu* 皇祖), a still earlier Ying Hou 應侯.

> 惟正二月初吉，王歸自成周。應侯見工遺王于周。辛未，王各于康。榮白內右應侯見工，賜彤弓一、彤百、馬四匹。見工敢對揚天子休，用作朕皇祖應侯大林鐘，用賜眉壽永命，子子孫孫永寶用。

> It was the official second month, first auspiciousness, the king returned from Chengzhou. Xiangong, Lord of Ying, escorted the king to Zhou. On *xinwei* (day 8), the king entered into Kang. Rongbo entered at the right of Xiangong, Lord of Ying, who was awarded one black bow, one hundred black arrows, and four horses. Xiangong dares in response to extol the Son of Heaven's beneficence, herewith making for my august ancestor Ying Hou this great stand of bells, herewith to award me long life and an eternal mandate. May sons' sons and grandsons' grandsons eternally treasure and use it.

An extensive cemetery from the state of Ying has been excavated over the last several decades at Pingdingshan, though apparently some of the most important tombs had been looted. A pair of *gui*-tureens has recently been acquired by the Poly Museum of Beijing. Like the *Ying Hou Xiangong zhong*, the inscriptions on these vessels show that they too were cast for Xiangong, Lord of Ying, and—like the *Ying Hou Xiangong zhong*—they too show Xiangong as having had a very intimate relationship with the Zhou king, here sharing a banquet with him and receiving even more lavish gifts:

惟正月初吉丁亥，王才某鄉醴。應侯見工友，賜玉五瑴、馬四匹、矢三千。見工敢對揚天子休釐，用作皇考武侯尊簋，用賜眉壽永令，子子孫孫永寶。

It was the first month, first auspiciousness, *dinghai* (day 24), the king was at Mou feasting wine. Xiangong, Lord of Ying, serving as friend, was awarded five items of jade, four horses, and three thousand arrows. Xiangong dares in response to extol the Son of Heaven's beneficent gift, herewith making for my august deceased-father Wu Hou this offertory *gui*-tureen, herewith to award me long life and an eternal mandate. May sons' sons and grandsons' grandsons eternally treasure it.[64]

These inscriptions leave no doubt that the lords of Ying—once again, "Ying Hou" 應侯—not only had a close relationship with the Zhou kings but were fully capable of producing, if not "highly accurate records of words and deeds," as Schaberg has put it, then certainly reasonably eloquent testimonies of that relationship.

I suggest that the poem "Xia Wu" is the same sort of testimony. To understand better the context of its creation—and the structure of the poem—it will be helpful to examine one other bronze inscription:[65] the *Shi Qiang pan* 史牆盤 (*Jicheng* 10175), which was discovered in December 1975 and is already well known. The flat surface of the pan-basin bears a lengthy inscription (284 graphs) that is neatly divided into two halves (for the inscription, see fig. 7.1), the first half commemorating the achievements of the Zhou kings and the second half commemorating the service that Scribe Qiang 史牆, for whom the basin was cast, and his ancestors provided to those kings. The inscription is too lengthy

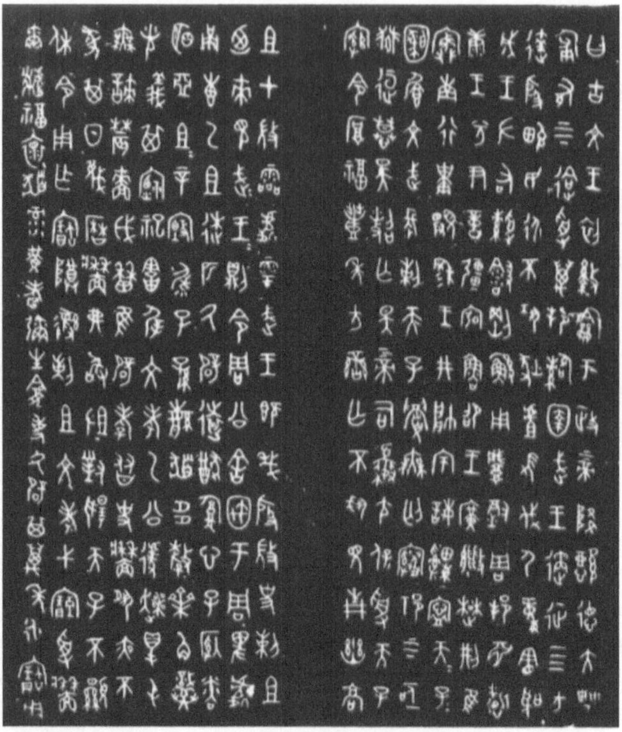

Figure 7.1. *Shi Qiang pan* 史牆盤 inscription. From Zhongguo Shehui kexueyuan Kaogu yanjiusuo, ed., *Yin Zhou jinwen jicheng*, 10175.

to quote in its entirety; I quote here just the encomia for the first two ancestors, King Wen of Zhou and the High Ancestor (*Gaozu* 高祖) of Qiang's Wei 微 family.

> 曰古文王，初𢾭龢于政，上帝降懿德大甹，匍有上下，迨受萬邦。. . . 青幽高祖，才微靈處。雩武王既𢦏殷，微史剌祖迺來見武王，武王則令周公舍㝣于周卑處。

Accordant with antiquity was King Wen! He first brought harmony to government. God on High sent down fine virtue and great security. Extending to the high and low, he joined the ten thousand states.

. . .

Pure and retiring was the High Ancestor, at the numinous place of Wei! When King Wu had already defeated Yin, the Wei scribes and valiant ancestors then came to present themselves to King Wu. King Wu then commanded the Duke of Zhou to dispense domicile at a low place of Zhou.

I cite this inscription on the *Shi Qiang pan* simply to show that there were precedents in the Western Zhou dynasty for juxtaposing praises of the Zhou kings and the ancestors of another family.

Given this context, if we look again at the poem "Xia Wu," this time looking more carefully at the structure of the poem, I think we may find echoes of the *Shi Qiang pan* inscription. This time I provide my own translation of the poem.

"Xia Wu" 下武 "Descending from Wu" (trans. Shaughnessy)

下武維周，	Descending martially is Zhou,
世有哲王！	Generations have had wise kings!
三后在天，	The three lords are up in heaven,
王配于京。	The king matches in the capital.
王配于京，	The king matches in the capital,
世德作求。	Worldly virtue being a mate.
永言配命，	Eternal the matching mandate,
成王之孚。	The Completing King's trustfulness.
成王之孚，	The Completing King's trustfulness,
下土之式。	A model for the lands below.
永言孝思，	Eternal the filial thoughts,
孝思維則。	Filial thoughts are the standard.
媚茲一人，	Beloved is this Unique Man,
應侯順德。	The Lord of Ying obeys in virtue.
永言孝思，	Eternal the filial thoughts,
昭哉嗣服。	Radiant the successive service!
昭茲來許，	Radiant this coming forward,
繩其祖武。	Extending the ancestor's feats.

於萬斯年	Oh, ten thousand should be the years
受天之祐！	Of receiving Heaven's blessings!
受天之祐，	Of receiving Heaven's blessings,
四方來賀。	The four quarters come in tribute.
於萬斯年，	Oh, ten thousand should be the years,
不遐有佐。	Not putting off their assistance.

Looking at the structure of the poem, the first thing that we might notice is that the last line of stanza 1 is repeated as the first line of stanza 2. Such repetition also occurs between stanzas 2 and 3, between stanzas 5 and 6, and nearly so between stanzas 4 and 5. The only two stanzas not linked in this way are the third and fourth stanzas; stanza 3 ends, "Filial thoughts are the standard" (*xiao si wei ze* 孝思維則) and stanza 4 begins, "Beloved is this Unique Man" (*mei si yi ren* 媚茲一人). For this reason, I have inserted an extra space between these two stanzas because I suggest that the poem breaks into two halves at this point.

Now looking more carefully at these two halves of the poem, we can see that the word "king" (*wang* 王) appears prominently in each of the three stanzas in the first half, but the term is conspicuously absent in the second half, where it is replaced by the early mention of the Lord of Ying (*Ying hou* 應候). Looking still more carefully at the content of the two halves, we find that the first half—the royal half, if you will—is about the king being in his capital, completing his trust, and serving as a model for all the lands of the four quarters—the sorts of things for which the *Shi Qiang pan* praises the Zhou kings. In the second half of the poem, stanzas 4 through 6, however, the tenor changes. We now have mention of "obedient virtue" (*shun de* 順德), "service" (*fu* 服), and "assistance" (*zuo* 佐), as well as the statement, "The four quarters come in tribute" (*si fang lai he* 四方來賀). These are precisely the sorts of qualities that Xiangong, Lord of Ying, claimed for himself, "escorting" (*yi* 遣, lit. "to leave") the king to Zhou and "befriending" (*you* 友) him there, and the qualities for which Qiang praised his own ancestors.

Whatever the literary qualities of my translation of "Xia Wu" might be, I am confident that mine better reflects the original structure and purpose of the poem than does that of the traditional interpretation, as reflected by the translation of James Legge. My contribution derives from awareness of a range of bronze inscriptions from the Western Zhou dynasty—especially the *Ying Hou Xiangong zhong* and *gui* as well as the *Shi Qiang pan*.

Conclusion

I began this study by citing Stephen Owen who argued for the importance of orality in the composition, transmission, and even editing of the *Shi*. I have adduced various types of evidence to show that at each of the three stages in the creation of the *Shi jing* that we have today—composition, early transmission, and redaction—writing was *also* very important. Of this evidence, the most compelling has come to light only in the last few years: several Warring States–period manuscripts from the Shanghai Museum and Tsinghua University collections with both systematic references to the *Shi* and also early versions of individual poems. These manuscripts are most assuredly evidence that the poems could be written in the Warring States period.

But there is also other evidence—less direct, to be sure—that strongly suggests writing was involved in every step of the creation and transmission of the *Shi*. Inscriptions on bronze vessels show that at least some of the social elites of the Western Zhou and the Spring and Autumn periods were fully capable of writing texts very similar to the poems we see in the received *Shi jing*. Graphic variants and errors seen in the received text of the *Shi jing*—plausibly caused by changes in the script or in the idiom of usage over the course of the centuries before the Common era—suggest that at least some of the transmission of the *Shi* was accomplished by copying from one manuscript to another. Moreover, the conflation in the received Mao version of the *Shi jing* of what were elsewhere two separate poems or stanzas of poems suggests that an editor or editors of that text was working with a text written on bamboo slips. All of this evidence should suffice to remind readers that, unlike the Homeric epics, the *Shi* was created within a fully literate context. By the end of the Western Zhou period, the time to which the poems "Jiang Han" and "Xia wu" probably date, scribes had been writing at the Shang and Zhou courts for some four hundred years.

Before concluding let me be explicit about two claims that I am *not* making. First, none of the evidence I have adduced here should be taken to exclude the role an oral context may have played at any of the moments in the creation of the received *Shi jing*. These were songs, after all, so surely they were sung and recited far more often than they were written and read. Even when they were written and read, the music and the lyrics doubtless resounded in the heads of the readers and the writers—and doubtless also affected the way they read and wrote. Second, I am most certainly not claiming that the entire *Shi jing* as we know it was written in the Western Zhou period and has been transmitted flawlessly down to the present. I suggest that two poems of the *Da ya* section of the *Shi jing* display the sort of wording and structure seen in Western Zhou bronze inscriptions and that, by analogy, other poems of this section would seem to be more or less contemporary.[66] Other poems, including most of the poems in the *Guo feng* section, were surely created later and in different contexts.

Moreover, I have shown that in the course of both transmission and final editing during the Han, changes of various sorts were introduced into the text. The first stanza of the suite of poems attributed to King Cheng in the Tsinghua manuscript *Zhou gong zhi qin wu* is surely identifiable with the poem "Jing zhi" from the *Zhou Song* section of the *Shi jing*, and yet even it contains several more or less important differences vis-à-vis the received text. Other poems surely differed as much as the poem "Xishuai" found in the Tsinghua manuscript *Qiye* does from the *Shi jing* poem of the same title. And this is evidence from the Warring States period. Poetry in still earlier periods doubtless differed even more from the *Shi jing* of the Han dynasty and today. But this is not evidence that they were not originally written or also transmitted in writing.

The much-quoted analogy used by William Baxter that the *Shi jing* "is a Zhou text in Han clothing" strikes me as not quite right.[67] The clothing in which we find the *Shi jing* was surely hemmed during the Spring and Autumn period, patched during the Warring States period, and mended again during the Han, but for all that I suggest it still remains Zhou clothing.

Chapter Eight

A First Reading of the Anhui University Bamboo-Slip *Shi Jing*

At the beginning of 2015, Anhui University acquired a cache of bamboo-slip manuscripts. These slips, like so many of the slips that have entered Chinese museum and university collections in recent years, are the result of tomb robbing, such that their archaeological provenance is unknown. Nevertheless, the slips have been subjected to various authentication tests, which have produced a scholarly consensus in China that they are authentic.[1] First, three specimens from the slips and the lacquer basket in which they were packed were sent to Peking University's carbon 14 testing lab, which determined a date for them of 2,280 years ago. Next, the National Cultural Artifacts Bureau (國家文物局) conducted infrared spectroscopy and X-ray diffraction analysis, determining that the slips date to the early to mid–Warring States period. The writing on the slips was also examined by various paleographers, both at Anhui University and also from elsewhere in China, and they have all determined the slips to be authentic manuscripts from the Warring States state of Chu 楚.

The Anhui slips include a number of different types of manuscripts, with volume 1 being devoted exclusively to a fragmentary manuscript in ninety-three slips that corresponds to portions of the received *Shi jing* 詩經

This chapter was originally published as "A First Reading of the Anhui University Bamboo-Slip *Shi Jing*," *Bamboo and Silk* 4 (2021): 1–44. I have deleted here the strict transcriptions of the manuscript provided in the *Bamboo and Silk* article; readers interested in seeing those transcriptions should consult that publication.

Classic of Poetry. Complete slips of this manuscript are 48.5 cm long and 0.6 cm wide. The slips were originally bound with three binding straps, the top strap about 2 cm from the top of the slip, the middle strap in the very middle of the slip, and the bottom strap also about 2 cm from the bottom of the slip. The space above the top binding strap is left blank, while beneath the bottom binding strap is a number, written in small graphs to the right side of the slip, from 1 to 117; these indicate the sequence of the slip. However, twenty-four of the slips—18, 19, 23, 24, 26, 30, 56–58, 60–71, 95–97—are missing, such that there are only ninety-three slips extant in the cache. Most of the slips are complete or nearly so (for instance, some are missing the top portion above the top binding strap), though there are also several slips that are quite fragmentary. The backs of the slips are reported to have diagonal markings of the sort that are now known for most Warring States bamboo slips, though they are difficult to see on the full-size photographs of the slips that have been included in a packet together with the volume. However, these photographs do show that the backs of many of the slips reveal impressions from the fronts of other slips that pressed on them within the scroll. All of this renders the sequence of the slips, often disputed with other Warring States manuscripts, quite transparent.

Slips contain between twenty-eight and thirty-seven characters per slip, representing fifty-seven poems from several different portions of the *Guo feng* 國風 *Airs of the States* section of the *Shi jing*. These are (according to the names given to the sections in the manuscript): *Zhou nan* 周南 (ten poems[2]), *Shao nan* 召南 (fourteen poems), *Qin* 秦 (ten poems), *Hou* 侯 (six poems), *Yong* 鄘 (seven poems), and *Wei* 魏 (ten poems). Each individual poem is written consecutively across one or more slips. In some, but not all, poems, the ends of individual lines are marked with small horizontal lines to the bottom right of the last character of the line. Invariably, the end of a poem is marked by a small black square to the lower right of the last character. The next poem then follows immediately after it, through the end of each individual section. New sections begin on new bamboo slips. For instance, after the last poem of the "Zhou nan" section (slip 20), there is a blank of about three characters followed by the notation "Zhou nan *shiyouyi*" 周南十又一 "*Zhou nan*: 11," followed by a black hook-shaped mark indicating the end of a section; this indicates both the name of the section and also the number of poems in it. The remainder of the slip is left blank except for the slip number (slip 20 [廿]) at the very bottom. In the case of the *Shao nan*, the last poem, known in the received text of the *Shi jing* as "Zouyu" 騶虞 (Mao 25) but written in the manuscript as "Cong hu" 從虖 (slips 40–41), and doubtless having a different meaning from that usually understood by the received tradition (for which, see the following discussion), is quite fragmentary, so that any section label is no longer extant. The last poem of the *Qin* section (slip 59), "Quan yu" 權輿 "Sprouts" (Mao 135), is also fragmentary, so that in this case too there is no section label extant. The last poem of the *Hou* section (slip 83), "Shi mou zhi jian" 十畝之間 "Within Ten Acres" (Mao 111), is followed by a blank space and then the notation "Hou liu" 侯六 "*Hou* 6," apparently indicating the number of poems in the section; it is followed by a hook-shaped mark indicating the end of a section. This is then followed, after another blank space that would correspond to three characters, by the three characters (plus one duplication mark) 作魚寺, followed by another space, what appears to be a solid black mark (of the sort indicating the end of a poem), another space, and then the thirteen characters 魚者索人見佳心虫之喬者虫之 (the last three characters of which are very faint, as if some attempt was made to erase them) that seem not to correspond to any poem in the received text of the *Shi jing*. Xu Zaiguo 徐在國, the coeditor in chief of the Anhui slips, suggests that they were practice writings on the part of a scribe.[3] The six poems in this *Hou* section, the title of which does not correspond to any section in the received text, correspond to six of the seven poems in the received version of the *Wei Feng* 魏風 (Mao 108–113).[4] The next section is *Yong* 甬 (i.e., 鄘), slips 84–99, with nine poems in all; slip 99 ends, after a blank space, with the notation "Yong jiu" 甬九 "*Yong* 9," and then after another blank space, with the notation "Bai zhou" 白舟, which appears to refer to the first poem in the section, known in the received *Shi jing* as "Bai zhou" 柏舟 "The Cypress Boat" (Mao 45). The Anhui editors suggest that this is an indication that even though most poems in the manuscript do not include a title, nevertheless individual poems were known by title. The final section included within the Anhui corpus is *Wei* (slips 100–117) with ten poems. The final slip ends with the notation "Wei jiu" 魏九 "*Wei* 9" and then "Ge lou" 葛婁, which is the title of the first poem in the section and corresponds to the poem "Ge ju" 葛屨 "Fiber Slippers" (Mao 107), the first poem in the received *Wei Feng*. While this poem is indeed found in the *Wei Feng* section of the received text of the *Shi jing*, the other poems in that section, as noted earlier, are included in the manuscript in the *Hou* section, whereas the other nine poems in this section are found in the received *Tang Feng* 唐 風. Moreover, the number "nine" here is clearly a mistake, since there are ten poems in the section, none of which is readily combinable with another poem. The identification of the *Hou* and *Wei* sections is, as the editors say, an issue requiring further study.⁵

The manuscript is written throughout in the orthography of the Warring States state of Chu. As such, it contains numerous variants vis-à-vis the received text of the *Shi jing*. Many of these variants are simply different ways of writing the same word as understood in the received text, though many may also indicate different nuances from that or those usually understood in the exegeses of the received text.⁶ There are also not a few variants that seem clearly to represent completely different words. Rather than trying to give any sort of statistical accounting of these variants, it seems better for the purposes of this first reading of the Anhui manuscript to give a few examples that reflect different degrees of similarity or difference between the manuscript and the received text. I will examine six separate poems, one from each of the six different sections of the manuscript (the titles of the poems necessarily being as given in the received text). I have selected these poems both because they illustrate certain features concerning the manuscript and also because of their importance within the greater *Shi jing* exegetical tradition. Nevertheless, I believe they are broadly illustrative of the manuscript as a whole.

I present the manuscript text rendered in current *kaishu* transcription side by side with the received text of the *Shi jing*, as well as translations of how I understand both the manuscript text and the received text. I highlight in bold lexical differences between the manuscript and the received text (though not all of the graphic differences). For the purposes of the present discussion, I forgo detailed annotation of either translation, though following this initial presentation I provide some discussion of the variants and how they may affect our understanding of the *Shi jing*.

"Guan Ju" 關雎 "J-o-i-n, the Osprey" (Mao 1)

Anhui University Manuscript	Received *Shi Jing*
關關雎鳩，才河之州。 J-o-i-n J-o-i-n cries the osprey, On the island of the river.	關關雎鳩，在河之洲。 J-o-i-n J-o-i-n cries the osprey, On the island of the river.

要嬥淑女，君子好逑。 Slender and shy is the chaste girl, A loving mate for the lord's son. 參沙芫菜，左右流之。 Up and down the water lilies, To the left and right drifting them. 要嬥淑女，痦寑求之。 Slender and shy is the chaste girl, Awake and **asleep** seeking her. 求之弗得，痦寑思倍。 Seeking her without **getting her**, Awake and asleep thinking **to pair**. 悠哉悠哉，輾轉反昃。 Longing, oh, longing oh, Tossing and turning to and fro. 參沙芫菜，左右采之。 Up and down the water lilies, To the left and right picking them. 要嬥淑女，琴瑟友之。 Slender and shy is the chaste girl, With harp and lute befriending her. 參沙芫菜，左右教之。 Up and down the water lilies, To the left and right **selecting** them. 要嬥淑女，鐘鼓樂之。 Slender and shy is the chaste girl, With bell and drum pleasuring her.	窈窕淑女，君子好逑。 Slender and shy is the chaste girl, A loving mate for the lord's son. 參差荇菜，左右流之。 Up and down the water lilies, To the left and right drifting them. 窈窕淑女，寤寐求之。 Slender and shy is the chaste girl, Awake and **asleep** seeking her. 求之不得，寤寐思服。 Seeking her without **success**, Awake and asleep thinking **of her**. 悠哉悠哉，輾轉反側。 Longing, oh, longing oh, Tossing and turning to and fro. 參差荇菜，左右采之。 Up and down the water lilies, To the left and right picking them. 窈窕淑女，琴瑟友之。 Slender and shy is the chaste girl, With harp and lute befriending her. 參差荇菜，左右芼之。 Up and down the water lilies, To the left and right **choosing** them. 窈窕淑女，鍾鼓樂之。 Slender and shy is the chaste girl, With bell and drum pleasuring her.

"Guan Ju" is the first and is generally regarded as the most important poem in the *Shi jing* (and perhaps in all of Chinese poetry), and thus readers will surely be interested to know if and how the Anhui University manuscript offers any new information about its early interpretation. Although a strict transcription of the manuscript would show numerous orthographic differences with the received text, most of these differences are probably simply different ways of writing the same words. There may be only two substantive variants, both in the second stanza: the manuscript's 寑, surely to be read as *qin* 寢 "to sleep," as opposed to the received text's *mei* 寐 "to sleep" in the second and third couplets; and the last word of the third couplet, written *bei* 伓: 倍 in the manuscript, and *fu* 服 in the received text. In the first case, *qin* 寢 and *mei* 寐 are clearly synonymous; in fact, the *Mao Zhuan* 毛傳 *Mao Tradition* commentary defines *mei* as *qin* (寐，寢也). While it is possible that there were graphically similar ways of writing the two words in the Warring States period,[7] there is certainly no phonetic contact between them, and thus they would seem to constitute two different words. In the second case, in Chu orthography 伓 routinely stands for the word *bei* 倍,[8] referring to multiples of persons, whereas the *fu* of the received text is variously glossed as *shi* 事 "service" or as *si zhi* 思之 "to think of it." The translation that I offer, "to pair" (understanding *bei* 倍 as cognate with *pei* 陪), may be too strong, but it does seem that something of this meaning approximates the protagonist's desire (which, it should be noted, is explicitly expressed with the verb *si* 思 "to wish for") to "seek" (*qiu* 求) the girl.[9] This is a topic to which I will return in the concluding section of this study.

There is also one other word (or words) that the Anhui University editors suggest should be understood as different from the reading of the received text: this concerns the recurrent 要翟, which they understand as *yao tiao* 腰嬥 "slender of waist,"[10] as opposed to *yaotiao* 窈窕, usually understood as a compound word meaning something like "Slender and shy," as I have translated it.[11] The editors' interpretation, which focuses on the physical attractiveness of the girl in question, seems to be consistent with a number of other unearthed documents that show that people in the Warring States and Western Han read the "Guan ju" poem as being concerned with sexual desire.[12] Nevertheless, two features render it unconvincing. First, one would expect an expression such as "slender of waist" to be written as *tiao yao* 嬥腰, with the adjective preceding the noun. Second, 要翟, though written differently than *yaotiao* 窈窕, is certainly homophonous with it, or at least nearly so: *ʔiau *liâuk as opposed to *ʔiûʔ *liûʔ,[13] especially considering that such rhyming binomial words are often written with different graphs and slight differences in pronunciation. Therefore, suggestive though the editors' interpretation is, it is likely that the manuscript writing of this word does not constitute a lexical variant vis-à-vis the received text. I will address this further in the concluding section of this study.

"Zouyu" 騶虞 "The Zouyu" (Mao 25)

Anhui University Manuscript	Received *Shi jing*
彼茁者葭，一發五豝。于嗟從呼！ Sprouting those many bulrushes; One volley shooting five sows. Aha, **after them**, ho!	彼茁者葭，壹發五豝。于嗟乎騶虞！ Sprouting those many bulrushes; One volley shooting five sows. Aha, oh ho, **what a *zouyu*.**
彼茁者蓬，一[發五豵]。于嗟從呼！ Sprouting those many raspberries; One volley shooting five . . . Aha, **after them**, ho!	彼茁者蓬，壹發五豵。于嗟乎騶虞！ Sprouting those many raspberries; One volley shooting five shoats. Aha, oh ho, **what a *zouyu*.**
彼茁者葭，一發五麇。[于嗟從呼]！ **Sprouting those many yarrow stalks; One volley shooting five elks. [Aha, after them, ho!]**	

The poem "Zouyu" is the last poem of the *Shao nan* section of both the Anhui manuscript and the received *Shi jing*. The poem is similar in structure in the two different texts, but in the Anhui manuscript it includes three stanzas whereas the received text includes only two. There is also an important lexical difference (or two) that may influence the overall interpretation of the poem. For the word *zou* 騶 "groom; to run" in the received text, the manuscript reads *cong* 從 "to follow," though, as we will see, the Anhui editors suggest reading it as *zong* 縱 "to release; relaxed." Also, the last character of each stanza (though not present in the third stanza, because of a broken bamboo slip) is written 虍, which the editors suggest reading, as customary in Warring States Chu manuscripts, as the final particle *hu* 乎.[14] *Hu* 乎 (archaic *hâ) and the corresponding character in the received text, *yu* 虞 (archaic *ngwa), are both written with a "tiger" 虎 component that serves as their phonetic, so it would be a simple matter to regard either as a phonetic loan for the other. However, as the Anhui University editors suggest, it is not necessary to posit a phonetic loan relationship between them; rather, they could simply represent two different readings of the poem.[15]

In the received exegetical tradition, there are two predominant explanations of the poem, centering on the word or words *zou yu* 騶虞. One tradition treats it as the name of a mythical animal, while another tradition treats it as the name of an officer or officers in charge of the hunt: "groom" and/or "warden." The *Mao Zhuan* is representative of the former interpretation, saying of the *zouyu* that it is "a righteous beast; a white tiger with black markings, which does not eat living things, such that the most sincere virtue responds to it" (騶虞，義獸也，白虎黑文，不食生物；有至信之德則應之).[16] On the other hand, the Lu 魯 and Han 韓 traditions of the *Shi*, though both lost, are quoted as saying that *zou yu* is "the officer of the Son of Heaven in command of fowling and hunting" (騶虞，天子掌鳥獸官).[17]

Both the *Shi Xu* 詩序 *Preface to the Poetry* and the commentary of Zheng Xuan 鄭玄 (127–200) seem to conflate these two interpretations, stating:

《騶虞》，《鵲巢》之應也。《鵲巢》之化行，人倫既正，朝廷既治，天下純被文王之化，則庶類蕃殖，蒐田以時，仁如騶虞，則王道成也。

"The Game Warden" is a response to "The Magpie's Nest." With the transforming effect of "The Magpie's Nest," human relations being correct and the royal court being well governed, all the world was affected by King Wen's transformative influence. The various plants ripened profusely and the hunts were timely, as humane as the *zouyu*, and then the royal way was complete.[18]

君射一發而翼五犯者，戰禽獸之命；必戰之者，仁心之至

That the lord shoots one shot and chases off five sows is being fearful for the lives of the beasts of prey; being necessarily fearful for them is the epitome of a humane heart.[19]

The Anhui editors interpret the manuscript in line with the *Preface to the Poetry* and Zheng Xuan, reading the *cong* 從 of 于嗟從呼, as *zong* 縱 "to relax, to release," perhaps meaning something like "let them go."[20] This in turn concerns the interpretation of the second line of each stanza: *yi fa wu ba/zong/mi* 一發五豝/豵/麋, which literally means "one shot five sows/shoats/elk." The interpretation turns on both the meanings of *yi fa* 一發, literally "one shot," and of the three different types of animals. *Yi fa* can mean that a team of hunters brings down five animals with one volley, as I have translated here, or it can mean that a single hunter shoots only one in five animals, allowing the others to escape, as Zheng Xuan seems to suggest. The *Mao Zhuan* offers no help in this case, stating simply, "a female swine is called a *ba*; the warden drives the animals together to await the lord's shot" (豕牝曰豝；虞人翼五豝以待公之發).[21] As for the animals, as noted, the received text is in only two stanzas, the first concerning the hunting of "sows" (*ba* 豝) and the second of "shoats" (*zong* 豵). The *Mao Zhuan* makes a point of defining *ba* 豝 as a "female pig" (豕牝曰豝) and *zong* 豵 as a one-year-old pig (一歲曰豵), which might not be appropriate targets of a hunt, whence the suggestion that the herd should simply be culled.[22] On the other hand, the manuscript adds a third stanza in which the prey is "elk" (*mi* 麋), which the *Er ya* 爾雅 *Approaching Eloquence*, among other texts, explicitly defines as a "male elk" (麋，牡麐).[23] Whereas the hunting of sows and shoats might be questionable, male elk would certainly seem to be a legitimate target of a hunt.

In a lecture at the Institute of History and Philology at Academia Sinica in Taiwan, Yan Shixuan 顏世鉉 proposed reading this poem as a simple hunting song.[24] He resisted Huang Dekuan's interpretation of *cong* 從 as *zong* 縱 "to relax, to release" and suggested that it is more straightforward to read it as the character itself in the sense of "to follow" or "to chase after." Also arguing that the animals mentioned in the poem were legitimate prey, he suggested that it is important to differentiate between the "original" intent of a poem and the intent and understanding of subsequent transmitters and editors. This, of course, is an old topic in the interpretation of the *Shi jing*,[25] but the Anhui manuscript provides important new evidence with which to debate the meaning of the *Shi jing* poem "Zouyu," and perhaps other poems of the collection as well.

"Huang Niao" 黃鳥 "Yellow Birds" (Mao 131)

Anhui University Manuscript	Received *Shi Jing*
鮫鮫黃鳥，止于桑。 ***Kriâu-kriâu*** the yellow birds, Stopping on the mulberry tree.	交交黃鳥，止于棘。 **To and fro flit** the yellow birds, Stopping on the bush of thorns.

誰從穆公？子車仲行。
Who will follow Duke Mu?
Junior Hang of the Zi Ju clan.
惟此仲行，口夫之方。
Let it be this Junior Hang,
A **model one** of a hundred.
臨其穴，惴惴其慄。
Looking down upon his pit,
Trembling, trembling is his shaking.
彼蒼者天，殲我良人。
That azure heaven up above,
How it cuts off our finest men.
如可贖也，人百其身。
Ah, if we could but ransom him,
A hundred men would give their lives.

鴥鴥黃鳥，止于楚。
Kriâu-kriâu the yellow birds,
Stopping on the hardwood tree.
誰從穆公？子車鍼虎。
Who will follow Duke Mu?
Zhen Hu of the Zi Ju clan.
惟此鍼虎，百夫之御。
Let it be this Zhen Hu,
A defender of a hundred.
臨其穴，惴惴其慄。
Looking down upon his pit,
Trembling, trembling is his shaking.
彼蒼者天，殲我良人。
That azure heaven up above,
How it cuts off our finest men.
如可贖也，人百其身。
Ah, if we could but ransom him,
A hundred men would give their lives.

誰從穆公？子車奄息。
Who will follow Duke Mu?
Yan Xi of the Zi Ju clan.
維此奄息，百夫之特。
Let it be this Yan Xi,
A **special one** of a hundred.
臨其穴，惴惴其慄。
Looking down upon his pit,
Trembling, trembling is his shaking.
彼蒼者天，殲我良人。
That azure heaven up above,
How it cuts off our finest men.
如可贖兮，人百其身。
Oh, if we could but ransom him,
A hundred men would give their lives.

交交黃鳥，止于桑。
To and fro flit the yellow birds,
Stopping on the mulberry tree.
誰從穆公，子車仲行。
Who will follow Duke Mu?
Junior Hang of the Zi Ju clan.
維此仲行，百夫之防。
Let it be this Junior Hang,
A **stalwart one** of a hundred.
臨其穴，惴惴其慄。
Looking down upon his pit,
Trembling, trembling is his shaking.
彼蒼者天，殲我良人。
That azure heaven up above,
How it cuts off our finest men.
如可贖兮，人百其身。
Oh, if we could but ransom him,
A hundred men would give their lives.

鮫鮫黃鳥，止于棘。 **Kriâu-kriâu** the yellow birds, Stopping on the bush of thorns. 誰從穆公？子車奄思。 Who will follow Duke Mu? Yan Si of the Zi Ju clan. 惟此奄思，百夫之德。 Let it be this Yan Si, A **virtuous one** of a hundred. 臨其穴，惴惴其慄。 Looking down upon his pit, Trembling, trembling is his shaking. 彼蒼者天，殲我良人。 That azure heaven up above, How it cuts off our finest men. 如可贖也，人百其身。 Ah, if we could but ransom him, A hundred men would give their lives.	交交黃鳥，止于楚。 **To and fro flit** the yellow birds, Stopping on the hardwood tree. 誰從穆公？子車鍼虎。 Who will follow Duke Mu? Zhen Hu of the Zi Ju clan. 維此鍼虎，百夫之禦。 Let it be this Zhen Hu, A defender of a hundred. 臨其穴，惴惴其慄。 Looking down upon his pit, Trembling, trembling is his shaking. 彼蒼者天，殲我良人。 That azure heaven up above, How it cuts off our finest men. 如可贖兮，人百其身。 Oh, if we could but ransom him, A hundred men would give their lives.

"Huang Niao" 黃鳥 "Yellow Birds" or "The Orioles" (Mao 131) is another of the most famous songs in the *Shi jing*, particularly important for its historical reference. It purports to describe the scene at the tomb of Duke Mu of Qin 秦穆公 (r. 659–621), as three noblemen of the Zi Ju 子車 clan prepared to follow him in death.[26] The Anhui manuscript version of this poem is almost identical with the received text, except that the order of the three stanzas is different. In the received text, Zi Ju Yan Xi 子車奄息 is the subject of the first stanza, Zi Ju Zhong Hang 子車仲行 of the second, and Zi Ju Zhen Hu 子車鍼虎 of the third. By contrast, the manuscript places Zi Ju Zhong Hang first, followed by Zi Ju Zhen Hu, and then Zi Ju Yan Si 子車奄思.[27] It may also be noted that one of these names, Yan Si 奄思 in the manuscript as opposed to Yan Xi 奄息 in the received text, is different, but differences in the writing of proper names are very common in all pre-Qin sources and the two words are almost homophonous.[28] Indeed, the only immediate difference between the two texts is in the first line of each stanza, in which the manuscript writes *ming* 鳴 "to call" where the received text writes *niao* 鳥 "bird." This seems clearly to be a simple miswriting on the part of the manuscript scribe (that it is a miswriting is clear from the adjective *huang* 黃 "yellow" before it, certainly not an appropriate modifier for a bird call). Nevertheless, this miswriting may reveal how the scribe understood another issue that has divided readers of this poem. The reduplicative that opens this first line of each stanza is written 駮 (i.e., 駮駮) in the manuscript and 交交 in the received text. Although the *Mao Zhuan* seems to understand *jiao jiao* as descriptive of the birds' flying to and fro from one type of tree to another, other readers have understood it to be onomatopoeia for the call of the birds.[29] I suspect that the manuscript's scribe's writing *niao* 鳥 "bird" as *ming* 鳴 "to call" may have been the result of his subconscious voicing of the birds' calls.

"Shuo Shu" 碩鼠 "Big Rat" (Mao 113)

Anhui University Manuscript	Received *Shi Jing*
碩鼠碩鼠，毋食我麥。 Big rat, big rat, Don't eat my wheat. 三歲戀女，莫我肯德。 For three years I was **linked to** you; You don't deign to treat me proper. 逝將去女，適彼樂國。 Now I am about to leave you, And go off to that happy state. 樂國樂國，爰得我直。 The happy state, the happy state, Where I will get what I deserve.	碩鼠碩鼠，無食我黍。 Big rat, big rat, Don't eat my grain. 三歲貫女，莫我肯顧。 For three years I was **pierced by** you; You don't deign to **look back** at me. 逝將去女，適彼樂土。 Now I am about to leave you, And go off to that happy land. 樂土樂土，爰得我所。 The happy land, the happy land, Where I will get where I belong.
碩鼠碩鼠，無食我黍。 Big rat, big rat, Don't eat my grain. 三歲戀女，莫我肯與。 For three years I was **linked to** you, You don't deign to **join** with me. 逝將去女，適彼樂土。 Now I am about to leave you,	碩鼠碩鼠，無食我麥。 Big rat, big rat, Don't eat my wheat. 三歲貫女，莫我肯德。 For three years I was **pierced by** you, You don't deign to treat me proper. 逝將去女，適彼樂國。 Now I am about to leave you,

And go off to that happy land. 樂土樂土，爰得我所。 The happy land, the happy land, Where I will get where I belong. 碩鼠碩鼠，無食我苗。 Big rat, big rat, Don't eat my sprouts. 三歲戀女，莫我肯勞。 For three years I was **linked to you**, You don't deign to give me credit. 逝將去女，適彼樂郊。 Now I am about to leave you, And go off to that happy fringe. 樂郊樂郊，維其永號。 The happy fringe, the happy fringe, **It is the place** long to call out.	And go off to that happy state. 樂國樂國，爰得我直。 The happy state, the happy state, Where I will get what I deserve. 碩鼠碩鼠，無食我苗。 Big rat, big rat, Don't eat my sprouts. 三歲貫女，莫我肯勞。 For three years I was **pierced by you**, You don't deign to give me credit. 逝將去女，適彼樂郊。 Now I am about to leave you, And go off to that happy fringe. 樂郊樂郊，誰之永號。 The happy fringe, the happy fringe, **Who is it who will** long call out.

"Shuo shu" 碩鼠 "Big Rat," which is a poem in the *Wei Feng* 魏風 section of the *Shi jing*, is found in the *Hou* 侯 section of the Anhui University manuscript.[30] As noted in the introduction to this study, the *Hou* section of the manuscript is anomalous within the *Shi jing* tradition; several studies have already been published, either formally or online, suggesting identifications of it,[31] but none of these would seem to be conclusive. Like "Shuo shu," the other five poems in the *Hou* section are also found in the *Wei Feng* section of the *Shi jing*, though in a different order.[32]

Like the poem "Huang niao," the sequence of the first two stanzas of "Shuo shu" is different from that of the received *Shi jing*. Nevertheless, also like "Huang niao," although there are numerous orthographic differences between the manuscript version of the poem and the received text, there are in fact very few differences of wording between the two versions of the poem. The Anhui University editors suggest that the *luan* 戀 found in the second couplet of each stanza should be regarded as a phonetic loan for the *guan* 貫 "to penetrate; to link" of the received text; *luan* 戀, which is the phonetic component of and probably the protoform of *luan*

挛 (*rôn) "to link," is in the same rhyme class as *guan* (*kôns), and thus by most standards of textual criticism constitutes an acceptable phonetic loan.³³ On the other hand, it seems to me that *luan* 挛 "to entangle; to link" is a reasonable reading within this line, such that there is no need to posit a phonetic relationship with the *guan* of the received text. It is just as likely that the two words are synonyms. The same is more or less true of the only other words that differ between the two versions: the last word of the same couplet in the second stanza (the first stanza of the received text), *yu* 與 "to join with; to give to" and the corresponding *gu* 顧 "to look back upon"; the Anhui editors simply note that the two words are similar both in meaning and pronunciation.³⁴ Again, either word is suitable in the context.

There is, however, one important feature of the manuscript version of this poem that may also have affected the transmission of the poem in later times: this has to do with punctuation. The final two characters of the third couplet of each stanza are followed by repetition marks: 樂 ₌或₌, 樂₌土₌, and 樂₌蒿₌. The Anhui editors note that in the *Mao Shi*, the corresponding characters are repeated three times: 適彼樂土, 樂土樂土 "And go off to that happy land. The happy land, the happy land"; 適彼樂國, 樂國樂國 "And go off to that happy state. The happy state, the happy state"; 適彼樂郊, 樂郊樂郊 "And go off to that happy fringe. The happy fringe, the happy fringe." However, they state that since such a triple repetition function for this repetition mark has not been seen in other unearthed manuscripts, they also suggest that the manuscript might read instead as 適彼樂國, 樂國, "And go off to that happy land, Happy land." This means that the first line of the following couplet would have only two characters,³⁵ which the editors say might preserve an early reading. Given the standard four-character lines of the Guo Feng poems, this is extremely unlikely. Indeed, Liu Gang 劉剛, a member of the Anhui University editorial team, has released a study of a *Shi jing* poem not found in the Anhui manuscript, the poem "You bi" 有駜 "They Are Stout" (Mao 298) of the *Lu Song* 魯頌 Lu Hymns section, in which he discusses this duplication mark and its attendant problems.³⁶ He notes first of all that Wu Kejing 鄔可晶 has pointed out that in the Tsinghua University "Qi ye" 耆夜 manuscript there are several places where duplication marks have to be understood as double duplicatives.³⁷ To give just one example, slip 3 reads: 作歌一終曰樂₌脂₌酉₌. This should be read as 作歌一終, 曰《樂樂脂酒》: 樂樂脂酒 "makes a song in one stanza, called 'Pleasing, pleasing the tasty wine'; 'Pleasing, pleasing the tasty wine." The duplication mark after *le* 樂 "pleasing" indicates that it is first to be read twice (i.e., 樂樂), and then the same duplication mark together with the duplication marks after *zhi jiu* 脂酒 indicate that the entire (four-character) phrase is to be repeated. Thus, the one character *le* 樂 is to be read four times. In this way, there is precedent—even if it is not at all common—for reading the duplication marks after 樂或, 樂土, and 樂䔪 in the Anhui manuscript version of "Shuo shu" as indicating that both characters are to be repeated and then repeated again.[38]

This suggests that in this line too, the Anhui manuscript and the *Mao Shi* share the same reading. However, of interest for the transmission of the *Shi jing*, the *Han Shi waizhuan* 韓詩外傳 reveals a different reading of this poem:

逝將去女，適彼樂土。 Now I am about to leave you,
 And go off to that happy land.
適彼樂土，爰得我所。 Going off to that happy land,
 Would that I get where I belong.

Over one hundred years ago, Yu Yue 俞樾 (1821–1907) suggested that the difference between the *Mao Shi* and the *Han Shi waizhuan* reading was doubtless brought about by different understandings of duplication marks.[39] While Yu concluded that the *Han Shi waizhuan* reading should be preferred, the Anhui manuscript now seems to give support to the *Mao Shi* reading. In either event, if Yu Yue (and Liu Gang) are correct in their analysis of the function of these duplication marks, and there would seem to be no better explanation of the marks in the "Shuo shu" poem, this means that at some point in the course of transmission of the *Shi*, different scribes were looking at duplication marks and understanding them differently.[40] This would seem necessarily to be evidence of visual copying from a written source text.

"Qiang you Ci" 牆有茨 "On the Wall
There Are Prickly Vines" (Mao 46)

Anhui University Manuscript	Received *Shi Jing*
牆有蛓蝥，不可欵也。 On the walls there are **vermin**, Which cannot be **coughed** off, oh.	牆有茨，不可埽也。 On the walls there is **star-thistle**, Which cannot be **swept** off, oh.

中冓之言，不可讀也。 What is said **at the midnight hour**, Cannot be stated out loud, oh. 口口讀也，言之辱也。 (What can be) stated out loud, oh, Are the most shameful of words, oh. 牆有蒺藜，不可毄也。 On the walls there are **vermin**, Which cannot be **spat** off, oh. 中冓之言，不可詳也。 What is said **at the midnight hour**, Cannot be made explicit, oh. 所可詳也，言之長也。 What can be made explicit, oh, Are the commonest of words, oh. 牆有蒺藜，不可啼也。 On the walls there are **vermin**, Which cannot be **puffed** off, oh. 中冓之言，不可道也。 What is said **at the midnight hour**, Cannot be stated outright, oh. 所可道也，言之猷也。 What can be stated outright, oh, Are the filthiest of words, oh.	中冓之言，不可道也。 What is said **within the walls**, Cannot be stated outright, oh. 所可道也，言之醜也。 What can be stated outright, oh, Are the filthiest of words, oh. 牆有茨，不可襄也。 On the walls there is **star-thistle**, Which cannot be **brushed** off, oh. 中冓之言，不可詳也。 What is said **within the walls**, Cannot be made explicit, oh. 所可詳也，言之長也。 What can be made explicit, oh, Are the commonest of words, oh. 牆有茨，不可束也。 On the walls there is **star-thistle**, Which cannot be **baled up**, oh. 中冓之言，不可讀也。 What is said **within the walls**, Cannot be stated out loud, oh. 所可讀也，言之辱也。 What can be stated out loud, oh, Are the most shameful of words, oh.

This poem corresponds to the poem "Qiang you Ci" 牆有茨 "On the Walls There Is Star-thistle" of the *Yong Feng* section of the *Shi jing*. The *Shi Xu* provides a historical context for this poem: "A man of Wei satirized his superior. The Ducal Son Wan was incestuous with the Dowager Mother. The people of the state were pained by it, but could not speak of it out loud" (衛人刺其上也。公子頑通乎君母，國人疾之，而不可道也). In fact, this was one of the more sordid tales of the Spring and Autumn period.[41] It began during the reign of Duke Xuan of Wei 衛宣公 (r. 718–700 BCE). Prior to becoming ruler of Wei, Duke Xuan had sired a son, Gongzi Ji 公子伋, with one of the secondary consorts of his father. When the duke in turn came to power, he named this son the crown prince. Later he arranged for Duke Xi of Qi 齊僖公 (r. 729–698 BCE) to send his daughter, Xuan Jiang 宣姜, to be Gongzi Ji's wife. However, when Xuan Jiang arrived in Wei, Duke Xuan, smitten with her beauty, took her as his own consort. Together they sired two sons: Gongzi Shou 公子壽 and Gongzi Shuo 公子朔. Late in Duke Xuan's life, Xuan Jiang, realizing that she was the legitimate wife of the crown prince Gongzi Ji, feared that he would take revenge on her when he came to power. She conspired with her younger son, Gongzi Shuo, to have Ji killed, so that her elder son, Shou, would become crown prince. According to the story, the plan was to send Ji to Qi, and to have him killed on the road. However, Shou and Ji were bosom buddies, and when Shou became aware of the plot, he attempted to stop it. When Ji persevered in going despite the threat to his life, Shou went along with him. Getting Ji drunk the night before the ambush, Shou stole his clothes and travel documents, and went off the next morning to be killed himself. When Ji heard of this, he too went to the assassins and was also put to death. At the loss of his two favorite sons, the elderly Duke Xuan took to his bed and died. This left Gongzi Shuo, the only remaining son, as Duke Xuan's successor, known posthumously as Duke Hui of Wei 衛惠公 (r. 699–696, 686–669 BCE).

The story does not end with his succession. Shortly after he came to power, two associates of Gongzi Ji and Gongzi Shou, both of them half-brothers by other consorts of Duke Xuan, joined forces to overthrow Duke Hui, driving him into exile, in Qi, in 696 BCE. They installed one of Ji's younger brothers, Qianmou 黔牟, as ruler of Wei. However, after Qianmou ruled for ten years, Duke Xiang of Qi 齊襄公 (r. 697–686 BCE), patron of the exiled Duke Hui of Wei, invaded Wei and ousted Qianmou, who went to the royal Zhou capital for protection. Duke Xiang of Qi arranged for Gongzi Ji's other younger brother, Gongzi Wan 公子頑, to be the new husband of Xuan Jiang. Although the people of the state apparently viewed this relationship as a scandal, Xuan Jiang and Gongzi Wan together sired five children. This poem, "Qiang you ci" 牆有茨, is supposed to satirize their relationship.

The Anhui University manuscript of this poem is generally similar to that of the received text, but it does contain certain differences that may reveal different meanings, at least of detail if not of general interpretation. Perhaps least important of these, the order of stanzas is once again different, with the first and third stanzas reversed. Perhaps more important, the first line of each stanza reads differently: for the received text's *ci* 茨 "star-thistle" clinging to the walls, the manuscript reads *jili* 蝍蟄, a type of small insect such as "vermin" (I would almost want to translate it as "creepy-crawler," if only for the alliterative effect).⁴² The Anhui University editors read 蝍蟄 as a phonetic loan for *jili* 蒺藜 "prickly vine," noting that the *Mao Zhuan* glosses *ci* as *jili* 蒺藜, and that both the *Er ya* and *Shuo wen jie zi* 說文解字 *Discussing Pictographs and Explaining Composite Graphs* equate *jili* 蒺藜 and *ci* 茨.⁴³ In my translation, I have translated the manuscript "literally." I would not wish to claim that *jili* 蝍蟄 "vermin" is necessarily the "correct" or "original" reading, but I would suggest it is a possible reading. Clearly, whether it is to be read as *jili* 蝍蟄 "vermin" or as *jili* 蒺藜 "prickly vine," or even as *ci* 茨 "star-thistle," whatever is on the wall(s) is meant to symbolize the problems that cannot be talked about. "Prickly vine" and "star-thistle" may well be appropriate botanical symbols of such prickly problems, but surely "vermin" would also be an apt metaphor. What is more, I would suggest too that there is some evidence that the manuscript scribe intended a meaning such as this; whereas all three verbs in the following lines of the received text, *sao* 埽 "to sweep off," *xiang* 襄 (usually understood as *rang* 攘) "to brush off," and *shu* 束 "to bind, to bale," are usually understood to involve brushing aside something (such as a plant), the verbs in the manuscript are written with significs having to do with the mouth: *shuo* 欶, usually "to suck," but also "to cough; to spit" (as if dispelling something poisonous, cognate with *sou* 嗽); 嗀; and 啹. Although the latter two of these characters are apparently unknown in the received lexicography, and it is not entirely clear (at least to me) why it would be necessary to use one's mouth to get rid of vermin (or some similar small insect), it is at least notable that all three verbs are written consistently.⁴⁴ (It might be interesting to note too that the verbs in the following lines, *du* 讀 "to recite," *xiang* 詳 "to specify," and *dao* 道 "to state," all have to do with "speech," which of course is also a function of the mouth.) The Anhui University editors do not even consider the possibility of reading these lines literally, apparently assuming that the received text is more or less "correct" in its botanical symbolism.

There is one other orthographic difference concerning which the Anhui University editors do depart from the Mao text, even if they adopt a reading that is at least attested by the Han 韓 tradition of the *Shi*. This is found in the phrase 中㑰之言, which recurs in the second couplet of each stanza, and which corresponds with the phrase *Zhong gou zhi yan* 中冓之言 of the received text. There have been three predominant interpretations of the term *zhong gou* 中冓: the "inner chamber," which is the reading of the *Mao Zhuan*;[45] "(illicit) sexual relations," presumably understanding *gou* 冓 as the protograph for *gou* 媾, which seems to be the interpretation of Zheng Xuan;[46] and "midnight," which is the reading of the *Han Shi*.[47] The Anhui editors transcribe the manuscript graph 🀰 as 㑰, and say that it derives directly from the oracle-bone graph 🀰, which has been identified by Huang Tianshu 黃天樹, as the term for midnight.[48] This need not suggest that the other readings are unsupported, but only that the scribe responsible for the Anhui manuscript understood this line to refer to "midnight."

"Xishuai" 蟋蟀 "Cricket" (Mao 114)

Anhui University Manuscript	Received *Shi jing*
蟋蟀在堂，歲矞其逝。 A cricket is in the hall, The year-star is about to be gone. 今者不樂，日月其邁。 Now it is that we are not pleased, The sun and moon will be going. 毋已內康，猶思其外。 **Do not** yet be at ease **within**, **Still** think of what is outside it. 好樂毋無，良士蹶蹶。 Love and pleasure **ought not** be **wasted**, The fine man so halting halting. 蟋蟀在堂，歲矞其暮。 A cricket is in the hall, The year-star is about to be dark.	蟋蟀在堂，歲聿其莫。 A cricket is in the hall, The year-star is about to be dark. 今我不樂，日月其除。 Now it is that we are not pleased, The sun and moon will be removed. 無已大康，職思其居。 **There are none** yet greatly at ease, **Only** think of where it **resides**. 好樂無荒，良士瞿瞿。 Love and pleasure **are without waste**, The fine man so fearful fearful.

今者不樂，日月其除。 Now it is that we are not pleased, The sun and moon will be removed. 毋已大康，猶思其懼。 **Do not** yet be greatly at ease, **Still** think of what it **fears**. 好樂毋無，良士懼懼。 Love and pleasure **ought not** be **wasted**, The fine man so fearful fearful. 蟋蟀在堂，役車其休。 A cricket is in the hall, War chariotlike is its grace. 今者不樂，日月其慆。 Now it is that we are not pleased, The sun and moon will be past. 毋已大康，猶思其憂。 **Do not** yet be greatly at ease, **Still** think of what worries it. 好樂毋無，良士浮浮。 Love and pleasure **ought not** be **wasted**, The fine man so **floating floating**.	蟋蟀在堂，歲聿其逝。 A cricket is in the hall, The year-star is about to be gone. 今我不樂，日月其邁。 Now it is that we are not pleased, The sun and moon will be going. 無已大康，職思其外。 **There are none** yet greatly at ease, **Only** think of what is outside. 好樂無荒，良士蹶蹶。 Love and pleasure **are without waste**, The fine man so halting halting. 蟋蟀在堂，役車其休。 A cricket is in the hall, War chariotlike is its grace. 今我不樂，日月其慆。 Now it is that we are not pleased, The sun and moon will be past. 無已大康，職思其憂。 **There are none** yet greatly at ease, **Only** think of what worries it. 好樂無荒，良士休休。 Love and pleasure **are without waste**, The fine man so **graceful graceful**.

Once again, the Anhui University manuscript poem corresponds very closely with the received *Shi jing* poem "Xishuai," even if the first and second stanzas are reversed in the two poems. There are several other variants, of greater or lesser lexical significance. For instance, the *yu* 喬 of the first couplet of the manuscript's first stanza and the *yu* 聿 of the corresponding second stanza of the received text are essentially different instantiations, different spellings if you will, of the same word; the nominalizing agent *zhe* 者 of the second couplet of each stanza is certainly different from the *wo* 我 "we" of the received text, but does not entail much difference of meaning; the third couplet of each stanza in the manuscript begins with the prescriptive negative *wu* 毋 "don't," whereas the received text has the descriptive negative *wu* 無 "there is not"; the *nei* 內 "inner" of the same couplet differs from the received text's *da* 大 "great" in the corresponding second stanza;[49] the second phrase of that couplet begins with the word *you* 猶 "still" in the manuscript and *zhi* 職 "only" in the received text; the last word of that couplet in the second stanza reads *ju* 懼 "fearful" in the manuscript and the homophonous *ju* 居 "to reside" in the received text; the first phrase of the last couplet of each stanza has *wu* 無 "not" where the received text has *huang* 荒 "waste";[50] and the very last words of the poem are *fu fu* 浮浮 "floating floating" in the manuscript as opposed to *xiu xiu* 休休 "graceful graceful" in the received text.[51] Any one of these variants is doubtless worthy of extended discussion. However, the manuscript version and the received version have exactly the same number of phrases, in the same order (other than the reversal of the first two stanzas), have the same perspective of speech, the same rhymes, and exactly the same content. It is hard to deny that the two texts reflect essentially one and the same poem.

Tentative Conclusions

I think that there can be little doubt that the publication of the Anhui University manuscript of the *Shi jing* will come to be viewed as a momentous event in the long history of scholarship on this classic. It is much to be regretted that the manuscript has come to light by way of a tomb robbing.[52] It is unfortunate too that it is fragmentary.[53] Nevertheless, it will surely be the subject of study for decades to come. Much of this study will be devoted, at least initially, to the paleography of the text. As our understanding of the text itself becomes more mature, other studies will take up the thorny question of how to integrate this new evidence into our evolving understanding of the *Shi* and its tradition. For now, I will offer just two preliminary thoughts on the basis of the preceding survey of six different poems as seen in the manuscript. Both of these thoughts concern questions of similarity and difference, first on a microlevel—

to what extent is the wording of the Anhui manuscript similar to or different from that of the received text, and then on a macrolevel—to what extent can this Anhui manuscript be identified with the received text of the *Shi jing* in general? I will restrict my comments to just the analyses of the six poems introduced earlier. Just as those analyses were tentative, so too should these thoughts be viewed as tentative, meant more to raise questions than to state conclusions.

The script in which the manuscript is written is obviously different from the *kaishu* 楷書 script in which the received text of the *Shi jing* has come to us. Nevertheless, within this difference, there are varying degrees of similarity. In some cases, there is a one-to-one correspondence between the characters of the manuscript and the characters of the received text; in some cases, there is no apparent relationship between the characters of the two texts; and in other cases, the characters are superficially different but appear to refer to the same underlying words in the two different writing systems. It is the last of these categories that is often ambiguous, requiring judgment on the part of the reader: to what extent do the differences mask the same underlying word, or to what extent do the differences indicate different words?

In his study of the poem "Zouyu" discussed earlier, Yan Shixuan quotes Qiu Xigui 裘錫圭 as warning of two pernicious tendencies in the way that scholars relate manuscript versions of ancient texts to received versions of those texts: an "urge to equate" (*qu tong* 趨同) and a desire to "establish difference" (*li yi* 立異).

> 在將簡帛古書與傳世古書（包括同一書的簡帛本和傳本）相對照的時候，則要注意防止不恰當的「趨同」和「立異」兩種傾向。前者主要指將簡帛古書和傳世古書意義本不相同之處說成相同，後者主要指將簡帛古書和傳世古書中彼此對應的、意義相同或很相近的字說成意義不同。

When correlating bamboo and silk ancient texts and transmitted ancient texts (including bamboo and silk versions and transmitted versions of the same text), it is important to resist two inappropriate tendencies: "the urge to equate" and "establishing difference." The former is primarily to conflate content of bamboo and silk texts and received texts that is basically different; the latter is to explain as different corre-

sponding graphs in bamboo and silk texts and received texts
the meaning of which is similar or very close.[54]

In the article from which this passage is drawn, Qiu examines mistakes of both of these kinds that he claims to have made in his own work explicating manuscripts with either corresponding received texts or with similar wording. While he is careful to call out the harmful effects of both tendencies, if I am not mistaken in my reading, he is more concerned with the latter tendency, the desire to "establish difference," than he is with the former.[55] As opposed to one "mistake" that he made due to accepting the reading of the received text—an example of the "urge to equate"—Qiu cites three examples in which he proposed a different reading from a received text (or in which he did not identify a corresponding received text) but for which he subsequently became convinced that the correct reading was in fact that of a received text.

Scott Cook has also discussed the same two tendencies.[56] In his review of essays deriving from an international conference on the Guodian 郭店 *Laozi* 老子 manuscript, Cook begins by identifying the problem:

> For the purposes of this review, I would like to focus my attention on one particular aspect of working with certain excavated texts that goes most centrally to the core of what makes them valuable to us, but which, if not properly understood and treated with caution, can constitute a potential source of harm as well. This is the issue of "reading" these texts against their received counterparts—an issue that is discussed, from various angles, most prominently in the essays by William Boltz, Qiu Xigui, and Gao Ming.[57]

After paying due deference to the contributions that unearthed manuscripts can make to the reading of received literature, and after acknowledging that there are countless problems with the received literature, Cook nevertheless concludes this portion of his discussion with the following plea for the "intrinsic authority" of the received texts.

So, while we must certainly recognize and be prepared to correct the countless errors and misreadings that these early editors have left us with, we should not go so far as to strip them altogether of that "intrinsic authority" they seem to carry due to their venerable age.

Indeed, in some respects the source of their authoritativeness—limited as it is—is akin to that of the archaeologically excavated texts themselves: they each represent determinations of the text made at a time much closer to the source than any we are able to make today (to the extent, of course, that these early editions themselves have not been subject to later corruption). The value of the early received editions vis-à-vis the excavated texts is simply that they were written down in standardized graphs in which lexical ambiguity is no longer as much of an issue—we can at least be reasonably sure of what those early editors thought the text meant, which is more than we can say in the case of the excavated texts.[58]

As evidence of the authoritative nature of received texts, Cook then spends five pages critiquing an argument by William G. Boltz that the Guodian manuscript of the *Zi yi* 緇衣 *Black Jacket* provides a preferable reading of the first chapter of that text to the corresponding reading in the received text in the *Li ji* 禮記 *Record of Ritual*. Employing both paleography and also traditional textual criticism, Cook argues instead that the received text is still to be preferred. Finally, referring to a parallel text in the *Xunzi* 荀子, he concludes that this parallel "reflects the received version of the 'Zi yi' line in question so neatly that we are almost compelled to give the latter greater weight because of it—unless, of course, we find that it just makes *too much sense* for our tastes."[59] Despite his *cri de coeur* for the authority of received texts, Cook's qualification of making "*too much sense* for our tastes" would seem to leave great leeway for each individual reader to arrive at her own reading.

Be this as it may, Cook is surely right that it is "the 'reading' of manuscripts against their received counterparts" "that goes most centrally to the core of what makes [unearthed manuscripts] valuable to us." Among scholars who work with unearthed manuscripts, he and Qiu are the two leading authorities in the West and in China respectively, and in their own work they have both explored the problems involved with considerable subtlety, subtlety that the preceding quotations cannot adequately reflect. However, these quotations do suffice to raise the issue. I propose to pursue it here only with respect to the Anhui University manuscript of the *Shi* vis-à-vis the received text of the *Shi jing*, and indeed only with respect to the six poems that I introduced in this chapter. My discussion will perhaps inevitably take issue with some of the decisions the Anhui University editors have made in "reading" the manuscript. Even though they have occasionally been ready to challenge the received text, as in the case of their reading the 要翟 of the manuscript version of "Guan ju" as *yao tiao* 腰嬥 "slender of waist," as opposed to the *yaotiao* 窈窕 "slender and shy" of the received text, there are also numerous places where I feel they have been all too ready to accommodate the text of the manuscript to the reading of the received text. Despite the critical nature of what I will say in the next few paragraphs, let me say at the outset that I very much appreciate the work that the editors have done; it forms the basis of any interpretation that I might offer.

The Anhui editors' reading of 要翟 in the manuscript version of "Guan ju" as *yao tiao* 腰嬥 "slender of waist" would seem to be a classic example of what Qiu Xigui refers to as "establishing difference." As previously noted, it would be unproblematic to read these two characters as homophonous with the *yaotiao* 窈窕 of the received text: *ʔiau *liâuk as opposed to *ʔiû? *liû?. After all, the writing of this rhyming binomial expression was quite fluid in early texts: it is written *jiaoshao* 茭芍 (*krâu *diauk[60]) in the Mawangdui 馬王堆 *Wu xing* 五行 manuscript, and, as Ma Ruichen 馬瑞辰 (1782–1835) has argued, *yaojiao* 窈糾 (*ʔiû? *kiuʔ[61]) in the *Shi jing* poem "Yue chu" 月出 "The Moon Comes Out" (Mao 143),[62] so using two other characters to write the word is not unusual. The editors were doubtless influenced by the meanings of the separate characters of which the binome is composed: 要, which the editors note is a pictograph of two hands cinching the waist, and thus the protograph for *yao* 腰 "waist"; and 翟, which the editors interpret, reasonably, as *tiao* 嬥, defined in the *Shuo wen jie zi* as *zhi hao mao* 直好皃 "straight (or more probably slender) and beautiful appearance," and in the *Guang yun* 廣韻 as *xi yao mao* 細腰貌 "thin waisted appearance."[63] However, as Martin Kern has noted, "such descriptive rhyming, alliterative, or reduplicative binomes cannot be decoded based on the meaning of each character. Instead, they constitute indivisible words."[64]

Whereas in this reading of 要翟 the editors adopt an implicitly sexual reading of this most important of poems of the *Shi jing*, nevertheless in another one of their readings from the same poem they revert all too easily to the received text. For the line 求之弗得，寤寐思怀, although they note that the final character 怀 is routinely used in Chu script to write the word *bei* 倍 "to pair," which would seem to be a natural desire of the poet's persona "to pair" with the girl of his (or perhaps her) desire (and thus an appropriate object of the verb *si* 思 "to wish for" preceding it), still they gloss the character as *fu* 服, the corresponding word in the received text, stating simply that the pronunciations of the two words were close and that they could be interchanged in antiquity.⁶⁵ In so stating, they simply accept the reading of the received text: 求之弗得，寤寐思服, even though the reading of this word *fu* is quite uncertain in the received tradition of the *Shi jing*. Usually meaning either "clothing," "service, responsibility," or even "to surrender, to submit," the *Mao Zhuan* glosses *fu* 服, almost inexplicably—though certainly influentially—as "to think about it/her" (思之也).⁶⁶ Zheng Xuan, with somewhat better lexical support, defines the word as "service, duty" (事也), and then almost comically goes on to describe its meaning for this poem: "In seeking the sagely woman but not getting her, when she wakes up then she thinks of her own official duty, and with whom she should share it" (求賢女而不得，覺寐則思己職事，當誰與共之乎).⁶⁷ Is it not easier to imagine that the sleepless poet was wishing "to pair" (*bei* 倍 or *pei* 陪) with the young woman, whether she was slender of waist or not? What is more, this would make an appropriate response to the last line of the preceding stanza: 君子好逑 "A loving mate for the lord's son," *qiu* 逑 and *pei* 陪 being virtually synonymous. In short, at the risk of being accused of wishing to "establish difference," I would suggest that the reading of the Anhui manuscript is far preferable to the reading of the received *Shi jing*, despite whatever authority the *Mao Zhuan* might have.

In the presentation of the poem "Zouyu" earlier, I have already surveyed the traditional interpretations of the poem, which though they differ in important details are in agreement at least that this is a hunting poem. As we have seen, both the *Shi Xu* and the *Mao Zhuan* interpret the characters 騶虞 to refer to a righteous animal (*yi shou* 義獸) that is so humane (*ren* 仁) that it does not eat the flesh of other living animals. On the other hand, Zheng Xuan reads the characters separately as *zou* 騶 "grooms" and *yu* 虞 "warden," referring to the huntsmen assisting the lord in the hunt. In the Anhui manuscript, these two characters are written as 從虍. As previously discussed, the Anhui editors note that in Chu script 虍 regularly stands for *hu* 乎, and they read it here unproblematically as a sentence final exclamation, even though, as we have also seen, it would certainly be possible to demonstrate a phonetic connection between *hu* 乎 (*hâ) and *yu* 虞 (*ngwa). This might be another instance of "establishing difference." On the other hand, for the manuscript's 從, the base meaning of which when read as *cong* is "to follow," but which also has numerous attested uses as "to chase,"⁶⁸ and which is thus synonymous with the base meaning of the received text's *zou* 騶, "to rush; to chase" (also written as *qu* 趨 or 趣), the editors follow Huang Dekuan 黃德寬 in reading the word as zong 縱 "to relax, to release."⁶⁹ This is entirely informed by the interpretation of the received text; according to this interpretation, although this is a hunting song, it is about a hunt that culls only one in every five animals. I would submit, as has Yan Shixuan, that such a moralistic reading is more reflective of Han dynasty interpretations than it would be of any earlier hunting song.

As evidence of such an earlier hunting song, one might look to one of the Qin Stone Drums (秦石鼓) as a poem more or less contemporary with the Anhui copy of the "Zouyu" poem.⁷⁰ The "Tian che" 田車 "Hunting Chariot" poem engraved on one of the ten drums reads as follows (in the translation of Gilbert Mattos; note that parts of the last portion of the poem are illegible) (see fig. 8.1).⁷¹

田車孔安,   The hunting chariot is ever so steady;
鋚勒馵馵   The metal-ornamented reins are X-ly.

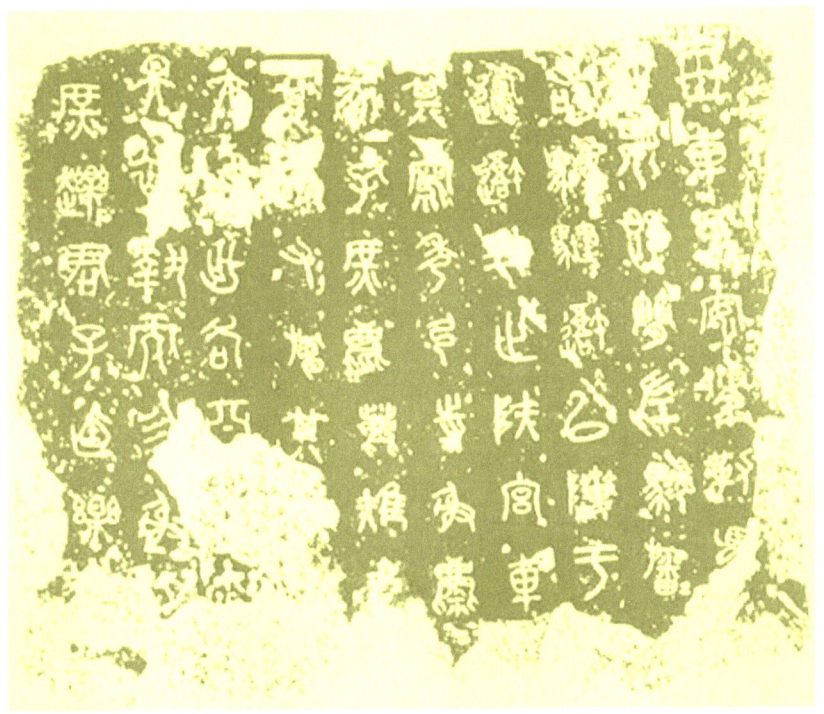

Figure 8.1. Qin Stone Drums poem "Tian che" 田車. From Ma Xulun 馬敘倫, Shi gu wen shuji 石鼓文疏記 (Shanghai: Shangwu yinshuguan, 1935), 20.

四衆既簡，	The mailed four-horse teams are completely select.
左驂旛旛。	The left outer-steed is spirited;
右驂騤騤，	The right outer-steed is robust.
吾以隮於邍	We hereby ascend the plain.
吾戎止阞	Our war-chariots come to a halt on a knoll;
宮車其寫	The palace-chariot is unhitched.
秀弓待射	We draw our bows and wait to shoot.
麋豕孔庶	The tailed-deer and wild boars are ever so numerous;
麀鹿雉兔	Stags and hinds, pheasants and hares.
其 . . . 又申	Their [flight] is helter-skelter;
其 . . . 趨大	Their [movement?] is flurried and X.
. . . 出各亞	. . . coming out, approach (?) . . .
. . . 畀 . . .	. . . tire? . . .
執而勿弞	Grasping [the bows] they vigorously shoot.
多庶趢趢	The throngs [of hunters and footmen] go romping about,
君子攸樂	Where the noblemen find pleasure.

According to this poem, the "pleasure" the noblemen find resides entirely in their "vigorously shoot[ing]"; the hunt was not an exercise in morality. Read in the light of this poem, I would submit that the 從 of the Anhui manuscript of "Zouyu" should certainly be read literally as the word *cong*: "after them."

Finally, I have also had occasion earlier to discuss in some detail the poem "Qiang you ci." There we have seen that the first line of each stanza reads 牆有蒺蛭, but that the Anhui editors have stated that *jili* 蒺蛭, usually understood to be a type of small insect or vermin, is a loan character for the homophonous *jili* 蒺藜 "prickly vine." They go on to explain that *jili* 蒺藜 "prickly vine" is in turn synonymous with *ci* 茨 "star-thistle," which is the reading of the received text. Moreover, consistent with this loan interpretation, they read each of the verbs in the following lines of the first couplet of each stanza as having to do with clearing vegetation, in line with the received text, even though in the manuscript these verbs are supplied with different signifies that refer to blowing or coughing. I will not repeat the argument made earlier for the appropriateness of reading 蒺蛭 literally as vermin. Instead, while I am happy to admit that *jili* 蒺藜 "prickly vine" can certainly be understood as an appropriate metaphor for something bad, I would suggest that "vermin" might be just as good a metaphor for something vile and perhaps even untouchable.

More to the point, I would also suggest that there is no need to choose between these two metaphors. It is possible—even likely—that at some stage in the written transmission of this poem, the metaphor was written simply 疾利, which is to say without any explicit signific. Subsequent readers of the poem would have been free to supply whatever signific they determined to be appropriate in order to make sense of these two graphs. (Indeed, they would have had to supply a signific in order to make appropriate sense of the characters.) This would have been true too of anyone who might have copied the poem, especially if making use of a new or more explicit script. I would submit that it is entirely possible that one copyist—and thus also one writer of the poem (in the sense that in a manuscript culture, a copyist is also a writer, in the full sense of the word)—might have understood the metaphor to be about creepy-crawly insects, and so added an "insect" 虫 signific to both graphs, while another copyist—and thus also another writer—understood it to be about prickly vegetation, and so added a "grass" 艹 signific to both graphs. This "prickly vine" or "star-thistle" reading and writing is not necessarily more "correct" just because it happens to stand on the authority of the Mao text of the *Shi jing*, though I should hasten to add as well that neither is the "vermin" reading and writing more "correct" because it is now the earliest attested form. Nevertheless, I would submit that by too readily accepting the authority of the *Mao Shi*, the Anhui editors have missed an excellent opportunity to explore some of the contributions that the Anhui manuscript might make to our understanding of how the poetry was created and transmitted prior to the Han dynasty. Finally, with all due respect to those editors, and also to Qiu Xigui and Scott Cook, I would suggest that in interpreting unearthed manuscripts with received counterparts, the "urge to equate" is generally a more pernicious problem than the desire to "establish difference."

Having made this point, let me now turn to the second topic that I would like to address in these concluding thoughts: what the Anhui manuscript might tell us about how the *Shi* was created and transmitted prior to the Han dynasty. The *Shi* 詩 *Poetry* was certainly the most important collection of ancient literature during the pre-Qin period. Aside from its intrinsic literary value, its importance within the literary tradition of ancient China is attested by the hundreds of quotations of the poems in pre-Qin works. It is quoted over 150 times in just the *Zuo zhuan* alone, and hundreds of times more in such early sources as the *Lunyu* 論語, *Mozi* 墨子, *Mengzi* 孟子, *Xunzi* 荀子, *Li ji* 禮記, and *Lü shi Chunqiu* 呂氏春秋.[72] By no later than the Warring States period, the *Shi* was routinely cited as the first of the Six Classics. Nevertheless, over the last twenty years or so, it has become increasingly popular in the Western world to question the textual status of the *Shi* during this period. Although such doubts about the written nature of the *Shi* are by now widespread among Western scholars, there is little doubt that the driving force behind them has been Martin Kern. Beginning with his first publication concerning a poem in the *Shi jing* in the year 2000,[73] he has published a long series of studies arguing that both the original creation and subsequent transmission of the poetry owed largely—even primarily—to the oral culture of ancient China.

Probably the most authoritative statement of Kern's position is to be found in his contribution to *The Cambridge History of Chinese Literature*. One paragraph of this passage was already quoted in the introduction to this book. It bears repeating here, together with the paragraph that follows it.

> Quoting and reciting the *Poetry* was primarily a matter of oral practice. Regardless of the writings excavated from a small number of elite tombs, the manuscript culture of Warring States China must have been of limited depth and breadth. The available stationery was either too bulky (wood and bamboo) or too expensive (silk) for the extensive copying of texts and their circulation over vast distances. . . . While local writing of technical, administrative, legal, economic, military, and other matters existed in the different regions of the Warring States, the extensive circulation of the Classics probably did not depend on writing. No pre-imperial source speaks of the circulation of the Classics as writings, or of the profound difficulties involved in transcribing them among distinctly different calligraphic and orthographic regional traditions. Not one of the numerous invocations of the *Poetry* in the *Zuo Tradition* and the *Discourses of the States* mentions the use of a written text; invariably, they show the ability of memorization and free recitation—in the literary koine mentioned above—as the hallmark of education.

> In Warring States times, no particular written version of the *Poetry* (or the *Documents*) was considered primary or authoritative. Only the institutionalization of official learning (*guanxue*) at the Qin and Han imperial courts led to written versions of the Classics taught at court, especially at the Imperial Academy founded in 124bc, and called for textual stabilization and standardization. Meanwhile, the sheer amount of graphic variation combined with archaic poetic idiom of the *Poetry* would have made private reading impossible.[74]

In his most recent contribution to this topic, expanding upon his comments about early manuscripts, Kern has examined a poem in the Tsinghua University manuscript *Qi ye* 耆夜 *Toasting Qi* that contains a poem corresponding in much of its wording with the poem "Xishuai" in the received *Shi jing*, but also showing manifest differences.[75] Kern argues that the two poems could not have been produced by "a simple model of consistent visual copying from a written original."

> A simple model of consistent visual copying from a written original cannot explain why one text has more phrases than the other, why shared phrases and entire lines appear in different places in the two poems, why the two poems differ in their perspectives of speech, why they have different rhymes, why they are contextualized and historicized in different ways, and why they contain phrases and lines of entirely different content. Whatever textual practices led to the two texts we now have (and possibly numerous others we no longer have, or have yet to discover), they must have included acts beyond those performed by faithful scribes. . . . What can be ruled out for the two "Xi shuai" poems, however, is clear: there is no direct line from one version to the other where a scribe copied the former from the latter, if by "copied" we mean an attempt to reproduce an existing model with some degree of fidelity.[76]

This conclusion concerning these two poems would seem to be unproblematic. Indeed, the great majority of scholars who have written on the two poems do in fact view them as two different poems such that there would be no "consistent visual copying" from one to the other.[77]

However, when Kern goes on to say, a few pages later, "It is easy to imagine how other 'Xi shuai' poems, were they to be discovered, would likewise be different," and "If this is true of 'Xi shuai,' it will also be true of other texts in the *Poetry*,"[78] it is not so easy to agree with him. As we have seen, the Anhui manuscript does contain another "Xishuai" poem. To be sure, there are differences between the Anhui manuscript version of "Xishuai" and the received *Classic of Poetry* version of the poem: as with several other poems that we have examined, the order of stanzas is different, and there are also several words that are different in the two different texts. Nevertheless, I would submit that the Anhui manuscript version of the poem is not so different as to constitute an entirely different poem. What is more, at least one of the differences between the two versions is almost certainly the result of visual copying at some point in the course of the transmission of the text.[79]

"Xishuai" is in no way exceptional within the Anhui University manuscript of the *Classic of Poetry*. Among just the poems introduced in this essay, "Guan ju," "Huang niao," "Shuo shu," and "Qiang you ci" are also essentially the same as the corresponding poems in the received text, notwithstanding the sorts of differences just examined. There are, of course, other types of differences between the Anhui manuscript and the received text, principal among which are the different order in which the various Airs (*Feng* 風) of the states appear, as well as the sequences of poems within some of them. Different people will attribute different weight to these differences; it may be a classic "glass half full, glass half empty" question regarding the developing canonical status of the poetry or *Shi*. For me, the Anhui University manuscript shows the metaphorical glass that is the canonical status of the *Shi* to be well more than half full. However, regardless of how one might view the contents of this glass, I am certain that all future studies of the early history of the *Shi jing* will have to take account of it, and that past conclusions should be rethought in the light of it.

Part III

Manuscripts

Chapter Nine

The *Mu Tianzi Zhuan* and King Mu–Period Bronzes

The *Mu tianzi zhuan* 穆天子傳 is one of the most famous and important of all of China's unearthed texts, even if it was unearthed so long ago that it is often not treated as an unearthed text at all.[1] Describing the western journeys of King Mu of Zhou 周穆王 (r. ca. 956–918 BCE) and especially his meeting with Xiwangmu 西王母 (Western Queen Mother), it was placed—together with numerous other texts—in a tomb in the Warring States–period state of Wei 魏 (in present-day Jixian 汲縣, Henan) in the very first years of the third century BC. This tomb was then robbed in AD 279. Although the bamboo strips on which the texts were written sustained considerable damage in the course of this robbery, nevertheless a great many of them were salvaged and sent to Luoyang 洛陽, the capital of the Western Jin dynasty. The emperor, Jin Wudi 晉武帝 (r. 265–289), ordered Xun Xu 荀勖 (d. 289), the head of the imperial library, and a committee of officials under him to edit these bamboo-strip texts. The *Mu tianzi zhuan* seems to have been the first of the texts to have been completed, extant editions containing a preface written by Xun Xu himself in 282 CE, and providing a description of the editorial work done on the text.

This chapter was originally published as "The *Mu tianzi zhuan* and King Mu–Period Bronzes," *Rao Zongyi Guoxueyuan yuankan* 饒宗頤國學院院刊 1 (2014): 55–75. The present version incorporates several minor revisions.

The *Mu tianzi zhuan* quickly became known to scholars of the time; for instance, in his *Bo wu zhi* 博物志, Zhang Hua 張華 (230–300) used materials from it as historical evidence concerning the time of King Mu. Bibliographies in the standard histories of the Sui and Tang dynasties all classified the *Mu tianzi zhuan* as "Qi ju zhu" 起居注 (rising-and-sitting notes), implying that it was a sort of veritable record of King Mu's reign. However, with the advent of iconoclastic attitudes toward ancient history during the Qing dynasty, doubts began to be expressed regarding the historicity of the text, and in the *Siku quanshu* 四庫全書 the *Mu tianzi zhuan* was placed instead in the "Xiaoshuo lei" 小說類 (fiction category). The "Simplified Index" to this work said of the text: "It records events concerning King Mu of Zhou's western travels that are not seen in the classic literature and contains many discrepancies with the texts of King Mu's time, so that it seems to be a miscellaneous record of contemporary rumors that circulated. Because it included exact dates, past histories placed it among the 'rising-and-sitting notes,' but based on its contents we now put it in the fiction category."[2] Similarly, the "Comprehensive Record of the *Siku quanshu*" says of the *Mu tianzi zhuan*:

> Not only is the text extremely corrupt, but many scholars have not been very careful in reading it. For instance, for "*feng* Mozhou *yu he shui zhi yang*" 封膜畫于河水之陽 (enfeoff Mozhou on the north side of the Yellow River), seen in the second *juan*, in which Mozhou 膜畫 is of course a person's name and *feng* 封 means "to enfeoff," Zhang Yanyuan 張彥遠 in his *Lidai minghua ji* 歷代名畫記 *Record of Famous Paintings through the Ages* mistakenly read *zhou* 書 as *hua* 畫, and then further mistook *feng mo* 封膜 to be the name of the ancestor of painters.[3]

After the *Siku quanshu* editors published this negative assessment, the received wisdom has been that the *Mu tianzi zhuan* has no historical value, at most providing a bit of information concerning Warring States–period literature and mythology.[4] Despite this, the twentieth century brought numerous archaeological discoveries, including actual bronze vessels from the time of King Mu of Zhou, the inscriptions on which mention the names of some of his important officials. When historians compared the information in these inscriptions with that in the *Mu tianzi zhuan*, they discovered that some of these names matched. The first scholar to compare the *Mu tianzi zhuan* with bronze inscriptions was probably Yu Xingwu 于省吾 (1896–1984), who in 1937 published an article entitled "*Mu tianzi zhuan* xinzheng" 穆天子傳新證 "New Evidence for the *Mu tianzi zhuan*." In this article, Yu pointed out that the figure Jing Li 井利 seen in the text should be read as Xing Li 邢利, and that in bronze inscriptions the name Xing 邢 is always written as Jing 井.[5] Moreover, with respect to the record "*ming* Mao Ban Feng Gu xian *zhi yu* Zhou" 命毛班逢固先至于周 "commanded Mao Ban and Feng Gu to arrive first in Zhou," Yu cited several passages in the Western Zhou bronze vessel *Ban gui* 班簋 to argue that Mao Ban "was a person of the time of King Mu, whereas Guo Moruo 郭沫若 and Wu Qichang 吳其昌 have both been mistaken in dating the *Ban gui* to the time of King Cheng."[6] After this, both Yang Shuda 楊樹達 (1885–1956) and Tang Lan 唐蘭 (1901–1979) provided more detailed discussions of the *Ban gui* inscription and of its implications for the authenticity of the *Mu tianzi zhuan*. Yang Shuda said: "Past scholars have viewed the *Mu tianzi zhuan* as fiction, and have said that its records are nonsensical and not to be believed, but now seeing that names in it are also seen in bronze inscriptions, there must be some basis for the book and it cannot be entirely groundless."[7] Tang Lan added: "Although [the *Mu tianzi zhuan*] contains exaggerations and the date of its composition is rather late, still other than the single chapter concerning Sheng Ji 盛姬, it generally has a historical basis and can be corroborated by this *gui* vessel."[8] Given these assessments, the *Mu tianzi zhuan* would seem to be something of a historiographical enigma: on the one hand, its date of composition is "rather late" and it is filled with records that are "nonsensical and not to be believed" and "exaggerations"; on the other hand, some of its content is not altogether without historical basis. As an unearthed document in its own right, the date that the *Mu tianzi zhuan* was copied is probably not in question: it was doubtless about 300 BC or slightly earlier, just before it was put into the tomb. However, the date and nature of the text's original composition still need to be clarified. I hope in the future to be able to devote a comprehensive study to these questions.[9] For present purposes, however, I will be able only to extend the work of Yu Xingwu, Yang Shuda, Tang Lan, and other scholars in examining the names in the text and comparing them with names seen in King Mu–period bronze inscriptions.

The identification of the "Mao Ban" 毛班 in the *Mu tianzi zhuan* with the Mao Ban of the *Ban gui* is by now accepted by virtually all scholars of Western Zhou bronze inscriptions, and would seem to require no further elaboration. However, there has recently surfaced some new evidence to consider in conjunction with this name. Aside from the *Mu tianzi zhuan*, the name of Mao Ban or Ban, Duke of Mao 毛公班, was also contained in another traditional text, but because of a textual corruption and other reasons its reading was never clear. At the end of 2010, the Research and Conservation Center for Unearthed Texts of Tsinghua University published the first volume of the Warring States bamboo-strip texts in its collection. Among the texts included in this volume was the *Zhai Gong zhi gu ming* 祭公之顧命 *Retrospective Command of the Duke of Zhai*, which corresponds to the "Zhai Gong" 祭公 "Duke of Zhai" chapter of the *Yi Zhou shu* 逸周書 *Leftover Zhou Scriptures*. The most important discovery in the bamboo-strip text is its mention of the "three dukes" (*san gong* 三公): Bi Huan 畢䮨 and Jing Li 井利, in addition to Mao Ban 毛班.

Whether as the *Zhai Gong zhi gu ming* or the "Zhai Gong," the text purports to be the last will and testament of Moufu Duke of Zhai 祭公謀父, a senior minister to King Mu of Zhou, presented to King Mu while the duke was on his deathbed. In the manuscript, the passage in question reads:

公懋拜＿頴＿曰允哉乚乃召䮨䮨 乚萊利毛班乚曰三公懋父朕疾惟不瘳敢告天子

The duke earnestly saluted with his hands and touched his head to the ground, saying: "Truly, indeed," and then summoned Bi Huan, Jing Li and Mao Ban, saying: "Three dukes, as for Moufu, my illness being incurable, I dare to report to the Son of Heaven."[10]

In the "Zhai Gong" chapter, on the other hand, the corresponding passage reads:

祭公拜手稽首，曰："允乃詔畢桓于黎民般"。公曰："天子，謀父疾維不瘳，敢告天子。"

The Duke of Zhai saluted with his hands and touched his head to the ground, saying: "True is your summons, entirely to bring about wholeness in the common people's service." The duke said: "Son of Heaven, Moufu's illness being incurable, I dare to report to the Son of Heaven."

Traditional readers of the "Zhai Gong" text had no way of understanding the meaning of the six characters *bi huan yu li min ban* 畢桓于黎民般, translated here as "entirely to bring about wholeness in the common people's service" in line with the explanation given by Kong Chao 孔 晁 (fl. 265 CE), the earliest commentator on the *Yi Zhou shu*:

般，樂也。言信如王告盡治民樂政也

Ban is "to enjoy"; it means it is really as the king has reported "completely to rule the people and to enjoy the government."

Kong Chao seems to have understood the *bi* 畢 of the passage as an adverb, meaning "completely" (expressed in his comment as *jin* 盡), *li* 黎 as a verb meaning "to rule" (*zhi* 治), and *ban* 般 as "to enjoy" (*le* 樂). This could only be regarded as nothing more than a guess on his part, but based on the passage as found in the received text there is probably no better reading. With the publication of the *Zhai Gong zhi gu ming* manuscript, we find that these six characters originally read *bi huan jing li mao ban* 繹䢜㭟利毛班. In the course of the text's transmission, the passage—and especially its last four characters—has been miscopied to such an extent that there is almost no way to recognize it as the same text. The character *jing* 㭟 was doubtless first simplified as *jing* 井, and then must have been subsequently miscopied as *yu* 于; whereas the character *li* 利 must have been elaborated as *li* 黎; *mao* 毛 miscopied as the graphically similar *min* 民; and *ban* 班 read as a phonetic loan for *ban* 般. The four characters *jing li mao ban* 㭟利毛班 of the bamboo-strip text are relatively easy to understand as two names, as the Tsinghua editors have pointed out; Jing Li and Mao Ban are the names of two important officials at the time of King Mu, both of their names appearing in bronze inscriptions of that period. If we examine the text of the bamboo strip further, we see that there is a punctuation mark (𠃊) added after the preceding two characters 繹䢜, indicating that these two characters should be read separately from the following characters. Moreover, the following sentence in the manuscript mentions the "three dukes," making it clear that these two characters are almost certainly the name of another minister of King Mu, that is, Bi Huan 畢桓. It is possible that this latter name also appears in bronze inscriptions from the time of King Mu, as I will examine later in more detail.

Because of the textual corruptions in the transmission of the "Zhai Gong" chapter of the *Yi Zhou shu*, the name of King Mu's minister Mao Ban was lost from the stage of history, not to be resurrected again until Yu Xingwu read the *Mu tianzi zhuan* together with the *Ban gui*. Now, the *Zhai Gong zhi gu ming* text links this name with that of Jing Li, which the Tsinghua editors note is a name that also "appears in Western Zhou bronze inscriptions." Chen Mengjia 陳夢家 (1911–1966) had already suggested this in connection with the *Mu tianzi zhuan*. In the new edition of his *Xi Zhou tongqi duandai* 西周銅器斷代 *The Periodization of Western Zhou Bronzes*, he pointed out with respect to the *Li ding* 利鼎 (*Jicheng* 2804): "The patron of this vessel is perhaps none other than the Jing Li of the *Mu tianzi zhuan*, though this is a point that still requires further verification."[11] The inscription of the *Li ding* 利鼎 (*Jicheng* 2804) reads as follows:

> 唯王九月丁亥，王客于般宮。丼白內右利立中廷北鄉。王乎乍命內史冊命利曰：易女赤市、旂，用事。利拜首，對揚天子不顯皇休，用作朕文考白鼎，利其萬年子孫永寶用。

> It was the ninth month, *dinghai* (day 24), the king entered into the Ban Palace. Jing Bo entered at the right of Li and stood in the central courtyard facing north. The king called out to the Maker of Commands the Interior Secretary to command Li in writing, saying: "I award you red kneepads, a bridle and pennant; use them to serve." Li bowed and touched his head to the ground, daring to respond to the Son of Heaven's illustriously august beneficence, herewith making for my deceased-father Zi Bo this offertory caldron; may Li for ten thousand years have sons and grandsons eternally to treasure and use it.

Because the inscription mentions "Jing Bo" 丼白 as the court guarantor (the so-called *youzhe* 右者), most scholars have assumed that this vessel should be dated to the mid-Western Zhou period, the time when Jing Bo was the most prominent official at the royal court. Although a vessel bearing the same inscription that has recently surfaced in the Historical Museum of Capital Normal University has a standard late Western Zhou vessel shape making it unlikely that the vessel could date as early as the reign of King Mu,[12] Li Xueqin subsequently published a more positive discussion of this question. In his article "The *Mu Gong gui gai*-cover and Its Significance for the Periodization of Bronze Vessels," Li first transcribed one unclear character in the inscription on the *Mu Gong gui gai* 穆公簋蓋 (*Jicheng* 4191) as *li* 利 (the entire sentence thus reading *wang hu Zai Li ci Mu Gong bei nian peng* 王乎宰利易穆公貝廿朋, "the king called out to Steward Li to award Mu Gong twenty strands of cowries"), and then went on to provide the following extended discussion of this name:

> Among the bamboo texts discovered in the Western Jin at the Ji Tomb is the received version of the *Mu tianzi zhuan* (including what the "Shu Xi zhuan" 束皙傳 of the *Jin shu* 晉書 refers to as "Zhou Mu wang meiren Sheng Ji si shi" 周穆王美人盛姬死事 (The Death of King Mu of Zhou's Beauty Sheng Ji), in which are mentioned such different individuals as Mao Ban 毛班, Jing Li 井利 and Feng Gu 逢固. Mao Ban was a real historical figure, as has already been demonstrated by the King Mu–period bronze vessel *Ban gui*, so that even though the *Mu tianzi zhuan* has some mythological flavor, it is not entirely imaginary. Jing Li was also an important official at the time of King Mu. According to the *Mu tianzi zhuan*, he and Feng Gu "commanded the six armies."

Comparing the sixth chapter of the *Mu tianzi zhuan* with the *Zhou li* 周禮 *Rites of Zhou*, it is clear that Jing Li's office was that of *zai* 宰 "Steward." The *Zhou li* mentions a *da zai* 大宰 "Great Steward," *xiao zai* 小宰 "Minor Steward," and *zaifu* 宰夫 "Steward," which in other texts are all called simply "steward." The description given for the responsibility of "Steward" states: "In all of the textual matters of state, he handles the admonishments as well as the furnishings and implements, in all cases making them available. For great and minor funerals, he handles the admonishments for the minor officers, and is in charge of performances. At the funerals of the Three Dukes and Six Ministers as well as those of officials, he is in charge of the officers and supervisors." The commentary of Zheng Xuan 鄭玄 states: "'Great funerals' are those of the king, queen, and heir apparent. 'Minor funerals' are for consorts and lower. 'Minor offices' are of the 'sire' rank, while for 'great offices' the Chief Steward handles the admonishments." Chapter 6 of the *Mu tianzi zhuan* records the funeral of King Mu's consort, who had gone with the king on a procession but caught a cold and died. The funeral was presided over by the crown prince Yi Hu 伊扈 (the future King Gong) as the master-of-mourning, with the king's eldest daughter as the mistress-of-ceremony. After the ritual wailing, the master-of-mourning Yi Hu came out of the shed crying, with his family members and kinsmen, as well as all present following him. Those in attendance wailed and then cleared away the food and serving implements. All of the officers each attended to his task, all wailing in exit. Jing Li managed the affair, leaving last and gathering all together. The commentary of Guo Pu 郭璞 says: "The reason that Jing Li was the last to leave by himself is because he was in charge of all of the funerary goods and needed to collect them. Someone has said that Jing Li was dilatory and out of rank in his exit, and therefore was put in fetters." At the time of the burial, King Mu commanded that the "burial rules for a queen were to be observed," and "before and after the funeral and among all the mourners, Jing Li was in charge of bells and flags and all of the accoutrements." From King Mu on down, everyone gave presents and "Jing Li then accepted them," which is to say that he placed the presented items into the tomb. These records suggest that the role played by Jing Li in the funeral was at the head of the supervisors and that he was in charge of the funerary goods, perfectly consistent with the responsibilities of the steward. For this reason, Steward Li in the inscription on the *Mu Gong gui gai* is very possibly the Jing Li of the text.[13]

Professor Li's discussion is very suggestive. The *Mu Gong gui gai* 穆公簋蓋 (*Jicheng* 4191) is without question a vessel of King Mu's reign, and so if the inscription did mention Jing Li as steward it would be very important information.[14] However, this too is by no means certain. Not only is the steward's lineage name (i.e., Jing 井) not given, but what is more Professor Li's transcription of his name, 🗌, as *li* 利 is perhaps open to question.[15] Thus, suggestive as it is, Professor Li's argument must remain inconclusive, at least in this regard. Nevertheless, elsewhere in his article he mentions another inscription, on the *Shi Ju fangyi* 師遽方彝 (*Jicheng* 9897), which does in fact mention a "Steward Li," and for which the characters are not at all in doubt. The inscription reads:

隹正月既生霸丁酉，王才周康寢，鄉醴。師遽蔑曆，侑。王乎宰利易師遽圭一、環章四。師遽拜頴首，敢對揚天子不顯休，用乍文且它公寶彝，用匄萬年無彊，百世孫子永寶。

> It was the first month, after the growing brightness, *dingyou* (day 34), the king was at the Kang Dormitory in Zhou, feasting wine. Captain Ju was praised for his accomplishments and attended. The king called out to Steward Li to award Captain Ju a jade scepter and four jade tablets. Captain Ju bows and touches his head to the ground, daring in response to extol the Son of Heaven's illustrious beneficence, herewith making for Ancestor Ta Gong this treasured offertory vessel, with which to entreat ten thousand years without limit, and a hundred generations of descendants eternally to treasure it.

Although "Li" here is again only a personal name and there is no way to be sure what lineage he belonged to, since this vessel was certainly cast at the time of King Mu, and indeed it is probably even possible to say that it was cast early in his reign, therefore just as Professor Li Xueqin has argued, it is quite likely that Steward Li is none other than the Jing Li of the *Mu tianzi zhuan*. In this way, of the three names mentioned in the *Zhai Gong zhi gu ming* text, at least "Jing Li" and "Mao Ban" are "seen in Western Zhou bronze inscriptions," just as the Tsinghua editors of *Zhai Gong zhi gu ming* have suggested.

Although there is no way to be sure that the first of the three names in *Zhai Gong zhi gu ming*, Bi Huan, is similarly attested in Western Zhou bronze inscriptions, the Tsinghua editors state cautiously, "The *Mu tianzi zhuan* also has a Bi Ju, but we do not know whether he is to be related with this Bi Huan."[16] By this, they seem to be referring to the following passage, found in chapter 4 of that text:

己巳，至于文山，西膜之所謂囗。觴天子于文山。西膜之人乃獻食馬三百、牛羊二千、穄米千車。天子使畢矩受之，曰：囗天子三日游于文山。於是取采石。

> On *dingsi* (day 54), arriving at Mount Wen, which in the western regions is called. . . . They feasted the Son of Heaven on Mount Wen. The men of the western region then presented three hundred feed horses, two thousand cows and sheep, and a thousand cartloads of grain. The Son of Heaven sent Bi Ju to accept them, saying: . . . Son of Heaven for three days traveled on Mount Wen, there collecting colored stones.[17]

In fact, this Bi Huan, written as 䢅䮃 in the Tsinghua manuscript, very possibly refers to the same person as the Bi Ju 畢矩 of the *Mu tianzi zhuan*. The lower right-hand element of 䢅 is *bi* 畢, and should be the main component of this character, which is to say that the other components are mere elaborations or decorations. "Bi" was an important lineage in the Western Zhou period, often seen in contemporary bronze inscriptions. Among just mid-Western Zhou period, members of the Bi lineage are mentioned in inscriptions on several vessels, including one, the *Wang gui* 壅簋, which refers to the "Bi royal family" 畢王家.[18] It is clear that the Bi lineage and the Zhou royal house had a very close relationship. It is also possible to show a connection between the names given in the two sources: Huan 䮃 in the Tsinghua manuscript and Ju 矩 in the *Mu tianzi zhuan*. Although the "bird" signific (i.e., 鳥) of 䮃 and the "arrow" signific (i.e., 矢) of 矩 seem to be very different, in the received text of the "Zhai Gong" chapter the corresponding character is written as *huan* 桓, which is to say with a "wood" signific (i.e., 木); an "arrow" signific and a "wood" signific can be easily mistaken.[19] As for the difference between 亘 and 巨, the two right-hand components, they are so close in form that if they are not two different transcriptions of the same archaic character, then they may simply be a later scribal corruption.[20]

In addition to the three names discussed earlier, the "Zhai Gong" text, whether the chapter of the *Yi Zhou shu* or the Tsinghua manuscript version, also supplies one other bit of extremely important information concerning the officials mentioned in the *Mu tianzi zhuan* and especially their relationship with King Mu–period bronze inscriptions. However, once again because of problems involved with the transmission of the text and the decipherment of bronze inscriptions, until recently this information has also been overlooked by scholars. This information concerns the main figure mentioned in the text: Moufu, the Duke of Zhai 祭公謀父. The Duke of Zhai is also mentioned several times in the *Mu tianzi zhuan*, even though his lineage name is written as *kui* 郊 rather than *zhai* 祭, and his personal name is not recorded. However, as the *Mu tianzi zhuan*'s earliest commentator, Guo Pu 郭璞 (276–324 CE), had already pointed out, Kuifu 郊父 is almost certainly none other than Zhai Gong Moufu, whom Guo Pu further identified as the author of the *Shi jing* 詩經 poem "Qi zhao" 祈招.[21] The Duke of Zhai is also well known from other texts, including the *Zuo zhuan* 左傳 *Zuo Tradition* and the *Guo yu* 國語 *Stories of the States*. In the *Zuo zhuan* (twelfth year of Lord Zhao 昭公), we read: "In the past when King Mu wanted to expand his desires and travel throughout the world, so that his wagon tracks and horse prints would be found everywhere, Moufu, the Duke of Zhai, wrote the poem 'Qi zhao' in order to put a brake on the king's desires." Elsewhere in the same text, at the twenty-fourth year of Lord Xi 僖公, where it records that "Zhai was descended from the Duke of Zhou" (祭周公之允也), and at the first year of Lord Yin 隱公, where it says that "Zhai the Elder came" (祭伯來), the commentary by Du Yu 杜預 (222–284 CE) reads: "Zhai was a lineage with the rank of royal official of the state level" (祭國伯爵諸侯王卿士者). The "Junguo zhi" 郡國志 "Record of Commanderies and States" of the *Han shu* 漢書 states:

中牟有蔡亭，即祭伯國，在今鄭州東北十五里，蓋圻內之國家也。

In Zhongmou, there is a Cai Pavilion, which is from the state of Zhai the Elder; it is fifteen *li* northeast of present-day Zhengzhou, a state within the territory of Qi.

The *Zhushu jinian* 竹書紀年 *Bamboo Annals*, which was discovered in the same tomb as the *Mu tianzi zhuan*, not only contains records of Moufu, the Duke of Zhai, but also mentions another Duke of Zhai 祭公 as an official of the preceding King Zhao. The record for the nineteenth year of King Zhao states, "The Duke of Zhai and Xin Bo followed the king to attack to Chu" (祭公辛伯從王伐楚), to which the Qing dynasty commentator Lei Xueqi 雷學淇 (*jinshi* 1814) remarked: "This Duke of Zhai, who was a younger brother of Bo Qin 伯禽, drowned together with the king in the Han River; his son was Moufu, and King Mu referred to him as his Ancestor Duke of Zhai."[22]

While all of this shows beyond doubt that the Duke of Zhai was an important official of King Mu, until about ten years ago it had seemed that his name was unknown in Western Zhou bronze inscriptions. However, in 1998 new evidence surfaced when the Guodian 郭店 manuscripts were published. Among these texts was the *Zi yi* 緇衣 *Black Jacket*, which quotes the following passage from the *Zhai Gong zhi gu ming*:

叡公之顧命曰毋以小謀敗大圖，毋以卑御人疾莊後，毋以卑御士息士大夫卿士

The Duke of Zhai's Retrospective Command states: "Do not use petty . . . to defeat great . . . , do not use favored consorts to pain the queen, and do not use favored comrades to trouble the officers and ministers.²³

Shortly after this text was made public, Li Xueqin published an article entitled "Explaining the Guodian Bamboo-Text *Zhai Gong zhi gu ming*," in which he pointed out that the graph ▨ should in fact be read as *zhai* 祭.²⁴ More than this, Professor Li also related this graph to the graph ▨ seen in Western Zhou bronze inscriptions. This graph, seen for instance in the *Hou Chuo fangding* 厚趠方鼎 (*Jichen* 2730) and *Lüe ding* 寽鼎 (*Jicheng* 2740) inscriptions, was previously generally transcribed as *lian* 溓, but it would seem that Professor Li's new transcription as *zhai* is certainly correct. These inscriptions read as follows:

隹王來各于成周年，厚趠又于 公。趠用乍氒文考父辛寶，其子子孫永寶。束

It was the year that the king came from entering into Chengzhou; Hou Chuo was rewarded by the Duke of Zhai. Hou Chuo makes for his cultured deceased-father Xin this treasured offertory caldron; may sons' sons and grandsons eternally treasure it. Clan sign

隹王伐東尸， 公令寽眔史旅曰： 以師氏眔有司後國栽伐貊。孚貝， 用乍饗公寶鼎。

It was when the king attacked the eastern Yi; the Duke of Zhai commanded Lüe and Secretary Lü saying: "Take the Captains of the Guards and the supervisors of the rear countries to hit and attack Mo." Lüe captured cowries, and Lüe herewith makes for Lord Yuan this treasured offertory caldron.

These two vessels both seem to date to about the time of King Kang or King Zhao, and it would seem from the *Lüe ding* inscription that the Duke of Zhai was a commander of the Zhou army, in line with the record in the *Zhushu jinian* that a Duke of Zhai was a lieutenant of King Zhao in his attack on Chu; from this, it seems quite possible that these two Dukes of Zhai refer to one and the same person. Of course, this is not direct bronze inscriptional evidence for the King Mu–period official Moufu, Duke of Zhai. However, since Moufu was only one generation removed from this evidence, it should at least corroborate that this name recorded in the *Zhushu jinian* was in fact an important personage of the reign of King Mu.

There can be little doubt that all of these figures mentioned in the *Mu tianzi zhuan* are also seen in Western Zhou bronze inscriptions. In addition to these important officers, there is another name that appears several times in the *Mu tianzi zhuan*, either as Feng Gu 逢固 or Feng Gong 逢公. In his article on the *Mu Gong gui gai* quoted earlier, Li Xueqin already mentioned this figure. The name appears in chapters 2, 4, and 5 of the *Mu tianzi zhuan*:

> 辛巳，入于曹奴之人戲，觴天子于洋水之上，乃獻食馬九百，牛羊七千，穋米百車。天子使逢固受之。

On *xinsi* (day 18), we entered into the Caonu people's games, and they feasted the Son of Heaven on the bank of the Yang River, and then contributed nine hundred feed horses, seven thousand cattle and sheep, and one hundred cartloads of grain. The Son of Heaven sent Feng Gu to receive them.[25]

> 丙寅，天子至于鈃山之隊，東升于三道之隥，乃宿于二邊，命毛班、逢固先至于周，以待天子之命。

On *bingyin* (day 3), the Son of Heaven arrived at the ridge of Jian Mountain, and climbed eastwardly to the ascent of the Three Roads and then camped at the Two Sides, commanding Mao Ban and Feng Gu to arrive first at Zhou in order to await the Son of Heaven's command.[26]

> 天子筮獵苹澤，其卦遇訟，逢公占之，曰：訟之繇，藪澤蒼蒼，其中□，宜其正公。戎事則從，祭祀則喜，畋獵則獲。□飲逢公酒，賜之駿馬十六，絺紵三十篋。逢公再拜稽首。

The Son of Heaven divined about hunting at Duckweed Marsh, the result met with being *Song* hexagram. Feng Gong prognosticated it, saying: "*Song*'s oracle is: 'Duckweed swamp is so verdant, It's midst so. . . . Appropriate for the upright duke.' Military affairs will be accordant, sacrifices will be happy, and hunts will have catches." . . . toasted Feng Gong with liquor, and awarded him sixteen fine horses and thirty cases of fine gauze. Feng Gong bowed twice and touched his head to the ground.[27]

It is also possible that this "Feng Gu" is also to be seen in a King Mu–period bronze inscription, though the evidence is admittedly less certain than in the other cases. The Shanghai Museum has in its collection a vessel that Chen Peifen 陳佩芬 refers to as *Feng Mofu you* 夆莫父卣 (*Jicheng* 5245), which she says is a "mid-Western Zhou vessel."[28] The vessel's most striking feature is the recumbent long-tailed birds filling the entirety of both the vessel and its lid. As Ms. Chen points out, this feature "mainly belongs to the period of Kings Mu and Gong, so that this *you*-bucket should also belong to this period, more or less at the beginning of the mid-Western Zhou period." This *Feng Mofu you* shows at least that there was a Feng 夆 (i.e., 逢) lineage active at the time of King Mu.[29]

Before closing I would like to offer one more piece of evidence connecting the *Mu tianzi zhuan* with King Mu–period Western Zhou bronzes. This evidence was unearthed only in 2004–2005, when archaeologists excavated a very large cemetery in Hengbei 橫北 Village, Jiangxian 絳縣, Shanxi.[30] In tombs M1 and M2 of this cemetery they found inscribed bronze vessels commissioned by a Peng Bo 倗伯. The following two vessels are fairly representative:

Pengbo zuo Bi Ji ding 倗伯作畢姬尊鼎

倗伯作畢姬尊鼎，其萬年寶。

Peng the Elder makes for Bi Ji this offertory caldron; may for ten thousand years it be treasured.

Peng Bo Cheng gui 倗伯偁簋

隹廿又三年初吉戊戌，益公蔑倗伯偁曆。右告令金車旂。偁拜手稽首，對揚公休，用作朕考寶尊。偁其萬年永寶用享。

It is the twenty-third year, first auspiciousness, *wuxu* (day 55); Yi Gong praised Peng Bo Cheng's accomplishments, and also reported to command him a bronze chariot and pennant.

Cheng salutes with his hands and touches his head to the ground, in response extolling the duke's beneficence, herewith making for my deceased-father this treasured *zun*-vase. May Cheng for ten thousand years eternally treasure and use it to make offerings.

The archaeologists dated these bronzes to the time of King Mu, a dating that seems to be at least generally accurate. On the other hand, they suggested that this Peng 倗 was unknown in the traditional literary record, which seems not to be accurate. Li Xueqin soon pointed out that this name should correspond to the place-name Peng 鄌 seen in the *Mu tianzi zhuan*.[31] The name appears already in chapter 1 of that text:

> 辛丑，天子西征至于鄌。河宗之子孫栢絮且逆天子于智之□，先豹皮十、良馬二六。天子使井利受之。癸酉，天子舍于漆澤，乃西釣于河，以觀□智之□。 . . . 天子飲于河水之阿。天子屬六師之人于鄌邦之南、滲澤之上。

On *xinchou* (day 38), the Son of Heaven campaigned, arriving at Peng. Peng Bo Zhao, the descendant of the River Ancestor, met the Son of Heaven at Zhi's . . . , ten leopard skins and twelve fine horses. The Son of Heaven sent Jing Li to accept them. On *guiyou* (day 10), the Son of Heaven resided at Poison Oak Marsh, and then to the west of it went fishing in the River, in order to view . . . Zhi's . . . The Son of Heaven toasted at the bluff over the River's water. The Son of Heaven assembled the men of the six armies at the Oozing Marsh to the south of Peng country.[32]

This passage follows immediately after entries mentioning that the "Son of Heaven campaigned northward and then cut across the Zhang 漳 River," that he "arrived at the foot of Jian 鈃 Mountain," and that the "Son of Heaven campaigned westward and then cut across the ascent at Yu 隃 Pass." Professor Li has pointed out that based on these locations, the *Mu tianzi zhuan*'s Peng 鄌, composed as it is of "mountain" 山 and "city" 邑 components with the phonetic *peng* 朋, should be the same place as the Peng 倗 state mentioned in bronzes from Jiangxian, which also features the *peng* 朋 phonetic.[33] From the inscription on the *Peng Bo zuo Bi Ji ding*, it is clear that Peng Bo was married to a woman of the Bi 畢 lineage, the same lineage as the Bi Huan of the Tsinghua *Zhai Gong zhi gu ming* manuscript or the Bi Ju of elsewhere in the *Mu tianzi zhuan*. This inscription also shows that the Bi lineage was part of the royal Ji 姬 family, attesting to a likely close relationship between Peng and the Zhou king. The inscription on the *Peng Bo Cheng gui* shows that Peng Bo Cheng received an award from the important royal official Yi Gong 益公. This is all consistent with the *Mu tianzi zhuan*'s narrative concerning King Mu's visit to Peng, such that it would seem that this record too cannot possibly be entirely fictional.

Conclusion

At the beginning of this chapter, I pointed out that the *Mu tianzi zhuan* seems to be a historiographical enigma: on the one hand, its contents are "nonsensical and not to be believed" and full of "exaggerations," such that it seems to be a *chuanqi* 傳奇 "legendary" sort of text from the Warring States period, but on the other hand its contents are not at all without historical basis. Having compared several of the names that appear in the *Mu tianzi zhuan* with names of royal officials that appear in bronze inscriptions from the time of King Mu, we have seen that it is by no means the case that only the name Mao Ban appears in both; in fact, these two different sources share at least three or four other names in common. While it is certainly not impossible that the legend of a single such official could have been transmitted through six or seven centuries, it is hard to imagine that a cluster of four or five such names could have been remembered—all together—over such a long period. It seems that we have to conclude that the core of this text should be traced back to some sort of contemporary source in the Western Zhou period. What this source may have been and how it may have been transmitted to the Warring States period are important questions that remain to be answered.

Chapter Ten

The Tsinghua Manuscript *Zheng Wen Gong wen Tai Bo and the Question of the Production of Manuscripts in Early China

In 2016, the Tsinghua University Research and Conservation Center for Unearthed Texts published the sixth volume of Warring States bamboo slips in its collection, with five new texts in six manuscripts.[1] Three of these texts concern the early history of the state of Zheng 鄭: *Zheng Wu furen gui ruzi 鄭武夫人規孺子 *Duke Wu's Wife's Admonition for the Heir Apparent*, two versions of *Zheng Wen Gong wen Tai Bo 鄭文公問太伯 *Duke Wen of Zheng Asks Tai Bo*, and *Zi Chan 子產. The other two texts are *Guan Zhong 管仲, a dialogue between Duke Huan of Qi 齊桓公 (r. 685–643 BCE) and his celebrated minister Guan Zhong 管仲, in which Guan Zhong elaborates on his political philosophy; and *Zi Yi 子儀, which concerns the Chu 楚 emissary Zi Yi 子儀 and his return to Chu from Qin 秦 after the Qin war with Jin 晉 during the reign of Duke Mu of Qin 秦穆公 (r. 659–621 BCE). All five of these texts present important new information concerning the history of the early

---

This chapter was originally published in Chinese as "Zheng Wen Gong wen Taibo yu Zhongguo gudai wenxian chaoxie de wenti" 《鄭文公問太伯》與中國古代文獻抄寫的問, *Jianbo* 簡帛 14 (2017): 11–15; the English translation, by the author, was published as "The Tsinghua Manuscript *Zheng Wen Gong wen Taibo and the Question of the Production of Manuscripts in Early China," *Bamboo and Silk* 3 (2020): 54–73. It is reprinted here with only minimal changes.

Spring and Autumn period, and each one will surely command scholarly attention in the coming years.² Of these texts, *Zheng Wen Gong wen Tai Bo is unique in being available in two separate manuscripts that were copied by a single scribe on the basis of two different source texts. As the editor of this text, Ma Nan 馬楠, notes, this is the first time we have seen such evidence of scribal practice, and it is crucial for the question of manuscript production in early China. In the present study, I will first describe these two manuscript versions of *Zheng Wen Gong wen Tai Bo, and then I will go on to consider their implications for the question of manuscript production in ancient China. Transcriptions of the two manuscripts as well as a consolidated translation of the text is included in the appendix to the chapter.³

*Zheng Wen Gong wen Tai Bo exists in two copies that are extremely similar, but which also reveal important differences. The Tsinghua editors refer to these two different manuscripts as Jia 甲 and Yi 乙, which I will translate here as manuscripts A and B. Manuscript A consists of fourteen bamboo slips 45 cm long by .06 cm wide; slip 3 is broken, with only the bottom half of the slip surviving. Other slips also show some damage,⁴ but in general the manuscript is very well preserved. Manuscript B must have originally consisted of twelve bamboo slips, though only eleven survive. These slips are also 45 cm long by .06 cm wide. Slip 3 is missing, and slips 2 and 4 are both broken in the middle with only the bottom halves surviving. The very top portions of slips 1, 9, and 12 are also broken, in the case of slip 1 with the loss of one character and in the cases of slips 9 and 12 probably two or three characters. Both manuscripts were bound with three binding straps. Although the editor does not provide measurements for the placement of these binding straps, the photographs indicate that the top strap was at about 3.5 cm from the top, just above the place of the topmost character; the middle strap at 22.5 cm, with space left for the binding strap to pass without covering a character; and the bottom strap at 3.5 cm from the bottom, just below the bottom character of the slip. Only a few notches to secure the binding straps are visible in the photographs, but they do appear on both manuscripts in the expected positions. Both manuscripts also make use of punctuation marks, though sparingly: the standard duplication marks for both repeating characters (chongwen 重文) and combined characters (hewen 合文); a black dot after the character ci 宩 on slip 2 and a similar black dot following the character ye 也 on slip 9 of manuscript A, as well as a similar black dot after the character chu 出 (and, perhaps more important, before the character *ze* 則) on slip 11 of manuscript B; and both manuscripts end with the standard 乙-shaped hook mark that routinely marks the end of a text. Both manuscripts also show evidence of proofreading, with characters added between graphs in three different places of manuscript A and in one place of manuscript B, as well as one apparently mistaken character blacked out on manuscript A.[5] Neither manuscript bears a title (the title having been given by the editors), nor are the slips numbered.

The manuscript purports to report a conversation between Duke Wen of Zheng 鄭文公 (r. 672–628 BCE) and a Tai Bo 太伯, the identification of whom is not certain.[6] However, since Tai Bo is portrayed as being on his deathbed and offering advice to the newly installed duke, he must certainly have been an elderly statesman of Zheng. Duke Wen was the son of Duke Li of Zheng 鄭厲公 (r. 701–697, 680–673), whose own succession to power had been quite problematic, as his dates of reign suggest. Duke Li was a younger son of Duke Zhuang of Zheng 鄭莊公 (r. 743–701 BCE) by a secondary consort. When Duke Zhuang died, he was initially succeeded by the eldest son, Duke Zhao 鄭昭公 (r. 701, 697–695 BCE). Duke Zhao was quickly deposed by Zhai Zhong 祭仲, the main power in the state of Zheng, in favor of Duke Li. However, when a few years later Duke Li's attempt to wrest control from Zhai Zhong ended in failure, he was forced into exile for seventeen years, during which time the nominal ruler of Zheng was Zhengzi Ying 鄭子嬰 (r. 694–680), a younger brother of Duke Li. Zhengzi Ying was eventually assassinated, and Duke Li welcomed back to power. Thus, when Duke Li died eight years after his second assumption of power, the succession of his own son Duke Wen was by no means assured.

Tai Bo recounts events in the history of Zheng, beginning with the move east under Duke Huan of Zheng 鄭桓公 (r. 806–771 BCE[7]), and further military successes under his son Duke Wu 鄭武公 (r. 770–744 BCE), at which time Zheng was acknowledged by other states in north China as a paramount power. Even under Duke Zhuang, the state remained powerful but, as noted earlier, the succession after Duke Zhuang was extremely troubled.

Although the text *Zheng Wen Gong wen Tai Bo* does not contain a date, indications are that it pertains to an event very early after Duke Wen's succession. Early in the text of the A manuscript, Duke Wen says that it was through the support of Tai Bo that he was able to attend to his 宋, which regularly stands for the word *ci* 次, which in this context refers to the shed where a son in mourning was supposed to reside after the death of his father.⁸ That Duke Wen would then remain in power for forty-five years suggests that he must have been quite young upon his succession. During his reign, Zheng came increasingly under the influence of the state of Chu 楚. Indeed, his principal consort, a Lady Mi 芈氏, was from Chu.⁹ Tai Bo seems also to allude to this marriage, criticizing Duke Wen for losing himself in the pleasures of the harem and "enlarging his palace" (*da qi gong* 大其宮) through the aid of Chu. The final history lesson recalled by Tai Bo hearkens back to the Shang dynasty, reminding Duke Wen that whereas people still speak of the virtuous founder of the dynasty, Tang 湯 (ca. 16th c. BCE), they also still speak of Zhou 紂 (r. 1086–1045 BCE), the paradigmatically evil last king of the dynasty.

The Question of Manuscript Production in Ancient China

As previously noted, Ma Nan, the Tsinghua University editor of *Zheng Wen Gong wen Tai Bo*, has pointed out that these manuscripts mark the first evidence of a single scribe making two copies of a single text based on two different source texts. Unfortunately, she does not elaborate on this insight. In my experience, this is representative of the scholarly attitude in China, where most scholars simply assume that in antiquity manuscripts were copied as a result of visual copying from one manuscript to another. As we will see, this assumption is both reasonable and also well grounded in the available evidence. However, it is an important enough assumption to deserve fuller scrutiny. For their part, Western scholars found the topic more worthy of discussion even before there was much hard evidence with which to discuss it.

In the West, the first and still the most influential discussion of this topic was Martin Kern's "Methodological Reflections on the Analysis of Textual Variants and the Modes of Manuscript Production in Early China," published in the *Journal of East Asian Archaeology* in 2002.¹⁰ Examining variations in the way quotations of the *Shi jing* 詩經 *Classic of Poetry* were written in unearthed manuscripts, primarily from the area of the ancient state of Chu 楚, as opposed to their form in the received text, he found that as many as one-third of all characters were "graphically different but phonologically interchangeable," essentially different "spellings" of the same words.¹¹ Kern proposed three scenarios for how ancient manuscripts may have been produced: "the scribe reproduces an earlier written text in front of him and is thus able to compare his own writing to the text he is copying"; "somebody reads a text aloud to the scribe, who then writes it down"; or "the scribe writes the text from memory, or how he hears it recited without any written copy at hand."[12] The first of these scenarios is of course the scenario assumed by most Chinese scholars currently working in this field, while the second also has a long tradition behind it in China, as well as some compelling artifactual evidence.[13] Nevertheless, Kern argued that the third of these scenarios best explains the incidence of variants that he found in these manuscripts. He concluded that they were copied without recourse to a written model at hand.

> Assuming both a certain degree of script standardization and the great number of homophonous words in early Chinese, a manuscript that in two-thirds of its characters would match any of its counterparts, and that in one-third—usually in the more difficult words—would differ from it, is probably what one would expect from manuscript production not immediately based on a written model.[14]

Kern's hypothesis about manuscript production was presented within an impressive statistical framework and has been much cited in the years since it was published. For instance, Dirk Meyer has cited it in various articles, and adapted the hypothesis in his book *Philosophy on Bamboo: Text and the Production of Meaning in Early China*, published in 2012.

> When producing a new copy of a written manuscript, the scribe worked from the sound he heard, not from the graph he saw.[15]

Unfortunately, the only evidence Meyer adduced in support of this far-reaching claim is "analogy to Early European manuscript production." Fortunately, in the years between when Kern published his original study and when Meyer's book was published, there appeared both new sorts of direct evidence for the way manuscripts were produced in antiquity and also new studies by Western scholars of that and other evidence. It will be helpful for our understanding of the importance of *Zheng Wen Gong wen Tai Bo to survey some of this evidence and some of these studies.[16]

From a later period, the manuscripts discovered at Dunhuang 敦煌 in the opening years of the twentieth century of course constitute a great resource to understand how manuscripts were produced. In 2007, Christopher Nugent published a study of eight different copies of the long poem "Qin fu yin" 秦婦吟 "Lament of the Lady Qin" by Wei Zhuang 韋莊 (836–910) that were found at Dunhuang.[17] We know, or at least are pretty sure, that Wei Zhuang wrote this poem with 238 lines of seven characters each in 886. Of the eight manuscripts containing the poem found at Dunhuang, five are dated (P3381 is dated to 905, P3780 to 955 or 957, P3910 to 979, S692 to 919, and P2700+S5834 to 920). Nugent compared these eight manuscripts in two-by-two pairs. Employing much the same sort of analysis as used by Martin Kern, he concluded that "the concrete evidence from the texts primarily indicates scribes working from written sources."[18]

Two years later, Matthias L. Richter took up the same question in an essay entitled "Faithful Transmission or Creative Change: Tracing Modes of Manuscript Production from the Material Evidence."[19] Richter first examined manuscript evidence of two different texts discovered in 1973 at Mawangdui 馬王堆: the two *Xingde* 刑德 *Punishment and Virtue* texts and the two *Laozi* 老子 texts. With respect to the *Xingde* texts, in particular, he noted that Marc Kalinowski had demonstrated how a copyist's error in one of the two manuscripts was due to an eye-skip on the part of the scribe copying from the other manuscript,[20] a sure sign of visual copying. He then turned his attention to two Warring States manuscripts unearthed in the early 1990s and now housed in the Shanghai Museum: *Tianzi jian zhou* 天子建州 *The Son of Heaven Establishes the Regions*.[21] These two manuscripts, clearly written in different hands, both preserve almost exactly the same text, though the second of the two manuscripts is missing two bamboo slips. According to Richter, the first manuscript is a fair copy made from the second, "which was at some point found inadequate."[22] In support of this conclusion, he examined the forms of particular characters:

> The first peculiarity that stands out when one compares the physical appearance of this identical text in the two manuscripts is a peculiar shape and structure of the first character for the word *ye* {也}. This word occurs only four times in the entire text, and only the first time it is written with a hitherto unattested, though still easily recognisable, form of the character 也. The last stroke of 也 is as a rule written as an extra stroke. It is sometimes merged with either the right or the left downward stroke, but never is it in any way connected with the horizontal stroke as it is in the peculiar

form. Remarkably, this peculiarity occurs in both manuscripts. The scribe of one of the manuscripts could have made such a mistake. This would be odd enough, since one would expect a well-developed routine in writing one of the simplest and most frequent characters. It is even more extraordinary that the scribe of the other manuscript repeated this mistake, and both scribes wrote the character correctly in the following cases, one of them being the very next sentence. From this example alone it is impossible to decide which manuscript is the copy and which the model. But that one of them is influenced by the other seems certain.[23]

In fact, the similarity between the two manuscripts goes far beyond just the shape of this one character. Richter cites unpublished work of Daniel Morgan demonstrating in great detail that the two manuscripts "are starkly identical."[24] Not only do both manuscripts write individual characters the same ways in different places in the text, but there are also forms of writing that are unique to just these manuscripts even within Chu orthography. More important, even nonlinguistic information in the manuscripts, by which Morgan means certain calligraphic decorations and accent marks, "coincides with startling fidelity." While Morgan prefers not to speculate on which manuscript copied which, or what the ultimate source text may have looked like, his conclusion is stated with the assurance of a rich evidentiary basis: "What *is* certain, is that there can be no other explanation for these coincidences than the two MSs are connected through unbroken visual copying."[25]

With the Tsinghua *Zheng Wen Gong wen Tai Bo* manuscripts, we now have a very different situation from that of the two copies of *Tianzi jian zhou*, which were evidently copied by two different scribes, very probably one copying from the other. As Ma Nan has said, whether in terms of "page design" or of the execution of individual characters, there can be no doubt that the two manuscripts of *Zheng Wen Gong wen Tai Bo* were in fact copied by a single scribe. The evidence of this is so pervasive that one need but compare two similarly placed slips from the two manuscripts (fig. 10.1 juxtaposes slip 1 of manuscript A with slip 1 of manuscript B). Nevertheless, as Ma Nan has also pointed out, it seems likely that this scribe was copying two different source texts. This can be seen in the different writing of certain characters: for example, *gu* 穀 is written 🖿 (㝅) in A and 🖿 (敦) in B; *you* 幽 is written 孝 (學) in A and 幺 (幽) in B; *ran* 然 is written 肰 (肽) in A and 然 (然) in B; *gu* 股 is written 服 (服) in A and 胠 (胠) in B; and *tang* 唐 is written 庚 (庚) in A and 康 (康) in B, and so forth. Perhaps most tellingly, manuscript A invariably writes the "city" signific (i.e., *yi* 邑) on the left side of characters, whereas the B manuscript writes it on the right side of the same characters; the following are just three from among numerous examples:

	邟	鄙	鄫
A			
B			

This difference may reflect orthographic traditions of different states: Chu orthography consistently wrote the "city" signific on the left side of characters, while Qin 秦 orthography, at least, as well as that of Zheng, wrote it on the right.[26] Of course, it is also possible that it simply reflects the idiosyncrasies of two different individual scribes. However, it is inconceivable that a single experienced scribe, such as the scribe of these two manuscripts obviously was, would write characters differently in this way unless he was seeking to reflect a difference in his source texts.[27]

It seems to me that the *Zheng Wen Gong wen Tai Bo* manuscripts demonstrate beyond any reasonable doubt that visual copying from one manuscript to another was a customary method of manuscript production in Warring States China. Of course, we cannot conclude from this evidence that visual copying was the only method or even *the* customary method of manuscript production, nor can we rule out such other methods of manuscript production as those hypothesized by Martin Kern in 2002. However, especially given the other manuscript evidence surveyed earlier, visual copying should now be the default assumption for textual reproduction in ancient China (see fig. 10.1).

The Tsinghua Manuscript *Zheng Wen Gong wen Tai Bo | 261

Figure 10.1. Slip 1 of the two *Zheng Wen Gong wen Tai Bo 鄭文公問太伯 manuscripts. From Li Xueqin, ed. in chief, and Qinghua daxue Chutu wenxian yanjiu yu baohu zhongxin, eds., *Qinghua daxue cang Zhanguo zhujian (Lu)* (Shanghai: Zhong Xi shuju, 2016), 10, 12. Used with permission.

Appendix

*Zheng Wen Gong wen Tai Bo 鄭文公問太伯:
Transcriptions and Translation

Manuscript A	Manuscript B
子人成子既死，太伯當邑。太伯有疾，吾公往問之。君若曰：	□人成子既死，太伯當邑。太伯有疾，文公往問之。君若曰：
"伯父，不穀幽弱。閔喪﹝一﹞吾君，譬若雞雛，伯父實被複不穀，	"伯父，不穀幽弱。閔喪吾君，譬﹝一﹞□□□□□□被複不穀，以能與

以能與就次。今天為不惠，或援然，與不穀争伯父所。【二】天不豫伯父，伯父而□□□□□□□□□穀"

太伯曰："君老臣□□□□【三】毋言而不當。古之人有言曰：'為臣而不諫，譬若饋而不釀'。昔吾先君桓公後出【四】自周，以車七乘徒世人，鼓其腹心，奮其股肱，以協於庸偶。攝胄擐甲，攜戈盾以造勛，戰於魚麗，吾獲函、瞀、轅車襲介克鄶。迢迢如容社之處，亦吾先君之力也。

世及【六】吾先君武公，西城伊、澗，北就鄔、劉，縈軹蔦、邢之國。魯、衛、蓼、蔡來見。

及吾先【七】君莊公，乃東伐齊虢之戎為徹，北城溫、原，遺陰、鄂次，東啟隕、樂。吾逐王於葛。【八】

世及吾先君昭公、厲公，抑天也，其抑人也。為是牢鼠不能同穴，朝夕鬥闋，亦不逸斬【九】伐。

今及吾君，弱幽而滋長，不能慕吾先君之武徹、莊功，色淫媱于庚，獲彼荊寵，【十】為大其宮。君而狃之不善哉。君如由彼孔叔、佚之夷、師之佢鹿、堵之俞彌，是四人者，【十一】方諫吾君於外，茲詹父內謫於中，君如是之不能茅，則譬若疾之亡醫。君之亡聞也，【十二】則亦亡問也。君之亡出也，則亦亡入也。戒之哉君。吾若聞夫殷邦，庚為語而受亦【十三】為語。"【十四】

就樆。今天為不惠，或援然，與不穀請伯父所。天不豫伯父，伯父【二】..."

"...自周，以車七乘徒世人，鼓其腹心，奮其股肱，【四】以協於庸偶。攝胄擐甲，攜戈盾以造勛，戰於魚麗，吾獲函、瞀、轅車襲介克鄶。迢迢如容社【五】之處，亦吾先君之力也。

世及吾先君武公，西城伊、澗，北就鄔、劉，縈軹蔦、邢之國。魯、衛、蓼、蔡【六】來見。

及吾先君莊公，乃東伐齊虢之戎為徹，北城溫、原，遺陰、鄂次，東啟隕、樂。吾逐王於葛。【七】

世及吾先君昭公、厲公，抑天也，其抑人也。其為是牢鼠不能同穴，朝夕鬥闋，亦不逸斬伐。

今【八】□□君，弱幽而滋長，不能慕吾先君之武徹、莊功，浮淫媱于庚，獲彼荊寵，為大其宮。君而【九】狃之不善哉。君如由彼孔叔、佚之夷、師之佢鹿、堵之俞彌，是四人者，方諫吾君於外，茲詹父【十】內謫於中，君如是之不能茅，則譬若疾之亡醫。君之亡聞也，則亦亡問也。君之亡出也，則亦亡入【十一】也。□□□君。吾若聞夫殷邦，曰庚為語而受亦為語。"【十二】

Ziren Chengzi having died, Tai Bo was in charge of the city. Tai Bo being ill, Duke Wen went to ask after him. The lord said to the effect: "Father Bo, I, the Unworthy One, am young and weak. Having unhappily lost [A1] my lord when I was like [B1] a hen's chick, Father Bo was really my protector, making it possible for the Unworthy One to be able to assume place in the mourning shed.[28] Now Heaven is being unkind, now sadly battling[29] with the Unworthy One over Father Bo's place. [A2] Heaven is discomfiting Father Bo, and Father Bo [B2] then . . . [Un]worthy One." Tai Bo said: "My lord, your old servant . . . [A3] not said anything that did not match.[30]

The ancients had a saying: "To be a minister and yet not to remonstrate is like a food offering being unsauced." In the past our former lord Duke Huan latterly went out [A4] from Zhou, taking seven chariots and thirty foot soldiers,[31] drumming their bellies and hearts and beating their arms and legs [B4] to align them in ranks, and taking up helmets and putting on armor, and wielding dagger-axes and shields in order to show [A5] valor, battling at Yuli, we then gained Han and Zi, and axling our chariots and strapping on mail conquered Hui. Even so distant as the place of Rong She [B5] was also under the power of our former lord.

"Coming [A6] to the generation of our former lord Duke Wu, to the west he walled Yi and Jian, and to the north advanced to Wu and Liu, tightly hitching the states of Hui and Yu. Lu, Wei, Lao, and Cai [B6] all came to pay court.

"Coming to the generation of our former [A7] lord Duke Zhuang, then to the east he attacked the warriors of Qi Quan as an opening, to the north walled Wen and Yuan, and ceding the Yin and E Camps to the east opened Tui and Le, and we drove the king out to Ge. [A8, B7]

"Coming to the generation of our former lords Duke Zhao and Duke Li, pressed by heaven and pressed by man, because of this caged rats could not share the same burrow, morning and evening grappling with each other, not even being free to [A9] attack.

"Now [B8] coming to my lord, he is young and still growing, unable to imitate our former lords' martial openings and valiant efforts, adrift[32] in the ease of pleasures and awards received from Chu, [A10] to enlarge his palace. For the lord to have [B9] drawn near to them is not good indeed. If the lord had followed those four men Kong Shu, Yi zhi Yi, Shi zhi Zhulu, and Du zhi Yumi, [A11] who remonstrated with our lord from without, or this Zhanfu [B10] who criticized from within, if my lord in this way were unable to strive, then it would be like an illness for which there is no doctor. If my lord has not heard of this, [A12] then it is also that he has not asked of it. If my lord has nothing to send out, then neither is there anything to send in [B11]. Be warned of it, indeed, my lord. I have heard that with such as the country of Yin, it is said that Tang is talked about but Shou is also [A13] talked about."[33] [A14, B12]

Chapter Eleven

The Eighth Century BCE Civil War in Jin as Seen in the *Bamboo Annals*

On the Nature of the Tomb Text and Its Significance for the "Current" *Bamboo Annals*

One of the most celebrated of the Warring States manuscripts in the collection of Tsinghua University is the *Xinian 繫年 (*Annals).[1] Li Xueqin 李學勤 (1933–2019), who was the director of the Center for the Study and Preservation of Unearthed Manuscripts at the university and the man primarily responsible for the acquisition of the collection, describes his first encounter with this manuscript:

> In the process of my encountering these precious bamboo slips, when I first saw hand-drawings of a small number of

---

The substance of this chapter was originally published as Xia Hanyi 夏含夷, "You Qinghua jian *Xinian* lun *Zhushu jinian* muben he jinben de tili" 由清華簡《繫年》論《竹書紀年》墓本和今本的體例, *Jianbo* 簡帛 22 (2021): 45–73. It has become standard in the field of Early China studies in the West to refer to the Tsinghua manuscript in question by the Chinese name *Xinian*, and so I do so here (though marking it as *Xinian to indicate that the title was supplied by the Tsinghua editors). However, since the other text under study here, the *Zhushu jinian* 竹書紀年, is better known in the West by the name *Bamboo Annals*, it seems preferable to mix the two languages of reference, even though elsewhere in this book I refer to texts by romanization of the Chinese title. Moreover, this avoids possible confusion between referring to *Xinian as *Annals and the frequently shortened name of the *Bamboo Annals* as either just *Jinian* or *Annals*.

slips, there was one that belonged to the *Xinian. Although at the time I didn't know what sort of text it was, I could see that its content was similar to that of the "Ancient Text" Bamboo Annals, and so I strongly felt its importance. Coming now to having edited this lengthy 138-slip *Xinian, due to the need to work with it I have come ever more to study in detail the "Ancient Text" Bamboo Annals; not only has this increased my understanding of the manuscript text, but it has also deepened my recognition of the Bamboo Annals as a text.[2]

Li subsequently went on to say that the reason he associated the *Xinian with the Bamboo Annals (Zhushu jinian 竹書紀年) is because he argues that the "Ancient Text" (guben 古本) of the Bamboo Annals more resembled the narrative history form of the Zuo zhuan 左傳 Zuo Tradition than it did the annalistic format of the Chunqiu 春秋 Springs and Autumns.

> Given that the *Xinian is totally different from the annalistic form of the Chunqiu, is the (Bamboo) Annals that type of annalistic history? If we look at the "Current Text" (jinben 今本) (Bamboo) Annals, which appeared late in history, it certainly is a standard annalistic history with events recorded according to years. However, after reading the *Xinian and then reexamining some quotations of the "Ancient Text" (Bamboo) Annals, one can see opposite traces in very many places, which is to say that the "Ancient Text" (Bamboo) Annals (or at least a portion of it) was not the sort of annalistic history like the Chunqiu, but is much more similar in form to the *Xinian.[3]

In support of this conclusion, Li compared a single passage in the Zhengyi 正義 Correct Significance commentary to the Chunqiu and Zuo zhuan quoting the Ji zhong shu Jinian 汲冢書紀年 Annals from the Ji Tomb Texts with one of the chapters of the newly discovered *Xinian.

> 《汲冢書紀年》云："平王奔西申，而立伯盤以為太子，與幽王俱死於戲。先是，申侯、魯侯及許文公立平王于申，以本大子，故稱天王。幽王既死，而虢公翰又立王子余臣于攜，周二王並立。二十一年，攜王為晉文公所殺。以本非適，故稱攜王。"

The Annals of the Texts from the Ji Tomb says: "King Ping fled to Western Shen, and they installed Bo Pan as crown prince; he died together with King You at Xi. Prior to this, the Lord of Shen, the Lord of Lu and Duke Wen of Xu had installed King Ping at Shen because he was originally the eldest son, and therefore called him Heavenly King. After King You had died, Han, the Duke of Guo, also installed the royal son Yuchen at Xie, and Zhou had two kings simultaneously in place. In the twenty-first year, the King of Xie was killed by Lord Wen of Jin. Because he was originally not the heir, therefore he was called the King of Xie."[4]

The *Xinian passage reads as follows:

周幽王取妻于西申,生平王,王或取褒人之女,是褒姒,生伯盤。褒姒嬖于王,王與伯盤逐平王,平王走西申。幽王起師,圍平王于西申,申人弗畀。曾人乃降西戎,以攻幽王,幽王及伯盤乃滅,周乃亡。邦君諸正乃立幽王之弟余臣于虢,是攜惠王。立廿又一年,晉文侯仇乃殺惠王於虢。周亡王九年。邦君諸侯焉始不朝于周,晉文侯乃逆平王于少鄂,立之於京師。三年,乃東徙,止于成周。

King You of Zhou took a wife from Western Shen, and she bore King Ping. The king then took a woman from the people of Bao; this was Bao Si, who bore Bo Pan. Bao Si was beloved by the king, and the king and Bo Pan drove out King Ping. King Ping ran off to Western Shen. King You raised the army and surrounded King Ping at Western Shen, but the people of Shen would not hand him over. The people of Zeng then surrendered to the Western Warriors in order to attack King You, and King You and Bo Pan were then wiped out, and Zhou was then lost. The rulers of the states and the many governors then installed King You's younger brother Yuchen in Guo; this was King Hui of Xie. Having been installed twenty-one years, Chou, Lord Wen of Jin, then killed King Hui at Guo. Zhou was without a king for nine years. With that the rulers of the states and the many governors began not to come to court at Zhou. Lord Wen of Jin then met King Ping at Shao'e, installing him at Jingshi. In the third year, then he transferred eastwards, stopping in Chengzhou.[5]

There is no doubt that the *Xinian passage and the Chunqiu Zuo zhuan zhengyi "quotation" of the "Annals of the Texts from the Ji Tomb" share important information about this famous event in Chinese history. However, there is considerable doubt that the *Chunqiu Zuo zhuan zhengyi* quotation reflects the original format of the *Bamboo Annals*, despite Li Xueqin's statement that "the 'Ancient Text' (*Bamboo*) *Annals* (or at least a portion of it) was not the sort of annalistic history like the *Chunqiu*, but is much more similar in form to the *Xinian." In making this statement, not only does Li dismiss the "Current Text" *Bamboo Annals*, saying that it "appeared late in history,"[6] but he also disregards literally hundreds of other quotations of the *Bamboo Annals* showing its format to have been precisely that of an "annalistic history like the *Chunqiu*."[7] In fact, Li's entitling the *Xinian as an "annals" has been roundly criticized by Chinese scholars, and his characterization of the (*Bamboo*) *Annals* is also certainly mistaken. Nevertheless, this may well be one of those kinds of seminal mistakes that points the way to a new understanding of a long-held misconception, in this case of the original nature of the tomb text of the *Bamboo Annals*. In the following study, I will examine in detail the portion of the *Bamboo Annals* concerning the downfall of the Western Zhou and its immediate aftermath, and I will show that the earliest—and still most influential—descriptions of the text were just as mistaken as Li Xueqin's description. Perhaps more important, I will also show that the "Current Text" *Bamboo Annals*, though clearly reflecting an editorial revision, derives ultimately from the first editors of the tomb text.

The *Bamboo Annals*

Du Yu 杜預 (222–284) of the Western Jin dynasty, the famous commentator on the *Chunqiu* and the *Zuo zhuan*, was one of the first eyewitnesses to the *Bamboo Annals*, which were part of a large cache of manuscripts from the Warring States period that were robbed from an ancient tomb in Ji Commandery 汲郡 in 279. In 281, Emperor Wu of the Jin dynasty 晉武帝 (r. 265–290) commanded Xun Xu 荀勗 (ca. 220–289), the director of the imperial library, to organize an editorial team to edit and transcribe into current script the "tadpole characters" (*kedou wenzi* 科斗文字) in which the manuscripts were written. Du Yu, having just taken part in the military campaign against Wu 吳 that unified Jin control of all of China in 280, and having just finished his commentary on the *Chunqiu* and *Zuo zhuan* at his home in present-day Xiangyang 襄陽, Henan, was not part of this editorial effort. However, on a visit to the capital in 282, he was shown the bamboo slips, and he included a brief description of them in a postface to his commentary, written in that year. This postface constitutes the earliest description of the text's contents.

> 其《紀年》篇起自夏、殷、周，皆三代王事，無諸國別也。唯特記晉國，起自殤叔，次文侯、昭侯，以至曲沃莊伯。莊伯之十一年十一月，魯隱公之元年正月也，皆用夏正建寅之月爲歲首。編年相次，晉國滅，獨記魏事，下至魏哀王之二十年。蓋魏國之史記也。推校哀王二十年，大歲在壬戌，是周赧王之十六年，秦昭王之八年，韓襄王之十三年，趙武靈王之二十七年，楚懷王之三十年，燕昭王之十三年，齊湣王之二十五年也。上去孔丘卒百八十一歲，下去今大康三年五百八十一歲。哀王，於《史記》襄王之子、惠王之孫也。惠王三十六年卒，而襄王立，立十六年卒，而哀王立。古書《紀年》篇惠王三十六年改元，從一年始至十六年，而稱「惠成王卒」，即惠王也。疑《史記》誤分惠之世以爲後王年也。哀王二十三年乃卒，故特不稱諡，謂之今王。其著書文意，大似《春秋》經，推此足見古者國史策書之常也。

Its *Annals* text begins from Xia, Yin, and Zhou, all of which are royal affairs of the Three Dynasties, without any differentiation of the many states. It only specially records the state of Jin beginning from Shangshu, followed by Lord Wen and Lord Zhao down to Zhuangbo of Quwo. Zhuangbo's eleventh month of his eleventh year was the first month of the first year of Lord Yin of Lu, in all cases using the *Yin* first month of the Xia calendar as the beginning of the year. Putting years in sequence one after the other, when Jin was wiped out, it only records Wei affairs, down to the twentieth year of King Ai of Wei. This was probably the historical record of the state of Wei. Calculating King Ai's twentieth year, its designation would have been *renxu*, the sixteenth year of King He of Zhou, the eighth year of King Zhao of Qin, the thirteenth year of King Xiang of Han, the twenty-seventh year of King Wuling of Zhao, the thirtieth year of King Huai of Chu, the thirteenth year of King Zhao of Yan, and the twenty-fifth year of King Min of Qi. It was eighty-one years after the death of Confucius, and 381 before the present third year of Great Peace (i.e., 282). According to the *Shi ji*, King Ai was the son of King Xiang, the grandson of King Hui. King Hui died in his thirty-sixth year, and King Xiang was installed, dying in the sixteenth year of his reign, when King Ai was installed. According to the ancient manuscript *Annals*, King Hui changed his "first year" in his thirty-sixth year, and began anew from the first year through the sixteenth year, saying that "King Huicheng died," which is King Hui. I suspect that the *Shi ji* mistakenly conflated Huicheng's generation with the following king's reign. King Ai died in his twenty-third year, and therefore was not called by his posthumous title, but was called "current king." The nature of the text is largely similar to that of the *Chunqiu* classic, from which it suffices to see the standard form of the historical texts of the ancient states.⁸

There is much that is right about this first eyewitness report, not least that "the nature of the text is largely similar to that of the *Chunqiu* classic." However, like Li Xueqin's first report concerning the *Xinian, there are also some basic mistakes in it. For instance, it describes the text as beginning "from Xia, Yin, and Zhou," though the editor of the text, Xun Xu, specifically stated that it began with Huangdi 黃帝,⁹ and indeed there are numerous quotations of the text pertaining to the period from Huangdi through Yao 堯 and Shun 舜, that is, prior to Xia.¹⁰ He mistakes the last king of the annals as "King Ai of Wei" 魏哀王, a king mentioned by Sima Qian 司馬遷 (145–ca. 89 BCE) in the *Shi ji* 史記 *Records of the Historian*, but who actually never existed; the last king of the *Bamboo Annals* was King Xiang'ai 襄哀王, generally known just as King Xiang 襄王 (r. 318–296 BCE). I have discussed these and other problems with Du Yu's report elsewhere, and there is no need to revisit them here.¹¹ Instead, I will focus just on his description of the end of the Western Zhou and beginning of the Eastern Zhou portion of the annals. He says that the annals used the reign years of the rulers of Jin 晉 "beginning from Shangshu 殤叔 (784–781 BCE), followed by Lord Wen 晉文侯 (780–746 BCE) and Lord Zhao 晉昭侯 (745–739 BCE) down to Zhuangbo 莊伯 of Quwo 曲沃 (730–716 BCE)." I will show that this portion of the tomb text was not arranged in this way at all. The years 781–771 BCE were certainly denominated according to the reign years of King You of Zhou 周幽王 (r. 781–771 BCE), and it is also likely that the first twenty-odd years thereafter continued to be given according to the Zhou kings. Sometime in the second half of the eighth century

BCE, the annals did begin to be denominated according to the reigns of the rulers of Jin, but not Lords Wen and Zhao, the "legitimate" lords in the Jin capital of Yi 翼, as Du Yu said, but rather with the rebel lords of Quwo 曲沃, probably beginning with Huanshu 桓叔 (745–731 BCE), and then certainly continuing with Zhuangbo and Duke Wu 武公 (r. 715–679/677 BCE). It was Duke Wu who finally killed the last of the mainline Jin rulers, Min, Lord of Jin 晉侯緡 (r. 706–679 BCE); sacked the capital of Yi; and brought the sixty-five-year-long Jin civil war to an end. It stands to reason that the annals of the civil war should be denominated in the years of the victors: the Quwo lords. I will also show that although the "Current Text" *Bamboo Annals* dates the records of these years according to the years of the Zhou kings, and thus marks a restructuring of the tomb text, nevertheless it reflects the viewpoint of the Quwo lords, and thus presumably derives from the tomb text.

According to the standard history of the state of Jin, Shangshu was a younger brother of Lord Mu of Jin 晉穆侯 (r. 812–785) who usurped power after his brother's death, forcing the crown prince Chou 仇, the future Lord Wen, to flee into exile. Four years later, Lord Wen returned and attacked his uncle, taking his place as ruler of Jin.[12] It would be totally incongruous to imagine that an annals of Jin would begin with such a usurper, and indeed there is not a single quotation dated according to his reign years. However, there is one quotation apparently dated to the reign of Lord Wen of Jin. This has led numerous scholars, including the most influential proponents of the "Ancient Text" Bamboo Annals, to argue that the Jin annals began at least with his first year: 780 BCE.[13] The *Shui jing zhu* 水經注 (*Commentary to the Classic of Rivers*) of Li Daoyuan 酈道元 (d. 527) contains the following quotation:

《竹書紀年》：晉文侯二年，同惠王子多父伐鄶，克之，乃居鄭父之丘，名之曰鄭，是曰桓公。

Bamboo Annals: second year of Lord Wen of Jin, together with Duofu, the son of King Hui of Zhou, attacked Kuai and defeated it, then locating at the Mound of Zhengfu, named it Zheng; this was Duke Huan.[14]

Despite a number of obvious mistakes in this quotation, it would seem to be incontrovertible evidence that an early text of the *Bamboo Annals* denominated events in the reign years of Lord Wen of Jin. But this is not so straightforward. For one thing, the reference to "Duofu, the son of King Hui" is inexplicable; King Hui of Zhou 周惠王 (r. 677–652 BCE) reigned a century or so after the time of Duke Huan of Zheng 鄭桓公 (r. 806–771 BCE) and so couldn't possibly be his father.[15] What is more, the sentence as written does not have a subject; this too is anomalous for the *Bamboo Annals*. Two other quotations, or perhaps better, paraphrases, that include the same material and are attributed to Xue Zan 薛瓚 or Minister Zan 臣瓚 (fl. late 3rd c.), a member of the team responsible for editing the *Ji zhong* texts, complicate the matter. One of these quotations is also found in the *Shui jing zhu*, while the second quotation is in the commentary to the *Han shu* 漢書 by Yan Shigu 顏師古 (581–645).

鄭桓公友之故邑也。《漢書》薛瓚《注》言：周自穆王已下都于西鄭，不得以封桓公也。幽王既敗，虢、會又滅，遷居其地，國于鄭父之丘，是為鄭桓公。無封京兆之文。

The former city of You, Duke Huan of Zheng. Xue Zan's commentary to the *Han shu* says: "From King Mu on, Zhou made its capital at Western Zheng; it would not have been possible to enfeoff Duke Huan there. After King You had been defeated, Guo and Kuai were also wiped out, and he transferred to reside in their land, with the citadel at the Mound of Zhengfu; this was Duke Huan of Zheng. There is no language about him being enfeoffed at Jingzhao.[16]

臣瓚曰：周自穆王以下都於西鄭，不得以封桓公也。初桓公為周司徒，故謀於史伯而寄帑與賄於虢會之間。幽王既敗，二年而滅會，四年而滅虢，居於鄭父之丘，是以為鄭桓公。無封京兆之文。

Minister Zan said: "Zhou from King Mu on made its capital at Western Zheng, so that Duke Huan could not have been enfeoffed there. At first, Duke Huan was the Zhou Supervisor of Infantry, and therefore plotted with Secretary Bo to place the treasury and wealth in Guo and Hui. After King You had been defeated, in the second year he wiped out Hui, and in the fourth year wiped out Guo, residing at the Mound of Zhengfu; this was Duke Huan of Zheng. There is no language about him being enfeoffed at Jingzhao.[17]

Zan's quotations are also garbled. The second implies that Duke Huan of Zheng "wiped out Hui" (*mie* Hui 滅會) the second year after King You had been defeated (i.e., 769 BCE), whereas all traditional sources concur that Duke Huan died together with King You in 771.

The key to reconciling the mistakes in these quotations would seem to be in the "Current Text" *Bamboo Annals*. The entry for the second year of King You (i.e., 780 BCE) reads as follows:

二年，涇、渭、洛竭。岐山崩。初增賦。晉文侯同王子多父伐鄶，克之，乃居鄭父之丘。是為鄭桓公。

Second year, the Jing, Wei, and Luo (rivers) dried up. Mount Qi crumbled. (They) first increased the taxes. Lord Wen of Jin together with the royal son Duofu attacked Ceng, defeating it, and then resided at the Mound of Zhengfu; this was Duke Huan of Zheng.[18]

Not only does this entry not mention "King Hui," but it also makes Lord Wen of Jin the subject of the sentence, thus clarifying the grammar of the sentence involving the "royal son Duofu's attack," in this case on Ceng 鄶 rather than Kuai 鄶 or Hui 會.[19] Perhaps more important, it shows that the "second year" of this entry pertains to the reign of King You, and not that of Lord Wen. This was nine years before Duke Huan died together with King You, resolving the anomalous chronology in the two quotations of Xue Zan or Minister Zan. Most important of all, it is also consistent with all other quotations for King You's reign, all of which date events according to King You's reign years. The following comparison correlates the "Current Text" *Bamboo Annals* record of King You's reign with early quotations of the *Bamboo Annals*.

King You Annals in the *Bamboo Annals*

Year BCE	"Current" *Bamboo Annals*	*Bamboo Annals* Quotations	Year BCE
781	元年，春正月，王即位。晉世子仇歸于晉，殺殤叔。晉人立仇，是為文侯。王錫太師尹氏、皇父命。		

	First year, spring, first month, the king assumed position. The Jin heir Chou returned to Jin and killed Shangshu. The people of Jin installed Chou; this was Lord Wen. The king bestowed commands on the Grand Captains Yinshi and Huangfu.		
780	二年，涇、渭、洛竭。岐山崩。初增賦。晉文侯同王子多父伐鄶，克之，乃居鄭父之丘。是為鄭桓公。 Second year, the Jing, Wei, and Luo (rivers) dried up. Mount Qi crumbled. (They) first increased the taxes. Lord Wen of Jin together with the royal son Duofu attacked Ceng, defeating it, and then resided at the Mound of Zhengfu; this was Duke Huan of Zheng.	《竹書紀年》：晉文侯二年，同惠王子多父伐鄶，克之，乃居鄭父之丘，名之曰鄭，是曰桓公。(《水經洧水注》) *Bamboo Annals*: Second year of Lord Wen of Jin, together with Duofu, the son of King Hui of Zhou, attacked Kuai and defeated it, then locating at the Mound of Zhengfu, named it Zheng; this was Duke Huan. (*Shui jing zhu*: Weishui) 鄭桓公友之故邑也。《漢書》薛瓚《注》言：周自穆王已下都于西鄭，不得以封桓公也。幽王既敗，虢、儈又滅，遷居其地，國于鄭父之丘，是為鄭桓公。無封京兆之文。(《水經渭水注》) The former city of You, Duke Huan of Zheng. Xue Zan's commentary to the *Han shu* says: "From King Mu on, Zhou made its capital at Western Zheng; it would not have been possible to enfeoff Duke Huan there. After King You had been defeated, Guo and Kuai were also wiped out, and he transferred to	

The Eighth Century BCE Civil War in Jin | 275

		reside in their land, with the citadel at the Mound of Zhengfu; this was Duke Huan of Zheng. There is no language about him being enfeoffed at Jingzhao. (*Shui jing zhu*: Weishui) 臣瓚曰：周自穆王以下都於西鄭，不得以封桓公也。初桓公為周司徒，故謀於史伯而寄帑與賄於虢會之間。幽王既敗，二年而滅會，四年而滅虢，居於鄭父之丘，是以為鄭桓公。無封京兆之文。(《漢書地理志注》 Minister Zan said: "Zhou from King Mu on made its capital at Western Zheng, so that Duke Huan could not have been enfeoffed there. At first, Duke Huan was the Zhou Supervisor of Infantry and therefore plotted with Secretary Bo to place the treasury and wealth in Guo and Hui. After King You had been defeated, in the second year he wiped out Hui, and in the fourth year wiped out Guo, residing at the Mound of Zhengfu; this was Duke Huan of Zheng. There is no language about him being enfeoffed at Jingzhao. (*Han shu zhu*, "Dilizhi")	
779	三年，王變褎姒。冬，大震電。 Third year, the king was enamored with Bao Si. In winter, there was great lightning and thunder.		
778	四年，秦人伐西戎。夏六月，隕霜。陳夷公蒐。 Fourth year, the people of Qin attacked the Western		

	Warriors. In summer, sixth month, there fell frost. Lord Yi of Chen passed away.		
777	五年，王世子宜臼出奔申。皇父作都于向。 Fifth year, the royal heir Yiqiu went out fleeing to Shen. Huangfu made a capital at Xiang.		
776	六年，王命伯士帥師伐六濟之戎，王師敗逋。西戎滅蓋。冬十月辛卯朔，日有食之。 Sixth year, the king commanded Boshi to lead an army to attack the Warriors of Liuji; the royal troops were defeated in a rout. The Western Warriors wiped out Gai. Winter, tenth month, on *xinmao*, the first day of the month, the sun was eclipsed.	後十年，幽王命伯士伐六濟之戎，軍敗，伯士死焉。(《後漢書西羌傳》) Ten years later, King You commanded Boshi to attack the Warriors of Liuji; the army was defeated and Boshi died there. (*Hou Han shu*, "Xi Qiang zhuan")	775
775	七年，虢人滅焦。 Seventh year, the people of Guo wiped out Jiao.		
774	八年，王錫司徒鄭伯多父命。王立褒姒之子曰伯服為太子。 Eighth year, the king bestowed command as Supervisor of Infantry on Duofu, the Elder of Zheng. The king installed Bao Si's son Bofu to be crown prince.	《紀年》曰：幽王八年，立褒姒之子曰伯服為太子。(《太平御覽》卷147) The *Jinian* says: King You eighth year, installed Bao Si's son Bofu to be crown prince. (*Taiping yulan*, *j*. 147)	774

The Eighth Century BCE Civil War in Jin | 277

773	九年，申侯聘西戎及鄫。 Ninth year, the Lord of Shen hosted the Western Warriors and Ceng.		
772	十年，春，王及諸侯盟于太室。秋九月，桃杏實。王師伐申。 Tenth year, spring, the king joined with the many lords in covenant at the Grand Chamber. Autumn, ninth month, the peach trees and almond trees bore fruit. The royal army attacked Shen.	盟于太室。《紀年》(《北堂書》卷21) Covenant at the Grand Chamber. (*Beitang shuchao*, j. 21) 書紀年》曰：幽王十年九月，《桃杏實。(《太平御覽》卷968) The text *Annals* says: King You tenth year, ninth month, the peach trees and almond trees bore fruit. (*Taiping yulan*, j. 968)	772
771	十一年，春正月，日暈。申人、鄫人及犬戎入宗周，弒王及鄭桓公。犬戎殺王子伯服，執褒姒以歸。申侯、魯侯、許男、鄭子立宜臼于申，虢公翰立王子余臣于攜。 Eleventh year, spring, first month, the sun had a halo. The people of Shen and the people of Ceng joined with the Dog Warriors to enter Zongzhou, assassinating the king and Duke Huan of Zheng. The Dog Warriors killed the royal son Bo Fu, and took prisoner Bao Si and returned. The Lord of Shen, the Lord of Lu, the Male of Xu, and the son of Zheng installed Yiqiu at Shen, and Han, Duke of Guo installed the royal son Yuchen at Xie.	《汲冢竹書紀年》："平王奔西申，而立伯盤以為太子，與幽王俱死於戲。先是，申侯、魯侯及許文公立平王於申，以本太子，故稱天王。幽王既死，而虢公翰又立王子余臣於攜。周二王並立。(《春秋左傳正義》，昭公26年). The *Annals of the Texts from the Ji Tomb* says: "King Ping fled to Western Shen, and they installed Bo Pan as crown prince; he died together with King You at Xi. Prior to this, the Lord of Shen, the Lord of Lu and Duke Wen of Xu had installed King Ping at Shen, because he was originally the eldest son, and therefore called him Heavenly King. After King You had died, Han, Duke of Guo, also installed the royal son Yuchen at Xie, and Zhou had two kings simultaneously in place. (*Chunqiu Zuo zhuan zhengyi*, twenty-sixth year of Lord Zhao)	771

As this comparison shows, quotations in the *Taiping yulan* 太平御覽 *Imperial Conspectus of the Great Peace Era*, from the early Northern Song dynasty, explicitly quote the *Annals* as dating events to the eighth and tenth years of King You's reign. Thus, there is no doubt that the record of the attack by Duofu, that is, Duke Huan of Zheng, on Ceng 鄫 or Kuai 鄶 (or Hui 會 or Zeng 曾), whatever the name of the state should be, and which certainly took place during the reigns of King You and Lord Wen of Jin, and which is explicitly dated to a "second year" of reign, should have taken place in 780 BCE, the second year of King You's reign. This eliminates the only quotation of the *Bamboo Annals* apparently dated according to a reign year of Lord Wen of Jin. In short, there is no evidence whatsoever that the tomb text of the *Bamboo Annals* dated events according to years of Lord Wen's reign. This too is as we would expect: despite having been vanquished in 771 BCE, King You has always been considered as the last legitimate king of the Western Zhou period. It is inconceivable that events during his reign would not be denominated according to his reign years.

The Opening Years of the Eastern Zhou as Seen in the *Bamboo Annals*

There are only two quotations of the *Bamboo Annals* for the opening years of the Eastern Zhou period, one of them just quoted and one of them alluded to at the beginning of this study. In the interest of clarity, it will be helpful to examine them again. The first is Minister Zan's quotation of the text concerning Duke Huan of Zheng's attack on Ceng (which Minister Zan refers to as Hui 會). The quotation mentions a second attack, this one on Guo 虢, explicitly dated to a fourth year.

> 臣瓚曰：... 初桓公為周司徒，故謀於史伯而寄帑與賄於虢會之間。幽王既敗，二年而滅會，四年而滅虢，居於鄭父之丘，是以為鄭桓公。

> Minister Zan said: ". . . At first, Duke Huan was the Zhou Supervisor of Infantry, and therefore plotted with Secretary Bo to place the treasury and wealth in Guo and Hui. After King You had been defeated, in the second year he wiped out Hui, and in the fourth year wiped out Guo, residing at the Mound of Zhengfu; this was Duke Huan of Zheng."

I have already discussed Chen Zan's apparent mistake in dating Duke Huan's attack on Hui (i.e., Ceng) two years after the death of King You (i.e., 769 BCE), instead of in the second year of his reign (i.e., 780). However, the second attack, that against Guo 虢, certainly would have taken place after the death of King You as part of the factional fighting at the time.[20] There is, in fact, just such a record in the "Current Text" *Bamboo Annals*, for the fourth year of King Ping 周平王 (trad. r. 770–720 BCE; i.e., 767 BCE).

四年，燕傾侯卒。鄭人滅虢。

Fourth year, Lord Qing of Yan died. People of Zheng wiped out Guo.

There is no need to accept literally that the people of Zheng "wiped out" (*mie* 滅) Guo; we routinely find states that have been "wiped out" continuing to play a role in ancient Chinese history. But the convergence of the date between Minister Zan saying that it happened in the fourth year "after King You had been defeated" (i.e., 767 BCE) and the "Current Text" *Bamboo Annals* date of the fourth year of King You is notable. The only explanation of this date would seem to be that some early text of the *Bamboo Annals*, whether the tomb text or not, dated this event according to the regnal calendar of a Zhou king, presumably King Ping, or perhaps King Hui of Xie 攜惠王 (r. 770–750 BCE).[21]

The second quotation of the *Bamboo Annals* provides further evidence that some early text was dated according to the reign of a Zhou king of this period. It occurs at the end of the early Tang dynasty *Chunqiu Zuo zhuan zhengyi* "quotation" that Li Xueqin cited to justify his name for the *Xinian. Here I will cite just the relevant portion.

汲冢書《紀年》云："...幽王既死，而虢公翰又立王子余臣于攜，周二王並立。二十一年，攜王為晉文公所殺。以本非適，故稱攜王。"

The *Annals* of the Texts from the Ji Tomb says: "... After King You had died, Han, the Duke of Guo, also installed the royal son Yuchen at Xie, and Zhou had two kings simultaneously in place. In the twenty-first year, the King of Xie was killed by Duke Wen of Jin. Because he was originally not the heir, therefore he was called the King of Xie."

The record of the killing of the royal son Yuchen 余臣, also known as the King of Xie 攜王 (or King Hui of Xie), in a twenty-first year, was assumed by both Wang Guowei 王國維 (1877–1927) and also Fang Shiming 方詩銘 (1919–2000) to be dated according to the reign years of Lord Wen of Jin (r. 780–746 BCE; i.e., 760 BCE). Nevertheless, as noted at the beginning of this study, the *Xinian confirms both the installation of Yuchen as the king at Xie 攜 immediately after the death of King You (i.e., 770 BCE), and also that he was killed by Lord Wen of Jin in the twenty-first year of his, that is, Yuchen's reign (i.e., 750 BCE), not Lord Wen's reign. Once again, I quote just the relevant portion of the passage.

> 幽王及伯盤乃滅,周乃亡。邦君諸正乃立幽王之弟余臣于虢,是攜惠王。立廿又一年,晉文侯仇乃殺惠王於虢。

> King You and Bo Pan were then wiped out, and Zhou was then lost. The rulers of the states and the many governors then installed King You's younger brother Yuchen in Guo; this was King Hui of Xie. His having been installed twenty-one years, Chou, Lord Wen of Jin, then killed King Hui at Guo.

The *Xinian chronology is not at all ambiguous in at least this respect. King Hui of Xie was killed in 750 BCE according to the logic of the quotation. This matches an entry in the "Current Text" *Bamboo Annals* for the twenty-first year of King Ping (i.e., 750 BCE).

> 二十一年,晉文侯殺王子余臣于攜。

> Twenty-first year, Lord Wen of Jin killed the royal son Yuchen at Xie.

This is the one point for which Li Xueqin admits that the "Current Text" *Bamboo Annals* "is correct."[22] It is strong evidence for the historicity of the "Current Text" *Bamboo Annals*. But more than this, for the "Current Text" *Bamboo Annals* to be correct concerning this point also necessarily entails that this portion of some early text of the *Bamboo Annals*, whether the tomb text or not, continued to be dated according to the reigns of the Zhou kings and was not dated according to the reign of Lord Wen of Jin.

The Jin Civil War as Seen in the *Bamboo Annals*

The foregoing discussion is not intended to suggest that the "Current Text" *Bamboo Annals* is correct in dating all of the remaining entries in the text according to the reigns of the successive Zhou kings. Early quotations of the text show without a doubt that the remainder of the text was organized first according to the reigns of the lords of Jin, and then when that state had fractured into three parts, according to the rulers of its successor state Wei 魏. I have argued elsewhere that this organization according to the Zhou kings may have been produced by the original editors under the leadership of Xun Xu as a sort of "crib" to help them keep track of the chronology; in the absence of a standard chronology such as years BCE, the years of the Zhou kings would doubtless have been the most convenient standard.[23] I still think that this is likely,[24] but it is not particularly relevant for my discussion here, in which I am attempting to suggest what this portion of the tomb text of the *Bamboo Annals* may have been like.

The years after the initial years of the Eastern Zhou saw a fraternal struggle between two royal sons both claiming to be Zhou kings: Yuchen 余臣 (i.e., King Hui) in Xie and Yiqiu 宜臼 (i.e., King Ping) at Western Shen 西申. As we have seen, this was resolved by Lord Wen of Jin killing King Hui of Xie in 750 BCE. According to the traditional chronology, as given, for instance, in the *Shi ji*, Lord Wen lived only another four years after this battle. When he died in 746 BCE, his own state of Jin was beset by a civil war, this one between his son Bo 伯, posthumously known as Lord Zhao 昭侯 (r. 745–739 BCE), based in the Jin capital city Yi 翼 (located at present-day Yicheng xian 翼城縣, Shanxi), and Lord Wen's younger brother Cheng Shi 成師, known as Huanshu of Quwo 曲沃桓叔 (r. 745–731 BCE), based at the neighboring Quwo 曲沃 (present-day Quwo xian 曲沃縣, Shanxi), just some twenty kilometers to the southwest. This civil war would prove to be much longer lasting than that between the two Zhou kings; it would persist, with off-and-on fighting, until Huanshu's grandson, Duke Wu 武公 (r. 715–679/77 BCE), finally succeeded in sacking the capital Yi and killing the last of the "legitimate" Jin rulers, Min, Lord of Jin 晉侯緡 (r. 706–679 BCE). The chronology of the two sets of Jin rulers is as follows:

Mainline Jin Lords (based at Yi 翼)	Quwo 曲沃 Jin Lords
Zhao Hou 昭侯 (745–740)	Huan Shu 桓叔 (745–731)
Xiao Hou 孝侯 (739–724)	
E Hou 鄂侯 (723–718)	Zhuang Bo 莊伯 (730–716)
Ai Hou 哀侯 (717–710)	
Xiaozi Hou 小子侯 (707–707)	Wu Gong 武公 (715–679/677)
Jin Hou Min 晉侯緡 (706–679)	

Since the *Bamboo Annals* is at least in part an annals of the state of Jin, it goes without saying that this civil war is the focus of most of its entries for this period. As we have seen, Du Yu, who has given us the earliest eyewitness account of the manuscript, states that it was arranged according to the years of Lord Wen, followed by Lord Zhao, and then apparently switching to Zhuangbo 莊伯 of Quwo (r. 730–716).

唯特記晉國，起自殤叔，次文侯、昭侯，以至曲沃莊伯。

It only specially records the state of Jin beginning from Shangshu, followed by Lord Wen and Lord Zhao down to Zhuangbo of Quwo.

We have already seen that Du Yu's report that the Jin portion of the annals began with Shangshu is certainly mistaken, as is almost certainly the ascription to Lord Wen. Not only this; there is absolutely no evidence that any events were recorded according to the reign years of Lord Zhao. What is more, it makes no sense that the records should have switched chronologies from the mainline rulers at Yi to the rebel rulers at Quwo in the middle of the civil war, before the result had been decided.[25] As I will try to show in the following portion of this study, the "Current Text" *Bamboo Annals* once again points toward the nature of the *Bamboo Annals* tomb text. Let me again correlate all quotations of the *Bamboo Annals* with the text of the "Current Text" *Bamboo Annals*, before then going on to discuss several important features of the quotations.

Jin Civil War Annals in the Bamboo Annals, 745–679 BCE

Year BCE	"Current Text" *Bamboo Annals*	*Bamboo Annals* Quotations	Year BCE
745	二十六年，晉封其弟成師于曲沃。 Twenty-sixth year, Jin installed its younger brother Cheng Shi at Quwo.		
739	三十二年，晉潘父弒其君昭侯，納成師，不克，立昭侯之子孝侯。晉人殺潘父。 Thirty-second year, Panfu of Jin assassinated his ruler Lord Zhao and took in Cheng Shi, who not being victorious, they installed Lord Zhao's son Lord Xiao. The men of Jin killed Panfu.		
731	四十年（自是晉侯在翼，稱翼侯），齊莊公卒。晉曲沃桓叔成師卒，子鱓立，是為莊伯。 Fortieth year, Lord Zhuang of Qi died. Cheng Shi, Huanshu of Quwo, died; his son Shan was installed; this was Zhuangbo.		
730	四十一年春（辛亥莊伯元年），大雨雪。 Forty-first year, spring, it greatly rained snow.	晉莊伯元年，不雨雪。（《太平御覽》卷879引《史記》） First year of Zhuangbo, it did not rain snow. (*Taiping yulan*, j. 879, quoting *Shi ji*)	730
729	四十二年，狄人伐翼，至于晉郊。宋襄公薨。魯惠公使宰讓請郊廟之禮，王使史角如魯諭止之。 Forty-second year, a Di man attacked Yi, reaching as far as the Jin suburbs. Lord Xiang of	二年，翟人俄伐翼，至於晉郊。（《太平御覽》卷879引《史記》） Second year, the Di men E attacked Yi, reaching as far as the Jin suburbs. (*Taiping yulan*, j. 879, quoting *Shi ji*)	729

	Song passed away. Lord Hui of Lu sent Steward Rang to request the rites of the Suburban Temple, and the king sent Scribe Jiao to go to Lu to instruct and stop him.		
724	四十七年，晉曲沃莊伯入翼，弒孝侯，晉人逐之，立孝侯子郄，是為鄂侯。 Forty-seventh year, Zhuangbo of Jin's Quwo entered Yi and assassinated Lord Xiao. The men of Jin expelled him and installed Lord Xiao's son Xi; this was Lord E.		
723	四十八年，無雲而雷。魯惠公卒。 Forty-eighth year, there were no clouds but it thundered. Lord Hui of Lu died.	《史記》曰：晉莊伯八年，無雲而雷。十年，莊伯以曲沃叛。而雷。十年，莊伯以曲沃叛。(太平御覽》卷876引《史記》) Eighth year of Zhuangbo of Jin, there were no clouds but it thundered. In the tenth year, Zhuangbo took Quwo to revolt. (*Taiping yulan*, j. 876, quoting *Shi ji*)	723
719	桓王元年壬戌，十月，莊伯以曲沃叛，伐翼。公子萬救翼，荀叔軫追之，至于家谷。翼侯焚曲沃之禾而還。翼侯伐曲沃，大捷。武公請成于翼，至相而還。 First year of King Huan, *renxu*, in the tenth month, Zhuangbo took Quwo to rebel, attacking Yi. Prince Wan rescued Yi, and Xunshu Zhen pursued them, reaching as far as Jiagu. The Lord of Yi burned Quwo's grain and returned. The Lord of Yi attacked Quwo and was	《竹書紀年》曰：莊伯十二年，翼侯焚曲沃之禾而還。(《水經‧澮水注》) Twelfth year of Zhuangbo, the Lord of Yi burned Quwo's grain and returned. (*Shui jing zhu*: "Huishui") 竹書紀年》曰：莊伯以曲沃叛，《伐翼，公子萬救翼，荀叔軫追之，至於家穀。 Zhuangbo took Quwo to rebel, attacking Yi. Prince Wan	719

	greatly victorious. Lord Wu requested peace from Yi, reaching Xiang and returning.	rescued Yi, and Xunshu Zhen pursued them, reaching as far as Jiagu. (*Shui jing zhu*: "Huishui") 竹書紀年曰：翼侯伐曲沃，大捷，武公請成于翼，至桐而返。（《水經·涑水注》） The Lord of Yi attacked Quwo and was greatly victorious. Duke Wu requested peace from Yi, reaching Tong and turning back. (*Shui jing zhu*: "Sushui")	
718	二年，王使虢公伐晉之曲沃。晉鄂侯卒。曲沃莊伯復攻晉，立鄂侯子光，是為哀侯。公子萬救翼，荀叔軫追之，至于家谷。 Second year, the king sent the Lord of Guo to attack Jin's Quwo. Lord E of Jin died. Zhuangbo of Quwo again struck Jin, who installed Lord E's son Guang; this was Lord Ai. Prince Wan rescued Yi, and Xunshu Zhen pursued them reaching as far as Jiagu.		
716	四年，曲沃莊伯卒，子稱立，是為武公，尚一軍。 Fourth year, Zhuangbo of Quwo died; his son Cheng was installed; this was Lord Wu, still a single army.	晉武公元年，尚一軍。芮人乘京、荀人董伯皆叛曲沃。（《水經·河水注》） First year of Duke Wu of Jin, still a single army. Cheng Jing, a man of Rui, and Dongbo, a man of Xun, both rebelled against Quwo. (*Shui jing zhu*: "Heshui")	715
715	五年，芮人乘京、荀人董伯皆叛曲沃。		

	Fifth year, Cheng Jing, a man of Rui, and Dongbo, a man of Xun, both rebelled against Quwo.		
709	十一年，曲沃獲晉哀侯。晉人立哀侯子為小子侯。芮伯萬出奔魏。(萬之毋逐萬) Eleventh year, Quwo seized Lord Ai of Jin. The men of Jin installed Lord Ai's son, who was Lord Xiaozi. Ruibo Wan left fleeing to Wei.	紀年》又云：晉武公七年，芮伯《萬之母薑逐萬，萬出奔魏。(《水經·河水注》) Seventh year of Lord Wu of Jin, Ruibo Wan's mother Jiang drove out Wan, and Wan left fleeing to Wei. (*Shui jing zhu*: "Heshui") 《紀年》：晉武公七年，芮伯萬之母芮姜逐萬，萬出奔魏。(《路史·國名紀·戊注》) Seventh year of Lord Wu of Jin, Ruibo Wan's mother Rui Jiang drove out Wan, and Wan left fleeing to Wei.	709
708	十二年，王師秦師圍魏，取芮伯萬而東之。 Twelfth year, the royal army and Qin army surrounded Wei, taking Ruibo Wan and moving him east.	八年，周師、虢師圍魏，取芮伯萬而東之。(《水經·河水注》) Eighth year, the Zhou army and Guo army surrounded Wei, taking Ruibo Wan and moving him east. (*Shui jing zhu*: "Heshui") 《紀年》(晉武公) 八年，周師、虢師圍魏，取芮伯萬而東之。(《路史國名紀戊注》) Eighth year, the Zhou army and Guo army surrounded Wei, taking Ruibo Wan and moving him east. (*Lu shi*: "Guoming ji, Wu zhu")	708

		(《紀年》) 又云：桓王十二年，秋，秦侵芮。冬，王師秦師圍魏，取芮伯萬而東之。(《路史國名紀戊注》) Twelfth year of King Huan, autumn, Qin invaded Rui. Winter, the royal army and Qin army surrounded Wei, taking Ruibo Wan and moving him east. (*Lu shi*: "Guoming ji, Wu zhu")	
707	十三年，冬，曲沃伯誘晉小子侯殺之。晉曲沃滅荀，以其地賜大夫原氏黯，是爲荀叔。戎人逆芮伯萬于郊。 Thirteenth year, winter, the elder of Quwo enticed Lord Xiaozi of Jin and killed him. Quwo of Jin wiped out Xun, taking its lands to bestow on the great officer Yuanshi Yin; this was Xunshu. The Rong men met Ruibo Wan in the suburbs.	九年，戎人逆芮伯萬于郊。(《水經·河水注》) The Rong men met Ruibo Wan in the suburbs. (*Shui jing zhu*: "Heshui") 汲塚古文》：晉武公滅荀，以賜《大夫原氏。(水經·汾水注) Duke Wu of Jin wiped out Xun, taking its lands to bestow on the great officer Yuanshi. (*Shui jing zhu*: "Fenshui") 《汲塚古文》：晉武公滅郇，以賜大夫原黯，是為郇叔。(《文選·北征賦》) Duke Wu of Jin wiped out Xun, to bestow on the great officer Yuan Dian; this was Xunshu. (*Wen xuan*: "Bei zheng fu")	707
706	十四年，王命虢仲伐曲沃，立晉哀侯弟緡于翼爲晉侯。 Fourteenth year, the king commanded Guozhong to		

	attack Quwo, installing Lord Ai of Jin's younger brother Min to be lord of Jin.		
704	十六年，春，滅翼。 Sixteenth year, spring, wiped out Yi.		
696	莊王元年，曲沃尚一軍，異于晉。 King Zhuang, first year, Quwo still a single army, was different from Jin.		
679	三年，曲沃武公滅晉侯緡，以寶獻王。王命武公以一軍爲晉侯。 Third year, Duke Wu of Quwo wiped out Lord Min of Jin, taking the treasures to present to the king. The king commanded Duke Wu with a single army to be lord of Jin.		
677	五年，晉武公卒。子詭諸立爲獻公。王陟。 Fifth year, Duke Wu of Jin died. His son Guizhu was installed as Duke Xian. The king passed away.		

There are no quotations of the text before 730, the first year of Zhuangbo, and so there is no basis on which to determine how the years between 750 and 731 may have been denominated. However, for the half century thereafter all evidence suggests that the records were in the regnal calendars of the two Quwo rulers: Zhuangbo and his son Duke Wu. This is as we might expect, since it was Duke Wu who finally won the civil war, making his line of the family the legitimate rulers of Jin. There are several things to note in this comparison. First, every single quotation has a corresponding entry in the "Current Text" *Bamboo*

Annals, almost always with exactly the same wording.[26] Second, while the quotations are dated according to the reign years of the Quwo rulers and the "Current Text" *Bamboo Annals* entries are dated according to the reign years of the Zhou kings, and with but two possible exceptions they all refer to the same year in an absolute chronology. The first of these exceptions comes in a *Taiping yulan* quotation, obviously misattributed to the *Shi ji*,[27] of two different records, the first dated to the eighth year of Zhuangbo of Quwo (i.e., 723 BCE), and the second either to a "tenth month" (*shi yue* 十月, and thus implicitly to the same 8th year) or to a "tenth year" (*shi nian* 十年; i.e., 721 BCE).[28]

晉莊伯八年，無雲而雷。十月/十年，莊伯以曲沃叛。

Eighth year of Zhuangbo of Jin, there were no clouds but it thundered. In the tenth month / tenth year, Zhuangbo took Quwo to revolt.

The "Current Text" *Bamboo Annals* has records for the forty-eighth year of King Ping of Zhou (i.e., 723) and for the first year of King Huan (i.e., 719) that match these two quotations.

四十八年，無雲而雷。魯惠公卒。

Forty-eighth year, there were no clouds but it thundered. Lord Hui of Lu died.

桓王元年壬戌，十月，莊伯以曲沃叛，伐翼。公子萬救翼，荀叔軫追之，至于家谷。翼侯焚曲沃之禾而還。翼侯伐曲沃，大捷。武公請成于翼，至相而還。

First year of King Huan, *renxu*, in the tenth month, Zhuangbo took Quwo to rebel, attacking Yi. Prince Wan rescued Yi, and Xunshu Zhen pursued them reaching as far as Jiagu. The Lord of Yi burned Quwo's grain and returned. The Lord of Yi attacked Quwo and was greatly victorious. Lord Wu requested peace from Yi, reaching Xiang and returning.

Whereas the *Taiping yulan* either implicitly attributes the second record to the tenth month of the "eighth year" (*ba nian* 八年) of Zhuangbo or explicitly to his "tenth year," the "Current Text" *Bamboo Annals* record for the first year of King Huan reads "tenth month (*shi yue* 十月), Zhuangbo took Quwo to rebel." This would be either four or two years later than the implied date of the *Taiping yulan* quotation. However, an undated quotation in the *Shuijing zhu* explicitly attributed to the *Bamboo Annals* that combines this record with the following record of that year's annals as seen in the "Current Text" *Bamboo Annals* suggests that these records all belong to the same year, which another *Shuijing zhu* quotation does date to the twelfth year of Zhuangbo, 719 BCE.

《竹書紀年》曰：莊伯以曲沃叛，伐翼，公子萬救翼，荀叔軫追之，至於家穀。

Zhuangbo took Quwo to rebel, attacking Yi. Prince Wan rescued Yi, and Xunshu Zhen pursued them, reaching as far as Jiagu.

《竹書紀年》曰：莊伯十二年，翼侯焚曲沃之禾而還。

Twelfth year of Zhuangbo, the Lord of Yi burned Quwo's grain and returned.

It is worth noting that the *Shi ji*, which dates events of this period according to the reign years of the mainline rulers at Yi, seems to date this attack by Zhuangbo to the sixth year of Lord E of Jin 晉鄂侯 (r. 723–718 BCE; i.e., 718 BCE).[29] Despite the one-year discrepancy with the *Bamboo Annals*, this is the only attack by Zhuangbo on Yi recorded in the *Shi ji*, and so it would seem to confirm the later date for the attack.

The second apparent discrepancy is seen in another *Shuijing zhu* quotation:

晉武公元年，尚一軍。芮人乘京、荀人董伯皆叛曲沃。

First year of Duke Wu of Jin, still a single army. Cheng Jing, a man of Rui, and Dongbo, a man of Xun, both rebelled against Quwo.

The first year of Duke Wu of Quwo was 715 BCE. In the "Current Text" *Bamboo Annals* these two records are split between two different years, the fourth and fifth years of King Huan of Zhou (i.e., 716 and 715 BCE).

四年，曲沃莊伯卒，子稱立，是為武公，尚一軍。

Fourth year, Zhuangbo of Qu died; his son Cheng was installed; this was Lord Wu, still a single army.

五年，芮人乘京、荀人董伯皆叛曲沃。

Fifth year, Cheng Jing, a man of Rui, and Dongbo, a man of Xun, both rebelled against Quwo.

The meaning of *shang yi jun* 尚一君, explained by commentators as meaning that the Quwo ruler was still entitled to muster only a single army, is unclear, and so it is also unclear whether it should properly come at the end of one year or at the beginning of the succeeding year.[30] But the chronological confusion here is easy to understand: in ancient China, rulers were "installed" (*li* 立) in the same year that their predecessors died, but their own "first year" (*yuannian* 元年) of reign was the following year. Thus, not only do these two apparent discrepancies not suggest any historiographical inaccuracies on the part of the "Current Text" *Bamboo Annals*, but they in fact suggest that it preserves accurate historical information that a putative forger working from *Shui jing zhu* quotations would have had no way of knowing.

Since the time of the *Siku quanshu zongmu* 四庫全書總目 *Outline of the Complete Texts of the Four Repositories* in the late eighteenth century, the predominant view among Chinese historians has been that the *Bamboo Annals* text found in the Tianyi ge 天一閣 library in Wuxi 無錫, Jiangsu, does not correspond with earlier quotations of the text and therefore is not authentic.[31] This view became ever more dominant with the *Jinben Zhushu jinian shuzheng* 今本竹書紀年疏證 *Current Text of the Bamboo Annals, Analyzed and Verified* of Wang Guowei 王國維 (1877–1927), in which he argued that the text is a "worthless" sixteenth-century forgery assembled on the basis of quotations of the *Bamboo Annals* found in such early sources as the *Shuijing zhu*, the *Shi ji suoyin* 史記索隱 commentary of Sima Zhen 司馬貞 (fl. 8th c.), and the *Taiping yulan*.[32] Influential though this view has been for the last century, there are many features of the text and its quotations that it does not explain.

For example, two features of the quotations call into question this received wisdom concerning the authenticity, or what we might call the provenance, of the "Current Text" *Bamboo Annals*. The first three quotations in the right-hand columns, for the first, second, and eighth years of Zhuangbo of Quwo, all come from the *Taiping yulan*, but rather than being attributed to the *Bamboo Annals*, as are most other quotations in the *Taiping yulan*, all three are attributed to the *Shi ji* 史記, presumably the *Records of the Historian* of Sima Qian. These are among several other *Taiping yulan* quotations of the *Shi ji*, none of which is found in the *Shi ji* but all but one of which are found in the "Current Text" *Bamboo Annals*.³³ Most important, the three quotations quoted here are all dated according to the reign years of Zhuangbo of Quwo, and—as the *Shui jing zhu* quotations show—the *Bamboo Annals* is the only text that gives dates in this manner; the "Jin shijia" 晉世家 "Genealogy of Jin" chapter of the *Shi ji* dates events for this period according to the mainline rulers of Jin, ruling in the capital of Yi.³⁴ These quotations, all but one of which match entries in the "Current Text" *Bamboo Annals*, once again calls into question the hypothesis that a putative forger of that text worked from earlier quotations of the text; it strains credulity to imagine that this forger could have known that these *Taiping yulan* quotations mistakenly attributed to the *Shi ji* actually come from the *Bamboo Annals*.

A second point to note about the quotations is that two of them found in the *Lu shi* 路史 *Exposed History* of Luo Bi 羅泌 (1131–1189) concerning an attack on Wei 魏 in which Ruibo Wan 芮伯萬 was captured feature two different forms of reign-year notation: one in the eighth year of Duke Wu of Jin and one in the twelfth year of King Huan of Zhou, in both cases corresponding to 708 BCE.

> (《紀年》（晉武公）八年，周師、虢師圍魏，取芮伯萬而東之。

> (Of the [Bamboo] Annals), eighth year (of Duke Wu of Jin), the Zhou army and Guo army surrounded Wei, taking Ruibo Wan and moving him east.³⁵

> (《紀年》）又云：桓王十二年，秋，秦侵芮。冬，王師秦師圍魏，取芮伯萬而東之。

> (The [Bamboo] Annals) also says: Twelfth year of King Huan, autumn, Qin invaded Rui. Winter, the royal army and Qin army surrounded Wei, taking Ruibo Wan and moving him east.³⁶

The *Lu shi*, begun by Luo Bi's father Luo Liangbi 羅良弼 (1108–1165) and completed in 1170, is a synoptic history of China from the time of Yao 堯 and Shun 舜, produced by quoting literature available at the time. As Fang Shiming and Wang Xiuling note in their *Guben Zhushu jinian jizheng*, the second of these quotations, that dated to the twelfth year of King Huan of Zhou, shows that a text very much like the "Current Text" *Bamboo Annals* had to be extant already by the middle of the twelfth century, some four hundred years before Fan Qin's Tianyi ge edition.[37] Indeed, the "Current Text" *Bamboo Annals* record for the twelfth year of King Huan matches the final portion of the second *Lu shi* quotation exactly, including reflecting even the royal bias in referring to the Zhou army as the "royal army" (*wang shi* 王師) instead of "Zhou army" (*Zhou shi* 周師).[38]

(周桓王) 十二年，王師秦師圍魏，取芮伯萬而東之。

(King Hui of Zhou) twelfth year, the royal army and Qin army surrounded Wei, taking Ruibo Wan and moving him east.

Conclusion

I think there is no doubt that Li Xueqin's characterization of the Tsinghua manuscript **Xinian* and the *Bamboo Annals* was fundamentally flawed. Although the title that he gave the manuscript, **Xinian*, on the basis of this misunderstanding is by now probably too well entrenched in the scholarly literature to be revised, his characterization of the nature of the text has proved much less influential; indeed, most Chinese scholars have simply disregarded it without mention, and the few Western scholars who have studied the text simply note that the text is not an "annals" at all.[39] On the other hand, his view of the *Bamboo Annals*, and especially of the "Current Text" *Bamboo Annals*, is still very much in the mainstream of Chinese scholarship. Nevertheless, I hope to have shown in this study that Li Xueqin was not the only scholar to mischaracterize that text; he was simply following other great Chinese historians, from Du Yu in the years immediately after the text's discovery to Wang Guowei writing in 1917. Unfortunately, their misperceptions have proved to be much more influential, such that the great majority of Chinese scholars regard Wang Guowei's conclusions about the texts to be the final word, even though some of his basic claims can readily be shown to be wrong.[40]

The most obvious of these mistakes is that Wang, like Du Yu before him, argued that the Jin annals begin even before the end of the

Western Zhou period, either with Shangshu or Lord Wen of Jin, despite there being clear evidence that the annals of Zhou kings continued at least through the reign of King You of Zhou, as we should surely expect. This is not just a trivial matter of a few years difference, but it ramifies over the course of the next hundred years of annals. The tomb text of the *Bamboo Annals* did indeed switch to denominating years according to the reigns of Jin rulers at some point during this time, but unlike Du Yu and Wang Guowei's assertions that these rulers were the mainline rulers at the Jin capital of Yi, all of the evidence shows that the text was organized according to the reign years of the rebel Quwo faction in the Jin civil war. This too is as we should expect, since it was the Quwo faction that ultimately defeated the mainline rulers; the victors wrote the history.

This too is not a trivial difference, since I have demonstrated that the "Current Text" *Bamboo Annals*, argued by Wang Guowei and Li Xueqin to be a worthless forgery,[41] reflects the same underlying annalistic structure as the tomb text. True, the "Current Text" *Bamboo Annals* is denominated according to the reign years of the Zhou kings rather than the Jin rulers, but its chronology is exactly the same as that of all early quotations of the *Bamboo Annals*, even though the chronology of those early quotations is by no means transparent. What is more, the "Current Text" also reflects the Quwo bias of the original Jin annals. No late forger, no matter when he may have been working, could have produced such a text.

Instead, the simplest explanation is that the original editors of the *Ji zhong* manuscripts, who most assuredly did not include Du Yu, despite occasional assumptions to the contrary, produced the "Current Text," or at least a text very much like it, in the course of editing the tomb text of the *Bamboo Annals*. For them, the reign years of the Zhou kings would have served as a common standard, more or less akin to the modern use of years BCE and CE. The edition of the text denominated according to the reign years of the Zhou kings was probably intended only as a reference guide as the editors attempted to reconstruct the chronology of the Jin (and then the Wei) rulers.[42] Nevertheless, there is also evidence that this version circulated beyond just the team of editors, it being quoted already just a few decades after the original editorial work was completed.[43]

Now, the discovery of the Tsinghua manuscript *Xinian has not only demonstrated yet again that the *Bamboo Annals*, including also the

"Current Text" *Bamboo Annals*, is an important source for the history of ancient China but, perhaps even more important, it provides a clue concerning the nature and organization of the text that was found in the tomb at Jixian some 1,750 years ago. What is more, mistakes made in the course of editing the *Xinian also suggest how mistakes might have been made both in the editing of the *Bamboo Annals* and also in the long history of scholarship on it. We are fortunate that new evidence provides the means to undo these mistakes, and we have every reason to hope for even more evidence in the future.

Chapter Twelve

The Qin *Bian Nian Ji and the Beginnings of Historical Writing in China

The recently published *Xinian 繫年 Annals that is part of the corpus of Warring States bamboo-slip manuscripts acquired by Tsinghua University 清華大學 has once again focused scholarly interest on the role that "annals" (jinian 紀年) played in early Chinese historical writing.[1] As described in the preceding chapter, Li Xueqin 李學勤 (1933–2019), then director of that university's Center for the Study and Preservation of Unearthed Manuscripts, argued that the *Xinian is a comprehensive "pan-state" type of annals, unlike such year-by-year annals as the Chunqiu 春秋 Springs and Autumns, but similar to, again according to Li, the Zhushu jinian 竹書紀年 Bamboo Annals.[2] As I have argued in the preceding chapter, this characterization of the *Xinian is open to challenge, as is Li's characterization of the Zhushu jinian. Nevertheless, it is surely the case that there were different types of annals available in early China, and they played a very significant role in the development of Chinese historical writing. I propose here first to survey the evidence for annals as a genre in early China; then to provide a detailed introduction to an

---

This chapter was initially published as "Jinian xingshi yu shi shu zhi qiyuan" 紀年形式與史書之起, in Jian bo, jingdian gu shi 簡帛、經典、古史, ed. Chen Zhi 陳致 (Shanghai: Shanghai Guji chubanshe, 2013), 39–46; a revised and expanded English version was published as "The Qin Bian Nian Ji and the Beginnings of Historical Writing in China," in Beyond the First Emperor's Mausoleum: New Perspectives on Qin Art, ed. Liu Yang (Minneapolis: Minneapolis Institute of Art, 2014), 115–36. In the version presented here, I delete the copious notes given for the appended translation; interested readers should consult my chapter in Beyond the First Emperor's Mausoleum.

annals called by its editors *Bian nian ji* 編年記 *Annalistic Record*, that was discovered in 1975 in tomb 1 at Shuihudi 睡虎地, Yunmeng 雲夢, Hubei;[3] and finally to consider the influence of annals on the beginnings of historical consciousness in China.

The most famous annals in the Chinese literary tradition is without question the *Chunqiu* 春秋 *Springs and Autumns* of the state of Lu 魯. This is the text that Confucius (551–479 BCE) is supposed to have edited, an attribution that no later than the late fourth century BCE caused it to be regarded as one of the Chinese classics. However, there are numerous other *chunqiu* 春秋 or annals known in the received literary tradition, and many more have since been discovered buried in ancient tombs. A simple listing of these annals would include at least the following titles:

- A *chunqiu* of Zhou 周 (apparently referring to the Western Zhou state)

- A *chunqiu* of the state of Yan 燕

- A *chunqiu* of the state of Song 宋

- A *chunqiu* of the state of Qi 齊[4]

- The *Chunqiu* 春秋 *Springs and Autumns* of the state of Lu 魯, spanning the years 722–481 BCE

- The *Sheng* 乘 of the state of Jin 晉

- The *Taowu* 檮杌 of the state of Chu 楚[5]

- An annals of the state of Qin 秦, apparently available to Sima Qian 司馬遷 (145–ca. 89 BCE) in his writing of the *Shi ji* 史記[6]

- The *Zhushu jinian* 竹書紀年 or *Bamboo Annals*, reportedly discovered in 279 in a tomb in Ji 汲 commandery (in present-day Henan)[7]

- An annals, called by its editors *Bian nian ji* 編年記, discovered in 1975 in tomb 1 at Shuihudi 睡虎地, Yunmeng 雲夢, Hubei

- Two different sorts of annals, one referred as *Da shi ji* 大事記 and the other as *Nianbiao* 年表, discovered in 1977 in tomb 1 at Shuanggudui 雙古堆, Fuyang 阜陽, Anhui[8]

The Qin *Bian Nian Ji and the Beginning of Historical Writing | 299

Although not all of these annals are still extant, there is enough evidence to suggest that they can be divided into at least two major sub-genres: one a year-by-year account, often devoted to a single state; and the other a synoptic form of annals combining information from several different states, without necessarily privileging any single regnal or calendrical tradition. This latter subgenre, evidenced especially by the *Nianbiao text discovered at Shuanggudui, would have given rise to the various nianbiao 年表 found in the Shi ji of Sima Qian: the "San dai shibiao" 三代世表 "Generation Table of the Three Dynasties," "Shi'er zhuhou nianbiao" 十二諸侯年表 "Annalistic Table of the Twelve Lords," "Liu guo nianbiao" 六國年表 "Annalistic Table of the Six States," "Qin Chu zhi ji yuebiao" 秦楚之際月表 "Monthly Table of Qin and Chu," "Han xing yilai zhuhou nianbiao" 漢興以來諸侯年表 "Annalistic Table of the Lords since the Rise of Han," and "Gao Zu gong chen houzhe nianbiao" 高祖功臣侯者年表 "Annalistic Table of the Ministers and Lords of Gaozu."[9] However, since the Shuanggudui *Nianbiao was not compiled until the Han dynasty and evidence for the text is fragmentary at best, I propose herewith simply to note the early existence of this format, and to focus my attention on the better known and better attested year-by-year annals format.

The best known of the year-by-year annals is the Chunqiu, which provides an account of events in the state of Lu from the first year of Lord Yin 隱 of Lu (r. 722–712 BCE; i.e., 722 BCE) to the fourteenth year of Lord Ai 哀 (r. 494–477 BCE; i.e., 481 BCE).[10] To select one year, more or less at random, the entry for the first year of Lord Zhao 昭 (r. 541–510 BCE; i.e., 541 BCE) gives some idea as to its contents (I here divide the text by entries, though traditional editions of the text do not do so; it is unclear how the original text may have been organized):

元年春王正月：公即位。叔孫豹會晉趙武、楚公子圍、齊國弱、宋向戌、衛齊惡、陳公子招、蔡公孫歸生、鄭罕虎、許人、曹人于虢。

三月：取鄆。

夏：秦伯之弟鍼出奔晉。

六月丁巳：邾子華卒。晉荀吳帥師敗狄于大鹵。

秋：莒去疾自齊入于莒。莒展輿出奔吳。叔弓帥師疆鄆田。葬邾悼公。

冬十有一月己酉：楚子麇卒。楚公子比出奔晉。

First year, spring, the royal first month: Our lord assumed position. Shusun Bao convened Zhao Wu of Jin, Gongzi Wei of Chu, Guo Ruo of Qi, Xiang Xu of Song, Qi E of Wei, Gongzi Zhao of Chen, Gongsun Guisheng of Cai, Han Hu of Zheng, someone of Xu, and someone of Cao in Guo.

Third month: We took Jun.

Summer: Zhen, younger brother of the elder of Qin, fled into exile in Jin.

Sixth month, *dingsi*: Prince Hua of Zhu died. Xun Wu of Jin led troops, defeating the Di at Dayan.

Autumn: Qu Ji of Ju came from Qi and entered into Ju; Zhan Yu of Ju fled into exile in Wu. Shu Gong led troops to defend the borders of the fields of Jun. Duke Dao of Zhu was buried.

Winter, the eleventh month, *jiyou*: Prince Jun of Chu died. Gongzi Bi of Chu fled into exile in Jin.

The records of this one year include many of the types given in other years as well: accessions of new rulers; meetings of the "many lords" (*zhuhou* 諸侯) of the various independent states; military campaigns, especially those of Lu itself (never referred to by name, but always as "we" or "our" [*wo* 我]), but also, though much less systematically, those of other states as well; exiles of nobility; and the deaths and burials of rulers. As here, throughout the *Chunqiu* multiple events are recorded for any single year, divided first into the seasons ("spring" [*chun* 春], "summer" [*xia* 夏], "autumn" [*qiu* 秋], and "winter" [*dong* 冬]), and then by month (enumerated sequentially in the Lu calendar). Occasionally, as in the sixth and eleventh months here, the days of particularly important events are indicated, invariably in the sexagesimal *ganzhi* 干支 system used to record days in all known calendars of ancient China.

Not all year-by-year annals of ancient China were as detailed as the *Chunqiu* by any means. Perhaps more representative would be the annals discovered at Shuihudi and called by its editors *Bian nian ji*. This text, found in the tomb of a third-century BCE Qin local magistrate named Xi 喜 (262–217 BCE), was written in two separate registers on fifty-three bamboo slips. It contains year entries for each year beginning with the first year of King Zhao 昭 of Qin (i.e., King Zhaoxiang 昭襄; r. 306–251 BCE) through the thirtieth year of the then "current" (*jin* 今) king (i.e., King Zheng 政 of Qin, later known as Shi huangdi 始皇帝; r. 246–210

BCE; i.e., 217 BCE), with many of the years supplied with records of major events in the state of Qin, especially military campaigns.¹¹ In addition to these official records, the bulk of which are written in one hand, the Shuihudi *Bian nian ji also includes mention of major events in the life of Xi himself, including his birth at cockcrow (*ji ming* 雞鳴) of the day *jiawu* 甲午 in the twelfth month of the forty-fifth year of King Zhao (i.e., 10 November 262 BCE), as well as various appointments and promotions, the deaths of his own parents, as well as the births of three children; these are written in a separate handwriting.¹² Annals for the last ten years of King Zhao's reign (i.e., 260–251 BCE) are more or less representative of the entire text and include most of its different features; I write the personal records pertaining to Xi in italics to differentiate them from the public records.

卌七年攻長平十一月敢產。

卌八年攻武安。

. . .

五十年攻邯鄲

五十一年攻陽城

五十二年王稽張祿死

五十三年吏誰從軍

五十四年

五十五年

五十六年後九月昭死正月遬產

Forty-seventh year: Attacked Changping.¹³ *Eleventh month: Gan was born.*¹⁴

Forty-eighth year: Attacked Wu'an.

. . .¹⁵

Fiftieth year: Attacked Handan.

Fifty-first year: Attacked Yangcheng.

Fifty-second year: Wang Qi and Zhang Lu died.

Fifty-third year: *The officer was selected to join the army.*

Fifty-fourth year:

Fifty-fifth year:

Fifty-sixth year, the latter ninth month: Zhao died. *First month: Su was born.*

The format and calligraphy of the text suggest that the main portion may have been copied in or shortly after 231 BCE from some sort of "official" annals, with the addition, in a different hand, of the family matters, and that entries for years after that date were added gradually, perhaps year by year, probably by Xi himself.[16] If it is the case that a local official in a relatively remote location in what is now Hubei Province, far removed from the Qin capital, made such a copy, then it is safe to assume that this annals was widely available throughout the Qin kingdom, and thus that the entries in it would have been known to all or almost all officials. In this way, the entries for individual years could have served as a sort of shorthand notation for the year in question; in other words, the year that "Wang Qi and Zhang Lu died" would have been known to all as the fifty-second year of King Zhao, or in effect 255 BCE.[17]

Indeed, we find various kinds of paleographic sources from this period in which dates are given in this sort of anecdotal fashion, presumably keyed to some annals or another. For instance, the first significant discovery of Warring States texts written on bamboo slips came in January 1987 from tomb 2 at Baoshan 包山, Hubei, the tomb of one Shao Tuo 邵疸 (d. 316 BCE), a magistrate of the state of Chu. The 288 bamboo slips in the tomb contained records of court cases over which Shao Tuo presided and also records of divinations performed on his behalf during the last several years of his life, as well as an inventory of the grave goods placed in the tomb. As the following two records show, both the court records and the personal divination records are routinely dated according to major events that occurred within the state of Chu.

> 大司馬邵陽敗晉師于襄陵之歲夏㫝之月庚午之日，命尹子士、大師子繡命龔陵公䢼鼉為鄩郢貣越異之錄金一百益二益四兩。

> In the year that Grand Marshall Zhao Yang defeated the Jin army at Xiangling, the Xiayi month, the *gengwu* day, Commandant Foreman Prince Tu and Grand Captain Prince Pei commanded Duke Yu Mao of Xunling to borrow 102 *yi* and 4 *liang* of Yue Yi gold dust on behalf of the suburban district.[18]

> 東周之客䛨緷歸胙于䊹郢之歲爂月己酉之日，䢼朕以少寶為左尹邵𧧟貞：既又病，病心疾，少氣，不內飤，爂月期中尚毋又桑。

> In the year that the East Zhou envoy Xu Ying brought offerings to Detached Ying, in the Cuan month, on day *jiyou*, Nong Qiang used the Small Treasure to divine on behalf of Zuoyin Shao Tuo: Having been pained, pained with heart problems, shortness of breath, and an inability to eat, within the Cuan month would that he not have anxiety.[19]

It is important to note that there is no intrinsic relationship between the event used to indicate the year in question and the content of the record. In the Baoshan corpus, there are seven different such year notations, some of them recurring repeatedly. Some of these, such as Grand Marshall Zhao Yang's 邵陽 defeat of the Jin army at Xiangling 襄陵, are well known from the traditional historical record (this particular event occurred in 322 BCE[20]); others, such as the offerings brought to the Chu capital by the East Zhou envoy Xu Ying 䛨緷, are unknown from the traditional historical record. However, on the basis of the content of the Baoshan records, it is possible to put them in sequence and even to date them securely to the years 322–316 BCE.

> 大司馬邵陽敗晉師于襄陵之歲

> The year that the Great Supervisor of the Horse Zhao Yang defeated the Jin army at Xiangling (i.e., 322 BCE)

齊客陳豫賀王之歲

The year that the Qi envoy Chen Yu greeted the king (i.e., 321 BCE)

魯陽公以楚師後城鄭之歲

The year that Duke Yang of Lu took the rearguard of the Chu army to wall Zheng (i.e., 320 BCE)

□客監固遇楚之歲

The year that the ... envoy Jian Gu met Chu (i.e., 319 BCE)

宋客盛公䩗聘于楚之歲

The year that the Song envoy Bian Duke Sheng presented himself at Chu (i.e., 318 BCE)

東周之客䛒緹歸胙于葴郢之歲

The year that the East Zhou envoy Xu Ying brought offerings to Detached Ying (i.e., 317 BCE)

大司馬悼愲將楚邦之師以救郙之歲

The year that Great Supervisor of the Horse Dao Hua led the army of the Chu state to relieve Fu (i.e., 316 BCE)

Similar dating notations are seen also in various kinds of bronze artifacts: weapons, weights and measures, and tallies. For instance, the *E Jun Qi jie* 鄂君啟節 is one of several bronze tallies that the king of Chu ordered to be made for Qi 啟, the lord of E 鄂, to ensure safe passage for him and his cargo as he passed through the Chu realm. Before providing a detailed itinerary of Qi's pathways, the tallies record the time and place of the Chu king's command:

大司馬卲陽敗晉師於襄陵之歲夏㞕之月乙亥之日，王處於葴郢之遊宮。大攻尹睢台王命命集尹悤糈、裁尹逆、裁敔阢為鄂君啟之賸造鑄金節

The Qin *Bian Nian Ji* and the Beginning of Historical Writing | 305

> In the year that Grand Marshall Zhao Yang defeated the Jin army at Xiangling, in the Xiayi month, on the day *yihai*, the king was located in the Traveling Palace in Detached Ying. Sui, the Great Foreman of Artisans, used the king's command to command the group foreman Shao Zhu, the foreman of tailors Ni, and the commandant of tailors Qi to create and cast metal tallies on behalf of Lord Qi of E's treasury.[21]

By a happy coincidence, these tallies were cast in the same year as many of the records included in the Baoshan corpus: "the year that Grand Marshall Zhao Yang defeated the Jin army at Xiangling," which is to say 322 BCE. It is again worth noting that the event used to indicate the year had no necessary relationship with the content of the tallies; it is simply a generic time marker. Moreover, the formula used in the *E Jun Qi jie* is word-for-word identical with those that occur in the Baoshan records made in the same year. This would seem to suggest, as also suggested earlier for the state of Qin, that there existed in the state of Chu an official annals, copies of which were widely available throughout the realm. This annals, keyed to important events in the state of Chu, was doubtless not simply a means of indicating dates of events, but must have served as something of an official history of the state.

There is some evidence that similar date notations were used much earlier than the late fourth century BCE and that they too may have been tied to some form of annals. Although the records in the *Chunqiu* are routinely dated numerically to the years of reign of the various lords of Lu, its canonical commentary the *Zuo zhuan* 左傳 includes several "great-event" year notations, including the following two examples that suggest that these year notations were well known and used within a calendrical context.[22]

> 公送晉侯，晉侯以公宴于河上，問公年。季武子對曰："會于沙隨之歲，寡君以生。"晉侯曰："十二年矣，是謂一終，一星終也。"

> Our lord (i.e., Lord Xiang of Lu) was escorting the Lord of Jin, and the Lord of Jin entertained our lord at the River. [The Lord of Jin] asked our lord's age. Jiwuzi responded: "In the year of the meeting at Shasui, my lord was born." The Lord of Jin said: "Twelve years, this is called one cycle, one planetary cycle." (Lord Xiang 襄 9; i.e., 564 BCE)

二月癸未，晉悼夫人食輿人之城杞者。絳縣人或年長矣，無子，而往與於食。有與疑年，使之年。曰："臣小人也，不知紀年。臣生之歲，正月甲子朔，四百有四十五甲子矣。其季於今，三之一也。"吏走問諸朝。師曠曰："魯叔仲惠伯會郤成子於承筐之歲也。是歲也，狄伐魯，叔孫莊叔於是乎敗狄于鹹，獲長狄僑如及虺也、豹也，而皆以名其子。七十三年矣。"

In the second month on *guiwei*, Consort Dao of Jin was feeding the men who had walled Ji. There was a man of Jiang district, who was aged and without children, and who went and joined in the meal. There were those who were suspicious about his age and had him tell it. He said: "I am but a petty person, and don't know how to count years. The year in which I was born, the day of the new moon of the first month was a *jiazi*, and there have been 445 *jiazi*s since, with one-third [of a cycle] left over today." The officers ran to ask at court. Master Kuang said: "It was the year that Shuzhong Huibo of Lu met Que Chengzi at Chengkuang. In that year, the Di attacked Lu, and Shusun Zhuangshu thereupon defeated the Di at Xian, capturing their leaders Qiaoru and Hui and Bao, which he used to name his sons. It has been seventy-three years." (Lord Xiang 襄 30; 543 BCE)

The "meeting at Shasui" 沙隨, a city in the state of Song 宋 located in present-day northeastern Henan, is recorded in the *Chunqiu* under the sixteenth year of Lord Cheng 成 (575 BCE). The meeting was convened by the lord of Jin at the time of a war between Jin and Chu, and included his allies from Qi 齊, Wei 衛, Song 宋, and Zhu 邾. The lord of Lu did not attend, apparently waiting to see which army would prove victorious, and was reproached for his absence. These circumstances would ensure that this event was well known throughout north China, and certainly to the rulers of Lu and Jin, the protagonists of the first passage cited earlier. It may be that the lord of Jin counted the years between that year and the year of his present meeting with the lord of Lu (564 BCE) extemporaneously (after all, twelve years should not be too hard to remember), but it seems possible also that he would have had reference to some sort of annals to confirm the number of years that had passed. In the case of the second passage, in which the interval between the two years was fully seventy-three years, it seems almost inconceivable that anybody—including even the perspicacious Master Kuang 師曠—would have been able to make such a calculation without a written record in front of him. In fact, the *Chunqiu* entry for the eleventh year of Lord Wen of Lu 魯文公 (r. 626–609 BCE), that is, 616 BCE, records both the meeting of Shuzhong Huibo 叔仲惠伯 and Que Chengzi 郤成子 at Chengkuang 承筐, though it does not use their posthumous names as does Master Kuang, and also the defeat of the Di 狄 by Shusun Zhuangshu 叔孫莊叔 (Master Kuang again referring to him by his posthumous epithet while the *Chunqiu* used the style-name he used during his lifetime, Dechen 得臣):

夏叔仲彭生會晉郤缺于承筐。. . .

冬十月甲午叔孫得臣敗狄于鹹。

In summer, Shuzhong Pengsheng met Que Que of Jin at Chengkuang. . . .

In winter, tenth month, *jiawu*, Shusun Dechen defeated the Di at Xian.

It is possible that written records such as these existed at much earlier times. As mentioned briefly at the beginning of this essay, the *Mozi* 墨子 begins its recounting of the *chunqiu* of the various states with the mention of a *chunqiu* of Zhou.

> 今執無鬼者言曰："夫天下之為聞見鬼神之物者，不可勝計也。亦孰為聞見神鬼有無之物哉？"子墨子曰："若以眾之所同見，與眾之所同聞，則若昔者杜伯是也。周宣王殺其臣杜伯而不辜，杜伯曰：'吾君殺我而不辜，若以死者為無知則止矣。若死而有知，不出三年必使吾君知之'。其三年，周宣王合諸侯而（用）〔田〕於圃田，車數百乘，（從）〔徒〕數千，人滿野。日中，杜伯乘白馬素車，朱衣冠，執朱弓，挾朱矢，追周宣王，射入車上，中心折脊，殪車中，伏弢而死。當是之時，周人從者莫不見，遠者莫不聞，著在周之《春秋》。"

Nowadays those who hold that there are no ghosts say: "Those under heaven who have heard and seen the things of ghosts and spirits are innumerable, but who has heard or seen the things that ghosts and spirits have or not?" Zi Mozi says: "If we take that which everyone has seen and everyone has heard, then it would be like the case of Dubo in the past. King Xuan of Zhou was about to kill his minister Dubo, who was innocent. Dubo said: 'My lord will kill me even though I am innocent. If the dead are without sentience, then it will stop at that. But if the dead are sentient, within three years I will certainly let my lord know it.' In the third year, King Xuan of Zhou together with the many lords was hunting in the fields of Pu. There were many hundreds of chariots and many thousands of followers, people filling the wilds. In the middle of the day, Dubo, riding in a plain chariot drawn by white horses, wearing a crimson jacket and hat, and holding a crimson bow and clutching crimson arrows, pursued King Xuan of Zhou and shot him in his chariot, breaking his breastbone and hitting his heart; [the king] died in his chariot, toppling over dead. At this time, among the Zhou followers there was none who did not see it, and none in distant parts who did not hear of it. It is recorded in the Zhou *Springs and Autumns*."

The event to which Mozi alludes, the killing of King Xuan of Zhou 周宣王 (r. 827/25–782 BCE), the penultimate king of the Western Zhou dynasty, by one Dubo 杜伯 probably ought not serve as evidence for the existence of ghosts (it is easy enough to imagine explanations for the sudden appearance of a "Dubo" other than the resurrection of a man who had been executed), but the explicit statement that this story "is recorded in the Zhou *Springs and Autumns*" (著在周之春秋) should certainly count as valuable evidence in the history of Chinese historiography.

At the beginning of the Western Zhou period, many bronze vessels include, often at the very beginning of the inscription, a sort of "great event" date notation. One of these inscriptions, on the *Zhong fangding* 中方鼎 (*Jicheng* 2751), formally resembles the date notations recorded in Warring States paleographic sources and in the *Zuo zhuan*.

惟王令南宮伐反虎方之年，王令中先省南或貫行，埶王位在夔陣真山。中乎歸生鳳于王，埶于寶彝。

It was the year in which the king commanded Nangong to attack the rebelling Hufang; the king commanded Zhong to advance and examine the southern states and connect the route, setting up the king's quarters at Huzhen Mountain in Kui. Zhong called out to return a live pheasant to the king, setting it out in this precious vessel.

Other examples are strikingly similar, even if they refer to different events. For instance, the *Lü ding* 旅鼎 (*Jicheng* 2728) is doubtless a generation or two older than the *Zhong fangding*, and so the rebellion that it refers to is certainly different, but the form is similar.

惟公大保來伐反尸年，在十又一月庚申，公在盩師。公賜旅貝十朋。旅用作父尊彝。

It was the year that the duke Grand Protector came from attacking the rebelling Yi, in the eleventh month, *gengshen*; the duke was at the Zhou Garrison. The duke awarded Lü ten strands of cowries. Lü herewith makes for his father this sacrificial vessel.

The *Qin gui* 禽簋 (*Jicheng* 4041) and *Gang Qie zun* 䎉劫尊 (*Jicheng* 5977) are closely contemporary with the *Lü ding*, and their inscriptions may even refer to the suppression of the same general rebellion. The inscriptions both begin with what, but for the lack of the word "year" (*nian* 年), would certainly be construed as a great event date notation.

王伐蓋侯。周公某，禽祝。禽又敗祝。王賜金百鋝。禽用作寶彝。

The king attacked the lord of Gai. The Duke of Zhou made plans and Qin prayed. Qin again prayed exorcistically, and the king awarded [him] one hundred measures of metal. Qin herewith makes this treasured vessel.

王征蓋，賜䎉劫貝朋，用作朕高祖缶尊彝。

The king campaigned against Gai, and awarded Gang Qie cowries. [He] herewith makes for my high ancestor this treasured sacrificial vessel.

It seems probable that in all of these cases, the great event notations are intimately connected with the events commemorated in the inscriptions and so may not constitute evidence of an independent dating convention; that is to say, in the first case, that Zhong's service was very much involved when the "the king commanded Nangong to attack the rebelling Hufang," in the second case, the Grand Protector's award to Lü was doubtless for services rendered in aiding his "attack [on] the rebelling Yi," and that both the third and fourth cases commemorate services rendered in the king's campaign against Gai 蓋. However, there are other inscriptions where the connection between the date notation and the content of the inscription is less direct. For instance, the *Hou Chuo fangding* 厚趠方鼎 (*Jicheng* 2730) commemorates an award to Hou Chuo 厚趠 by the Duke of Zhai 祭公, a state located in present-day northeastern Henan. The inscription begins by mentioning a royal visit to the eastern capital at Chengzhou 成周, even though the king seems not to be involved in Hou Chuo's relationship with the Duke of Zhai (of course, it may well be that Hou Chuo was dispatched by the king to pay a visit to the Duke of Zhai, perhaps even in the context of his royal visit to the eastern capital).

惟王來各于成周年，厚趠又價于祭公。趠用作厥文考父辛寶尊齋，其子子孫永寶。束

It was the year in which the king came from entering into Chengzhou. Hou Chuo had an award from the Duke of Zhai. Chuo herewith makes for his cultured deceased-father Father Xin this treasured, sacrificial caldron; may sons' sons and grandsons eternally treasure it. Clan sign

While there is of course no direct evidence showing that these great event year notations were ever correlated to any sort of annals kept at the Zhou court, it may not be entirely unreasonable to speculate that there may have been such a Zhou court annals. In making this suggestion, allow me to return to the inscription on the *Zhong fangding*, with which I opened this discussion of Western Zhou bronze inscriptions. The inscription begins: "It was the year in which the king commanded Nangong to attack the rebelling Hufang; the king commanded Zhong to advance and examine the southern states and connect the route." The vessel on which the inscription was cast was one of six vessels discovered during the reign of Song Hui zong 宋徽宗 (r. 1101–1125; the vessel was discovered in 1118) in Xiaogan 孝感, Hubei. It is generally dated to the time of a southern military campaign led by King Zhao of

Zhou 周昭王 (r. 977/75–957 BCE), a campaign that led to a defeat on the part of the Zhou army, with King Zhao himself dying. Despite the disastrous result of this campaign, in the earliest "history" of the dynasty, the inscription on the Shi Qiang pan 史墻盤 (Jicheng 10175), this event is used to identify, albeit indirectly, King Zhao's reign.

弘魯邵王：廣辝楚刑，惟寏南行。

Vast and substantial was King Zhao: he broadly tamed Chu and Jing; it was to connect the southern route.

Notice that the purpose of this southern campaign is said to have been "to connect the southern route," reminiscent of the wording of the Zhong fangding inscription: "to advance and examine the southern states and connect the route."[23] I think it goes without saying that Secretary Qiang 史墻, the "author" of the Shi Qiang pan inscription, did not have direct access to the Zhong fangding inscription (after all, the vessel that carried the inscription was buried in Hubei, far to the south of the Zhou capital). What better way to explain the coincidence of wording between these two sources than some sort of intermediary annalistic account kept at the Zhou royal court and to which Secretary Qiang, who was an official secretary at that court, would have had easy access by virtue of his position?

Let me not close with a question, but rather with an affirmation. I do not mean to say, as I once did, that the Shi Qiang pan inscription itself marks the "first conscious attempt in China to write history,"[24] though I certainly continue to believe that it reflects a historical consciousness.[25] As I and several others have noted, the narrative of events included in some bronze inscriptions is but a tertiary record, a copy of a copy of a "command document" (ming shu 命書) stored in the archives of the royal palace.[26] These command documents were primary records that the secretaries not only composed but also had the responsibility to store and to consult—both practices that are surely in the repertoire of any historian. Unfortunately, we do not now have access to these archives, and may never have it. Nevertheless, what I wish to argue is that the Western Zhou bronze inscriptions, including some from the very beginning of the Western Zhou period, reflect—albeit at yet one further remove—this record-keeping practice that contributed directly to the making of annals. This certainly would have been an important step—if not the "first" step—in the writing of history in China.

Appendix

Translation of Shuihudi 睡虎地 Qin Bamboo-Strip Manuscript *Bian Nian Ji* 編年紀 Annals

The *Annals* are written on fifty-three bamboo slips in two registers, an upper register starting just below the top binding strap, and a lower register starting just below the middle binding strap.[27] The upper register runs from the first year of King Zhao of Qin 秦昭王 (i.e., King Zhaoxiang of Qin 秦昭襄王, r. 306–251 BCE; i.e., 306 BCE) through the fifty-third year (254 BCE), while the bottom register runs from the fifty-fourth year of King Zhao through thirty-seven slips to the thirtieth year of the "Current" (*Jin* 今) King, Qin Wang Zheng 秦王政 (i.e., Qin Shi huangdi 秦始皇帝, r. 246–210 BCE; i.e., 217 BCE), with the lower register of the last sixteen slips blank. In the following translation, I strive to preserve this two-register layout, though in a horizontal format. As I did earlier in the main body of this essay, I write the personal records concerning events in the life of Xi 喜 in italics to differentiate them from the official public annals. The original published version of this essay is supplied with copious notes identifying place-names and indicating correspondences between the Shuihudi *Annals* and the *Shi ji* 史記 (as well as occasional discrepancies); interested readers should consult the original publication for these notes.

Slip	Top Register	Bottom Register
01	昭王元年 King Zhao first year	五十四年 Fifty-fourth year
02	二年攻皮氏 Second year: Attacked Pishi	五十五年 Fifty-fifth year
03	三年 Third year	五十六年後九月昭死正月速產 Fifty-sixth year, the latter ninth month: Zhao died. *First month: Su was born*

The Qin *Bian Nian Ji* and the Beginning of Historical Writing | 313

04	四年攻封陵 Fourth year: Attacked Fengling	孝文王元年立即死。 King Xiaowen first year: Having taken his place immediately died
05	五年歸蒲反 Fifth year: Returned Pufan	莊王元年 King Zhuang first year
06	六年攻新城 Sixth year: Attacked Xincheng	莊王二年 King Zhuang second year
07	七年新城陷 Seventh year: Xincheng fell	莊王三年莊王死 King Zhuang third year: The king died
08	八年新城歸 Eighth year: Xincheng was returned	今元年喜傅 The Current (King) first year: *Xi was instructed*
09	九年攻析 Ninth year: Attacked Xi	二年 Second year
10	十年 Tenth year	三年卷軍八月喜揄吏 Third year: The Juan Army. *Eighth month: Xi was drafted as secretary*
11	十一年 Eleventh year	〔四年〕囗軍十一月喜囗安陸囗史 Fourth year: . . . Army. *Eleventh month: Xi . . . Anlu . . . secretary*
12	十二年 Twelfth year	五年 Fifth year
13	十三年攻伊闕 Thirteenth year: Attacked Yique	六年四月為安陸令史 Sixth year, *fourth month: Became Commandant Secretary of Anlu*
14	十四年伊闕 Fourteenth year: Yique	七年正月甲寅鄢令史 Seventh year, *first month, jiayin: Commandant Secretary of Yan*

15	十五年攻魏 Fifteenth year: Attacked Wei	八年 Eighth year
16	十六年攻宛 Sixteenth year: Attacked Wan	九年 Ninth year
17	十七年攻垣枳 Seventeenth year: Attacked Yuan and Zhi	
18	十八年攻蒲反 Eighteenth year: Attacked Pufan	十一年十一月獲產 Eleventh year, *eleventh month*: Hu was born
19	十九年 Nineteenth year	十二年四月癸丑喜治獄鄢 Twelfth year, *fourth month*, guichou: Xi governed lawsuits at Yan
20	廿年攻安邑 Twentieth year: Attacked Anyi	十三年從軍 Thirteenth year: *Joined the army*
21	廿一年攻夏山 Twenty-first year: Attacked Xiashan	十四年 Fourteenth year
22	廿二年 Twenty-second year	十五年從平陽軍 Fifteenth year: *Joined the Pingyang Army*
23	廿三年 Twenty-third year	十六年七月丁巳公終自占年 Sixteenth year, *seventh month*, dingsi: *Father met his end. The year I registered*
24	廿四年攻林 Twenty-fourth year: Attacked Lin	十七年攻韓 Seventeenth year: Attacked Han
25	廿五年攻茲氏 Twenty-fifth year: Attacked Zishi	十八年攻趙正月恢生 Eighteenth year: Attacked Zhao. *First month: Hui was born*

26	廿六年攻離石	十九年□□□□南郡備敬
	Twenty-sixth year: Attacked Lishi	Nineteenth year: ... Southern Commandery prepared the alarm
27	廿七年攻鄧	廿年七月甲寅嫗終韓王居□山
	Twenty-seventh year: Attacked Deng	Twentieth year, *seventh month, jiayin*: Mother met her end. The king of Hann resided at ... Mountain
28	廿八年攻[鄢]	廿一年韓王死昌平君居其處有死□屬
	Twenty-eighth year: Attacked Yan	Twenty-first year: The king of Hann died. The Lord of Changping occupied his place; there were dying ... adherents
29	廿九年攻安陸	廿二年攻魏梁
	Twenty-ninth year: Attacked Anlu	Twenty-second year: Attacked Wei's Liang
30	卅年攻□山	廿三年興攻荊□□守陽□死四月昌文君死
	Thirtieth year: Attacked ... shan	Twenty-third year: Raised to attack Jing ... Shouyang ... died. Fourth month: Lord Changwen died
31	卅一年□	□□□王□□
	Thirty-first year: ...	... king ...
32	卅二年攻啟封	廿五年
	Thirty-second year: Attacked Qifeng	Twenty-fifth year
33	卅三年攻蔡中陽	廿六年
	Thirty-third year: Attacked Cai and Zhongyang	Twenty-sixth year

34	卅四年攻華陽 Thirty-fourth year: Attacked Huayang	廿七年八月己亥廷食時產穿耳 Twenty-seventh year, *eighth month*, jihai, *just at the hour of breakfast was born Chuan Er*
35	卅五年 Thirty-fifth year	…年今過安陸 …year: The Current (King) passed through Anlu
36	卅六年 Thirty-sixth year	廿九年 Twenty-ninth year
37	卅七年口寇剛 Thirty-seventh year: … robbed Gang	卅年 Thirtieth year
38	卅八年闕輿 Thirty-eighth year: Yanyu	
39	卅九年攻懷 Thirty-ninth year: Attacked Huai	
40	卌年 Fortieth year	
41	卌一年攻邢丘 Forty-first year: Attacked Xingqiu	
42	卌二年攻少曲 Forty-second year: Attacked Shaoqu	
43		
44	卌四年攻大行·口攻 Forty-fourth year: Attacked Taihang … attacked	
45	卌五年攻大野王十二月甲午雞鳴時喜產	

	Forty-fifth year: Attacked Dayewang. *Twelfth month, jiawu, at the hour of Cockcrow, Xi was born*	
46	卌六年攻□亭 Forty-sixth year: Attacked . . . -ting	
47	卌七年攻長平十一月敢產 Forty-seventh year: Attacked Changping. *Eleventh month: Gan was born*	
48	卌八年攻武安 Forty-eighth year: Attacked Wu'an	
49	. . .	
50	. . . 攻邯單 (Fiftieth year): Attacked Handan	
51	五十一年攻陽城 Fifty-first year: Attacked Yangcheng	
52	. . . 年王稽張祿死 (Fifty-second) year: Wang Qi and Zhang Lu died	
53	. . . 三年吏誰從軍 (Fifty)-third year: *The officer was selected to join the army*	

Notes

Introduction

1. David Schaberg, "Review of *Before Confucius: Studies in the Creation of the Chinese Classics*, by Edward L. Shaughnessy," *Journal of Asian Studies* 57, no. 4 (1998): 1137–38.

2. David Schaberg, "Texts and Artifacts: A Review of *The Cambridge History of Ancient China*," *Monumenta Serica* 49 (2001): 474–75.

3. For quotations of these scholars' views vis-à-vis orality and the *Shi jing*, see Edward L. Shaughnessy, "The Origin and Development of Western Sinologists' Theories of the Oral-Formulaic Nature of the *Classic of Poetry*," *Bulletin of the Jao Tsung-i Academy of Sinology* 3 (2016): 133–35.

4. Martin Kern, "Early Chinese Literature, Beginnings through Western Han," in *The Cambridge History of Chinese Literature, Vol. 1: To 1375*, ed. Kang-I Sun Chang and Stephen Owen (Cambridge: Cambridge University Press, 2011), 27–28.

5. Edward L. Shaughnessy, *Before Confucius: Studies in the Creation of the Chinese Classics* (Albany: State University of New York Press, 1997), 3.

6. Zhu Hanmin 朱漢民 and Chen Songchang 陳松長, ed., *Yuelu shuyuan cang Qin jian* 岳麓書院藏秦簡 (Shanghai: Shanghai Cishu chubanshe, 2010–), five volumes published to date. For an introduction to these materials in English, see Robin D. S. Yates, "The Qin Slips and Boards from Well No. 1, Liye, Hunan: A Brief Introduction to the Qin Qianling County Archives," *Early China* 35–36 (2012–2013): 291–329.

7. Dirk Meyer, *Philosophy on Bamboo: Text and the Production of Meaning in Early China* (Leiden: Brill, 2012), 241–47, argues that bamboo-slip manuscripts first became broadly diffused in the second half of the first millennium BCE, and that this prompted the philosophical innovations associated with that period, though he admits that "mere technological availability therefore was not the sole factor in the development of these new forms of text."

8. Li Xueqin 李學勤, ed. in chief, and Qinghua daxue Chutu wenxian yanjiu yu baohu zhongxin 清華大學出土文獻研究與保護中心, eds., *Qinghua daxue cang Zhanguo zhujian* 清華大學藏戰國竹簡 (Shanghai: Zhong Xi shuju, 2010–).

9. Li Feng, "Literacy and the Social Contexts of Literacy in the Western Zhou," in *Writing and Literacy in Early China: Studies from the Columbia Early China Seminar*, ed. Li Feng and David Prager Branner (Seattle: University of Washington Press, 2011), 272. While I would not wish to make a similar claim for the still earlier Shang dynasty, Li's comment uncannily echoes a statement made by David N. Keightley (1932–2017) many years before about the means by which the Shang royal court was able to govern:

> It should be noticed that the large-scale mobilization of labor for warfare and agriculture, and the existence of a proto-bureaucracy to administer it, far precedes any hydraulic role by the government. Historical reasons, rather than the theories of the geographical determinists, explain the development of Shang public work and its continuance by the Chou. The survival of both dynasties, surrounded by hostile tribes, depended upon strong military forces, which in turn required efficient manpower conscription and weapons production. The Shang were the first group to organize their subjects in this way because they were the first group in China to possess the indispensable bureaucratic tool—a written language.

David Noel Keightley, "Public Work in Ancient China: A Study of Forced Labor in the Shang and Western Chou," PhD diss., Columbia University, 1969, abstract.

10. Li Feng, "Literacy and the Social Contexts of Literacy in the Western Zhou," 301, 280.

11. Jingzhou shi bowuguan, ed. *Guodian Chu mu zhu jian* 郭店楚墓竹簡 (Beijing: Wenwu chubanshe, 1998).

12. In chapter 7, p. 174, I note that as of 2005 Kern characterized his conclusions as tentative and subject to revision based on new evidence; Martin Kern, "The *Odes* in Excavated Manuscripts," in *Text and Ritual in Early China*, ed. Martin Kern (Seattle: University of Washington Press, 2005), 150–51. Kern's most recent statement that I have seen concerning this topic, which was published only after this book was well in press, does seem to revise his earlier statements about the centrality of orality:

> Before turning to artifacts of *literary writing*, something must be said about the prehistory of literature before writing, or rather, the absence of any evidence for such a prehistory in ancient China. In

contrast to, say, Greece, India, or Mesopotamia, there is no trace of a grand Chinese narrative or epic that may first have existed orally before finally being committed to writing, nor can we point to an early culture of song that preceded the arrival of writing and then was continued in written form. This does not mean that such things did not exist; in China just as everywhere else, people would have told their stories and sung their songs long before they knew or cared about how to write them. But none of these songs and stories is visible in the early documented stages of Chinese writing. Instead, the known traces of mythical narratives—all of them small fragments and often contradictory—that point to the dawn of history postdate the emergence of writing by several centuries and hence may not reflect that ancient oral culture at all.

The literary teleology from orality to writing, perhaps still a valid paradigm elsewhere, thus does not apply to early China.

Martin Kern, "Chinese," in *How Literatures Begin: A Global History*, ed. Joel B. Lande and Denis Feeney (Princeton, NJ: Princeton University Press, 2022), 22–23.

13. Wooden slips bearing writing were first discovered in Central Asia in 1900, with additional discoveries there coming over the subsequent several decades, though it is the case that ancient bamboo slips bearing writing had been unearthed occasionally during Six Dynasties, Tang, and Song periods.

Chapter One: History and Inscriptions

1. Throughout this book, dates are as given in Michael Loewe and Edward L. Shaughnessy, eds., *The Cambridge History of Ancient China: From the Origins of Civilization to 221 BCE* (New York: Cambridge University Press, 1999), 25, with the exception of revising the dates for King Xiao of Zhou 周孝王 from 872?–866 to 882?–866; the question mark indicates the particularly uncertain nature of this date. Indeed, all of these dates are uncertain and are intended primarily to provide a convenient timeline.

2. Most Shang oracle-bone inscriptions are now routinely cited according to their entry number in Guo Moruo and Hu Houxuan, *Jiaguwen heji*.

3. In the original publication of this essay, I also indicated that Yue 戉 shared the same trajectory from an initial adversarial relationship with the Shang court to one of their allies. I am no longer sure Yue was an enemy in the same way as Fou and Xuan, and so I have deleted comments about it.

4. David N. Keightley, "The Diviners' Notebooks: Shang Oracle-Bone Inscriptions as Secondary Sources," in *Actes du Colloque International Commémo-*

rant le Centenaire de la Découverte des Inscriptions sur Os et Carapaces (Paris: Langages Croisés, 2001), 23.

5. The reverse side of the bone contains a *ganzhi* 干支 "stem-and-branch" chart, but only about one-third of the sixty days of a complete chart survive; see fig. 1.1. Thus, it stands to reason that only about one-third of the inscription on the obverse survives.

6. Keightley, "The Diviners' Notebooks," 11.

7. This assumes that the three inscriptions all refer to the same bone on which they were inscribed.

8. Keightley, "The Diviners' Notebooks," 14.

9. The earliest inscriptions on bronze vessels, usually just a single graph in the form of a clan insignia, date to the reign of Shang king Wu Ding and therefore are roughly contemporary with the earliest oracle-bone inscriptions.

10. The *corpus inscriptionum* of record is Zhongguo Shehui kexueyuan Kaogu yanjiusuo, ed., *Yin Zhou jinwen jicheng* 殷周金文集成, 18 vols. (N.p.: Zhonghua shuju, 1984–1994); it will be cited hereafter, in the text, as *Jicheng*. For the most recent catalogs, including both more recently unearthed bronzes and also those held in private collections that were previously unpublished, see Wu Zhenfeng 吳鎮烽, *Shang Zhou qingtongqi mingwen ji tuxiang jicheng* 商周青銅器銘文暨圖像集成, 35 vols. (Shanghai: Shanghai Guji chubanshe, 2012), and Wu Zhenfeng, *Shang Zhou qingtongqi mingwen ji tuxiang jicheng xubian* 商周青銅器銘文暨圖像集成續編, 4 vols. (Shanghai: Shanghai Guji chubanshe, 2016).

11. In the original version of this essay, I accepted the consensus view that the *Da Yu ding* 大盂鼎 should be dated to the reign of King Kang. I now suspect that this date is two generations too early, and that the vessel should instead date to the reign of King Mu. For a study by me supporting this revisionist view, see Xia Hanyi 夏含夷, "Cong *Zeng Gong Qiu bianzhong* mingwen chongxin kaolü *Da Yu ding* he *Xiao Yu ding* de niandai" 從《曾公求編鐘》銘文重新考慮《大盂鼎》和《小盂鼎》的年代, in *Zhang Changshou Chen Gongrou xiansheng jinian wenji* 張長壽、陳公柔先生紀念文集, ed. Li Feng 李峰 and Shi Jingsong 施勁松 (Shanghai: Zhong-Xi shuju, 2022), 373–83.

12. This *yi* 已, like *er* 爾, are routinely assumed to be sentence-opening ejaculations, perhaps similar to "hey" or "you" in English.

13. Shaanxi sheng Kaogu yanjiusuo, Baoji shi kaogu gongzuodui and Meixian wehuaguan, "Shaanxi Meixian Yangjia cun Xi Zhou qingtongqi jiaocang fajue jianbao" 陝西眉縣楊家村西周青銅器窖藏發掘簡報, *Wenwu* 文物 2003.6, 25–27.

14. For a translation and study of this important vessel inscription, see Li Feng, "Literacy and the Social Contexts of Writing in the Western Zhou," 287–92.

15. For the inscription, see Ma Chengyuan 馬承源, "Jin Hou Su bianzhong" 晉侯蘇編鐘, *Shanghai bowuguan guankan* 上海博物館館刊 7 (1996): 1–17; and Beijing daxue Kaoguxuexin et al., "Tianma Qucun yizhi Beizhao Jin Hou mudi di erci fajue" 天馬曲村遺址北趙晉侯墓地第二次發掘, *Wenwu* 1994.1, 20–22. The

translation follows, with minor revisions, that of Jaehoon Shim, "The 'Jinhou Su Bianzhong' Inscription and Its Significance," *Early China* 22 (1997): 49–56.

16. The identification of Su 蘇 as the name of the lord known posthumously as Lord Xian 獻侯 is accepted by virtually all scholars. However, the dates of his reign, and therefore the dates of the events recorded in the *Jin Hou Su bianzhong*, are much debated. For studies by me showing that his dates of reign were 795–785 BCE instead of 822–812 BCE, as given in the *Shi ji* 史記 *Historian's Records* of Sima Qian 司馬遷 (ca. 145–89 BCE), and that the events recorded by the bells inscription took place in 794 BCE, see David S. Nivison and Edward L. Shaughnessy, "The Jin Hou Su Bells Inscription and Its Implications for the Chronology of Early China," *Early China* 25 (2001): 29–48, and for a subsequent—and more decisive—study, see Xia Hanyi 夏含夷, "You Meixian Shan shi jiazu tongqi zai lun Shanfu Ke tongqi de niandai: Fudai zai lun Jin Hou Su bianzhong de niandai" 由眉縣單氏家族銅器再論膳夫克銅器的年代：附帶再論晉侯蘇編鐘的年代, in *Zhongguo gudai qingtongqi guoji yantaohui lunwenji* 中國古代青銅器國際研討會論文集, ed. Shanghai bowuguan and Xianggang Zhongwen daxue wenwuguan (Shanghai: Shanghai bowuguan and Xianggang Zhongwen daxue wenwuguan, 2010), 165–78.

17. This statement now needs to be modified somewhat: beginning in 2007, two separate cemeteries in southwestern Shanxi, one at Dahekou 大河口, Yicheng 翼城, associated with the state of Ba 霸, and one at Hengbei 橫北, Jiangxian 降縣, associated with the state of Peng 倗, have been excavated with numerous tombs dating to the mid-Western Zhou. Other bronzes from the same period have been unearthed, whether by archaeologists or tomb robbers, from the state of Ying 應 located at Pingdingshan shi 平頂山市 in central Henan and from the state of Zeng 曾 in Suizhou 隨州, Hubei. However, while the inscriptions on these vessels attest to ongoing relations with the Zhou royal family, they suggest even more strongly the growing independence of the local rulers.

18. Jessica Rawson, "Statesmen or Barbarians? The Western Zhou as Seen through Their Bronzes," *Proceedings of the British Academy* 75 (1989): 71–95.

19. David S. Nivison, "Western Zhou History Reconstructed from Bronze Inscriptions," in *The Great Bronze Age of China: A Symposium*, ed. George Kuwayama (Los Angeles: Los Angeles County Museum of Art, 1983), 49–50.

20. Herrlee Glessner Creel, "Bronze Inscriptions of the Western Chou Dynasty as Historical Documents," *Journal of the American Oriental Society* 56, no. 3 (1936): 342. In the introduction to *Before Confucius*, I made much the same point as that to be made here: that bronze inscriptions were but tertiary documents. The evidence I used there was the same evidence cited by Creel: the *Song gui* 頌簋 (*Jicheng* 4332) and other inscribed vessels made for Song 頌. I went one step beyond Creel's discussion by noting that the inscriptions on the *First-year* and *Third-year Shi Dui gui* 師兌簋 (*Jicheng* 4274, 4319) show that the original command documents (*ming shu* 命書) were kept in a royal archive

to be consulted in the event of later commands to the same recipient. See Shaughnessy, *Before Confucius*, 3–5.

21. For the vessels and their inscriptions, see Shaanxi sheng wenwuju and Zhonghua Shiji tan yishuguan, eds., *Sheng shi jijin: Shaanxi Baoji Meixian qingtongqi jiaocang* 盛世吉金：陕西寶雞眉縣青銅器窖藏 (Beijing: Beijing chubanshe, 2003). The original version of the present study included a more detailed treatment of these three inscriptions. Since they are translated and discussed in full in chapter 3 of the present book, I have abbreviated the discussion here.

22. Keightley, "The Diviners' Notebooks," 11.

23. Herrlee Glessner Creel, *The Birth of China* (New York: John Day, 1937), 255.

24. The following discussion of early archives, drawing largely on Cheng Hao 程浩, "Cong 'Mengfu' dao 'Xingtan': Xian-Qin 'shu' lei wenxian de shengcheng jieji yu liubian" 從"盟府"到"杏壇"：先秦"書"類文獻的生成、結集與流變, *Qinghua daxue xuebao (Zhexue Shehui kexue ban)* 清华大学学报 (哲學社會科學版) 6 (2021): 85–106, has been newly added to the original version of this study.

25. Huang Huaixin 黃懷信, Zhang Maorong 章懋鎔, and Tian Xudong 天旭, eds., *Yi Zhou shu huijiao jizhu* 逸周書彙校集注 (Shanghai: Shanghai Guji chubanshe, 1995), 800.

26. *Zuo zhuan* 左傳, fourth year of Lord Ding 定公; Stephen Durrant, Wai-yee Li, and David Schaberg, *Zuo Zhuan* 左傳: Commentary on the "Spring and Autumn Annals" (Seattle: University of Washington Press, 2016), vol. 3, 1745–51, with minor emendations: primarily adding a title mark (《》) around 伯禽 in the first Chinese paragraph, and quotation marks (indicative of chapter titles) around "Bo Qin," "Kang Proclamation," and "Tang Proclamation" in the first three paragraphs of the English translation. The "Kang Proclamation" (*Kang gao* 康誥) is, of course, the chapter by that title in the received *Shang shu*, the "Tang Proclamation" (*Tang gao* 唐誥) is mentioned in the *Shu xu* 書序 *Preface to the Scriptures* as a chapter in the *Shang shu*, though it is no longer extant. It stands to reason that the "Bo Qin" 伯禽 was also the title of a document, as the translators' note (1748, n. 47) had been suggested by Gu Yanwu 顧炎武 (quoted at Yang Bojun 楊伯峻, *Chunqiu Zuo zhuan zhu* 春秋左傳注 [Beijing: Zhonghua shuju, 1990], vol. 4, 1537). I have also changed the final sentence from "It is stored in the Zhou archive and can be consulted" to "They are stored in the Zhou Repository (i.e., archive) and can be consulted," understood as referring to all five of the texts quoted. Finally, and less consequentially, I have also changed "Zhou Duke" to "duke of Zhou" for *Zhou gong* 周公, and "Investiture Document" to "Command Scripture" for *mingshu* 命書.

27. David Schaberg, "Speaking of Documents: *Shu* Citations in Warring States Texts," in *Origins of Chinese Political Philosophy: Studies in the Composition and Thought of the* Shangshu (*Classic of Documents*), ed. Martin Kern and Dirk Meyer (Leiden: Brill, 2017), 345.

28. Schaberg, "Speaking of Documents," 340.

29. Sarah Allan, "On *Shu* (Documents) and the Origin of the *Shang Shu* (Ancient Documents) in Light of Recently Discovered Bamboo Slip Manuscripts," *Bulletin of the School of Oriental and African Studies* 75, no. 3 (2012): 555; see too Sarah Allan, "What Is a *Shu* 書," *EASCM Newsletter* 4 (2011): 4. The only caveat I would raise regarding this "hypothesis" is that the expression *wang ruo yue* 王若曰 ought not be understood as "the king seemingly said," but rather as "the king approved of saying" (understanding *ruo* 若 in its standard verbal sense of "to approve"). Nevertheless, as Allan says, this expression "marked the fact of their performance by someone other than the purported author."

30. Li Xueqin 李學勤, ed. in chief, and Qinghua daxue Chutu wenxian yanjiu yu baohu zhongxin 清華大學出土文獻研究與保護中心, eds., *Qinghua daxue cang Zhanguo zhujian (wu)* 清華大學藏戰國竹簡 (伍) (Shanghai: Zhong Xi shuju, 2014), 4–5 (full-size photographs), 39–44 (enlarged photographs), 117–23 (transcription and notes). For this translation, see Edward L. Shaughnessy, *The Tsinghua University Warring States Bamboo Manuscripts*, vol. 1: *The Yi Zhou Shu and Pseudo-Yi Zhou Shu Chapters* (Beijing: Tsinghua University Press, 2022).

31. Although the Tsinghua editors argue for the early Western Zhou date, Zi Ju 子居, "Qinghua jian *Feng Xu zhi Ming* jiexi" 清華簡《封許之命》解析, https://www.ctwx.tsinghua.edu.cn/info/1081/2226.htm (posted 28 April 2015) notes several lexical items in the text that do not otherwise appear until the late Western Zhou. On the other hand, Cheng Hao 程浩 and Su Jianzhou 蘇建洲 both point out numerous orthographic features attesting to the text's antiquity, at least within the context of Warring States Chu scribal practices; see Cheng Hao 程浩, "*Feng Xu zhi ming* yu ceming 'shu'" 《封許之命》與冊命"書", *Chutu wenxian* 出土文獻 7 (2015): 134; and Su Jianzhou 蘇建洲, "Qinghua jian di wu ce zici kaoshi" 清華簡第五冊字詞考釋, *Chutu wenxian* 出土文獻 7 (2015): 159–60.

Chapter Two: The *Bin Gong Xu* Inscription and the Origins of the Chinese Literary Tradition

1. For discoveries through 1996, the most convenient general survey is Pian Yuqian 駢宇騫 and Duan Shu'an 段書安, eds., *Ben shiji yilai chutu jian bo gaishu* 本世紀以來出土簡帛概述 (Taipei: Wanjuanlou tushu youxian gongsi, 1999).

2. For these texts, see Jingzhou shi bowuguan, *Guodian Chu mu zhu jian*.

3. For the proceedings of this conference, see Sarah Allan and Crispin Williams, ed., *The Guodian Laozi: Proceedings of the International Conference, Dartmouth College, May 1998* (Berkeley: Society for the Study of Early China and the Institute of East Asian Studies, University of California, Berkeley, 2000).

4. For a comprehensive discussion of this debate, providing full documentation, see Edward L. Shaughnessy, "The Guodian Manuscripts and Their

Place in Twentieth-Century Historiography on the *Laozi*," *Harvard Journal of Asiatic Studies* 65, no. 2 (December 2005): 417–57.

5. This view is usually associated with Li Xueqin 李學勤 (1933–2019), though he himself usually preferred to use the term *shi gu* 釋古 "interpreting antiquity"; for probably the most influential of his many statements on this issue, see "Zou chu yi gu shidai" 走出疑古時代, *Zhongguo wenhua* 中國文化 7 (1993); reprinted as the introduction to a volume of Li's essays bearing the same title: *Zou chu yigu shidai* 走出疑古時代 (1994; rev. 2nd ed. Shenyang: Liaoning daxue chubanshe, 1997), 1–19.

6. E. Bruce Brooks and A. Taeko Brooks, *The Original Analects: Sayings of Confucius and His Successors* (New York: Columbia University Press, 1998). The Brookses work has, to be sure, also met with criticism on the part of Western Sinologists; see, among other critical reviews, those of John Makeham, *China Review International* 6, no. 1 (1999): 1–33, and David Schaberg, "'Sell It! Sell It!' Recent Translations of *Lunyu*," *Chinese Literature: Essays, Articles, Reviews* 23 (2001): 115–39. However, I think it is no exaggeration to say that the *yi gu* spirit continues to dominate Western sinology. For a still more radical suggestion that the *Lunyu* was not only not composed until the Western Han, in the second century BCE, but that its thought also reflects that period, see Michael Hunter, *Confucius beyond the Analects* (Leiden: Brill, 2017).

7. This was originally stated as E. Bruce Brooks, Warring States Project, Archive Messages nos. 791 and 985, which no longer seem to be active. For a very brief statement to this effect, see http://wsproject.org/archive/books/overview.html#04c.

8. Stephen Owen, "Interpreting *Sheng Min*," in *Ways with Words: Writing about Reading Texts from Early China*, ed. Pauline Yu, Peter Bol, Stephen Owen, and Willard Peterson (Berkeley: University of California Press, 2000), 25.

9. For one concise survey of the history of the text, see Edward L. Shaughnessy, "*Shang shu* 尚書 (*Shu ching* 書經)," in *Early Chinese Texts: A Bibliographical Guide*, ed. Michael Loewe (Berkeley: Society for the Study of Early China and Institute of East Asian Studies, University of California, Berkeley, 1993), 376–89.

10. For an early indication of Gu Jiegang's view of the "Zhou shu" *gao* chapters, interestingly enough for the discussion that will follow in this chapter, in a discussion concerning the antiquity of legends about Yu 禹, see Gu Jiegang, "*Gu shi bian* di yi ce zixu" 古史辨第一冊自序, in *Gu shi bian* 古史辨, vol. 1, ed. Gu Jiegang (1924; rpt. Shanghai: Shanghai Guji chubanshe, 1980), 62. A more developed indication of his views at that time can be seen in the work of a student of his at Zhongshan daxue 中山大學 in Guangzhou where Gu was teaching a course on the *Shang shu*; He Dingsheng 何定生, "*Shang shu* de wenfa ji qi niandai" 尚書的文法及其年代, *Guoli Zhongshan daxue yuyan lishixue yanjiusuo zhoukan* 國立中山大學語言歷史學研究所週刊5, nos. 49–51 (17 October

1928): 1793–1979. These chapters remained an abiding interest of Gu's. In 1960, he began to work on a comprehensive study and translation, which, however, as far as I know, was never completed and has been published only piecemeal; for the first publication of it, see Gu Jiegang, "Wu Wang de si ji qi niansui he jiyuan" 武王的死及其年歲和紀元, *Wenshi* 文史 18 (1983): 1–32. For an outline of his research activities at this later time, see Gu Chao 顧潮, *Gu Jiegang nianpu* 顧頡剛年譜 (Beijing: Zhongguo Shehui kexue chubanshe, 1993), 578ff. Gu's work on the *Shang shu* was subsequently completed by another of his students: Liu Qiyu 刘起釪; see *Shang shu yuanliu ji chuanben kao* 尚書源流及傳本考 (Shenyang: Liaoning daxue chubanshe, 1987) and, *Shang shu xueshi* 尚書學史 (Beijing: Zhonghua shuju, 1989).

11. David Keightley, "Review of Herrlee G. Creel, *The Origins of Statecraft in China: The Western Chou Empire*," *Journal of Asian Studies* 30, no. 3 (May 1971): 656; Schaberg, "Texts and Artifacts," 477–81 and 506–08.

12. Schaberg, "Texts and Artifacts," 481.

13. Schaberg, "Texts and Artifacts," 507.

14. In a later publication, Schaberg seems to accept that the *Zhou shu* chapters were written in a language much older than that of the classical texts of the Warring States period; Schaberg, "Speaking of Documents," 320; for the quotation, see, chapter 5, n. 54, in this volume.

15. For one demonstration of the similarity of the language used in the *Zhou shu* chapters of the *Shu* and in Western Zhou bronze inscriptions, see W. A. C. H. Dobson, *Early Archaic Chinese: A Descriptive Grammar* (Toronto: University of Toronto Press, 1962). For another effort, see Xia Hanyi 夏含夷, "Lüelun jinwen Shangshu Zhoushu gepian de zhuzuo niandai" 略論今文尚書周書各篇的著作年代, in *Di er jie Guoji Zhongguo guwenzi yantaohui lunwenji, xubian* 第二屆國際中國古文字研討會論文集續編 (Collected Papers of the Second International Conference on Chinese Paleography) (Hong Kong: Chinese University of Hong Kong, 1996), 399–404. For a long study that has argued that the language of the five *gao* chapters is, in fact, different from that seen in Western Zhou bronze inscriptions, see Kai Vogelsang, "Inscriptions and Proclamations: On the Authenticity of the 'Gao' Chapters in the *Book of Documents*," *Bulletin of the Museum of Far Eastern Antiquities* 74 (2002): 138–209. However, the methodology used in this study is open to question.

16. The most recent catalogs of bronze inscriptions, Wu Zhenfeng, *Shang Zhou qingtongqi mingwen ji tuxiang jicheng* and *Shang Zhou qingtongqi mingwen ji tuxiang jicheng xubian*, include over eighteen thousand individual vessels with inscriptions.

17. Creel, *The Birth of China*, 255.

18. The Poly Museum has issued a catalog devoted to just this one vessel: *Sui Gong xu: Da Yu zhi shui yu wei zheng yi de*; the romanization "Sui Gong" is given on the title page.

19. The original publication of this essay included translation together with extensive annotations as an appendix to the essay proper. For the purposes of the present volume, this degree of annotation is unnecessary; readers interested in the annotations should consult the original publication.

20. *Shang shu zhengyi* 尚書正義, in *Shisan jing zhu shu* 十三經注疏, ed. Ruan Yuan 阮元 (Beijing: Zhonghua shuju, 1980), 146.

21. *Shang shu zhengyi*, 146.

22. *Shang shu zhengyi*, 176.

23. *Shang shu zhengyi*, 251. Of course, while these comparisons show that the *Bin Gong xu* inscription derives from the same general literary context as the chapters of the *Shu*, they do not necessarily show in reverse that all of these chapters of the *Shu* must date as early as the *Bin Gong xu* (indeed, the *Shu xu* almost certainly dates to the Han period).

24. The *Jin Hou Su bianzhong* 晉侯蘇編鐘 bells and a cache of 1,200 bamboo slips from the Warring States period, both now in the possession of the Shanghai Museum, are two of the most notable recent purchases on the Hong Kong antiques market. For the *Jin Hou Su bianzhong* inscriptions, see chapter 1, pp. 30–31.

25. Ma Chengyuan, personal communication, December 2002; Lu Liancheng 廬連成, personal communication, February 2003.

26. For a discussion of the role that spacers play in demonstrating the authenticity of bronze inscriptions, see Edward L. Shaughnessy, *Sources of Western Zhou History: Inscribed Bronze Vessels* (Berkeley: University of California Press, 1991), 58–62.

Chapter Three: The Writing of a Late Western Zhou Bronze Inscription

1. Shortly after the discovery of the cache, the vessels were sent to Beijing for a special exhibition at the Chinese Century Altar Museum (Zhonghua Shiji tan yishuguan 中華世紀壇藝術館), which issued a catalog: Shaanxi sheng wenwuju and Zhonghua Shiji tan yishuguan, *Sheng shi jijin*. The vessels have subsequently been included in Wu Zhenfeng, *Shang Zhou qingtongqi mingwen ji tuxiang jicheng*, no. 14543 (Qiu pan), nos. 2501–2502 (Forty-Second Year Qiu ding), nos. 2503–2512 (Forty-Third Year Qiu ding).

For initial reports of the discovery in the scholarly press, see Shaanxi sheng Kaogu yanjiusuo, Baoji shi kaogu gongzuodui and Meixian wehuaguan, "Shaanxi Meixian Yangjia cun Xi Zhou qingtongqi jiaocang fajue jianbao"; Liu Huaijun 劉懷君 and Liu Junshe 劉君社, "Shaanxi Meixian Yangjia cun Xi Zhou qingtongqi jiaocang" 陝西眉縣楊家村西周青銅器窖藏, *Kaogu yu wenwu* 考古與文物 2003.3, 3–12. Also of interest are "Shaanxi Meixian chutu jiaocang tongqi bitan" 陝西眉縣出土窖藏銅器筆談, *Wenwu* 2003.6, 43–65, and "Baoji Meixian

Yangjiacun jiaocang Shan shi jiazu qingtongqi qun zuotan jiyao" 寶鷄眉縣楊家村窖藏單氏家族青銅器群座談紀要, *Kaogu yu wenwu* 2003.3, 13–16. Western studies that appeared too late to be considered during the original writing of this study include Lothar von Falkenhausen, "The Inscribed Bronzes from Yangjiacun: New Evidence on Social Structure and Historical Consciousness in Late Western Zhou China (c. 800 BC)," *Proceedings of the British Academy* 139 (2006): 239–96, and David Sena, "Arraying the Ancestors in Ancient China: Narratives of Lineage History in the 'Scribe Qiang' and 'Qiu' Bronzes," *Asia Major* (3rd series) 25, no. 1 (2012): 63–81.

2. The initial publications transcribed the name of the patron of the vessel as Lai 逨 (read as "Mai" in Lothar von Falkenhausen, "Issues in Western Zhou Studies: A Review Article," *Early China* 18 [1993]: 158–59). Other transcriptions have been suggested as well: Qiu 逑, for which see Chen Jian 陳劍, "Ju Guodian jian shi du Xi Zhou jinwen yi li" 據郭店簡釋讀西周金文一例, *Beijing daxue Guwenxian yanjiu zhongxin jikan* 北京大學古文獻研究中心集刊 2 (2001): 378–96, and Dong Shan 董珊, "Lüe lun Xi Zhou Shan shi jiazu jiaocang qingtongqi mingwen" 略論西周單氏家族窖藏青銅器銘文, *Zhongguo lishi wenwu* 中國歷史文物 2003.4, 42; Zuo 佐, for which see Li Xueqin 李學勤, "Meixian Yangjia cun xin chu qingtongqi yanjiu" 眉縣楊家村新出青銅器研究, *Wenwu* 文物 2003.6, 66–73, and Tang Yuhui 湯余惠, "Du jinwen suoji (ba pian)" 讀金文鎖記（八篇）, *Chutu wenxian yanjiu* 出土文獻研究 1998.1, 60–61; Bi 祕, for which see Zhang Zhenglang 張政烺, "He zun mingwen jieshi buyi" 何尊銘文解釋補遺, *Wenwu* 1976.1, 66; and Su 速, for which see Noel Barnard, in association with Cheung Kwong-yue, *The Shan-fu Liang Ch'i Kuei and Associated Inscribed Vessels* (Taipei: SMC, 1996), 336–41. It should also be noted that the inscriptions are sometimes also referred to by the patron's title: Yu 虞 "Warden."

3. For my own contribution to this effort, see Xia Hanyi 夏含夷, "42 nian 43 nian liangge Yu Lai ding de niandai" 42年43年兩個吳逨鼎的年代, *Zhongguo lishi wenwu* 中國歷史文物2003.5, 49–52; for my most comprehensive study, see "'Xia Shang Zhou duandai gongcheng' shi nian hou zhi pipan: Yi Zhou zhu wang zai wei niandai wei lizheng" "夏商周斷代工程"十年後之批判：以西周諸王在位年代為例證, in *Di si jie Guoji Hanxue huiyi lunwenji: Chutu cailiao yu xin shiye* 第四屆國際漢學會議論文集：出土材料與新視野 (Taipei: Academia Sinica, 2013), 341–80.

4. See David Sena, "Reproducing Society: Kinship and Social Organization in Western Zhou China," PhD diss., University of Chicago, 2005, chapter 1: "What's in a Name? Appellations of the Living and the Dead in the Inscriptions of the Shan Lineage."

5. Unfortunately, this wishful thinking has not been borne out; tomb robbing has remained rampant in China over the twenty years since the Meixian peasants reported their discovery.

6. To my knowledge, the first person to have discussed the importance of this transfer of the king's address from the royal scribe to the guest at audience, and subsequently from the slips to the bronze vessel, is Creel, "Bronze

Inscriptions of the Western Chou Dynasty as Historical Documents," 342. Creel cited as evidence the inscription of the *Song ding* 頌鼎 (*Jicheng* 2827–29) as well as a description of court audiences in the *Yi li* 儀禮 (*Yi li zhushu* 儀禮注疏 [*Sibu beiyao* ed.], 27.3a–b).

7. For a discussion of the differing usage of *wang* and *tianzi* in just the dedicatory prayer portion of inscriptions, see Musha Akira 武者章, "Sei Shū satsu mei kinbun bunrui no kokoromi" 西周冊命金文分類の試み, in *Sei Shū seidōki to sono kokka* 西周青銅器とその國家, ed. Matsumaru Michio 松丸道雄 (Tokyo: Tokyo daigaku shuppankai, 1980), 293–300.

8. For a translation of the *Li fangyi* / *fangzun* inscription, together with a discussion presenting this analysis, see Edward L. Shaughnessy, "Western Zhou History," in *The Cambridge History of Ancient China: From the Origins of Civilization to 221 B.C.*, ed. Michael Loewe and Edward L. Shaughnessy (New York: Cambridge University Press, 1999), 325.

9. Other inscriptions that mention Shang Di are found on the possibly preconquest *Tian Wang gui* 天亡簋 (*Jicheng* 4261), and that of the *Xing zhong* 𤼈鐘 (*Jicheng* 0247–56), the latter of which however derives in very large measure from the *Shi Qiang pan* inscription, Xing probably having been the son of Qiang 牆.

10. Shaughnessy, *Sources of Western Zhou History*, 181.

11. In addition to bronze inscriptions, such as that on the *Shi X gui* 師顈 簋 (*Jicheng* 4312), that seem to show Gong Bo He 共伯和 in charge of the Zhou government, thus confirming the tradition of a Gonghe 共和 interregnum during King Li's exile, the inscription of the *Ran xu* 塑盨 (*Jicheng* 4469) has generally been dated to the following reign of King Xuan because of its mention that the "men of the country, men of the offices, and men of the legions" (*bang ren zheng ren shishi ren* 邦人正人師氏人) had "rebelled and driven off their ruler" (*nüe zhu jue jun* 虐逐厥君). As I will argue in chapter 5 with similar reasoning, it is also possible that this *Ran xu* should date instead to the reign of King Xiao 孝 (r. 882?–866 BCE), the successor to King Yih.

12. Sima Qian 司馬遷, *Shi ji* 史記 (Beijing: Zhonghua shuju, 1959), 140.

13. *Zhushu jinian* 竹書紀年 (*Sibu congkan* ed.), 2.11a. The *Shi ben* 世本 also mentions this removal, stating that King Yih *xi* 徙 to Quanqiu 犬邱 (another name for Huaili). While *xi* is synonymous with the *qian* 遷 used by the *Zhushu jinian*, it seems to carry the nuance of a forced removal; thus, the *Guangya* 廣雅 defines it as *bi* 避 "to flee."

14. Nivison, "Western Chou History Reconstructed from Bronze Inscriptions," 49–50.

15. The *Qiu pan* inscription's praise for Kings Xiao and Yi may also support this hypothesis: *you cheng yu Zhou bang* 又成于周邦. It is certainly possible to interpret *you* 又 as *you* 有 "to have," as have all published studies that I have seen, and to read this phrase as an innocuous statement that these kings "had success in the Zhou state." However, with the historical context outlined ear-

lier, it also seems possible to read *you* as "again," with the statement meaning something like the kings "again succeeded in the Zhou state."

16. I here adapt an insight first made in Sena, "Reproducing Society," 95–98.

17. This description needs to be qualified in that the high ancestor of a family or lineage is said to have occupied a central position between the *zhao* and *mu* ancestors. In the case of the Shan lineage, the high ancestor would be Shan Gong.

18. See n. 4 in this chapter.

19. For a similar case in which a king refers to a previous command issued to the same individual, see the *First* and *Third Year Shi Dui gui* 師兌簋 inscriptions (*Jicheng* 4275 and 4318); for partial translations of the inscriptions, see Shaughnessy, *Sources of Western Zhou History*, 281–82.

20. Two other bells have made their way into American collections, one in the Cleveland Gallery of Art, and one in the collection of George Fan of Ossining, New York. For a detailed study of these bells, see Barnard, *The Shan-fu Liang Ch'i Kuei*, 324–56.

21. The bell in the Cleveland Gallery of Art also bears the same 117-character inscription, while the bell in the Fan collection contains 20 characters of the dedicatory portion of the complete inscription. There is some overlap between this portion and the 23-character inscription on the bell in the Meixian Country Cultural Relics Control Station, but they are not exactly the same.

22. Indeed, as previously noted, n. 2, the graph of his name was variously transcribed as Lai or Mai 逨, or Su 速.

23. Falkenhausen, "Issues in Western Zhou Studies," 158.

24. Among other types of vessels, inscriptions that begin by quoting the patron include (in rough chronological order) the *Dong fangding* 㺇方鼎 (*Jicheng* 2824), *Meng gui* 孟簋 (*Jicheng* 4162), *Xing gui* 㝬簋㝬 (*Jicheng* 4170–4177), *Yu ding* 禹鼎 (*Jicheng* 2834), and *Da Ke ding* 大克鼎 (*Jicheng* 2836), as well, of course, as the *Qiu pan*. Western Zhou bell inscriptions that begin similarly include the *Jingren Ren Ning zhong* 井人人妄鐘 (*Jicheng* 0109–10, 0111), *Xing zhong* 㝬鐘 (*Jicheng* 0247–0250), *Guoshu Lü zhong* 虢叔旅鐘 (*Jicheng* 0238–0244), *Liang Qi zhong* 梁其鐘 (*Jicheng* 0187–0192), and *Shanbo Yi Sheng zhong* 單白昊生鐘 (*Jicheng* 0082). This last vessel doubtless derives from the Shan family of which Qiu was also a member, and the wording is so similar as to suggest some cross-influence between them:

單白昊生曰。不顯皇且剌考逑匹先王。爵堇大命。
余僅肇帥井朕皇且考敫德。用保䠧。

Shanbo Yi Sheng said: "Illustrious august ancestors and the valiant deceased-father joined and aided the prior kings, having merit and taking care with the great mandate. I the young son have begun to follow the example of my august ancestors' and deceased-father's fine virtue, herewith protecting and stabilizing it."

25. Barnard, *The Shan-fu Liang Ch'i Kuei*, 346–47. Barnard goes on to attribute this "textual attenuation," "effected by the artisan/scribe," to "certain technical problems." In a lengthy note to this idea, he discusses the process of an inscription's composition but concludes that a number of questions "constitute the unknowns which limit our powers of assessment." It is not clear, to me at least, who he thinks was responsible for composing the inscription (as opposed to engraving it [in the clay model]), the term "artisan/scribe" allowing a considerable range of possibilities.

26. Other counts, that count characters with duplication marks as two characters, give the total number of characters as 129.

27. Olivier Venture, "Étude d'un emploi rituel de l'écrit dans la Chine archaïque (XIIIe–VIIIe siècle avant notre ère): Réflexion sur les matériaux épigraphiques des Shang et des Zhou occidentaux," PhD diss., Université Paris 7, 2002, 99, 101, 134, makes observations on how inscriptions were influenced by their visibility.

28. As previously noted (pp. 75–76), Qiu's description of his deceased-father as "capable of making clear and bright his heart" is found in the *pan* inscription attributed not to Gongshu but rather to Gongshu's own grandfather Lingbo 零伯. However, as discussed there, since Gongshu and Lingbo would have been arrayed on the same side of the Shan family ancestral temple, it is possible that they shared this sort of epithet.

It is also worth noting that whereas the *pan* inscription is dedicated generically to "my august ancestors and deceased-father" (*zhen huang zu kao* 朕皇祖考), which is appropriate given the lengthy narrative extolling the seven generations of ancestors that begins the inscription, the *zhong* inscription is dedicated only to "my august deceased-father Gongshu" (*zhen huang kao* Gongshu 朕皇考龔叔).

29. It is perhaps worthy of note that in the *pan* inscription, the character *xia* 下 "below" apparently failed to register in the bronze, though there is a space for it. This might lead one to imagine that the person responsible for preparing the text of the *zhong* inscription, what Barnard calls the "artisan/scribe," had the actual *pan* inscription before him as he was writing the *zhong* inscription, was confused by the failure of the graph to register, and thus deleted this phrase *yi zai xia* 廙才下. However, such a scenario seems entirely improbable to me. I suspect instead that the text of the inscription was written by a scribe on bamboo or wooden slips, and it was this medium in which it was conducted to the artisan responsible for carving the inscription block. For an important study of how bronze inscriptions were prepared and copied onto the inscription block, see Ondřej Škrabal, "Writing before Inscribing: On the Use of Manuscripts in the Production of Western Zhou Bronze Inscriptions," *Early China* 42 (2019): 273–332.

30. It is interesting to note that the two published English translations of this inscription diverge on this point, Falkenhausen offering "many times bestowed his munificence on me. He charged me . . ." ("Issues in Western Zhou Studies," 159), while Barnard gives "Su [has been] favoured with [royal] commands [= appointments]" (*The Shan-fu Liang Ch'i* Kuei, 346).

31. However, this would be the only case where *xiu ling* would be the object of the verb *ci* "to award"; all other cases involve the patron extolling (*yang* 揚) the Son of Heaven's "beneficent command."

32. I suppose that with the new understanding of duplication marks mentioned later in chapter 6, p. 347–48 n. 27, in which a single duplication mark can entail multiple duplications, it may be possible to read 天子孫 as *tianzi zizi sunsun* 天子子子孫孫 "the Son of Heaven, and sons' sons and grandsons' grandsons" (i.e., understanding the duplication mark after *zi* 子 to indicate that the character is to be read three times). However, I continue to believe that it is anomalous in this context and derives from an awkward cut-and-paste editorial effort.

33. For a study of inexpert editing of Western Zhou bronze inscriptions, see Li Feng, "Literacy Crossing Cultural Borders: Evidence from the Bronze Inscriptions of the Western Zhou Period (1045–771 BCE)," *Bulletin of the Museum of Far Eastern Antiquities* 74 (2002): 210–42.

34. The present study has been primarily concerned with how bronze inscriptions were written, by which I mean composed. In a recent study that appeared too late to be incorporated here, Ondřej Škrabal has demonstrated how they were actually written—physically. He shows that the texts were first written on bamboo or wood—which he terms a "master-layout"—before being transferred to the bronze vessel. Noting the preponderance of inscriptions in symmetrical columns, and especially of inscriptions having exactly one hundred character spaces, he argues that "all such inscriptions must have been planned with the utmost care, anticipating the desired symmetry of the layout" ("Writing before Inscribing," 286), and concludes: "I believe we have good reason to assume that the final outcome of the composition or compilation process, i.e., the master copy, visually reflected the intended master-layout of the inscriptions, specifying instances of ligatures, sharing of character-spaces, reduplications and, in a few cases, paragraph spacing" ("Writing before Inscribing," 293).

Chapter Four: On the Casting of the Art Institute of Chicago's *Shi Wang Ding*

1. Wu Dacheng 吳大澂, *Kezhai jigulu* 愙齋集古錄 (N.p.: Hanfenlou, 1918), 5.7.

2. Zou An 鄒安, *Zhou jinwen cun* 周金文存 (Shanghai: Haiguancang xuejun boliban yinyishu congbian, 1916), 2.22.

3. Chen Rentao 陳仁濤, *Jinkui lun gu chuji* 金匱論古初集 (Hong Kong: Yazhou chubanshe, 1952), 7–61.

4. For both of these vessels, see Shaanxi sheng wenwuju and Zhonghua Shiji tan yishuguan, *Sheng shi jijin*.

5. Guo Moruo 郭沫若, *Liang Zhou jinwenci daxi kaoshi* 兩周金文辭大系考釋 (Tokyo: Bunkyodo shoten, 1935), 80.

6. Shirakawa Shizuka 白川靜, *Kimbun tsushaku* 金文通釋 (Kobe: Hakutsuru bijustukan, 1968), fasc. 22, 71–80; Ma Chengyuan 馬承源, ed., *Shang Zhou qingtongqi mingwen xuan* 商周青銅器銘文選 (Beijing: Wenwu chubanshe, 1988), vol. 3, 146–47.

7. Wang Shiming 王世民, Chen Gongrou 陳公柔, and Zhang Changshou 張長壽, *Xi Zhou qingtongqi fenqi duandai yanjiu* 西周青銅器分期斷代研究 (Beijing: Wenwu chubanshe, 1999), 31–32.

8. Jessica Rawson, *Western Zhou Ritual Vessels from the Arthur M. Sackler Collections* (Washington, DC: Arthur M. Sackler Foundation, 1990), 295.

9. Wu Zhenfeng 吳鎮烽 and Luo Zhongru 雒忠如, "Shaanxi sheng Fufeng xian Qiangjia cun chutu de Xi Zhou tongqi" 陝西省扶風縣強家村出土的西周銅器, *Wenwu* 文物1975.8, 57–62.

10. Li Xueqin 李學勤, "Xi Zhou zhongqi qingtongqi de zhongyao biaochi: Zhouyuan Zhuangbai Qiangjia liang chu qingtongqi jiaocang de zonghe yanjiu" 西周中期青銅器的重要標尺：周原莊白、強家兩處青銅器窖藏的綜合研究, *Zhongguo lishi bowuguan guankan* 中國歷史博物館館刊 1979.1, 29–36; Zhu Fenghan 朱鳳瀚, *Shang Zhou jiazu xingtai yanjiu* 商周家族形態研究 (Tianjin: Tianjin guji chubanshe, 1990), 374.

11. See, for example, Zhang Maorong 張懋鎔, "Shilun Xi Zhou qingtongqi yanbian de feijunhengxing wenti" 試論西周青銅器演變的非均衡性問題, *Kaogu xuebao* 考古學報2008.3, 340; Han Wei 韓巍, "Zhouyuan Qiangjia Xi Zhou tongqiqun shixi wenti bianxi" 周原強家西周銅器群世系問題辨析, *Zhongguo lishi wenwu* 中國歷史文物 2007.3, 70–76; Xia Hanyi, "You Meixian Shan shi jiazu tongqi zailun Shanfu Ke tongqi de niandai."

12. Wu Dacheng, *Kezhai jigulu*, 14.17.

13. Wang Shimin, Chen Gongrou, and Zhang Changshou, *Xi Zhou qingtongqi fenqi duandai yanjiu*, 133.

14. Suzanne R. Schnepp, "Condition Report on Arrival," December 6, 2005, Art Institute of Chicago internal memorandum.

15. Xia Hanyi 夏含夷, "Wu wudu qingtongqi mingwen" 勿誤讀青銅器銘文, *Zhongguo Shehui kexuebao* 中國社會科學報, 12 August 2012, 4.

16. Su Rongyu 蘇榮譽, "Ershi shiji dui Xian Qin qingtong liqi zhuzao jishu de yanjiu" 二十世紀對先秦青銅禮器鑄造技術的研究, in *Quanwu toushang: Quanwu boguguan qingtongqi toushe saomiao jiexi* 泉屋透賞：泉屋博古館青銅器透射掃描解析, ed. Quanwu boguguan he Jiuzhou Guoli bowuguan 泉屋博古館和九

州國立博物館, and trans. Huang Rongguang 黃榮光 (Beijing: Kexue chubanshe, 2015), 387–445.

17. Su Rongyu, "Ershi shiji dui Xian Qin qingtong liqi zhuzao jishu de yanjiu," 440, citing Li Ji 李濟 and Wan Jiabao 萬家保, *Yinxu chutu qingtong dingqi zhi yanjiu* 殷墟出土青銅鼎形器之研究, *Gu qiwu yanjiu zhuankan* 古器物研究專刊 4 (Taibei: Zhongyang yanjiuyuan Lishi yuyan yanjiusuo, 1970), 30 and 31.

18. Su Rongyu, "Ershi shiji dui Xian Qin qingtong liqi zhuzao jishu de yanjiu," 441, citing Hua Jueming 華覺明 et al., *Fu Hao mu qingtong qiqun zhuzao jishu de yanjiu* 婦好墓青銅器群鑄造技術的研究, *Kaoguxue jikan* 考古學集刊 1 (Beijing: Zhongguo Shehui kexue chubanshe, 1981), 270.

19. Niwa Takafumi 丹羽崇史, "CT jiexi yu zhongguo qingtongqi zhizuo jishu de yanjiu" CT 解析與中國青銅器製作技術的研究, in *Quanwu toushang: Quanwu boguguan qingtongqi toushe saomiao jiexi* 泉屋透賞：泉屋博古館青銅器透射掃描解析, ed. Quanwu boguguan he Jiuzhou Guoli bowuguan 泉屋博古館和九州國立博物館, and trans. Huang Rongguang 黃榮光 (Beijing: Kexue chubanshe, 2015), 452–59.

20. Niwa Takafumi, "CT jiexi yu zhongguo qingtongqi zhizuo jishu de yanjiu," 454.

21. Noel Barnard, "Chou China: A Review of the Third Volume of Cheng Te-k'un's *Archaeology in China*," *Monumenta Serica* 24 (1965): 400.

22. Zhang Shixian 張世賢, "Cong Shang Zhou tongqi de neibu tezheng shilun Mao Gong ding de zhenwei wenti: 1981 nian shiyi yue Aozhou Guoli daxue 'Keji ziliao zai kaogu he lishi yanjiu shang de yingyong' toulunhui lunwen" 從商周銅器的內部特徵試論毛公鼎的真偽問題：1981年十一月澳洲國立大學「科技資料在考古和歷史研究上的應用」討論會論文, *Gugong jikan* 故宮季刊 1982.16.4, 62.

23. Zhang Shixian, "Cong Shang Zhou tongqi de neibu tezheng shilun Mao Gong ding de zhenwei wenti," 63–64.

24. Martin Kern, "Review of Mark Edward Lewis, *Writing and Authority in Early China*," *China Review International* 7, no. 2 (2000): 338–39.

25. Kern, "Review of Mark Edward Lewis, *Writing and Authority in Early China*," 339.

26. Falkenhausen, "Issues in Western Zhou Studies," 147–48 (*Sources* referring to Shaughnessy, *Sources of Western Zhou History*).

Chapter Five: A Possible Lost Classic

1. Li Xueqin 李学勤, ed. in chief, and Qinghua daxue chutu wenxian yanjiu yu baohu zhongxin, eds., *Qinghua daxue cang Zhanguo zhujian (ba)* 清華大學藏戰國竹簡 (捌) (Shanghai: Zhong-Xi shuju, 2018), 2–5 (full-size photographs), 25–48 (enlarged photographs), and 110–20 (transcription and notes). The editor for this text was Ma Nan 馬楠. However, since she is not explicitly credited

with the editorial work, and since that work was clearly a group effort, I refer throughout this essay to the "Tsinghua editors" in the plural.

2. Among Western Zhou bronze inscriptions, the *Xun gui* 訇簋 (*Jicheng* 4321) and *Shi Xun gui* 師訇簋 (*Jicheng* 4342), both of which date to the mid-Western Zhou, slightly earlier than the putative date of the *She ming* appointment, also have the investiture record at the end of the inscription, though in both of these cases it is more abbreviated than found in the *She ming*. I am grateful to Ondřej Škrabal for pointing this out.

3. In addition to a brief discussion in *Qinghua daxue cang Zhanguo zhushu*, the editor of the *She ming* manuscript, Ma Nan, presents a fuller exposition of this argument in "Qinghua jian *She ming* chudu" 清華簡《攝命》初讀, *Wenwu* 2018.9, 46–49, where she credits Li Xueqin with first making this suggestion. For a fuller comparison of the graphic compositions, see Jia Lianxiang 賈連翔, "'She ming' ji *Shu xu* 'Jiong ming' 'Jiong ming' shuo" "攝命"即《書序》"冏命""囧命"說, *Qinghua daxue xuebao (Zhexue shehui kexue ban)* 清華大學學報 (哲學社會科學班) 2018.5, 49–53.

4. Li Xueqin et al., *Qinghua daxue cang Zhanguo zhujian (ba)*, 112 n. 1.

5. Li Xueqin et al., *Qinghua daxue cang Zhanguo zhujian (ba)*, 112 n. 1.

6. Sima Qian, *Shi ji*, 4.140.

7. Sima Qian, *Shi ji*, 13.503.

8. The text repeatedly refers to She as Bo She 伯攝 "Elder She," indicative of the first-born son of a generation. This would be consistent with a status as a potential king, but of course it could also refer to the eldest son of a nonroyal lineage.

9. Given the redundancy between the meanings of *chenzi* 沈子 and *xiaozi* 小子, literally "young son," I suspect that *xiaozi* is a sort of gloss that was introduced into this text at some point in its transmission as a way to clarify the meaning of the more or less unusual *chenzi*.

10. Li Xueqin et al., *Qinghua daxue cang Zhanguo zhujian (ba)*, 110.

11. Li Xueqin 李学勤, ed. in chief, and Qinghua daxue chutu wenxian yanjiu yu baohu zhongxin, eds., *Qinghua daxue cang Zhanguo zhujian (yi)* 清華大學藏戰國竹簡 (壹). Shanghai: Zhong Xi shuju, 2010, 158.

12. *Shangshu Kong zhuan* 尚書孔傳 (*Sibu beiyao* ed.), 7.9b–10a.

13. For multiple uses of *chenzi* 沈子, see the *Ta gui* 它簋 (*Jicheng* 4330). For a use of *chensun* 沈孫, in this case to refer to a Zhou king (King Li 厲王 [r. 857/853–842/828]), see the *Hu zhong* 鈇鐘 (*Jicheng* 260).

14. For a recent study demonstrating the point conclusively, see Dong Shan 董珊, "Shi Xi Zhou jinwen de 'chenzi' he *Yi Zhou shu Huangmen* de 'chenren'" 釋西周金文的'沈子'和《逸周書皇門》的'沈人,' *Chutu wenxian* 出土文獻 2 (2016): 29–34.

15. Sima Qian, *Shi ji*, 4.135.

16. Jingzhou shi bowuguan, *Guodian Chu mu zhujian*, 20 (slip 45). The line quoted from the *Shi jing* (from "Ji zui" 既醉 [Mao 247]), reads: "How associates treat each other, / They treat each other with comportment 朋友攸攝, 攝以威義."

17. Ma Chengyuan 馬承源, ed., *Shanghai bowuguan cang Zhanguo Chu zhushu (yi)* 上海博物館藏戰國楚竹書 (一) (Shanghai: Shanghai guji chubanshe, 2001), 67 (slip 23).

18. *Shangshu Kong zhuan*, 12.4b; Sima Qian, *Shi ji*, 5.215.

19. Cheng Hao 程浩, "Qinghua jian *She ming* de xingzhi yu jiegou" 清華簡《攝命》性質與結構 (哲學社會科學班), *Qinghua daxue xuebao (Zhexue shehui kexue ban)* 2018.5, 54.

20. *Shangshu Kong zhuan*, 12.4b–6a. For an English translation, see James Legge, *The Chinese Classics*, Volume III: *The Shoo King or the Book of Historical Documents* (1865; rpt. Hong Kong: Hong Kong University Press, 1960), 583–87.

21. By my count, some 120 of the 237 characters of the text are found in four-character phrases.

22. *Shangshu Kong zhuan*, 2.6a.

23. *Lunyu zhushu* 論語注疏, in *Shisan jing zhushu* 十三經注疏, ed. Ruan Yuan 阮元 (Beijing: Zhonghua shuju, 1980), 1/3, 5/25, 15/27, and 17/17.

24. For Wu Yu and Wu Cheng's views of the ancient-script chapters of the *Shangshu*, see Benjamin Elman, "Philosophy (*I-Li*) versus Philology (*K'ao-Cheng*): The Jen-hsin Tao-Hsin Debate," *T'oung Pao* 69 (1983): 182–83 (for Wu Yu) and 187 (for Wu Cheng).

25. Among inscriptions that command recipients to "take out and report on the king's commands" 出納王命 are those on *Shi Wang ding* 師望鼎 (*Jicheng* 2812), *Da Ke ding* 大克鼎 (*Jicheng* 2836), and *Mao Gong ding* 毛公鼎 (*Jicheng* 2841: 出納敷命于外); in all three of these cases, the recipients of the royal commands would appear to have been of the highest rank in the officialdom.

26. It is somewhat frustrating that the notes to the text primarily cite parallel passages in other sources and do not attempt to explain the text in its entirety. There are many passages—and many of the most opaque passages—for which there are no notes at all, leaving the reader with the suspicion that the editors were no more successful in making sense of them.

27. In the original publication of this study, I presented the Chinese text, slip-by-slip, in three registers: the first line giving scans of the original characters with the yellow background of the bamboo slip removed; the second line representing a more or less strict transcription, with components of the Chu script written into standard *kaishu* 楷書 components (though not always in the same position within the character); and the third line representing an interpretive transcription, translating the Chu script into modern equivalents, and also adding punctuation. Useful though this style of presentation is for a paleographic study, for the purposes of the present study, it seems unnecessarily

cumbersome. Therefore, I retain only the third register and arrange the text so as to illustrate the structure of the king's address, with the Chinese text followed by the English translation. For ease of comparison with the original publication, I provide the slip number in [ ] brackets in both the Chinese and English texts.

The translation, unchanged from the original publication, is as literal as possible, often sacrificing smooth English expression so as to be as transparent as possible in my choices of translation. The original publication provided copious footnotes substantiating my translation. Again for the purposes of the present book, I have dispensed with all but the most important annotations; readers interested in this level of detail should consult either the original publication of this article or essentially the same presentation in Shaughnessy, *The Tsinghua University Warring States Bamboo Manuscripts*, vol. 2.

28. Whereas the Tsinghua editors read the character 𦐇 as *xiang* 鄉 and interpret it to mean "in the past," I read it as *qing* 卿 "officer" (as in the *Fan Sheng gui* 番生簋 [*Jicheng* 4326]).

29. The graphs 丕 and 不, which can both be read either as *bu* 不 "not" or as *pi* 丕 "very," are clearly differentiated in the manuscript and would seem to require that the first character be read as *pi* 丕 and the second as *bu* 不. However, note that in slip 20, 丕 would seem to be sensible only as *bu* 不 "not."

30. This phrase *yue nai yu* 曰乃毓 ("speaking of your parentage") presents no problems in terms of paleography (the reading of 㐬, i.e., 㐬, as *yu* 毓 is straightforward), but its significance seems to have escaped the Tsinghua editors. In their published comments, they note only that the term *yuzi* 毓子 "nurtured son" occurs later (slip 28; however, in an unpublished vernacular translation, they render it as "yourself are a royal relative" 自己是王室宗親). These two uses would seem to be clearly differentiated. *Yu* 毓 here, literally "birth" or "nurturance," seems to refer to She's royal parentage.

31. For the editors' reading of 彖 as *tuan* 彖 "lazy," see the later discussion, p. 134.

32. *Zhen* 朕 is typically the first-person possessive pronoun ("my"), though it can sometimes be used in the subject position ("I"). It rarely, if ever, comes in the object position ("me"). However, the following phrase that begins with *ru wu gan* 如毋敢 ("you ought not dare") is a perfectly normal way to begin a sentence, so that *zhen* cannot be read with it. As noted later, the final three characters on this slip (13) also seem to be extraneous. This has caused some readers to suggest that this slip is out of sequence. However, attempts to produce other sequences have also been unsatisfying. It seems that we just have to accept that there were problems in the copying of this particular slip.

33. The Tsinghua editors note that *qi yi wei* 其亦隹 here is unintelligible, and they suspect that it is extraneous, presumably copied twice with the same characters at the beginning of slip 14. Others argue that the order of the slips here should be revised to 11, 13, 12, 14; see Wang Ning 王寧, "Qinghua jian

She ming chudu" 清華簡攝命初讀, http://bsm.org.cn/forum/forum.php?mod=view-thread&tid=4352&extra=& (posted 18 November 2018). Attractive though this suggestion is in terms of content, not only are the slips clearly numbered on their backs, but the scoring on the backs of the slips also indicates that the sequence is as the editors have given it. It does seem that *qi yi wei* was simply written twice.

34. As opposed to my earlier comment in n. 29, the graph 不 seems here to be *bu* 不, "not."

35. For a fuller explication of this suggestion, see Shaughnessy, "Western Zhou History," 323–28.

36. For evidence of such penetration, see the inscriptions on the *Dong gui* 㢬簋 (*Jicheng* 4322) and *Dong fangding* 㢬方鼎 (*Jicheng* 2824).

37. *Yi Zhou shu* (*Sibu beiyao* ed.), 8.1a–3b. For a study of the text and this translation, see Edward L. Shaughnessy, "Texts Lost in Texts: Recovering the 'Zhāi Gōng' Chapter of the *Yí Zhōu Shū*," in *Studies in Chinese Language and Culture: Festschrift in Honour of Christoph Harbsmeier on the Occasion of His 60th Birthday*, ed. Christoph Anderl and Halvor Eifring (Oslo: Hermes Academic, 2006), 31–47; for this translation, see 39–40.

38. Nivison, "Western Chou History Reconstructed from Bronze Inscriptions," 49. Nivison's discussion of the reign of King Xiao comes on page 50. For the *Shi ji*, see Sima Qian, *Shiji*, 4.140.

39. *Zhushu jinian* 竹書紀年 (*Sibu congkan* ed.), 2.6b.

40. For the reference to Dog-mound or Waste-mound, the see *Shi ji suoyin* 史記索隱 commentary in Sima Qian, *Shi ji*, 4.140–41, n. 8.

41. For a detailed discussion of the chronology of this period, see Shaughnessy, *Sources of Western Zhou History*, 256–66.

42. Lü Dalin 呂大臨, *Kaogu tu* 考古圖 (Yizheng tang 亦政堂, 1752 ed.), 3, 24a–25b.

43. For a study of the vessel and inscription, and especially of its publication history, see Li Feng, "Textual Criticism and Western Zhou Bronze Inscriptions: The Example of the Mu Gui," in *Tao li cheng xi ji: Qingzhu An Zhimin xiansheng bashi shouchen* 桃李成蹊集：慶祝安志敏先生八十壽辰, ed. Deng Cong 鄧聰 and Chen Xingcan 陳星燦 (Hong Kong: Chinese University of Hong Kong Press, 2004), 280–97.

44. This date is one of the keys to the dating of this vessel and inscription. It is consistent with the regnal calendar required by the full dates on the *Shi Chen ding* 師晨鼎 (third year, third month, first auspiciousness, *jiawu* [day 11]; *Jicheng* 2817), and the *Jian gui* 諫簋 (fifth year, third month, first auspiciousness, *xinhai* [day 27]; *Jicheng* 4285). Both of these inscriptions feature two figures, Sima Gong 司馬共 and Secretary Nian 史年, as participating in the investiture ceremony, who are certainly dateable to this period. However, the dates are incompatible with the calendars required by vessels certainly dateable to the reigns of Kings

Gong, Yih, or Yi. Therefore, a process of elimination, if nothing else, requires that they date to the reign of King Xiao.

45. The vessels are the *Shi Hu gui* 師虎簋 (*Jicheng* 4316) and *Shi Yun gui gai* 師𧽙簋蓋 (*Jicheng* 4283, 4284).

46. There is one other bronze inscription recorded in the *Kaogu tu* that is especially reminiscent of the inscription on the *Mu gui*; this is the *Ran xu* 冉盨 (*Kaogu tu* 3.34; *Jicheng* 4469):

" . . . 又進退，于邦人、足人、師氏，人又辠又故，迺協朋即汝，迺繇宕卑復虐逐厥君厥師，迺作余一人夶。王曰：冉，敬明乃心，用辟我一人，善效乃友內辟，勿事暴虐從獄，爰奪劇行道。厥非正命迺敢疾訊人，則惟輔天降喪，不囗 唯死。賜汝秬鬯一卣、乃父市、䝙赤舄、駒車，賁較、朱虢、靷靳、虎冟、熏裏、畫轉、畫輻、金甬、馬四匹、鑾勒。敬夙夕勿廢朕命。冉拜稽首，敢對天子丕顯魯休，用作寶盨。叔邦父、叔姞萬年子子孫孫永寶用。

" . . . having advanced and retreated, with respect to the countrymen, assistant men, captains who are criminal and guilty. Then resist associates who approach you, and then lead to excess, causing them to return to abuse and expel their lords and their captains, and then causing me the One Man trouble." The king said: "Ran, respectfully make bright your heart, with which to serve me the One Man. Teach well your friends to contribute service, not to cause violence or abuse, or lenience in court cases, going on to thievery and stopping travel on the roads. If they negate correct commands and then dare to harm and sue people, then it will be assisting heaven that will send down destruction, not . . . only death. (I) award you one bucket of black millet sweet wine, your father's kneepads, crimson slippers, a colt chariot with decorated side rails, a covering of the front rail and chest-trappings made of scarlet leather, a tiger-skin canopy with brown lining, a bronze bell, and four horses with bits and bridles. Respectfully from morning to evening do not neglect my command."

Ran saluted and touched his head to the ground, in response extolling the Son of Heaven's illustriously fine beneficence, herewith making this treasured *xu*-tureen. Shu Bangfu and Shu Ji will for ten thousand years have sons' sons and grandsons' grandsons eternally to treasure and use it.

Kaogu tu notes that, like the *Mu gui*, this too was found in the vicinity of present-day Xi'an (Jingzhao 京兆). Both the wording and calligraphy are extremely similar to those of the *Mu gui* (though the similar calligraphy may be a matter that both were hand carvings by the *Kaogu tu*). The *Kaogu tu* preserves only the second half of the *Ran xu* inscription, so that the initial portion recording the investiture ceremony is not extant. Unfortunately, because of this, there are no personal names with which the inscription can be dated. In the past, this inscription has been associated with the inscription on the *Mao Gong ding* and dated to the reign of King Xuan of Zhou 周宣王 (r. 827/25–782 BCE) on that basis. I suspect that it should instead be dated to the reign of King Xiao. However, since there is no firm evidence to support this dating, I only mention this here as a possibility.

47. *Shangshu Kong zhuan*, 7.10b.
48. *Shangshu Kong zhuan*, 7.10b.
49. *Shangshu Kong zhuan*, 8.2b.
50. *Shangshu Kong zhuan*, 10.13b.
51. For this graph in Warring States orthography, see He Linyi 何琳儀, *Zhanguo guwen zidian* 戰國古文字典 (Beijing: Zhonghua shuju, 1998), 1225. He Linyi suspects that the graph should be read as *sui* 遂.
52. In this reading, the editors follow Chen Jian 陳劍, "Jinwen 'tuan' zi kaoshi" 金文「彖」字考釋, in his *Jiagu jinwen kaoshi lunji* 甲骨金文考釋論集 (Shanghai: Xianzhuang shuju, 2007), 243–72.
53. Schaberg, "Speaking of Documents," 321–22.
54. Schaberg, "Speaking of Documents," begins his essay by highlighting the distinct difference between "texts associated with the Western Zhou" and Warring States texts:

> Considered—naively—as a record of linguistic development, the canonical early Chinese texts imply a strikingly discontinuous sort of evolution. Between texts associated with the Western Zhou, such as the older portions of the *Shang shu* 尚書 and of the *Shi jing* 詩經, and Warring States texts like the *Zuo zhuan* 左傳, there lies a dark age of change, in which syntax and vocabulary were transformed. Some words dropped out of regular use or took on new meanings. Some syntactical patterns emerged while others disappeared. Even on the level of rhetoric and logic, a disjointed, haranguing style of address common for the early period seems to have given way to the structured arguments of large-scale Warring States speeches and essays. (320)

55. Schaberg, "Speaking of Documents," 321.
56. See Xia Hanyi, "Cong *Zeng Gong Qiu bianzhong* mingwen chongxin kaolü *Da Yu ding* he *Xiao Yu ding* de niandai." For published English translations of the *Da Yu ding* inscription, see Dobson, *Early Archaic Chinese*, 221–26; and Constance A. Cook, in *A Source Book of Ancient Chinese Bronze Inscriptions*, ed.

Constance A. Cook and Paul R. Goldin (Berkeley, CA: Society for the Study of Early China, 2016), 30–35. See, too, Jeffrey R. Tharsen, "Chinese Euphonics: Phonetic Patterns, Phonorhetoric and Literary Artistry in Early Chinese Narrative Texts," PhD diss., University of Chicago, 2015, 103–27.

57. I refer here to the manifest similarities between the text of the *She ming* and the text of Western Zhou bronze inscriptions and do not intend the sort of naïve blanket statement once made by Bernhard Karlgren: "It is important to remember that . . . the early *book* in China was the *ritual bronze* . . . lengthy and important documents were preserved by being inscribed in ritual bronzes. The genuine *Shu ching* chapters and the odes of the *Shih* . . . may well have been cast in bronze long before they were transcribed into ordinary wooden documents." See Karlgren, "Yin and Chou in Chinese Bronzes," *Bulletin of the Museum of Far Eastern Antiquities* 8 (1936): 13–14.

58. For the Qiu vessels, see Shaanxi sheng Kaogu yanjiusuo, Baoji shi kaogu gongzuodui and Meixian wehuaguan, "Shaanxi Meixian Yangjia cun Xi Zhou qingtongqi jiaocang fajue jianbao."

59. Cheng Hao, "Cong 'Mengfu' dao 'Xingtan,'" based on a classic study by Luo Genze 羅根澤, "You *Mozi* yin jing tuice Ru Mo liang jia yu jingshu zhi guanxi" 由《墨子》引經推測儒墨兩家與經書之關係, in *Gu shi bian* 古史辨, vol. 4, ed. Luo Genze (1933; rpt. Shanghai: Shanghai Guji chubanshe, 1982), 278–81, and a more recent study by Gao Huaping 高華平, "'San Mo' xueshuo yu Chu guo Moxue" "三墨" 學說與楚國墨學, *Wenshizhe* 文史哲 2013.5, 14–28, makes a strong case that Mozi 墨子 (ca. 468–376 BCE) and his disciples were instrumental in transmitting the *Scriptures* (*shu* 書) to Chu. His argument involves several types of evidence, some negative and some positive. The negative evidence is that the *Scriptures*-related texts that have been unearthed in Hubei (or assumed to have been robbed from tombs in Hubei), that is, the former territory of Chu, exhibit notable differences in texts, titles, and wording from the *Scriptures* usually understood to be Confucian (e.g., quoted by Mencius 孟子, Xunzi 荀子, or included in such sources as the *Li ji* 禮記 *Record of Ritual*). The positive evidence is more abundant, even if largely circumstantial. Among these, four points seem noteworthy. First, of all Warring States texts, the *Mozi* contains the greatest number of quotations of the *Scriptures* (forty-seven in all, as opposed to thirty-eight in the *Mencius* and twenty-eight in the *Xunzi*), though many of these quotations are quite different from the received text of the *Shangshu*, but similar in many respects to the unearthed Chu texts. There is evidence, both in the received text of the *Mozi* and also in medieval quotations of the text, that Mozi went to Chu late in his life, taking "scriptures" with him, and presented them to King Hui of Chu 楚惠王 (r. 488–432 BCE). Third, several prominent disciples of Mozi either served as officials in Chu or were from Chu. Finally, a quotation of the lost "Yue ming" 說命 chapter in the *Mozi* differs from a quotation of what is obviously the same passage in the "Zi yi" 緇衣 chapter

of the *Li ji*, but is more similar with the same passage in the recently recovered Tsinghua manuscript *Fu Yue zhi ming* 傅說之命:

墨子： 唯口出好興戎。

Mozi: It is only the mouth that produces good but arouses warfare.

緇衣： 惟口起羞。

"Zi yi": It is the mouth that causes shame to arise.

傅說之命： 惟口起戎出好。

Fu Yue zhi ming: It is the mouth that causes warfare to arise and produces good.

60. Li Xueqin 李學勤, "Qinghua jian yu *Shang shu Yi Zhou shu* de yanjiu" 清華簡與《尚書》《逸周書》的研究, *Shixue shi yanjiu* 史學史研究 2011.2, 106.

Chapter Six: Varieties of Textual Variants

1. Li Xueqin 李學勤, ed. in chief, and Qinghua daxue Chutu wenxian yanjiu yu baohu zhongxin, eds., *Qinghua daxue cang Zhanguo zhujian (Wu)* 清華大學藏戰國竹簡 (伍) (Shanghai: Zhong Xi shuju, 2015).
I am grateful to Christoph Harbsmeier, David Lebovitz, and Boqun Zhou, with whom I read this text and whose ideas inform much of the translation.

2. *Mengzi* 孟子 1B ("Liang Hui Wang xia" 梁惠王下)/3 includes the following passage:

《書》曰： 天降下民，作之君，作之師，惟曰其助上帝寵之。

The *Scriptures* says: "Heaven sent down the lower people and made for them rulers and made for them teachers, and said: 'Would that they help the Lord on High cherish them.'"

Compare the following passage in the Tsinghua manuscript *Houfu* (slip 5):

古天降下民設萬邦作之君作之師隹曰其助上帝亂下民之匿

In antiquity, Heaven sent down the lower people and set up the ten thousand countries, and made for them rulers, and made for them teachers, and said: "Would that they help the Lord on High untangle the lower people's flaws."

Although the correspondence is not exact, it is certainly close enough to suggest the identity of the two passages. Since the *Houfu* purports to be a discussion between an unnamed king of the Xia dynasty and his minister Houfu 厚父, and shares both wording and tone with chapters in the received text of the *Shang shu*, it would seem to be a reasonable inference that it is the text quoted by the *Mencius*. For a study and translation of this manuscript, see Shaughnessy, *The Tsinghua University Warring States Bamboo Manuscripts*, volume 2, chapter 6: "Houfu."

3. For a translation and study of this manuscript, see Shaughnessy, *The Tsinghua University Warring States Bamboo Manuscripts*, volume 1, chapter 9: "*Feng Xu zhi Ming* 封鄦之命 The Command Enfeoffing Xu."

4. For translations and studies of all of these texts related to Yi Yin 伊尹, see Boqun Zho, *The Tsinghua University Warring States Bamboo Manuscripts*, volume 3: Shang Kings and Ministers (Beijing: Tsinghua University Press, 2023).

5. For *Ming xun, see Li Xueqin et al., *Qinghua daxue cang Zhanguo zhujian (Wu)*, 6–9 (full-size photographs), 45–57 (enlarged photographs), 124–133 (transcription and commentary by Liu Guozhong 劉國忠).

6. For instance, in a position where it would ordinarily quote a chapter of the *Shang shu*, the "Zi yi" 緇衣 "Black Jacket" chapter of the *Li ji* 禮記 *Record of Ritual* quotes the "She Gong zhi gu ming" 葉公之顧命 "Retrospective Command of the Duke of She," which both the Guodian 郭店 and Shanghai Museum manuscripts of the *Zi yi* write as *Zhai Gong zhi gu ming* 祭公之顧命 *Retrospective Command of the Duke of Zhai*. There is a Tsinghua manuscript self-titled as *Zhai Gong zhi gu ming* 祭公之顧命 that corresponds very closely with the "Zhai Gong" 祭公 "Duke of Zhai" chapter of the *Yi Zhou shu*, and which contains the same quotation. It is clear that for the author of the "Zi yi," the *Zhai Gong zhi gu ming* or "Zhai Gong" chapter had the same status as texts included in the *Shang shu*. What is more, there is reason to believe that when Mencius 孟子 objected to the *Shang shu* for its inclusion of a text portraying the Zhou conquest of Shang as a bloody affair (*Mengzi* 7B/3), he was referring to the text "Shi fu" 世俘 "World's Capture" now found as a chapter in the *Yi Zhou shu*. For a brief discussion of these points and their implications for the complementary statuses of the *Shang shu* and *Yi Zhou shu*, see Edward L. Shaughnessy, *Rewriting Early Chinese Texts* (Albany: State University of New York Press, 2006), 58–60.

7. Lu Wenchao's critical edition, simply entitled *Yi Zhou shu*, was originally published in his *Baojingtang congshu* 抱經堂叢書 (1786), and is reprinted in the *Sibu beiyao* 四部備要 edition. For the others, see Ding Zongluo丁宗洛, *Yi Zhou shu guanjian* 逸周書管箋 (1830 woodblock edition); Wang Niansun王念孫, *Du Yi Zhou shu za zhi* 讀逸周書書雜志 (included in his *Du shu za zhi* 讀書雜志 [Huang Qing jingjie xubian ed.]); Chen Fengheng 陳逢衡, *Zhou shu buzhu* 周書

補注 (1825 Xiumei shan guan ed.); Zhu Youzeng 朱右曾, *Zhou shu ji xun jiaoshi* 周書集訓校釋 (1846 woodblock edition); Yu Yue俞樾, *Zhou shu pingyi* 周書平議 (Huang Qing jingjie xubian ed.); Sun Yirang孫詒讓, *Zhou shu jiaobui* 周書斠補 (1894 woodblock edition); Liu Shipei 劉師培, *Zhou shu buzheng* 周書補正, included in *Liu Shenshu xiansheng yishu* 劉申叔先生遺書 (Taipei: Daxin shuju, 1965).

8. In 1976, Huang Peirong 黃沛榮 completed a PhD dissertation entitled "*Zhou shu* yanjiu" 周書研究, Taiwan University, 1976. For a brief introduction to the *Yi Zhou shu*, see Edward L. Shaughnessy, "*I Chou shu* 逸周書," in *Early Chinese Texts: A Bibliographical Guide*, ed. Michael Loewe (Berkeley: Society for the Study of Early China and Institute of East Asian Studies, University of California, Berkeley, 1993), 229–33. In English, for monographic treatments of the *Yi Zhou shu*, Robin McNeal, *Conquer and Govern: Early Chinese Military Texts from the Yizhou Shu* (Honolulu: University of Hawai'i Press, 2012), which provides a translation of five chapters of the text (chapter 6–10), and Yegor Grebnev, *Mediation of Legitimacy in Early China: A Study of the Neglected Zhou Scriptures and the Grand Duke Traditions* (New York: Columbia University Press, 2022), which provides the most thorough account currently available. For a study that provides a comprehensive introduction to the *Yi Zhou shu*, and especially to all of the Tsinghua manuscripts that correspond to chapters in it, see Shaughnessy, *The Tsinghua University Warring States Bamboo Manuscripts*, volume 1: *The Yi Zhou Shu and Pseudo-Yi Zhou Shu Chapters*.

9. Huang Huaixin 黃懷信, *Yi Zhou shu jiaobu zhuyi* 逸周書校補注譯 (Xi'an: Xibei daxue chubanshe, 1996); Huang Huaixin, Zhang Maorong, and Tian Xudong, *Yi Zhou shu huijiao jizhu*.

10. As will be noted later (n. 16), whereas the manuscript writes *chi* 恥 "shame," the received text systematically writes *chou* 醜 "disgrace."

11. *Lunyu* 論語, 13/23.

12. For perhaps the most eloquent statement of this argument, see Bernard Cerquiglini, *Éloge de la variante: Histoire critique de la philology* (Paris: Éditions du Seuil, 1989). I myself have made a similar argument with respect to variants in the *Zhou Yi* 周易 or *Zhou Changes* and its tradition; see Xia Hanyi 夏含夷, "Jianlun 'Yuedu xiguan': Yi Shangbo Zhou Yi Jing gua wei li" 簡論"閱讀習慣": 以上博《周易・彔》卦為例, *Jianbo* 簡帛 4 (2009): 385–94.

13. When this study was first published, an anonymous referee for *Early China* objected to any notion of text criticism that prefers one variant over another. Conceptually interesting though such an objection may be—especially for temporally parallel texts—it has been well documented for centuries that when texts are transmitted by scribal copying, variants are almost invariably introduced into the copies. It seems worthwhile studying how these variants may have been produced.

14. For a systematic presentation of variants between the two texts, see Shaughnessy, *The Tsinghua University Warring States Bamboo Manuscripts*, volume 1.

15. The variation between *wang* 亡 and *wu* 無 is common in Chinese excavated texts. Indeed, many readers simply read 亡 as *wu* and unproblematically

transcribe it as 无 or 無. The *Ming xun* manuscript may offer some support for this reading practice. On slip 11, there is a passage written as 𥘺 (秎) 之以季 but read, primarily on the basis of the received text, as *fu zhi yi hui* 撫之以惠 "soothe them with generosity." If 秎 is indeed to be read as *fu* 撫 "to soothe," then it would demonstrate phonetic contact between 亡 and *wu* 無.

16. *Chi* 恥 "ashamed" and *chou* 醜 "disgraced" are synonyms, and the variation between them does not influence the meaning, at least very much. It is, however, interesting to note that in the "Chang xun" chapter of the *Yi Zhou shu*, the "six limits" (*liu ji* 六極) are enumerated as "command" (*ming* 命), "hearing" (*ting* 聽), "good fortune" (*fu* 福), "awards" (*shang* 賞), "misfortune" (*huo* 禍), and "punishment" (*fa* 罰), with *ting* 聽 taking the place of *chou* 醜 in the received text's enumeration of the "six limits." In his critical edition, Lu Wenchao emended *ting* 聽 to *chou* 醜, presumably on the basis of other usage throughout this and the other two related chapters. Now with the corresponding word in the *Ming xun* manuscript being *chi* 恥,written as 佴, it seems possible to explain this variant: some early version of the "Chang xun" chapter doubtless also read either 佴 or, more likely 恥, and the "ear signific" (耳) caused this to be mistaken for *ting* 聽.

17. Actually, the manuscript itself seems slightly incorrect here, in that it seems to be missing a question particle *hu* 乎 at the end of the phrase *ren neng ju* 人能居 "can mankind be content?" While it is the case that question particles are not essential in rhetorical questions such as this, that *hu* occurs in the following four parallel questions in the text strongly suggests that it should occur here as well. A very similar phrase, *min neng ju hu* 民能居乎 "can the people be content?," appears in the "Du xun" chapter of the *Yi Zhou shu*, *Yi Zhou shu* 1.1b.

18. For these pronunciations, see Axel Schuessler, *Minimal Old Chinese and Later Han Chinese: A Companion to* Grammata Serica Recensa (Honolulu: University of Hawai'i Press, 2009), 138, 328. Whereas the archaic pronunciations are quite distinct, the respective medieval pronunciations became much closer: according to Schuessler, *zheng* 正 had a later Han pronunciation something like *tśeŋ, while *zhen* 震 had a medieval pronunciation like *tśjen (as given for 振). This perhaps suggests that the variant entered the text sometime after the Han dynasty.

19. Lu Wenchao emended the apparently meaningless *qie* 且 here to read *ji* 冀 "to hope for," an emendation accepted by all subsequent editors.

20. Elsewhere in the manuscript (e.g., at slip 8), *shang* is written simply as 上, that is, 上. It is unclear to me whether the different orthography carries any semantic distinction.

21. For this form of *shang* 上, see Gao Ming 高明 and Tu Baikui 涂白奎, ed., *Guwenzi leibian* 古文字類編 (2nd rev. ed.; Shanghai: Shanghai Guji chubanshe, 2008), 367.

22. Both Chen Fengheng and Tang Dapei silently read the *wu* as *shang*, but neither provides any explanation.

23. For these forms of *ge* 戈 and *jie* 戒, see Gao Ming and Tu Baikui, *Guwenzi leibian*, 619 and 213.

24. For similar examples, see, for example, *Zuo zhuan* 左傳 "Yin" 隱 3:

君義，臣行，父慈，子孝，兄愛，弟敬，所謂六順也。

The lord being proper, the minister behaving, the father being loving, the son being filial, the older brother being caring, and younger brother being respectful are what are called the six compliances.

See *Chunqiu Zuo zhuan zheng yi*, 1724. See also *Lunyu* 15/5:

子張問行。子曰：「言忠信，行篤敬，雖蠻貊之邦，行矣。言不忠信，行不篤敬，雖州裏，行乎哉？

Zi Zhang asked about (good) behavior. The Master said: "If one speaks loyally and credibly and one behaves generously and respectfully, then even abroad in the countries of the barbarians it certainly counts as (good) behavior. If one does not speak loyally and credibly and one does not behave generously or respectfully, then even at home would it count as (good) behavior?

Lunyu zhushu, 2516. I am grateful to Christoph Harbsmeier for suggesting these parallels.

25. For *gan* 干 "to strive," here, some editions of the received text write *yu* 于 "in," which however hardly makes any sense in the context.

26. Li Xueqin et al., *Qinghua daxue cang Zhanguo zhujian (yi): Cheng wu*: 6–7, 47–51, 135–41; *Huang men*: 18–21, 87–96, 163–72; *Zhai Gong zhi gu ming*: 22–25, 99–113, 173–79. For translations and studies of all of these texts, see Shaughnessy, *The Tsinghua University Warring States Bamboo Manuscripts*, volume 1.

27. In the original published version of this chapter, I translated the sentence 大命殜罰少命_身 as "The great mandate for generations punishes; the minor mandates command the person," understanding the duplication mark after *ming* 命 "command" as meaning that *ming* was to be read twice, as is normal in all early Chinese manuscripts. However, after subsequently reading Meng Yuelong 孟躍龍, "Qinghua jian *Ming xun* 'Shao ming _ shen' de dufa: Jianlun gudai chaoben wenxian zhong chongwen fuhao de teshu yongfa" 清華簡《命訓》"少命_身"的讀法：兼論古代抄本文獻中重文符號的特殊用法, *Jian bo* 简帛 13 (2017): 71–77, I learned that duplication marks can occasionally refer to some

other word or words prior to the mark. In this case, the mark should clearly refer to *fa* 罰 "punish," as in the received text of "Ming xun." I subsequently published a note concerning this topic, correcting the original translation, and providing a full discussion of the feature; see Edward L. Shaughnessy, "To Punish the Person: A Reading Note Regarding a Punctuation Mark in the Tsinghua Manuscript *Ming Xun,*" *Early China* 40 (2017): 303–10.

Chapter Seven: Unearthed Documents and the Question of the Oral versus Written Nature of the *Shi Jing*

1. "Yuwen Suo'an tan wenxueshi de xiefa" 宇文所安谈文学史的写法, *Dongfang zaobao* 東方早報, 8 March 2009, 2–3.

2. "Yuwen Suo'an tan wenxueshi de xiefa," 2 (ellipsis in the original).

3. Owen, "Interpreting *Sheng Min,*" 25.

4. In the remaining discussion, I focus on Martin Kern's work, mentioned by Owen as a scholar many of whose ideas he agrees with. Kern's and Owen's view can be taken as representative of much of the field. For a review of other Western scholars' views over the course of the last century, focusing primarily upon Marcel Granet (1884–1940) and C. H. Wang (Wang Jingxian 王靖獻), but including also quotations of the views of many contemporary Sinologists, see Shaughnessy, "The Origin and Development of Western Sinologists' Theories of the Oral-Formulaic Nature of the *Classic of Poetry.*"

5. Marcel Granet, *Fêtes et chansons anciennes de la Chine* (1919; 2nd ed., Paris: Leroux, 1929); *Festivals and Songs of Ancient China,* trans. E. D. Edwards (London: Routledge and Kegan Paul, 1932). Ching-hsien Wang, "'Shih Ching': Formulaic Language and Mode of Creation," PhD diss., University of California, Berkeley, 1971, subsequently published as C. H. Wang, *The Bell and the Drum: Shih Ching as Formulaic Poetry in an Oral Tradition* (Berkeley: University of California Press, 1974).

6. Martin Kern, "Methodological Reflections on the Analysis of Textual Variants and the Modes of Manuscript Production in Early China," *Journal of East Asian Archaeology* 4, nos. 1–4 (2002): 143–81; "Early Chinese Poetics in the Light of Recently Excavated Manuscripts," in *Recarving the Dragon: Understanding Chinese Poetics,* ed. Olga Lomová (Prague: Charles University, Karolinum Press, 2003), 27–72; "The *Odes* in Excavated Manuscripts," 149–93; "Excavated Manuscripts and Their Socratic Pleasures: Newly Discovered Challenges in Reading the 'Airs of the States,'" *Études Asiatiques / Asiatische Studien* 61, no. 3 (2007): 775–93; "Bronze Inscriptions, the *Shangshu,* and the *Shijing*: The Evolution of the Ancestral Sacrifice during the Western Zhou," in *Early Chinese Religion, Part One: Shang through Han (1250 BC to 220 AD),* ed. John Lagerwey and Marc Kalinowski (Leiden: Brill, 2009), 143–200; "Lost in Tradition: The *Classic*

of Poetry We Did Not Know," *Hsiang Lectures on Chinese Poetry* 5 (Montreal: Centre for East Asian Research, McGill University, 2010), 29–56.

7. Kern, "Methodological Reflections."

8. Kern, "Methodological Reflections," 167; see also 171.

9. Kern, "Methodological Reflections," 165–66. See too 175: "The *Odes* enjoyed a particular cultural status, and they were organized in poetic form; for both reasons, their wide-spread memorization and oral-exchange among the members of the cultural elite distinguished their overall presence from that of other texts. Yet as noted above, their textual variants are not fundamentally different from those found in other texts with a history."

10. Kern, "Methodological Reflections," 164; cf. Kern, "The *Odes* in Excavated Manuscripts," 160.

11. Kern, "The *Odes* in Excavated Manuscripts," 158.

12. This difference might well indicate that one edition was published before 1955 and the other after that date, or that one was published in Taiwan or Hong Kong while the other was published in the People's Republic of China (PRC), but it does not indicate anything about the original nature of the text.

In the original publication of this study, I provided a more or less extensive discussion of evidence for copying manuscripts from earlier written versions, citing work by Matthias Richter and Daniel Patrick Morgan concerning duplicate versions of four different Shanghai Museum manuscripts, and Christopher Nugent concerning multiple Dunhuang 敦煌 manuscripts of the single text "Qinfu yin" 秦婦吟 "Lament of the Lady Qin" by Wei Zhuang 韋莊 (836–910). In the meantime, more compelling evidence concerning this question has come to light in the two Tsinghua University manuscripts *Zheng Wen Gong wen Tai Bo* 鄭文公問太伯 *Duke Wen of Zheng Asks Tai Bo*. Since these manuscripts are the topic of chapter 10 in the present volume, and the discussion of the earlier evidence is more appropriate there, I have deleted it here.

13. Kern, "The *Odes* in Excavated Manuscripts," 150–51.

14. Ma Chengyuan 馬承源, ed., *Shanghai bowuguan cang Zhanguo Chu zhushu (yi)*) 上海博物館藏戰國楚竹書 (一) (Shanghai: Shanghai guji chubanshe, 2001), 13–41 (plates), 121–65 (transcription and appendices). For a recent study and complete translation, including full references to prior scholarship, see Thies Staack, "Reconstructing the *Kongzi Shilun*: From the Arrangement of the Bamboo Slips to a Tentative Translation," *Asiatische Studien / Études Asiatiques* 64, no. 4 (2010): 857–906.

15. For an overview of this debate, see Shaughnessy, *Rewriting Early Chinese Texts*, 19–23.

16. No paleographer in China working in the field of Warring States manuscripts has expressed any doubt about the authenticity of the Shanghai Museum manuscripts.

17. See, especially, Ji Xusheng 季旭昇, ed., "*Shanghai bowuguan cang Zhanguo Chu zhushu (yi)" duben*《上海博物館藏戰國楚竹書（一）》讀本 (Taipei: Wanjuanlou tushu gongsi, 2004), 60–61, and the appendix "Ode title synopsis," in Staack, "Reconstructing the *Kongzi Shilun*," 901–2.

18. Kern, "The *Odes* in Received Manuscripts," 153.

19. Li Xueqin et al., *Qinghua daxue cang Zhanguo zhujian (yi)*.

20. "Qi ye" 耆夜, in Li Xueqin et al., *Qinghua daxue cang Zhanguo zhujian (yi)*, 10–13 (full-size photos), 63–72 (enlarged photos), 149–56 (transcription).

21. This poem by the Duke of Zhou begins at the end of slip 9 and continues through the end of the manuscript (slip 14). For convenience of presentation, I transcribe the characters of the manuscript into standard *kaishu* 楷書 orthography, writing, for instance, *xishuai* 蟋蟀 where the manuscript writes 䗪蠶. For the purposes of this article, a functional transcription method seems adequate.

22. "Cricket" (*Xishuai* 蟋蟀, Mao 114), in *Mao Shi zhengyi* 毛詩正義, in *Shisan jing zhushu* 十三經注疏, ed. Ruan Yuan 阮元 (Beijing: Zhonghua shuju, 1980), 361.

23. After this chapter was first published, Martin Kern published a study of the Tsinghua manuscript "Xishuai" 蟋蟀 poem: "'Xi Shuai' 蟋蟀 ('Cricket') and Its Consequences: Issues in Early Chinese Poetry and Textual Studies," *Early China* 42 (2019): 39–74. In this study, he says that the two poems (i.e., the poem "Xishuai" of the *Shi jing* and the Tsinghua manuscript *Xishuai*) could not have been produced by "a simple model of consistent visual copying from a written original" (52). Kern then goes on to say, "It is easy to imagine how other 'Xi shuai' poems, were they to be discovered, would likewise be different" (57) and "if this is true of 'Xi shuai,' it will also be true of other texts in the *Poetry*" (58). While the first of these statements is doubtless true, as has been accepted by most scholars who have studied the issue, the latter two statements have already been called into question by the Anhui University manuscript of the *Shi*.

This manuscript, which appeared after both the original publication of this chapter and also of Kern's study, also contains a version of the poem "Xishuai" that, despite occasional orthographic differences, is certainly identifiable with the Mao version of the poem. For a discussion of this poem and a line-by-line comparison of the Anhui University manuscript version with the Mao version, see chapter 8, pp. 221–22.

24. See p 170.

25. Of course, with the publication of the Anhui University manuscript of the *Shi*, there is now artifactual evidence for at least fifty-six other poems (in addition, that is, to the poem "Xishuai" "Cricket" mentioned in n. 24) from the Warring States period.

26. For instance, the "Yiwen zhi" 藝文志 chapter of the *Hanshu* 漢書 says of the *Shi jing*: "The reason that, having met with Qin, it remained intact is

because it was sung and chanted and was not only on bamboo and silk"; Ban Gu 班固, *Hanshu* 漢書 (Beijing: Zhonghua shuju, 1964), 1708.

27. For this text, see Hu Pingsheng 胡平生 and Han Ziqiang 韓自強, *Fuyang Han jian Shijing yanjiu* 阜陽漢簡詩經研究 (Shanghai: Shanghai guji chubanshe, 1988).

28. The evidence is of two sorts, positive and negative. The negative evidence is the clearer: the manuscript freely writes the word *bang* 邦 "country," and thus does not observe a taboo on the name of Liu Bang 劉邦, the founding emperor of the Han dynasty (r. 202–195 BCE). The positive evidence is less clear: Hu Pingsheng notes that one of the divination formulas, *lin guan li zhong* 臨官立眾 "to oversee an office and to take governance," is written elsewhere as *lin guan li zheng* 臨官立正 (or 政), and that this may suggest that the scribe was intentionally avoiding the name of Ying Zheng 嬴政, the First Emperor of Qin; Hu Pingsheng 胡平生, "Fuyang Han jian Zhou Yi gaishu" 阜陽漢簡周易概述, *Jian bo yanjiu* 簡帛研究 3 (1998): 265–66.

29. See, for instance, Tsuen-hsuin Tsien, *Written on Bamboo and Silk: The Beginnings of Chinese Books and Inscriptions*, 2nd ed. (Chicago: University of Chicago Press, 2004), 204. For a more far-ranging argument regarding the effect of bamboo slips on the content of early Chinese texts, see William G. Boltz, "The Composite Nature of Early Chinese Texts," in *Text and Ritual in Early China*, ed. Martin Kern (Seattle: University of Washington Press, 2005), 50–78.

30. Hu Pingsheng and Han Ziqiang, *Fuyang Han jian Shijing yanjiu*, 90.

31. Shaughnessy, "Rewriting the *Zi yi*," 63–130. For the manuscripts, see *Ziyi*, in Jingzhou shi bowuguan, *Guodian Chu mu zhujian*, 17–20 (photographs), and 129–37 (transcription and notes); and Li Xueqin et al., *Shanghai bowuguan cang Zhanguo Chu zhushu (yi)*, 45–68 (photographs) and 171–200 (transcription and notes). For the received text, see "Ziyi," in *Liji zhengyi* 禮記正義, in *Shisan jing zhushu* 十三經注疏, ed. Ruan Yuan 阮元 (Beijing: Zhonghua shuju, 1980), 1647–51.

32. "Zi yi," in Jingzhou shi bowuguan, *Guodian Chu mu zhujian*, 18, 130 (slip 17); Li Xueqin et al., *Shanghai bowuguan cang Zhanguo Chu zhushu (yi)*, 53–54, 183–85 (slips 9–10, however, all but the last two characters, *suo xin* 所信, are lost in this latter manuscript due to a broken bamboo slip).

33. *Liji zhengyi*, 1648.

34. *Mao Shi zhengyi*, 493–94.

35. Zheng Xuan, *Liji Zheng zhu* 禮記鄭注, quoted in *Liji zhengyi*, 1648.

36. *Chunqiu Zuo zhuan zhengyi* 春秋左傳正義, in *Shisan jing zhushu* 十三經注疏, ed. Ruan Yuan 阮元 (Beijing: Zhonghua shuju, 1980), 1959.

37. Quoted at *Mao Shi zhengyi*, 493.

38. This argument derives from Wu Rongzeng 吳榮曾, "*Zi yi* jianben, jin ben yin *Shi* kaobian" 《緇衣》簡、今本引《詩》考辨, *Wenshi* 文史 60 (2002): 15–16.

39. Wang Xianqian 王先謙, *Shi san jia yi jishu* 詩三家義集疏 (N.p.: Xushou tang, 1915), 20.9a–b.

40. James Legge, *The Chinese Classics*, vol. 4, *The She King* (Oxford: Oxford University Press, 1871), 409–11; brackets in Legge's original.

41. There are numerous poems in the *Shi jing* that have identical titles, with six separate titles shared by two poems and two other titles shared by three poems each: "Bo zhou" 柏舟 (Mao 26; *Bei Feng* 邶風) and (Mao 45; *Yong Feng* 鄘風); "Gu feng" 谷風 (Mao 35; *Bei Feng* 邶風) and (Mao 201; *Xiao Ya* 小雅); "Yang zhi shui" 揚之水 (Mao 68; *Wang Feng* 王風), (Mao 92; *Zheng Feng* 鄭風) and (Mao 116; *Tang Feng* 唐風); "Gao qiu" 羔裘 (Mao 80; *Zheng Feng* 鄭風), (Mao 120; *Tang Feng* 唐風) and (Mao 146; *Gui Feng* 檜風); "Fu tian" 甫田 (Mao 102; *Qi Feng* 齊風) and (Mao 211; *Xiao Ya* 小雅); "Di du" 杕杜 (Mao 119; *Tang Feng* 唐風) and (Mao 169; *Xiao Ya* 小雅); "Wu yi" (Mao 122; *Tang Feng*) and (Mao 133; *Qin Feng* 秦風); and "Huang niao" 黃鳥 (Mao 131; *Qin Feng* 秦風) and (Mao 187; *Xiao Ya* 小雅).

42. Shaughnessy, *Rewriting Early Chinese Texts*, 54 n. 108.

43. Li Xueqin has recently suggested a similar scenario to explain one of the anomalous titles in the **Kongzi Shi lun* that the Shanghai Museum editors were unable to identify: "Zhong Shi" 中氏 "The Second-Born," which appears on slip 27 along with the all-too-brief characterization that describes a *junzi* 君子 as a "noble person." Li suggests that this title may well correspond to the fourth stanza of the received Mao version of the poem "Yanyan" 燕燕 "Swallows" (Mao 28); Li Xueqin, "*Shi lun* yu *Shi*" 《詩論》與《詩》, *Zhongguo zhexue* 中國哲學 24 (2002), 123; translated as Li Xueqin, "'Comments on the *Poetry*' (Shilun) and 'The *Poetry*' (Shi)," *Contemporary Chinese Thought* 39, no. 4 (2008): 20–21. If Li Xueqin is correct, it would show once again that a lost stanza of a poem could be grafted onto a different poem.

44. Kern, "Methodological Reflections," 155–56.

45. Kern, "Methodological Reflections," 171.

46. Yu Xingwu, *Shuang jian chi Shijing xinzheng* 雙劍誃詩經新證 (1935); reprinted as *Shijing Chuci xinzheng* 詩經楚辭新證 (Beijing: Zhonghua shuju, 1982); this publication served as the inspiration for numerous subsequent *xin zheng* 新證 studies. For recent *xinzheng* studies modeled upon that of Yu Xingwu, see, for instance, Ji Xusheng 季旭昇, *Shijing guyi xinzheng* 詩經古義新證 (1994; Beijing: Xueyuan chubanshe, 2001); and Feng Shengjun 冯胜君, *Ershi shiji gu wenxian xinzheng yanjiu* 二十世纪古文献新证研究 (Ji'nan: Qilu shushe, 2006).

47. *Mao Shi zhengyi*, 520.

48. Both Bernhard Karlgren, *The Book of Odes: Chinese Text, Transcription and Translation* (1950; rpt. Stockholm: The Museum of Far Eastern Antiquities, 1974), 194, and Wang Li 王力, *Shijing yun du* 詩經韻讀 (Shanghai: Shanghai guji chubanshe, 1980), 342, indicate that *bi* 比 (given as **piər* [Karlgren] or

*piei [Wang]) is a cross-rhyme with *lei* 類 (given as *liwəd [Karlgren] or *liuət [Wang]) three lines ahead.

49. Yu Xingwu, *Shijing Chuci xinzheng*, 52–53.

50. See "Cai shu" 采菽 (Mao 222), in *Mao Shi zhengyi*, 490, and "Bi gong" 閟宮 (Mao 300), in *Mao Shi zhengyi*, 617.

51. See, for instance, He Linyi, *Zhanguo guwen zidian*, v. 1, 429.

52. *Mao Shi zhengyi*, 584.

53. For example, Pang Sunjoo 方善柱 suggests that the famous mention of a tenth-month (*shi yue* 十月) solar eclipse in the poem "Shi yue zhi jiao" 十月之交 "Intersection of the Tenth Month" (Mao 193) is a graphic error for a "seventh-month" (*qi yue* 七月) eclipse, the archaic character for "seven" (十) being essentially identical with the clerical script form of the character for "ten" (十); see Pang Sunjoo (Fang Shanzhu), "Xi Zhou niandai xue shang de jige wenti" 西周年代學上的幾個問題, *Dalu zazhi* 大陸雜誌 51, no. 1 (1975): 17–23. The Han dynasty redactors of the *Shi* could have introduced this error simply by doing nothing other than transcribing the text of the poem exactly in the archaic characters of the Warring States period.

54. Schaberg, "Texts and Artifacts," 507, quoted also earlier, p. 50.

55. Indeed, Arthur Waley treated the poem essentially as an inscription on a bronze vessel, understanding the word *kao* 考 "deceased-father" of the line *Zuo Shao gong kao* 作召公考 "Making for father Duke of Shao" to be a mistake for the phonetically similar *gui* 簋 "tureen" (rendered by Waley as "urn": "He made the Duke of Shao's urn"); see Arthur Waley, *The Book of Songs: The Ancient Chinese Classic of Poetry* (1937; rpt. New York: Grove Press, 1987), 281. I think Waley is probably correct in this reading, but since there is no explicit textual evidence to support the emendation I translate the line as found in the received text.

Ondřej Škrabal has pointed out to me (personal communication, 13 October 2014) that Zhu Xi 朱熹 (1130–1200) had already noted the similarity between the wording of this poem and ancient bronze inscriptions:

言穆公既受賜，遂答稱天子之美命，作康公之廟器，而勒王策命之詞，以考其成。且祝天子以萬壽也。古器物銘云：'郘拜稽首，敢對揚天子休命，用作朕皇考龏伯尊敦。郘其眉壽，萬年無疆。'語正相類。但彼自祝其壽，而此祝君壽耳。

This speaks of Duke Mu having already received the award, then in answer praising the Son of Heaven's fine command, making a vessel for the temple of Duke Kang and engraving the words of the king's written appointment in order to show his accomplishments and also to pray for the Son of Heaven's longevity. An inscription on an ancient vessel says: "Bian bows and touches his head to the ground, daring in response to extol the Son of Heaven's beneficent command, herewith making for my august deceased-father Gongbo this sacrificial tureen. May Bian have long life of ten thousand years without limit." The language is just the same type, only that that one prays for his own longevity and this one prays for the lord's longevity.

See Zhu Xi 朱熹, *Shi jing ji zhu* 詩經集註 (Taipei: Qunyutang chuban gongsi, 1991), 171. The inscription that Zhu Xi quotes was first published in the *Kao gu tu* 考古圖 of Lü Dalin 呂大臨 (1040–1092), published in 1092 (3.10), and was also included in the *Lidai zhong ding yiqi kuanzhi fatie* 歷代鐘鼎彝器款識發帖 of Xue Shanggong 薛尚功 (fl. ca. 1140), published in 1144 (14.10).

56. Waley adds the following note to his translation of the line *Zuo Shao gong kao* 作召公考 "He made the Duke of Shao's urn" of the poem "Jiang Han": "Not necessarily the same one as Karlgren, B.104." It is not clear to me just what this reference is supposed to mean, though I suspect it refers to the two *Diao Sheng gui* vessels, formerly better known as the *Shaobo Hu gui* 召伯虎簋. For the fifth-year *Diao Sheng gui*, see *Jicheng* 4292; for the sixth-year *Diao Sheng gui*, see *Jicheng* 4293. In 2006, two *Diao Sheng zun* with identical inscriptions that fit neatly in between the fifth-year and sixth-year inscriptions on the two *gui* 簋 vessels were discovered in Wujun xicun 五郡西村, some five kilometers to the west of the county seat of Fufeng 扶風 County, Shaanxi; see Baoji shi kaogudui and Fufeng xian bowuguan, "Shaanxi Fufeng xian xin faxian yipi Xi Zhou tongqi" 陝西扶風縣新發現一批西周青銅器, *Kaogu yu wenwu* 考古與文物 2007.4, 3–12.

57. *Zhushu jinian*, 2.9a.
58. "Jiang Han" (Mao 262), in *Mao Shi zhengyi*, 573–74.
59. Karlgren, "Yin and Chou in Chinese Bronzes," 13–14.
60. Legge, *The Chinese Classics*, vol. 4, 458–60 (changing Legge's romanization to pinyin). In the original version of this essay, I presented the translation of Arthur Waley: Waley, *Book of Songs*, 240–41. Because of copyright issues, I here use Legge's translation, which is almost identical to that of Waley in terms of its structural interpretation.
61. Qu Wanli 屈萬里, *Shi jing shi yi* 詩經釋義 (Taipei: Zhongguo wenhua daxue chubanbu, 1983), 336.
62. I first presented the following analysis of the poem "Xia Wu" to the conference "Qu Wanli xiansheng bai sui danchen guoji xueshu yantaohui" 屈萬里先生百歲誕辰國際學術研討會 (Taiwan daxue, 15 September 2006), and the paper was published in the conference volume as Xia Hanyi 夏含夷, "You tongqi mingwen chongxin yuedu *Shi Da Ya Xia Wu*" 由銅器銘文重新閱讀《詩大雅下武》, in *Qu Wanli xiansheng bai sui danchen guoji xueshu yantaohui lunweiji* 屈萬里先生

百歲誕辰國際學術研討會論文集, ed. Guojia tushuguan et al. (Taipei: N.p., 2006), 65–69. At the conference I learned that Zhao Boxiong 趙伯雄 had previously published a similar analysis: "Shi Xia Wu 'Ying hou shun de' jie" 《詩·下武》應侯順德解, Guji zhengli yanjiu 古籍整理研究 (June 1998): 1–3.

63. The Mao commentary (in Mao Shi zhengyi, 525) defines the two words ying 應 and hou 侯 as dang 當 "to match" and wei 維 "to be," while the commentary of Zheng Xuan (Mao 525) states: "King Wu is able to match this obedient virtue, meaning that he is able to complete his ancestors' achievements" 武王能當此順德，謂能成其祖考之功也.

64. Baoli cang jin xu 保利藏金續 (Guangzhou: Lingnan meishu chubanshe, 2001), 124–27.

65. In the original published version of this study, I also compared the poem "Xia Wu" to the inscription on the Qiu pan 逑盤. Since I have already provided a complete translation and study of this lengthy inscription in chapter 3, it can be dispensed with here, though it suffices to say that it confirms the points regarding the Shi Qiang pan.

66. In an earlier study, I argued that similar comparisons with the language of bronze inscriptions suggest that poems of the "Zhou Hymns" section of the Shi can also be dated to the Western Zhou period, some to the first half of the period and others to after the "Ritual Reform" that took place over the course of its middle period; see Edward L. Shaughnessy, "From Liturgy to Literature: The Ritual Contexts of the Earliest Poems in the Book of Poetry," Hanxue yanjiu 漢學研究 (Chinese Studies) 13, no. 1 (1995): 133–64; reprinted in Shaughnessy, Before Confucius, 165–96.

67. See William H. Baxter, "Zhou and Han Phonology in the Shijing," in Studies in the Historical Phonology of Asian Languages, ed. William G. Boltz and Michael C. Shapiro (Amsterdam: John Benjamins, 1991), 30.

Chapter Eight: A First Reading of the Anhui University Bamboo-Slip Shi Jing

1. The slips have been published in Anhui daxue Hanzi fazhan yu yingyong yanjiu zhongxin, ed., Anhui daxue cang Zhanguo zhujian 安徽大學藏戰國竹簡 1 (Shanghai: Zhongxi shuju, 2019). General information concerning the slips is drawn from the preface (前言) to this volume; 1–7. For general studies of the Anhui University Shi jing manuscripts, see Huang Dekuan 黃德寬, "Anhui daxue cang Zhanguo zhujian gaishu" 安徽大學藏戰國竹簡概述, Wenwu 文物 2017.9, 56–58, and Huang Dekuan, "Lüelun xinchu Zhanguo Chu jian Shi jing yiwen ji qi jiazhi" 略論新出戰國楚簡《詩經》異文及其價值, Anhui daxue xuebao (Zhexue Shehui kexue ban) 安徽大學學報(哲學社會科學版) 2018.3, 71–77. See too eight articles in a special section of the journal Hanzi Hanyu yanjiu 漢字漢語

研究 (2020.2) and the special issue of *Bamboo and Silk* (4 [2021]) with seven articles, in addition to the original version of the present chapter, addressing the Anda *Shi jing*. See too Dirk Meyer and Adam Craig Schwartz, *Songs of the Royal Zhōu and the Royal Shào: Shī 詩 of the Ânhuī University Manuscripts* (Leiden: Brill, 2022). Since these latter three sources were all published after the original writing of this chapter, it is possible here only to take note of them in notes (as for example in n. 6).

2. There is a notation at the end of this section "Zhou Nan *shi you yi*" 周南十又一 "*Zhou Nan*: 11," indicating that the manuscript included eleven poems, matching the number in the received *Shi jing*. However, two slips, 18 and 19, are missing from the manuscript. These slips would have contained the last four characters of the poem that corresponds to the *Shi jing* poem "Han guang" 漢廣 "The Han Is Broad" (Mao 9), the entirety of the poem "Ru fen" 汝墳 "Banks of the Ru" (Mao 10), and the first fourteen characters of the poem "Lin zhi zhi" 麟之趾 "Hooves of the Doe" (Mao 11).

3. *Anhui daxue cang Zhanguo zhujian (yi)*, 125, n. 2. Xia Dazhao 夏大兆, "Anda jian *Shi jing* 'Hou liu' kao" 安大簡《詩經》"侯六"考, *Guizhou Shifan daxue xuebao (Shehui kexueban)* 貴州師範大學學報(社會科學版) 2018.4, 119–25, esp. 124, argues that *yu* 魚 is a phonetic loan for *wu* 吾 "I," and is a self-referential comment on the part of the scribe referring to his writing of "this poem" (*zhi shi* 之詩). Because he identifies this *Hou* 侯 as referring to the state of Jin 晉, he suggests that the scribe was from Jin but had migrated to the southern state of Chu (whence the Chu orthography of the manuscript). In a subsequent study, he suggests further that this scribe was instead a refugee from Chu 楚 living in Jin; Xia Dazhao 夏大兆, "Anda jian *Shi jing* 'Hou liu' xukao" 安大簡《詩經》"侯六"續考, *Zhanguo wenzi yanjiu* 戰國文字研究 1 (2019): 93–108. In this context, he reads the final thirteen graphs as "The old friends seeing me: Whose heart is thumping? It is mine that is thumping" (昔人見吾者，誰心蟲之，余者蟲之). This is certainly a creative reading, but perhaps no more satisfying than Xu Zaiguo's suggestion that this is merely a scribe practicing his calligraphy.

4. The sequence of the poems in the manuscript is different from that in the received text of the *Shi jing*. The poems correspond to the following poems in the received text: "Fen ju ru" 汾沮洳 (Mao 108), "Zhi hu" 陟岵 (Mao 110), "Yuan you tao" 園有桃 (Mao 109), "Fa tan" 伐檀 (Mao 112), "Shi shu" 碩鼠 (Mao 113), and "Shi mu zhi jian" 十畝之間 (Mao 111).

5. *Anhui daxue cang Zhanguo zhujian*, 3.

6. In a fascinating example of paleographic exegesis, Adam Schwartz points out that references to my "horse" (*ma* 馬) in the final three stanzas of the poem "Juan er" 卷耳 "Curly-Ears" (i.e., cockleburs; Mao 3) are written in three different ways, first with all four legs visible in the pictograph, then with

the legs wavering, and finally with the legs abbreviated entirely, as the poem recounts the horse's progressive fatigue; see Meyer and Schwartz, *Songs of the Royal Zhōu and the Royal Shào*, 12–13 and 78.

7. The Anhui University editors note that there is evidence that in Warring States Chu script *mei* was variously written as 寐 and as 㮴, both of which feature 帚 components and both of which resemble 寐 and 寢; *Anhui daxue cang Zhanguo zhujian*, 70–71, n. 7. Jiang Wen 蔣文, "A Re-examination of the Controversy over the Oral and Written Nature of the *Classic of Poetry*'s Early Transmission, Based on the Anhui University Manuscript," *Bamboo and Silk* 4, no. 1 (2021): 142–43, shows evidence that 寐 could stand for either 寢 "to sleep" or *mei* 寐 "asleep," depending on context.

8. The Anhui University editors note that 伓 is often seen in Warring States Chu manuscripts, in which it routinely serves as an alternative form of *bei* 倍 "double; to add to; to join together with"; *Anhui daxue cang Zhanguo zhujian*, 71, n. 9. *Bei* 倍 is also cognate with *pei* 陪 "to accompany," which it strikes me is also an appropriate reading here.

9. It is perhaps worth noting in this context that *pei* 陪 (and perhaps *bei* 倍) is synonymous with *qiu* 逑 "mate, match," used to describe the girl in the preceding stanza.

10. The Anhui University editors note that the original form of the graph *yao* 要, still apparent in its Chu form, is of two hands cinching the waist; they understand it as the protograph for *yao* 腰 "waist." *Tiao* 嬥 is defined in the *Shuo wen jie zi* 說文解字 as *zhi hao mao* 直好皃 "straight (or more probably slender) and pretty appearance." The *Guang yun* 廣韻 defines it as *xi yao mao* 細腰貌 "thin waisted appearance." For these definitions, see *Anhui daxue cang Zhanguo zhujian*, 70 n. 3.

11. For an excellent discussion of the meaning of *yaotiao* in the received text, see Kern, "Lost in Tradition," 41–47.

12. For the first of these unearthed documents, the *Wu xing* 五行 manuscript from Mawangdui 馬王堆, see Jeffrey Riegel, "Eros, Introversion, and the Beginnings of *Shijing* Commentary," *Harvard Journal of Asiatic Studies* 57, no. 1 (1997): 149–59. For a similar reading in the Shanghai Museum *Kongzi Shi lun* 孔子詩論 manuscript, see Kern, "Lost in Tradition," 33–36.

13. For these archaic reconstructions, see Schuessler, *Minimal Old Chinese and Later Han Chinese*, 197, 207, 173, and 199. Subsequent reconstructions of archaic pronunciations will also be taken from this work. I am grateful to several friends for convincing me that this is best understood as a different writing of the same word: Ondřej Škrabal, Jiang Wen 蔣文, and Jeffrey Tharsen.

14. For 虖 read as the final particle *hu* 乎 or *hu* 呼 "to call out," see Teng Rensheng 滕壬生, *Chu xi jianbo wenzibian* 楚系简帛文字编 (Wuhan: Hubei jiaoyu chubanshe, 2008), 121–22.

15. The editors here explicitly credit Huang Dekuan 黃德寬 with this interpretation. For details, see Huang Dekuan, "Lüelun xinchu Zhanguo Chu jian *Shi jing* yiwen ji qi jiazhi," 73.

16. *Mao Shi Zheng jian* 毛詩鄭箋 (*Sibu beiyao* ed.), 1.18b.

17. This was quoted in Xu Shen 許慎, *Wu jing yi yi* 五經異義; see Chen Shouqi 陳壽祺, *Wu jing yi yi shuzheng* 五經異義疏證 (rpt. Shanghai: Shanghai guji chubanshe, 2012), 223.

18. Chen Shouqi, *Wu jing yi yi shuzheng*, 223.

19. Chen Shouqi, *Wu jing yi yi shuzheng*, 223. Zheng Xuan's meaning is not very clear; the translation given here reflects the interpretation of the *Mao Shi zhengyi*, 294:

> 戰之者，不忍盡殺令五豝；止一發，中則殺一而已。

> Being fearful for them, he cannot bear to kill all five sows, so he only shoots once, and hitting it then kills one and that is all.

20. *Anhui daxue cang Zhanguo zhujian*, 98 n. 4.

21. *Mao Shi Zheng jian*, 1.18b.

22. For instance, James Legge suggested that these animals are "inconsistent with the benevolence which the piece is understood to celebrate"; Legge, *The Chinese Classics*, vol. 4, 37.

23. *Er ya Guo zhu* 爾雅郭注 (*Sibu beiyao* ed.), 11.1a. For another statement of this, see Zheng Xuan's gloss to the *Zhou li* 周禮: *Zhou li Zheng zhu* 周禮鄭注 (*Sibu beiyao* ed.), 29.9a.

24. Yan Shixuan 顏世鉉, "*Shi* Shao nan 'Zou yu' 'zou yu' jie: Jianlun duidai Han Ru *Shi* shuo de taidu" 《詩·召南·騶虞》"騶虞"解：兼論對待漢儒《詩》說的態度, paper presented to the Institute of History and Philology, Academia Sinica, 7 May 2018.

25. Yan Shixuan quotes Wei Yuan 魏源 (1794–1856), *Shi gu wei* 詩古微, as making this point:

> 夫詩有作詩者之心，而又有采詩、編詩者之心焉。有說詩者之義，而又有賦詩、引詩者之義焉。作詩者自道其情，情達而止，不計聞者之如何也。. . . 作詩者意盡於篇中，序詩者事徵於篇外。是毛傳仍同三家，不以序詩為作詩。

> With the *Shi*, there is the intention of the ones who made the poems, and there is also the intention of those who collected the poems and who edited the poems. There is the meaning of those who explain the poems, and there is also the meaning of those who recited the poems and quoted the poems. Those who made the

poems simply stated their feelings, and with the feelings expressed they stopped, without taking into account how the listener might react. . . . The thought of those who made the poems is entirely within the poems, while the affairs documented by those who put the poems in sequence is outside of the poems. In this, the *Mao Zhuan* is just the same as the other Three Schools; we should not consider the sequencing of the poems to be the making of the poems.

26. This event is narrated also in the *Zuo zhuan* 左傳 (6th year of Duke Wen 文公); see *Chunqiu Zuo zhuan zhengyi*, 1844.

27. Different ordering of the stanzas vis-à-vis the Mao version of the *Shi* is a fairly pervasive feature of the Anhui University manuscript, occurring in fifteen of the fifty-seven poems; for a complete listing and study of the feature, see Yuasa Kunihiro 湯淺邦弘, "On the Question of Inverted Stanzas in the Anda-Slip *Shi jing* Poem 'Si tie,'" *Bamboo and Silk* 4, no. 1 (2021): 149–71. It seems to me likely that this difference in the sequence of stanzas may be due to a codicological feature seen, for instance, in the Fuyang 阜陽 manuscript of the *Shi jing*, whereby whole stanzas were written on individual bamboo slips. As these slips came undone, it would have been natural for different readers—and thus different editors—to put them in different orders. For the Fuyang manuscript, see Hu Pingsheng and Han Ziqiang, *Fuyang Han jian* Shi jing *yanjiu*.

28. *Si* 思 (*sə) is in the *zhi* 之 rhyme class and *xi* 息 (*sək) is in the *zhi* 職 rhyme class, members of which were commonly interchanged.

29. See, for instance, Waley, *The Book of Songs*, 103. See, too, Yuan Mei 袁梅, Shi jing yizhu (Guo feng bufen) 詩經譯注(國風部分) (Jinan: Qi-Lu shushe, 1983), 340.

30. The top portion of slip 81 is broken, with about eight characters missing. The top portion of slip 82 is broken, with one character missing.

31. Xia Dazhao, "Anda jian *Shi jing* 'Hou liu' kao"; Xia Dazhao, "Anda jian *Shi jing* 'Hou liu' xukao"; Wang Ning 王寧, "Anda jian *Shi jing* 'Hou' yijie 安大簡《詩經》"侯"臆解, http://www.gwz.fudan.edu.cn/Web/Show/4411, posted 6 April 2019; Hu Pingsheng 胡平生, "Anda jian *Shi jing* 'Hou' wei 'Wei feng' shuo" 安大簡《詩經》"矦"爲"魏風"說, http://wxs.swu.edu.cn/s/wxs/index52/20190930/3782252.html, posted 30 September 2019.

32. In the received *Shi jing*, there are seven poems in the *Wei Feng*: the six found in the *Hou* section of the Anhui manuscript, and also the poem "Ge ju" 葛屨 (Mao 107), which is the first poem in the *Wei Feng*. In the Anhui manuscript, "Ge ju" is likewise the first poem of the *Wei* 魏 section, though the other nine poems in that section are found in the *Tang Feng* 唐風 section of the received text of the *Shi jing*.

33. *Anhui daxue cang Zhanguo zhujian (yi)*, 123 n. 3.

34. *Anhui daxue cang Zhanguo zhujian (yi)*, 123 n. 8.

35. *Anhui daxue cang Zhanguo zhujian (yi)*, 123 n. 4.

36. Liu Gang 劉剛, "A Reconstruction of the Text of the Poem 'You Bi' of the *Liturgies of Lu* Section of the *Classic of Poetry*," *Bamboo and Silk* 4, no. 1 (2021): 189–99.

37. Posted to the site "Anda jian *Shi jing* chudu" 安大簡《詩經》初讀, http://www.bsm.org.cn/forum/forum.php?mod=viewthread&tid=12409&extra=&page=17, accessed 24 October 2019.

38. For discussion of other anomalous uses of duplication marks in early maunscripts, see Meng Yuelong, "Qinghua jian *Ming xun* 'Shao ming ̣ shen' de dufa"; Liu Xinfang 劉信芳, *Shangbo cang liu* shi jie zhi san" 上博藏六試解之三, www.bsm.org.cn, posted 9 August 2007; Yang Xiquan 楊錫全, "Chutu wenxian 'shi ̣' ju qian xi" 出土文獻 '是 ̣' 句淺析, http://www.gwz.fudan.edu.cn/old/SrcShow.asp?Src_ID=958, posted 3 November 2009; "Chutu wenxian 'shi ̣' ju qian xi buzheng yi ze" 出土文獻 '是 ̣' 句淺析補證一則, http://www.gwz.fudan.edu.cn/old/SrcShow.asp?Src_ID=1004, posted 2 December 2009; "Chutu wenxian 'shi ̣' ju qian xi zai bu yi ze: Jianlun xici 'shi' laiyuan wenti" 出土文獻 '是 ̣' 句淺析' 再補一則：兼論係詞 "是" 來源問題, http://www.gwz.fudan.edu.cn/old/SrcShow.asp?Src_ID=1028, posted 26 December 2009; "Chutu wenxian chongwen yongfa xin tan" 出土文獻重文用法新探, http://www.gwz.fudan.edu.cn/old/SrcShow.asp?Src_ID=1145, posted 10 May 2010. See too chapter 6, n. 27, in the present volume for implications concerning the Tsinghua manuscript *Ming xun*.

39. Yu Yue 俞樾, *Gu shu yi yi juli* 古書疑義舉例 (rpt. Beijing: Zhonghua shuju, 1956), 105.

40. Of course, it is also possible that different manuscript versions of the text used duplication marks differently, but without any further evidence we can only speculate about this.

41. This story is first alluded to in both the *Chunqiu* 春秋 and *Zuo zhuan* 左傳 in the sixteenth year of Duke Huan 桓公 (696 BCE) and then more fully in the *Zuo zhuan* for the second year of Duke Min 閔公 (660 BCE); see *Chunqiu Zuo zhuan zhengyi*, 1758, 1788; see too Durrant, Li, and Schaberg, *Zuo Tradition*, vol. 1, 127, 241.

42. I thank Ondřej Škrabal again for suggesting that it might be interesting to read these two graphs in the manuscript "literally."

43. *Anhui daxue cang Zhanguo zhujian (yi)*, 118 n. 1. For the *Mao Zhuan* gloss, see *Mao Shi Zheng jian*, 2.1a. For the *Er ya* and *Shuo wen jie zi* glosses, see *Er ya Guo zhu*, 8.10b; Duan Yucai 段玉裁, *Shuo wen jie zi Duan zhu* 說文解字段注 (*Sibu beiyao* ed.), 1B.15b (writing the word *ci* as 薺 and quoting this line of the *Shi* as 牆有薺).

44. David Lebovitz reminds me that *xiang* 襄 is also written with two "mouth" components, so it may well be that this character should be read as *xiang*.

45. The *Mao zhuan* says simply *nei gou ye* 內冓也 "inner chamber"; see *Mao Shi Zheng jian*, 3.1b–2a; see too, for instance, Legge, *The Chinese Classics*, vol. 4, 75.

46. *Mao Shi Zheng jian*, 3.1b–2a. It must be admitted that Zheng Xuan's explanation is open to different interpretations in its own right.

47. The *Han Shi* 韓詩 states: "*Zhong gou* is midnight, and refers to words of licentious talk" (中冓，中夜，謂淫辭之言也); see Yuan Mei 袁梅, *Shi jing yiwen huikao bianzheng* 詩經異文彙考辯證 (Jinan: Qi-Lu shushe, 2013), 69.

48. *Anhui daxue cang Zhanguo zhujian*, 118, citing Huang Tianshu 黃天樹, *Huang Tianshu guwenzi lunji* 黃天樹古文字論集 (Beijing: Xueyuan chubanshe, 2006), 185–88.

49. The Anhui University editors suggest that because of the two characters' graphic similarity, *nei* 內 may be a mistake for *da* 大. I suspect that it is more likely that *da* would be a mistake for *nei*, which contrasts nicely with the concluding *wai* 外 "outside, outer" of the couplet.

50. It seems likely that this *wu* 無 "not" in the manuscript was a transformation of *wang* (*mang) 亡 "not; nonexistent," which in turn is essentially homophonous with the *huang* (*hmâng) 荒 "waste" of the received text.

51. Although these two words would seem to have nothing in common, and the characters for them in *kaishu* 楷書 form are quite distinct, the right sides of the two characters may be similar enough to have been easily mistakeable: *fu* 𦥑 versus *xiu* 𦥯.

52. As noted in chapter 7, n. 14, there are preliminary reports that from July 2014 through January 2015, archaeologists affiliated with the Jingzhou Museum 荊州博物館 excavated cemeteries at Xiajiatai 夏家台 and Liujiatai 劉家台, just to the north of Jingzhou 荊州 and south of Yingnan 郢南 village, respectively. Xiajiatai tomb 106, dated to the Warring States period, is said to have contained more than one hundred bamboo slips, including the first fourteen poems from the *Bei Feng* 邶風 section of the *Shi jing*; see "Zui zao de *Shi jing* chutu yu Jingzhou." There is a still more recent report that another manuscript of the *Shi* has been unearthed from tomb 798 at Wangjiazui 王家嘴, also in the vicinity of Jingzhou; see "Xixun: Jingzhou Wangjiazui 798 hao Zhanguo Chu mu ronghuo '2021 nian Hubei liu da kaogu xin faxian'" 喜訊！荊州王家咀798號戰國楚墓榮獲"2021年湖北六大考古新發現，" http://wlj.jingzhou.gov.cn/xxdt/dtyw/202206/t20220610_737887.shtml.

53. Because of the unprovenanced nature of the Anhui University manuscripts, there is no way to know how many more, if any, slips the manuscript of the *Poetry* may have originally contained in addition to the 117 numbered slips.

54. Qiu Xigui 裘錫圭, "Zhongguo gudianxue chongjian zhong yinggai zhuyi de wenti" 中國古典學重建中應該注意的問題, in Qiu Xigui, *Qiu Xigui xueshu wenji: Jiandu boshu juan* 裘錫圭學術文集：簡牘帛書卷 (Shanghai: Fudan daxue chubanshe, 2015), 339.

55. This statement follows upon several pages where Qiu was at pains to show how he misread lines in the Guodian 郭店 manuscripts by not paying sufficient attention to corresponding passages in the received literature. It is then followed in turn by one simple example of a mistake he made in too readily accommodating his reading of a passage in the Guodian *Laozi* 老子 to the received *Laozi*, occupying a little over half a page, and then one more example, but covering a page and a half, of how he went wrong by trying to "establish difference." Of course, the number of characters devoted to one problem is not necessarily indicative of the importance accorded to that problem, but the overall tenor of Qiu's argument shows, to me at least, that he is more concerned with the problems pertaining to "establishing difference" than with those stemming from an "urge to equate."

56. See Scott Cook, "Review of Sarah Allan and Crispin Williams, ed., *The Guodian* Laozi: *Proceedings of the International Conference, Dartmouth College, May 1998*," *China Review International* 9, no. 1 (2002): 54–64.

57. Cook, Review of Allan and Williams, *The Guodian* Laozi, 54.

58. Cook, Review of Allan and Williams, *The Guodian* Laozi, 56.

59. Cook, "Review of Allan and Williams, *The Guodian* Laozi," 61 (emphasis in the original).

60. Schuessler, *Minimal Old Chinese and Later Han Chinese*, 195, 206.

61. Schuessler, *Minimal Old Chinese and Later Han Chinese*, 173, 171.

62. Ma Ruichen 馬瑞辰, *Mao Shi zhuan jian tongshi* 毛詩傳箋通釋 (rpt. Beijing: Zhonghua, 1989), 417–18, cited in Kern, "Lost in Tradition," 46.

63. For these definitions, see *Anhui daxue cang Zhanguo zhujian*, 70 n. 3.

64. Kern, "Lost in Tradition," 45, citing George A. Kennedy, "A Note on Ode 220," in *Studia Serica Bernhard Karlgren Dedicata: Sinological Studies Dedicated to Bernhard Karlgren on His Seventieth Birthday*, ed. Søren Egerod and Else Glahn (Copenhagen: E. Munksgaard, 1959), 190–98.

65. *Bei* 倍 *bəʔ is in the *zhi* 之 rhyme class, while *fu* 服 *bəʔ is in the *zhi* 職 rhyme class.

66. *Mao Shi Zheng jian*, 1.3a. It is unclear why *fu* 服, which follows *si* 思 "to think, to wish for," should mean "to think." Others have gotten around this problem by explaining *si* 思 as an "empty particle" without meaning (for which, see, for instance, Yuan Mei, *Shi jing yizhu*, 78 n. 13), even though the very next gloss of the *Mao Zhuan* uses *si* 思—very much as a full word—to define *you* 悠.

67. *Mao Shi Zheng jian*, 1.3a. Although most modern readers view the persona of the poet as a male, both the *Mao Zhuan* and Zheng Xuan regard it as the queen (*houfei* 后妃); hence the use of female pronouns here. For a study that explores the gender of the poet's persona, see Tamara Chin, "Orienting Mimesis: Marriage and the *Book of Songs*," *Representations* 94 (Spring 2006): 53–79.

68. For just some of these uses, see Yan Shixuan, "*Shi* Shao nan 'Zou yu' 'zou yu' jie," 10.

69. While it is easy to see how *cong* 從 "to follow; to chase" and *zou* 驟 or *qu* 趨 "to rush; to chase" are related, it would be more difficult to see any relationship between *zong* 縱 "to relax; to release" and *zou* (or *qu*). Indeed, a substitution of *cong* 從 for *zou* 驟 might be seen as a classic example of *lectio facilior*, a word "easier" to write and understand replacing a more difficult word (though recognizing that this principle does not apply as predictably with Chinese as with some other languages).

70. The Qin Stone Drums probably date to the fifth century BCE; see Gilbert L. Mattos, *The Stone Drums of Ch'in*, Monumenta Serica Monograph Series 19 (Nettetel: Steyler Verlag, 1988), 75–112; see, too, Qiu Xigui 裘錫圭, "Guanyu Shi Gu Wen de shidai wenti" 關於石鼓文的時代問題, *Chuantong wenhua yu xiandaihua* 傳統文化與現代化 1 (1995): 40–48.

71. Mattos, *The Stone Drums of Ch'in*, 220–21.

72. For a compendium of these quotations, see Ho Che Wah 何志華 and Chan Hung Kan 陳雄根, *Xian-Qin Liang Han dianji yin Shi jing ziliao huibian* 先秦兩漢典籍引《詩經》資料彙編 (added English title: *Citations from the Shijing to Be Found in Pre-Han and Han Texts*) (Hong Kong: Chinese University Press, 2004).

73. Martin Kern, "*Shi Jing* Songs as Performance Texts: A Case Study of 'Chu ci' ('Thorny Caltrop')" *Early China* 25 (2000): 49–111.

74. Kern, "Early Chinese Literature, Beginnings through Western Han," 27–28.

75. Kern, "'Xi Shuai' 蟋蟀 ('Cricket') and Its Consequences."

76. Kern, "'Xi Shuai' 蟋蟀 ('Cricket') and Its Consequences," 52.

77. Kern cites ten different studies that he consulted: Li Xueqin 李學勤, "Lun Qinghua jian *Qi ye* de *Xi shuai shi*" 論清華簡《耆夜》的《蟋蟀》詩, *Zhongguo wenhua* 中國文化 33 (2011), 7–10; Li Feng 李峰, "Qinghua jian *Qi ye* chudu ji qi xiangguan wenti" 清華簡《耆夜》初讀及其相關問題, in *Disijie guoji hanxue huiyi lunwenji: Chutu cailiao yu xin shiye* 第四屆國際漢學會議論文集:出土材料與 新視野, ed. Li Zongkun 李宗焜 (Taipei: Zhongyang yanjiuyuan, 2013), 461–91; Huang Huaixin 黃懷信, "Qinghua jian *Qi ye* jujie" 清華簡《耆夜》句解, *Wenwu* 文物 2012.1, 77–93; Chen Minzhen 陳民鎮, "*Xi shuai* zhi 'zhi' ji qi shixue chanshi: jianlun Qinghua jian *Qi ye* Zhou Gong zuo *Xi shuai* benshi" 《蟋蟀》之"志"及其詩學闡釋——兼論清華簡《耆夜》周公作《蟋蟀》本事, *Zhongguo shige yanjiu* 中國詩歌研究 9 (2013): 57–81; Cao Jianguo 曹建國, "Lun Qinghua jian zhong de *Xi shuai*" 論清華簡中的《蟋蟀》, *Jiang Han kaogu* 江漢考古 2011.2, 110–15; Li Rui 李銳, "Qinghua jian *Qi ye* xutan" 清華簡《耆夜》續探, *Zhongyuan wenhua yanjiu* 中原文化研究 2014.2, 55–62; Chen Zhi 陳致, "Qinghua jian suo jian gu yinzhi li ji *Qi ye* zhong gu yishi shijie" 清華簡所見古飲至禮及《夜》中古佚詩試解, *Chutu wenxian* 出土文獻 1 (2010): 6–30; Hao Beiqin 郝貝欽, "Qinghua jian *Qi ye* zhengli yu yanjiu" 清華簡《耆夜》整理與研究, MA thesis, Tianjin Normal University 天津師範 大學, 2012; Marcel Schneider, "The '*Qí yè* 耆夜' and '*Zhōu Gōng zhī qín wǔ* 周公之琴舞' from the Qīnghuá Bamboo Manuscripts:

An Annotated Translation," Licentiate dissertation, University of Zurich, 2014, as well as my own study "Unearthed Documents and the Question of the Oral versus Written Nature of the *Classic of Poetry*," *Harvard Journal of Asiatic Studies* 75, no. 2 (December 2015): 331–75, esp. 342 (reprinted as chapter 7 in this volume; see esp. pp. 176–78). Of these, those by Hao Beiqin 郝貝欽 and Marcel Schneider are not available to me. However, despite Kern's statement that "nearly all studies contend it is just one poem" (49), in fact quite the opposite is the case. Other than the studies by Li Xueqin 李學勤 and two of his students (Huang Huaixin 黃懷信 and Chen Minzhen 陳民鎮), all of the other studies (those by Li Feng 李峰, Cao Jianguo 曹建國, Li Rui 李銳, Chen Zhi 陳致, as well as that by myself) draw precisely the opposite conclusion: that we are dealing here with two different poems.

78. Kern, "'Xi Shuai' 蟋蟀 ('Cricket') and Its Consequences," 57, 58.

79. This concerns the *nei* 內 "inner" of the third couplet of the first stanza of the manuscript version of the poem, which differs from the received text's *da* 大 "great" in the corresponding second stanza. The two characters are visually quite similar, but very different in terms of pronunciation (*nûts vs. *dâs). I have also suggested (n. 52 in this chapter) that the difference between the manuscript's *fu* 浮 and the received text's *xiu* 休 may also be due to the graphic similarity of the two characters. Needless to say, this does not entail any direct influence between the Anhui University manuscript, which after all has been underground for the last 2,300 or more years, and the received *Shi jing*. However, we can surely assume that there were other similar manuscripts circulating above ground during the Warring States period, both in the ancient state of Chu and also in other states of northern China, and that some at least of these manuscripts survived long enough to have a direct influence on the Mao 毛 version of the *Shi jing*.

Chapter Nine: The *Mu Tianzi Zhuan* and King Mu–Period Bronzes

1. For the text, see *Mu tianzi zhuan* 穆天子傳 (*Sibu congkan* ed.). For a brief introduction to the text, see Rémi Mathieu, *Mu t'ien-tzu chuan* 穆天子傳, in *Early Chinese Texts: A Bibliographical Guide*, ed. Michael Loewe (Berkeley: The Society for the Study of Early China and the Institute of East Asian Studies, University of California, 1993), 342–46.

2. Ji Yun 紀昀 et al., eds., *Qinding Siku quanshu jianming mulu* 欽定四庫全書簡明目錄 (Shanghai: Shanghai Guji chubanshe, 1985), 552.

3. Ji Yun 紀昀 et al., eds., *Qinding Siku quanshu zongmu tiyao* 欽定四庫全書總目提要 (Taibei: Taibei Shangwu yinshuguan, 1985), vol. 1042, 246.

4. Mathieu, *Mu t'ien-tzu chuan*, 342, reflects well this appraisal: "If historical facts are mentioned, they serve no more than as a pretext for presenting a

romantic tale, which is marked by exaggeration, grandiloquence and sentiment. Possibly the work should be regarded as one of the few successful attempts to produce an epic in ancient Chinese literature."

5. Yu Xingwu 于省吾, "*Mu tianzi zhuan* xin zheng" 穆天子傳新證, *Kaogu she kan* 考古社刊 6 (1937): 277.

6. Yu Xingwu, "*Mu tianzi zhuan* xin zheng," 283. For the dating given by Guo Moruo and Wu Qichang, see Guo Moruo, *Liang Zhou jinwenci daxi kaoshi*, 20; Wu Qichang 吳其昌, *Jinwen lishuo shuzheng* 金文曆朔疏證 (Wuhan: Guoli Wuhan daxue congshu, 1936), 1.28.

7. Yang Shuda 楊樹達, "Mao Bo Ban gui ba" 毛伯班簋跋, in Yang Shuda, *Jiweiju jinwen shuo* 積微居金文說 (Changsha: Hunan jiaoyu chubanshe, 2007), 124.

8. Tang Lan 唐蘭, *Xi Zhou qingtongqi mingwen fendai shizheng* 西周青銅器銘文分代史徵 (Beijing: Zhonghua shuju, 1986), 355.

9. A first installment toward this hope is Edward L. Shaughnessy, "On the Editing of the *Mu Tianzi Zhuan*," in *In Between the Lines: The Narration of Ancient China: A Festschrift in Honor of William H. Nienhauser*, ed. Chen Zhi (Leiden: Brill, 2023).

10. Li Xueqin et al., *Qinghua daxue cang Zhanguo zhujian* (yi), 173.

11. Chen Mengjia 陳夢家, *Xi Zhou tongqi duandai* 西周銅器斷代 (Beijing: Zhonghua shuju, 2004), 149.

12. The vessel has traditionally been dated to the mid-Western Zhou based in part on the calligraphy of the inscription and especially due to its mention of Jing Bo, one of the most important figures at the courts of Kings Mu, Gong 共, and Yih 懿; see, for instance, Zhongguo shehui kexueyuan kaogu yanjiusuo 中國社會科學院考古研究所, ed., *Yin Zhou jinwen jicheng shiwen* 殷周金文集成釋文 (Hong Kong: Chinese University of Hong Kong, Institute of Chinese Studies, 2001), 2804; Shanghai bowuguan Shang Zhou qingtongqi mingwen xuan bianxiezu 上海博物館商周青銅器銘文選編寫組, ed., *Shang Zhou qingtongqi mingwenxuan* 商周青銅器銘文選 (Beijing: Wenwu chubanshe, 1986), 200. However, the shape of this vessel would seem to call this early date into question. The vessel has a deep hemispherical belly typical of late Western Zhou. It is unclear how to reconcile the evidence of the inscription with that of the vessel.

13. Li Xueqin, "Mu Gong gui gai zai qingtongqi fenqi shang de yiyi" 穆公簋蓋在青銅器分期上的意義, *Wenbo* 文博 1984.2: 7.

14. For the vessel and its inscription, see *Jicheng* 4191. Although only the cover of the vessel is extant, it features the facing long-tailed birds that are characteristic of King Mu–period ornamentation.

15. Although the transcription of the character as *li* 利 seems to be questionable, it is found also in Zhongguo shehui kexueyuan kaogu yanjiusuo, *Yin Zhou jinwen jicheng shiwen*, 4191.

16. Li Xueqin et al., *Qinghua daxue cang Zhanguo zhujian*, (Yi), 177 n. 23.

17. *Mu tianzi zhuan*, 4.2a.

18. For the *Wang gui* 望簋, see *Jicheng* 4272. Other mid–Western Zhou vessels that mention members of the Bi family include the *Peng Zhong ding* 倗仲鼎, which mentions a woman named Bi Huai 畢媿 (*Jicheng* 2462); the *Bi Xian gui* 畢鮮簋, the patron of which is a man named Bi Xian 畢鮮 (*Jicheng* 4061); the *Duan gui* 段簋, which mentions a Bi Zhong 畢中 (*Jicheng* 4208); and the *Yong yu* 永盂, which mentions Captain Tong, man of Bi 畢人師同 (*Jicheng* 10322).

19. See, for instance, He Linyi, *Zhanguo guwen zidian*, 1217.

20. He Linyi, *Zhanguo guwen zidian*, 1050, 459.

21. *Mu tianzi zhuan*, 1.2b.

22. Lei Xueqi 雷學淇, *Zhushu jinian yizheng* 竹書紀年義證 (1810; rpt. Taibei: Yiwen yinshuguan, 1971), 308 (20.53b).

23. Jingzhou shi bowuguan, *Guodian Chu mu zhujian*, strip 22.

24. Li Xueqin, "Shi Guodian jian Zhai Gong zhi gu ming" 釋郭店簡祭公之顧命, *Wenwu* 文物 1998.7, 44–45.

25. *Mu tianzi zhuan*, 2.3b.

26. *Mu tianzi zhuan*, 4.4a.

27. *Mu tianzi zhuan*, 5.4b.

28. Chen Peifen 陳佩芬, *Xia Shang Zhou qingtongqi yanjiu* 夏商周青銅器研究 (Shanghai: Shanghai Guji chubanshe, 2004), vol. 2b, 370–71.

29. In the original published version of this chapter, I suggested that the name Gu 固 of the *Mu tianzi zhuan*'s Feng Gu might represent some sort of distortion of the name of the patron of the bronze vessel: 䚡. It is possible that *gu* 固 is but an elaboration of 古, which is more or less similar to 䚡. However, it now seems to me that this is too speculative to present with any conviction.

30. Shanxi sheng kaogu yanjiusuo 山西省考古研究所, Yuncheng shi wenwu gongzuozhan 運城市文物工作站, and Jiangxian wenhuaju 絳縣文化局, "Shanxi Jiangxian Hengshui Xi Zhou mu fajue jianbao" 山西絳縣橫水西周墓發掘簡報, *Wenwu* 2006.8, 4–18. For an in-depth study of this cemetery, its bronzes, and its relationship with the Zhou royal capital, see Maria Khayutina, "The Tombs of the Rulers of Peng and Relationships between Zhou and Northern Non-Zhou Lineages (Until the Early Ninth Century B.C.)," in *Imprints of Kinship: Studies of Recently Discovered Bronze Inscriptions from Ancient China*, ed. Edward L. Shaughnessy (Hong Kong: Chinese University of Hong Kong Press, 2017), 71–132.

31. Li Xueqin 李學勤, "Jiangxian Hengbei cun mudi yu Peng guo" 絳縣橫北村墓地與國, *Zhongguo wenwu bao* 中國文物報, 14 September 2007, 5.

32. *Mu tianzi zhuan*, 1.1b–2a.

33. For traditional evidence placing Peng in the Hedong 河東 area of southern Shanxi province, see Shaughnessy, "On the Editing of the *Mu Tianzi Zhuan*." See, too, Khayutina, "The Tombs of the Rulers of Peng," Map 4.1: Geographical situation of Peng.

Chapter Ten: The Tsinghua Manuscript *Zheng Wen Gong wen Tai Bo* and the Question of the Production of Manuscripts in Early China

1. Li Xueqin 李學勤, ed. in chief, and Qinghua daxue Chutu wenxian yanjiu yu baohu zhongxin, eds., *Qinghua daxue cang Zhanguo zhujian (Lu)* 清華大學藏戰國竹簡 (陸) (Shanghai: Zhong Xi shuju, 2016).

2. In addition to the information given in the introduction and notes to *Zheng Wen Gong wen Tai Bo* in *Qinghua daxue cang Zhanguo zhujian (Lu)*, see too Ma Nan 馬楠, "Qinghua jia *Zheng Wen Gong wen Taibo* yu Zheng guo zaoqi shishi" 清華簡《鄭文公問太伯》與鄭國早期史實, *Wenwu* 文物 2016.3, 84–87. For translations of *Zheng Wu furen gui ruzi*, the two versions of *Zheng Wen Gong wen Tai Bo*, and *Zi Yi* 子儀, see Rens Krijgsman, *The Tsinghua University Warring States Bamboo Manuscripts*, vol. 6 (Beijing: Tsinghua University Press, 2023); for translations of *Zi Chan* 子產 and *Guan Zhong* 管仲, see Vincent Leung, *The Tsinghua University Warring States Bamboo Manuscripts*, vol. 8 (Beijing: Tsinghua University Press, in press).

3. The original publications of this study (i.e., both the Chinese and English versions) presented the texts first in scanned versions of the individual characters, followed by a strict transcription of the *kaishu* 楷書 components, and then finally by a transcription into modern Chinese characters complete with modern punctuation. While I believe this is the ideal format to present early Chinese manuscripts, it is unnecessary for the purposes of the present book (especially since the fuller original versions are available). Instead, I present simply the texts of the two manuscripts side by side in modern Chinese characters followed by a consolidated annotated translation pointing out syntactic differences between the two texts.

4. Slip 1 is broken in two about a third of the way down from the top, resulting in the loss of most of one character (which however can be retrieved based on content and comparison with manuscript B); slip 2 is broken vertically at about the same point, with the loss of half of three separate characters; slip 6 is also broken at the same point, with the loss of one character.

5. For the A manuscript, see the character *yu* 與 on slip 2, *ye* 也 on slip 9, and the character *ze* 則 on slip 10; for the B manuscript, see the character *er* 而 just before the end of slip 12. The single blacked-out character is found on slip 5 of manuscript A just before the character 敓.

6. The editor of the text, Ma Nan 馬楠, identifies Ziren Chengzi 子人成子, the first person mentioned in the text, as Ziren Yu 子人語, a younger brother of Duke Li of Zheng and the founder of the Ziren 子人 lineage of Zheng. Wang Ning 王寧, "Qinghua jian *Zheng Wen Gong wen Tai Bo* shiwen jiaodu" 清華簡《鄭文公問太伯》釋文校讀, www.gwz.fudan.edu.cn/Web/Show/2809, suggests that

Tai Bo was the next counselor of Duke Wen of Zheng: Yi Jia 駕, but there is no firm evidence to support this identification.

7. Manuscripts that have recently come to light, including this *Zheng Wen Gong wen Tai Bo, have called into question the traditional end date of Duke Huan's reign. This is a question that requires much further research.

8. For this meaning of ci 次, see the gloss by Du Yu 杜豫 to the word's use in the Zuo zhuan 左傳 (9th yr. of Duke Xi僖): Ci, sang qin 次，喪寢 "Ci is a mourning bedroom." The B manuscript at the same point reads instead xi 樨 "a type of tree," but here obviously either a phonetic loan for ci 次 or an alternative writing for qi (or xi) 棲 "to reside for a short term."

9. For Lady Mi, see Zuo zhuan 左傳, Duke Xi 僖 22 (638 BCE).

10. Kern, "Methodological Reflections."

11. For some discussion of the nature of these variants, see chapter 7, p. 173, in this volume.

12. Kern, "Methodological Reflections," 167.

13. The best known of this artifactual evidence is a porcelain figurine, unearthed in 1958 from tomb 9 at Jinpenling 金盆岭, Changsha 長沙, Hunan, depicting two scribes facing each other, one holding a text that he is apparently reading, while the other is holding a brush and document on which he is writing. The figurine is currently in the Hunan Provincial Museum; for a photograph, see https://baike.baidu.com/item/西晋青瓷对书俑/465544?fromtitle=青瓷对书俑&fromid=4053537. It is also reproduced as the cover of Shaughnessy, Rewriting Early Chinese Texts.

14. Kern, "Methodological Reflections," 171.

15. Meyer, Philosophy on Bamboo, 150.

16. The following discussion is slightly revised from that found in the original published version of this chapter.

17. Christopher M. B. Nugent, "The Lady and Her Scribes: Dealing with Multiple Dunhuang Copies of Wei Zhuang's 'Lament of the Lady Qin,'" Asia Major 3rd ser. 20, no. 2 (2007): 25–73. This study was based on Nugent's doctoral dissertation: Christopher Nugent, "The Circulation of Poetry in Tang Dynasty China," PhD diss., Harvard University, 2004.

18. Nugent, "The Lady and Her Scribes," 71.

19. Matthias L. Richter, "Faithful Transmission or Creative Change: Tracing Modes of Manuscript Production from the Material Evidence," Asiatische Studien / Études Asiatique 63, no. 4 (2009): 895–903.

20. Marc Kalinowski, "La production des manuscrits dans la Chine ancienne: Une approche codicologique de la bibliothèque funéraire de Mawangdui," Asiatische Studien / Études Asiatiques 59, no. 1 (2005): 131–68.

21. For *Tianzi jian zhou 天子建州, see Ma Chengyuan 馬承源, ed., Shanghai bowuguan cang Zhanguo Chu zhu shu (liu) 上海博物館藏戰國楚竹書 (六) (Shanghai: Shanghai guji chubanshe, 2007), 125–39 (*Tianzi jian zhou A

photographs), 143–53 (*Tianzi jian zhou* B photographs), 309–38 (*Tianzi jian zhou* A/B transcription).

22. Richter, "Faithful Transmission or Creative Change," 897.

23. Richter, "Faithful Transmission or Creative Change," 897.

24. Richter refers to Morgan's study as "a comprehensive codicological study" of the *Tianzi jian zhou* manuscripts; Richter, "Faithful Transmission or Creative Change," 896 n. 22. A Chinese version of Morgan's work has been posted online: Mo Zihan 墨子涵, "Tianzi jian zhou zhong suojian fanyinwen, weishizi ji jidian jiduan" 《天子建州》中所見反印文、未釋字及幾點臆斷, http://www.bsm.org.cn/show_article.php?id=764>, posted 25 December 2007. Morgan also produced an English-language version of his study: "A Positive Case for the Visuality of Text in Warring States Manuscript Culture," paper presented at the Creel-Luce Paleography Forum, Chicago, 24–25 April, from which the quotation here and the following quotations are taken (3–4).

25. As both Richter and Morgan also point out, the Shanghai Museum has also published three other pairs of manuscripts bearing the same texts: *Zheng Zijia sang* 鄭子家喪 *Mourning for Zijia of Zheng*, *Junren zhe he bi an zai* 君人者何必安哉 *Must Rulers Be at Rest*, and *Fan wu liu xing* 凡物流型 *All Things Flow into Form*; for these manuscripts, see Ma Chengyuan, *Shanghai bowuguan cang Zhanguo Chu zhu shu (qi)* 上海博物館藏戰國楚竹書 (七), 33–39 (*Zhengzi jia sang* A photographs), 43–49 (*Zhengzi jia sang* B photographs); 53–61 (*Junren zhe he bi an zai* A photographs), 65–73 (*Junren zhe he bi an zai* B photographs); 77–107 (*Fan wu liu xing* A photographs), 111–32 (*Fan wu liu xing* B photographs); 171–88 (*Zhengzi jia sang* A/B transcription); 191–218 (*Junren zhe he bi an zai* A/B transcription); 221–300 (*Fan wu liu xing* A/B transcription). All three of these pairs of manuscripts, and especially *Fan wu liu xing*, also reveal clear evidence of visual copying of one from the other. See Richter, "Faithful Transmission or Creative Change," 905 n. 27; Morgan, "A Positive Case for the Visuality of Text," 4–5.

26. For Chu practice, see Li Shoukui 李守奎, ed., *Chu wenzi bian* 楚文字編 (Shanghai: Huadong Shifan daxue chubanshe, 2003), 391–415, and Zhang Guangyu 張光裕, ed., *Baoshan Chu jian wenzi bian* 包山楚簡文字編 (Taibei: Yiwen yinshuguan, 1992), 383–410. For Qin practice, see, for instance, Chen Zhenyu 陳振裕 and Liu Xinfang 劉信芳, eds., *Shuihudi Qin jian wenzi bian* 睡虎地秦簡文字編 (Wuhan: Hubei Renmin chubanshe, 1993), 181–84. For Zheng practice, see, for instance, the character *bang* 邦 "country" in the *Ai Chengshu ding* 哀成叔鼎 (*Jicheng* 2782) inscription.

27. It is also possible that the scribe had only a single source text, written in the script of some foreign state (such as the state of Qin 秦) and copied one text as a facsimile while intentionally converting some characters—as I will point out later, the way that place-names were written was systematically different in the states of Qin and Zheng as opposed to Chu—into the forms familiar to the state of Chu.

28. The A manuscript here reads *ci* 次 "mourning shed," while the B manuscript reads *xi* 欅 "a type of tree," but here it is almost certainly a loan of some sort for the same idea as the A manuscript.

29. For *zheng* 爭 "to contend; to battle," the B manuscript here reads *qing* 請 "to request." Both readings are sensible in the context.

30. The B manuscript is lacking one entire slip at this point.

31. Zi Ju 子居, "Qinghua jian *Zheng Wen Gong wen Tai Bo (Jiaben)* jiexi" 清華簡《鄭文公問太伯 (甲本) 解析, xianqinshi.blogspot.com/2017/09/blog-post_34.html, suggests that "seven" (*qi* 七) here is a mistake (in both manuscripts) for "ten" (*shi* 十), a mistake frequently seen in ancient texts based on the similarity of the ancient forms of *shi* and *qi*, and given the standard understanding of chariotry as combining ten foot-soldiers per chariot. This is a reasonable conjecture, but there is no text evidence to support such an emendation.

32. The A and B manuscripts here read differently, the A manuscript giving 𢒈, *se* 色 "color; appearance," as opposed to the B manuscript's 𢑘, *fu* 孚 "sincerity," but here doubtless to be read as *fu* 浮 "to float, to drift." It is easy to see that the two characters are visually very similar, such that one could easily be a miswriting for the other. In this case, *fu* 浮 "to drift" seems to make the best sense of the sentence.

33. The two manuscripts display several minor differences in this passage: both Yin 殷 and Tang 唐 are written differently in the two manuscripts (A: 𥃩, i.e., 營 vs. B: 𥃫, i.e., 鄯, and A: 𣅠, i.e., 庚 vs. B: 𣅱, i.e., 康), and the B manuscript also includes the word *yue* 曰 "to say."

Chapter Eleven: The Eighth Century BCE Civil War in Jin as Seen in the *Bamboo Annals*

1. Li Xueqin et al., *Qinghua daxue Zhanguo zhujian (er)*.

2. Li Xueqin 李學勤, "You Qinghua jian *Xinian* lun *Jinian* de tili" 由清華簡《繫年》論《紀年》的體例, *Shenzhen daxue xuebao (Renwen Shehui kexueban* 深圳大學學報》(人文社會科學版) 2012.2, 42–44, 42.

3. Li Xueqin, "You Qinghua jian *Xinian* lun *Jinian* de tili," 43.

4. Li Xueqin, "You Qinghua jian *Xinian* lun *Jinian* de tili," 43, quoting *Chunqiu Zuo zhuan zhengyi*, 2114 (26th year of Lord Zhao 昭公). It may be that Li Xueqin ends this quotation two characters too soon. The text continues that (the King of Xie) had "arrogated command" (*jian ming* 奸命). The commentary then concludes: "It used to be said that the King of Xie was Bo Fu 伯服. Bo Fu was written as Bo Pan 伯盤 in ancient script; he was not the King of Xie. Bo Fu was installed as king for several years before the many lords deposed him and installed King Ping. This is perhaps consistent with reality."

5. Li Xueqin et al., *Qinghua daxue Zhanguo zhujian (er)*, 138. I have translated the passage literally, including the sentence *Zhou wang wang jiu nian* 周亡王九年, which has prompted a great outpouring of discussion concerning the implications for the chronology of the period. That discussion, important though it is, is not particularly relevant to the topic of the current study. For English-language introductions, see Jae-hoon Shim, "The Eastward Relocation of the Zhou Royal House in the *Xinian* Manuscript: Chronological and Geographical Aspects, *Archiv Orientální* 85 (2017): 67–97; Chen Minzhen and Yuri Pines, "Where Is King Ping: The History and Historiography of the Zhou Dynasty's Eastward Relocation," *Asia Major* 3rd ser. 31, no. 1 (2018): 1–27.

6. Despite dismissing the "Current Text" *Bamboo Annals* as a late forgery, Li Xueqin elsewhere admits that the *Xinian* passage corroborates information found only in the "Current Text" *Bamboo Annals*:

> With respect to "Yuchen," the manuscript (i.e., the *Xinian*) explains that he was "King You's younger brother," that he was "installed at Guo," that he was called "King Hui of Xie," that he reigned twenty-one years, and that he was killed by Lord Wen of Jin, all of which is consistent with what is recorded in the ("Current Text" *Bamboo*) *Annals*. The *Annals*' "twenty-first year" should also refer to the twenty-first year of the King of Xie's twenty-first year, and not to the twenty-first year of Lord Wen of Jin. On this point, the "Current Text" *Bamboo Annals* is correct and the *Guben Zhushu jinian jijiao* 古本竹書紀年輯校 of Wang Guowei 王國維 is mistaken.

Li Xueqin, "Qinghua jian *Xinian* ji youguan gu shi wenti" 清華簡《繫年》及有關古史問題, *Wenwu* 文物 2011.3, 71. It is hard to understand how a "late forgery" could anticipate information found only in a manuscript unearthed hundreds of years after its creation.

7. Two early collections of these quotations, generally referred to as the "Ancient Text" (*Guben* 古本) *Bamboo Annals*, are Zhu Youzeng 朱右曾, *Ji zhong jinian cunzhen* 汲冢紀年存真 (N.p.: Guiyan zhai, 1846), and Wang Guowei 王國維, *Guben Zhushu jinian jijiao* 古本竹書紀年輯校 (1917), in *Haining Wang Jing'an xiansheng yishu* 海寧王靜安先生遺書, vol. 36 (N.p.: n.p., 1936). For the most complete collection, see Fang Shiming 方詩銘 and Wang Xiuling 王修齡, *Guben Zhushu jinian jizheng* 古本竹書紀年輯證 (Shanghai: Shanghai Guji chubanshe, 1981), which builds upon the works of Zhu Youzeng and Wang Guowei. Quotations of the *Bamboo Annals* in the remainder of this study will all be taken from this latter collection.

8. Du Yu, "*Chunqiu jingjie jijie* Houxu," 1a–b. The postface continues with comparisons of records in the *Annals* with the *Chunqiu*, "just a few of very many"

(諸若此輩甚多，略舉數條) "to show that the ancient historians in all cases relied on reports based on actual events to write the affairs of the time" (以明國史皆承告據實而書時事); other records similar to the *Zuo zhuan* but different from the *Gongyang* 公羊 and Guliang 穀梁 commentaries, showing that these latter two commentaries were inconsistent with the original meaning of the *Chunqiu*; and differences with the *Shang shu* 尚書, showing that "old man Fu Sheng may well have come to be senile" (老叟之伏生或致昏忘), all of which "can somewhat add to the *Zuo zhuan*" (爲其粗有益於《左氏》). It is clear that Du Yu made more than just a cursory inspection of the manuscript, but it is also clear that his primary interest was with how it corresponded with the *Chunqiu* and *Zuo zhuan*.

9. The *Shi ji jijie* 史記集解 commentary of Pei Yin 裴駰 quotes Xun Xu as saying: "He Qiao said: 'The *Annals* starts from Huangdi and ends with Wei's 'Current King'" (和嶠云："《紀年》起自黃帝，終於魏之'今王'"); see Sima Qian, *Shi ji*, 1849. It is possible that Xun Xu was responsible for the entire editorial project, while He Qiao 和嶠 (d. 292) was in charge of editing the *Bamboo Annals* in particular.

10. For these quotations, see Fang Shiming and Wang Xiuling, *Guben Zhushu jinian jizheng*, 62–65, 170–71.

11. For an overview of the confused chronology of the state of Jin, and how the *Bamboo Annals* resolved it, see Shaughnessy, *Rewriting Early Chinese Texts*, 237–39.

12. See Sima Qian, *Shi ji*, 1637–38.

13. For the views of Zhu Youzeng and Wang Guowei, see Wang Guowei, *Guben Zhushu jinian jijiao*, 10b.

14. Li Daoyuan 酈道元, *Shui jing zhu jiao* 水經注校, ed. Wang Guowei 王國維 (Shanghai: Shanghai Renmin chubanshe, 1984), 22.703.

15. Fang Shiming and Wang Xiuling, *Guben Zhushu jinian jizheng*, 66–67, note that the Yongle dadian 永樂大典 version of the *Shui jing zhu* reads as given here, but they accept an emendation by Dai Zhen 戴震 (1724–1777) changing *tong hui* 同惠 to *zhou xuan* 周宣, such that Duofu is said to be the son of King Xuan of Zhou, rather than the son of King Hui of Zhou. Fang and Wang note too that others, including both Zhu Youzeng and Wang Guowei, have emended the text to read *zhou li* 周厲, such that Duofu is said to be the son of King Li of Zhou 周厲王, as he is said to be in the *Shi ji*. Neither of these emendations has any textual support. The *Shui jing zhu* passage quoted immediately following goes on to quote the *Shi ben* 世本 as saying, "In his twenty-second year, King Xuan of Zhou enfeoffed his younger half-brother You at Zheng" (周宣王二十二年，封庶弟友于鄭); Li Daoyuan 酈道元, *Shui jing zhu shu* 水經注疏 (N.p.: Jiangsu Guji chubanshe, 1989), 19.1652. This would seem to corroborate the *Shi ji*'s identification of You, that is, Duke Huan of Zheng, as a son of King Li, not of King Xuan. It is worth noting too that the *Shi tong* 史通 of Liu Zhiji 劉

知幾 (661–721) explicitly quotes the *Bamboo Annals* as saying: "Duke Huan of Zheng was the son of King Li" (鄭桓公，厲王之子); Liu Zhiji 劉知幾, *Mingben Shi tong* 名本史通 (Beijing: Guojia Tushuan chubanshe, 2019), 16.4a (133). Commentators have sought to emend this to "son of King Xuan" (宣王子); see, for instance, Fang Shiming and Wang Xiuling, *Guben Zhushu jinian jizheng*, 66, however, there is again no textual support for doing so.

16. Li Daoyuan, *Shui jing zhu shu*, 19.1651–52.

17. Ban Gu, *Han shu*, 1544. It is curious that Fang Shiming and Wang Xiuling's *Guben Zhushu jinian jizheng* does not cite these quotations in its normal manner, but only mentions them in its discussion of the first *Shui jing zhu* quotation; Fang Shiming and Wang Xiuling, *Guben Zhushu jinian jizheng*, 66.

18. *Bamboo Annals* 竹書紀年 (Sibu congkan ed.), Xia 下, 16b. All subsequent quotations from the "Current Text" *Bamboo Annals* will be from this text; since all editions are arranged by years, and thus readily found, I will not provide further citations.

19. The name of the state attacked by Lord Wen and Duke Huan has drawn the attention of scholars. The *Guoyu* 國語 and *Shi ji* both write the name of the state as Zeng 繒, while the *Xinian writes it as Zeng 曾, whereas the *Shui jing zhu* quotation gives it as Kuai 鄶 and the two quotations of Xue Zan give it as Hui 會. It is clear that all four of these characters derive from a single original, 曾 and 會 being easily mistaken one for the other. Li Feng, *Landscape and Power in Early China: The Crisis and Fall of the Western Zhou, 1045–771 B.C.* (New York: Cambridge University Press, 2006), 202, argues convincingly for the "Current Text" *Bamboo Annals*' reading of Ceng 鄶 (though he refers to it as Zeng).

20. For an excellent discussion of this factionalism, pitting Zheng and Jin against Guo, see Li, *Landscape and Power in Early China*, 203–15, 242–45.

21. As noted earlier, both Zhu Youzeng and Wang Guowei date the first of the two attacks mentioned by Chen Zan, that against Hui (i.e., Ceng), to the second year of Duke Wen of Jin (i.e., 779). Fang Shiming and Wang Xiuling argue, without any textual evidence, that the date should be emended to "twelfth year" (十二年), assuming that a "ten" (*shi* 十) has fallen out of the text; Fang Shiming and Wang Xiuling, *Guben Zhushu jinian jizheng*, 67. Curiously, neither Zhu nor Wang address at all the attack against Guo. Fang Shiming and Wang Xiuling, *Guben Zhushu jinian jizheng*, 164, note that it "seems as if it comes from the *Jinian*" (似出《紀年》) but because there is no certain evidence (以乏確據), they relegate it to their "Doubtful" (*cun yi* 存疑) cases.

22. See n. 4 in this chapter. Writing prior to the discovery of the *Xinian, Fang Shiming and Wang Xiuling, *Guben Zhushu jinian jizheng*, 67, provide the following very brief comment on the *Chunqiu Zuo zhuan zhengyi* quotation of the *Bamboo Annals* record:

《輯校》以二十一年屬晉文侯，是。《存真》以為周平王二十一年，誤從今本。

Jijiao (i.e., Wang Guowei, *Guben Zhushu jinian jijiao*) takes "twenty-first year" as belonging to Lord Wen of Jin (i.e., 760), which is right. *Cunzhen* (i.e., Zhu Youzeng, *Ji zhong Jinian cunzhen*) considers it to be the twenty-first year of King Ping, mistakenly following the Current Text.

This is not the only place that Wang Guowei was mistaken in his studies of the *Bamboo Annals*.

23. Reading Du Yu's postface to his *Chunqiu jing zhuan jijie* commentary (see pp. 269–70), one gets some sense of the complexity of determining the chronology:

Calculating King Ai's twentieth year, its designation would have been *renxu*, the sixteenth year of King He of Zhou, the eighth year of King Zhao of Qin, the thirteenth year of King Xiang of Han, the twenty-seventh year of King Wuling of Zhao, the thirtieth year of King Huai of Chu, the thirteenth year of King Zhao of Yan, and the twenty-fifth year of King Min of Qi. It was eighty-one years after the death of Confucius, and 381 before the present third year of Great Peace (i.e., 282).

24. Several quotations of the *Bamboo Annals* well before the emergence of the "Current Text" *Bamboo Annals* in the Tianyi ge 天一閣 library in the mid-sixteenth century show that a text organized according to the reign years of the Zhou kings, similar to the structure of the "Current Text" *Bamboo Annals*, was already extant. For evidence of such a text in the twelfth century, see p. 293 and especially n. 37 in this chapter.

25. It should be noted that this would also leave a gap of nine years (739–730) between the death of Lord Zhao and the installation of Zhuangbo of Quwo, during which time Lord Zhao's son Ping 平, known posthumously as Lord Xiao 孝侯, ruled in Yi.

26. There are occasional differences, but almost all are the sorts of textual variants one might expect in an age of copying from one manuscript to another. For instance, the *Taiping yulan* quotation for the first year of Zhuangbo (i.e., 730 BCE) says that "it did not rain snow" (*bu yu xue* 不雨雪) while the "Current Text" *Bamboo Annals* record for the same year says that "it greatly rained snow" (*da yu xue* 大雨雪). While the *Taiping yulan* quotation is ostensibly from the *Shi ji*, it is clear that this is a mistake for the *Bamboo Annals*, as I will discuss in more detail later in this chapter. One *Shui jing zhu* quotation for the twelfth

year of Zhuangbo (i.e., 719) refers to Jiagu 家穀 while the "Current Text" *Bamboo Annals* record for that year writes Jiagu 家谷, and another *Shuijing zhu* quotation for the same year refers to Tong 桐 while the "Current Text" *Bamboo Annals* refers to Xiang 枏. Undated quotations in the *Shuijing zhu* and *Wenxuan zhu* 文選注 refer, in the first case, to Yuanshi 原氏 and, in the other case, to Yuan Dian 原點, while the corresponding record in the "Current Text" *Bamboo Annals* for the thirteenth year of King Huan of Zhou 周桓王 (i.e., 707 BCE) refers to Yuanshi Yin 原氏黶.

27. For discussion of these *Taiping yulan* misattributions to the *Shi ji*, see n. 33 in this chapter.

28. Fang Shiming and Wang Xiuling, *Guben Zhushu jinian jizheng*, 165. Fang and Wang note that both Zhu Youzeng and Wang Guowei read "tenth month," presumably based upon the Bao Chongcheng 鮑崇城 edition of *Taiping yulan*. The 1960 Zhonghua shuju edition, which is a photo-reprint of a Southern Song edition, reads "tenth year" instead of "tenth month"; *Taiping yulan* 876.3891. In either case, the date would be different from that of the "Current Text" *Bamboo Annals*, which puts this entry into the first year of King Huan of Zhou, which corresponds to the twelfth year of Zhuangbo of Quwu.

29. Sima Qian, *Shi ji*, 1639.

30. A subsequent record, which occurs only in the "Current Text" *Bamboo Annals*, for the third year of King Zhuang of Zhou 周莊王 (i.e., 679 BCE) mentions the king's recognition of Duke Wu as the ruler of Jin with a single army after having wiped out (*mie* 滅) Lord Min 侯緡 of the Yi faction of Jin.

三年，曲沃武公滅晉侯緡，以寶獻王。王命武公以一軍爲晉侯。

> Third year, Duke Wu of Quwo wiped out Lord Min of Jin, taking the treasures to present to the king. The king commanded Duke Wu with a single army to be lord of Jin.

31. Ji Yun et al., *Qinding Siku quanshu zongmu tiyao*, j. 47, 52–54.

32. Wang Guowei 王國維, *Jinben Zhushu jinian shuzheng* 今本竹書紀年疏證 (N.p.: n.p., 1936), vol. 36.

33. There are ten such quotations in the *Taiping yulan*, all bunched in four *juan* of the text: three in *juan* 876, one quoting the eighth year of Zhuangbo of Jin, one quoting the twelfth and eighteenth years of Duke You of Jin 晉幽公, and one attributed to the reign of Qin Ershi Huangdi 秦二世皇帝; two in *juan* 877, the first quoting the second and sixth years of Duke Hui of Jin 晉惠公, and the second quoting the eighth year of King Huicheng of Wei 魏惠成王; one in *juan* 878, quoting the seventh year of King Xiao of Zhou 周孝王; and four in *juan* 879, the first paraphrasing records of the Gonghe 共和 interregnum

between the reigns of King Li of Zhou 周厲王 and King Xuan of Zhou 周宣王, the second and third quoting the first and second years of Zhuangbo of Jin, and the last quoting the twenty-third and twenty-fourth years of Duke Lie of Jin 晉烈公; for these, see Fang Shiming and Wang Xiuling, *Guben Zhushu jinian jizheng*, 161–66. Although both Zhu Youzeng and Wang Guowei attribute all of these *Taiping yulan* quotations to the *Bamboo Annals*, Fang and Wang dismiss them, primarily because the one paraphrase from the time of Qin Ershi Huangdi could not possibly be in the *Bamboo Annals*. This is certainly true, but since not only do all of the other quotations match the "Current Text" *Bamboo Annals*, but at least two of them (that for the Gonghe interregnum and that for the eighteenth year of Duke You of Jin) explicitly contradict statements of the *Shi ji*, it is clear that they must come from the *Bamboo Annals*.

34. The "Jin yu" 晉語 chapter of the *Guo yu* 國語 mentions only that Duke Wu of Quwo killed Lord Ai, but without a date in either reign, and the *Xinian does not contain a pericope dealing with the Jin civil war.

35. Luo Bi 羅泌, *Lu shi* 路史 "Guoming ji, Wu" 國名紀戊, quoted at Fang Shiming and Wang Xiuling, *Guben Zhushu jinian jizheng*, 181.

36. Luo Bi 羅泌, *Lu shi* 路史 "Guoming ji, Wu" 國名紀戊, quoted at Fang Shiming and Wang Xiuling, *Guben Zhushu jinian jizheng*, 181.

37. Fang Shiming and Wang Xiuling, *Guben Zhushu jinian jizheng*, 182. Fang and Wang also note that the *Lu shi* contains another quotation of the *Jinian* dated to the seventeenth year of King Huan, which however is not seen in the "Current Text" *Bamboo Annals*, but also showing that a text with this organization was extant.

There are also earlier precedents for a text of the *Bamboo Annals* organized according to years of the Eastern Zhou kings. The *Zizhi tongjian waiji* 資治通鑑外紀 of Liu Xu 劉恕 (1032–1078) contains a quotation, implicitly dated to the reign of King Kao of Zhou 周考王 (r. 440–426 BCE):

(周考王) 二年，河水赤於龍門三日。

(King Kao of Zhou) second year, the water of the River was red at Dragon-Gate for three days.

The *Shui jing zhu* also quotes the same record, but attributes it to the fourth year of King Huicheng of Wei (Liang) 魏 (梁) 惠成王 (r. 370–334/319 BCE):

梁惠成王四年，河水赤於龍門三日。

King Huicheng of Liang, fourth year, the water of the River was red at Dragon-Gate for three days.

The "Current Text" *Bamboo Annals* also quotes the same text but attributes it to the second year of King Xian of Zhou 周顯王 (r. 368–321):

(周顯王) 二年，河水赤於龍門三日。

(King Xian of Zhou), second year, the water of the River was red at Dragon-Gate for three days.

What is interesting is that the second year of King Xian of Zhou corresponds to the fourth year of King Huicheng of Wei (Liang): 367 BCE. It is apparent that during the Northern Song dynasty there were two different versions of the text, one denominated according to rulers of Wei 魏, and one denominated according to the kings of Zhou, but that Liu Shu misattributed the "second year" record to King Kao of Zhou instead of to King Xian of Zhou.

The earliest such quotation is found in the *Sou shen ji* 搜神記 of Gan Bao 干寶 (286–336), a scholar working just decades after the initial editing of the *Ji zhong* manuscripts.

周隱王二年，齊地暴長，長丈餘，高一尺。

King Yin of Zhou, second year (i.e., 313 BCE), the land of Qi violently grew, growing more than a *zhang* long and a foot high.

See Liu Qi 劉琦 and Liang Guofu 梁國輔, *Sou shen ji Sou shen houji yizhu* 搜神記搜神後記譯注 (Changchun: Jilin Wenshi chubanshe, 1997), 145. Although this passage does not make explicit its source, the *Bamboo Annals* is the only text that refers to this Zhou king as King Yin 隱王; all other sources refer to him as Yan, King of Nan 赧王延, or as King He of Zhou 周赧王 (r. 314–256 BCE). The "Current Text" *Bamboo Annals* for the second year of King Yin matches this exactly. This shows that a text very much like the "Current Text" *Bamboo Annals* was extant shortly after the discovery of the manuscript.

38. On the other hand, another difference between the two *Lu shi* quotations seems to suggest that the one dated to the reign of Duke Wu preserves more accurate historical information. That quotation says that a "Qin army" (Qin *shi* 秦師) rather than a "Guo army" (Guo *shi* 虢師) surrounded Wei 魏. According to the "Jin shijia" chapter of the *Shi ji*, Han Wan 韓萬, referred to in the *Bamboo Annals* as Ruibo Wan 芮伯萬 (Han 韓 was the capital city of the small state of Rui 芮), was sent by Duke Wu of Quwo to kill Lord Ai of Jin 晉哀侯 (r. 717–709 BCE) in 709; Sima Qian, *Shi ji*, 1639. Four years later, Duke Wu then enticed Lord Ai's successor Lord Xiaozi 小子侯 to Quwo, where he killed him. With this, King Huan dispatched Guo Zhong 虢仲 to attack

Duke Wu. This would seem to corroborate the *Lu shi* quotation denominated according to the reign year of Duke Wu.

39. Yuri Pines, "Zhou History and Historiography: Introducing the Bamboo Manuscript *Xinian*," *T'oung Pao* 100, nos. 4–5 (2014): 287–324, focuses exclusively on the relationship of the **Xinian* with the *Zuo zhuan*, while Olivia Milburn says simply, "The name chosen for this text is a misnomer; "The *Xinian*: An Ancient Historical Text from the Qinghua University Collection of Bamboo Books," *Early China* 39 (2016): 55.

40. Chen Li 陳力, "Wang Guowei xiansheng zhi *Zhushu jinian* yanjiu pingyi" 王國維先生之《竹書紀年》研究評議, *Wenxian* 文獻 (2 March 2022): 4–16, is a refreshing departure from the usual uncritical reception of Wang's scholarship. Chen shows that Wang produced his two studies in a matter of weeks, that his *Guben Zhushu jinian jijiao* is largely derivative of Zhu Youzeng's previous work, and that his *Jinben Zhushu jinian shuzheng* in particular is marred by slipshod scholarship.

41. In the preface to his *Jinben zhushu jinian shuzheng*, Wang Guowei had the following to say of the "Current Text" *Bamboo Annals*:

今本所載殆無一不襲他書。其不見他書者，不過百分之一，又率空洞無事實，所增加者年月而已。. . . 夫事實既具他書，則此書為無用；年月又多杜撰，則其說為無徵。無用無徵，則廢此書可。

There is probably not a single item that the Current Text contains that is not taken over from another text. There is no more than one in a hundred that is not seen in other texts, and these are empty and unfactual; what is added is nothing more than year and month dates. Since the facts are all available in other texts, this book is useless; and since the year and month dates are mainly made up, what it says is baseless. Being useless and baseless, it would be fine to throw this book in the garbage.

For Li Xueqin's view of the "Current Text" *Bamboo Annals*, see n. 6 in this chapter.

42. It is well known that the discovery of the *Bamboo Annals* revealed errors in Sima Qian's chronologies of ancient China, especially of both the Jin and Wei rulers. While it can be shown that the original editors of the manuscript were deeply influenced by Sima Qian in their editing of the text, important differences can still be seen in both early quotations of the *Bamboo Annals* and in the "Current Text." For one study of its evidence for the chronology of Jin, see Xia Hanyi 夏含夷, "Jin Chu Gong ben zu kao: Jianlun *Zhushu jinian* de liangge zuanben" 晉出公奔卒考：兼論竹書紀年的兩個纂本, *Shanghai bowuguan jikan* 上海博物館集刊 9 (2002): 186–94.

43. See n. 37 in this chapter for evidence that this version of the text was quoted already in the *Sou shen ji* of Gao Bao in the early fourth century.

Chapter Twelve: The Qin *Bian Nian Ji* and the Beginnings of Historical Writing in China

1. Li Xueqin et al., *Qinghua daxue cang Zhanguo zhu jian (er)*.

2. Li Xueqin 李學勤, "Qinghua jian *Xinian* ji youguan gu shi wenti" 清華簡《繫年》及有關古史問題, *Wenwu* 文物 2011.3, 70–74. The publication of the *Xinian* prompted a great outpouring of scholarship on it, the most recent contribution being Yuri Pines, *Zhou History Unearthed: The Bamboo Manuscript Xinian and Early Chinese Historiography* (New York: Columbia University Press, 2020); Pines notes that as of 2019, there had been published "no fewer than twelve monographs and more than two hundred articles (including very lengthy ones) in China, Japan, and the West" (37–38); see 251 n. 3 in Pines for more detail.

3. For the official publication of this text, see Shuihudi Qin mu zhu jian zhengli xiaozu, ed., *Shuihudi Qin mu zhujian* 睡虎地秦墓竹簡 (Beijing: Wenwu, 1990), 3–7 (photographs), 3–10 (transcription).

4. For the *chunqiu* of Zhou, Yan, Song, and Qi, see *Mozi* 墨子 (*Sibu beiyao* ed.), 8.2b, 3b, 4a, and 4b. None of these annals has survived.

5. For the *Sheng* of Jin and the *Taowu* of Chu, see *Mengzi*, 4B/21. Neither of these annals has survived, though Barry B. Blakeley, "On the Authenticity and Nature of the *Zuo Zhuan*," *Early China* 29 (2004): 238–39, suggests that parts of at least the *Taowu* are quoted in the *Zuo zhuan*.

6. Sima Qian states explicitly that he read a "Qin ji" 秦紀; see Sima Qian, *Shi ji*, 6, 293. It apparently serves as the core of the *Shi ji*'s "Qin benji" 秦本紀 and "Qin Shi huang benji" 秦始皇本紀 chapters.

7. There is a vast scholarship concerning the authenticity and nature of the *Zhushu jinian*. There is extant a two-*juan* 卷 edition of the text from the late Ming dynasty. Although many scholars view this as a late forgery, I have argued that it is a more or less faithful edition of one of the transcriptions prepared by the first team of editors charged with organizing the original bamboo-slip manuscript; see Shaughnessy, *Rewriting Early Chinese Texts*, 219–24. Nevertheless, I have also argued that this transcription (as also that of a second team of editors, working about one decade after the first team) included numerous errors. Of these, perhaps the most important was the conflation of two different annals, one a year-by-year account of the states of Xia 夏, Shang 商, Zhou 周, Jin 晉, and Wei 魏, and another, which can only be surmised from indirect evidence, a synoptic annals of the various states of the Springs and Autumns and Warring States periods. The first of these annals may have been divided into two or more sections, with at least some early reference to a *Xia Yin chunqiu* 夏殷春秋 and

a *Jin chunqiu* 晉春秋; see Liu Zhiji 劉知幾, *Shi tong tongshi* 史通通釋 (Shanghai: Shangwu yinshuguan, 1935), 1.3–4.

8. For these texts, see Hu Pingsheng 胡平生, "Some Notes on the Organization of the Han Dynasty Bamboo 'Annals' Found at Fuyang," translated by Deborah Porter, *Early China* 14 (1989): 1–25.

9. For a monographic treatment of these tables, see Grant Hardy, *Worlds of Bronze and Bamboo: Sima Qian's Conquest of History* (New York: Columbia University Press, 1999).

10. For the finest Western-language study of the *Chunqiu*, see Newell Ann van Auken, *Spring and Autumn Historiography: Form and Hierarchy in Ancient Chinese Annals* (New York: Columbia University Press, 2023).

11. One slip for one year, the forty-third year of King Zhao (i.e., 264 BCE), appears in the published photograph to be completely blank. It is unclear why this should be the case.

12. The published photographs of the manuscript are not sufficiently clear to be meaningfully reproducible here; see Shuihudi Qin mu zhu jian zhengli xiaozu, *Shuihudi Qin mu zhujian*, 3–7.

13. In cases in which no grammatical subject is expressed, it is assumed to be "we" or "Qin."

14. It is unclear who Gan 敢 was; perhaps he was Xi's younger brother.

15. The top of this slip, where the year record would come, is broken off.

16. Achim Mittag, "The Qin *Bamboo Annals* of Shuihudi: A Random Note from the Perspective of Chinese Historiography," *Monumenta Serica* 51 (2003): 543–70, esp. 556, argues convincingly that the core of the **Bian nian ji* is an official annals of the state of Qin, that has only been supplemented by entries concerning Xi and his family.

17. One problem that presents itself in this regard is how events that occurred late in the year could have been used to characterize the year in question. Of course, this would not have been a problem for subsequent reference to these events.

18. Hubei sheng Jing-Sha tielu kaogudui, ed., *Baoshan Chu jian* 包山楚簡 (Beijing: Wenwu chubanshe, 1991), no. 115. Huang Xiquan 黃錫全, "Shi shuo Chu guo huangjin huobi chengliang danwei 'ban yi'" 試說楚國黃金貨幣稱量單位半益, *Jiang Han kaogu* 江漢考古 2000.1, 56–62, shows that the Chu measure *yi* 益 equaled 251.3 grams, while one *liang* 兩 was 15.5 grams. There remain uncertainties concerning several of the other words in this record. For a concise synoptic explanation, see Chen Wei 陳偉 et al., *Chu di chutu Zhanguo jiance [shisi zhong]* 楚地出土戰國簡冊 [十四種] (Beijing: Jingji kexue chubanshe, 2009), 48–52.

19. *Baoshan Chu jian*, no. 221.

20. As will be seen later, this great event date notation also occurs in the inscriptions on the *E jun qi jie* 鄂君啟節 bronze tallies, which were discovered in 1957 in Shouxian 壽縣, Anhui. Based on records in the "Liu guo nianbiao" 六

國年表 and "Chu shijia" 楚世家 chapters of the *Shi ji* (15.730, 40.1721), which date this event to the sixth year of Chu Huai Wang 楚懷王 (r. 328–299), scholars had dated this event to 323 BCE. However, the Xiayi 夏層 month of the Chu calendar corresponds with the *mao* 卯 month, and the *mao* month of 323 BCE did not contain a *gengwu* 庚午 day (day 7 of the sixty-day cycle). Because of this, with the publication of the Baoshan records, Hirase Takao 平勢隆郎, *Shimpen Shiki Tō Shū nempyō* 新編史記東周年表 (Tokyo: Tokyo daigaku Tōyō bunka kenkyūjo, 1995), 176, and Chen Wei 陳偉, *Baoshan Chu jian chutan* 包山楚簡初談 (Wuhan: Wuhan daxue chubanshe, 1996), 11, have both argued that this event should actually date to 322 BCE. Because the record concerns a Chu attack on Wei 魏, both scholars suggest that the event may have occurred at the turn of the year, and that different calendars in Chu and Wei would ascribe it to different years. It seems to me that there is another possibility. Because the chronology Sima Qian 司馬遷 (145–ca. 89 BCE) gives for the state of Wei is mistaken by one year beginning in 370 BCE, dating events one year too early, if his record of this event originally derived from his Wei annals it would be one year too early.

21. For this inscription, see *Jicheng* 12210. For a study and complete translations of the various inscriptions, see Lothar von Falkenhausen, "The E Jun Qi Metal Tallies: Inscribed Texts and Ritual Contexts," in *Text and Ritual in Early China*, ed. Martin Kern (Seattle: University of Washington Press, 2005), 79–123.

22. Other similar year notations include:

會于夷儀之歲

The year of the meeting at Yiyi (Xiang 25)

齊人城郊之歲

The year that the men of Qi walled Jia (Xiang 26)

鑄刑書之歲

The year they cast the penal documents (Zhao 7)

晉韓宣子為政聘于諸侯之歲

The year that Han Xuanzi of Jin was ruling and entertained the many lords (Zhao 7)

蔡侯般弒其君之歲

The year that Ban, the lord of Cai, killed his ruler (Zhao 11)

23. Yuri Pines, "Chinese History Writing between the Sacred and the Secular," in *Early Chinese Religion, Part One: Shang through Han (1250 BC–220 AD)*, ed. John Lagerwey and Marc Kalinowski (Leiden: Brill, 2009), 315–40, esp. 317, also draws a connection between the inscription on the *Shi Qiang pan* and annalistic records, but his interpretation is far different from the formal association that I wish to suggest. More in line with what I have suggested here is the argument by Léon Vandermeersch that annals developed out of oracle-bone divination, the duties of the *shi* 史, rendered here as "secretary," originally encompassing both divination and (historical) writing; "Entre divination et écriture: Essai de clonage d'un texte des *Annales sur bamboo*," *Études chinoises* 18, nos. 1–2 (1999): 125–35. Interesting though this thesis is, it seems to me to give undue importance to Shang oracle-bone inscriptions, which I suspect are only by coincidence the earliest evidence we have for writing in China. As noted in chapter 1, pp. 23–24, Keightley, "The Diviners' Notebooks," shows that one oracle-bone inscription (*Heji* 13753) includes a verification written 175 days after the initial divination; from this he concludes: "Not only does this suggest the presence of some kind of filing system for retrieving the bone over this extended period, but it also suggests that, if the charge and verification had indeed been carved at the same time, the diviner had kept a 'notebook' record of his charges and prognostications which the engravers presumably consulted when they finally recorded the divination scenario after Shu's death" (14).

24. For this wording, see Shaughnessy, *Sources of Western Zhou History*, 1.

25. Despite Martin Kern's statement, "While there can be no doubt that the Western Zhou and their successors produced and kept historical records, no bronze inscription and no passage of the *Odes* (*Shi* 詩), *Documents* (*Shu* 書), or *Changes* (*Yi* 易)—our main sources of transmitted texts that presumably date in part from Western Zhou times—portrays a *shi* as 'writing history' in any meaningful later sense of the word, or as a person responsible for 'archiving' information" (see Martin Kern, "The Performance of Writing in Western Zhou China," in *The Poetics of Grammar and the Metaphysics of Sound and Sign*, ed. Sergio La Porta and David Shulman [Leiden: Brill, 2007], 117), there is substantial evidence that *shi* were responsible for archiving information. As for whether there is any text that "portrays a *shi* as 'writing history' in any meaningful later sense of the word," I suppose it all depends on what one views as "meaningful." I continue to view the *Shi Qiang pan* as a text full of meaning for the early history of historical writing in China.

26. For a discussion of this feature, showing some of the implications for the writing of the inscription itself, see chapter 3, pp. 76–80, in this volume.

27. For the text, see Shuihudi Qin mu zhu jian zhengli xiaozu, *Shuihudi Qin mu zhujian*, 3–7 (photographs), 3–10 (transcription).

Bibliography

Allan, Sarah. "On *Shu* (Documents) and the Origin of the *Shang Shu* (Ancient Documents) in Light of Recently Discovered Bamboo Slip Manuscripts." *Bulletin of the School of Oriental and African Studies* 75, no. 3 (2012): 547–57.
Allan, Sarah. "What Is a *Shu* 書." *EASCM Newsletter* 4 (2011): 1–5.
Allan, Sarah, and Crispin Williams, eds. *The Guodian Laozi: Proceedings of the International Conference, Dartmouth College, May 1998*. Berkeley: Society for the Study of Early China and the Institute of East Asian Studies, University of California, Berkeley, 2000.
"Anda jian *Shi jing* chudu" 安大简《詩經》初讀. http://www.bsm.org.cn/forum/forum.php?mod=viewthread&tid=12409&extra=&page=17. Accessed 24 October 2019.
Anhui daxue Hanzi fazhan yu yingyong yanjiu zhongxin 安徽大學漢字發展與應用研究中心, ed. *Anhui daxue cang Zhanguo zhujian* 安徽大學藏戰國竹簡 1. Shanghai: Zhongxi shuju, 2019.
Ban Gu 班固. *Hanshu* 漢書. Beijing: Zhonghua shuju, 1964.
"Baoji Meixian Yangjiacun jiaocang Shan shi jiazu qingtongqi qun zuotan jiyao" 寶雞眉縣楊家村窖藏單氏家族青銅器群座談紀要. *Kaogu yu wenwu* 2003.3, 13–16.
Baoji shi kaogudui and Fufeng xian bowuguan. "Shaanxi Fufeng xian xin faxian yipi Xi Zhou tongqi" 陝西扶風縣新發現一批西周青銅器. *Kaogu yu wenwu* 考古與文物 2007.4, 3–12.
Baoli cang jin xu 保利藏金續. Guangzhou: Lingnan meishu chubanshe, 2001.
Barnard, Noel. "Chou China: A Review of the Third Volume of Cheng Te-k'un's *Archaeology in China*." *Monumenta Serica* 24 (1965): 307–442.
Barnard, Noel, in association with Cheung Kwong-yue. *The Shan-fu Liang Ch'i Kuei and Associated Inscribed Vessels*. Taipei: SMC, 1996.
Baxter, William H. "Zhou and Han Phonology in the *Shijing*." In *Studies in the Historical Phonology of Asian Languages*, edited by William G. Boltz and Michael C. Shapiro, 1–34. Amsterdam: John Benjamins, 1991.

Behr, Wolfgang. *Reimende Bronzeinschriften und die Entstehung der chinesichen Endreimdichtung*. Edition Cathay 55. Bochum: Projekt Verlag, 2008.

Beijing daxue Kaoguxuexi et al. "Tianma Qucun yizhi Beizhao Jin Hou mudi di erci fajue" 天馬曲村遺址北趙晉侯墓地第二次發掘. *Wenwu* 1994.1, 20–22.

Blakeley, Barry B. "On the Authenticity and Nature of the *Zuo Zhuan*." *Early China* 29 (2004): 217–67.

Boltz, William G. "The Composite Nature of Early Chinese Texts." In *Text and Ritual in Early China*, edited by Martin Kern, 50–78. Seattle: University of Washington Press, 2005.

Brooks, E. Bruce, and A. Taeko Brooks. *The Original Analects: Sayings of Confucius and His Successors*. New York: Columbia University Press, 1998.

Cao Jianguo 曹建國. "Lun Qinghua jian zhong de *Xi shuai*" 論清華簡中的《蟋蟀》. *Jiang Han kaogu* 江漢考古 2011.2, 110–15.

Cerquiglini, Bernard. *Éloge de la variante: Histoire critique de la philology*. Paris: Éditions du Seuil, 1989.

Chen Fengheng 陳逢衡. *Zhou shu buzhu* 周書補注. 1825 Xiumei shan guan ed.

Chen Jian 陳劍. "Jinwen 'tuan' zi kaoshi" 金文「彖」字考釋. In Chen Jian, *Jiagu jinwen kaoshi lunji* 甲骨金文考釋論集, 243–72. Shanghai: Xianzhuang shuju, 2007.

Chen Jian 陳劍. "Ju Guodian jian shi du Xi Zhou jinwen yi li" 據郭店簡釋讀西周金文一例. *Beijing daxue Guwenxian yanjiu zhongxin jikan* 北京大學古文獻研究中心集刊 2 (2001): 378–96.

Chen Li 陳力. "Wang Guowei xiansheng zhi *Zhushu jinian* yanjiu pingyi" 王國維先生之《竹書紀年》研究評議. *Wenxian* 文獻 (2 March 2022): 4–16.

Chen Mengjia 陳夢家. *Xi Zhou tongqi duandai* 西周銅器斷代. Beijing: Zhonghua shuju, 2004.

Chen Minzhen 陳民鎮. "*Xi shuai* zhi 'zhi' ji qi shixue chanshi: jianlun Qinghua jian *Qi ye* Zhou Gong zuo *Xi shuai* benshi" 《蟋蟀》之"志"及其詩學闡釋——兼論清華簡《耆夜》周公作《蟋蟀》本事. *Zhongguo shige yanjiu* 中國詩歌研究 9 (2013): 57–81.

Chen Minzhen and Yuri Pines. "Where Is King Ping: The History and Historiography of the Zhou Dynasty's Eastward Relocation." *Asia Major* (3rd series) 31, no. 1 (2018): 1–27.

Chen Peifen 陳佩芬. *Xia Shang Zhou qingtongqi yanjiu* 夏商周青銅器研究. Shanghai: Shanghai Guji chubanshe, 2004.

Chen Rentao 陳仁濤. *Jinkui lun gu chuji* 金匱論古初集. Hong Kong: Yazhou chubanshe, 1952.

Chen Shouqi 陳壽祺. *Wu jing yi yi shuzheng* 五經異義疏證. Shanghai: Shanghai guji chubanshe, 2012.

Chen Wei 陳偉. *Baoshan Chu jian chutan* 包山楚簡初談. Wuhan: Wuhan daxue chubanshe, 1996.

Chen Wei 陳偉. "Du *Shangbo liu* tiao ji zhi er" 讀《上博六》條記之二. http://47.75.114.199/show_article.php?id=602. Posted 10 July 2007.

Chen Wei 陳偉, ed. in chief, and Wuhan daxue Jianbo yanjiu zhongxin, Hubei sheng bowuguan and Hubei sheng Wenwu kaogu yanjiusuo, eds. *Qin jiandu heji* 秦簡牘合集. Wuhan: Wuhan daxue chubanshe, 2014.

Chen Wei 陳偉 et al. *Chu di chutu Zhanguo jiance [shisi zhong]* 楚地出土戰國簡冊 [十四種]. Beijing: Jingji kexue chubanshe, 2009.

Chen Zhenyu 陳振裕 and Liu Xinfang 劉信芳, eds. *Shuihudi Qin jian wenzi bian* 睡虎地秦簡文字編. Wuhan: Hubei Renmin chubanshe, 1993.

Chen Zhi 陳致. "Qinghua jian suo jian gu yinzhi li ji *Qi ye* zhong gu yishi shijie" 清華簡所見古飲至禮及《夜》中古佚詩試解. *Chutu wenxian* 出土文獻 1 (2010): 6–30.

Cheng Hao 程浩. "Cong 'Mengfu' dao 'Xingtan': Xian-Qin 'shu' lei wenxian de shengcheng jieji yu liubian" 從"盟府"到"杏壇"：先秦"書"類文獻的生成、結集與流變, *Qinghua daxue xuebao (Zhexue Shehui kexue ban)* 清华大學學報 (哲學社會科學版) 2021.6: 85–106.

Cheng Hao 程浩. "Qinghua jian *She ming* de xingzhi yu jiegou" 清華簡《攝命》性質與結構. *Qinghua daxue xuebao (Zhexue shehui kexue ban)* 清華大學學報 (哲學社會科學班) 2018.5, 53–57.

Cheng Hao 程浩. "*Feng Xu zhi ming* yu ceming 'shu'" 《封許之命》與冊命"書." *Chutu wenxian* 出土文獻 7 (2015): 131–35.

Chin, Tamara. "Orienting Mimesis: Marriage and the *Book of Songs*." *Representations* 94 (Spring 2006): 53–79.

Chunqiu Zuo zhuan zhengyi 春秋左傳正義. In *Shisan jing zhushu* 十三經注疏, edited by Ruan Yuan 阮元, 1697–2188. Beijing: Zhonghua shuju, 1980.

Cook, Constance A., and Paul R. Goldin, eds. *A Source Book of Ancient Chinese Bronze Inscriptions*. Berkeley, CA: Society for the Study of Early China, 2016.

Cook, Scott. "Review of Sarah Allan and Crispin Williams, ed. *The Guodian Laozi: Proceedings of the International Conference, Dartmouth College, May 1998.*" *China Review International* 9, no. 1 (2002): 54–64.

Creel, Herrlee Glessner. *The Birth of China*. New York: John Day, 1937.

Creel, Herrlee Glessner. "Bronze Inscriptions of the Western Chou Dynasty as Historical Documents." *Journal of the American Oriental Society* 56, no. 3 (1936): 335–49.

Ding Zongluo 丁宗洛. *Yi Zhou shu guanjian* 逸周書管箋. 1830 woodblock ed.

Dobson, W. A. C. H. *Early Archaic Chinese: A Descriptive Grammar*. Toronto: University of Toronto Press, 1962.

Dong Shan 董珊. "Lüe lun Xi Zhou Shan shi jiazu jiaocang qingtongqi mingwen" 略論西周單氏家族窖藏青銅器銘文. *Zhongguo lishi wenwu* 中國歷史文物 2003.4, 40–50.

Dong Shan 董刪. "Shi Xi Zhou jinwen de 'chenzi' he *Yi Zhou shu Huangmen* de 'chenren'" 釋西周金文的'沈子'和《逸周書皇門》的'沈人.' *Chutu wenxian* 出土文獻 2 (2016): 29–34.

Du Yu 杜預. "*Chunqiu jingjie jijie* Houxu" 春秋經傳集解後序. In *Chunqiu Zuo zhuan zhengyi* 春秋左傳正義 (*Sibu beiyao* ed.), edited by Kong Yingda 孔穎達, "Jiaokan ji Houxu" 校勘記後序, 1a–2a.

Duan Yucai 段玉裁. *Shuo wen jie zi Duan zhu* 說文解字段注. *Sibu beiyao* ed.

Durrant, Stephen, Wai-yee Li, and David Schaberg. *Zuo Tradition* Zuozhuan 左傳: *Commentary on "The Spring and Autumn Annals."* Seattle: University of Washington Press, 2016.

Elman, Benjamin. "Philosophy (*I-Li*) versus Philology (*K'ao-Cheng*): The *Jen-hsin Tao-Hsin* Debate." *T'oung Pao* 69 (1983): 175–222.

Er ya Guo zhu 爾雅郭注. *Sibu beiyao* ed.

Falkenhausen, Lothar von. "The E Jun Qi Metal Tallies: Inscribed Texts and Ritual Contexts." In *Text and Ritual in Early China*, edited by Martin Kern, 79–123. Seattle: University of Washington Press, 2005.

Falkenhausen, Lothar von. "The Inscribed Bronzes from Yangjiacun: New Evidence on Social Structure and Historical Consciousness in Late Western Zhou China (c. 800 BC)." *Proceedings of the British Academy* 139 (2006): 239–96.

Falkenhausen, Lothar von. "Issues in Western Zhou Studies: A Review Article." *Early China* 18 (1993): 139–226.

Fang Shiming 方詩銘 and Wang Xiuling 王修齡. *Guben Zhushu jinian jizheng* 古本竹書紀年輯證. Shanghai: Shanghai Guji chubanshe, 1981.

Feng Shengjun 馮勝君. *Ershi shiji gu wenxian xinzheng yanjiu* 二十世紀古文獻新證研究. Ji'nan: Qilu shushe, 2006.

Gansu sheng Wenwu kaogu yanjiusuo, ed. *Tianshui Fangmatan Qin jian* 天水放馬灘秦簡. Beijing: Zhonghua, 2009.

Gao Huaping 高華平. "'San Mo' xueshuo yu Chu guo Moxue" "三墨"學說與楚國墨學. *Wenshizhe* 文史哲 2013.5: 14–28.

Gao Ming 高明 and Tu Baikui 涂白奎, eds. *Guwenzi leibian* 古文字類編. 2nd rev. ed. Shanghai: Shanghai Guji chubanshe, 2008.

Gordini, André. "Psychologie expérimentale et exégèse." *La Croix*, 3 February 1927, 4.

Granet, Marcel. *Festivals and Songs of Ancient China*. Translated by E. D. Edwards. London: Routledge and Kegan Paul, 1932.

Granet, Marcel. *Fêtes et chansons anciennes de la Chine*. 1919; 2nd ed., Paris: Leroux, 1929.

Grebnev, Yegor. *Mediation of Legitimacy in Early China: A Study of the* Neglected Zhou Scriptures *and the Grand Duke Traditions*. New York: Columbia University Press, 2022.

Gu Chao 顧潮. *Gu Jiegang nianpu* 顧頡剛年譜. Beijing: Zhongguo Shehui kexue chubanshe, 1993.

Gu Jiegang 顧頡剛. "*Gu shi bian* di yi ce zixu" 古史辨第一冊自序. In *Gu shi bian* 古史辨 1 (1924), edited by Gu Jiegang. Rpt. As *Gu shi bian zixu* 古史辨自序. Shijiazhuang: Hebei Jiaoyu chubanshe, 2003.

Gu Jiegang 顧頡剛. "Wu Wang de si ji qi niansui he jiyuan" 武王的死及其年歲和紀元. *Wenshi* 文史 18 (1983): 1–32.
Guang yun 廣韻. *Sibu beiyao* ed.
Guo Moruo 郭沫若. *Liang Zhou jinwenci daxi kaoshi* 兩周金文辭大系考釋. Tokyo: Bunkyodo shoten 文求堂書店, 1935.
Guo Moruo 郭沫若, ed. in chief, and Hu Houxuan 胡厚宣, ed. *Jiaguwen heji* 甲骨文合集. 13 vols. N.p.: Zhonghua shuju, 1982.
Han Wei 韓巍. "Zhouyuan Qiangjia Xi Zhou tongqiqun shixi wenti bianxi" 周原強家西周銅器群世系問題辨析. *Zhongguo lishi wenwu* 中國歷史文物 2007.3, 70–76.
Hao Beiqin 郝貝欽. "Qinghua jian *Qi ye* zhengli yu yanjiu" 清華簡《耆夜》整理與研究. MA thesis, Tianjin Normal University 天津師範大學, 2012.
Hardy, Grant. *Worlds of Bronze and Bamboo: Sima Qian's Conquest of History*. New York: Columbia University Press, 1999.
He Dingsheng 何定生. "*Shang shu* de wenfa ji qi niandai" 尚書的文法及其年代. *Guoli Zhongshan daxue yuyan lishixue yanjiusuo zhoukan* 國立中山大學語言歷史學研究所週刊 5, nos. 49–51 (17 October 1928): 1793–1979.
He Linyi 何琳儀. *Zhanguo guwen zidian: Zhanguo wenzi shengxi* 戰國古文字典—戰國文字聲系. Beijing: Zhonghua shuju, 1998.
He Youzu 何有祖. "Du *Shangbo liu* zhaji" 讀上博六札記. http://www.bsm.org.cn/show_article.php?id=601. Posted 9 July 2007.
Hirase Takao 平勢隆郎. *Shimpen Shiki Tō Shū nempyō* 新編史記東周年表. Tokyo: Tokyo daigaku Tōyō bunka kenkyūjo, 1995.
Ho Che Wah 何志華 and Chan Hung Kan 陳雄根. *Xian-Qin Liang Han dianji yin Shi jing ziliao huibian* 先秦兩漢典籍引《詩經》資料彙編. Added English title: *Citations from the Shijing to Be Found in Pre-Han and Han Texts*. Hong Kong: Chinese University Press, 2004.
Hu Pingsheng 胡平生. "Anda jian *Shi jing* 'Hou' wei 'Wei feng' shuo" 安大簡《詩經》"矦"爲"魏風"說. http://wxs.swu.edu.cn/s/wxs/index52/20190930/3782252.html. Posted 30 September 2019.
Hu Pingsheng 胡平生. "Fuyang Han jian Zhou Yi gaishu" 阜陽漢簡周易概述. *Jian bo yanjiu* 簡帛研究 3 (1998): 255–66.
Hu Pingsheng 胡平生. "Some Notes on the Organization of the Han Dynasty Bamboo 'Annals' Found at Fuyang." Translated by Deborah Porter. *Early China* 14 (1989): 1–25.
Hu Pingsheng 胡平生 and Han Ziqiang 韓自強. *Fuyang Han jian Shijing yanjiu* 阜陽漢簡詩經研究. Shanghai: Shanghai guji chubanshe, 1988.
Hua Jueming 華覺明 et al. *Fu Hao mu qingtong qiqun zhuzao jishu de yanjiu* 婦好墓青銅器群鑄造技術的研究. *Kaoguxue jikan* 考古學集刊 1. Beijing: Zhongguo Shehui kexue chubanshe 中國社會科學出版社, 1981.
Huang Dekuan 黃德寬. "Anhui daxue cang Zhanguo zhujian gaishu" 安徽大學藏戰國竹簡概述. *Wenwu* 文物 2017.9, 56–58.

Huang Dekuan 黃德寬. "Lüelun xinchu Zhanguo Chu jian *Shi jing* yiwen ji qi jiazhi" 略論新出戰國楚簡《詩經》異文及其價值. *Anhui daxue xuebao (Zhexue Shehui kexue ban)* 安徽大學學報 (哲學社會科學版) 2018.3, 71–77.

Huang Huaixin 黃懷信. "Qinghua jian *Qi ye* jujie" 清華簡《耆夜》句解. *Wenwu* 文物 2012.1, 77–93.

Huang Huaixin 黃懷信. *Yi Zhou shu jiaobu zhuyi* 逸周書校補注譯. Xi'an: Xibei daxue chubanshe, 1996.

Huang Huaixin 黃懷信, Zhang Maorong 張懋鎔, and Tian Xudong 田旭東. *Yi Zhou shu huijiao jizhu* 逸周書彙校集注. Rev. ed. Shanghai: Shanghai Guji chubanshe, 2007.

Huang Peirong 黃沛榮. "*Zhou shu* yanjiu" 周書研究. PhD diss., Taiwan University, 1976.

Huang Tianshu 黃天樹. *Huang Tianshu guwenzi lunji* 黃天樹古文字論集. Beijing: Xueyuan chubanshe, 2006.

Huang Xiquan 黃錫全. "Shi shuo Chu guo huangjin huobi chengliang danwei 'ban yi'" 試說楚國黃金貨幣稱量單位半益. *Jiang Han kaogu* 江漢考古 2000.1, 56–62.

Hubei sheng Jing-Sha tielu kaogudui, ed. *Baoshan Chu jian* 包山楚簡. Beijing: Wenwu chubanshe, 1991.

Hunter, Michael. *Confucius beyond the Analects*. Leiden: Brill, 2017.

Ji Xusheng 季旭昇, ed. *"Shanghai bowuguan cang Zhanguo Chu zhushu (yi)" duben* 《上海博物館藏戰國楚竹書 (一)》讀本. Taipei: Wanjuanlou tushu gongsi, 2004.

Ji Xusheng 季旭昇. *Shijing guyi xinzheng* 詩經古義新證. 1994; Beijing: Xueyuan chubanshe, 2001.

Ji Yun 紀昀 et al., eds. *Qinding Siku quanshu jianming mulu* 欽定四庫全書簡明目錄. Shanghai: Shanghai Guji chubanshe, 1985.

Ji Yun 紀昀 et al., eds. *Qinding Siku quanshu zongmu tiyao* 欽定四庫全書總目提要. Taibei: Taibei Shangwu yinshuguan, 1965.

Jia Lianxiang 賈連翔. "'She ming' ji *Shu xu* 'Jiong ming' 'Jiong ming' shuo" "攝命"即《書序》"臩命""囧命"說. *Qinghua daxue xuebao (Zhexue shehui kexue ban)* 清華大學學報 (哲學社會科學班) 2018.5, 49–53.

Jiang Wen 蔣文. "A Re-examination of the Controversy over the Oral and Written Nature of the *Classic of Poetry*'s Early Transmission, Based on the Anhui University Manuscript." *Bamboo and Silk* 4, no. 1 (2021): 128–48.

Jingzhou shi bowuguan, ed. *Guodian Chu mu zhu jian* 郭店楚墓竹简. Beijing: Wenwu chubanshe, 1998.

Kalinowski, Marc. "La production des manuscrits dans la Chine ancienne: Une approche codicologique de la bibliothèque funéraire de Mawangdui." *Asiatische Studien / Études Asiatiques* 59, no. 1 (2005): 131–68.

Karlgren, Bernhard. *The Book of Odes: Chinese Text, Transcription and Translation*. 1950; rpt. Stockholm: Museum of Far Eastern Antiquities, 1974.

Karlgren, Bernhard. "Yin and Chou in Chinese Bronzes." *Bulletin of the Museum of Far Eastern Antiquities* 8 (1936): 9–156.

Keightley, David N. "The Diviners' Notebooks: Shang Oracle-Bone Inscriptions as Secondary Sources." In *Actes du Colloque International Commémorant le Centenaire de la Découverte des Inscriptions sur Os et Carapaces*, edited by Yau Shun-chiu and Chrystelle Maréchal, 11–25. Paris: Langages Croisés, 2001.

Keightley, David Noel. "Public Work in Ancient China: A Study of Forced Labor in the Shang and Western Chou." PhD diss., Columbia University, 1969.

Keightley, David. "Review of Herrlee G. Creel, *The Origins of Statecraft in China: The Western Chou Empire*." *Journal of Asian Studies* 30, no. 3 (May 1971): 655–58.

Kennedy, George A. "A Note on Ode 220." In *Studia Serica Bernhard Karlgren Dedicata: Sinological Studies Dedicated to Bernhard Karlgren on His Seventieth Birthday*, edited by Søren Egerod and Else Glahn, 190–98. Copenhagen: E. Munksgaard, 1959.

Kern, Martin. "Bronze Inscriptions, the *Shangshu*, and the *Shijing*: The Evolution of the Ancestral Sacrifice during the Western Zhou." In *Early Chinese Religion, Part One: Shang through Han (1250 BC to 220 AD)*, edited by John Lagerwey and Marc Kalinowski. 143–200. Leiden: Brill, 2009.

Kern, Martin. "Chinese." In *How Literatures Begin: A Global History*, edited by Joel B. Lande and Denis Feeney, 19–42. Princeton, NJ: Princeton University Press, 2022.

Kern, Martin. "Early Chinese Literature, Beginnings through Western Han." In *The Cambridge History of Chinese Literature, Vol. 1: To 1375*, edited by Kang-I Sun Chang and Stephen Owen, 1–115. Cambridge: Cambridge University Press, 2011.

Kern, Martin. "Early Chinese Poetics in the Light of Recently Excavated Manuscripts." In *Recarving the Dragon: Understanding Chinese Poetics*, edited by Olga Lomová, 27–72. Prague: Charles University, Karolinum Press, 2003.

Kern, Martin. "Excavated Manuscripts and Their Socratic Pleasures: Newly Discovered Challenges in Reading the 'Airs of the States.'" *Études Asiatiques/Asiatische Studien* 61, no. 3 (2007): 775–93.

Kern, Martin. "Lost in Tradition: The *Classic of Poetry* We Did Not Know." *Hsiang Lectures on Chinese Poetry* 5, 29–56. Montreal: Centre for East Asian Research, McGill University, 2010.

Kern, Martin. "Methodological Reflections on the Analysis of Textual Variants and the Modes of Manuscript Production in Early China." *Journal of East Asian Archaeology* 4, nos. 1–4 (2002): 143–81.

Kern, Martin. "The *Odes* in Excavated Manuscripts." In *Text and Ritual in Early China*, edited by Martin Kern, 149–93. Seattle: University of Washington Press, 2005.

Kern, Martin. "The Performance of Writing in Western Zhou China." In *The Poetics of Grammar and the Metaphysics of Sound and Sign*, edited by Sergio La Porta and David Shulman, 109–76. Leiden: Brill, 2007.

Kern, Martin. "Review of Mark Edward Lewis, *Writing and Authority in Early China*." *China Review International* 7, no. 2 (2000): 336–76.

Kern, Martin. "*Shi Jing* Songs as Performance Texts: A Case Study of 'Chu ci' ('Thorny Caltrop')." *Early China* 25 (2000): 49–111.

Kern, Martin. "'Xi Shuai' 蟋蟀 ('Cricket') and Its Consequences: Issues in Early Chinese Poetry and Textual Studies." *Early China* 42 (2019): 39–74.

Khayutina, Maria. "The Tombs of the Rulers of Peng and Relationships between Zhou and Northern Non-Zhou Lineages (Until the Early Ninth Century B.C.)." In *Imprints of Kinship: Studies of Recently Discovered Bronze Inscriptions from Ancient China*, edited by Edward L. Shaughnessy, 71–132. Hong Kong: Chinese University of Hong Kong Press, 2017.

Krijgsman, Rens. *The Tsinghua University Warring States Bamboo Manuscripts*, vol. 6. Beijing: Tsinghua University Press, 2023.

Legge, James. *The Chinese Classics*, vol. 3: *The Shoo King or the Book of Historical Documents*. 1865; rpt. Hong Kong: Hong Kong University Press, 1960.

Legge, James. *The Chinese Classics*, vol. 4, *The She King*. Oxford: Oxford University Press, 1871.

Lei Xueqi 雷學淇. *Zhushu jinian yizheng* 竹書紀年義證. 1810; rpt. Taibei: Yiwen yinshuguan, 1971.

Leung, Vincent. *The Tsinghua University Warring States Bamboo Manuscripts*, vol. 8. Beijing: Tsinghua University Press, in press.

Lewis, Mark Edward. *Writing and Authority in Early China*. Albany: State University of New York Press, 1999.

Li Daoyuan 酈道元. *Shui jing zhu jiao* 水經注校, edited by Wang Guowei 王國維. Shanghai: Shanghai Renmin chubanshe, 1984.

Li Daoyuan 酈道元. *Shui jing zhu shu* 水經注疏. N.p.: Jiangsu Guji chubanshe, 1989.

Li Fang 李方 et al., eds. *Taiping Yulan* 太平御覽. Rpt. Beijing: Zhonghua shuju, 1960.

Li, Feng. *Landscape and Power in Early China: The Crisis and Fall of the Western Zhou, 1045–771 B.C.* New York: Cambridge University Press, 2006.

Li, Feng. "Literacy Crossing Cultural Borders: Evidence from the Bronze Inscriptions of the Western Zhou Period (1045–771 BCE). *Bulletin of the Museum of Far Eastern Antiquities* 74 (2002): 210–42.

Li, Feng. "Literacy and the Social Contexts of Literacy in the Western Zhou." In *Writing and Literacy in Early China: Studies from the Columbia Early China Seminar*, edited by Li Feng and David Prager Branner, 271–301. Seattle: University of Washington Press, 2011.

Li Feng 李峰. "Qinghua jian *Qi ye* chudu ji qi xiangguan wenti" 清華簡《耆夜》初讀及其相關問題 In *Disijie guoji hanxue huiyi lunwenji: Chutu cailiao yu xin shiye* 第四屆國際漢學會議論文集:出土材料與 新視野, edited by Li Zongkun 李宗焜, 461–91. Taipei: Zhongyang yanjiuyuan, 2013.

Li, Feng. "Textual Criticism and Western Zhou Bronze Inscriptions: The Example of the Mu Gui." In *Tao li cheng xi ji: Qingzhu An Zhimin xiansheng bashi shouchen* 桃李成蹊集：慶祝安志敏先生八十壽辰, edited by Deng Cong 鄧聰 and Chen Xingcan 陳星燦, 280–97. Hong Kong: Chinese University of Hong Kong Press, 2004.

Li Ji 李濟 and Wan Jiabao 萬家保. *Yinxu chutu qingtong dingxingqi zhi yanjiu* 殷墟出土青銅鼎形器之研究. *Gu qiwu yanjiu zhuankan* 古器物研究專刊 4. Taibei: Zhongyang yanjiuyuan Lishi yuyan yanjiusuo 中央研究院歷史語言研究所, 1970.

Li Rui 李銳. "Qinghua jian *Qi ye* xutan" 清華簡《耆夜》續探. *Zhongyuan wenhua yanjiu* 中原文化研究 2014.2, 55–62.

Li Shoukui 李守奎, ed. *Chu wenzi bian* 楚文字編. Shanghai: Huadong Shifan daxue chubanshe, 2003.

Li Xueqin. "'Comments on the *Poetry*' (Shilun) and 'The *Poetry*' (Shi)." *Contemporary Chinese Thought* 39, no. 4 (2008): 18–29.

Li Xueqin 李學勤. "Jiangxian Hengbei cun mudi yu Peng guo" 絳縣橫北村墓地與國. *Zhongguo wenwu bao* 中國文物報, 14 September 2007, 5.

Li Xueqin 李學勤. "Lun Qinghua jian *Qi ye* de *Xi shuai* shi" 論清華簡《耆夜》的《蟋蟀》詩. *Zhongguo wenhua* 中國文化 33 (2011): 7–10.

Li Xueqin 李學勤. "Meixian Yangjia cun xin chu qingtongqi yanjiu" 眉縣楊家村新出青銅器研究. *Wenwu* 文物 2003.6, 66–73.

Li Xueqin 李學勤. "Mu Gong gui gai zai qingtongqi fenqi shang de yiyi" 穆公簋蓋在青銅器分期上的意義. *Wenbo* 文博 1984.2: 6–8.

Li Xueqin 李學勤. "Qinghua jian *Xinian* ji youguan gu shi wenti" 清華簡《繫年》及有關古史問題. *Wenwu* 文物 2011.3, 70–74.

Li Xueqin 李學勤. "Qinghua jian yu *Shang shu Yi Zhou shu* de yanjiu" 清華簡與《尚書》《逸周書》的研究. *Shixue shi yanjiu* 史學史研究 2011.2, 104–09.

Li Xueqin 李學勤. "Shi Guodian jian *Zhai Gong zhi gu ming*" 釋郭店簡祭公之顧命. *Wenwu* 文物 1998.7, 44–45.

Li Xueqin 李學勤. "*Shi lun* yu *Shi*"《詩論》與《詩》. *Zhongguo zhexue* 中國哲學 24 (2002): 121–36.

Li Xueqin 李學勤. "Xi Zhou zhongqi qingtongqi de zhongyao biaochi: Zhouyuan Zhuangbai Qiangjia liang chu qingtongqi jiaocang de zonghe yanjiu" 西周中期青銅器的重要標尺：周原莊白、強家兩處青銅器窖藏的綜合研究. *Zhongguo lishi bowuguan guankan* 中國歷史博物館館刊 1979.1, 29–36.

Li Xueqin 李學勤. "You Qinghua jian *Xinian* lun *Jinian* de tili" 由清華簡《繫年》論《紀年》的體例. *Shenzhen daxue xuebao (Renwen Shehui kexueban* 深圳大學學報)（人文社會科學版）2012.2: 42–44.

Li Xueqin 李學勤. "Zou chu yi gu shidai" 走出疑古時代. *Zhongguo wenhua* 中國文化 7 (1993). In Li Xueqin, *Zou chu yigu shidai* 走出疑古時代, 1–19. 1994; rev. 2nd ed. Shenyang: Liaoning daxue chubanshe, 1997.

Li Xueqin 李學勤, ed. in chief, and Qinghua daxue chutu wenxian yanjiu yu baohu zhongxin, eds. *Qinghua daxue cang Zhanguo zhujian (yi)* 清華大學藏戰國竹簡 (壹). Shanghai: Zhong Xi shuju, 2010.
Li Xueqin 李學勤, ed. in chief, and Qinghua daxue Chutu wenxian yanjiu yu baohu zhongxin, eds. *Qinghua daxue cang Zhanguo zhu jian (er)* 清華大學藏戰國竹簡 (貳). Shanghai: Zhong Xi shuju, 2011.
Li Xueqin 李學勤, ed. in chief, and Qinghua daxue Chutu wenxian yanjiu yu baohu zhongxin, eds. *Qinghua daxue cang Zhanguo zhujian (wu)* 清華大學藏戰國竹簡 (伍). Shanghai: Zhong Xi shuju, 2014.
Li Xueqin 李學勤, ed. in chief, and Qinghua daxue chutu wenxian yanjiu yu baohu zhongxin, eds. *Qinghua daxue cang Zhanguo zhujian (lu)* 清華大學藏戰國竹簡 (陸). Shanghai: Zhong Xi shuju, 2016.
Li Xueqin 李學勤, ed. in chief, and Qinghua daxue chutu wenxian yanjiu yu baohu zhongxin, eds., *Qinghua daxue cang Zhanguo zhujian (ba)* 清華大學藏戰國竹簡 (捌). Shanghai: Zhong Xi shuju, 2018.
Liji zhengyi 禮記正義. In *Shisan jing zhushu* 十三經注疏, edited by Ruan Yuan 阮元, 1221–1696. Beijing: Zhonghua shuju, 1980.
Liu Gang 劉剛. "A Reconstruction of the Text of the Poem 'You Bi' of the *Liturgies of Lu* Section of the *Classic of Poetry*." *Bamboo and Silk* 4, no. 1 (2021): 189–99.
Liu Huaijun 劉懷君 and Liu Junshe 劉君社. "Shaanxi Meixian Yangjia cun Xi Zhou qingtongqi jiaocang" 陝西眉縣楊家村西周青銅器窖藏. *Kaogu yu wenwu* 考古與文物 2003.3, 3–12.
Liu Shipei 劉師培. *Zhou shu buzheng* 周書補正. In *Liu Shenshu xiansheng yishu* 劉申叔先生遺書. Ningwu Nan shi, 1934.
Liu Qi 劉琦 and Liang Guofu 梁國輔. *Sou shen ji Sou shen houji yizhu* 搜神記搜神後記譯注. Changchun: Jilin Wenshi chubanshe, 1997.
Liu Qiyu 劉起釪. *Shang shu xueshi* 尚書學史. Beijing: Zhonghua shuju, 1989.
Liu Qiyu 劉起釪. *Shang shu yuanliu ji chuanben kao* 尚書源流及傳本考. Shenyang: Liaoning daxue chubanshe, 1987.
Liu Xinfang 劉信芳. "*Shangbo cang liu shi jie zhi san*" 上博藏六試解之三. www.bsm.org.cn. Posted 9 August 2007.
Liu Xu 劉恕. *Zizhi tongjian waiji* 資治通鑑外紀. Taipei: Shangwu yinshuguan, 1977.
Liu Zhiji 劉知幾. *Mingben Shi tong* 名本史通. Beijing: Guojia Tushuan chubanshe, 2019.
Liu Zhiji 劉知幾. *Shi tong tongshi* 史通通釋. Shanghai: Shangwu yinshuguan, 1935.
Loewe, Michael, ed. *Early Chinese Texts: A Bibliographical Guide*. Berkeley: Society for the Study of Early China and Institute of East Asian Studies, University of California, Berkeley, 1993.
Loewe, Michael, and Edward L. Shaughnessy, eds. *The Cambridge History of Ancient China: From the Origins of Civilization to 221 B.C.* New York: Cambridge University Press, 1999.

Lü Dalin 呂大臨. *Kaogu tu* 考古圖. 1752 Yizheng tang 亦政堂 ed.
Lu Wenchao 盧文弨. *Yi Zhou shu*. *Sibu beiyao* ed.
Lunyu zhushu 論語注疏. In Ruan Yuan 阮元 ed. *Shisan jing zhushu* 十三經注疏, 2453–2536. Beijing: Zhonghua shuju, 1980.
Luo Bi 羅泌. *Lu shi* 路史. Shanghai: Shanwu yinshuguan, 1936.
Luo Genze 羅根澤. "You *Mozi* yin jing tuice Ru Mo liang jia yu jingshu zhi guanxi" 由《墨子》引經推測儒墨兩家與經書之關係. In *Gu shi bian* 古史辨, vol. 4., edited by Luo Genze, 278–81. 1933; rpt. Shanghai Shanghai Guji chubanshe, 1982.
Ma Chengyuan 馬承源. "Jin Hou Su bianzhong" 晉侯蘇編鐘. *Shanghai bowuguan guankan* 上海博物館館刊 1996.7, 1–17.
Ma Chengyuan 馬承源, ed. *Shanghai bowuguan cang Zhanguo Chu zhushu (yi)* 上海博物館藏戰國楚竹書 (一). Shanghai: Shanghai guji chubanshe, 2001.
Ma Chengyuan 馬承源, ed. *Shanghai bowuguan cang Zhanguo Chu zhu shu (liu)* 上海博物館藏戰國楚竹書 (六). Shanghai: Shanghai guji chubanshe, 2007.
Ma Chengyuan 馬承源, ed. *Shanghai bowuguan cang Zhanguo Chu zhu shu (qi)* 上海博物館藏戰國楚竹書 (七). Shanghai: Shanghai guji chubanshe, 2008.
Ma Chengyuan 馬承源, ed. *Shang Zhou qingtongqi mingwen xuan* 商周青銅器銘文選. Beijing: Wenwu chubanshe, 1988.
Ma Nan 馬楠. "Qinghua jian *She ming* chudu" 清華簡《攝命》初讀. *Wenwu* 2018.9, 46–49.
Ma Nan 馬楠. "Qinghua jia *Zheng Wen Gong wen Taibo* yu Zheng guo zaoqi shishi" 清華簡《鄭文公問太伯》與鄭國早期史實. *Wenwu* 文物 2016.3, 84–87.
Ma Ruichen 馬瑞辰. *Mao Shi zhuan jian tongshi* 毛詩傳箋通釋. Beijing: Zhonghua shuju, 1989.
Ma Xulun 馬敘倫. *Shi gu wen shuji* 石鼓文疏記. Shanghai: Shangwu yinshuguan, 1935.
Makeham, John. "Review of E. Bruce Brooks and A. Taeko Brooks, *The Original Analects: Sayings of Confucius and his Successors.*" *China Review International* 6, no. 1 (1999): 1–33.
Mao Shi Zheng jian 毛詩鄭箋. *Sibu beiyao* ed.
Mao Shi zhengyi 毛詩正義. In *Shisan jing zhushu* 十三經注疏, edited by Ruan Yuan 阮元, 259–629. Beijing: Zhonghua shuju, 1980.
Mathieu, Rémi. *Mu t'ien-tzu chuan* 穆天子傳. In *Early Chinese Texts: A Bibliographical Guide*, edited by Michael Loewe, 342–46. Berkeley: The Society for the Study of Early China and the Institute of East Asian Studies, University of California, 1993.
Mattos, Gilbert L. *The Stone Drums of Ch'in*. Monumenta Serica Monograph Series 19. Nettetel: Steyler Verlag, 1988.
McNeal, Robin. *Conquer and Govern: Early Chinese Military Texts from the Yizhou Shu*. Honolulu: University of Hawai'I Press, 2012.

Meng Yuelong 孟躍龍. "Qinghua jian *Ming xun* 'Shao ming _ shen' de dufa: Jianlun gudai chaoben wenxian zhong chongwen fuhao de teshu yongfa" 清華簡《命訓》"少命_身"的讀法：兼論古代抄本文獻中重文符號的特殊用法. *Jianbo* 簡帛 13 (2017): 71–77.

Mengzi 孟子. *Sibu beiyao* ed.

Meyer, Dirk. *Philosophy on Bamboo: Text and the Production of Meaning in Early China*. Leiden: Brill, 2012.

Meyer, Dirk, and Adam Craig Schwartz. *Songs of the Royal Zhōu and the Royal Shào: Shī* 詩 *of the Ânhuī University Manuscripts*. Leiden: Brill, 2022.

Milburn, Olivia. "The *Xinian*: An Ancient Historical Text from the Qinghua University Collection of Bamboo Books" *Early China* 39 (2016): 53–109.

Mittag, Achim. "The Qin *Bamboo Annals* of Shuihudi: A Random Note from the Perspective of Chinese Historiography." *Monumenta Serica* 51 (2003): 543–70.

Mo Zihan 墨子涵. "*Tianzi jian zhou* zhong suojian fanyinwen, weishizi ji jidian jiduan" 《天子建州》中所見反印文、未釋字及幾點臆斷. http://www.bsm.org.cn/show_article.php?id=764. Posted 25 December 2007.

Morgan, Daniel. "A Positive Case for the Visuality of Text in Warring States Manuscript Culture." Paper presented at the Creel-Luce Paleography Forum, Chicago, 24–25 April 2010.

Mozi 墨子. *Sibu beiyao* ed.

Mu tianzi zhuan 穆天子傳. *Sibu congkan* ed.

Musha Akira 武者章. "Sei Shū satsu mei kinbun bunrui no kokoromi" 西周冊命金文分類の試み. In *Sei Shū seidōki to sono kokka* 西周青銅器とその國家, edited by Matsumaru Michio 松丸道雄, 293–300. Tokyo: Tokyo daigaku shuppankai, 1980.

Nivison, David S. "Western Zhou History Reconstructed from Bronze Inscriptions." In *The Great Bronze Age of China: A Symposium*, edited by George Kuwayama, 44–55. Los Angeles: Los Angeles County Museum of Art, 1983.

Nivison, David S., and Edward L. Shaughnessy. "The Jin Hou Su Bells Inscription and Its Implications for the Chronology of Early China." *Early China* 25 (2001): 29–48.

Niwa Takafumi 丹羽崇史. "CT jiexi yu zhongguo qingtongqi zhizuo jishu de yanjiu" CT 解析與中國青銅器製作技術的研究. In *Quanwu toushang: Quanwu boguguan qingtongqi toushe saomiao jiexi* 泉屋透賞：泉屋博古館青銅器透射掃描解析, edited by Quanwu boguguan 泉屋博古館 and Jiuzhou Guoli bowuguan九州國立博物館, and translated by Huang Rongguang 黃榮光, 452–59. Beijing: Kexue chubanshe 科學出版社, 2015.

Nugent, Christopher. "The Circulation of Poetry in Tang Dynasty China." PhD diss., Harvard University, 2004.

Nugent, Christopher M. B. "The Lady and Her Scribes: Dealing with Multiple Dunhuang Copies of Wei Zhuang's 'Lament of the Lady Qin.'" *Asia Major* (3rd series) 20, no. 2 (2007): 25–73.

Owen, Stephen. "Interpreting *Sheng Min*." In *Ways with Words: Writing about Reading Texts from Early China*, edited by Pauline Yu, Peter Bol, Stephen Owen, and Willard Peterson, 25–31. Berkeley: University of California Press, 2000.

Owen, Stephen. "Reproduction in the *Shijing* (Classic of Poetry)." *Harvard Journal of Asiatic Studies* 61, no. 2 (2001): 287–315.

Pang Sunjoo 方善柱 (Fang Shanzhu). "Xi Zhou niandai xue shang de jige wenti" 西周年代學上的幾個問題. *Dalu zazhi* 大陸雜誌 51, no. 1 (1975): 17–23.

Pian Yuqian 駢宇騫 and Duan Shu'an 段書安, eds. *Ben shiji yilai chutu jian bo gaishu* 本世紀以來出土簡帛概述. Taipei: Wanjuanlou tushu youxian gongsi, 1999.

Pines, Yuri. "Chinese History Writing between the Sacred and the Secular." In *Early Chinese Religion, Part One: Shang through Han (1250 BC–220 AD)*, edited by John Lagerwey and Marc Kalinowski, 315–40. Leiden: Brill, 2009.

Pines, Yuri. "Zhou History and Historiography: Introducing the Bamboo Manuscript Xinian." *T'oung Pao* 100, no. 4–5 (2014): 287–324.

Pines, Yuri. *Zhou History Unearthed: The Bamboo Manuscript Xinian and Early Chinese Historiography*. New York: Columbia University Press, 2020.

Qiu Xigui 裘錫圭. "Guanyu Shi Gu Wen de shidai wenti" 關於石鼓文的時代問題. *Chuantong wenhua yu xiandaihua* 傳統文化與現代化 1 (1995): 40–48.

Qiu Xigui 裘錫圭. *Qiu Xigui xueshu wenji* 裘錫圭學術文集. 6 vols. Shanghai: Fudan daxue, 2015.

Qiu Xigui 裘錫圭. "Tantan guwenzi ziliao dui gu Hanyu yanjiu de zhongyaoxing" 談談古文字資料對古漢語研究的重要性. *Zhongguo yuwen* 中國語文 1979.6: 437–42. Rev. rpt. in *Qiu Xigui xueshu wenji: Yuyan wenzi yu gu wenxian juan* 裘錫圭學術文集：語言文字與古文獻卷 (Shanghai: Fudan daxue, 2015), 40–48.

Qiu Xigui 裘錫圭. "Zhongguo gudianxue chongjian zhong yinggai zhuyi de wenti" 中國古典學重建中應該注意的問題. In Qiu Xigui, *Qiu Xigui xueshu wenji: Jiandu boshu juan* 裘錫圭學術文集：簡牘帛書卷, 334–44. Shanghai: Fudan daxue chubanshe, 2015.

Qiu Xigui 裘錫圭, ed. in chief, Hunan sheng bowuguan 湖南省博物館 and Fudan daxue Chutu wenxian yu guwenzi yanjiu zhongxin 復旦大學出土文獻與古文字研究中心, eds. *Changsha Mawangdui Han mu jianbo jicheng* 長沙馬王堆漢墓簡帛集成. Shanghai: Shanghai Guji, 2015.

Qu Wanli 屈萬里. *Shi jing shi yi* 詩經釋義. Taipei: Zhongguo wenhua daxue chubanbu, 1983.

Rawson, Jessica. "Statesmen or Barbarians? The Western Zhou as Seen through Their Bronzes." *Proceedings of the British Academy* 75 (1989): 71–95.

Rawson, Jessica. *Western Zhou Ritual Vessels from the Arthur M. Sackler Collections*. Washington, DC: Arthur M. Sackler Foundation, 1990.

Richter, Matthias L. "Faithful Transmission or Creative Change: Tracing Modes of Manuscript Production from the Material Evidence." *Asiatische Studien / Études Asiatique* 63, no. 4 (2009): 895–903.

Riegel, Jeffrey. "Eros, Introversion, and the Beginnings of *Shijing* Commentary." *Harvard Journal of Asiatic Studies* 57, no. 1 (1997): 149–59.

Saussy, Haun. "Repetition, Rhyme, and Exchange in the *Book of Odes*." *Harvard Journal of Asiatic Studies* 57, no. 2 (1997): 519–42.

Schaberg, David. "Review of *Before Confucius: Studies in the Creation of the Chinese Classics*, by Edward L. Shaughnessy." *Journal of Asian Studies* 57, no. 4 (1998): 1137–38.

Schaberg, David. "'Sell It! Sell It!' Recent Translations of *Lunyu*." *Chinese Literature: Essays, Articles, Reviews* 23 (2001): 115–39.

Schaberg, David. "Speaking of Documents: *Shu* Citations in Warring States Texts." In *Origins of Chinese Political Philosophy: Studies in the Composition and Thought of the* Shangshu, edited by Martin Kern and Dirk Meyer, 320–59. Leiden: Brill, 2017.

Schaberg, David. "Texts and Artifacts: A Review of *The Cambridge History of Ancient China*." *Monumenta Serica* 49 (2001): 463–515.

Schneider, Marcel. "The '*Qí yè* 耆夜' and '*Zhōu Gōng zhī qín wǔ* 周公之琴舞' from the Qīnghuá Bamboo Manuscripts: An Annotated Translation." Licentiate diss., University of Zurich, 2014.

Schnepp, Suzanne R. "Condition Report on Arrival." Art Institute of Chicago internal memorandum, 6 December 2005.

Schuessler, Axel. *Minimal Old Chinese and Later Han Chinese: A Companion to Grammata Serica Recensa*. Honolulu: University of Hawai'i Press, 2009.

Sena, David. "Arraying the Ancestors in Ancient China: Narratives of Lineage History in the 'Scribe Qiang' and 'Qiu' Bronzes." *Asia Major* (3rd series) 25, no. 1 (2012): 63–81.

Sena, David. "Reproducing Society: Kinship and Social Organization in Western Zhou China." PhD diss., University of Chicago, 2005.

"Shaanxi Meixian chutu jiaocang tongqi bitan" 陝西眉縣出土窖藏銅器筆談. *Wenwu* 2003.6, 43–65.

Shaanxi sheng Kaogu yanjiusuo, Baoji shi kaogu gongzuodui and Meixian wehuaguan. "Shaanxi Meixian Yangjia cun Xi Zhou qingtongqi jiaocang fajue jianbao" 陝西眉縣楊家村西周青銅器窖藏發掘簡報. *Wenwu* 2003.6, 4–42.

Shaanxi sheng wenwuju and Zhonghua Shiji tan yishuguan, eds. *Sheng shi jijin: Shaanxi Baoji Meixian qingtongqi jiaocang* 盛世吉金：陝西寶雞眉縣青銅器窖藏. Beijing: Beijing chubanshe, 2003.

Shanghai bowuguan Shang Zhou qingtongqi mingwen xuan bianxiezu 上海博物館商周青銅器銘文選編寫組, eds. *Shang Zhou qingtongqi mingwenxuan* 商周青銅器銘文選. Beijing: Wenwu chubanshe, 1986.

Shang shu zhengyi 尚書正義. In *Shisan jing zhu shu* 十三經注疏, edited by Ruan Yuan 阮元, 109–258. Beijing: Zhonghua shuju, 1980.

Shangshu Kong zhuan 尚書孔傳. *Sibu beiyao* ed.

Shanxi sheng kaogu yanjiusuo 山西省考古研究所, Yuncheng shi wenwu gongzuozhan 運城市文物工作站, and Jiangxian wenhuaju 絳縣文化局. "Shanxi Jiangxian Hengshui Xi Zhou mu fajue jianbao" 山西絳縣橫水西周墓發掘簡報. *Wenwu* 2006.8, 4–18.

Shaughnessy, Edward L. *Before Confucius: Studies in the Creation of the Chinese Classics*. Albany: State University of New York Press, 1997.

Shaughnessy, Edward L. "The *Bin Gong Xu* Inscription and the Beginnings of the Chinese Literary Tradition." In *The Harvard-Yenching Library 75th Anniversary Memorial Volume*, edited by Wilt Idema, 1–19. Hong Kong: Chinese University Press, 2007.

Shaughnessy, Edward L. "A First Reading of the Anhui University Bamboo-Slip *Shi Jing*." *Bamboo and Silk* 42 (2021): 1–44.

Shaughnessy, Edward L. "From Liturgy to Literature: The Ritual Contexts of the Earliest Poems in the *Book of Poetry*." *Hanxue yanjiu* 漢學研究 (*Chinese Studies*) 13, no. 1 (1995): 133–64.

Shaughnessy, Edward L. "The Guodian Manuscripts and Their Place in Twentieth-Century Historiography on the *Laozi*." *Harvard Journal of Asiatic Studies* 65, no. 2 (2005): 417–57.

Shaughnessy, Edward L. "History and Inscriptions, China." In *The Oxford History of Historical Writing*, vol. 1: *Beginnings to AD 600*, edited by Andrew Feldherr and Grant Hardy, 371–93. Oxford: Oxford University Press, 2011.

Shaughnessy, Edward L. *I Chou Shu* 尚書 逸周書. In *Early Chinese Texts: A Bibliographical Guide*, edited by Michael Loewe, 229–33. Berkeley: Society for the Study of Early China and Institute of East Asian Studies, University of California, Berkeley, 1993.

Shaughnessy, Edward L. "On the Editing of the *Mu Tianzi Zhuan*." In *In Between the Lines: The Narration of Ancient China: A Festschrift in Honor of William H. Nienhauser*, edited by Chen Zhi. Leiden: Brill, in press.

Shaughnessy, Edward L. "The Origin and Development of Western Sinologists' Theories of the Oral-Formulaic Nature of the *Classic of Poetry*." *Bulletin of the Jao Tsung-i Academy of Sinology* 3 (2016): 133–49.

Shaughnessy, Edward L. "A Possible Lost Classic: The *She Ming* or *Command to She*." *T'oung Pao* 106 (2020): 266–308.

Shaughnessy, Edward L. "The Qin *Bian Nian Ji* and the Beginnings of Historical Writing in China." In *Beyond the First Emperor's Mausoleum: New Perspectives on Qin Art*, edited by Liu Yang, 115–36. Minneapolis: Minneapolis Institute of Art, 2014.

Shaughnessy, Edward L. "Rewriting the *Zi yi*: How One Chinese Classic Came to Be Read as It Does." In Edward L. Shaughnessy, 63–130. *Rewriting Early Chinese Texts*. Albany: State University of New York Press, 2006.

Shaughnessy, Edward L. *Shang shu* 尚書 (*Shu ching* 書經). In *Early Chinese Texts: A Bibliographical Guide*, edited by Michael Loewe, 376–89. Berkeley: Society for the Study of Early China and Institute of East Asian Studies, University of California, Berkeley, 1993.

Shaughnessy, Edward L. *Sources of Western Zhou History: Inscribed Bronze Vessels*. Berkeley: University of California Press, 1991.

Shaughnessy, Edward L. "To Punish the Person: A Reading Note Regarding a Punctuation Mark in the Tsinghua Manuscript *Ming Xun*." *Early China* 40 (2017): 303–10.

Shaughnessy, Edward L. "Texts Lost in Texts: Recovering the 'Zhāi Gōng' Chapter of the *Yí Zhōu Shū*." In *Studies in Chinese Language and Culture: Festschrift in Honour of Christoph Harbsmeier on the Occasion of His 60th Birthday*, edited by Christoph Anderl and Halvor Eifring, 31–47. Oslo: Hermes Academic, 2006.

Shaughnessy, Edward L. "The Tsinghua Manuscript *Zheng Wen Gong wen Taibo* and the Question of the Production of Manuscripts in Early China." *Bamboo and Silk* 3 (2020): 54–73.

Shaughnessy, Edward L. *The Tsinghua University Warring States Bamboo Manuscripts*, vol. 1: *The Yi Zhou Shu and Pseudo-Yi Zhou Shu Chapters*. Beijing: Tsinghua University Press, 2023.

Shaughnessy, Edward L. *The Tsinghua University Warring States Bamboo Manuscripts*, vol. 2: *The Shang Shu and Pseudo-Shang Shu Chapters*. Beijing: Tsinghua University Press, 2024.

Shaughnessy, Edward L. "Unearthed Documents and the Question of the Oral versus Written Nature of the *Classic of Poetry*." *Harvard Journal of Asiatic Studies* 75, no. 2 (2015): 331–75.

Shaughnessy, Edward L. "Varieties of Textual Variants: Evidence from the Tsinghua Bamboo-Slip *Ming Xun* Manuscript." *Early China* 39 (2016): 111–44.

Shaughnessy, Edward L. "Western Zhou History." In *The Cambridge History of Ancient China: From the Origins of Civilization to 221 B.C.*, edited by Michael Loewe and Edward L. Shaughnessy, 292–351. New York: Cambridge University Press, 1999.

Shaughnessy, Edward L. "The Writing of a Late Western Zhou Bronze Inscription." *Asiatische Studien / Études Asiatiques* 61, no. 3 (2007) 845–77.

Shim, Jae-hoon. "The Eastward Relocation of the Zhou Royal House in the Xinian Manuscript: Chronological and Geographical Aspects. *Archiv Orientální* 85 (2017): 67–97.

Shim, Jaehoon. "The 'Jinhou Su *Bianzhong*' Inscription and Its Significance." *Early China* 22 (1997): 43–75.

Shirakawa Shizuka 白川靜. *Kimbun tsushaku* 金文通釋. 54 fascicles. Kobe: Hakutsuru bijustukan 白鶴美術館, 1962–1984.

Shuihudi Qin mu zhujian zhengli xiaozu, eds. *Shuihudi Qin mu zhujian* 睡虎地秦墓竹簡. Beijing: Wenwu, 1990.

Sima Qian 司馬遷. *Shi ji* 史記. Beijing: Zhonghua shuju, 1959.

Škrabal, Ondřej. "Writing before Inscribing: On the Use of Manuscripts in the Production of Western Zhou Bronze Inscriptions." *Early China* 42 (2019): 273–332.

Smith, Adam Daniel. "The Evidence for Scribal Training at Anyang." In *Writing and Literacy in Early China: Studies from the Columbia Early China Seminar*, edited by Li Feng and David Prager Branner, 173–205. Seattle: University of Washington Press, 2011.

Staack, Thies. "Reconstructing the *Kongzi Shilun*: From the Arrangement of the Bamboo Slips to a Tentative Translation." *Asiatische Studien / Études Asiatiques* 64, no. 4 (2010): 857–906.

Su Jianzhou 蘇建洲. "Qinghua jian di wu ce zici kaoshi" 清華簡第五冊字詞考釋. *Chutu wenxian* 出土文獻 7 (2015): 148–62.

Su Rongyu 蘇榮譽. "Ershi shiji dui Xian Qin qingtong liqi zhuzao jishu de yanjiu 二十世紀對先秦青銅禮器鑄造技術的研究. In *Quanwu toushang: Quanwu boguguan qingtongqi toushe saomiao jiexi* 泉屋透賞：泉屋博古館青銅器透射掃描解析, edited by Quanwu boguguan 泉屋博古館 and Jiuzhou Guoli bowuguan九州國立博物館 and translated by Huang Rongguang 黃榮光, 387–445. Beijing: Kexue chubanshe, 2015.

Sui Gong xu: Da Yu zhi shui yu wei zheng yi de 燹公盨：大禹治水與為政以德. Beijing: Xianzhuang shuju, 2002.

Sun Yirang 孫詒讓. *Zhou shu jiaobui* 周書斠補. 1894 woodblock ed.

Tang Lan 唐蘭. *Xi Zhou qingtongqi mingwen fendai shizheng* 西周青銅器銘文分代史徵. Beijing: Zhonghua shuju, 1986.

Tang Yuhui 湯余惠. "Du jinwen suoji (ba pian)" 讀金文鎖記（八篇）. *Chutu wenxian yanjiu* 出土文獻研究 1998.1, 60–66.

Teng Rensheng 滕壬生. *Chu xi jianbo wenzibian* 楚系簡帛文字編. Wuhan: Hubei jiaoyu chubanshe, 2008.

Tharsen, Jeffrey R. "Chinese Euphonics: Phonetic Patterns, Phonorhetoric and Literary Artistry in Early Chinese Narrative Texts." PhD diss., University of Chicago, 2015.

Tsien, Tsuen-hsuin. *Written on Bamboo and Silk: The Beginnings of Chinese Books and Inscriptions*. 2nd ed. Chicago: University of Chicago Press, 2004.

van Auken, Newell Ann. *Spring and Autumn Historiography: Form and Hierarchy in Ancient Chinese Annals*. New York: Columbia University Press, 2023.

Vandermeersch, Léon. "Entre divination et écriture: Essai de clonage d'un texte des *Annales sur bamboo*." *Études chinoises* 18, nos. 1–2 (1999): 125–35.

Venture, Olivier. "Étude d'un emploi rituel de l'écrit dans la Chine archaique (XIIIe–VIIIe siècle avant notre ère): Réflexion sur les matériaux épigraphiques des Shang et des Zhou occidentaux." PhD diss., Université Paris 7, 2002.

Vogelsang, Kai. "Inscriptions and Proclamations: On the Authenticity of the "Gao" Chapters in the *Book of Documents*." *Bulletin of the Museum of Far Eastern Antiquities* 74 (2002): 138–209.

Waley, Arthur *The Book of Songs: The Ancient Chinese Classic of Poetry.* 1937; rpt. New York: Grove Press, 1987.

Wang Guowei 王國維. *Guben Zhushu jinian jijiao* 古本竹書紀年輯校. 1917. In *Haining Wang Jing'an xiansheng yishu* 海寧王靜安先生遺書, vol. 36, *juan* 3, 1–27. N.p.: n.p., 1936.

Wang Guowei 王國維. *Jinben Zhushu jinian shuzheng* 今本竹書紀年疏證. 1917. In *Haining Wang Jing'an xiansheng yishu* 海寧王靜安先生遺書, vol. 36, *juan* 3, 1–27, 1–32. N.p.: n.p., 1936.

Wang Li 王力. *Shijing yun du* 詩經韻讀. Shanghai: Shanghai guji chubanshe, 1980.

Wang Niansun 王念孫. *Du Yi Zhou shu za zhi* 讀逸周書雜志. In *Du shu za zhi* 讀書雜志. Huang Qing jingjie xubian ed.

Wang Ning 王寧. "Anda jian *Shi jing* 'Hou' yijie 安大簡《詩經》"侯"臆解. http://www.gwz.fudan.edu.cn/Web/Show/4411. Posted 6 April 2019.

Wang Ning 王寧. "Qinghua jian *Zheng Wen Gong wen Tai Bo* shiwen jiaodu" 清華簡《鄭文公問太伯》釋文校讀. www.gwz.fudan.edu.cn/Web/Show/2809. Posted 30 May 2016.

Wang Ning 王寧. "Qinghua jian *She ming* chudu" 清華簡播命初讀. http://bsm.org.cn/forum/forum.php?mod=viewthread&tid=4352&extra=&. Posted 18 November 2018.

Wang Shimin 王世民, Chen Gongrou 陳公柔, and Zhang Changshou 張長壽. *Xi Zhou qingtongqi fenqi duandai yanjiu* 西周青銅器分期斷代研究. Beijing: Wenwu chubanshe, 1999.

Wang Xianqian 王先謙. *Shi san jia yi jishu* 詩三家義集疏. N.p.: Xushou tang, 1915.

Wang, C. H. *The Bell and the Drum: Shih Ching as Formulaic Poetry in an Oral Tradition.* Berkeley: University of California Press, 1974.

Wang, Ching-hsien. "'Shih Ching': Formulaic Language and Mode of Creation." PhD diss., University of California, Berkeley, 1971.

Wang Fu 王黼 et al., eds. *Bogu tulu* 博古圖錄 (1123).

Wei Yihui 魏宜輝. "Zailun Mawangdui boshu zhong de 'shi ⌣' ju" 再論馬王堆帛書中的 "是⌣" 句. *Dongnan wenhua* 東南文化 2008.4, 56–57.

Wei Yuan 魏源. *Shi gu wei* 詩古微. 1840 woodblock ed.

Wu Dacheng 吳大澂. *Kezhai jigulu* 愙齋集古錄. 1918 Hanfenlou ed.

Wu Qichang 吳其昌. *Jinwen lishuo shuzheng* 金文曆朔疏證. Wuhan: Guoli Wuhan daxue congshu, 1936.

Wu Rongzeng 吳榮曾. "*Zi yi* jianben, jin ben yin *Shi* kaobian" 《緇衣》簡、今本引《詩》考辨. *Wenshi* 文史 60 (2002): 14–18.

Wu Zhenfeng 吳鎮烽. *Shang Zhou qingtongqi mingwen ji tuxiang jicheng* 商周青銅器銘文暨圖像集成. 35 vols. Shanghai: Shanghai Guji chubanshe, 2012.

Wu Zhenfeng 吳鎮烽. *Shang Zhou qingtongqi mingwen ji tuxiang jicheng xubian* 商周青銅器銘文暨圖像集成續編. 4 vols. Shanghai: Shanghai Guji chubanshe, 2016.

Wu Zhenfeng 吳鎮烽 and Luo Zhongru 雒忠如. "Shaanxi sheng Fufeng xian Qiangjia cun chutu de Xi Zhou tongqi" 陝西省扶風縣強家村出土的西周銅器. *Wenwu* 文物 1975.8, 57–62.

Xia Dazhao 夏大兆. "Anda jian *Shi jing* 'Hou liu' kao" 安大簡《詩經》"侯六"考. *Guizhou Shifan daxue xuebao (Shehui kexueban)* 貴州師範大學學報(社會科學版) 4 (2018): 119–25.

Xia Dazhao 夏大兆. "Anda jian *Shi jing* 'Hou liu' xukao" 安大簡《詩經》"侯六"續考. *Zhanguo wenzi yanjiu* 戰國文字研究 1 (2019): 93–108.

Xia Hanyi 夏含夷. "42 nian 43 nian liangge *Yu Lai ding* de niandai" 42年43年兩個吳來鼎的年代. *Zhongguo lishi wenwu* 中國歷史文物 2003.5, 49–52.

Xia Hanyi 夏含夷. "Cong *Zeng Gong Qiu bianzhong* mingwen chongxin kaolü *Da Yu ding* he *Xiao Yu ding* de niandai" 從《曾公求編鐘》銘文重新考慮《大盂鼎》和《小盂鼎》的年代. In *Jinian Zhang Changshou he Chen Gongrou liangwei xiansheng de lunwenji* 紀念張長壽和陳公柔兩位先生的論文集, ed. Li Feng 李峰 and Shi Jingsong 施勁松, 373–83. Shanghai: Zhong-Xi shuju, 2022.

Xia Hanyi 夏含夷. "Jianlun 'Yuedu xiguan': Yi Shangbo *Zhou Yi Jing* gua wei li" 簡論"閱讀習慣": 以上博《周易‧菜》卦為例. *Jianbo* 簡帛 4 (2009): 385–94.

Xia Hanyi 夏含夷. "Jin Chu Gong ben zu kao: Jianlun *Zhushu jinian* de liangge zuanben" 晉出公奔卒考：兼論竹書紀年的兩個纂本. *Shanghai bowuguan jikan* 上海博物館集刊 2002.9, 186–94.

Xia Hanyi 夏含夷. "Jinian xingshi yu shi shu zhi qiyuan" 紀年形式與史書之起源. In *Jian bo, jingdian gu shi* 簡帛、經典、古史, edited by Chen Zhi 陳致, 39–46. Shanghai: Shanghai Guji chubanshe, 2013.

Xia Hanyi 夏含夷. "Lüelun jinwen Shangshu Zhoushu gepian de zhuzuo niandai" 略論今文尚書周書各篇的著作年代. In *Di er jie Guoji Zhongguo guwenzi yantaohui lunwenji, xubian* 第二屆國際中國古文字研討會論文集續編 (Collected Papers of the Second International Conference on Chinese Paleography), 399–404. Hong Kong: Chinese University of Hong Kong, 1996.

Xia Hanyi 夏含夷. "Shilun Xi Zhou tongqi mingwen de xiezuo guocheng: Yi Meixian Shan shi jiazu tongqi wei li" 試論西周銅器銘文的寫作過程：以眉縣單氏家族銅器為例. In *Chutu wenxian yu Zhongguo sixiang yantaohui lunwenji* 新出土文獻與先秦思想重構論文集, edited by Guo Lihua 郭梨花, 119–30. Taipei: Taiwan Guji chuban youxian gongsi, 2007.

Xia Hanyi 夏含夷. "Wu wudu qingtongqi mingwen" 勿誤讀青銅器銘文. *Zhongguo Shehui kexuebao* 中國社會科學報, 12 August 2012, 4.

Xia Hanyi 夏含夷. "'Xia Shang Zhou duandai gongcheng' shi nian hou zhi pipan: Yi Zhou zhu wang zai wei niandai wei lizheng" "夏商周斷代工程"十年後之

批判：以西周諸王在位年代為例證. In *Di si jie Guoji Hanxue huiyi lunwenji: Chutu cailiao yu xin shiye* 第四屆國際漢學會議論文集：出土材料與新視野, 341–80. Taipei: Academia Sinica, 2013.

Xia Hanyi 夏含夷. "You Meixian Shan shi jiazu tongqi zailun Shanfu Ke tongqi de niandai: fudai zailun Jin Hou Su bianzhong de niandai" 由眉縣單氏家族銅器再論膳夫克銅器的年代——附帶再論晉侯蘇編鐘的年代. In *Zhongguo gudai qingtongqi guoji yantaohui lunwenji* 中國古代青銅器國際研討會論文集, 165–78. Shanghai: Shanghai bowuguan and Xianggang Zhongwen daxue wenwuguan, 2010.

Xia Hanyi 夏含夷. "You Qinghua jian *Xinian* lun *Zhushu jinian* muben he jinben de tili" 由清華簡《繫年》論《竹書紀年》墓本和今本的體例. *Jianbo* 簡帛 22 (2021): 45–73.

Xia Hanyi 夏含夷. "You tongqi mingwen chongxin yuedu *Shi Da Ya Xia Wu*" 由銅器銘文重新閱讀《詩大雅下武》. In *Qu Wanli xiansheng bai sui danchen guoji xueshu yantaohui lunweiji* 屈萬里先生百歲誕辰國際學術研討會論文, edited by Guojia tushuguan 國家圖書館 et al., 65–69. Taipei: n.p., 2006.

Xia Hanyi 夏含夷. "*Zheng Wen Gong wen Taibo* yu Zhongguo gudai wenxian chaoxie de wenti"《鄭文公問太伯》與中國古代文獻抄寫的問. *Jianbo* 簡帛 14 (2017): 11–15.

"Xixun: Jingzhou Wangjiazui 798 hao Zhanguo Chu mu ronghuo '2021 nian Hubei liu da kaogu xin faxian'" 喜訊！荊州王家咀798號戰國楚墓榮獲"2021年湖北六大考古新發現." http://wlj.jingzhou.gov.cn/xxdt/dtyw/202206/t20220610_737887.shtml.

Xue Shanggong 薛尚功. *Lidai zhong ding yiqi kuanzhi fatie* 歷代鐘鼎彝器款識法帖. Shanghai: Dianshi zhai, 1882.

Yan Shixuan 顏世鉉. "*Shi* Shao nan 'Zou yu' 'zou yu' jie: Jianlun duidai Han Ru *Shi* shuo de taidu"《詩·召南·騶虞》"騶虞"解：兼論對待漢儒《詩》說的態度. Paper presented to the Institute of History and Philology, Academia Sinica, 7 May 2018.

Yang Shuda 楊樹達. "Mao Bo Ban gui ba" 毛伯班簋跋. In Yang Shuda, *Jiweiju jinwen shuo* 積微居金文說, 123–24 Changsha: Hunan jiaoyu chubanshe, 2007.

Yang Xiquan 楊錫全. "Chutu wenxian chongwen yongfa xin tan" 出土文獻重文用法新探. http://www.gwz.fudan.edu.cn/old/SrcShow.asp?Src_ID=1145. Posted 10 May 2010.

Yang Xiquan 楊錫全. "Chutu wenxian 'shi ' ju qian xi buzheng yi ze" "出土文獻'是'句淺析"補證一則. http://www.gwz.fudan.edu.cn/old/SrcShow.asp?Src_ID=1004. Posted 2 December 2009.

Yang Xiquan 楊錫全. "Chutu wenxian 'shi ' ju qian xi zai bu yi ze: Jianlun xici 'shi' laiyuan wenti" "出土文獻'是'句淺析"再補一則：兼論係詞"是"來源問題. http://www.gwz.fudan.edu.cn/old/SrcShow.asp?Src_ID=1028. Posted 26 December 2009.

Yang Xiquan 楊錫全. "Chutu wenxian 'shi ' ju qian xi" 出土文獻 '是 '句淺析. http://www.gwz.fudan.edu.cn/old/SrcShow.asp?Src_ID=958. Posted 3 November 2009.

Yates, Robin D. S. "The Qin Slips and Boards from Well No. 1, Liye, Hunan: A Brief Introduction to the Qin Qianling County Archives." *Early China* 35–36 (2012–2013): 291–329.

Yi li zhushu 儀禮注疏. *Sibu beiyao* ed.

Yi Zhou shu 逸周書. *Sibu beiyao* ed.

"Yuwen Suo'an tan wenxueshi de xiefa" 宇文所安談文學史的写法. *Dongfang zaobao* 東方早報, 8 March 2009, 2–3.

Yu Xingwu 于省吾. *Mu tianzi zhuan* xin zheng 穆天子傳新證. *Kaogu she kan* 考古社刊 6 (1937): 277.

Yu Xingwu 于省吾. *Shuang jian chi Shijing xinzheng* 雙劍誃詩經新證. 1935; rpt. *Shijing Chuci xinzheng* 詩經楚辭新證, 275–85. Beijing: Zhonghua shuju, 1982.

Yu Yue 俞樾. *Gu shu yi yi juli* 古書疑義舉例. Beijing: Zhonghua shuju, 1956.

Yu Yue 俞樾. *Zhou shu pingyi* 周書平議. Huang Qing jingjie xubian ed.

Yuan Mei 袁梅. *Shi jing yiwen huikao bianzheng* 詩經異文彙考辯證. Jinan: Qi-Lu shushe, 2013.

Yuan Mei 袁梅. *Shi jing yizhu (Guo feng bufen)* 詩經譯注(國風部分). Jinan: Qi-Lu shushe, 1983.

Yuasa Kunihiro 湯淺邦弘. "On the Question of Inverted Stanzas in the Anda-Slip *Shi jing* Poem 'Si tie.'" *Bamboo and Silk* 4, no. 1 (2021): 149–71.

Zhang Chongli 張崇禮. "*Jing gong yao di jiu jian jiegu*" 競公瘧第九簡解詁. http://www.bsm.org.cn/show_article.php?id=678. Posted 29 July 2007.

Zhang Guangyu 張光裕, ed. *Baoshan Chu jian wenzi bian* 包山楚簡文字編. Taibei: Yiwen yinshuguan, 1992.

Zhang Maorong 張懋鎔. "Shilun Xi Zhou qingtongqi yanbian de feijunhengxing wenti" 試論西周青銅器演變的非均衡性問題. *Kaogu xuebao* 考古學報2008.3, 337–52.

Zhang Shixian 張世賢. "Cong Shang Zhou tongqi de neibu tezheng shilun Mao Gong ding de zhenwei wenti: 1981 nian shiyi yue Aozhou Guoli daxue 'Keji ziliao zai kaogu he lishi yanjiu shang de yingyong' toulunhui lunwen" 從商周銅器的內部特徵試論毛公鼎的真偽問題：1981年十一月澳洲國立大學「科技資料在考古和歷史研究上的應用」討論會論文. *Gugong jikan* 故宮季刊 16, no. 4 (1982): 55–77.

Zhang Zhenglang 張政烺. "He zun mingwen jieshi buyi" 何尊銘文解釋補遺. *Wenwu* 1976.1, 66.

Zhao Boxiong 趙伯雄. "*Shi Xia Wu* 'Ying hou shun de' jie" 《詩下武》應侯順德解. *Guji zhengli yanjiu* 古籍整理研究1998.2, 1–3.

Zheng Xuan 鄭玄. *Liji Zheng zhu* 禮記鄭注. *Sibu beiyao* ed.

Zheng Xuan 鄭玄. *Zhou li Zheng zhu* 周禮鄭注. *Sibu beiyao* ed.

Zhongguo shehui kexueyuan Kaogu yanjiusuo, ed. *Yin Zhou jinwen jicheng* 殷周金文集成. 18 vols. N.p.: Zhonghua shuju, 1984–1994.

Zhongguo shehui kexueyuan kaogu yanjiusuo 中國社會科學院考古研究所, ed. *Yin Zhou jinwen jicheng shiwen* 殷周金文集成釋文. Hong Kong: Chinese University of Hong Kong, Institute of Chinese Studies, 2001.

Zhou, Boqun. *The Tsinghua University Warring States Bamboo Manuscripts*, vol. 3: *The Yi Yin Texts*. Beijing: Tsinghua University Press, 2023.

Zhu Fenghan 朱鳳瀚. *Shang Zhou jiazu xingtai yanjiu* 商周家族形態研究. Tianjin: Tianjin guji chubanshe, 1990.

Zhu Fenghan 朱鳳瀚. *Zhongguo qingtongqi zonglun* 中國青銅器綜論. Shanghai: Shanghai Guji chubanshe, 2009.

Zhu Hanmin 朱漢民 and Chen Songchang 陳松長, eds. *Yuelu shuyuan cang Qin jian* 岳麓書院藏秦簡. Shanghai: Shanghai Cishu chubanshe, 2010–. Five volumes published to date.

Zhu Xi 朱熹. *Shi jing ji zhu* 詩經集註. Taipei: Qunyutang chuban gongsi, 1991.

Zhushu jinian 竹書紀年. *Sibu congkan* ed.

Zhu Youzeng 朱有曾. *Ji zhong jinian cunzhen* 汲冢紀年存真. N.p.: Guiyan zhai, 1846.

Zhu Youzeng 朱右曾. *Zhou shu ji xun jiaoshi* 周書集訓校釋. 1846 woodblock ed.

Zi Ju 子居. "Qinghua jian *Feng Xu zhi Ming* jiexi" 清華簡《封許之命》解析. https://www.ctwx.tsinghua.edu.cn/info/1081/2226.htm. Posted 28 April 2015.

Zi Ju 子居. "Qinghua jian *Zheng Wen Gong wen Tai Bo* (*Jiaben*) jiexi" 清華簡《鄭文公問太伯（甲本）》解析. xianqinshi.blogspot.com/2017/09/blog-post_34.html. Posted 23 September 2017.

Zou An 鄒安. *Zhou jinwen cun* 周金文存. Shanghai: Haiguancang xuejun boliban yinyishu congbian, 1916.

"Zui zao de *Shi jing* chutu yu Jingzhou" 最早的《詩經》出土於荊州. http://www.360doc.com/content/17/0429/09/8527076_649527308.shtml. Accessed 9 October 2019.

Index

Added or Deleted Text, 154–9
Alcohol, and *She ming 攝命, 127; injunctions against, 121
Allan, Sarah, 42
Analects, 120, 144
Ancestral temple, 88
Ancient Script (guwen 古文) Shang shu 尚書, 1–2
Ancient Text (Guben 古本) Bamboo Annals, 266; collections of, 371 n. 7
Anhui University, 203
Annals, 266, 268, 371–2 n. 8; and *Bian nian ji, 380 n. 16; and Shi Qiang pan, 382 n. 22; and Zhou court, 310; of Chu, 305
Anyang 安陽, 15, 18
Appointment document, 43
Archaeology, 2, 6, 24; advances in excavation techniques, 8; and Jin Hou Su bianzhong, 31; and Meixian bronzes, 57; Song-dynasty interest in, 24
Archaic pronunciations, 346 n. 18
Archives, 40, 43, 80, 106, 311, 323 n. 20, 382 n. 25; and *She ming, 137
Art Institute of Chicago, 89, 94, 97, 105
Artisan/scribe, 332 n. 25

Award document, 37, 39, 62

Ba 霸, 323 n. 17
"Bai zhou" 柏舟, 205
Bamboo Annals, 9, 265–95, 379–80 n. 7; and chronology, 280, 376–7 n. 37, 378 n. 42; and King Yih 懿王, 72, 129; and *She ming 攝命, 115; and Zhai Gong 祭公, 247, 248; tomb text of, 268, 294, 295
Bamboo slips, 5, 45, 319 n. 7; and binding straps, 114; and command scriptures, 58; and effect on the textual content, 351 n. 29; and Fuyang Shi manuscript, 181; and numbering, 114; and *She ming, 137; and textual transmission, 201; and Western Zhou period, 8
Ban gui 班簋, 239, 243
Baoshan 包山 manuscripts, 302–3
Barnard, Noel, 82, 102
Baxter, William, 202
Before Confucius: Studies in the Creation of the Chinese Classics, 1, 4, 6, 7, 8
Bei Feng 邶風, 361 n. 52
Believing Antiquity (xin gu 信古), 47–49
Bi Gong Gao 畢公高, 175
Bi Huai 畢媿, 366 n. 18

Bi Huan 畢龏, 240, 242, 245–6, 252
Bi Ju 畢矩, 246
Bi Xian gui 畢鮮簋, 366 n. 18
Bi Xian 畢鮮, 366 n. 18
Bi Zhong 畢中, 366 n. 18
Bi 畢 lineage, 246, 252
*Bian nian ji 編年記, 9, 298–317
Bin Gong 豳公, 51, 53
Bin Gong xu 豳公盨, 51–54; translation of, 52; authorship of, 53; shape and ornamentation of, 54; rubbing and photo of, 55
Bin 賓 Group, 17
Blow-holes, 98
Bo Pan 266, 267
Bo Qin 伯禽, 33, 247
"Bo Qin" 伯禽, 324 n. 26
Bo wu zhi 博物志, 238
Boltz, William G., 226
Bribes, 121, 128
Bronze inscriptions, 7, 24–32; and archival function, 108; and bamboo slips, 332 n. 29, 334 n. 34; and court audiences, 58; and full date notations, 36; and King Mu of Zhou 周穆王, 238; and literacy, 201; and orality, 82; and *Shang shu* 尚書 chapters, 50; and **She ming* 攝命, 114; and *Shi jing*, 353 n. 55; and spacers, 326 n. 26; and subjective view of history, 33; and surface area, 84; and tertiary record, 39, 51, 311; and written commands, 37; commemorative nature of, 106; earliest examples of, 13–14, 322 n. 9; legibility of, 109; placement of, 108
Bronze tools, 25
Bronze vessels, 5; and casting technology, 102, 106; and documents, 193–4; and King Mu reform, 34; and Ritual Reform, 35; recent discoveries of, 323 n. 17

Brooks, E. Bruce and A. Taeko, 48, 49
Brundage Rhino, 25
Bureaucratization, 34

Cai 蔡, 41
Captain Tong, man of Bi 畢人師同, 366 n. 18
Carbon-14 dating, 175
Ceng 鄫, 272, 273, 278, 373 n. 19
"Chang mai" 嘗麥, 40
"Chang xun" 常訓, 142, 152, 346 n. 16
Changes (*Yi* 易), 107; see too *Zhou Yi* 周易
Charge, 16, as paired divinations, 17, 24
Chen Fengheng 陳逢衡, 143
Chen Mengjia 陳夢家, 242
Chen Peifen 陳佩芬, 250
Chen Rentao 陳仁濤, 90
Cheng Hao 程浩, 119
Cheng Shi 成師; see Huanshu of Quwo 曲沃桓叔
*Cheng wu 程寤, 160
Chengkuang 承筐, 307
Chenzi 沈子, 117, 336 n. 9, n. 13
Chronology, 20, 80, 321 n. 1, 371 n. 5; and Western Zhou, 36; complexity of, 374 n. 23; mistakes of, 378 n. 42
Chu 楚, 6; script of, 173
Chunqiu 春秋, 266, 298, 299–300, 371–2 n. 8; and Du Yu, 268
"Chunqiu" 春秋 "annals," 298
Chunqiu of Zhou 周春秋, 298, 307–8
Chunqiu Zuo zhuan Zhengyi 春秋左傳正義, 266, 268, 279
Ci 茨 "star-thistle," 220
Classics, 1, 4, 6, 7, 49
Classifier Variation, 148–9
Command, 76–80; and bamboo slips, 87; *Qiu Zhong* 仇鐘 abbreviation of, 85

Command document (*ming shu* 命書), 16, 37, 39, 41, 45, 311, and archives, 40; as copy, 38, 323 n. 20
"Cong hu" 從曉, 205
Cook, Scott, 225–6, 231
Copyist, 4, 231; 186–7
Core, 98
Court cases, 121, 128, 130
Covenant Repository (*Meng fu* 盟府), 40
Covenant scripture, 42
Crack, 16
Creel, Herrlee, 37, 40, 51, 329 n. 6
Cui Shu 崔述, 2, 48
Current Text (*jinben* 今本) *Bamboo Annals*, 266, 268, accurate historical information of, 291; and *Bamboo Annals* tomb text, 282; Quwo bias of, 294

Da Ke ding 大克鼎, 90, 331 n. 24, 337 n. 25
*Da shi ji 大事記, 298
Da Yu ding 大盂鼎, 27–28, 35, 113, 135–6; revised dating of, 322 n. 11
Dahekou 大河口, 323 n. 17
Dai Zhen 戴震, 372 n. 15
Dai 殆 "danger," 159–60
Daisy-picking divination, 17
Di Xin 帝辛, 19–20; *see too* Zhou 紂
Di Yi 帝乙, 19, 20, 25
Diao Sheng gui 調生簋, 191
Diao Sheng zun 調生尊, 191, 354 n. 56
Ding Zongluo 丁宗洛, 143
Divination, 16, 303
Documents (*Shu* 書), 107; *see too Shang shu* 尚書
Dog-mound (Quanqiu 犬丘), 129
Dong fangding 㦰方鼎, 331 n. 24
Dong gui 㦰簋, 339 n. 36
Doubting Antiquity (*yi gu* 疑古), 47–49

Dragon bones, 15
"Du ren shi" 都人士, 183–6
"Du xun" 度訓, 142, 152
Du Yu 杜預, 247, 268–70, 282; and *Bamboo Annals*, 372 n. 8; and editors of Ji Zhong manuscripts, 294; mis-interpretation of, 293–4
Duan gui 段簋, 366 n. 18
Dubo 杜伯, 307–8
Duke Hu of Shao 召公虎, 193; and "Jiang Han" 江漢, 191
Duke Huan of Qi 齊桓公, 253
Duke Huan of Zheng 鄭桓公, 255, 263, 271, 272–3, 278–9; dates of, 368 n. 7; identity of, 372, n. 15
Duke Hui of Wei 衛惠公, 219
Duke Li of Zheng 鄭厲公, 255, 263
Duke Mu of Qin 秦穆公, 213, 253
Duke of Zhai 祭公, 119, 310
Duke of Zhou 周公, 33, 41
Duke Wen of Zheng 鄭文公, 255, 263
Duke Wu of Quwo 曲沃武公, 271, 288, 290; and Lord Ai of Jin 晉哀侯, 377 n. 38; and Lord Min of Jin 晉侯緡, 375 n. 30
Duke Wu of Zheng 鄭武公, 255, 263
Duke Xi of Qi 齊僖公, 219
Duke Xiang of Qi 齊襄公, 219
Duke Xuan of Wei 衛宣公, 219
Duke Zhao of Zheng 鄭昭公, 255, 263
Duke Zhuang of Zheng 鄭莊公, 255, 263
Dunhuang 敦煌, 257
Duofu 多父, 278, 372, n. 15
Duplication marks, 216–7, 332 n. 26, 333 n. 32, 347 n. 27, 360 n. 38, 360 n. 40

E Jun Qi jie 鄂君啟節, 304, 305, 380–1, n. 20
"Elder Qin" 伯禽, 42, 43

Elk (*mi* 麋), 211
Emperor Wu of Jin 晉武帝, 268
"Establish difference" (*li yi* 立異), 224–5, 227, 228, 231
Event notation, 302, 308–10

Falkenhausen, Lothar von, 82, 106, 108–9
Fan Ju sheng hu 番匊生壺, 96
Fan Qin 范欽, 293
Fan wu liu xing 凡物流型, 369 n. 25
Fang Shiming 方詩銘, 280, 293
Fen 汾 River, 18
Feng Gong 逢公; see Feng Gu 逢固
Feng Gu 逢固, 243, 249–50, 366 n. 29
Feng Mofu you 夆莫父卣, 250
Feng Xu zhi ming 封許之命, 43–45, 141; date of, 325 n. 31
Fengchu 鳳雛, 15
Fifth-year Diao Sheng gui 調生簋, 354 n. 56
Filing system, 24
First Year Shi Dui gui 師兌簋, 323 n. 20, 331 n. 19
Forty-Second Year Qiu ding 逑鼎, 37, 57; and bronze-vessel periodization, 94; and royal command, 77–79, 87; shape of, 90; translation of, 58–60
Forty-Third Year Qiu ding 逑鼎, 38, 57, 67, 137; and bronze-vessel periodization, 94; and royal command, 77–79; shape of, 90; translation of, 60–62
Fou 缶, 18–19
Fu Hao 婦好, 25
Fu Qian 服虔, 183, 185
Fu Sheng 伏勝, 49
Fu Yue zhi ming 傅說之命, 343 n. 59
Fuyang 阜陽 manuscript, 181, 359 n. 27

Gan Bao 干寶, 377 n. 37

Gang Qie zun 掆劫尊, 309
Gansu, 5
"Gao zong rong ri" 高宗肜日, 53
Gao Zong 高宗; see Wu Ding 武丁
"Gao Zu gong chen houzhe nianbiao" 高祖功臣侯者年表, 299
Gao 誥 "proclamation," 49
"Gaoyao mo" 皋陶謨, 120
Gas bubbles, 96, 98, 101, 103
Gas, 98
"Ge ju" 葛屨, 205
"Ge lou" 葛藟, 205
Giles, Herbert, 48
"Glass half full, glass half empty" question, 234
Gong Bo He 共伯和, 36, 330 n. 11
Gongshu 公叔, 84–85
Gongzi Ji 公子伋, 219
Gongzi Shou 公子壽, 219
Gongzi Shuo 公子朔, 219
Gongzi Wan 公子頑, 219
Granet, Marcel, 171, 348 n. 4
Graphic variants, 151–4, 186, 201; *She ming* 攝命, 134; and Shi jing 詩經, 233
Grave robbing, 175
Gu Jiegang 顧頡剛, 2, 49, 326 n. 10
Gu shi bian 古史辨, 2
"Guan Ju" 關雎, 206–8
Guan Zhong 管仲, 253
Guan Zhong 管仲, 253
Guangdong, 5
Guo Bi ding 虢比鼎, 96
Guo Bi xu 虢比盨, 95
Guo Feng 國風, 174, 204
Guo Moruo 郭沫若, 93, 239
Guo Pu 郭璞, 244, 246
Guo yu 國語, 4, 232, 246
Guo Zhong 虢仲, 377–8 n. 38
Guo 虢, 279
Guodian 郭店 manuscripts, 7, 47, 247; and Qiu Xigui 裘錫圭, 362 n. 55

Guoshu Lü zhong 虢叔旅鐘, 331 n. 24

Hain-teny, 171
Han Shi waizhuan 韓詩外傳, 217
Han Wei 韓魏, 105
"Han xing yilai zhuhou nianbiao" 漢興以來諸侯年表, 299
Harbsmeier, Christoph, 3, 347 n. 24
He Qiao 和嶠, 372 n. 9
He zun 何尊, 26
Heaven, cult of, 68–69
Hengbei 橫北, 323 n. 17
Hengshui 橫水, 366 n. 30
Historical epic, 364–5 n. 4
Historiography, 9, 14, 15, 16; beginning of, 24
History, writing of, 40, 382 n. 25
Hollows, 16
Homeric epics, 171, 201
Hong Kong antiques market, 32, 51, 53, 175
Hook-shaped mark, *see* 乙-hooked shape mark
Hou Chuo fangding 厚趠方鼎, 248, 310
Hou 侯, and Anhui University manuscript, 204, 215
Houfu 厚父, 141, 343 n. 2
Hu gui 默簋, 29, 68, 189
Hu zhong 默鐘, 29, 68, 336 n. 13
Hua Jueming 華覺明, 101
Huai Yi 淮夷, 128, 191, 193
Huaili 槐里, 129
Huang Dekuan 黃德寬, 211, 229
Huang Huaixin 黃懷信, 144
Huang men 皇門, 160, 161
"Huang Niao" 黃鳥, 211–4
Huang Tianshu 黃天樹, 221
"Huang yi" 皇矣, 187–8
Huangdi 黃帝, 270
Huanshu of Quwo 曲沃桓叔, 271, 281
Huayuanzhuang 花園莊, 15

Hui Dong 惠棟, 1
Hui 會, 273, 373 n. 19
Huizhong Lifu 惠仲盨父, 66, 73, 76
Hunan, 5

Iconoclasm, 1–2, 48–49
Impressions, 204
Inscriptions, and event records (*ji shi keci* 記事刻辭), 22; and religious ceremonies, 14; earliest known, 17
Institute of History and Philology, 15
Investiture ceremonies, 28
Investiture inscriptions, 58, 336 n. 2; and *She ming* 攝命, 114, 116, 121, 132
Invocator Tuo 祝佗, 41

Ji Commandery 汲郡, 268
Ji zhong 汲冢, 266
Jiaguwen 甲骨文, 16; *see too* Oracle-Bone Inscriptions
Jian gui 諫簋, 339 n. 44
"Jiang Han" 江漢, 190–2
Jiang Yougao 江有誥, 188
Jiangsu, 5
Jifu 吉甫, 193
Jili 蒺藜 "prickly vine," 230
Jili 蝍蛆 "vermin," 220
Jin Hou Su bianzhong 晉侯穌編鐘, 29–33, 36; archaeological provenance of, 31–32; date of, 323 n. 16
Jin 晉, chronology of, 282, 372 n. 11; civil war of, 271, 281–93
"Jin teng" 金滕, 117
Jin Wudi 晉武帝, 237
Jing Bo 井白, 242, 365 n. 12
Jing Li 井利, 239, 240, 242, 243, 244
"Jing zhi" 敬之, 178–80, 202
Jingren Ren Ning zhong 井人人妥鐘, 331 n. 24
Jinkui lun gu chuji 金匱論古初集, 90
Jinpenling 金盆嶺, 368 n. 13

"Jiong ming" 囧命, 113, 118; text of, 120–1; transmission of, 138
Jixian 汲縣, 237
Johnson, Samuel, 173
*Junren zhe he bi an zai 君人者何必安哉, 369 n. 25

Kaishu 楷書 script, 173
Kalinowski, Marc, 258
"Kang gao" 康誥, 42, 43, 324 n. 26
Kangshu Feng 康叔封, 33
Kao xin lu 考信錄, 2
Kaogu tu 考古圖, 130, 340 n. 46
Karlgren, Bernhard, 193–4; 342 n. 57
Keightley, David 20, 22–24, 37, 40, 49, 50; and writing as indispensable tool, 320 n. 9
Kern, Martin, 3–4, 8, 260; and function of inscribed bronze vessels, 106–8, 109; and *Kongzi Shi lun 孔子詩論, 175; and manuscript production, 256–7; and Shi jing 詩經, 169–70, 172–4, 186, 232–4; and writing of history, 382 n. 25; and "Xishuai," 363–4 n. 77; and yaotiao 腰嬲, 227; revisions of, 320–21 n. 12
Kezhai jigulu 愙齋集古錄, 89, 96
King Ai of Wei 魏哀王, 269, 270
King Cheng of Zhou 周成王, 26, 33, 117; and "Xia Wu" 下武, 195; and Ying 應, 196; and *Zhou Gong zhi qinwu 周公之琴舞, 178
King Gong of Zhou 共王, 29, 35, 72, 116; and date of Shi Wang ding 師望鼎, 93; and Mu tianzi zhuan 穆天子傳, 244
King Huan of Zhou 周桓王, 293
King Hui of Wei 魏惠王, 270
King Hui of Xie 攜惠王, 267, 279, 280, 281, 371 n. 6
King Hui of Zhou 周惠王, 272, 273

King Kang of Zhou 周康王, 27; and "Xia Wu" 下武, 195
King Li of Zhou 周厲王, 29, 36, 68, 72
King Mu of Zhou 周穆王, 27, 34; and "Jiong ming" 囧命, 113, 118, 119; and Mu tianzi zhuan 穆天子傳, 237; capital of, 272; problematic reign of, 128
King Ping of Zhou 周平王, 266, 267
King Wen of Zhou 周文王, 67–68, 69; and "Huang yi" 皇矣, 187; and Shi Qiang pan 史牆盤, 198
King Wu of Zhou 周武王, 26, 67–68; and *Qi ye 耆夜, 175; and "Xia Wu" 下武, 195
King Xiang of Wei 魏襄王, 270
King Xiang'ai of Wei 魏襄哀王, 270
King Xiao of Zhou 周孝王, 35, 36, 72, 128, 129, 330–1 n. 15; and date of Shi Wang ding 師望鼎, 94; and *She ming 攝命, 113–4, 116; revised dates of, 321 n. 1
King Xuan of Zhou 周宣王, 29, 36; and "Jiang Han" 江漢, 191; killing of, 307–8
King Yi of Zhou 周夷王, 36, 72, 116; and *She ming 攝命, 114, 116
King Yih of Zhou 周懿王, 35, 36, 72, 116; and date of Shi Wang ding 師望鼎, 94; and Quanqiu 犬邱, 330 n. 13
King Yin of Zhou 周隱王, 377 n. 37
King You of Zhou 周幽王, 36, 270, 272, 279; and Bamboo Annals entries and quotations, 273–7
King Zhao of Qin 秦昭王, 300, 312
King Zhao of Zhou 周昭王, 33, 71, 128, 311; and Zhai Gong 祭公, 248
King Zheng of Qi 秦王政, 300
Knechtges, David, 3

Kong Chao 孔晁, 151, 152, 241
Kong Yingda 孔穎達, 183
Kongzi Shi lun 孔子詩論, 174–5
Kongzi 孔子, 174
Korea, 5
Kuai 鄶, 273, 278, 373 n. 19

Lady Mi 羋氏, 256
Laozi 老子, 47–48, 258; and Guodian 郭店 manuscripts, 362 n. 55
Lawsuits, 128
Lectio facilior, 189, 363 n. 69
Legge, James, 183–4, 194–5, 200
Lei Xueqi 雷學淇, 247
Lewis, Mark Edward, 106
Li Daoyuan 酈道元, 271
Li ding 利鼎, 242
Li fangyi 盠方彝, 34, 66
Li fangzun 盠方尊, 66
Li Feng, 6
Li gui 利簋, 26
Li ji 禮記, 182
Li Xueqin 李學勤, 326 n. 5; and ancient-script *Shang shu* 尚書, 138–9; and date of *Shi Wang ding* 師望鼎, 94; and *She ming 攝命, 115; and Tsinghua manuscripts, 175; and *Xinian 繫年, 265–8, 297; and *Bamboo Annals*, 268; and Current *Bamboo Annals*, 280; 371 n. 6, 378 n. 41; and Feng Gu 逢固, 249; and Jing Li 井利, 243–4, 245; and Peng 倗, 251; and "Yan yan" 燕燕, 352 n. 43; and *Zhai Gong zhi gu ming* 祭公之顧命, 248; mistakes of, 270, 279, 293, 370 n. 4
Li 曆, 58
Li, Yung-ti 李永迪, 105
Lian Haiping 廉海萍, 105
Liang Qi zhong 梁其鐘, 82, 331 n. 24
Liaoning, 5
Linguistic turn, 24

Literate culture, 4, 7
Liu Gang 劉剛, 216
"Liu guo nianbiao" 六國年表, 299
Liu Guozhong 劉國忠, 142–3, 145, 151, 159
Liu Shipei 劉師培, 143–4
Liu Zhiji 劉知幾, 372–3 n. 15
Liye 里耶, 6
Local administration, 5, 7
Lord Ai of Jin 晉哀侯, 377 n. 38
Lord Min of Jin 侯緡, 375 n. 30
Lord Mu of Jin 晉穆侯, 271
Lord of Wèi 衛侯, 41
Lord Wen of Jin 晉文侯, 267, 269, 270, 278, 280–1, 294; and *Bamboo Annals*, 280, 371 n. 6; and Du Yu 杜預, 282
Lord Xian of Jin 晉侯獻, 31–32, 323 n. 16
Lord Xiao of Jin 晉孝侯, 374 n. 25
Lord Zhao of Jin 晉昭侯, 269, 270, 281
Lu 魯, 33, 36
Lu shi 路史, 292, 376 n. 37, 377–8 n. 38
Lu Wenchao 盧文弨, 143, 159–60
Lü Dalin 呂大臨, 130
Lü ding 旅鼎, 309
Lü Shangfu 呂尚父, 176
"Lü xing" 呂刑, 53
Lüe ding 䚄鼎, 248
Lunyu 論語, 48
Luo Bi 羅泌, 292
Luo Liangbi 羅良弼, 292
Luo Zhongru 雒忠如, 94

Ma Chengyuan 馬承源, 54, 93
Ma Nan 馬楠, 254, 256, 259, 335 n. 1, 367 n. 6
Ma Ruichen 馬瑞辰, 227
Maker of Slips Ren (*Zuoce Ren* 作冊任), 119

Manuscript culture, 4
Manuscripts, 3, 7, and Dunhuang 敦煌, 257–8; and nonlinguistic information, 259; and visual copying, 256, 260; pairs of, 369 n. 25; recent discoveries of, 47
Mao Ban 毛班, 239–40, 242, 243
Mao Commentary, 179, 195
Mao Gong ding 毛公鼎, 29, 102, 103–4, 134, 337 n. 25, 341 n. 46
Mao Shi Zhengyi 毛詩正義, 183
Mao Shi 毛詩, 208, 228; and Anhui University manuscript, 208; and creation of Shi jing 詩經, 359 n. 25; and "Shuo Shu" 碩鼠, 217; and "Zouyu," 210, 228
Master Kuang 師曠, 307
Mathieu, Rémi, 364–5 n. 4
Mattos, Gilbert, 229
Mawangdui 馬王堆, 48, 258
Meixian 眉縣, 87; and discovery of Qiu Zhong 仇鐘, 80; bronze vessels of, 66
Memorization, 4
Mencius 孟子, 343 n. 2, 344 n. 6
Meng gui 孟簋 (Jicheng 4162)
Meyer, Dirk, 257
Min, Lord of Jin 晉侯緡, 271, 281
Ming 命, 16; see too Charge
Ming shu 命書, 37; see too Command document
*Ming xun 命訓, 141–68
Minister Zan 臣瓚, 272, 278–9; see too Xue Zan 薛瓚
Misplaced slip (cuojian 錯簡), 182
Miswriting or Miscopying, 146–8
Mold assemblage, 98, 100
Morgan, Daniel, 259, 349 n. 12
Moufu, Duke of Zhai 祭公謀父, 240, 246
Mourning shed, 256

Mozi 墨子, 307; and transmission of Shang shu 尚書, 342 n. 59
Mu Gong gui gai 穆公簋蓋, 243–4, 249
Mu gui 牧簋, 130, 340 n. 46
Mu tianzi zhuan 穆天子傳, 237–52

National Palace Museum, 102
New Testament, 171
*Nianbiao 年表, 298, 299
Nivison, David, 36; and King Xiao 孝, 72, 129
Niwa Takafumi 丹羽崇史, 101
Notebooks, 22, 24, 382 n. 23
Nugent, Christopher, 257–8
Numbering of slips, 339 n. 33; and Anhu University manuscript, 204; and *Ming xun 命訓, 142; and *Zheng Wen Gong wen Tai Bo 鄭文公問太伯, 255

Odes (Shi 詩), 107; see too Shi jing 詩經
Old English poetry, 171
Oracle bones, 5
Oracle-bone inscriptions, 7, 13–24; as historical records, 14; as positive-negative questions, 17; as secondary documents, 37; carving of, 24; Preface of, 17, 20; Prognostication of, 17, 24; Verification of, 18, 19, 23, 24
Orality, 3–4, 8, 201–2; and bronze inscriptions, 108; and oral transmission, 187; and Shi jing 詩經, 232; theories of, 170–2
Orthography, 4, 172–3, 356–7 n. 6; and Anhui University manuscript, 206, 224; and *Tianzi jian zhou 天子建州, 259; differences of, 349 n. 12, 369 n. 26

Owen, Stephen, 3, 49, 169–70, 172, 178, 201
Oxen, 16

Pan Geng 盤庚, 18
Pang Sunjoo 方善柱, 353 n. 53
Penal scripture (xing shu 刑書), 40
Peng 倗, 251, 323 n. 17, 366 n. 33
Peng Bo 倗伯, 250
Peng Bo Cheng gui 倗伯偁簋, 250–1
Peng Zhong ding 倗仲鼎, 366 n. 18
Peng Zu 彭祖, 142
Pengbo zuo Bi Ji ding 倗伯作畢姬尊鼎, 250
Performance, 3, 43; and poetry, 171
Phonetic loans, 149–51, 215–6, 241; and Shi jing 詩經, 172
Phonetic reconstructions, 357, n. 13
Pit YH127, 15
Plastron, 16
Poetry, 171
Poets, and King Xiao 孝王, 35
Pointillism, 7
Poly 保利 Museum, 51, 53–54, 197
Prayers, 13
Proofreading, 115
Pseudo-variant, 159–60
Punctuation, and *Ming xun, 146; and *She ming 攝命, 115; and "Shuo Shu" 碩鼠, 216; and *Zheng Wen Gong wen Tai Bo 鄭文公問太伯, 254

Qi 耆, 176
*Qi ye 耆夜, 175–8, 202, 216, 233–4
"Qi zhao" 祈招, 246
"Qiang you Ci" 牆有茨, 217–21, 230
Qiangjiacun 強家村, 93
Qianmou 黔牟, 219
Qin 秦, 6, 172; and burning of the books, 178, 181, 185

Qin 秦, and Anhui University manuscript, 204
"Qin Chu zhi ji yuebiao" 秦楚之際月表, 299
"Qin fu yin" 秦婦吟, 257–8, 349 n. 12
Qin Gong gui 秦公簋, 189
Qin Gong zhong 秦公鐘, 188
Qin gui 禽簋, 309
Qin Shi Huangdi 秦始皇帝, 300, 312
Qin Stone Drums (秦石鼓), 229, 363 n. 70
Qin Wang Zheng 秦王政, 312; see Qin Shi Huangdi 秦始皇帝
Qiu 逑, 37; family of, 66; ancestors of, 67; other transcriptions of, 329 n. 2
Qiu pan 逑盤, 29, 37, 43, 57, 137, 331 n. 24; and King Yih's exile, 36; and Qiu zhong 逑鐘, 82–84; and royal command, 77–79; and Shi Qiang pan 史牆盤, 70, 87; and "Xia Wu," 355 n. 65; quasi-historical nature of, 71; translation of, 63
Qiu Wei gui 裘衛簋, 28–29, 34
Qiu Xigui 裘錫圭, 224–5, 227, 231, 362 n. 55
Qiu zhong 逑鐘, 75, 80–82; and Qiu pan 逑盤, 82–84; and royal command, 77–79
Qu Wanli 屈萬里, 195
"Quan yu" 權輿, 205
Que 雀, 18
Que Chengzi 郤成子, 307
Quwo 曲沃, 271; rulers of, 288

Ran xu 冉盨, 330 n. 11, 340 n. 46
Rawson, Jessica, 35; and date of Shi Wang ding 師望鼎, 93
Received texts, 3

Record-keeping, 7
Religion, and writing, 24
Renfang 人方, 20, 25
Research and Conservation Center for Unearthed Texts, 175
Rhyme, 188
Richter, Matthias L., 258–9, 349 n. 12
Ritual Reform, 35, 355 n. 66
Ruibo Wan 芮伯萬, 377 n. 38
Ruyin 汝陰, lord of, 181

Saga of Zhou kings, 69, 88
San shi pan 散氏盤, 29
Scapula bones, 16
Schaberg, David, 1, 2, 3, 6, 8, 42, 49–50, 190, 193–4, 197; and archaistic composition, 134–5; and texts associated with the Western Zhou, 341 n. 54
Schnepp, Suzanne R., 96, 99, 100
Schwartz, Adam, 356–7 n. 6
Scribes, 6, 7, 8, 9; and literacy, 51; and *Zheng Wen Gong wen Tai Bo* 鄭文公問太伯, 254; errors of, 186–7, 246, 258, 259, 353 n. 53, 370 n. 31, 370 n. 32; idiosyncrasies of, 260; self-reference of, 356 n. 3
Scriptures (*shu* 書), 9
Secret code, 8
Secretary Nian 史年, 339 n. 44
Secretary Qiang 史墻, 311
Sexual desire, 208, 227
Shan 單 family, 38, 57, 73–74
Shan Gong 單公, 67–68, 73
Shanbo Yi Sheng zhong 單白昊生鐘, 331 n. 24
Shandong, 5
Shanfu Shan ding 膳夫山鼎, 58
Shang Di 上帝, 68, 330 n. 9
Shang 商 kings, 18
Shang shu 尚書, 9, 27, 113, 160; ancient-script text of, 114; and archives, 40; and authenticity of ancient-script chapters, 120, 121; language of, 132
Shanghai Museum, 32, 101, 174; and bronze vessels, 54; manuscripts of, 349 n. 16, 369 n. 25
Shangshu 殤叔, 269, 270, 271, 282, 294
Shao Gong Shi 召公奭, 33, 175
Shao nan 召南, 204
Shao Tuo 邵㡱, 302
Shasui 沙隨, 306
She 攝, 113–14; identification of, 115–8
**She ming* 攝命, 113–39; physical characteristics of, 114–5; translation of, 121–7; transmission of, 137–8
Sheng 乘, 298
Sheng Ji 盛姬, 239, 243
Shi 史, 382 n. 25
Shi 師 Group, 17
Shi 詩 1, 3, 4, 6, 49; see too *Shi jing* 詩經
Shi Chen ding 師晨鼎, 339 n. 44
Shi Cheng zhong 師丞鐘, 94
"Shi fu" 世俘, 344 n. 6
Shi Hu gui 師虎簋, 340 n. 45
Shi ji 史記, 2, 270; and *Bamboo Annals*, 374 n. 26, 375 n. 27, 375 n. 33; and dating of Jin 晉, 290; and King Yih 懿王, 72; and **She ming* 攝命, 115; mis-quotations of, 289, 292
"Shi ji" 史記 chapter of the *Yi Zhou shu* 逸周書, 119
Shi jing 詩經, 9; Anhui University manuscript of, 203–23; and different order of stanzas, 359 n. 27; and Fuyang 阜陽 manuscript, 359 n. 27; and orality, 169–74; quotations of, 118, 256; and

poems with identical titles, 352 n. 41; and saga of Zhou kings, 69; and Xiajiatai 夏家台 manuscript, 361 n. 52; and Wangjiazui 王家嘴 manuscript, 361 n. 52; as sung and chanted, 350–1 n. 26; manuscript discoveries of, 174–80; Mao version of, 183; Qi 齊, Lu 魯 and Han 韓 traditions of, 183, 210, 221; quotations of, 232
Shi Ju fangyi 師遽方彝, 244–5
"Shi mou zhi jian" 十畝之間, 205
Shi Qiang pan 史墻盤, 29, 57, 68, 197–9, 201, 311, 330 n. 9; and annals, 382 n. 22; and Qiu pan, 70, 87; and writing of history, 382 n. 25; Wei 微 family of, 73; quasi-historical nature of, 71; translation of, 63–66
Shi Song ding 史頌鼎, shape of, 90
Shi Tangfu ding 師湯父鼎, 93
Shi Wang ding 師望鼎, 89–109, 337 n. 25; casting of, 97–106; date of, 93–97; inscription of, 91–92
Shi Wang gui 師望簋, 94–5
Shi Wang hu 師望壺, 96
Shi Wang xu 師望盨, 94–5
Shi X gui 師顈簋, 330 n. 11
Shi Xu 詩序, 179; and "Qiang you Ci" 牆有茨, 218; and "Zouyu" 騶虞, 210, 228
Shi Xun gui 師訇簋, 336 n. 2
Shi Yu zhong 師臾鐘, 94
Shi Yun gui gai 師𡪞簋蓋, 340 n. 45
"Shi'er zhuhou nianbiao" 十二諸侯年表, 299
Shirakawa Shizuka 白川靜, 93
Shu 書, 1, 49; see too *Shang shu* 尚書
Shu Xu 書序, 53; and "Jiong ming" 119
Shuanggudui 雙古堆, 181, 298
Shui jing zhu 水經注, 271

Shuihudi 睡虎地, 9, 298
Shun 舜, 270
"Shuo Shu" 碩鼠, 214–7
Shusun Zhuangshu 叔孫莊叔, 307
Shuzhong Huibo 叔仲惠伯, 307
Significs, 231
Siku quanshu 四庫全書, 238
Siku quanshu zongmu 四庫全書總目, 291
Sima Gong 司馬共, 339 n. 44
Sima Qian 司馬遷, 270; and Qin annals, 298; mistakes of, 378 n. 42
Simplified characters (*jiantizi* 简体字), 173
Six Classics, 232
Sixth-year Diao Sheng *gui* 調生簋, 354 n. 56
Skepticism, 1
Škrabal, Ondřej, 360 n. 42
Song ding 頌鼎, 58, 101, 330 n. 6
"Song Gao" 崧高, 193
Song gui 頌簋, 323 n. 20
Song Huizong 宋徽宗, 310
Song 頌 Hymns, 174
Songs, 202
Sou shen ji 搜神記, 377 n. 37
Source text, 369 n. 27
Spacers, 54
Spirit tablets, 88
Spoken pronouncement, 3
Sprue, 99, 101, 105, 106
Standard characters (*fantizi* 繁體字), 173
Stationery, 4
Su 蘇, 31
Su Rongyu 蘇榮譽, 100, 101
Sun Peiyang 孫沛陽, 105
Sun Yirang 孫詒讓, 143

Ta gui 它簋, 336 n. 13
Taboo, 351 n. 28
Tadpole characters (*kedou wenzi* 科斗文字), 268

Tai Bo 太伯, 255, 263
Taihang 太行 mountain range, 18
Taiping yulan 太平御覽, 278, 289, 292
Tang 唐, 142, 256, 264
*Tang chu yu Tang Qiu 湯處於湯丘, 142
Tang Dapei 唐大培, 148
Tang Feng 唐風, 206
"Tang gao" 唐誥, 42, 324 n. 26
Tang Lan 唐蘭, 239
*Tang zai Di Men 湯在啻門, 142
Tangshu 唐叔, 41
Taowu 檮杌, 298, 379 n. 5
Textual attenuation, 82, 332 n. 25, 332 n. 29
Textual corruptions, 241–2
Textual transmission, 145
Textualist prejudices, 2
The Cambridge History of Chinese Literature, 4
Third Year Shi Dui gui 師兌簋, 331 n. 19
Third-year Shi Dui gui 師兌簋, 323 n. 20
"Tian che" 田車, 229
Tian Wang gui 天亡簋, 330 n. 9
Tianma-Qucun 天馬曲村, 31
Tianyi ge 天一閣 library, 291, 293; and quotations of *Bamboo Annals*, 374 n. 24
Tianzi 天子, 62, 85, 330 n. 7
*Tianzi jian zhou 天子建州, 258–9
Tomb robbing, 31, 58, 203, 329 n. 5; and Anhui University *Shi jing* 詩經, 223
Traditional history, 2
Tsinghua (Qinghua) University, 6, 175, 297; manuscripts of, 113, 175, 265
Turtle shell, 14, 16
Turtles, 16

"Urge to equate" (*qu tong* 趨同), 224–5, 231

Vandermeersch, Léon, 382 n. 23
Variants, 145; and Anhui University manuscript, 206; and *Bamboo Annals*, 374 n. 26; and graphic similarity, 361 n. 49, 364 n. 79; and "Guan Ju" 關雎, 207–8; and manuscript, 173, 257, 345 n. 13; and "Qiang you Ci" 牆有茨, 221; and *Shi jing* 詩經, 172; and "Shuo Shu" 碩鼠, 215–6; and "Xishuai" 蟋蟀, 222–3; and "Zhai Gong" 祭公, 241
Vent, 99, 101, 105, 106
Verso scoring, 339 n. 33
Virtue, 52
Visual copying, 258

Waley, Arthur, 194, 195, 353 n. 55, 354 n. 56
Wan Jiabao 萬家保, 101
Wang 王, 62, 330 n. 7
Wang gui 望簋, 93, 246, 366 n. 18
Wang Guowei 王國維, 280, 291; and Current *Bamboo Annals*, 378 n. 40, 378 n. 41; mistakes of, 293–4, 374 n. 22
Wang Niansun 王念孫, 143
Wang ruo yue 王若曰, 43, 66, 115, 135, 325 n. 29
Wang, Tao 汪濤, 105
Wang Xianqian 王先謙, 183
Wang Xiuling 王修齡, 293
Wang Yirong 王懿榮, 15
Wang, C. H., 171–2, 348 n. 4
Wangjiazui 王家嘴, 361 n. 52
Waste Mound (Feiqiu 廢丘), 35, 129
Webster, Noah, 173
Wei Feng 魏風, 205, 359 n. 32

Wei 魏, 281; chronology of, 381 n. 20
Wei 魏, and Anhui University manuscript, 204
Wei 微 family, 73, 198
"Wei tian zhi ming" 維天之命, 188–9
Wei Yuan 魏源, 358 n. 25
Wei Zhuang 韋莊, 257–8
Well, 6
"Wen Wang" 文王, 69
Western Zhou, 32–9; chronology of, 80
Wooden slips, 5; discovery of, 321 n. 13
Wu Cheng 吳澄, 120
Wu Dacheng 吳大澂, 89, 96
Wu Ding 武丁, 13, 17, 25; and *Yin Gao Zong wen yu San Shou 殷高宗問於三壽, 142
Wu furen gui ruzi 鄭武夫人規孺子, 253
Wu Kejing 鄔可晶, 216
Wu Qichang 吳其昌, 239
*Wu xing 五行 manuscript, 357 n. 12
Wu Yu 吳棫, 120
Wu Zhenfeng 吳鎮烽, 94

X-ray, 96, 98, 102, 103–4
Xi 喜, 300, 301, 312
Xi Jia 兮甲, 192
Xi Jia pan 兮甲盤, 192–4
"Xia Wu" 下武, 194–201
Xiahou Zao 夏侯竈, 181
Xiajiatai 夏家台, 361 n. 52
Xiangling 襄陵, 303, 305
Xiangong, Lord of Ying 應侯見工, 196–7, 200
Xianyun 獫狁, 58, 193
Xiao Chen Yu zun 小臣余尊, 25
Xiao Ke ding 小克鼎, 93, 101; periodization of, 94; shape of, 90

Xiaotun 小屯, 15
Xiaotun Locus South (Xiaotun nandi 小屯南地), 15
Xibo Jifu 兮伯吉父, 192
Xie 燮, 267; and King Yi of Zhou 周夷王, 114
Xin Gong Quan Jia 辛公䚄廖, 175–6
Xing gui 㺇簋㺇, 331 n. 24
Xing Li 邢利, 239
Xing zhong 㺇鐘, 330 n. 9, 331 n. 24
Xing 行, 154–7
*Xingde 刑德, 258
*Xinian 繫年 *Annals, 265–8, 280, 294, 297; Li Xueqin's interpretation of, 293; name of, 378 n. 39; studies of, 379 n. 2
Xinjiang, 5
Xiping Stone Classics 熹平石經, 183
"Xishuai" 蟋蟀, 176–8, 202, 221–3, 233–4, 350 n. 23
Xiwangmu 西王母, 237
Xu Ying 譻經, 303
Xu Zaiguo 徐在國, 205
Xu 鄦/許, 43
Xuan 亘, 18–19
Xuan Jiang 宣姜, 219
Xue Zan 薛瓚, 272–3; see too Minister Zan 瓚
Xun gui 旬簋, 336 n. 2
Xun Xu 荀勖, 237, 268, 270; and editing of Bamboo Annals, 281, 372 n. 9
Xunzi 荀子, 226

Ya 雅, 174
Yan 炎, 20
Yan 燕, 33
Yan Ruoqu 閻若璩, 1
Yan Shigu 顏師古, 272
Yan Shixuan 顏世鉉, 211, 229
Yang Shuda 楊樹達, 239

Yangjiacun 楊家村, 57, 80, 87
"Yanyan" 燕燕, 352 n. 43
Yao 堯, 270
Yaotiao 窈窕, 208, 227
"Yaoyao zhijiu" 藥藥旨酒, 176
Yi 翼, 271
Yi 易 Changes, 1, 49; see too Zhou Yi 周易
Yi gu 疑古, 326 n. 6
Yi Hu 伊扈, 244; see too King Gong of Zhou 周共王
Yi Yin 伊尹, 142, 344 n. 4
Yi Zhou shu 逸周書, 40, 143, 160; and "Ming xun" 命訓, 142
*Yin Gao Zong wen yu San Shou 殷高宗問於三壽, 142
Ying 應, 196, 323 n. 17
Ying hou 應侯, 195, 200
Ying Hou Xiangong gui 應侯見工簋, 197
Ying Hou Xiangong zhong 應侯見工鐘, 196
Ying Zheng 嬴政, 351 n. 28; see too Qin Shi Huangdi 秦始皇帝
Yiqiu 宜臼, 281; see too King You of Zhou 周幽王
Yong 鄘, 204
Yong yu 永盂, 366 n. 18
"You bi" 有駜, 216
Yu 禹, 52, 326 n. 10
Yu ding 禹鼎, 331 n. 24
"Yu gong" 禹貢, 53
Yu Xingwu 于省吾, 187–8, 239, 242
Yu Yue 俞樾, 143, 217
Yuchen 余臣, 267, 280, 281, 371 n. 6
Yue 戉, 321 n. 3
"Yue chu" 月出, 227
"Yue ming" 說命, 343 n. 59
Yufang 盂方, 20
Yugoslavian ballads, 171

Zeng 曾, 267, 323 n. 17, name of, 373 n. 19

Zhai 祭, 247
"Zhai Gong" 祭公, 128, 160, 240–1; "Zi yi" 緇衣 quotations of, 344 n. 6
Zhai Gong Moufu 祭公謀父, 128; see too Moufu, Duke of Zhai
Zhai Gong zhi gu ming 祭公之顧命, 160, 161, 240–1, 247–8, 344 n. 6
Zhai Zhong 祭仲, 255
Zhang Hua 張華, 238
Zhang Nie 章蘖, 143
Zhang Shixian 張世賢, 102, 104, 105
Zhang Yanyuan 張彥遠, 238
Zhao Boxiong 趙伯雄, 355 n. 62
Zhao Yang 邵陽, 303, 305
Zhao 昭 - mu 穆 system, 76
"Zheng Min" 烝民, 193
*Zheng Wen Gong wen Tai Bo 鄭文公問太伯, 169, 253–64, 349 n. 12
Zheng Xuan 鄭玄, 183, 185, 228, 243, 361 n. 46; and "Zouyu" 騶虞, 210–1, 228
*Zheng Zijia sang 鄭子家喪, 369 n. 25
Zhengzi Ying 鄭子嬰, 255
Zhong fangding 中方鼎, 308, 310–11
Zhou 紂, 264; and *Zheng Wen Gong wen Tai Bo 鄭文公問太伯, 256
Zhou 周 conquest, 22, 32
Zhou Gong Dan 周公旦, 175, 176, 178; see too Duke of Zhou 周公
*Zhou Gong zhi qinwu 周公之琴舞, 178–80, 202
Zhou Song 周頌, 355 n. 66
Zhou jinwen cun 周金文存, 90
Zhou li 周禮, 243
Zhou Mu wang meiren Sheng Ji si shi 周穆王美人盛姬死事, 243
Zhou Nan 周南, 204
Zhou Repository (Zhou fu 周府), 41, 42
Zhou shu 周書, 143; see too Yi Zhou shu 逸周書
Zhou shu 周書 chapters, 49, 50

Zhou Wu wang you ji, Zhou Gong suo zi yi dai wang zhi zhi 周武王又疾，周公所自以弋王之志, 117
Zhou Ya 周亞, 101, 102
Zhou Yi 周易, 134; Fuyang manuscript of, 181
Zhou Yuan 周原, 57
Zhu Fenghan 朱鳳瀚, 94
Zhu Xi 朱熹, 353–4 n. 55
Zhu Youzeng 朱右曾, 143, 371 n. 7, 372 n. 13, 372 n. 15, 373 n. 21, 374 n. 22, 375 n. 28, 376 n. 33
Zhuangbo of Quwo 曲沃莊伯, 269, 270, 288
Zhushu jinian 竹書紀年; see *Bamboo Annals*
*Zi Chan 子產, 253
Zi Ju 子車 clan, 213

Zi yi 緇衣, 118, 182, 226, 247–8; and "Du ren shi" 都人士, 185
"Zi yi" 緇衣, and *Li ji* 禮記, 118; and "Yue ming" 說命, 343 n. 59
*Zi Yi 子儀, 253
Ziren Yu 子人語, 367 n. 6
Zou An 鄒安, 90
Zouyu 騶虞, 210
"Zouyu" 騶虞 "The Zouyu" 209–11, 205, 228
Zuo zhuan 左傳, 4, 40–1, 183, 246, 266; and annals, 372 n. 8; and Du Yu 杜預, 268; and event notations, 305; and *Shi jing* 詩經, 232
Zuo Zongtang 左宗棠, 89
Zuoce Yi 作冊逸, 176
乙-hook-shaped mark, 114, 115, 204, 205, 255

www.ingramcontent.com/pod-product-compliance
Lightning Source LLC
Chambersburg PA
CBHW020257240426
43673CB00039B/627